Exploring
Tech Careers

FOURTH EDITION

VOLUME 1

Ferguson
An imprint of Infobase Publishing

Exploring Tech Careers, Fourth Edition

Copyright © 2006 by Infobase Publishing

Ferguson
An imprint of Infobase Publishing
132 West 31st Street
New York NY 10001

Exploring tech careers.—4th ed.
    v. <1> p. cm.
    Includes bibliographical references and index.
    ISBN 0-8160-6447-4 (hc : alk. paper)
    1. Technology—Vocational guidance.
    T65.3.E95 2006
    602.3—dc22   2005019101

Ferguson books are available at special discounts when purchased in bulk quantities for businesses, associations, institutions, or sales promotions. Please call our Special Sales Department in New York at (212) 967-8800 or (800) 322-8755.

You can find Ferguson on the World Wide Web at
http://www.fergpubco.com

Text design by Mary Susan Ryan-Flynn
Cover design by Salvatore Luongo

Printed in the United States of America

VB MSRF 10 9 8 7 6 5 4 3 2 1

This book is printed on acid-free paper.

CONTENTS

ACKNOWLEDGMENTS

The editorial staff of Ferguson Publishing would like to express its appreciation to all of the individuals who gave of their time and experiences for the benefit of this book. Also, many thanks to all of the educators, employers, and associations whose additional comments and factual data helped to make this publication the most up-to-date reference of its kind.

INTRODUCTION
||||||||||||||||||||||||||||||||||||||||||||||||||||||||||||

Semiconductor technicians. Teacher aides. Medical record technicians. Physical therapy assistants. Had you looked in the help-wanted ads of the newspaper several years ago, you would not have seen any ads for these careers. But in today's increasingly busy and diversified workplace, these and other technicians and paraprofessionals represent some of the fastest-growing segments of the job market. Not only are most tech careers abundant, but they generally involve a relatively short training period, competitive salaries, and valuable work experience that could lead to a more advanced career in your field of interest. Whether you are interested in a future in business, science, health care, education, or communications (just to name a few), chances are there is a promising tech career waiting for you.

What Is a Technician?

Technicians, often called *paraprofessionals,* are highly specialized individuals who work with scientists, physicians, engineers, and other professionals, as well as with clients and customers. They assist these professionals in many activities, help clients and customers, and frequently direct skilled workers. Technicians work in factories, businesses, science labs, hospitals, law offices, schools, clinics, shops, and private homes. Some are self-employed as consultants. They are found in all facets of the work world and are one of the fastest-growing job ranks. *Exploring Tech Careers* seeks to motivate readers about this exciting job category through profiles of real technicians and technologists in more than 100 technical and paraprofessional jobs.

First and foremost, a technician is a specialist. When looking at the range of job classifications in the traditional, hierarchical sense, the technician is the middleman between the scientist in the laboratory and the worker on the floor; between the physician and the patient; between the engineer and the factory worker. In short, the technician's realm is where the scientific meets the practical application, where theory meets product.

Little by little, however, industries and businesses are expanding the traditional definition of technician. All workers, be they scientist, manager, technician, or line worker, are coming to be viewed as part of a team.

Competency and knowledge are the new standards by which workers are valued, not rank alone. Thus technicians are seen as valuable employees in their own right, not simply junior scientists or engineers or "wannabe" doctors. Although they by nature play a supporting role for their professional colleagues, the work of those professionals frequently could not be done without technicians. Think about it. Would you really want your radiologist operating the X-ray machine? Or your lawyer spending hours of time in the library researching your case? Or the automotive engineer fixing your car? Of course not. Assuming that the professional could even remember that far back in his or her training to perform the work, it is certain that he or she does not know the technician's specialty as well as the technician. Rather, the radiologist should be hard at work diagnosing health problems; the lawyer creating brilliant summations to win cases; the engineer designing more efficient, better cars. The technician's job is to make all of this possible.

One reason for the growing reliance on technicians is society's growing reliance on technology. As businesses switch to automated systems, as products become more technologically complex, technicians are needed to help design, implement, run, and repair such systems or equipment, be they automobiles, airplanes, X-ray machines, or computer networks. Even in areas that are not technological, there exists a certain expectation of speed, efficiency, and quality that is frequently the domain of the technician.

Another reason for the popularity of technicians is their overall cost when compared to that of highly paid professionals such as doctors, lawyers, engineers, and scientists. While in some industries technicians work alongside professionals as valued members of the team, contributing their unique knowledge and skills in areas professionals lack the time to fully develop, technicians in other industries are actually replacing professionals because they are cheaper. The field of nursing, for example, is one area in which the replacement of professionals with technicians is a hotly debated issue. Hospitals, on the one hand, are faced with the need to cut costs, while professional, registered nurses, on the other hand, argue that patient care will be compromised by relying on less highly trained staff.

Technician careers are appealing for another, very practical reason: They are a short track to a good job. Most technician careers initially require two years or less of postsecondary training. A few require a bachelor's degree to be competitive, and a very few do not require a high school diploma. For someone interested in medicine but who views with dread eight or more years of college—along with the tremendous responsibilities of being a doctor—a career as a medical technician may be just the ticket. For the aspiring engineer more interested in the day-to-day, practical applications of engineering rather than the theoretical side of science, a career as an engineering technician may be perfect. Technicians often work right alongside the professionals. They are present for and often directly involved in the groundbreaking discoveries, long-awaited advances, and cutting-edge leaps. For a comparatively small investment in time and money, a person can emerge with a practical, highly marketable career.

A tech career is a respectable one. Technicians are intelligent, highly skilled, and dynamic people who enjoy being on the cutting edge and lending their special kind of expertise to all areas of the work world. By reading what real technicians have to say about their careers, you can come to understand what it's really like to work in this segment of the job market. *Exploring Tech Careers* will help readers—primarily high school students, but in reality anyone interested in a new career—explore and evaluate some of the exciting possibilities a technician's career can offer.

How to Use This Book

Each chapter of *Exploring Tech Careers* is divided into 12 main sections (and their relevant subsections) that discuss specific aspects of each job. Integral to each chapter is an interview with a person who actually does the job. Some of the interviewees are just starting out; some have been in the business for several years or are even nearing the end of their careers. All are excited about their work and were glad to have the opportunity to share some advice with students and others who are just beginning to consider a career or a career change.

All of the career profiles in this newly revised edition of *Exploring Tech Careers* have been thoroughly updated with the latest salary, outlook, and other job information from the U.S. Department of Labor and professional organizations. All bibliographic listings have been updated with the most recent references available, and all contact information for professional organizations is the most current available at the time of publication. There are new and informative sidebars throughout the book, in addition

to new chapters on drafters, medical technologists, orthotic and prosthetic technicians, and teacher aides.

OPENING SIDEBAR

The opening sidebar of each chapter gives the reader an at-a-glance overview of the job being discussed: definition, alternative job titles, suggested high school courses, personal skills, salary range (begin-ning, experienced, and very experienced), work environment, minimum educational requirements, certiication or licensing, and outlook. Also given here are the *Dictionary of Occupational Titles* (DOT), *Guide for Occupational Exploration* (GOE), Canada's National Occupational Classification(NOC) system (new to this edition), and the Occupational Information Network-Standard Occupational Classification (O*NET-SOC) index numbers. The DOT, GOE, and O*NET-SOC indexes have been created by the U.S. government; the NOC index is Canada's career classification system. Readers can use the identification numbers listed in the opening sidebar to access further information about a career. Print editions of the DOT (*Dictionary of Occupational Titles*. Indianapolis, Ind.: JIST Works, 1991) and GOE (*Guide for Occupational Exploration*. 3d ed. Indianapolis, Ind.: JIST Works, 2001) are available at libraries. Electronic versions of the NOC (http://www23.hrdc-drhc.gc.ca) and O*NET-SOC (http://online.onetcenter.org) are available on the World Wide Web. When no DOT, GOE, NOC, or O*NET-SOC numbers are present, this means that the U.S. Department of Labor or Human Resources Development Canada have not created a numerical designation for this career. In this instance, you will see the acronym "N/A," or not available.

INTRODUCTION

The opening text section of each chapter is an introductory scene describing an aspect of the health care professional's workday. By appealing to readers on an emotional or imaginative level, the introduction provides a general feeling about the particular type of work.

WHAT DOES A TECHNICIAN DO?

This section describes in broad terms the basics of what the technician does. Any variations in job duties and titles are covered as well; actual job duties and titles may vary according to where a technician works, and an effort is made here to discuss some of the more common ones. Primary duties and secondary duties are also covered.

WHAT IS IT LIKE TO BE A TECHNICIAN?

In this section, the reader gets a first-person account of what it's like to do the job. This section prompts the reader to ask himself or herself, "Could I really do this?" and, more importantly, "Do I want to?" Here the reader formally meets the profiled person and sees him or her at work on a typical day or series of days. Typical tasks or duties are covered, and a distinction is made between primary duties and secondary ones. As the technicians describe what their work days are like, readers can begin asking themselves if this is something they really want to do. For example, jobs that sound glamorous on the surface may seem more monotonous after getting down to the details of the day; or, conversely, jobs that don't sound that exciting at first glance can be seen as very rewarding when viewed through the eyes of an enthusiastic technician. Readers should remember, however, that these are personal accounts; not all technicians will have similar situations and experiences.

DO I HAVE WHAT IT TAKES TO BE A TECHNICIAN?

In this section, the profiled person tells the reader what personal qualities are important for success in the job and discusses what he or she likes and dislikes about the job. Where appropriate, educators and employers of technicians add their own opinions about personal qualities and what they like to see in an employee.

Communication skills are the common and most basic requirement of all tech carers. This may be surprising at first because, when thinking technicians and technical work, one might consider computer skills to be first. Computer skills *are* critical in most of the jobs covered here, but the so-called soft skills— being able to clearly communicate ideas, problems, and solutions, both verbally and in writing; being able to take direction from superiors or coworkers; being able to get along well with coworkers and superiors (and frequently, clients or customers); as well as being able to think critically, that is, solve

problems—are what often make the difference between being qualified for a job and actually getting hired, not to mention being able to advance.

Another common trait important to being a successful technician is the willingness to commit to lifelong learning. Nearly every technician interviewed expressed frustration at the amount of information there is to keep up-to-date with (although most of them liked the challenge). Most of the technicians regularly read trade magazines and books, and they attend conferences and seminars to keep up with constantly changing technology and developments. Their dedication is demonstrated by the fact that such self-improvement is often done on the technician's own time.

HOW DO I BECOME A TECHNICIAN?

This section explores the educational path to the job, frequently giving examples from the profiled person's own experiences. A subsection on high school details important classes and activities to take in preparation for the job. It is important to note here that technicians' jobs are not for academic slouches. Many require complex math skills, as well as skills in a science such as physics or chemistry. Shop classes, such as auto shop, machine shop, and electronics shop, are also frequently very useful, and nearly everyone stressed taking English composition and speech classes to improve communication skills.

A subsection on postsecondary training discusses the options of community college, vocational/ technical schools, apprenticeships, armed forces training, and on-the-job training. Typical courses of study are outlined, including specific courses and any practical clinical or internship experience required. On-the-job training is the way most technicians hone their classroom skills, or for some, their primary method of training. Future technicians should be prepared to learn from a variety of sources and methods.

A section on certification or licensing outlines the options and requirements of the profession, whether voluntary or mandatory. Details about tests and information about contacting certifying or licensing agencies are also given. For most technicians' jobs that do not formally require certification, those interviewed recommended it as a way to show commitment and dedication to one's profession and to stand out from other job applicants or as a way to advance.

A section on scholarships and grants (if applicable) highlights any money available for those wishing to enter a particular profession. Readers are reminded to check with their high school guidance counselor and to contact schools' financial aid offices for additional information.

A section on internships and volunteerships (if applicable) details options for prejob experience. Many of the jobs covered here, or at least their settings, such as hospitals, can be explored first in volunteer situations. Enterprising students can often create their own "internships" by offering to work for experience alone at places such as churches or charitable organizations that can't afford to hire professional help.

Finally, a section on labor unions (if applicable) identifies any major unions that are affiliated with the profession.

WHO WILL HIRE ME?

This section gives the reader an idea about how to get a job in the particular field, frequently discussing how the profiled person got his or her first job in the field. Identified are the most likely places of employment (hospital, clinic, factory, airline, and so forth) and how to contact such places. Sources of employment, such as job lines, resume services, and trade magazine classifieds, are also discussed, as is the importance of making and maintaining contacts in one's field. Many of the technicians interviewed here got their first jobs through a personal contact.

WHERE CAN I GO FROM HERE?

This section tells the reader about advancement possibilities, illustrated with the profiled person's own goals about where he or she eventually sees himself or herself going in the field. Advancement usually connotes two things: an increase in responsibilities and an increase in pay. The same is true for technicians, for whom advancement usually means graduated salary increases up to a certain point, and corresponding changes in one's title, such as "Senior" or "Supervisor" added. In some fields earning potential for technicians is virtually unlimited, and these technicians are able to stay in their field and continue to enjoy respectable salaries (this includes those fields that are able to support "consulting technicians," those who are able to open their own businesses and hire out their services to the highest bidder). In other

fields, technicians' salaries eventually top off, so that no matter how many years of experience one has, as long as one remains a technician, one is never going to earn over a certain amount. (This scenario is not, of course, limited to technicians, but an experience of workers in all ranges of jobs.) For those technicians who require greater earning power, there is a choice. They can attempt to increase their salary by changing jobs, going to work for a bigger, more prestigious employer (or a smaller, more specialized employer) who pays more, perhaps even switching to a related technician career that has more earning potential; or they can go back to school to become a technologist or even a professional, such as an engineer or a doctor.

Many technicians are satisfied with being technicians; had they wanted to be engineers or doctors, they would have gone that route in the first place. Others, however, treat their experience as a technician as a sort of internship for a professional position. It is, after all, a way for a person to quickly begin working in their chosen field, making a decent income and having the opportunity to make important contacts and continue their education. Roughly 40 percent of licensed practical nurses, for example, go on to become registered nurses; on the other hand, few dental hygienists go on to become dentists.

WHAT ARE THE SALARY RANGES?

This section gives the reader an idea of the average beginning salary, experienced worker salary, and maximum salary. Where available, salaries in particular geographic regions or cities are indicated. When considering salaries, readers should keep the entire benefits package in mind—insurance, pension, tuition reimbursement, and vacation, sick, and holiday pay.

WHAT IS THE JOB OUTLOOK?

The purpose of this section is to get the reader thinking about the big picture and his or her long-term objectives. It relies heavily on the U.S. Department of Labor's *Occupational Outlook Handbook* to indicate the projected job growth (decline, slow, average, faster than average, and much faster than the average) for the particular job and explains to the reader how the future of the job is tied to the overall economy or subsections of the economy—in short, how it fits into the scheme of things.

HOW DO I LEARN MORE?

This section includes two subsections: professional organizations, which lists relevant organizations that provide information to students or their members on the profession, scholarships, employers, or education; and a bibliography, which lists a sampling of relevant books that students can begin looking through to learn about the jobs.

ADDITIONAL MATERIAL

Each chapter of *Exploring Tech Careers* also has several sidebars that provide useful "FYI" quick facts, "Lingo to Learn" (a glossary of terms relevant to the profession), advancement possibilities, personal traits necessary for success in the job, related jobs, and in-depth features on history, famous people, and events.

Indexes

At the end of Volume 2 are five indexes: DOT, GOE, NOC, O*NET-SOC, and Job Title. The DOT index lists careers by their three-digit DOT Occupational Group number. The GOE index lists careers by their six-digit GOE subgroups. The NOC index lists careers by their four-digit NOC unit groups. The O*NET-SOC index uses an organizational system that is based on the most current version of the Standard Occupational Classification system (SOC). The Job Title index lists all major jobs discussed in this work and their page numbers, with appropriate cross-references. (The Job Title index also appears in Volume 1.)

A Final Note

It should be obvious from reading the interviews on these pages that people love to talk about what they do. We encourage readers to take this a step further and seek out people who have jobs they are interested in. Talk to them about their work. Find out what they like and do not like and what they would do differently if they had to do it all over again. There is no better teacher than experience. Students would do well to learn from the experiences of those who have been there.

AGRICULTURAL FOOD AND PROCESSING ENGINEERS

||||||||||||||||||||||||||||||||||||||||||||||||||||||||||

What can you do with soybeans? If you're an agricultural food and processing engineer, you can make crayons. At least, that's what Jocelyn Wong and her classmate did. They created color crayons from soybean oil for a college competition seeking innovative uses of soybeans. Using their agricultural food and process engineering knowledge, they created prototypes of the environmentally friendly, nontoxic, biodegradable crayons. They conducted literature and patent searches, ran laboratory tests, completed cost analyses, and used a structured trial and error process to research and test their prototypes. Most problems that could arise did: some crayons were too brittle and broke too easily, some didn't transfer color well, some contained too much pigment and stained their hands, and others were too soft. Little did they know their work would go on to win first prize, reap heaps of publicity, and sell their crayons to a major manufacturer. On the Fourth of July, 1997, Jocelyn attended a kickoff party at the Indianapolis Zoo, where soybean farmers, children, and the media all gathered to celebrate her crayons. She's not kidding when she says, "Food engineering gives you a lot of possibilities."

What Does an Agricultural Food and Processing Engineer Do?

Agricultural food and processing engineers work in food processing and food manufacturing plants. This can include plants that make products such as potato chips and candy or plants that make intermediate products such as soybean oil. The agricultural food and processing engineer's job is to create new processes for the production of biological products such as food and biochemicals, design and plan how to successfully produce these products, including the layout of the processing lines, and assist in the building and maintenance of equipment and processes. These processes can involve mixing, storing, sterilizing,

Definition
Agricultural food and processing engineers design processes and systems for the efficient manufacturing and processing of food products.

Alternative Job Titles
Agricultural engineers
Food processing engineers
Process engineers
Research and development engineers

High School Subjects
Chemistry
Mathematics
Physics

Personal Skills
Mechanical/manipulative
Technical/scientific

Salary Range
$37,120 to $52,340 to $92,000+

Minimum Educational Level
Bachelor's degree

Certification or Licensing
Voluntary

Outlook
About as fast as the average

DOT
013

GOE
02.07.01

NOC
2123

O*NET-SOC
17-2021.00

refrigerating, packaging, extracting, and more. Very simply put, agricultural food and processing engineers figure out how to make food for our consumption.

Agricultural food and process engineering fits under the larger umbrella of agricultural engineering and is closely related to chemical and mechanical engineering. Agricultural engineers may work in natural resources conservation, environmental protection, food processing, and agricultural production. Often, they deal with a single commodity, such as wheat, and design equipment for farm operations and production. But while agricultural engineers may work on farms or in forests, agricultural food and processing engineers work primarily in offices, in laboratories, and on the floors of manufacturing plants. Food process engineering also involves less agricultural science and a lot more chemistry.

An extensive chain of various disciplines is involved with producing food and food products. The chain may start with the agricultural scientist, who deals with the science of growing the food. For example, the agricultural scientist may figure out how to improve the soil or control the pests that damage soybean crops. Next in line is the agricultural engineer, who may design the machinery and equipment needed to harvest those soybeans. The food science technologist or food scientist is involved with microbiology, biochemistry, and food chemistry and may develop ideas about what to do with the soybeans. The food scientist hands off to the agricultural food and processing engineer, who designs the equipment so the plant can produce the finished product. These areas often overlap and are dependent on one another.

Agricultural food and processing engineers usually fall into three primary categories: *research and development (R&D) engineer, project engineer,* and *plant or process engineer.*

The research and development engineer's task is to come up with new or improved food products and processes. Working in laboratories and offices with food scientists and chemists, R&D engineers are responsible for giving us baked potato chips, sugar substitutes, and fat-free salad dressings. They may also focus on improving existing products as well, such as studying and designing the shapes and sizes of macaroni noodles so they will cook and boil to the correct texture and consistency. Combining market research, engineering, and science, R&D engineers study and develop new processes and determine their feasibility and usefulness.

The project engineer takes what the R&D engineer has developed in the laboratory and designs the equipment and processes to make it happen on a larger scale. Relying upon chemical and hydraulic engineering principles, the project engineer has to consider every aspect of the process, such as the number of tanks that will be needed, the number of pumps that will be required, and so on.

The plant or process engineer is responsible for the actual process of producing the final product. After the project engineer has designed the processes and equipment and the installation is complete, the plant or process engineer handles the day-to-day supervision of the plant. This entails making sure

Lingo to Learn

Biochemistry The chemistry of chemical compounds and processes. Biochemistry is used in agricultural food and process engineering to develop new processes and compounds using natural products.

Equipment drawings These diagrams provide technical specifications of equipment and machinery.

Heat transfer Heat transfer refers to the amount of heat that is being lost or transferred through machinery and pipelines.

Piping and instrumentation design (P&ID) A diagram that maps out the entire flow and process of a system and provides details regarding pipelines and location specifics.

Process flow diagram (PFD) A flowchart that illustrates the progression and process of a system.

Upstream/downstream These terms are used to describe the direction and flow of control valves.

the plant is running the way it is designed to and is manufacturing product every day like it is supposed to. The plant or process engineer may supervise the technicians who run the plant, deal with personnel issues, and troubleshoot mechanical problems and equipment failures.

Closely related to the plant or process engineer is the *reliability engineer,* whose task is to ensure that the plant is running efficiently and producing a maximum percentage of product. Training employees, running reports, and setting up systems for measuring reliability are all responsibilities of the reliability engineer.

What Is It Like to Be an Agricultural Food and Processing Engineer?

Jocelyn Wong is a project engineer/reliability engineer for Procter & Gamble's (P&G) Oleanplant

An agricultural engineer tests a computer-directed scanning system used in chicken processing. *(Keith Weller/ U.S. Department of Agriculture)*

in Cincinnati, Ohio. She typically works a 40-hour week, but sometimes the hours can grow longer, depending on project deadlines. Her project engineer duties include designing equipment and processes and getting them into place. The start of her workday is devoted to checking e-mail and messages, making phone calls, and planning the day's activities. She reviews equipment drawings and piping and instrumentation designs (P&IDs), which are like blueprints or maps of the plant from a technical standpoint. If, for instance, they are installing a heat exchanger and a pump, Jocelyn reviews the appropriate P&IDs and drawings to determine how large the condenser is, the size of the motor, where the equipment needs to go, and what other pipelines must go in and out of it.

Jocelyn also meets with vendors or contractors, communicating with them about what needs to be accomplished, including how and when. Jocelyn then finds out about their needs—they may have to obtain specific permits to perform the job, or they may require that the plant be shut down for a certain number of hours in order to complete their tasks. It is Jocelyn's job to follow through on these requests and disseminate the appropriate information to all parties.

Sitting through meetings is another part of an agricultural food and processing engineer's job. Jocelyn usually attends several meetings each day, receiving direction on projects, taking on new assignments, or working on design issues. She always works as a team member, and each project may have about eight members. Sometimes she might lead the effort on a project, while other times she works on one portion.

Jocelyn's reliability engineer tasks include making sure the plant is running the way it was designed to 85 percent of the time. She must make sure that work systems are in place to measure the plant's reliability, and this can include writing reports, training employees, and receiving updates and progress reports from her staff.

Agricultural food and processing engineers work on many projects at once, so it is important to be able to prioritize. "You have to be smart about what you think the priorities are," emphasizes Jocelyn. "Sure I'll have six or seven different things to work on, but if something is more urgent at the time, then that becomes my first priority. It's not like in school where you have one project at a time." It all boils down to the same goal, however: Make sure the plant is running well and producing product. Working on different projects means Jocelyn is always learning something new and that there is plenty of variety in her job.

Jocelyn enjoys most every aspect of being an agricultural food and processing engineer. She likes seeing the fruits of her labor. She says, "You get to use your creativity and see it through to the end, which is very nice. You're working on things that you've designed and you've built." Jocelyn works with people from many different industries to accomplish her tasks, which she finds interesting. "I could work with construction workers, architects, business and accounting people, and cost engineers. It gives you an opportunity to work with many different facets."

> I could work with construction workers, architects, business and accounting people, and cost engineers.

Of course, being an agricultural food and processing engineer can be stressful. Jocelyn works with deadlines all the time, and if she is unable to deliver on a project, everyone else hits a snag as well

and the entire project may be held up. And engineering itself is no day at the park—it's very technical and difficult. Having this technical knowledge, however, is a big plus that can open a lot of doors. "A pro of being an engineer is you have a deep technical understanding of how things work," says Jocelyn, "which is wonderful because you can leverage that, and in 10 years I could go down a completely different path than engineering. I could go into advertising or sales, but I'll always have that technical foundation."

Do I Have What It Takes to Be an Agricultural Food and Processing Engineer?

Agricultural food and processing engineers must have problem-solving skills to analyze difficult concepts and communication skills to express their ideas clearly. Creativity is also critical in order to come up with design ideas and possible solutions to problems. It helps to have technical aptitude, and if you don't have it, you must work to get it. Jocelyn recalls, "I will not lie—college and engineering are very, very hard. You have to be determined and hard working."

An interest in mathematics and the sciences, particularly chemistry and physics, is also important if you are thinking about a career as an agricultural food and processing engineer. You need to be able to work well with others because all projects are team-based, and if you are easily rattled by deadlines, then engineering may not be the right choice. "Engineers work under pressure a lot, because you're always schedule driven," says Jocelyn.

Food and processing engineers work in offices and laboratories, as well as in food processing and manufacturing plants, so you must be willing to get your hands dirty and work with loud machinery in occasionally adverse environments or conditions. The plant Jocelyn works in is located outdoors, which means she must sometimes brave the rain and the cold to accomplish her work.

The technical aspect of engineering threw Jocelyn the biggest curve. "I was never very technical," she recalls. "I was never one of those people who was born to be an engineer. I had to work twice as hard as other engineers." Besides tenacity, Jocelyn possesses other qualities that have helped her succeed as an agricultural food and processing engineer, including

TO BE A SUCCESSFUL AGRICULTURAL FOOD AND PROCESSING ENGINEER, YOU SHOULD . . .

- ○ have good written and verbal communication skills
- ○ enjoy working with others on team-oriented projects
- ○ have problem-solving and analytical thinking skills
- ○ be detail oriented and well organized
- ○ be resourceful and creative

strong initiative and leadership skills. Jocelyn adds, "I'm very quick to say what I don't know, and I'm good at finding the resources to get what I don't know. I'm good at asking questions and being aware of my faults and being able to work on them, thinking of them as challenges rather than faults." Believing in your capabilities, as Jocelyn has proved, can carry you far.

How Do I Become an Agricultural Food and Processing Engineer?

Jocelyn hadn't planned to study engineering in college until her father suggested it. As Jocelyn recalls, "I was more interested in business and management, and it turns out that if you have an engineering degree, you're a much stronger manager." The idea of job security and the flexibility engineering can offer in career choices down the road appealed to her. Jocelyn chose food engineering as her major because "there was a lot of room for creativity," she says.

EDUCATION

High School

To prepare for a career as an agricultural food and processing engineer, focus on math and sciences, such as calculus, algebra, geometry, chemistry, and physics. All of these subjects will come into play as an engineer, and it is important to build up the knowledge base and analytical thinking skills. Jocelyn remembers being inspired by physics projects that required students to create solutions to problems, like how to drop an egg off of a building without having the egg smash on the ground.

Jocelyn suggests getting involved in science fairs and clubs, which will provide you with the opportunity to design and create science projects and compete against other schools. Activities such as these will also help you build up communication skills and learn the art of working as a team member.

Postsecondary Training

A bachelor's degree is required for agricultural food and processing engineers. Jocelyn attended Purdue University in Indiana, majoring in both biochemistry and food process engineering in the school of agricultural and biological engineering. Food engineering programs are often offered jointly by the departments of agricultural engineering, chemical engineering, and food science and technology.

Jocelyn enjoyed her upper-division classes more than her core engineering courses. "I hated my beginning college classes," she recalls, "like the basics, like physics and chemistry. But later on, in your junior and senior year, you start to take classes like plant engineering." These project-based courses gave Jocelyn the opportunity to work with fellow students, creating and designing plants. "We had to come up with an idea of a plant we wanted to build, and we came up with a winery. So we had to do lab scale tests to make wine, and then we had to get into the nitty gritty of actually building a plant that makes wine. So we had to get into what equipment you would use, and so on." Seeing a project through from start to finish was a rewarding learning experience for Jocelyn.

Joining a student chapter of a professional organization such as the American Society of Agricultural Engineers or the American Institute of Chemical Engineers is a good idea while you're in college. You are able to meet engineers working in the field, thus gaining the opportunity to establish contacts, build relationships with those in the industry, and learn more about the field. Jocelyn says, "I tried to be as involved as I could in the organizations so I could learn more about the job and what I was getting myself into." Jocelyn and a friend founded the Society of Biochemical and Food Process Engineers at Purdue University, which is still going strong.

CERTIFICATION OR LICENSING

There is no certification or licensing specifically geared toward agricultural food and processing engineers. Most employers require only that their engineers have graduated from an engineering program accredited by the Accreditation Board for Engineering and Technology (ABET). Engineers may, if they choose, earn a professional engineering license from the National Society of Professional Engineers. To begin the process, college students take a written examination during their senior year on fundamental engineering principles. If they pass and graduate from school, they gain the distinction of being an "engineer in training" (EIT). After four years in the workforce as an engineer, EITs take another written examination. If they pass, they become professional engineers (PEs). PEs can sign off on engineering plans and drawings or start their own businesses.

SCHOLARSHIPS AND GRANTS

Scholarship and grant opportunities are plentiful for students in engineering disciplines. It would be a good idea to contact various associations and professional organizations with engineers as members, such as the American Society of Agricultural Engineers, the National Society of Professional Engineers, or the American Chemical Society. Universities offer a wide variety of scholarships in various departments and with assorted eligibility requirements. Contact the financial aid office or a guidance counselor for further information.

Large companies are another source of financial aid. Companies that hire and employ engineers are likely to offer scholarship programs for aspiring engineers. Some may also provide summer work opportunities as part of a scholarship award. Your school advisor or guidance counselor should have access to this information, but you can also find this information at the library or on the Internet. In fact, most large companies have Web sites that list scholarship and grant information.

INTERNSHIPS AND VOLUNTEERSHIPS

Internships are common for agricultural food and processing engineers, and Jocelyn recommends them highly. "I would say that 75 percent of the people I graduated with had an internship or co-op experience." Jocelyn participated in a cooperative work-study program in which she alternated semesters and worked in the industry. She also had two summer internships where she worked for different companies and gained hands-on experience. Engineering internships usually pay well, which is another bonus.

Internships are an excellent way to learn what the job of an agricultural food and processing engineer may be like after graduation. Jocelyn enjoyed her internship experiences immensely, and they reminded her why she was in school studying engineering. "The classes are frustrating at first, but after you actually get a taste of what the industry is like, it is extremely satisfying."

Who Will Hire Me?

Agricultural food and processing engineers are needed in almost all facets of the food industry, and food manufacturing plants and food processing companies are the primary employers. Entry-level agricultural food and processing engineers often begin as plant or project engineers, and some may find positions in research and development. Jocelyn's fellow graduates landed jobs with companies such as General Mills, Kraft, Calistoga, Frito-Lay, Campbell Soup Company, and other large companies.

Consulting agencies also hire agricultural food and processing engineers. These agencies consult with a variety of food processing plants and offer solutions to manufacturing problems, suggest ways to make the plants more efficient and more productive, and design equipment and processes. Consulting jobs often involve travel. Some jobs may be available with companies that manufacture machinery or food-related equipment as well.

The best way to find a job if you are in college is to go through your school's career planning and placement center. Jocelyn found her job thanks to Purdue University's placement center, which, she says, offers a great placement program. Recruiters often visit campuses to meet with and interview prospective employees. Purdue, for example, hosts an industry roundtable every year, with hundreds of companies in attendance. Engineering students can go from table to table, passing out resumes, learning about the companies and what they can offer, networking, interviewing, and finding entry-level jobs. Many of Jocelyn's classmates landed jobs through the industry roundtable.

Networking and contacts are another avenue for finding jobs in the industry, so it is important to be involved with professional organizations and clubs. These organizations frequently publish trade magazines, and it is possible to find job openings listed. Many professional associations also host annual conferences or national meetings, which is another opportunity to find out about jobs. The American Chemical Society (ACS), for example, provides various career services to its members. ACS has a national database of job openings that matches members' qualifications with appropriate jobs, offers employment clearinghouses where members can interview with hiring companies at ACS meetings, and has career consultants on staff who can help you with your resume, provide interview tips, and get you on a career path.

Some agricultural food and processing engineers have found jobs through headhunters and placement agencies, while others have discovered job opportunities through classified advertisements in newspapers. Almost all professional organizations and major newspapers can be found on the Web, which is an excellent tool for finding job leads or openings and for researching companies you may be interested in working for. Large companies often list job opportunities on their Web sites, along with the option to apply directly online.

Where Can I Go from Here?

Jocelyn has been working for Procter & Gamble for more than two years, and she plans to continue working there, gaining more experience and working on as many projects as possible. Concurrently, she would like to attend school and earn a master's degree in business administration. Because Jocelyn enjoys interacting with others, she hopes to shift away from project engineering at some point: "I would like to go into manufacturing where I work more with people and see the day-to-day business."

Agricultural food and processing engineers typically advance within their companies as they gain more experience. Advancement usually entails additional responsibility, such as supervising more employees, including engineers, and overseeing larger-scale projects. A vice president of engineering may be in charge of an entire company function, such as engineering for all salted snacks, for example. The job of a vice president tends to focus on the business management end more heavily than the actual engineering end.

Section heads or department managers of companies manage entire divisions or sections of a plant. A section head, for example, may be in charge of all engineering projects for a specific product or oversee a plant start-up, which includes the design and building of a new plant. Section heads must plan, direct, and coordinate all activities and departments to accomplish the overall goals. Section heads report to vice presidents.

Also within a company, technical leaders or supervisors oversee large projects and delegate work to other engineers. Technical leaders typically tend to

---

ADVANCEMENT POSSIBILITIES

Vice presidents direct the operations of various company units, such as engineering or manufacturing.

Section heads or **department managers** supervise and manage divisions of manufacturing plants and oversee technical leaders.

Technical leaders or **supervisors** oversee teams of engineers and coordinate large-scale projects.

Consultants work on a contract basis for different companies, undertaking a variety of projects.

---

focus on the business management and finance end of projects, and they leave much of the engineering work to the engineers. Technical leaders report to section heads and may be in charge of a subsection, such as the controls portion of a project, the packing area, or specific unit operations.

Independent consultants visit different food companies and work on various projects on a contract basis. For example, a smaller food processing plant may not require a full-time agricultural food and processing engineer, or it may have a unique project or problem it is having trouble resolving.

Agricultural food and processing engineers can also go into teaching. Teaching at a two-year college may be possible with a master's degree, but teaching at a four-year university requires a doctoral degree.

What Are the Salary Ranges?

According to the *Occupational Outlook Handbook*, median annual earnings of agricultural engineers were $52,340 in 2003. Those in the middle 50 percent had salaries between $41,880 and $73,770, while those in the lowest paid 10 percent earned less than $37,120. Agricultural engineers in the highest paid 10 percent earned more than $89,910.

Earnings vary widely based on educational level, years of experience and type of employer. In its 2003 salary survey the Institute of Food Technologists states that the starting salary for those with a bachelor's degree was $40,000; with a master's degree the starting salary was $49,250; and with a Ph.D. the starting salary was $68,000. With more than five years experience salaries ranged from $57,148 to $75,000. With experience, those employed by food and beverage manufacturer/processors earned between $62,410 and $90,250 while those working for food ingredient manufacturer/suppliers earned between $70,800 and $92,000, depending on level of education. The IFT also notes employees in management, sales and marketing, and purchasing earn more than those employed in research and development or scientific/technical areas.

Agricultural food and processing engineers usually receive comprehensive benefits packages.

What Is the Job Outlook?

Agricultural food and processing engineering is a relatively young field, and specific outlook information is scarce. According to Jocelyn, however, the job outlook is extremely positive. She says, "If you think about it, food is a necessity. In today's age, people want more convenient foods and healthier foods. The need for food engineers and the ability to do that kind of work is increasing tremendously." As entire households enter the workforce, packaged and prepared foods are growing in popularity. In addition, the increasingly health-conscious public demands foods lower in fat and calories. The shelves of every grocery store are lined with fat-free and low-fat products, and new products appear regularly. Jocelyn also points to the worldwide population boom, noting that food processing engineers are needed to find ways to feed all the people.

The *Occupational Outlook Handbook* reports that employment of agricultural engineers is expected to grow about as fast as the average. As technology advances and competition increases, companies will be compelled to come up with new ideas and improve on old products and designs more rapidly. This, in turn, means companies must maximize production and make sure manufacturing processes are as efficient as possible, and this is where agricultural food and processing engineers will enter the picture.

Biochemistry is a growing field within agricultural food and process engineering, which is lucky for Jocelyn, who majored in it along with food processing

engineering. "Biochemistry," explains Jocelyn, "is using natural products, like soybeans, and using it for a variety of different purposes that we never have even dreamed of. The biochemistry field is going to be really hot." Olestra, the fat substitute used in potato chips and other snack foods, is an example of what biochemistry can provide the public.

Although there are few statistics concerning agricultural food and process engineering, Jocelyn feels her job is secure and that the industry she selected is growing. Jocelyn and her fellow graduates all work for well-established companies and are in demand. "We're contacted by headhunters all the time," she declares.

How Do I Learn More?

PROFESSIONAL ORGANIZATIONS

The following organizations provide information on careers, accredited schools and educational programs, scholarship opportunities, and employers:

American Chemical Society
1155 16th Street, NW
Washington, DC 20036
800-227-5558
http://www.acs.org

American Institute of Chemical Engineers
Three Park Avenue
New York, NY 10016-5991
212-591-7392
careerservices@aiche.org
http://www.aiche.org

American Society of Agricultural Engineers
2950 Niles Road
St. Joseph, MI 49085
269-429-0300
hq@asae.org
http://www.asae.org

Biochemical and Food Process Engineering Club
Purdue University
1146 ABE Building
West Lafayette, IN 47907
765-494-1167
elarson@purdue.edu
http://pasture.ecn.purdue.edu/~bfpe

Institute of Food Technologists
525 West Van Buren, Suite 1000
Chicago, IL 60607
312-782-8424

info@ift.org

http://www.ift.org

National Society of Professional Engineers
1420 King Street
Alexandria, VA 22314
703-684-2800
http://www.nspe.org

BIBLIOGRAPHY

The following is a sampling of materials relating to the professional concerns and development of agricultural food and processing engineers:

Connor, John M., and William A. Schiek. *Food Processing: An Industrial Powerhouse in Transition:* 2d ed. New York: John Wiley & Sons, 1997.

Heldman, Dennis R. *Encyclopedia of Agricultural, Food, and Biological Engineering.* New York: Marcel Dekker, 2003.

Mather, Robin. *A Garden of Unearthly Delights: Bioengineering and the Future of Food.* New York: E. P. Dutton, 1995.

Smith, P. G. *Introduction to Food Process Engineering.* New York: Plenum US, 2003.

AGRICULTURAL TECHNICIANS

L loyd Nelson walks across the farmer's field with a notebook in hand. He stops to dig the toe of his boot into the ground, checking to see how deeply the rain water has soaked into the soil. He glances out across the wide-open field. The only building in sight is a farmhouse alongside the winding gravel road. He catches the scent of sage in the wind and regrets having to go back to the office, where he'll have to sit behind a desk and report today's work.

Lloyd hasn't been to this spot of land for three months. He's here now to check that his conservation planning has worked for the land. He looks out across the dam he designed. Because of the recent rain, the water sits trapped in the dam, soaking into the soil. Pleased to see all his plans in place and successful, Lloyd marks down the results of another completed job.

What Does an Agricultural Technician Do?

If you've spent even one day on a farm, you've seen the variety of hard work that goes into keeping the farm productive. Raising livestock or crops requires a careful understanding of natural resources and animal, insect, and plant ecosystems. A farmer must know about complex machinery, structures, and irrigation systems. And different animals and crops have different demands: Someone with a pecan orchard in New Mexico must have a different understanding of the soil and irrigation systems than someone growing corn in Nebraska or tobacco in Virginia; a beekeeper in Oregon must understand different structures and controlled environments than a rancher raising Longhorn cattle in Texas. Agriculture offers diverse job opportunities for researchers, engineers, scientists, and technicians all across the country.

Agricultural technicians work with farmers and ranchers to help them use their resources and equipment for maximum efficiency and to keep up on the latest and most economical tools and designs in farming. With their knowledge of biology, the environment, engineering, and design, technicians bring together the work of many professionals. They study animals and

Definition
Agricultural technicians assist engineers, scientists, and conservationists in food, plant, soil, and animal research, production, and processing. Some perform tests and experiments to improve crop yield and quality, or to increase animal and plant resistance to diseases, insects and other hazards. Others work with animal breeding and nutrition projects.

Alternative Job Titles
Agricultural engineering technicians
Conservation technicians
Science technicians

High School Subjects
Agriculture
Biology
Chemistry

Personal Skills
Leadership/management
Technical/scientific

Salary Range
$18,700 to $29,200 to $47,300

Minimum Education Level
High school diploma

Certification or Licensing
Voluntary

Outlook
More slowly than the average

DOT
624

GOE
03.03.01

NOC
7316

O*NET-SOC
45-2091.00, 49-3041.00

their environments and help develop healthy facilities for raising them. They design electrical, irrigation, and food processing systems. They improve farm machinery, operate the equipment, and lay out plans for the conservation of natural resources.

Agricultural technicians can choose to specialize in one of four areas: food science, plant science, soil science, or animal science. The type of work performed varies according to the specialization.

Fruits, vegetables, grains, baked goods, candy, beverages, meat and dairy products, and other foods all require processing and preparation. Food and processing engineering involves using agricultural materials for food, feed, fiber, and industrial products. Technicians who specialize in food science devise ways to preserve the food's taste and nutrition and design systems for the proper shipment and storage of food. They study the physical properties of food materials and determine the best ways to heat, refrigerate, and dry the materials. They are also involved in handling, packaging, and product development. Agricultural technicians involved in food science may also enforce government regulations and inspect food processing plants to uphold the standards of sanitation, safety, quality, and waste management.

Plant science involves agronomy, crop science, entomology, and plant breeding. Agricultural technicians may conduct tests and experiments to improve the quality and yield of crops or study various ways to increase the resistance of plants to insects and disease. They may also work to improve seed quality and the nutritional value of crops. Agricultural technicians in plant science help farmers and scientists produce the largest, healthiest crops possible, factoring in variables such as pest control, disease, crop management, and genetic engineering to breed stronger plants.

Agricultural technicians who specialize in soil science study soil composition and its relationship to crop and plant growth. This includes the effects of various fertilizers, crop rotation, and plowing and sowing practices. Technicians may also conduct erosion studies and diagnose and solve soil problems. Conservation of natural resources is also the task of an agricultural technician. Technicians design and install irrigation systems and dams and lay out conservation plans.

Animal science involves the nutrition, genetics, growth, and reproduction of domestic farm animals. Agricultural technicians working in animal science study animals in relation to their environments and develop adequate ventilation, management, and sanitation systems so the animals will be healthy enough to produce high-quality, plentiful products, including milk and eggs. They may assist farmers in designing or upgrading animal housing structures, and they devise nutrition and feeding plans for livestock.

Agricultural technicians often work with power and machinery, designing equipment for the efficient harvesting of crops, the baling of hay, and other field operations. They help manufacturers and engineers develop and research the products that will make farm work easier and more economical, which may involve acquiring new machinery or upgrading existing products. Agricultural technicians also assist in the design of buildings, such as storage structures for grains or waste.

Electrical and electronic systems are also part of an agricultural technician's area of expertise. Farms and other agricultural producers require electrical systems to operate the variety of machines used in their daily work for storage, refrigeration, heating, irrigation, and grain and feed handling. Technicians provide farms with efficient electrical distribution systems, taking these systems from the design stages to installation.

What Is It Like to Be an Agricultural Technician?

Lloyd Nelson has been working for the U.S. Department of Agriculture (USDA) for over 23 years. As a technician for the Soil Conservation Service, he works in many different areas of agriculture, from engineering and conservation planning to pipeline design and concrete testing. "I'm a jack-of-all-trades,"

Lingo to Learn

Aquaculture Working with the quality, use, and discharge of water.

Biotechnology Working with living systems to aid in the development of commercial processes and products.

Cryopreservation The storage of cells in suspended animation at -196 degrees Celsius; used for the storage of plant species that produce seeds.

Field mapping Profiling a field on the basis of yield performance.

Microirrigation Irrigation distributing a small amount of water; irrigation by drip or trickle.

Watershed The region or area drained by a river or stream.

he says, referring to the diversity of projects he heads. His job involves soil and range conservation, work with irrigated crop land, water management, and dairy and waste management. And this list continues to grow as he learns more about agriculture and conservation.

Most of Lloyd's work hours are spent in the field, and his remaining hours are devoted to administrative duties, engineering work, and educating the public about conservation. "I spend about 70 percent of my time in the field, surveying and installing conservation systems for agricultural producers and landowners," Lloyd says. Another 20 percent of his time is devoted to paperwork and entering data in the computer. He spends the remaining 10 percent on design and engineering work.

A typical day begins early for Lloyd; he usually checks into the office at about 7:00 A.M. to read his mail and retrieve messages. The calls start coming in shortly after he arrives—calls from farmers and ranchers requesting conservation planning. Lloyd schedules meetings with these landowners, giving priority to those with land in specific areas. The Soil and Water Conservation District Board determines these priority areas based on conservation needs. "But I hate to have to keep somebody waiting a month," Lloyd says. "My job is to get out there and get conservation [practices started] on the land."

During his initial meeting with a farmer, Lloyd gathers information, including the farmer's thoughts, plans, and conservation objectives. "I have to be pretty thorough," Lloyd says. "I have to get involved in solving a problem. I approach the problem like it's my own, so I can provide the best solution." He not only tries to find the best solution for the farm, but the most cost-efficient one as well. "And I look for shortcuts," he says, "ways to get the job done as quickly as I can." He later visits the actual job site for layout, design, and surveying. Once the project is complete, and conservation practices are in place, Lloyd schedules follow-up visits to make sure everything is going as planned. Lloyd must also document all his work, providing full reports of his goals and achievements.

Though most jobs for agricultural technicians don't require certification, Lloyd is certified by the American Concrete Institute in field testing. With this certification, he has worked with the design and management of pipelines, and has served as concrete inspector and concrete surveyor on various projects.

Lloyd generally works a 40-hour workweek either in the field or in the office. He also spends some time traveling from farm to farm and from farm to office. The most active months are between April and October, when farmers use their land for summer crops.

Do I Have What It Takes to Be an Agricultural Technician?

Agricultural technicians must have the skills necessary to communicate ideas clearly and completely both in speech and writing. Farmers and agricultural professionals work closely with technicians and must be able to rely on the technician's perceptions, planning, and reports. They also must be able to trust a technician's creative solutions to complex problems in agricultural production.

Lloyd credits much of his success to working well alongside others. "I can get along with just about anybody I come into contact with," he says. This rapport makes it easier to gather information from the farmers and to get the answers to his many questions. With this clear line of communication, he can offer good solutions to a farmer's problems.

The problem solving itself can be difficult and requires a lot of creativity, but Lloyd enjoys these challenges. "I like solving other people's problems," he says, "and I like being responsible for getting the work done." Sometimes the challenges for an agricultural technician can involve design and engineering practices, so a background in math, mechanics, and the sciences is valuable.

> I like solving other people's problems, and I like being responsible for getting the work done.

A familiarity with and interest in farming can give a technician an understanding of the terminology and practices of farm work. Lloyd was hired at the USDA after having grown up on a farm, and he continues to pursue his agricultural interests at home as well as at work. "I love growing plants," he says. "I have a backyard that looks like a jungle." Although you don't have to have lived on a farm to get a job as an agricultural technician, you should have an interest in nature and the outdoors. You may be spending many hours in the field focusing on natural resources, plant growth, or animal life. A curiosity in one or all of these areas will direct you in your research and design.

Lloyd enjoys the variety of work available in agriculture, and he welcomes the challenges, but he wishes there were more opportunities for technicians to advance. The USDA offers many opportunities for advancement but has a basic education requirement for professional positions. Although Lloyd does work similar to that of professional farm planners, he can't move into that position without the minimum number of college credit hours.

How Do I Become an Agricultural Technician?

Before going to work for the USDA, Lloyd took some community college courses specific to his interests in agriculture. Having lived on a farm, he was familiar with farm practices and terminology, and this helped him with his course work and his on-the-job training. Lloyd fondly remembers his on-the-job training, made easier by the experienced and helpful engineers and employees he worked with.

EDUCATION

High School

Courses in the agricultural sciences will give you a good background in farm study and might also provide you with field experience. The National FFA (Future Farmers of America) Organization has chapters all over the nation and offers many programs for those interested in agriculture. You can learn about farm practices, agricultural issues, and business management. You can acquire hands-on experience operating farm machinery and equipment, raising livestock, and identifying plants and trees. Your school should be able to provide you with information about your local chapter.

If your high school doesn't offer courses specifically in agricultural science, any science courses can prepare you for agricultural work. Math courses will prepare you for design and engineering. Also, register for any course that will give you an

---

To Be a Successful Agricultural Technician, You Should . . .

○ be able to communicate and work well with people

○ enjoy working outdoors

○ be willing to accept responsibility

○ have an understanding of math and science

○ have a curiosity about plants, animals, or insects

---

understanding of electrical systems and electronics. Courses that require reading and composition can help you to develop the communication skills you need for working with farmers and agricultural professionals. And don't ignore computer classes—more and more farms are relying upon sophisticated computer systems for farm management.

Your state may have an education commission that can provide information about high school work-experience programs. These programs combine classroom study with on-the-job experience.

Postsecondary Training

While formal postsecondary training is not required to become an agricultural technician, more two-year schools are offering associate's degrees in agricultural technology and related fields. This schooling can provide you with a solid foundation and technical training that will be helpful in the field. Course work completed in an agricultural technology program can also be transferred and applied toward a four-year degree if you choose to continue your education. In fact, many of the two-year schools have cooperative programs with four-year colleges or universities, which means you can take classes at the four-year college while enrolled in the two-year school. Some of the courses you may take include science and management of range lands, forests and watersheds, fish and wildlife, local and regional landscapes, resource planning and design, agricultural mechanics, and computers.

Other postsecondary opportunities for agricultural technicians are emerging as well and can be

In-depth

Agriculture for Today and Tomorrow

Precision agriculture is the up and coming trend in agriculture and crop management. Precision agriculture, also known as precision farming, prescription farming, and site-specific farming, utilizes computers and technology to increase the efficiency and yield of crops and farms. Making use of satellites and global positioning systems (GPS), farmers can map fields, detect crop yields, study and assess the pH levels in the soil, and tailor the soil content and fertilizer in fields. For instance, a farmer drives an all-terrain vehicle equipped with a computerized card over a field. The vehicle is hooked into a satellite system that maps out the field as the farmer progresses across the field. This card can then be downloaded onto a computer system that will map out the field into grids. Soil samples can then be taken from each of the grids and tested for mineral content. The farmer or agricultural technician can then make fertilizer recommendations and program prescriptions for each grid, place the prescriptions on a computer card, insert the card into a spreader truck, and drive the truck over the field. The card will tell the truck how much lime or other minerals to spread into each grid, making the farmer's job much easier and more manageable.

|||||||||||||||||||||||||||||||||||||||||||||||||||||||||||||||||||

attributed to the increase in technological demands in farming and the proliferation of larger, commercial farms. For example, Hopkinsville Community College in Hopkinsville, Kentucky, offers a one-year certificate program for agricultural technicians. Credits can be used toward a two-year degree as well. The certificate program was developed out of a need for technicians trained in modern agricultural techniques. The program focuses on farm operations and management, emphasizing hands-on learning.

Many universities and colleges offer cooperative education programs that can give you full- or part-time work experience as you pursue a degree. This can sometimes lead directly to a professional position. Check with your adviser or career placement office. You may also want to look into continuing education. The National FFA offers a variety of programs for those who work in the agriculture industry.

CERTIFICATION OR LICENSING

Certification is generally not required for agricultural technicians. Technicians who apply herbicides or pesticides must be licensed, but most agricultural technicians need not seek licensing. The American Society of Agronomy (ASA) offers a Certified Crop Advisor (CCA) Program that requires you to pass international and local examinations. Applicants must also have up to four years of education and experience, although a college degree is not mandatory. The ASA, along with the Crop Science Society of America and the Soil Science Society of America, offers other certification programs. The programs require bachelor's degrees and professional work experience.

SCHOLARSHIPS AND GRANTS

The National FFA Organization offers scholarships to students in agriculture, as well as contests and monetary awards. Colleges offering instruction in agricultural technology and related fields may also offer scholarships, and you should also research large agricultural companies and farms for financial aid opportunities.

If you choose to pursue a degree in agricultural engineering or engineering technology, you can contact the American Society of Agricultural Engineers for scholarship information. The American Chemical Society and the American Institute of Biological Sciences can also direct you toward fellowships available in agricultural study Be sure to allow plenty of time for the application process.

INTERNSHIPS AND VOLUNTEERSHIPS

There are many opportunities for internships and volunteerships. The National FFA Organization and your local FFA chapter can provide you with information and resources. Some schools collaborate with farmers and provide summer fieldwork opportunities for high school students. You may wish to contact local farms or agricultural organizations to find out about internships or to volunteer your time.

Some two-year college programs require students to complete internships before granting degrees. Contact your adviser or placement office for information. You may also request information about internships in your area by writing to the USDA.

Who Will Hire Me?

Lloyd was recruited by the USDA just a few weeks out of high school. The Soil Conservation Service was looking for young workers with a farm background. Lloyd had already become familiar with the USDA, having met some of the engineers and conservationists through past farm business and also through the FFA.

Federal, state, and local governments are actively involved in protecting natural resources and regularly employ technicians. The USDA also hires technicians for work with the Agricultural Research Service, the Bureau of Land Management, the Fish and Wildlife Service, the Forest Service, and the National Park Service. Write the branch offices of USDA agencies for career information.

Technicians work with manufacturing companies, testing and selling tractors, farm implements, and other equipment. Agricultural supply organizations, grain and feed handling companies, and electrical utilities also hire technicians.

Agricultural workers are needed in most stages of food processing and are employed by meat packers, distribution companies, dairy companies, vegetable canning companies, and other food product and processing businesses. Large farms also employ agricultural technicians to help operate and manage all stages of farm production.

Where Can I Go from Here?

Lloyd has received some credit from the local community college, but he needs to take nine more credit hours to move into a professional position with the USDA. "There are good opportunities for advancement," he says, "if you've got the education."

> ### ADVANCEMENT POSSIBILITIES
>
> **Agricultural equipment design engineers** design agricultural machinery and equipment.
>
> **Agricultural equipment test engineers** conduct tests on agricultural machinery and equipment.
>
> **Agricultural research engineers** conduct research to develop agricultural machinery and equipment.
>
> **Agricultural scientists** study farm crops and animals, devising ways to improve quality and increase quantity through research and development.

By taking community college or university courses specific to agriculture, technicians can meet the basic education requirements for advancement and better pay. Lloyd plans to get the credit hours necessary to move into a farm planner position.

Agricultural technicians can continue with schooling and earn higher degrees, such as bachelor's and master's degrees. Technicians may become agricultural research engineers, agricultural scientists, agricultural equipment design engineers, or agricultural equipment test engineers, just to name a few. Technicians who earn bachelor's degrees often shift to more research-oriented positions.

Technicians can also move into farm management and administration, supervising personnel and overall operation of farms.

What Are the Salary Ranges?

According to the Occupational Outlook Handbook, in 2003 the average annual salary biological science technicians working for the federal government was $30,440. In 2002, the median hourly wage of agricultural technicians $13.74 or about $28,579 annually.

Wages vary depending on the region and the technician's educational background and experience. According to U.S. Department of Labor Career InfoNet, in 2003 the median annual earnings for agricultural technicians were $29,200. The lowest paid 10 percent earned $18,700, and the highest paid 10 percent earned $47,300. Technicians working for the USDA are eligible for benefits, including health, life, and retirement.

What Is the Job Outlook?

The U.S. Department of Labor predicts that while employment overall of science technicians should increase about as fast as the average; however, employment for agricultural technicians is projected to grow more slowly than the average through 2012, due in part to limited growth in agriculture. Despite the slow growth, biotechnology research will remain important as more people become concerned about the conservation of natural resources.

Agricultural technicians are needed to put conservation practices in place. Management of crops and pests without the use of harmful chemicals will create challenges for agricultural technicians. Environmentally sound production systems are also needed, meaning more jobs in service, sales, development, and application of mechanical systems.

Food product processing is another area expected to expand as engineers and scientists devise new ways to ship and preserve more kinds of foods. By keeping up on the latest in agricultural equipment and products, students can get a sense of which areas of agriculture are growing and developing.

Technicians considering work with the USDA should keep track of which areas receive the best funding. When a USDA program must cut back spending, it will sometimes phase out technician positions and rely only on the work of professionals. Also, because of the competitive job pool, the USDA's educational requirements are becoming more demanding, and technicians may have a difficult time securing a federal job without at least a bachelor's degree.

How Do I Learn More?

PROFESSIONAL ORGANIZATIONS

The following organizations can provide information regarding careers in agriculture, scholarship opportunities, accredited schools, and more:

American Chemical Society
1155 16th Street, NW
Washington, DC 20036

800-227-5558
http://www.chemistry.org

American Institute of Biological Sciences
1444 I Street, NW
Washington, DC 20005
202-628-1500
http://www.aibs.org

American Society of Agricultural Engineers
2950 Niles Road
St. Joseph, MI 49085
269-628-1500
hq@asae.org
http://asae.org

American Society of Agronomy
677 South Segoe Road
Madison, WI 53711
608-273-8080
http://www.agronomy.org

Crop Science Society of America
677 South Segoe Road
Madison, WI 53711
608-273-8080
http://www.crops.org

National FFA Organization
PO Box 68960
Indianapolis, IN 46268-0960
317-802-6060
http://www.ffa.org

Soil Science Society of America
677 South Segoe Road
Madison, WI 53711
608-273-8080
http://www.soils.org

U.S. Department of Agriculture
1400 Independence Avenue, SW
Washington, DC 20250
202-720-2791
http://www.usda.gov

BIBLIOGRAPHY

The following is a sampling of materials relating to the professional concerns and development of agricultural technicians:

Fasulo, Mike et al. *Careers in the Environment.* Lincolnwood, Ill.: VGM Career Horizons, 2000.

White, William C. et al. *Opportunities in Farming and Agricultural Careers.* Lincolnwood, Ill.: VGM Career Horizons, 1996.

AIR TRAFFIC CONTROLLERS

In addition to such low-tech equipment as binoculars, telephones, and boards with magnetic strips, air traffic controller Jim Weber uses a number of different kinds of computers. "Air traffic controllers in the tower use radar computers called ARTS, automated radar terminal systems," he says. "The ARTS displays aircraft identification and flight plan data, as well as speed and altitude."

Doppler weather radar in the tower can help make ground controllers aware of powerfully severe wind effects capable of knocking aircraft from the sky. Digital bright tower indicator equipment (D-BRITE) provides visual display in both day and night conditions and is used to direct aircraft on the runways and around the terminals.

What Does an Air Traffic Controller Do?

Like traffic cops at any busy intersection, *air traffic controllers (ATCs)* regulate the flow of airplane traffic into, out of, and around airports. With thousands of flights operating every day, safety is a primary concern, and the ATC makes certain that airplanes follow their designated flight paths and maintain safe distances from one another. The ATC keeps flights operating on schedule, helping to minimize delays. The ATC also provides pilots with information about weather conditions that will affect their landing or takeoff or even their ability to handle their planes. ATCs alert pilots to other factors, such as geographical terrain features, the presence and movement of other aircraft in the area, ground taxi instructions, and which air routes—the highways in the sky—the pilot should take. Other ATCs guide aircraft through emergency situations or conduct searches for late or lost planes.

Using radar, radio, computer automation, and their own eyes, ATCs usually coordinate a number of planes at once, preparing one plane for takeoff while advising another plane on its approach, and at the same time directing a third plane safely through the airport's airspace. As an airplane leaves an ATC's airspace—which can include up to 40 miles—the ATC passes control of the plane to an en route air traffic

controller farther along the plane's flight path. An ATC who is a radar controller accepts control from an en route controller for an airplane entering his or her airspace.

ATCs must be able to recognize, remember, and react to a great deal of information, often coming simultaneously, such as an airplane's registration number and flight plans, registration and flight plans of any other aircraft nearby (coming to them as blips on a radar screen), the airplane's speed and altitude, the type of craft, and the instructions they have already given to the pilots. ATCs must be able to respond quickly to every situation and issue clear and decisive instructions.

An ATC is also responsible for relaying a variety of information to other air traffic control positions

---

Definition
Air traffic controllers organize and direct the movement of aircraft into, out of, and between airports.

Alternative Job Title
Air traffic control specialists
Flight service specialists

High School Subjects
Computer science
Mathematics
Physics

Personal Skills
Communication/ideas
Leadership/management

Salary Range
$55,340 to $97,020 to $136,170

Minimum Educational Level
Some postsecondary training

Certification or Licensing
Required

Outlook
About as fast as the average

DOT
193

GOE
07.02.01

NOC
2272

O*NET-SOC
53-2021.00

Lingo to Learn

Altitude This describes the altitude above "mean sea level," not the altitude above the ground. Altitudes are also in hundreds and thousands of feet.

Call sign The unique emblem and three-letter code assigned to each airline that air traffic controllers must memorize. For example, America West's call sign is a cactus and its code AWE.

Flight number A number that always comes before an airline's call sign, usually associated with specific routes and airlines.

Heading (Direction) A spoken number that reflects the direction an airplane is traveling, such as 360 is north. The numbers correspond to a compass.

Speed How fast an airplane is traveling. It is measured in knots, not miles per hour with 100 knots equal to 115.2 miles per hour.

Wake turbulence Also called "wing-tip vortices," this is the shape of the air, which resembles a tornado on its side, that follows an airplane when lift is created by the wings. The larger the airplane the more wake turbulence it generates.

and centers. And, because it can often take an hour or more for an aircraft to pass through his or her airspace, an ATC must be able to maintain intense concentration over a long period of time.

The duties of an air traffic controller can vary from airport to airport and among the several types of traffic control centers. In a large (Class V) facility, such as an international airport where traffic is particularly heavy, an ATC may receive a specific assignment, for example, as a ground controller. At a combined facility, typically where traffic is less heavy, an ATC can be charged with all the various air traffic control functions. Controllers at an en route facility usually work in teams of three or more, with each team responsible for conducting traffic within a specific portion of the airway. Flight service stations link all the air traffic towers together, coordinating flight data and weather and terrain conditions. In all cases, ATCs

never work alone. Teamwork is an important part of maintaining the safety of our skies.

What Is It Like to Be an Air Traffic Controller?

From a tower in Atlantic City, New Jersey, Jim Weber guides aircraft on and off the airport runways. He begins his shift by reviewing changes in the work environment. "There are always notices and informational bulletins that come out for runway closures and openings, lights, equipment," Jim says. "You make sure you're up on all the changes." Jim may be scheduled either for the tower or the radar room. After receiving his assignment, he relieves the ATC, then works for an hour before his first break of approximately 30 minutes or more. "You'll continue that rotation through the day," he says. "The thing about controllers is they have no collateral duties. Their job is to talk to airplanes and that's it."

In the tower, Jim relies on a special radar scope which can be read in the daylight. "You're using binoculars, your eyes, your brain," he says. In the radar room, Jim uses a variety of computers. "You're still using radar, lots of phone lines, lots of different types of computers, whether it's a weather computer, or a flight plan computer." Jim describes the work as constant decision making. "Every time you sit down, you have to figure out which airplane's going to be first, which is going to be last. There isn't just one way to do something. There are many ways to skin that cat, but you have to decide what's best for that situation. Current winds, visibility, the type of airplane, the type of pilot. It pretty much always changes."

When a plane is departing the airport, the controllers first signal the pilot about the visibility, the direction and speed of the wind, weather, and other conditions that will affect the flight. The plane is then guided along the taxiways to the runway, where it is cleared for takeoff, and then directed through the airport's airspace. From there, en route controllers are notified and direct the pilot along the flight's designated air route. At all times during the flight, the plane is kept under the guidance and direction of the team of ATCs.

Generally, an airport's traffic schedule remains constant. The same flights arrive and depart on a schedule that doesn't vary. This helps controllers know what other airplanes are out there and allows them to act quickly when anything goes wrong. Because ATCs are highly trained, not only in the Federal Aviation Administration (FAA) Training Academy but on the job as well, they become instinctually aware of the skies around them.

Heather Kennedy works as an en route ATC. "I control en route traffic from over North Dakota to the western part of Nevada, from Canada down to the southern part of Nevada," she says. "We work en route traffic as well as clear aircraft off small airports that have no control towers." Still in the training stages, Heather works as a radar associate. "You're working all the non-radar parts of air traffic control: You're clearing the aircraft on and off the airport, you're taking care of the strips, the bay, looking for traffic that's coming ahead of you."

Though the work can be stressful at times, Heather believes the environment is relaxed and casual. "Everybody is very team-oriented," she says. "What goes on in the control room is completely different from what goes on in everybody's personal life. Everybody gets along really well."

Jim really likes the challenges of the work, but also appreciates the breaks and weekends. "The work is never the same," he says. "You never have the same weather, winds, and airplanes. Then, when you unplug that position and someone relieves you, it doesn't matter how long you go away for, there's no paperwork waiting for you, there's nothing left on your desk. The planes keep flying, somebody else takes over and you jump out of the loop, then you just jump back in."

Air traffic controllers typically work rotating shifts. The workweek is 40 hours, with four days on the job and two days off, with shifts changing from week to week. A shift can last eight to 10 hours, depending on the facility, the expected traffic at the airport, and the number of ATCs available. Overtime is available and can be paid out as extra days off.

Do I Have What It Takes to Be an Air Traffic Controller?

A good memory is important to an ATC, as well as a great deal of certainty. "It's a job where you know when you're doing bad and you know when you're doing good," Jim says. "You know inside of you. You can't fake it. You have to have confidence, and you have to be able to think on your feet." This means you can't get too locked into work habits and patterns.

TYPES OF CONTROLLERS

○ **Arrival controller** Regulates the flow of traffic entering the airspace, establishes holding patterns, and clears planes for landing.

○ **Departure controller** Coordinates the flow of traffic leaving the airport's airspace.

○ **En route air traffic control specialist** Coordinates the flow of traffic between airports' airspace.

○ **Flight data and clearance delivery specialist** Receives and communicates flight plans, airport weather conditions, and other data between pilots and other air traffic control towers along the pilot's route.

○ **Flight service station air traffic control specialist** Links the many air traffic control facilities, providing data on flight plans, type of plane, weather and terrain conditions, and other essential information.

○ **Ground controller** Maintains the smooth flow of traffic along the airport's taxiways leading to the runways.

○ **Local controller** Speaks directly to pilots, prepares them for takeoff, and guides them on the final landing approach.

"Sometimes your first plan may not work and you have to have a plan two and a plan three. You have to be able to shift on the fly pretty good."

You have to have confidence, and you have to be able to think on your feet.

ATCs must be able to express themselves clearly, recall instantly and act on large amounts of rapidly changing data. They must be able to perform many rapid calculations and understand the relationships among the many and constantly changing variables

In-depth

History

The goal of the first air traffic control efforts—beacon lights—was to guide airplanes along a specified airway. As airways and aircraft grew in number, radio communication and radio beacons were added to help planes navigate and to provide weather forecasts. In 1936, the federal government opened the first air traffic control center to regulate the increasing numbers of aircraft flying into and out of the country's growing airports. The Instrument Landing System, a method for signaling aircraft, was instituted in 1941. Airplanes were reaching higher speeds and altitudes, and the controllers' functions became more important to guard against collisions, to ensure safe landings, and to warn pilots of potential weather and geographic hazards in flights. Radar, developed during World War II, allowed air traffic controllers to track the movements of many aircraft and for longer distances. The air traffic control network was extended to include centers at airports, en route, and flight service stations, each of which performed specific tasks and controlled specific portions of the skies. After the war, more sophisticated communication systems were developed, including VOR (very high frequency omnidirectional range) transmission, which was used to signal flight path data directly to the plane. Computers were soon installed in order to provide still greater accuracy to the air traffic controller's instructions. Development of the global positioning system (GPS), however, has made it possible for airplanes to achieve greater control over their flight paths, so fewer air traffic controllers will be needed to protect the skies.

involved in safely conducting an airport's traffic. Because of the stress of maintaining such high levels of concentration, controllers need to possess a highly developed emotional self-control. This allows them to perform their duties while giving and receiving instructions calmly, clearly, and decisively.

Heather emphasizes the importance of good health and personal background in order to meet strict medical and security requirements. Because of a minor health problem when she was 15 years old, she had some trouble meeting basic medical requirements. "I had to go through quite a lot just to get hired, from that one illness," she says. Even traffic violations are scrutinized. "It's something you really have to plan ahead for."

How Do I Become an Air Traffic Controller?

Competition for ATC training is fierce, in part because of the high pay, generous benefits, and job security ATCs enjoy, but also because of the stringent requirements for this career. All candidates must have three to four years of progressive work experience (that is, work in which their responsibilities steadily increase) or four years of college, or a combination of both, and they must score highly on the federal civil service examination. Many candidates come from a military background, where they may even have functioned as an operations specialist, the equivalent of a civilian air traffic controller. Others enter with experience in a related field, including pilots and navigators. And some ATCs come into the job with no experience at all.

EDUCATION

High School

A high school diploma is an essential first step toward becoming an air traffic controller. Candidates at the FAA Academy need a solid understanding of mathematics. Some knowledge of aviation, meteorology, and computers is also helpful. Yet, says Rob Reedy, an air traffic controller at DuPage Airport in Illinois and the former National Training Coordinator for the National Air Traffic Controllers Association, "the FAA will teach you everything you need to know at the academy and on the job. In fact, they almost prefer an 'empty sponge,' someone who will do what they are told, when they are told. The ability to learn is an essential skill. Other than that, I would say that a high school student should concentrate on his communication skills," Rob adds, "because that is really the whole job."

Postsecondary Training

Three to four years of college or progressive work or military experience are required before you can be accepted into training at the FAA Academy. A college degree is also desirable. Equivalent work experience includes administrative, supervisory, professional, or technical positions that have prepared the candidate for the great responsibilities of air traffic control.

Only candidates who score high on the civil service exam are considered for training. This exam measures your aptitude for the skills you need to become a qualified air traffic controller. You then go through a four-day computer screening to determine if you have the alertness, decisiveness, motivation, emotional self-control, and ability to work under intense pressure that are essential to the work of an ATC. The pre-employment test is offered only to students enrolled in the FAA Air Traffic Collegiate Training Initiative (AT-CTI) Program or the Minneapolis Community and Technical College, Air Traffic Control Training Program. Candidates must be at least 18 years of age but not older than 31 and articulate, with eyesight correctable to 20/20. They must also pass a physical exam and routinely submit to drug testing, which continues after you become an ATC.

After you complete one of the FAA-approved training programs and pass the pre-employment test you are eligible for employment as an ATC and may attend an intensive eleven- to seventeen-week course at the FAA Academy in Oklahoma City. At this point, trainees are considered employees of the FAA and are paid as such. Training consists of the fundamentals of the airway systems, civil air regulations, radar, and aircraft performance characteristics. Emergency simulations, designed to test the candidates' emotional stability under pressure, contribute to the high (50 percent) failure rate among all candidates.

In recent years, efforts have been made to reduce the stress of the training period. "In the old days," Rob Reedy says, "you had to undergo a sixteen-week screening before you could even begin your actual training. You never knew if you'd wash out, up to the day of graduation. Now, with the four-day computer screening period, you know quickly if you'll be accepted into training. And the atmosphere at the academy has become more like a college campus, where people want you to succeed."

ATC candidates may join academic programs offered in the army, navy, and air force or at one of several private institutions. However, only candidates trained at the FAA/Department of Transportation or military academies are guaranteed jobs with the FAA, where they will receive their crucial on-the-job training.

CERTIFICATION OR LICENSING

On-the-job training, with increasing levels of responsibility and continued study, are required before you can become a fully certified air traffic controller. This training period can range between 18 months and six years, depending on the facility and the amount of traffic. Senior ATCs supervise and grade trainees' performance each day. Rob Reedy explains: "A new hire at an en route center can train from three to six years before he or she is fully certified there. Here at DuPage, where we direct mostly private and pilot training flights, someone beginning their training in the summer, when there is much more traffic, can expect to finish their on-the-job training much sooner than someone who begins in the winter, when traffic is light. Here, the training range is from 18 to 28 months." Candidates must be certified at each level of air traffic control, and failure to certify within a specific period of time results in dismissal. Yearly physical exams and twice-yearly job performance reviews are also part of the job.

A candidate fresh from the academy will typically be assigned to an available position in a specific region of the country. Persons with the highest grades will have the widest choice of assignments. This is important because everyone has his or her own career goals and preferences. "Personally, I like it here at DuPage Airport," Rob Reedy says. "At a place like O'Hare [in Chicago], you deal only with professional pilots. But here, where our pilots are mainly leisure flyers and student pilots, things don't always happen the way they're supposed to. That keeps you on your toes."

On-the-job training begins at the flight data and clearance delivery position. The next step is ground controller. "It's only on the job that a controller is really tested," Rob Reedy says. "They may know everything they need to know, but if they have what we call mike fright, that is, if they freeze when speaking to the pilots, they'll never be a good controller." From ground controller, the controller advances through the local controller and departure controller grades, before reaching the grade of arrival controller. The tower supervisor, finally, functions as an extra pair of eyes and ears, overseeing all of the activities of the tower, and is ready to offer assistance whenever the need arises. At an en route facility, a candidate begins by supporting the teams with printed flight data, then advances to the teams themselves as a radar associate and finally radar controller.

SCHOLARSHIPS AND GRANTS

Students enrolled in an air traffic control program at a school licensed or approved by the FAA may apply to the Air Traffic Control Association's scholarship program for financial support. Also eligible to apply are students working toward a bachelor's degree or higher in an aviation-related program.

Who Will Hire Me?

Air traffic controllers held about 26,000 jobs in 2002, according to the U.S. Department of Labor. The majority are employed by the federal government, mostly in the FAA. In addition to the nearly 450 airport control towers across the United States, there are also 24 en route air control centers, each with 300 to 700 controllers, and more than 275 flight service stations, which provide pilots with preflight or inflight assistance, linking the airways above the United States. Some air traffic controllers work for the U.S. Department of Defense, others are instructors at the FAA Academy. The FAA also employs some professional controllers as researchers at it experimental center in Atlantic City, New Jersey. A small number of ATCs are employed at privately owned, non-FAA towers.

ADVANCEMENT POSSIBILITIES

District supervisors coordinate and supervise the responsibilities of all air traffic control facilities in a given district.

FAA administrators work in a variety of administrative posts within the FAA, from policy development to statistical research to candidate recruitment.

Facility supervisors supervise and grade the performances of noncertified air traffic controllers and coordinate the schedules and responsibilities of controllers and other personnel working in air traffic control.

Where Can I Go from Here?

Promotion to each successive grade of ATC certification increases the complexity of the controller's responsibilities. At the higher grades, a controller may coordinate all of the traffic control activities at his or her facility, supervise and train controllers at the lower grades, or manage the various aeronautical agencies involved in air traffic control.

Controllers can reach supervisory and managerial positions, and assume responsibilities for wider and wider areas. Some controllers continue on to administrative positions within the Federal Aviation Administration. Controllers are granted civil service status upon completion of their first year on the job and career status at the end of their third year.

Advancement moves from assistant to fully qualified controller. When fully qualified, you may move into a chief controller position, air traffic control management, or FAA administration. There is a rapid turnover due to early retirement, yet job competition is stiff since there are more qualified personnel than there are jobs.

"There isn't really much of a chance for promotion unless you want to go into a supervisor position," Heather says. "You get raises on a time basis, whether you do a good job or you don't. Right now, all I see is doing air traffic control. When you're a supervisor, you only work traffic eight hours a month. I think it's pointless to be a controller and not control airplanes."

What Are the Salary Ranges?

The U.S. Department of Labor notes that, air traffic controllers had a median annual salary of $97,020 in 2003. Those in the lowest paid 10 percent had incomes of less than $55,340 annually, while those in the highest paid 10 percent earned more than $136,170 a year. Salaries vary widely with level of seniority, degree of responsibility, and type of facility. For example, an experienced air traffic controller working for the federal government earned a median salary of $97,500 annually, while those working for other agencies such as local governments and for scheduled air transportation facilities earned between $43,370 and $71,520. Generally, the higher the level of the air traffic facility, the higher the salary will be.

Air traffic controllers also receive special benefits, such as a higher pay scale than other civil service employees, more vacation days, and a liberal retirement program. Air traffic controllers receive life insurance and health benefits, 13 paid sick days, and, depending on their length of service, 13 to 26 paid vacation days. Air traffic controllers also enjoy job security; even during times of recession, they are rarely laid off.

What Is the Job Outlook?

The *Occupational Outlook Handbook* reports that employment of air traffic controllers will grow about as fast as the average through 2012. Technological advances that make it possible for controllers to perform their work more efficiently and federal budget restrictions may limit job opportunities. Most openings will come from controllers retiring or leaving for other jobs. The National Air Traffic Controllers Association reports that the biggest problem currently facing air traffic control is staffing. It expects more than half of the current workforce of air traffic controllers will retire by 2010.

Employment opportunities will be particularly strong for candidates with college degrees, a strong background of progressive work experience, or

FYI

The FAA reports that air traffic controllers manage about 87,000 flights per day with approximately 5,000 aircraft in the air at any given moment. Currently about 600 million people fly annually and the FAA projects that number to reach 1 billion by 2010.

related civil or military experience as controllers, navigators, or pilots. Recent years have seen the active recruitment of women and minorities into this career. Top scores on the civil service exam, excellent performance on the four-day computer screening, and high grades in training will improve your chances of becoming an ATC and ensure that you have a wide range of options when choosing the facility in which to begin your career.

How Do I Learn More?

PROFESSIONAL ORGANIZATIONS

The following organizations provide information on air traffic control training, scholarships, careers, and employers:

Air Traffic Control Association
1101 King Street, Suite 300
Alexandria, VA 22314
703-299-2430
info@atca.org
http://www.atca.org

Federal Aviation Administration
Office of Personnel and Training
800 Independence Avenue, SW
Washington, DC 20591
202-267-3229
http://www.faa.gov

National Association of Air Traffic Specialists
11303 Amherst Avenue, Suite 4
Wheaton, MD 20902
301-933-6228
http://www.naats.org

National Air Traffic Controller Association
1325 Massachusetts Avenue, NW
Washington, DC 20005
202-628-5451
http://www.natca.org

Canadian Air Traffic Control Association
162 Cleopatra Drive
Nepean, Ontario, Canada K2G 5X2
613-225-3553
catca@catca.ca
http://www.catca.ca

BIBLIOGRAPHY

The following is a sampling of materials related to the professional concerns and development of air traffic controllers:

Brenlove, Milovan S. *The Air Traffic System: A Common Sense Guide.* 2d ed. Ames, Iowa: Iowa State Press, 2003.

————. *Vectors to Spare: The Life of an Air Traffic Controller.* Ames, Iowa: Iowa State University Press, 1993.

Careers in Focus: Transportation. 2d ed. Chicago: Ferguson Publishing Company, 2003.

Nolan, Michael S. *Fundamentals of Air Traffic Control,* 4th ed. Belmont, Calif.: Brooks/Cole Publishing Company, 2003.

Power-Waters, Brian. *Margin for Error, None: Through the Skills of the Air Traffic Controllers, A Faulty System Is Made to Work.* Lincoln, Neb.: Authors Choice Press, 2001.

Wilkens, Christopher D. *The Future of Air Traffic Control: Human Operators and Automation.* Washington, D.C.: National Academies Press, 1998.

ANIMAL BREEDERS

IIIIIIIIIIIIIIIIIIIIIIIIIIIIIIIIIIIIIIIIIIIIIIIIIIIIIIIIIIIIIIIIIIII

It's so early, it's still pitch dark out, and Jill Dannelly arrives at the pig processing facility for her morning shift. As a department manager, she feels responsible for keeping things running smoothly. So when she sees that the electricity is out, she races into the building, quickly showers, then puts on her uniform. Every day, as she arrives and as she leaves, Jill must shower for biosecurity reasons, to prevent the spread of disease among the pigs. "We don't need an outbreak of anything right now," Jill thinks, the concern about animal sickness frequently on her mind. Scour, a diarrhea in pigs caused by intestinal infection, has been causing some of the pigs to die, and she must prepare for the veterinarian's visit later in the morning.

In the dark, Jill makes some calls, does some investigating, and learns that a fan broke down at a substation, causing the room to overheat and the generators to shut down. In the summertime, it's not unusual for heat to make the work at the facility miserable; animal smells, mingled with the heavy humidity, can make every task a major chore.

After the electricity returns, Jill walks through the 28-room facility with a handheld computer, recording the number of pigs to each litter. When the vet arrives later in the day, she discusses particular problems. Together they discuss solutions, and they examine a pig that has died from the recent outbreak. At the vet's side as he performs an autopsy, Jill helps to cut away lymph nodes, lungs, and parts of intestines and helps him prepare the organs for delivery to a lab.

What Does an Animal Breeder Do?

Selective breeding is usually intended to improve the genetic makeup of common animals such as cattle, horses, sheep, poultry, dogs, and cats, along with more exotic species such as llamas and monkeys. Some breeding programs help preserve threatened or endangered species; these efforts often take place at zoos or facilities that raise animals to be released into the wild.

Definition
Animal breeders breed and raise animals to improve traits, to develop new breeds, to maintain standards of existing breeds, or to preserve threatened or endangered species.

Alternative Job Titles
Animal husbandry technicians
Artificial inseminators
Livestock production technicians

High School Subjects
Agriculture
Biology
Computer science

Personal Skills
Helping/teaching
Leadership/management

Salary Range
$16,160 to $25,560 to $53,310

Minimum Education Level
High school diploma

Certification or Licensing
None available

Outlook
More slowly than the average

DOT
410

GOE
03.02.01

NOC
N/A

O*NET-SOC
45-2021.00

By mating males and females with preferred traits, breeders encourage the production of young with the best traits of both. For example, a *cattle breeder* might mate a bull whose offspring have lean meat with a cow who is uncommonly large. The calf would most likely be a large animal with more than the average amount of lean meat. Cattle breeders typically try to develop animals that are large, have less fat than in the past, give birth easily, eat less, and are not very susceptible to diseases. Strong, healthy, meaty cattle bring higher profits for their owners.

Horse breeders also try to develop strong, healthy animals, but for a different reason. Horse breeders are always trying to find ways to make horses jump higher, run faster, or ride more smoothly.

Some *dog* or *cat breeders* want animals that meet the standards of a breed association. They might aim for a collie with a perfect, long nose and small, dainty feet or a Persian cat with eyes of a certain shape and fur of a certain color. Other breeders want working dogs with a natural ability and desire to perform a certain job, such as herding sheep.

Domestic animals are usually bred to please humans. Animals in zoos are bred mainly to maintain their populations, both in zoos and in the wild. Pandas, gorillas, Chinese alligators, and the Arabian oryx (a graceful antelope) are just a few of the species that have been bred in captivity in an attempt to save them from extinction. The breeding of exotic animals requires special skills and training, but it is done in basically the same way as livestock breeding.

Like other animal breeding endeavors, zoo breeding now relies heavily on artificial insemination, although it is also still common to bring the animals together and let nature take its course. Artificial insemination is often easier, cheaper, and more predictable than the old-fashioned method. In vitro fertilization (which produces "test-tube babies") is also becoming more common, particularly for zoo breeding and other work with endangered species.

Modern technology has also affected the way breeders decide which animals to mate. Computers are used to keep track of schedules and to enter and analyze data about each animal. A computer can generate pictures that show how the offspring of any two animals would be apt to look. Computers are essential tools for laboratory specialists who do genetic work.

Artificial-breeding laboratory technicians usually focus on laboratory tests, measuring, and other procedures to improve the quality of stored semen. *Artificial-breeding technicians* collect and package semen for artificial insemination, but they rarely perform the actual insemination. *Artificial insemination technicians* inseminate female animals and sometimes collect semen from males. *Poultry inseminators* collect semen from roosters and use it to fertilize the eggs of chickens and other fowl.

Animal breeders often spend time on preparatory tasks and follow-up visits to animals that have been inseminated. Before they begin work on an animal, they make sure the equipment is sterile and functioning properly and that the semen is stored at the optimum temperature. They work closely with the owners and handlers of the animals, sometimes visiting the site ahead of time to make sure the procedure will go as

Lingo to Learn

Calving ease The ease or difficulty with which a cow delivers her calves; it depends to some degree on the calf's size.

Dam A female animal that is or will be a mother.

Daughter The female offspring of bulls whose semen is sold for breeding purposes.

Linear traits Confirmation characteristics of bull's daughters, such as how tall they are or what mammary structure they have.

Semen straws The container in which semen is stored in preparation for inseminating dams. The straws are approximately four inches long and three-sixteenths of an inch in diameter and are inserted into the dam using an insemination gun.

planned. When it's time for the animals to give birth, breeders frequently assist with the delivery and make sure the babies get a healthy start in life.

What Is It Like to Be an Animal Breeder?

At a breeding facility called Beaver Valley Pork (BVP) in central Nebraska, Jill Dannelly oversees the farrowing department. Though she manages employees, which includes training, she also works actively with the pigs. "I'm involved with the treating of animals," Jill says, "diagnosing their diseases or sicknesses. I assist sows when they're farrowing [giving birth], kind of like a nurse does when a woman's having a baby." This can involve reaching into the sow's birth canal in cases of emergency. Jill was recently promoted into a managerial position, but she still frequently must get down in the muck and be involved with the everyday care of the animals.

Jill is one of the first ones to work every morning, arriving at 5:30 A.M. Because of the number of diseases carried by pigs, many of which are airborne or in manure, employees are required to shower when they arrive and then change into their uniforms. (They must also shower and change when leaving the facility.) Ten minutes later, Jill heads out to the barns. The facility has 28 rooms, with 30 crates per room. With a handheld computer, Jill visits every room to check on the sows and the farrowing process. When a sow has completed farrowing, Jill records the number of pigs born alive and the number of those stillborn. "We sort litters according to numbers and size," Jill says, "so that every sow has the same number and every pig is the same size."

The BVP farrowing department has many well-established processes in place, but the work still requires that Jill constantly examines current practices. She contributes ideas for increasing production and for keeping work habits efficient. She recently discovered that having employees at the facility at night led to more pigs being born alive. With a high rate of stillborns, the facility was willing to take a chance on bringing in a night crew. As a result, the number of stillborns dropped, thereby helping production. "It's just trial and error," Jill says. "We're always trying something new."

To keep close track of how the facility operates, Jill assists with processing and feeding. "Processing involves giving the iron shot," Jill says. "You process the pigs that are three days old. We put a tattoo in their ear which says 'BVP' and the day of birth." At 21 days of age, the pigs are sent to another facility across the state, where they are raised up to market.

To feed the animals, Jill pushes a large cart around the room, with a separate cart for each room. The cart contains grains of corn, with protein and fat added. After feeding the pigs, Jill returns the cart to the feed line where it can be refilled without requiring the workers to carry bags of feed around. "We also have a system to determine how many times a sow has been off feed," Jill says. "If they're off three times—we feed them three times during the day—we treat them with penicillin. Usually, if they're off feed, it's because they have an infection going through them."

Jill must stay aware of the health of the animals. A vet visits regularly, and Jill escorts the vet on his rounds. She asks him questions, as well as takes his suggestions for better conditions. When treating animals, Jill uses syringes and hypodermic needles. She also uses very sharp blades for the castrating of pigs.

Jill and the other technicians work a rotation of seven days on, then one day off. This is followed by four days on, and a weekend off. Because her day starts so early, Jill is able to leave work by 2:30 P.M.

FYI

Breeder's Online (http://www.breedersonline.com) is a site devoted to livestock and animal breeders. With chat rooms, question and answer boards, and classifieds, the site sets out to serve the varied interests of animal breeders by putting them in touch with other technicians, professionals, and employers. The site features sections focusing on cattle, horses, sheep, goats, exotic animals, bison, dogs, cats, poultry, and swine.

every afternoon, allowing for some daylight hours to enjoy.

Do I Have What It Takes to Be an Animal Breeder?

Animal breeders need to enjoy animals and feel comfortable and confident working with them. You must also be comfortable around human beings. Jill stresses the importance of being a team player. "Everything we do is intertwined," Jill said about the facility. "If one department doesn't get the animals bred they need to, then my department doesn't get the litters it needs, and we are short on production." Part of the teamwork requires contributing ideas. "You can't be shy and quiet about it. If you've got an idea, you have to toss it out there." The work can also be fast-paced, and you may be required to learn quickly on the job. "A lot of people just quit and don't give their two weeks [notice], so sometimes we're short-handed," Jill says. "Every once in a while, a person doesn't get enough training time." This can add to the demands of work already stressful for a manager. "I've got a lot to do, and I have a lot of people around me relying on me to do a good job."

For a livestock breeder, it is also essential to enjoy meeting and visiting new people. By contrast, technicians may need to be prepared for opposition. "We get protesters all the time," Jill said, referring to

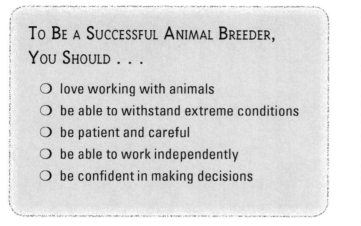

neighbors of the facility who complain of the stench. "But it's a farming community—there are going to be farm smells."

Self-discipline is important for those animal breeders who work mostly on their own. It is up to them to complete their breeding calls and then make sales calls. Livestock breeders need to be able to handle a regular workday (visiting farms, meeting with farmers, inseminating cows, calling into the center for assignments, making sales calls), as well as any emergencies that come their way.

How Do I Become an Animal Breeder?

Jill grew up on a farm and received a bachelor's degree in agricultural education, with an emphasis on training and development. She started at BVP in a part-time position one summer. "You just kind of pick it up," she says of the work. "It's hands-on training." She did receive close supervision in the process, however. Her trainer demonstrated how to perform certain tasks, left her alone to work, then later went over her processes and how to improve.

EDUCATION

High School

Nearly all animal breeding organizations require that their new hires have a high school diploma, and a growing number require some postsecondary training. Without a high school diploma, it is possible to start out as a stable hand and move up through experience, although at some point along the way you won't be able to advance further without some

formal training. Stable hands work for an hourly wage that is not much higher than the minimum wage, but with time and effort it is possible to earn much more.

If you have spent time around animals, you have an advantage over those with no experience. Future Farmers of America (FFA) and 4-H offer useful opportunities to learn about animals and the future of the industry. You can also work a summer job at a horse or cattle farm or ranch, an animal shelter, or a zoo to gain experience. Raising a pet is a good way to become familiar with animals and their needs. It is also advisable to read books about animals.

In school, the more classes you have with an agricultural base, the better prepared you will be. Courses in genetics, biology, health, mathematics, chemistry, communications, mechanics, natural science, and the environment are helpful. In case you end up owning a business or moving into management of a company some day, it is also wise to take some business classes.

Postsecondary Training

Nine months to two years of technical schooling provides the basic training for an animal breeder. A four-year degree in animal science or animal husbandry is recommended if you plan to become a farm or ranch manager eventually. For zoo careers, on-the-job experience is sometimes enough for an entry-level position, but usually a four-year degree in animal science, zoology, marine biology, conservation biology, wildlife management, or animal behavior is necessary. Significant experience in the care of exotic animals is also required for many zoo positions.

College will help you gain a background in animal sciences, and you'll also learn business skills that will be helpful if you need to sell a product or if you move into management. Courses in animal science tend to cover a range of subjects. For example, at the University of California's Animal Science Horse Facility, students work with a herd of about 30 mares, four stallions, and five to 10 foals. Classes cover feeding, breeding, unsoundness, health management, physiology, sports medicine, biology, pharmacology, equine nutrition, equine exercise, law, and marketing. The program also features internships that include experience with studs, broodmares, and foals.

In-depth

Pedigreed Animals

Raising pedigreed animals, such as dogs and cats, differs from the multimillion-dollar industries of horse and livestock breeding. State agencies regulate the care and breeding of animals to some extent, but because of the large number of breeders and the wide variety of pedigreed animals, this is often difficult. Clubs organize and set standards for each type and breed of animal. They also officially document and confirm each animal's lineage, or pedigree. Pedigreed animals, because of the purity of their breeding, are more expensive than nonpedigreed animals, and breeders often can make several hundred dollars per animal. Unfortunately, this has led some individuals to enter the field purely for monetary reasons. The result is what Ed Kilby of Daytona Beach, Florida, calls "puppy mills," which generate large numbers of unwanted dogs.

Ed has been breeding, showing, and judging bloodhounds for 35 years, and today he serves as secretary of the American Bloodhound Club. "Someone interested in dog breeding, or any other kind of breeding in which the animals are pedigreed, should know it's serious business, not fun and games," he says. "Too many folks already get into it for all the wrong reasons. You don't just slap two animals together. You have to know what you're doing. You have to care about the breed."

Ed says dog breeders should be familiar with genetics and how to research a pedigree, have a basic knowledge of veterinary procedures, and understand the anatomy of dogs. "If you lack any of these, you're just wasting your time and perhaps helping ruin the breed," he adds.

The goal of a reputable dog breeder is always to breed the perfect dog and to improve the breed by taking the best female, or dam, and matching her with the best male, or sire. Each club defines the ideal dog, establishing a standard by which every generation of the breed is judged. "If you can look at a dog and he looks exactly like the standard, you know you've not only bred a great dog, but you've helped maintain the breed," Ed says.

For example, weight and color are among the standard requirements for bloodhounds. Bloodhounds should weigh, on the average, from 90 to 110 pounds and be black and tan, red, or liver and tan—the only accepted colors.

Ed explains the purpose of the standard: "Over one thousand years ago, the bloodhound was bred to find things and people. Of all the canines in the world, this dog has the best nose. It's the only dog whose scent trail to a criminal can be used as evidence in a court of law. Today, if he can't find anything, he's not a bloodhound."

Researching a dog's lineage is crucial to improving the breed. "You want to go back at least three generations and know each individual relative of both the sire and the dam. You don't want to pass along any medical or behavioral problems to the next generation, so you have to be extremely careful," Ed says.

The pedigree is important because, although the breeder is not registered with the state, the puppies he raises are. The American Kennel Club can refuse to register a dog if the breeder has not tried to follow the standard or, in trying to cut costs, has actually harmed or mistreated the animal. Without registration, the breeder cannot sell the animal as an officially pedigreed dog.

"Breeding is hard work. It takes a lot of research and study before the dog is born and then more hard work to train it. You've got to love the breed and respect the standard," Ed says.

INTERNSHIPS AND VOLUNTEERSHIPS

At some junior colleges you can participate in an apprenticeship program that combines course work and on-the-job training. The college provides classroom studies, and an employer pays you for part-time work at a facility that produces livestock or other animals.

Many artificial insemination organizations offer internships to help prospective animal breeders learn about the industry before they commit to it as a career. Most are summer positions, although some are offered during the school year. You might also find work in veterinary clinics, animal hospitals, and animal shelters. Although artificial insemination internships will give you the most valuable insights into a career as an animal breeder, any job that involves working with animals will provide relevant experience.

Zoos sometimes offer internships and most accept volunteers. If you'd like to volunteer at a zoo or aquarium, inquire at a local facility or contact the Association of Zoo and Aquarium Docents through its Web site, http://www.azadocents.org, for information.

Who Will Hire Me?

Animal breeders work in various settings. Some travel to various farms and ranches. Others work for large operations, such as a zoo or the hatchery of a poultry farm. Some work in laboratories, where they develop better products and techniques for the industry. Some people with degrees in animal science use their training as a springboard into other animal-related careers, such as livestock sales, selling horses on video or over the telephone, professional horse photography, or working in advertising that features animals.

Finding a job is sometimes easier for college students, who can take advantage of the placement offices at universities and technical colleges. Many of these offices place at least 85 percent of their graduates in their fields of expertise; some companies recruit directly from the campuses. Companies also sometimes offer permanent employment to outstanding technicians who have completed internships there. Additional information on the industry and possible employment is often available in trade magazines, such as *Farm Journal* (http://

ADVANCEMENT POSSIBILITIES

Conservation biologists/zoologists provide scientific expertise in the management of zoo animals and participate in research and conservation projects.

Herd evaluators offer advice on sires to help producers improve their herds.

Production managers are responsible for overall sire management and semen production.

Sales managers supervise technicians and direct herd sales representatives for specific geographic areas.

Zoo keepers/aquarists care for animals and fish; they prepare food, clean animals and their quarters, maintain exhibits, and keep records.

---

www.farmjournal.com) and *Successful Farming* (http://www.agriculture.com).

Where Can I Go from Here?

Jill enjoys instructing people in farm work, but doesn't want to teach school. "My goal is to someday work in an extension office," she says, "as a 4-H youth assistant, possibly."

Most breeders begin their careers by working for established companies. Some go into business for themselves after they gain enough experience. You could operate a freelance animal breeding venture, or if you could raise the money, you could own a farm or ranch. With sufficient education, you could advance to manager of a stud farm or other livestock operation. You could also become a feedlot manager, supervisor, or distributor of artificial breeding products.

What Are the Salary Ranges?

According to the U.S. Bureau of Labor Statistics, employees with agricultural science degrees earned as much as $86,930 in 2003. The median earnings for animal breeders in 2003 were $25,560. The lowest paid 10 percent earned less than $16,600 while the highest paid 10 percent earned $53,310.

Farm Journal magazine reports that in 2004, feedlot managers earned about $66,000 annually, while assistant managers earned between $40,000 and $50,000. Other positions paid between $30,000 and $40,000.

Some companies offer food and housing allowances that can add up to a value of several thousand dollars annually. Other benefits vary, but often they include health insurance, paid vacation time, and pension plans.

What Is the Job Outlook?

According to the U.S. Department of Labor, employment of animal breeders is expected to grow more slowly than the average through 2012. In 2002 there were 9,000 animal breeders holding jobs nationwide and that is expected to increase by only about 6 percent to 9,500 in 2012.

The animal production industries have been going through a period of change recently, and the way animals are raised and marketed is expected to continue changing rapidly in coming years. There is great emphasis on uniform products. In addition, animal husbandry operations must cope with small profit margins and competition from foreign markets. In agricultural endeavors, such as the breeding of sheep and cattle, it is now almost impossible for a one-person business to remain solvent; large corporations and cooperatives of consultants are becoming the norm.

How Do I Learn More?

PROFESSIONAL ORGANIZATIONS

The following organizations may provide information about the industry, scholarships, education, training, and career opportunities:

American Dog Breeders Association
PO Box 1771
Salt Lake City, UT 84110
801-936-7513

bstofshw@adba.cc
http://www.adba.cc

American Society of Animal Science
1111 North Dunlap Avenue
Savoy, IL 61874
217-356-3182
asas@assochq.org
http://www.asas.org

Humane Society of the United States
2100 L Street, NW
Washington, DC 20037
202-452-1100
http://www.hsus.org

National Pedigreed Livestock Council
177 Palermo Place
The Villages, FL 32159
352-259-6005
http://www.nplc.net

United States Animal Health Association
8100 Three Chopt Road, Suite 203
Richmond, VA 23288
804-285-3210
usaha@usaha.org
http://www.usaha.org

BIBLIOGRAPHY

The following is a sampling of materials relating to the professional concerns and development of animal breeders:

Bourdon, Richard M. *Understanding Animal Breeding.* 2d ed. Paramus, N.J.: Prentice Hall, 1999.

Careers in Focus: Animal Care. 2d ed. Chicago: Ferguson Publishing Company, 2001.

Collins, Donald N. and William C. White. *Opportunities in Farming and Agriculture Careers.* Lincolnwood, Ill.: NTC/Contemporary Publishing Group, 1995.

Jurgens, Marshall H. *Animal Feeding and Nutrition.* 9th ed. Dubuque, Iowa: Kendall Hunt Publishing, 2001.

Lee, Richard and Mary Price Lee. *Opportunities in Animal and Pet Care Careers.* Lincolnwood, Ill.: VGM Career Books, 2001.

Pavia, Audrey. *Careers with Animals.* Hauppauge, N.Y.: Barrons Educational Series, 2001.

ANIMAL CARETAKERS

||||||||||||||||||||||||||||||||||||||||||||||||||||||||||||||||||||||||||||||||||||||||

" I'm on the cutting edge of scientific breakthroughs and health care," says Deborah Donohoe. "I gown up, assist in the operating room, and look out for the welfare of the patient before and after surgery." Then she smiles and adds, "But none of our patients are human. Instead, as an animal laboratory technologist, I work with pigs, monkeys, rabbits, cats, dogs, mice, turtles, rats, and chinchillas." Donohoe explains that research physicians, M.D.'s with experience caring for people, often are not familiar with the medical needs of animals. It is the animal lab technologist's job to read up on the biology of other species, inform the research team, and then make sure that each different animal is cared for properly during the procedure.

"This morning," she says, "we're working with rabbits in order to test a new technology involving lasers. Everything that's done for humans in a hospital setting is done for these animals. For instance, I make sure that the rabbits fast properly before the procedure, inject them with antibiotics, test the equipment we use, and after advising the physicians about rabbit behavior and physiology, assist in surgery. That's a lot of responsibility, but I thrive on it. I have to use my brain every day and no two days are ever the same."

What Does an Animal Caretaker Do?

People and animals have coexisted for millions of years. In exchange for a warm place by the fire and a few bones to chew on, dogs helped prehistoric people hunt. Later, cats kept grain storehouses free of rodents and pet birds cheered people with their beautiful songs. Throughout history, humans have used and enjoyed animals, and throughout history, someone took responsibility for the health and welfare of the animals that lived side-by-side with people.

Today *animal caretakers* work with animals in a variety of settings. They are responsible for the basic welfare of these creatures. They feed, water, groom, and exercise animals. They clean the animals' living quarters and provide companionship. They watch for signs of ill health and inform medical staff when necessary.

Definition
Animal caretakers feed, water, exercise, and monitor the general health of animals. They also clean and repair cages and provide companionship for animals. Those involved with veterinary medicine or research may assist during animal surgery or medical testing procedures.

Alternative Job Titles
Animal laboratory technicians
Animal laboratory workers

High School Subjects
Agriculture
Biology
Health

Personal Skills
Helping/teaching
Technical/scientific

Salary Range
$12,810 to $17,470 to $28,490+

Minimum Educational Level
Some postsecondary training

Certification or Licensing
Required by certain states

Outlook
Faster than the average

DOT
410

GOE
03.02.01

NOC
6483

O*NET-SOC
39-2021.00

Animal caretaking is a broad field that may be divided into six major categories: animal laboratory workers, veterinary hospital employees, animal shelter workers, zookeepers, stable and farm workers, and groomers and kennel employees.

Animal laboratory workers are employed by institutions that use live animals for research, testing, or educational purposes. Laboratory workers are classified according to their education levels and job duties. *Assistant animal laboratory technicians,* the entry-level position for this branch of animal caretakers, provide the most basic animal care. They clean cages and feed animals. They help with general animal husbandry and handling. In the second tier position, *animal laboratory technicians* take on additional responsibilities. They provide more direct care. They may give prescribed medications, take medical specimens, perform lab tests, record daily scientific observations, and help with minor surgeries.

Animal laboratory technologists work at the highest level and supervise the work of lab assistants and technicians. They oversee the advanced care of animals and assist in surgery and other complicated medical procedures.

Veterinary hospital employees also may be classified according to job duties and educational level. *Veterinary technicians* have the most responsibility. While they do not diagnose illnesses or prescribe medicines, they prepare animals for surgery, assist during medical procedures and examinations, perform lab tests, dress wounds, take specimens, and keep records. *Veterinary assistants* feed and bathe animals, administer medications as directed, and assist veterinarians and veterinary technicians. *Animal attendants* (often part-time, entry-level workers) clean cages, exercise animals, and observe sick and recovering animals for signs of illness.

Another type of animal caretaker is employed by private or city-run shelters. *Animal shelter workers* are in charge of general husbandry, vaccinating new arrivals, arranging for adoptions or animal foster care, and when necessary, euthanizing sick, injured, or unwanted animals.

Zookeepers work in zoological parks or aquariums. Every day they clean and maintain the animal enclosures. They prepare the animals' food and observe their behavior in order to detect signs of illness. They are often concerned with conservation issues and may be involved in breeding loans with other zoos, with public educational projects, and with other programs dedicated to preserving threatened and endangered species.

Some animal caretakers work in stables or on farms. *Stable workers* may saddle and unsaddle horses, feed and groom them, muck out stalls, and organize tack rooms, supplies, and feed. Others exercise or help train racehorses. Stable workers may also assist other professionals who care for horses, such as farriers and veterinarians. *Farm workers* perform similar animal husbandry functions on a variety of domestic animals. They may feed and water chickens, sheep, pigs, or goats. They also clean and maintain their coops, stalls, corrals, or pens.

Kennel workers care for pet animals such as dogs or cats. They may bathe, groom, and exercise animals

> # Lingo to Learn
>
> **Animal husbandry** The general care and raising of animals, including feeding and watering, maintenance of clean living areas, and monitoring animal health.
>
> **Euthanasia** The act of causing death painlessly. Also known as "putting an animal down" or "putting an animal to sleep."
>
> **Mammalogy** A branch of zoology dealing with the warm-blooded, usually hairy, class of animals who drink their mothers' milk when young.
>
> **Ornithology** The branch of zoology dealing with birds.
>
> **Spay/neuter** Medical procedures that prevent animals from reproducing. Males are neutered (castrated) and females are spayed (ovaries removed).
>
> **Zoology** A science dealing with the biology of animals.

while their owners are out of town or while the pets are under the care of veterinarians. Kennel workers also feed and water the animals and clean their cages or enclosed runs. Some kennel workers move up to overseeing other employees while others become small business owners and manage their own kennels.

Groomers specialize in maintaining the appearance of animals, usually dogs. They bathe and clip the dogs according to standards for each specific breed. Groomers may own their own businesses or work for kennels or pet supply firms. Other animal caretakers may work for pet stores or teach animal obedience classes.

What Is It Like to Be an Animal Caretaker?

Deborah Donohoe works for the Medical College of Wisconsin as an animal laboratory technologist. One of her projects involved testing the effectiveness of using shock waves to break apart gallstones. In the United States about 20 million people have problems with gallstones. "Because surgery can be dangerous," she says, "we wanted to investigate a new, less invasive procedure." Her research team used 200-pound domestic pigs as substitutes for human subjects.

"But pigs can be peculiar," she notes, "because they have an enormous amount of body fat. Consequently, anesthesia may collect in the fat and the animal can be overdosed very easily." Her job involved providing researchers with up-to-date information on pig biology as well as watching over the pigs before, during, and after laboratory tests. Thanks to her efforts, four hours after the first surgery, the pigs were on their feet and eating and drinking like—well, pigs.

But not all of Deborah's work occurs in the operating room, and it involves much more than just feeding and cleaning animals. She spends a lot of time sterilizing, preparing, and testing equipment. She also contacts other departments within her institution to set up collaborative research projects in order to decrease the total number of experimental animals used. In addition, Deborah has the opportunity to write professional papers and train other animal caretakers. "All that I do keeps me on my toes," she says. "Plus, I'm the first person to see the animals in the morning. I know my job is important. Animal care technologists are what make the research go."

Jewel Waldrip works in another branch of animal caretaking, and her job is quite different from laboratory research. She works at the Tucson Humane Society in Tucson, Arizona. She meets anxious pet owners searching for lost cats and dogs, receives pets from people who can no longer keep them, and arranges for animal adoptions.

On a typical day she may also vaccinate new arrivals, clean kennels, feed and water the animals, train coworkers, or write press releases, newsletter articles, or informational handouts.

Jewel loves animals. "I've worked with them for 23 years," she says. "I started as a kennel worker, then moved on to grooming. I've shown dogs and done a bit of desktop publishing about handling horses and dogs. For a while I volunteered at the Humane Society and then when a job opened up, I applied for it and got it. Now I can use all my skills and experience in one place."

Another Tucson resident, Taylor Edwards, works as a zookeeper at the Arizona-Sonora Desert Museum. Taylor works in mammalogy and ornithology. His duties include cleaning, feeding, and servicing the bird and mammal enclosures. For instance, he puts out fresh drinking water and makes sure that all the bird perches are stable in the museum's walk-through aviary. If any of the birds' "furniture" needs replacing, he fixes it. He also feeds the birds, but not by simply pouring pellets into a trough. "Keepers are also in charge of providing enrichment activities for the animals," he explains. "So I scatter the food around the aviary so that the birds will have to search for it. Sometimes I stack logs or move rocks into interesting positions and place the food there. This keeps the birds mentally healthy and active."

"I also write daily reports on the behavior of the animals," Taylor says. "But one of my very favorite things to do as a keeper is to talk to museum visitors, especially children. There's a connection people can make with animals whether it's at home with their dog or with animals in the zoo. I help people understand the purpose of zoos and teach them a little bit about each animal."

> I help people understand the purpose of zoos and teach them a little bit about each animal.

Because they are dealing with live animals, caretakers often work flexible hours. Some shelter employees, for instance, must arrive early to feed and water the animals and clean their cages. Others must stay late or work weekends to accommodate extended adoption and receiving hours. Research laboratory technicians and technologists monitoring ongoing research projects also put in some night and weekend hours. Dog groomers, kennel workers, veterinary assistants, stable workers, and farm workers also work evenings and weekends according to the needs of their employers. Much of their work may also be seasonal and tied to the horseracing calendar or to the vacations of clients.

Do I Have What It Takes to Be an Animal Caretaker?

"I've touched tigers," says Taylor Edwards. "I have a chance to be with animals that many people never get close to." In addition, by being involved with captive breeding and reintroduction programs like the Mexican wolf study at the Arizona-Sonora Desert Museum, Taylor has found a way to make sure that those animals can continue to have a place in the wild. He says, "Compared to Ph.D. scientists who work on population genetics but mostly sit before computer terminals, zookeepers are on the forefront of each project."

Jewel Waldrip agrees. "It's so gratifying to see that what you're doing makes a difference. One time some people brought a standard poodle into the Humane Society. He'd been a cute puppy once, but as he grew up they ignored and neglected him. By the time we saw him his fur was matted to the skin and his ears were all infected and full of foxtails. I knew the shelter would have to put him down if I couldn't find a foster family to care for him." Jewel smiles as she relates the story's happy ending. "The foster family groomed the poodle, took him to obedience school, and last week brought him in to sign his adoption papers. That dog is now one of the happiest, most well-trained animals I've ever seen."

However, working with animals and being involved with the general public does have its downside. Animal shelter workers must deal with distraught people who have lost their pets. Also they must try not to be judgmental when people deliver unwanted pets to the shelter for what may seem like selfish reasons. It can be easy to get depressed when confronted with so many unwanted pets. Shelter workers try to combat the pet overpopulation problem through educational campaigns and by providing low-cost spay and neuter services.

Dog groomers should be aware that theirs is a physically demanding job. Occasionally, they may be bitten or scratched by frightened dogs. Pet hair and dander along with the chemicals used in flea dips, sprays, and shampoos can irritate humans. Some groomers also suffer from carpal tunnel syndrome due to the repetitive nature of their work.

The hardest aspect of animal caretaking is one that most workers must deal with at some point— euthanasia. Animal caretakers are usually the ones to put animals to death humanely. Shelters can't keep every animal forever, hoping for adoptions that never come. Besides, some animals are simply too sick or too young or too old to be adopted successfully. In addition, the end point for all animal research is also euthanasia. "Intellectually you know that there's a termination plan," says Deborah Donohoe. "You put it to the back of your mind and yet you can't help but form an attachment. Even at the completion of

---

TO BE A SUCCESSFUL ANIMAL CARETAKER, YOU SHOULD . . .

○ enjoy working with animals
○ have at least a high school diploma for basic animal caretaking
○ have a bachelor's degree for zookeeping
○ be able to take direction and work independently
○ be able to lift heavy animals, supplies, or equipment

---

short studies, I've cried." Maintaining compassion while doing what's best—or necessary—is often quite difficult.

How Do I Become an Animal Caretaker?

Taylor Edwards began his career at his hometown zoo in Albuquerque, New Mexico, as a high school volunteer. He worked in the petting zoo, showing baby animals to schoolchildren, and then moved up to junior zookeeper. "Ever since I was 10 or 11 years old," he says, "I knew I liked animals. Volunteering at the Rio Grande Zoo helped me to see different job possibilities: zookeeper, veterinarian, research

An animal caretaker gives a bottle to a baby elephant. *(David Hosking / Photo Researchers Inc.)*

scientist." After high school, he attended college and received a bachelor's degree in zoology. His hands-on experience combined with a college education earned him a job at the Arizona-Sonora Desert Museum.

EDUCATION

High School

Entry-level animal caretakers often begin their careers with only a high school diploma. Classes in biology, math, and English, along with additional courses in other sciences, are helpful. Computer literacy, business skills, and verbal and written proficiency are also recommended. In addition, if you plan to work as a zookeeper or work toward professional certification, you need to fulfill the entrance requirements of the college or university you plan to attend.

Postsecondary Training

On-the-job training is a large part of the education of all animal caretakers. People working in kennels, animal shelters, stables, farms, pet stores, and as dog groomers are almost exclusively trained on the job. Most dog groomers, for instance, begin by practicing on their own pets. Then they groom dogs belonging to their friends and neighbors. They may also attend a dog grooming school. Finally they apprentice to a professional groomer and learn more about the business while on the job. In addition, the American Boarding Kennel Association and the National Dog Groomers Association provide workshops and educational videos for their members.

Several colleges offer course work in animal health, usually leading to an associate's degree after two years of study. Future animal caretakers at Harnell College in Salinas, California, for instance, take classes in anatomy, physiology, biology, chemistry, mathematics, clinical procedures, animal care and handling, clinical pharmacology, infectious diseases, pathology, radiology, surgical assisting, anesthesia, and current veterinary therapy. These students go on to work in veterinary practices, zoos and marine mammal parks and for wildlife rehabilitators, humane societies, pharmaceutical companies, and laboratory animal research institutions.

Zookeepers need a college degree in zoology, biology, or an animal-related field. Experience as a zoo volunteer, animal intern, or veterinary assistant is also very beneficial.

FYI

ABKA members provide dog and cat boarding, and dog daycare services to more than 15 million pets annually.

CERTIFICATION OR LICENSING

Licensing or certification for animal caretakers varies according to the job performed and the state of residence. For example, some states require veterinary technicians to be licensed while others do not, and no state regulates the dog grooming industry. Animal caretakers should check with their municipalities to determine local governmental regulations.

While many states do not regulate animal caretakers, several professional organizations offer certification. Professional certification, combined with work experience, helps animal caretakers earn higher pay and obtain better jobs.

Through correspondence courses, the American Boarding Kennel Association (ABKA) offers three levels of educational programs for its members: pet care technician, advanced pet care technician, and certified kennel operator. The National Dog Groomers Association offers a two-tiered voluntary certification program for its members, basic and master groomer, as well as periodic, one-day, intensive workshops. Certification requires completing a written test and hands-on performance. The applicant's work is critiqued by dog grooming professionals.

To determine certification for its members, the American Association for Laboratory Animal Science (AALAS) combines on-the-job work experience with college courses and rigorous AALAS examinations. AALAS certifies three categories: assistant laboratory animal technician, laboratory animal technician, and laboratory animal technologist. The AALAS also offers a manager of animal resources certification.

INTERNSHIPS AND VOLUNTEERSHIPS

Colleges and universities, along with professional organizations, are sources of information on work-study projects and student internships. Any type of volunteer work with animals is beneficial for future animal caretakers. Often, it is the only way for entry-level personnel to get important hands-on experience. Most cities have local divisions of the Humane Society, which are frequently in need of volunteers.

LABOR UNIONS

Most animal caretaker positions are not unionized. The exceptions are zookeepers who work for city or state zoos or aquariums that are under union contract. In these places, zookeepers may become union members.

Who Will Hire Me?

Deborah Donohoe began her career in laboratory animal science following a job layoff. While she enjoyed her work as a receptionist, it seemed a logical time to make a change. She began talking to lots of people about career alternatives. She already had an associate's degree in business when she decided to take the Purina Laboratory Animal Care Course. Her first job as a laboratory technician involved caring for 70 old world macaques and 20 squirrel monkeys at the Yerkes Primate Center in Atlanta.

Deborah believes in setting goals. When she started in laboratory animal science, she was determined to learn as much as she could about her new career and to advance as far as possible. "After my regular job duties were done, I asked if I could watch animal autopsies," she says. "I knew I didn't want to stay on the lowest rung of the career ladder, so I talked to pathologists,

veterinarians, microbiologists—anyone who would listen to my questions! Everyone was very receptive and I learned a lot." She also credits her American Association of Laboratory Animal Science certifications with helping her move forward. Now, more than 14 years after her first job with laboratory animals, she has reached the highest rung on the professional ladder and is a certified laboratory animal technologist.

Animal caretaking is a very broad field. Technical personnel work for research laboratories. Others may be employed by pharmaceutical and chemical companies, food production companies, medical schools, teaching hospitals, federal and state governments, or a branch of the armed forces. The majority of animal caretakers work in veterinary offices or boarding kennels. Zookeepers are employed by both private and public zoos. Some animal caretakers, especially those who are dog groomers or pet store owners, may operate their own businesses.

Business directories listing professional organizations and major employers may be obtained from local libraries. Federal job centers and state employment services may have information on jobs in animal caretaking.

Where Can I Go from Here?

Because the field is so varied, there is no typical career path for animal caretakers. Dog groomers or pet store workers may become store managers. Kennel workers may move up to kennel supervisor, assistant manager, or manager. With enough capital, groomers, kennel workers, and pet store caretakers may open their own businesses. Animal shelter workers may be promoted to animal control officers, assistant shelter managers, or shelter directors. Laboratory staff may advance from assistant laboratory animal technician to laboratory animal technician to technologist.

Beginning zookeepers start as animal attendants and may move to lead keeper in one area of the zoo. After that, they may become senior keepers and oversee the entire routine for an animal. They may also supervise the work of other employees. From there, zookeepers can move to administrative positions. These positions, though salaried, are less hands-on and require additional education. Curators, zoo registrars (people who keep track of breeding loans and animal stud books), and reproductive and behavior physiologists are examples of other salaried positions at zoos.

ADVANCEMENT POSSIBILITIES

Animal shelter directors run animal shelters and, if the shelter is a private organization, determine and enforce policy regarding adoptions and euthanasia; they also hire and supervise other workers.

Laboratory animal technologists supervise lab assistants and technicians and oversee the advanced care of animals, assisting in surgery and other complicated medical procedures.

Senior animal keepers oversee the entire routine and care of a particular zoo animal.

What Are the Salary Ranges?

Experience, level of education, employer, and work performed determine the salary ranges for animal caretakers. According to the *Occupational Outlook Handbook,* animal care and service workers had median annual earnings of $17,470 in 2003. Those in the middle 50 percent earned between $14,770 and $21,990. The lowest paid 10 percent earned less than $12,810, while the highest paid 10 percent earned more than $28,490.

The U.S. Department of Labor Occupational Information Network reports that in 2003 nonfarm animal caretakers earned $17,500 annually, with the lowest paid 10 percent earning $12,800 and the highest paid earning $28,500. Salary.com found that in 2005, the annual earnings nationwide for animal groomers were between $21,825 and $33,347; animal technicians earned from $32,811 to $36,971.

Information on the AALAS Web site includes several occupations and salary ranges for animal caretakers in 2005: cagewashers, $17,000 to $28,000; laboratory animal technicians, $18,000 to $38,000; animal health technicians, $28,000 to $39,000; and facility supervisors, $34,000 to $49,000. The highest paid are facility directors, who may earn from $110,000 to $148,000 annually.

What Is the Job Outlook?

According to the U.S. Department of Labor, job opportunities for animal care and service workers are expected to grow faster than the average through 2012. Most animal caregivers work in boarding kennels, animal shelters, animal hospital, and veterinary clinics. Others are employed by circuses and theme parks, and dog or horse race tracks. Zoos and similar facilities also offer employment opportunities; however, positions as animal caretakers in zoos, aquariums, and wildlife rehabilitation centers are scarce. Far more people want to work with wild and exotic animals than there are positions available.

Funding for both private and public research with animals is less now than what it has been in the past. Fewer research dollars means fewer animal caretaker jobs. Nevertheless, there remains a shortage of qualified laboratory animal research technicians and technologists. Veterinary practices and animal shelters often can't find enough staff. And almost every area of the country has pet stores, dog groomers, and kennels. Turnover, especially among part-time workers in these businesses, is high. Dedicated and qualified animal caretakers, particularly those with a lot of hands-on experience, are in high demand.

How Do I Learn More?

PROFESSIONAL ORGANIZATIONS

Following are organizations that provide information on animal caretaker careers, accredited schools, and employers.

American Association for Laboratory Animal Science
9190 Crestwyn Hills Drive
Memphis, TN 38125
901-754-8620
info@aalas.org
http://www.aalas.org

American Boarding Kennels Association
1702 East Pikes Peak Avenue
Colorado Springs, CO 80909
719-667-1600
info@abka.com
http://www.abka.com

Humane Society of the United States
2100 L Street, NW
Washington, DC 20037-1525
202-452-1100
http://www.hsus.org

National Dog Groomers Association of America
PO Box 101
Clark, PA 16113
724-962-2711
ndga@nationaldoggroomers.com
http://www.nationaldoggroomers.com

BIBLIOGRAPHY

The following is a sampling of materials relating to the professional concerns and development of animal caretakers:

Careers in Focus: Animal Care. 2d ed. Chicago: Ferguson Publishing Company, 2001.

Lee, Richard and Mary Price Lee. *Opportunities in Animal and Pet Careers.* Lincolnwood, Ill.: VGM Career Books, 2001.

Miller, Louise. *Careers for Animal Lovers & Other Zoological Types.* Lincolnwood, Ill.: VGM Career Horizons, 2000.

Pavia, Audrey. *Careers With Animals.* Hauppauge, N.Y.: Barron's Educational Series, 2001.

AUDIOMETRIC TECHNICIANS

"I can hear!" the client keeps repeating as he walks around the office, marveling at the effectiveness of his new hearing aid. For 10 years he has been missing out on many of the sounds in the world. Finally he has come to Don Sutton to purchase an assistive device

The client was concerned about the price, but Don has helped him select a reliable, inexpensive model that fits behind his ear. The customer is overjoyed, and his wife is also relieved that he can hear again.

She is perhaps not as relieved as another client who comes to Don because she has accidentally broken off the head of a cotton swab inside her ear canal. As he examines her ear, Don can see the cotton swab through his video otoscope, an instrument with a camera so tiny that it can be placed inside the patient's ear canal. He is advising the woman to consult a medical doctor when the instrument happens to touch the cotton swab, sticks to it, and pulls it out.

Although the remedy was unexpected, Don is glad to have solved the woman's problem. Helping people is a big part of an audiometric technician's job.

What Does an Audiometric Technician Do?

A hearing disorder can result from trauma at birth or other injury, an infection, the overuse of antibiotics or aspirin, smoking, a genetic defect, exposure to loud noises, unhealthy teeth, or other causes. People of all ages can suffer from hearing impairment, but it is most common among the elderly. To help people cope with hearing problems, *audiometric technicians* test clients' hearing, fit and clean hearing aids, and teach clients how to use assistive listening devices. They make ear mold impressions, prepare charts and graphs to track each patient's progress, teach clients about hearing and hearing disorders, and sell assistive listening devices and accessories.

To test hearing, the technician might have clients sit in a soundproof booth, where they listen through earphones to sounds such as human voices, automobiles, birds, and rain. The technician

Definition
Audiometric technicians conduct hearing screenings, test and clean hearing aids, and make ear mold impressions. They often also sell hearing aids and accessories.

Alternative Job Titles
Audiology assistants
Audiometrists
Auditory prosthologists
Hearing aid dispensers
Hearing instrument specialists
Licensed hearing specialists

High School Subjects
Biology
Speech

Personal Skills
Communication/ideas
Technical/scientific

Salary Range
$31,560 to $39,450 to $41,250+

Minimum Educational Level
Some postsecondary training

Certification or Licensing
Required by certain states

Outlook
Faster than the average

DOT
N/A

GOE
N/A

NOC
N/A

O*NET-SOC
N/A

pronounces various words and uses an audiometer to determine how well the customer can discern them. Audiometric technicians also use other types of sophisticated equipment to measure a person's sensitivity to pitch, intensity, and loudness.

To see inside a client's ears, the technician may use a video otoscope. The camera creates a magnified picture that the patient and technician can observe on a video screen. If a medical problem or significant blockage from ear wax is detected, the technician refers the client to a physician.

If a patient simply needs a hearing aid, the technician makes an ear mold impression by combining a special oil and powder to make liquid

Lingo to Learn

Acoustic trauma Hearing loss caused by a blow to the ear or by excessive noise.

Binaural Relating to or involving both ears.

Conductive hearing loss Hearing loss caused by interference with the way sound is carried into the inner ear.

Otosclerosis Hearing loss caused by new bone growth in the middle ear. This condition is usually hereditary.

Presbycusis Hearing loss associated with normal aging, that is, the gradual degeneration of sensory cells in the inner ear that leads to the inability to discriminate sounds.

Sensorineural (perceptive) hearing loss Hearing loss caused by degeneration of the organ of hearing, of the nerve that transmits impulses from the inner ear to the brain, or of the brain itself.

Tinnitus The perception of sound in the ear when there is no sound, commonly known as "ringing in the ears."

in conjunction with medical doctors. Requirements for this specialization vary from state to state, but in general a hearing instrument specialist has earned a license by passing a rigorous examination. An *auditory prosthologist* is a hearing instrument specialist with advanced certification.

Other audiometric technicians are employed as *audiology assistants*. They perform basic duties under the direction of certified audiologists, who hold master's or doctoral degrees. *Audiologists* have completed years of graduate-level studies in subjects such as anatomy, neuroanatomy, human perception of language, and the medical causes of hearing loss. They scientifically measure hearing ability, test for diseases in the middle ear, fit hearing aids, teach lip reading, and perform other rehabilitative services. Audiology assistants typically gather information that will be assessed by the audiologist, but they do not interpret test results or discuss evaluation and treatment with patients. The American Speech-Language-Hearing Association (ASHA) was founded in 1925 as the American Academy of Speech Correction. The organization standardized the requirements for audiology assistants in 1969 and adopted its current name in 1978.

What Is It Like to Be an Audiometric Technician?

wax. The technician inserts cotton and a string in the ear canal and pours the liquid wax over the cotton. The wax instantly hardens into a perfect duplicate of the ear canal. It is pulled out with the string and sent to the hearing aid manufacturer to be used as a model for making an assistive listening device that will fit comfortably inside the client's ear.

After fitting a hearing aid, the technician usually helps the client become oriented to the often overwhelming array of new sounds. The technician typically performs various follow-up services, such as changing batteries, monitoring for infection, adjusting the fit to eliminate any soreness, and checking periodically to ensure that the device is functioning properly.

Audiometric technicians who perform hearing examinations and who fit, dispense, clean, repair, and sell hearing aids and accessories are called *hearing instrument specialists, hearing aid dispensers,* or *licensed hearing specialists*. Often, they work in retail hearing aid stores. Sometimes they operate

Don Sutton is a hearing instrument specialist for Hearing Aid Counselors, a company that operates a chain of hearing aid outlets in Oregon. He is the office manager and the only audiometric technician in the store at Albany, where he works with one assistant and two telemarketers. He sees about 15 clients each day, mostly elderly people. The customers are generally friendly and often entertaining, but they can sometimes be difficult. Don is patient, chatting with them and learning each person's unique story.

Some customers visit only briefly to have their hearing aids cleaned, adjusted, or repaired. Don or his assistant scrub dust and wax out of the openings on the hearing aid with a small brush, then coat the device with a lubricating lotion that makes it easier to place in the ear. If the hearing aid is still not working properly, Don cleans it with a special vacuum or partially dismantles it and cleans the inside. The battery usually needs to be changed, and sometimes Don performs minor repairs on the hearing aid or ships it back to the manufacturer for more extensive repairs.

Don also tests people's hearing, using a video otoscope and an audiometer. As he performs the tests, he explains how the ear functions, what the test results reveal about the individual's hearing, how a hearing aid could help, and what types are available. Most new clients ask numerous questions, and Don can spend anywhere from 30 minutes to two hours talking with each of them.

In addition to his work at the store, Don sometimes makes house calls, an unusual service for an audiometric technician. In addition to his regular visits to six retirement homes in the community, he occasionally performs hearing tests at the homes of shut-in clients who cannot come to the store.

Another hearing aid specialist, Grant Gording, manages the Hearing Aid Counselors office at a shopping mall in Eugene, Oregon. He and his secretary open the store at about ten in the morning, take an hour for lunch, and go home at five or five-thirty. Working six- or seven-hour days and not having to work outside in bad weather are two things he says he loves about his job.

In a typical day Grant sees about four to six clients with appointments and perhaps a few walk-ins. He spends about an hour with each one. New customers fill out paperwork that details the history of their hearing, and then they are escorted to Grant's office for a hearing examination. If a client needs a hearing aid, Grant discusses the options and helps them select an appropriate model. About 60 percent of his customers already have hearing aids that need be examined, cleaned, adjusted for a proper fit, repaired in the office, or shipped away for repair.

Grant does much more than merely sell hearing aids. He explains, "Sometimes someone will say, 'My ear hurts,' and I have to find out where the problem is." With experience, he has become more adept at handling that type of challenge.

Grant talks to the owner of the Hearing Aid Counselors' chain of stores every few days but is basically in charge of the store in Eugene. It is almost like being self-employed, except that the home office pays the overhead.

Unlike Don and Grant, Fran Cosgrove is a licensed hearing aid specialist who operates her own store and sets her own working hours. She agrees that although retail sales are important for her business, customer service is her primary responsibility: "You can't just sell hearing aids. You need to offer service, too. A person can make a lot of money in this field, but we're here to help people hear better, not to sell someone something they don't want or need." Since manufacturers recommend replacing a hearing aid every four to six years, Fran knows that she will have continuing business as satisfied customers return to purchase new models.

> ... we're here to help people hear better, not to sell someone something they don't want or need.

Fran offers the same basic services as Don and Grant. She begins her examination by using a video otoscope to check for blockage from ear wax or other physical problems that should be referred to a medical doctor. She checks each ear separately, since hearing loss is not necessarily the same in both ears. All the while, she explains what tests she is conducting and why. "You need to gain the confidence of your client, so it's important to keep them informed about each procedure," she says.

Do I Have What It Takes to Be an Audiometric Technician?

Audiometric technicians need to be great communicators who are tactful and sensitive to the needs and feelings of their customers. They should also be patient, because some clients will probably be children or senior citizens who have special needs and comfort levels. A genuine desire to help people is perhaps a technician's most important quality.

Grant Gording says he entered the field "to be able to help people hear better. I knew a few people that needed help with their hearing." Most of his customers are elderly, and he notes, "You have to be good with people, with seniors particularly."

It is also important to be thorough and pay attention to detail. Many tests need to be repeated time and again, and some patients progress slowly. The technician must demonstrate perseverance and self-confidence. "It takes time for people to get used to wearing a hearing aid," Fran says. "I like working with people, and that's what you have to do. Find the right aid and make a good fit for the patient."

An aptitude for math and science is valuable in this field. Some knowledge of electronics, anatomy, physiology, linguistics, and psychology is also helpful.

How Do I Become an Audiometric Technician?

Grant Gording had two other careers before he became an audiometric technician more than 10 years ago. He began investigating the profession by talking to hearing instrument specialists in his community. When he knew that he wanted to obtain a license in the field, he began studying to prepare for the examination.

There is no standardized program of study for audiometric technicians, and requirements for licensure vary from state to state. In many states, hearing instrument specialists need only learn enough to pass the licensing examination. In other states, some experience, such as an apprenticeship, is required. In contrast, to become an audiology assistant, you must be sponsored by a certified audiologist.

EDUCATION

High School

You will probably not be allowed to apply for a license as an audiometric technician without a high school diploma or GED. To begin preparing for a career in the hearing sciences, you should take high school classes in biology, mathematics, electronics, psychology, speech, linguistics, and perhaps music. Some knowledge of computers will be helpful, since computer interactive programs are often part of a patient's course of treatment. Some high schools also offer classes that give students an opportunity to interact with children in a classroom; experience with children would be helpful if you became an audiometric technician who works at a school.

Postsecondary Training

Usually some training beyond high school is required to become an audiometric technician, but preparation for the career can be as simple as reading library books independently to prepare for the often rigorous licensing tests. This is what Grant Gording did, studying at home for about four months. He also completed an optional, two-day, preparatory course offered by a private company in Portland.

Don Sutton enrolled in a training program sponsored by a company that manufactures hearing aids. These programs can last from several months to a year and include instruction in human anatomy, with emphasis on topics such as the nerves within and around the ears.

The International Hearing Society National Board for Certification in Hearing Instrument Sciences (NBC-HIS) offers a home-study program for people interested in the hearing health care field. The course covers the human ear, audiometric testing, hearing instruments, and fitting.

You could also prepare by studying communication sciences and disorders, audiology, or speech pathology at a college or university. A general background in liberal arts would serve you well in various speech and language fields. After earning a bachelor's degree, you could work as an audiometric technician, return to school at some later time, and obtain the master's degree required to become an audiologist or speech pathologist.

Regardless of how you trained to enter the profession, you might be required to complete continuing education to retain your license. For example, in North Carolina audiometric technicians must complete eight to 12 hours of continuing education annually.

CERTIFICATION OR LICENSING

A license or certification is required to practice in this field, but licensing requirements vary from state to state. Grant Gording earned his certification by passing a written and practical test administered by the state. He and Fran Cosgrove both found that their licensing examinations were demanding and required intensive preparation.

Certification and licensing is typically handled through state departments of regulation and licensing. Those departments often provide candidates with study guides to help them prepare for the examinations. The exams typically consist of a written test and a hands-on demonstration of your skills in the trade. For example, in Wisconsin you have to perform hearing tests for all types and degrees of hearing loss during the examination.

You also are required to demonstrate your skills in audiometry and in making ear molds.

The International Hearing Society National Board for Certification and Hearing Instrument Sciences offers a certification program. Applicants must have two years experience in testing and fitting hearing instruments and must pass the National Competency Exam. This certification is not required but demonstrates professionalism.

Your state's licensing and regulatory board can provide specific information about obtaining credentials in your region. If you expect to relocate to another state some day, it might be wise to investigate reciprocity agreements; some states do not accept credentials granted in other states.

SCHOLARSHIPS AND GRANTS

Some grants are available through hearing aid manufacturers, such as Beltone, Starkey, and Miracle Ear, but most scholarships and grants are given to students pursuing a master's degree in audiology or speech pathology. Most graduate programs administer their own financial aid programs. The American Speech-Language-Hearing Association offers a few scholarships and grants for college and university students at the undergraduate, master's, and doctoral levels.

INTERNSHIPS AND VOLUNTEERSHIPS

Volunteering at a nursing home, community center, hospital, or public agency can help you decide whether you enjoy working with the public and, in particular, the elderly who make up the largest percentage of an audiometric technician's clientele. In some states you will need more structured on-the-job experience to pass the licensing examinations, because candidates must demonstrate their ability to perform the work of an audiometric technician. This gives you insights into the career and helps you prepare for the practical and written licensing examinations.

In some states you can learn this profession through an apprenticeship. For example, in Alabama an apprentice permit is granted in certain circumstances, but apprenticeship training is not required. In North Carolina candidates are required to complete 750 hours of on-the-job training under the supervision of a licensed hearing aid dealer and

ADVANCEMENT POSSIBILITIES

Audiologists determine the type and degree of hearing impairment and provide a range of services to help clients cope with impaired hearing. They also test noise levels where people work, and they conduct hearing protection programs for businesses, schools, and communities.

Speech pathologists, also known as **speech therapists,** work with people who cannot speak; those who cannot speak clearly, smoothly, and at the proper pitch; and those who cannot understand language. For example, they work with patients who stutter or have had a stroke. Sometimes they also diagnose and treat patients who have difficulty in swallowing and eating.

Speech, language, and hearing scientists study the complexities of human communication; investigate the way social and psychological factors influence communication; and help develop new ways to treat speech, language, and hearing disorders.

Otolaryngologists, also known as **otorhinolaryngologists,** are medical doctors who specialize in treating diseases of the ear, nose, and throat.

fitter before applying for a license through the state Hearing Aid Dealers and Fitters Board. In Wisconsin candidates can obtain trainee permits and practice the trade for one year under the supervision of a licensed hearing instrument specialist before taking the examination to obtain a permanent license.

Fran Cosgrove learned the trade by assisting another audiometric technician on the job. "He really took me under his wing and taught me the things I needed to know," she says. She adds that a formal training program, such as the one offered by the International Hearing Society National Board for Certification and Hearing Instrument Sciences, is useful, but "there is nothing that helps as much as practical experience. It certainly helped me."

In-depth

Parts of the Ear

The *outer ear* includes cartilage from which earrings are hung and the *external auditory canal,* a tunnel leading from the ear's opening to the *tympanic membrane* or *eardrum.*

The middle ear includes the inner surface of the eardrum and the three tiny, bony ossicles. They are named for their shape: the hammer, anvil, and the stirrup. In Latin, they are called the malleus, incus, and the stapes. When a sound causes the air to vibrate, these bones vibrate in response, and their vibrations are transmitted to the inner ear.

The *inner ear* includes chambers that are completely filled with fluid, which is jostled by the ossicles vibrating against a thin membrane called the *oval window.* This membrane separates the middle ear from the inner ear. Another flexible membrane, the *round window,* prevents the motion of the inner ear fluid from becoming too violent. The cochlea (Latin for snail or snail shell, which the organ resembles) is a bony structure about the size of a pea. Behind it is the *organ of Corti,* thousands of specialized nerve endings that are the individual sense receptors for sound. These are in the form of tiny hairs projecting from the membrane lining the cochlea; they wave like stalks of underwater plants in response to the oscillating currents of the inner ear fluid. There are some 20,000 of these hairs within the cochlea. They merge at the core of the cochlea and exit from its floor as the *auditory nerve.*

Who Will Hire Me?

Grant Gording found a job by calling hearing aid dealers on the telephone and explaining that he was a licensed hearing aid specialist in search of employment. Some of them invited him to be interviewed, and Hearing Aid Counselors offered him the position he now holds. That is an acceptable and fairly common way to find employment in this field. "Once you have a license, a lot of companies will have room for you," Grant notes.

Audiometric technicians have a wide range of potential employers. They work for the federal government, the Department of Veterans Affairs, the National Institutes of Health, the Department of Health and Human Services, and the Department of Education.

Audiometric technicians also work at city and county public health departments, community clinics, psychiatric institutions, retirement homes, nursing homes, universities, research laboratories, and private offices. Many audiometric technicians work in hospitals or rehabilitation centers. Others work for public schools and in offices where hearing aids are sold. Manufacturers of hearing aids, including the Beltone, Starkey, and Danavox companies, also employ audiometric technicians.

To find job openings in the field, watch the classified advertising sections of newspapers. This is how Fran Cosgrove found her first position and the mentor who taught her the basics of the profession. Some associations in the field maintain job banks on the Internet and publish newsletters that list employment opportunities.

Job seekers can also send resumes to audiologists; they are listed in the yellow pages of local telephone books. Many technicians learn of job openings through friends in the field, professors, and other personal contacts.

Where Can I Go from Here?

Grant Gording likes his job and plans to stay where he is indefinitely. He doesn't expect to be promoted since he works in a small office with no positions to which he could advance, but he will be paid more as the office does more business. He could operate his own store, but he says he has no desire to do that.

In contrast, Fran Cosgrove learned the trade by working under the tutelage of another audiometric technician, and then went into business for herself. She could expand on her success as an entrepreneur and eventually own a chain of hearing aid stores.

On the other hand, for an audiology assistant, the probability of advancement is small. Slight raises in pay would come with experience, but the American Speech-Language-Hearing Association strictly limits the scope of an assistant's responsibilities. The assistant would always have to work under the supervision of a certified audiologist. Any audiometric technician has the option of advancement, however, by obtaining a master's degree and becoming an audiologist, a speech pathologist, or a speech, language, and hearing scientist.

What Are the Salary Ranges?

An audiometric technician can invest a relatively small amount of money for training and a license, then earn a substantial income. The salary range is wide, however; some technicians get paid a salary, others work on commission, and others own their own businesses.

According to the American Speech-Language-Hearing Association (ASHA), technicians make approximately 60 to 75 percent of the salaries earned by audiologists and speech-language pathologists. Applying this percentage to the salaries listed in a 2003 ASHA survey would place the average technician's salary at between $31,560 and $41,250. Those with their own businesses, however, may make as much as $150,000 a year.

What Is the Job Outlook?

According to the *Occupational Outlook Handbook,* careers in audiology will grow faster than the average through 2012, largely because the number of elderly people will increase during the next few decades. There is also a growing awareness of childhood hearing problems and of the need to help people who have suffered a hearing loss on the job.

Most audiologists work in the offices of physicians, hospitals, and educational services, including elementary schools. The number of audiologists and speech-language pathologists in private practice is small, but it is expected to increase rapidly as schools, hospitals,

nursing homes, and managed care practices use more contract services. Audiometric technicians will be hired as assistants at many of those private offices.

There will be continued demand for hearing aids, but Grant Gording remarks, "With all the competition out there, it's getting harder and harder in this field." In addition to competing with numerous people entering the profession, he has seen profits drop as hearing aids are discounted. Third, he says, some hearing aids being built now are priced lower because their quality is not as high as it could be. "Unfortunately, a lot of consumers are buying into that," he notes.

Still, a large number of people will purchase hearing aids, particularly as technology improves the looks, quality, reliability, and comfort of assistive devices. Audiometric technicians will be needed to sell and service hearing aids until cures are found for the many causes of hearing impairment.

How Do I Learn More?

PROFESSIONAL ORGANIZATIONS

The following organizations provide information on audiometric technician careers, accredited schools, and employers:

American Academy of Audiology
8300 Greensboro Drive, Suite 750
McLean, VA 22102
703-790-8466
http://www.audiology.org

American Speech-Language-Hearing Association
10801 Rockville Pike
Rockville, Maryland 20852
800-638-8255
actioncenter@asha.org
http://www.asha.org

International Hearing Society National Board for
    Certification and Hearing Instrument Sciences
16880 Middlebelt Road
Livonia, MI 48154
734-522-2900
http://www.hearingnbc.org

BIBLIOGRAPHY

The following is a sampling of materials relating to the professional concerns and development of audiometric technicians:

Clark, John Greer, and Frederick N. Martin. *Introduction to Audiology: A Review Manual,* 5th ed. Needham Heights, Mass.: Allyn & Bacon, 2000.

Gelfand, Stanley A. *Essentials of Audiology.* 2d ed. New York: Thieme Medical Publishers, 2001.

Hicks, Patricia Larkins. *Opportunities in Speech-Language Pathology Careers.* Lincolnwood, Ill.: VGM Career Horizons, 1996.

Pearson, Lynea. *Competencies and Strategies for Speech-Language Pathologist Assistants.* Clifton Park, N.Y.: Singular, 2002.

AUTOMATIC TELLER MACHINE TECHNICIANS

||||||||||||||||||||||||||||||||||||||||||||||||||||||||||||||||||||

Guns, armored trucks, stacks of money, electronics. A day in the life of an ATM servicer can often appear to be something out of a high-tech heist movie.

Some years ago, the only way to make a transaction from your car was at the bank's drive-thru window via a series of pneumatic tubes. Today, there are ATM machines within blocks of each other. Some ATM technicians repair these machines, while others perform the daily duties of collecting deposits and replenishing the cash. Those handling the money often drive armored trucks and carry a gun, and may service 40 machines during one shift.

Obviously, security is a major issue, and technicians must pass security clearance and remain very honest. "To me, the best part of the job," says ATM technician Julie Hann, "is knowing that I'm trusted to be put into this kind of position. I like to know that people have such confidence in me."

What Does an ATM Technician Do?

How many times have you been frustrated to find that the nearest automated teller machine was blinking "temporarily out of service" across its screen? We tend to rely on those machines to be available 24-hours-a-day, seven days a week. But despite the fact that it is called an "automatic teller," each machine requires daily service—it certainly doesn't print the money and file the deposits on its own! ATMs are essentially computers that are connected to a central computer through a data network. To service ATMs may be as simple as clearing paper jams and situating cash properly, or it may require an understanding of electronics and computer programming.

The work of *ATM technicians* varies according to the position. *First line technicians* are those who replenish the money, replace receipt paper, remove any obstructions in the machine, balance the machine, and remove deposits and deliver them to a central office. When an ATM seems not to be working

Definition
Automatic teller machine (ATM) servicers maintain and repair the ATMs at banks, grocery stores, convenience stores, and other locations.

Alternative Job Titles
ATM field service technician
ATM network specialist
ATM servicer

High School Subjects
Computer science
Mathematics
Technical/shop

Personal Skills
Following instructions
Technical/scientific

Salary Range
$20,700 to $33,950 to $53,470+

Minimum Educational Level
Some postsecondary training

Certification or Licensing
Required by certain states

Outlook
About as fast as the average

DOT
N/A

GOE
09.09.01

NOC
N/A

O*NET-SOC
49-2011.00

properly, technicians troubleshoot and attempt to define the problem. They may also check security equipment, such as cameras and VCRs, to ensure they are working properly. Depending on the size of the city in which they work, ATM technicians may service 30 to 40 machines a day. These technicians are usually armed and drive armored trucks to and from the ATM locations. First line technicians are also stationed in the office to dispatch technicians, count the money, and fill out forms for the banks. Processing deposits involves opening envelopes and documenting the contents. Supervisors train and schedule technicians. They also send out *second line technicians* when the first line technicians are unable to fix particular problems with the machines.

Second line technicians are typically on call and are paged when a repair is necessary. With an understanding of particular machines, networks, and electronic systems, they perform maintenance on the machines, replacing parts when necessary. They also test the machines as preventive maintenance. If the dispenser (the part of the machine that contains the money) needs to be serviced, first line technicians will stand guard while the second line technicians make any necessary adjustments. A technician may be called in if a machine is unable to properly read bank cards because of worn magnetic heads, or if it has a "fail" that prevents it from dispensing the requested amount of cash. If a problem is too extensive to be corrected on site, the technician may take the machine, or parts of it, to a *bench technician*.

Some technicians are trained to install ATMs, which can involve securing the ATM at a particular site and programming the machine. They may put up signs and awnings over the machines. They may also remove or relocate machines.

Both first line and second line technicians can work odd hours. Technicians may work day or night shifts, or they may be on call over long periods of time. ATMs may need servicing late at night, on weekends, and on holidays.

What Is It Like to Be an ATM Technician?

Julie Hann is a first line technician for an armored truck service. As a night-shift supervisor, she oversees the work of other first line technicians and assigns them their routes. She also goes out on runs when they are short-staffed. "My major responsibility is paperwork," she says, "because they're bringing back money and they've got to count it. I've got to report what we bring back to the bank, so I have to fill out all kinds of forms on the computer, print them out, and fax them over."

Julie believes the work of a first line ATM technician is fairly simple, but that some people do have problems following the procedures as closely as they need to. When her crew of technicians service an ATM, they replenish money, replace paper rolls, and perform other routine maintenance. "You've got to remember to check all the paper. You've got to make sure the money is in right, make sure no sensors are blocked. If you've got a part that's actually broken

or a part that needs to be replaced, you have to call second line." The most successful technicians are those who can follow closely all the required steps.

Richard Wesley is a second line technician for an ATM overhaul and service company that contracts with an area bank. "I have to do whatever it takes to get the ATM back in service," he says. "ATMs can't stay down very long." He works a regular 8:00 A.M. to 5:00 P.M., Monday through Friday workweek, and is also on call every other weekend and after 5:00 P.M. every other week. He is stationed at home and receives calls via cell phone and pager. "When I get a call, I go to the branch or off-site, like a grocery store, that has the bank's ATMs." With his understanding of electronics, Richard performs repairs on site after speaking to the first line technician about the ATM's problems. "After each repair, I have to call the host, which electronically talks to the site and also to the bank via the ATM. I do that to close out the service call and to make sure that the ATM is working properly."

Though Richard doesn't like being on call so much and having to drive between 400 and 1,200 miles a week, he does like working out of his home rather than an office. "You're your own boss," he says. "As long as you do your job and keep the ATMs operational, the company doesn't interfere." Some days he doesn't have to answer a single call, while other days he may work for 12 hours straight.

Lingo to Learn

Armored car A truck with plates of armor and strong locks for the transporting of large sums of money.

Debit card A plastic card with identification encoded into its electromagnetic strip; used in ATMs for bank service.

Dispenser The compartment of the ATM that holds and distributes the cash.

Proprietary network A network that is only accessible by one particular bank's customers.

Shared network A network that links together a number of different banks and accounts.

Frank Ryan has been with Brink's, the armored truck service, for more than 32 years and has seen firsthand how ATM technology has developed. When he first started working as an ATM technician over 18 years ago, the crews made three runs with 25 stops a day. "Now we do probably 15 runs and 40 stops a day. There used to be a mile or two between ATMs, now you've got four or five in the same block." The number of different data networks has also increased. "There are about 50 different networks, and we have to know how each network is balanced and what could go wrong."

Do I Have What It Takes to Be an ATM Technician?

Trustworthiness is probably the main quality you should have. "You have to be very responsible because you're dealing with money," says Julie. "The armored people bring in money too, but theirs is packaged. We actually have our hands on the money. So responsibility is very important." To ensure that you're trustworthy, employers will put you through extensive security clearance. "They have credit checks, background checks, driving record checks," Julie says. Some employers also require polygraph and drug tests.

You should also be dependable. If an employer is going to rely on you to be on call, you'll need to be prepared to service a machine at odd, inconvenient hours. You must also be able to work without close supervision. Richard says, "You have to have the desire to make sure the work is done right since no one is looking over your shoulder."

Problem-solving skills are important, and if supervising other technicians, you'll need people skills and the ability to coordinate the work of others. If doing second line service, you'll need some mechanical and computer skills, as well as finger dexterity and good vision.

How Do I Become an ATM Technician?

Richard developed electronics training and supervisory skills before going to work as a second line technician. He found the job listing in the local newspaper. "I was hired because of my electronics

FYI

Although a patent for an automated-type cash machine was registered by George Simjian in New York in the 1930s, John Shepherd-Barron is recognized as the machine's inventor. The National Cash Register Co. (NCR) produced and installed the first ATM in a Barclays Bank in the London Borough of Enfield on June 27, 1967.

training for work on the ATMs," he says, "and my supervisor skills to satisfy the banking personnel whenever the ATMs were down and customers got mad." He recommends that students take courses that deal with both electronics and mechanics, because ATM repair requires skill in both areas.

EDUCATION

High School

Take any computer and electronics courses available, including programming. Being familiar with some

To Be a Successful Automatic Teller Machine Technician, You Should . . .

○ be exceedingly trustworthy and responsible

○ have good mechanical and computer skills, as well as finger dexterity

○ be dependable, since you may be on call to work at odd or irregular hours

○ have good vision

○ be able to work without close supervision

○ enjoy troubleshooting and solving complex problems

○ be a good problem-solver

FYI

According to the ATM Industry Association, in 2005 there were almost 1.5 million ATMs worldwide. In 2004, the average number of transactions per ATM were 2,400 a month.

ATMs are known by a variety of names around the world, including Bankomat (Continental Europe), Bank Machine (Canada), Geldautomat (Germany), Postomat (Switzerland), and Telebanco and Cajero Automtico (Spain). Other names used to describe ATMs are "hole-in-the-wall," "ugly teller," and "robotic teller."

computer languages may give you an edge as ATMs become more complex. By taking English courses, you'll develop the communication skills that can be necessary in supervising other technicians and dealing with the clients of the ATM service.

Postsecondary Training

First line technicians typically get their training on the job, but second line technicians often must have electronics experience before being hired. Some positions require an associate's degree, or equivalent experience, in electronics or electronic equipment repair. Manufacturers of machines also provide training, and employers may require that technicians have an understanding of specific ATMs and data networks.

Electronics technology programs are available at community colleges and vocational schools and offer courses in such subjects as electrical circuits, technical mathematics, mechanics, electrical drafting, and industrial electronics.

CERTIFICATION OR LICENSING

Various manufacturers, such as NCR, Triton Systems, and Diebold, offer certification in the use of their machines. This certification may be required

by some employers. Some states also require that technicians driving armored trucks or carrying guns be licensed as security guards.

Who Will Hire Me?

While banks and credit unions do hire technicians, the majority of work is available from businesses that contract with banks for the maintenance of ATMs. Armored truck services such as Brink's hire first and second line technicians, as do suppliers of ATMs and parts. Most technicians will find jobs with ATM installation and service companies that maintain the many ATMs in grocery and convenience stores, malls, department stores, and at other citywide locations. These jobs are frequently advertised in the newspaper, or you can check for area services in the yellow pages under "Automated Teller Machines." By typing "ATM services" in an Internet search engine, you'll be directed to installation companies that hire technicians from all across the country. ATMmarketplace.com offers free membership and allows you to search current job postings; it also links you to the sites of ATM manufacturers.

ADVANCEMENT POSSIBILITIES

Software engineers create computer software programs tailored to the needs of specific businesses.

Database administrators design, install, and update computer databases of business information.

Sales managers oversee sales staff in direct interaction with customers.

Computer and office machine service technicians install, calibrate, maintain, troubleshoot, and repair equipment such as computers and their peripherals, office equipment, and specialized electronic equipment used in many factories, hospitals, airplanes, and numerous other businesses.

Where Can I Go from Here?

Julie worked as a first line technician in various shifts before advancing into a supervisor position. Some day she'd like to go back to college, but she likes the close-knit community that the small armored truck business provides. Richard plans to continue to repair ATMs or to explore other opportunities in electronics.

Within an installation and repair service, a technician may move on to become a bench technician who handles the more complex repairs that can't be made on site. Technicians may also go to work for manufacturers to assist engineers in designing equipment. Some technicians also start their own services, contracting with banks and credit unions to install and maintain their ATMs.

What Are the Salary Ranges?

According to the *Occupational Outlook Handbook*, computer, automated teller, and office machine repairers had an annual median salary of $33,950 in 2003. Those in the lowest paid 10 percent earned less than $20,700, and those in the highest paid 10 percent made more than $53,470. Technicians sometimes draw overtime, and may also have benefits such as medical, dental, paid vacation, and 401(k). They may be allowed a company car or van for personal and work use.

What Is the Job Outlook?

The U.S. Department of Labor expects that employment of computer, automated teller, and office machine repairers will grow about as fast as the average through 2012. Job growth for repairers is expected to come from the dependence of businesses on more advanced computers and office equipment that will need maintenance and repairs. Workers who complete the most advanced training will be in high demand.

According to ATMmarketplace.com, some industry leaders don't believe there is much of a shortage of technicians because of the self-

sufficiency of the machines themselves. ATMs are becoming more reliable and in less need of second line maintenance. Others in the industry, however, believe the hardware is becoming more complex and computer based, requiring more second line technicians with programming knowledge and more extensive training.

ATM manufacturers are constantly exploring new technology and developing ATMs that require less service while offering more features. ATMs will soon be offering more than just money; additional dispensers will be added to offer stamps, phone cards, and even tickets for travel by bus, train, or plane. Some ATMs being developed have Web capabilities, allowing for more direct marketing. Though manufacturers promote these ATMs as requiring less maintenance, these machines may actually require the services of more extensively trained technicians to maintain all the various systems and hardware.

In addition, as banks and financial institutions look for methods to improve their economics they are beginning to outsource the ATM portion of their businesses to independent companies and third-party providers, which may lead to new job opportunities for repairers.

How Do I Learn More?

PROFESSIONAL ORGANIZATIONS

To learn more about the ATM industry, contact
ATM Industry Association
1 Sterling Ridge Drive
Rensselaer, NY 12144
888-208-1589
http://www.atmianortham.com

BIBLIOGRAPHY

Ibe, Oliver C. *Essentials of ATM Networks and Services.* Boston: Addison-Wesley, 1997.

Karim, M. R. *ATM Technology and Services Delivery.* Upper Saddle River, N.J.: Pearson Education, 2000.

Keyes, Jessica. *Handbook of Technology in Financial Services.* Boca Raton, Fla.: CRC Press, 1999.

McDyson, David E. and Darren L. Spohn. *ATM Theory and Applications.* New York: McGraw-Hill, 1998.

AUTOMOBILE MECHANICS

The problem seemed simple—the customer had brought the car to the Toyota dealership, reporting that the "check engine light" was on. Kelly Pennington, the auto technician, brought the car into his stall and hooked up the computer. "It had 15 codes," Kelly says, "which is way out of the ordinary." Usually the computer brings up only a few codes, which direct the technician in repair. Kelly called in the shop foreman, and they began working on the car. "I pulled the entire engine wiring harness out of this car trying to find an open wire, a wire that had broken or been severed inside the shielding where you couldn't see it." When he saw that everything was fine, he put the car back together.

The same 15 computer codes came up. "So we went to work on it again," he says. "By then I had the wiring schematics out, and we were tracing each and every wire on this wiring schematic. This car has 17 onboard computers, there are wires everywhere." Eventually, Kelly discovered that all the circuits affected had a common ground point beneath the carpeting and up under the dash. The customer had neglected to tell them that water had been running on the floorboard whenever he ran the air-conditioner. Moss had plugged the drain hole, and the running water had corroded the ground connector for all the different circuits. "I pulled this little 10 millimeter screw out, cleaned it up, plugged it back in, erased the codes, and the car ran great. It took me 10 minutes."

What Does an Automobile Mechanic Do?

Americans have become dependent upon their vehicles. Each year we buy more cars and trucks and vans, which in time require routine services and repairs. In addition, almost everyone has experienced the frustration and inconvenience of an automobile breakdown. Whether we are dealing with a complete breakdown or a routine oil change, we bring our vehicles to automobile mechanics, who service and repair automobiles and other gasoline-powered vehicles.

When mechanical or electrical troubles occur, mechanics either discuss the nature of the trouble with the vehicle owner or, if they work in a dealership or large repair shop, they may consult a *repair service estimator* or access the information on a computer system. Relying on solid analytical and troubleshooting skills and a thorough knowledge of automobiles, mechanics diagnose the source of the problem with the aid of test equipment such as engine analyzers, scanners, spark plug testers, and compression gauges. Most mechanics value the challenge of making an accurate diagnosis, counting it among their favorite duties.

After the cause of the problem has been established, mechanics make adjustments or repairs. If the part

---

Definition
Automobile mechanics repair, service, and overhaul the mechanical, electrical, hydraulic, and electronic parts of automobiles, light trucks, vans, and other gasoline-powered vehicles.

Alternative Job Titles
Automotive service technicians
Bus mechanics
Truck mechanics

High School Subjects
Mathematics
Physics
Technical/shop

Personal Skills
Leadership/management
Mechanical/manipulative

Salary Range
$17,510 to $31,570 to $53,550+

Minimum Educational Level
Some postsecondary training

Certification or Licensing
Voluntary

Outlook
About as fast as the average

DOT
620

GOE
05.03.01

NOC
7321

O*NET-SOC
49-3023.00

in question is damaged or worn beyond repair, it is ordered, often with the use of a computer system, and replaced, usually with the authorization of the vehicle owner.

During routine service and preventive maintenance—an oil change, for instance—mechanics consult a checklist to ensure they service all important items. They inspect a vehicle's belts, hoses, steering system, fuel injectors, air filter, battery, spark plugs, transmission fluid, and brake systems. They lubricate and adjust engine components and repair or replace parts to avoid future breakdowns.

In their work, mechanics use a variety of power tools, such as pneumatic wrenches, machine tools, such as lathes and grinders to rebuild brakes, and hand tools. Most mechanics furnish their own hand tools, acquired gradually during the first several years of their careers. They may spend between $2,000 and $15,000 for a complete set of tools. In addition, they use welding equipment to repair exhaust systems, jacks and hoists to lift vehicles, and a growing variety of sophisticated electronic equipment, such as infrared analyzers and computerized diagnostic devices.

Most mechanics are able to perform a wide array of repairs, but as automobiles have become increasingly sophisticated, mechanics have become specialized.

Electrical systems mechanics service and repair batteries, starting and charging systems, lighting and signaling systems, electrical instruments, and accessories.

Automotive radiator mechanics flush radiators with chemical solutions, locate and solder leaks, install new radiator cores, and replace old radiators with new ones.

Automotive exhaust technicians conduct tests on vehicles to ensure that exhaust emission levels comply with state regulations.

Engine performance mechanics perform general and specific engine diagnosis and service and repair ignition systems, fuel and exhaust systems, emission control systems, and cooling systems.

Automotive field-test technicians work in manufacturing, research, and development, preparing vehicles for road tests in field proving grounds.

Brake mechanics inspect and repair drum, disc, and combination brake systems, parking brake systems, power assist units, and hydraulic application systems. Some perform front-end work as well.

What Is It Like to Be an Automobile Mechanic?

Kelly Pennington works for Toyota as an automotive technician. When customers bring their cars to the dealership for repair, they explain the problems they're experiencing to a service writer, who then enters the complaint into the computer. The service writer also goes out to the vehicle to verify the problem to the best of his or her ability. Once this verification is made, the computer prints out a ticket for the dispatcher. Each morning, the dispatcher distributes these tickets to the mechanics on duty.

Kelly has his own assigned stall, which includes two lifts. After reading the complaint from the ticket, Kelly brings the car in and begins to diagnose the problem. "They're all different," Kelly says. "One could be that a brake light is out, the next one could be that the engine's knocking."

One of his first responsibilities is to fill out a price and availability sheet. "I figure out what the car needs and how much labor time it's going to take to

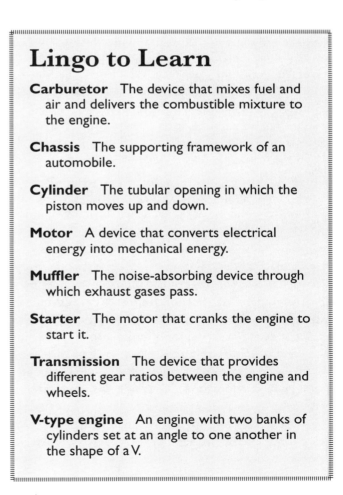

Lingo to Learn

Carburetor The device that mixes fuel and air and delivers the combustible mixture to the engine.

Chassis The supporting framework of an automobile.

Cylinder The tubular opening in which the piston moves up and down.

Motor A device that converts electrical energy into mechanical energy.

Muffler The noise-absorbing device through which exhaust gases pass.

Starter The motor that cranks the engine to start it.

Transmission The device that provides different gear ratios between the engine and wheels.

V-type engine An engine with two banks of cylinders set at an angle to one another in the shape of a V.

fix it," he says. The service writer then takes the sheet and contacts the customer. If the customer okays the repairs, Kelly starts work; even if the customer declines the work, Kelly must enter a report into the computer. "We have to do a computer story on every car we work on," Kelly says.

Kelly relies a great deal on reference materials. "At the Toyota dealership," he says, "I bet if there's one, there's a thousand service manuals back there on all different kinds of Toyotas."

In dealing with a particular problem, Kelly is only paid for a certain amount of time. Toyota puts out a manual that mechanics must consult, detailing how many hours of labor it will pay for a certain kind of repair. "The Toyota book says it pays six-and-a-half hours' labor to do a clutch in a Four-Runner with a three liter V6," Kelly explains. "If it takes you nine hours to do that job, you only get paid for six-and-a-half hours. If it takes you three hours to do that job, you still get paid six-and-a-half hours. The more you learn, the faster you get, the more money you make."

Automobile mechanics do most of their work indoors, in well-ventilated, lighted repair shops, though some make outdoor service calls to perform emergency repairs on vehicles that have broken down on the road. Mechanics often work in awkward, cramped positions, beneath vehicles or under the hoods, handling greasy and dirty parts. Design, test, research, and development technicians often work in engineering departments or in laboratories that are cleaner than repair shops.

While mechanics must be able to work independently, they must also have the ability to function as members of a team. Above all, technicians must understand the basic scientific and mathematical theories that support their work. As the field changes and automobiles become more complex, technicians need a clear understanding of the underlying science in order to keep abreast of the industry.

Computers have become important to automotive work. Kelly uses a "scan tool" that allows him to plug into the computer programs built into the Toyotas he services. "You can talk directly to the computer," he says. "The computer will tell you what the car's doing, why it's doing it." The handheld computer tool allows Kelly to pull a "snapshot" depicting exactly what the car was doing when it died.

Kelly works a regular five-day workweek, which includes every other Saturday. "I love my job," Kelly says. "I like working on cars. You get

gratification from it, because a car comes in broken and it leaves fixed." The job also allows Kelly to work independently, while also providing a team on which to rely. "On some things I get stumped," he says, "and there are always guys to talk to. A lateral support group, I guess you'd call it."

One drawback Kelly cites is the expense of the tools. "Most places don't provide tools, or they only provide a very limited supply," he says. "You must buy your own, and they're not cheap." He estimates conservatively that he has $25,000 invested in tools. "And I don't have nearly as many tools as most of the guys in my shop who have been there 15 or 20 years."

Do I Have What It Takes to Be an Automobile Mechanic?

"You have to be able to think through a problem," Kelly says. "Problem solving, on today's cars, is probably more important than being mechanically inclined."

> Problem solving . . . is probably more important than being mechanically inclined.

In addition, mechanics need strong interpersonal and customer service skills. They are often required to listen to customers explain automotive problems and, in turn, they must be able to explain diagnostic results and required repairs, translating technical language into lay terms. Dealing with customers who do not understand the basic functions of an automobile can be a challenging experience.

Individuals with a desire to learn new service and repair techniques are excellent candidates for postsecondary automotive training programs. Mechanics must be disciplined, systematic, and analytical and have careful work habits. They must understand every detail of every part, how the parts work together, and what would happen if all parts were not assembled or working properly. Technicians today also must have a working knowledge of electronics, because a growing variety of automotive components are using electronic devices. In automotive vehicles, electrical systems crank the engine for starting, furnish high voltage sparks to the cylinders to fire compressed fuel-air charges, and operate the lights, the heater motor, and other accessories. Mechanics must be able to determine when an electronic malfunction is responsible for a problem.

How Do I Become an Automobile Mechanic?

Kelly first learned about cars as a kid hanging out in his grandfather's repair shop. Since going to work for Toyota, his training has been on the job. As part of the training process, he was sent to a regional center for classes. "If you pursue an associate's degree in automotive technology," Kelly says, "you will learn so much so fast, and you'll be three times as marketable coming out of the gate as you would if you just went and applied for a job." He recommends that students take any kind of electrical training, in order to learn how to read map circuits and voltage flow.

EDUCATION

High School

Chuck Bowen is the director of the Transportation Technology Department at the Dunwoody College of Technology in Minneapolis, Minnesota. He recommends that high school students interested in pursuing a diploma in automotive technology take mathematics, physics, and English courses. "Applied math and applied science courses are ideal," he says. In order to keep up with new technology and understand technical manuals, high school students are told to take courses in algebra, plane geometry, chemistry or another laboratory science, basic drafting, automotive technology, electronics, and metals. Strong reading, grammar, and writing skills are essential.

Postsecondary Training

Chuck Bowen's postsecondary program is typical of those offered by vocational-technical schools and community colleges. While there are some four-year programs, most institutions spread the training over two years, after which you earn a

---

TO BE A SUCCESSFUL AUTOMOBILE MECHANIC, YOU SHOULD . . .

○ be patient and have excellent troubleshooting skills

○ have a mechanical aptitude

○ be comfortable talking to strangers

○ have excellent customer service and communication skills

○ have a working knowledge of computers

---

diploma. Some community colleges supplement the technical training with courses in English, speech, composition, and social science, awarding an associate's degree at the end of two years. High school programs in automotive technology offer an introduction to the field, but they vary in quality, and it is difficult to get the necessary science background and the hands-on experience that a formal program offers.

In order to be admitted to the Dunwoody program, you must have graduated in the top half of your high school classes; otherwise you must pass an entrance exam. Students may enroll in either the Automotive Technician Apprenticeship Cooperative program or the Automotive Service Technology program. Each is two years long and covers all aspects of automotive repair, including engine performance analysis, automatic transmissions, brake operation and service, fuel systems, ignition systems, and computer control systems. Students also take courses in math, science, English, and computers.

FYI

According to the U.S. Department of Transportation, there were 129,748,704 passenger cars in the United States in 1997. In 2004 the number of registered passenger cars and motorcycles had increased to 140,924,833.

An automotive mechanic inspects and changes brake pads.   (David R. Frazier / Photo Researchers Inc.)

The Dunwoody College of Technology programs are certified by the National Automotive Technicians Education Foundation (NATEF), an affiliate of the National Institute for Automotive Service Excellence (ASE). While certification is voluntary for training institutions, it ensures that a program meets uniform standards for instructional facilities, equipment, staff credentials, and curriculum. Over 1,200 high schools and postsecondary automotive service technician training programs are certified by NATEF.

Several automobile manufacturers sponsor two-year training programs in automotive service technology. For more information contact the following organizations:

Ford Motor Company ASSET Program
http://www.fordasset.com

Chrysler Dealer Apprenticeship Program
800-722-7666
http://www.sunyrockland.edu/auto/cap.htm

General Motors Automotive Service Educational
   Program
800-828-6860
http://www.gmasepbsep.com

CERTIFICATION OR LICENSING

Voluntary certification by ASE is recognized as a standard of achievement for automotive mechanics, who become certified in one or more of eight different areas—the same eight units by which the Dunwoody College of Technology organizes its educational program.

Certification requires at least two years of experience and the passing of the examination. Completing an automotive mechanics program in high school or community or junior college may be substituted for one year of experience. Individuals who pass all eight tests earn the title General Automobile Mechanic. Certified mechanics must retake the examinations at least every five years.

LABOR UNIONS

Some automobile mechanics belong to the International Association of Machinists and Aerospace Workers or the International Brotherhood of Teamsters, Chauffeurs, Warehousemen and Helpers of America. Another union is the United

Automobile, Aerospace, and Agricultural Implement Workers of America.

Who Will Hire Me?

Typically, trainee mechanics work one or two years, acquiring the proficiency to perform the more difficult types of diagnostic testing, service, and repairs. Some specialists, such as automotive radiator and brake mechanics, learn the skills quickly, while the more difficult specialties, such as automatic transmission repair, take a great deal of time to learn. "When a shop hires someone on," Kelly says, "they hire them on as a lube tech. You do oil changes all day long, every day. Then sooner or later, a master tech [position] comes open and they sign the new hire on as an apprentice. Then he's got to be an apprentice for two years. He's paid a minimum wage working under a master tech so that the master tech can watch him, teach him what he needs to know."

The majority of mechanics work in franchised dealerships, such as Chrysler, Honda, GM, and Saturn. Other jobs exist in service stations, auto body repair shops, tire stores, parts supply stores, and department store automotive service centers. Federal, state, and local governments hire technicians to service their vehicles, as do taxi cab companies, trucking firms, and bus lines. Technical program students can learn more about job openings from their department heads, teachers, or placement officers. Graduating students may also apply directly to the personnel office of any auto, truck, or tractor dealership or to the many related industries.

Where Can I Go from Here?

With Toyota, mechanics advance through a three-step process. They hire on as technicians, move up to pro technicians, then master technicians. Kelly is working toward a position as a master tech. "That's where the money is," he says. "That's where you're marketable."

As mechanics gain practical experience and become ASE-certified in one or more specialties, they become more valuable to their employers. Experienced mechanics with demonstrated leadership skills may advance to garage supervisor positions or service management. Mechanics adept at working with customers may become automotive repair estimators

> **ADVANCEMENT POSSIBILITIES**
>
> **Automobile collision repairers** repair, replace, and repaint damaged body parts of automobiles, buses, and light trucks.
>
> **Automatic transmission technicians** service power trains, couplings, hydraulic pumps, mechanical systems, and other parts of automatic transmissions.
>
> **High-performance engine technicians** analyze, test, and maintain high-performance engines in the auto racing industry. They also redesign parts to enhance engine performance.
>
> **Sales representatives** advise customers and recommend the parts or vehicles best suited to their needs.
>
> **Service managers** manage automobile dealership service departments, hire and train employees, select equipment, and assist in diagnosing customer automotive problems.

or salespersons. Many mechanics, in time, open their own independent shops.

What Are the Salary Ranges?

According to the U.S. Department of Labor, the median earnings in 2003 for automobile mechanics were $31,570. Those in the middle 50 percent earned between $22,850 and $42,220. The lowest paid 10 percent earned $17,510 annually, while the highest paid 10 percent earned $53,550.

Salaries also are dependent upon the geographic location and type of shop. Automotive mechanics employed by maintenance and repair facilities averaged $29,690 annually; auto dealers, $39,180; auto parts and tire stores, $28,460; gas stations, $30,860; and local governments, $38,960. The main factors affecting earnings are experience and training. The key to getting a good-paying job is good training. Salary.com reports that the median earnings nationwide in 2005 for an automotive mechanic with two to five years of experience were $38,673.

What Is the Job Outlook?

In general, it is important to remember the simple fact that machinery and equipment eventually break down, and thus skilled repair technicians will always be in demand. The *Occupational Outlook Handbook* reports that employment for automobile mechanics is expected to increase as fast as the average for all occupations through 2012. The best jobs will go to those with some automotive training.

Kelly expects technician jobs to become more plentiful, as shops are having trouble finding good mechanics. "They're hard to come by these days," Kelly says, "because nobody wants to get dirty and greasy, and nobody wants to sweat in the summer. And nobody wants to go through all the rigamarole it takes to be a good technician."

Federal, state, and local regulations governing safety and pollution control, along with more extensive warranties on new cars and trucks, will create jobs for skilled technicians. In addition, the overall economic climate has little effect on the automobile repair business. Vehicles break down irrespective of an increase in interest rates or a sharp dive by the Dow Jones industrial average.

Opportunities are expected to increase for technicians with experience in the area of alternative fuels vehicles. In efforts to decrease U.S. reliance on foreign oil as well as decrease air pollution, auto manufacturers are producing more vehicles fueled by alternatives to gasoline and diesel. With more alternative fuel vehicles on the road, there will be more demand for technicians with special training in their repair.

How Do I Learn More?

PROFESSIONAL ORGANIZATIONS

The following are organizations that provide information on automobile mechanic careers, accredited schools and scholarships, and employers:

Automotive Service Association
PO Box 929
Bedford, TX 76095-0929
800-272-7467
asainfo@asashop.org
http://www.asashop.org

Motor and Equipment Manufacturers Association
PO Box 13966
10 Laboratory Drive
Research Triangle Park, NC 27709-3966
919-549-4800
info@mema.org
http://www.mema.org

National Institute for Automotive Service Excellence
101 Blue Seal Drive, Suite 101
Leesburg, VA 20175
703-669-6650
http://www.iatn.net/ase

National Automotive Technician Education Foundation
101 Blue Seal Drive, Suite 101
Leesburg, VA 20175
703-669-6650
http://www.natef.org

BIBLIOGRAPHY

The following is a sampling of materials relating to the professional concerns and development of automobile mechanics:

Careers in Focus: Mechanics. Chicago: Ferguson Publishing Company, 2001.

Lee, Richard S. and Mary Price Lee. *Careers for Car Buffs and Other Freewheeling Types.* 2d ed. New York: McGraw-Hill, 2003.

McShane, Clay. *The Automobile: A Chronology of Its Antecedents, Development, and Impact.* Chicago: Fitzroy Dearborn Publishers, 1997.

Weber, Robert M., Philip A. Perry, and Ronald H. Weiner. *Opportunities in Automotive Service Careers.* Lincolnwood, Ill.: VGM Career Horizons, 2001.

AUTOMOTIVE BODY REPAIRERS

Shawn Bosolo looks over the white Toyota pickup truck and rereads the estimate. The truck had hit a deer, the most common accident on the highways in and around Missoula, Montana, where Shawn works as an automotive body repairer.

Yesterday he finished up a white Chevrolet pickup that had also hit a deer, but he's glad this one is a Toyota. He needs to take most of the truck apart to get at the repairs, and he could probably do it all with a 10- and 12-millimeter socket. "Working on domestic cars takes five times the number of tools needed to work on foreign cars," Shawn says. "And the tools change every year because the cars change every year."

After Shawn gets the hood and radiator off the car, he'll put the entire body up on the frame rack to straighten it out. The right front corner was seriously squashed, and the whole front end bent sideways as a result. "Must have been a buck," Shawn muses. Then he gets to work.

What Does an Automotive Body Repairer Do?

Automotive body repairers fix all kinds of vehicles, but cars and small trucks make up the bulk of their work load. Some repair buses, large trucks, and tractor trailers. Thousands of motor vehicles are damaged in traffic every day, and although some are scrapped for salvage, most can be made to look and drive like new again.

Automotive body repairers use alignment machines to straighten out bent vehicle bodies and frames. They chain or clamp frames and sections to the machines, which use hydraulic pressure to straighten the damaged parts. "Unibody vehicles," where the body and frames are welded together, must be restored precisely to their original specifications, just as they left the factory, in order to run properly. To do this, repairers use bench systems to measure exactly how much each section is out of alignment, then use hydraulic machines to return it to its original shape. Most cars are unibodies. Trucks, on the other hand, are built with separate frames and bodies.

Definition
Automotive body repairers straighten bent automobile bodies, remove dents, and replace the crumbled parts of cars that have been damaged in traffic accidents. They repair all types of vehicles to look and drive like new.

Alternative Job Titles
Automobile collision repairers
Collision-repair technicians

High School Subjects
Computer science
Mathematics
Technical/shop

Personal Skills
Following instructions
Mechanical/manipulative

Salary Range
$18,640 to $33,360 to $57,830

Minimum Educational Level
High school diploma

Certification or Licensing
None available

Outlook
About as fast as the average

DOT
620

GOE
05.03.01

NOC
7321

O*NET-SOC
49-3023.00

Automotive body repairers remove the badly damaged sections of vehicles, like hoods, grills, and bumpers, and weld on or install new replacement parts. Less serious dents are banged or hammered out, usually with a hand-prying bar, a pneumatic hammer, a hydraulic jack, or some other hand tool. Small dents and creases in the metal are repaired by holding a small anvil on one side of the dent and hammering from the opposite side. Very small pits and dimples are removed with pick hammers and punches by a process called metal finishing.

Usually, a dent is never completely knocked out so it's flush with the undamaged area, and the technician must fill in the gaps with special fillers that

Lingo to Learn

Bench system A rack that sets and locks a vehicle into position so nothing moves except the piece you're trying to straighten out or align.

Brass and bronze These are alloys of copper. Metal alloys are used more extensively than pure metals.

Frame rack A bench system run by hydraulic pressure. Frame rack is an older term for a bench system, which now straightens complete unibodies, not just frames.

Hydraulic pressure A machine run by hydraulic pressure is pumped by oil that's run by an electric motor.

Metal alloy A combination of metals and nonmetals fused together to make a substance. Alloys of carbon and iron are among the most widely used and include cast iron and steel.

Pneumatic sander, hammer, and other tools Air-powered tools that plug into an air line in order to run.

bond to the car. Called "bondo," these fillers come in different consistencies and makes, depending on what material they're being used with. Some bondos are made for metal, some for fiberglass and plastic, and some for sheet-metal compound. Some are harder than others, and some need a sealer on the metal before the bondo is applied. After the bondo goes on and dries, the technician sands down the repaired area till it's flush and smooth with the undamaged area. The repaired dent is usually sent over to the *painter* for the final touches, who does his or her best to match the car's original color. "I know how to do painting and could if I had to," says Shawn, "but we like to have our own painter who specializes in that field." In small shops, repair technicians often do the painting as well as the repairing.

Technicians also fix the electrical wiring in headlamps, blinkers, and taillights if it gets damaged. After they find the break in the current, they can usually splice the wires together to make the repair. In large shops, body repairers sometimes specialize in a certain type of repair, such as frame straightening or door repair. Some exclusively replace glass windshields and windows.

Automotive body repairers face challenges with each new car. Every job is unique and requires a different solution. Usually, the repairer is given the estimate of damage and must go from there to make sure the actual damage matches the appraised damage. "Sometimes it's very different," says Shawn, "because you never know what's going on till you get some pieces off and take a look."

What Is It Like to Be an Automotive Body Repairer?

Shawn arrives at his job at 8:00 A.M., Monday through Friday. He usually finishes around 5:00 P.M., then returns home to do a little automotive body repair on the side. His day begins with inspections of the work he did the previous day and the work he needs to do today. New stuff that comes in? "Well," says Shawn, "that'll come to me eventually."

Shawn first takes a look at the new door skin he put on a Volvo the day before and at a few other repairs he made on the car. "When you put a door skin on, you have to bend it around the old door frame with a hammer. I looked to make sure I didn't put any dents in the door when I fixed it. Sometimes that happens because the door skin is so flexible." Shawn, in fact, had put a few minor dents in the new door, so he gently pulled them out. He inspected the other damage he repaired the day before: three dents in the front fender and a broken blinker and park light. "I replaced the lenses," says Shawn. "It was not an electrical job at all." When Shawn fixes a dent, he tries to use as little bondo as possible, and that means getting the dent almost completely out. "A car is made of metal, not bondo," says Shawn. "You ruin the structural integrity of the car if you use too much filler."

After inspecting his work, Shawn writes up the order for the painter. The door is ready to be edged, and the painter will have to blend the inside edge of the old door with the new door skin, which came already painted from the factory.

By the time Shawn gets the Volvo door over to the painter, the white Toyota pickup he finished the day before, the one that hit the deer, is back from the painter. Its owner is coming in the afternoon to pick up the car, and Shawn needs to get a new radiator in and install the bumper and grill that just arrived from the factory. This takes him until lunch.

"I work on about 50 cars or pickups a month," says Shawn, "and sometimes up to five a day, depending on what needs to be done to them." The hardest part of Shawn's job is working on dirty, trashed vehicles. "You can tell when the owners don't take care of their rig," says Shawn. "If they don't care, why should I?"

"When a new car comes in, I'm the first person to deal with fixing it," says Shawn. "I look at the estimate and evaluate the damage and how to go about the repair. There's never one way to make a repair. Every repairer develops their own technique." Shawn finds it incredibly rewarding to fix a damaged car and make it so new looking you can't even tell where the repair was made. "That's always my goal," Shawn says, "and I take pride in my work."

Do I Have What It Takes to Be an Automotive Body Repairer?

Today's advanced technology has greatly changed the structure, materials, and parts used in automobiles. Because of this, repair technicians need to know the newest techniques in repairs and be skilled at implementing them. For example, the bodies of cars are now made of a combination of metals, alloys, and plastics, each one requiring different techniques and materials to smooth out dents and pits and repair damaged parts. Restoring unibody cars to their original state requires a precise measuring and synchronization of body parts. Therefore, being able to read and follow complex instructions, diagrams, and three-dimensional measurements in technical manuals is essential for an automotive body repair technician. Basic math and computer skills are also needed to use the manuals that come with today's sophisticated vehicles. It has been estimated that technicians must be able to interpret 500,000 pages of technical text to repair any car on the road, and new information is being produced at a rate of 100,000 pages a year. Today's automotive technicians, besides being good with their hands, must also have a solid understanding of math, science, and electronics. These skills are necessary because most of a vehicle's functions are now controlled by computer.

Repair technicians need to be organized, detail-oriented, and neat. Sloppy work is unacceptable. Shawn believes taking pride in one's work is the most

In-depth

Henry Ford

On January 14, 1914, Henry Ford did the inconceivable. He raised the wages of his Ford Motor Company employees to an unheard of amount of $5 a day. Then he decided to earmark 10 million of his company's $25 million dollar earnings to an employee profit-sharing plan. His critics went wild. This will ruin the industry, they cried! We'll all have to pay workers more! But Ford remained undaunted. "I like to see folks who work hard get their fair share," he said in response. To remain a Ford employee, however, the workers had certain standards they had to abide by. For one, they had to live in a comfortable house and were forbidden to take in a large number of boarders, a common practice for making additional income in Ford's day. Workers had to prove they were saving their money and often had to report how they were spending it! Ford became so adamant about how he wanted his employees to live their lives, he sent inspectors out to their homes. If you didn't follow the rules, you were fired.

important trait a repair technician can have. The technician usually works alone, unsupervised, and must manage his or her time well to be productive on the job. Obviously, liking cars and understanding cars are primary traits to have. Along with that comes the dirt. "You can't mind getting dirty," says Shawn.

Some drawbacks to being an automotive body repairer include working with toxic chemicals. Repairers are exposed to materials that contain hazardous fumes and substances, and Shawn often wears a face mask and gloves for protection when he works. "That's the one part of the job I can do without," says Shawn. "The mask filters out about 99 percent of the fumes, but health-wise, there aren't

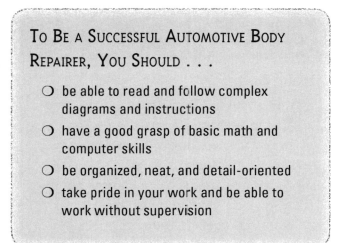

To Be a Successful Automotive Body Repairer, You Should . . .

○ be able to read and follow complex diagrams and instructions

○ have a good grasp of basic math and computer skills

○ be organized, neat, and detail-oriented

○ take pride in your work and be able to work without supervision

many pros. I'm on my knees a lot, too. This job is just hard on the body."

How Do I Become an Automotive Body Repairer?

Automotive body repairers do not need formal training to become technicians. Most employers prefer to hire repairers who have completed a training program, however, because of the highly sophisticated advances that have been made in automotive technology. Having an education in automotive body repair could help your chances of getting a job and speed up promotion and salary increases.

Some employers, though, favor hiring helpers, or people with little or no experience, and training them on the job. Most employers look for helpers who are high school graduates, know how to use hand tools, and are quick to learn. Shawn worked in the restaurant business before he got hired on as a helper at Jax Auto Body & Paint Inc. "My first question was, are you willing to hire someone who knows very little?" says Shawn. His supervisor, and the owner of Jax, was willing.

"I prefer to hire people with no formal training. They don't come in with set ideas about how to do something," says Keith Koch, who has owned the business for 13 years. "But there are requirements. I look for people who have a good mechanical sense and a genuine desire to learn. In today's technical world, you also need a high school diploma."

Helpers begin by assisting body repairers with small dents and the removal and installation of body parts. They observe technicians doing the bigger jobs, such as repairing a car on a frame rack. Then they begin their own projects, starting with small dents and moving into more complicated repairs. It usually takes three to four years to become a skilled automotive repair technician. Shawn has been learning for three years now. "I'm amazed at what I've learned on the job," says Shawn. "And I picked it up really fast."

EDUCATION

High School

In high school, you should pay attention in math, English, and computer science to get the skills you need to read technical car manuals and work on computerized cars. Shawn took woodshop in high school, a class that taught him to appreciate the finished product and take pride in his work. Shawn wishes he had taken welding and metals class in high school and recommends that would-be repair technicians select both these classes if available. Auto shop is also a must, and many high schools offer vocational training programs in automotive repair.

When Shawn was little, he remembers watching and helping his older brother renovate a classic Chevrolet. In high school, Shawn continued to tinker around with cars. "All my friends came to me when they had car problems. They still do," says Shawn. He believes any work you can do on cars is good experience. "Most of what I've learned," says Shawn, "I couldn't get from a book."

Postsecondary Training

Most vocational and technical schools and community colleges offer training programs in automotive body repair. If you attend a vocational school or community college to learn the automotive body repairer trade, you can expect to take courses in structural analysis and damage repair, mechanical and electrical components, plastics and adhesives, and painting and refinishing. Many schools offer a separate training program in painting and refinishing for those interested in that part of the trade.

Because the trade is becoming so technical, schools are now starting to recommend or require academic course work along with vocational training. Classes in computer science, communication, mathematics, and English are becoming more common requirements for those who want to graduate from a collision-repair technician program.

CERTIFICATION OR LICENSING

Certification for automotive body repairers is offered by the National Institute for Automotive Service Excellence. Although voluntary, it is the recognized standard of achievement for repair technicians. To be certified, you must pass a written exam and have at least two years of experience working as a technician. You can take exams in a variety of subject areas to become certified, for example, in painting and refinishing. If you complete a postsecondary training program, it may be substituted for one year of experience. Every five years, you must take a recertification exam.

I-CAR, a nonprofit training organization, offers educational classes nationwide for automotive body repairers in such subjects as electronics collision repairs, electrical repairs, and structural work. They also do qualification testing in welding. Shawn's employer has paid for him and other employees to take several courses, for which they receive certificates of completion. I-CAR offers a toll-free technical assistance number to anyone who has taken their courses.

SCHOLARSHIPS AND GRANTS

Sometimes large companies, such as NAPA Auto Parts, offer scholarships or apprenticeships to vocational schools and training programs in their area for students learning the trade. Specific automobile dealerships also offer opportunities for students to learn how to work on Ford Assets, for example, or Toyota T-10s. Usually these scholarships are more for collision than repair. For information about scholarship and opportunities for automotive body repairers, contact large companies in the industry directly or your school's financial aid office.

INTERNSHIPS AND VOLUNTEERSHIPS

Automotive repair technicians who begin as helpers are paid to train on the job. Shawn began his career as a helper at $6 an hour. It is not unusual for repair shops to accept apprentices, or helpers, even though no formal apprenticeship exists for the automotive repair technician field.

School programs often have apprenticeships and internships as part of their course requirements. The school usually sets up internships with area dealers and shops so students have the chance to practice on-the-job skills.

LABOR UNIONS

Some automotive body repairers are members of unions, including the International Association of Machinists and Aerospace Workers; the International Union, United Automobile, Aerospace and Agricultural Implement Workers of America; the Sheet Metal Workers' International Association; and the International Brotherhood of Teamsters. Most auto body technicians in a union work for large automobile manufacturers, trucking companies, and bus lines.

Who Will Hire Me?

Automotive body repairers held about 220,000 jobs in 2002. Most repairers work for automobile and truck dealers who specialize in body repairs and painting or privately owned auto repair shops. Some body workers are employed by bus lines, trucking companies, and other organizations like car rental companies that have a frequent need for body work done on their vehicles. A few work for motor vehicle manufacturers. About one out of six automotive body repairers is self-employed.

A recent survey done by the Automotive Service Association (ASA) found that auto body repairer shops find the majority of their employees through referrals made by other employers. Sixteen percent find new technicians through vocational and technical schools, and another 13 percent advertise and hire new positions through newspaper want ads.

Shawn knew the owner of Jax from the restaurant where he worked. "He knew I was good at woodworking, and I knew he had an automotive repair shop. He needed some carpentry work done, and I needed some repair work done, so we traded," Shawn remembers. "He liked my work so much he offered to train me on the job."

Where Can I Go from Here?

Shawn likes working on cars so much, he would hesitate to do anything that would take him away from that. He believes he could supervise someday, but for now he wouldn't want to stop repairing cars. "Why stop doing something if you're good at it?" says Shawn. Someday, though, he would like to operate his own automotive body repair shop.

Most automotive repair technicians have the opportunity to continue to learn and train on the job, both by taking education courses offered by I-CAR and working with experienced people. By doing so, automotive body repairers can earn journeyman status and eventually work into production management and supervisory positions in their shop. They can also become estimators, estimating car repair costs, or automobile damage appraisers for insurance companies. Owning your own repair shop business, as Shawn would like to do someday, is another option.

What Are the Salary Ranges?

According to the *Occupational Outlook Handbook*, the median annual salary of automotive body repairers was $33,360 in 2003. The middle 50 percent earned between $24,930 and $44,590 a year. The lowest paid 10 percent made less than $18,640 a year while the highest paid 10 percent earned $57,830.

Many collision-repair technicians are paid on an incentive basis for the work they finish. Under this method, body repairers are paid a predetermined amount for various tasks, and what they earn depends on the amount of work assigned to them and how fast they get it done. Some shops guarantee their repairers a minimum amount of work or weekly salary. Helpers and trainees usually receive an hourly wage until they gain the skills and experience to take on their own projects. Body repairers who work for bus and trucking companies usually receive an hourly wage.

The ASA 2004 survey reports that 28 percent of all repair shops pay their technicians an hourly wage, while 36 percent pay a flat rate, 8 percent pay a percentage-of-labor rate, and 15 percent pay a combination of hourly wage plus commission. Only about 15 percent pay an annual salary. Among the survey respondents, 95 percent of the shops now provide paid vacations, 89 percent offer paid holidays, and 74 percent provide employees health insurance benefits. Shawn is paid an hourly wage and feels commission pay inspires quantity instead of quality work.

What Is the Job Outlook?

Employment opportunities for automotive body repairers are expected to increase about as fast as the average through 2012, according to the *Occupational Outlook Handbook*. Opportunities for those with formal training will probably be better than for those with no training or experience. This is mainly due to the sophisticated technology of cars now being produced and the numerous changes made to cars each year. With automotive technology changing at such a rapid pace, the most knowledgeable and up-to-date repair technician is going to get the job.

FYI

The following are some online automotive periodicals:

Autobody Online. Daily. Resource for collision repair specialists. (http://www.autobodyonline.com)

Autobody Pro. Daily. Product and service listings, discussion boards, and industry news. (http://www.autobodypro.com)

Car and Driver. Magazine for auto lovers and auto professionals. (http://www.caranddriver.com)

Collision Repair Industry Insight. Insider's guide to collision repair, including a shop finder index with reviews. (http://www.collision-insight.com)

The U.S. Department of Labor cites the nation's population growth as the main factor for such a healthy job outlook for automotive body repairers. As the number of people increases, the number of vehicles is expected to grow as well and with that growth will come a greater number of cars in accidents, getting damaged and needing repairs. Another important factor is the automobile itself. The new, lighter materials now being used in automobiles, such as plastics, aluminum, and metal alloys, are more prone to damage than the heavier steel car parts of the past. These materials are also harder to repair and take more time than those of older cars. The majority of jobs will be replacement jobs as automotive body repairers retire, move on to management positions, or go on to other occupations.

Economic conditions also account for the job market in the collision-repair industry. Most repairs are paid by car insurance, which is mandatory in a majority of states. And since most cars need to be restored in order to operate safely, people usually bring their cars in to be fixed. Minor dents and fender benders, however, are more subject to the economy. If the economy is slow, people tend to defer these repairs, reasoning that they can live with the dent rather than pay a hefty insurance deductible.

How Do I Learn More?

PROFESSIONAL ORGANIZATIONS

The following associations and organizations offer information on automotive body repairer schools, training sessions, and ASE-accredited programs as well as opportunities for a career as a collision-repair technician:

Accrediting Commission of Career Schools and Colleges of Technology
2101 Wilson Boulevard, Suite 302
Arlington, VA 22201
703-247-4212
info@accsct.org
http://www.accsct.org

Automotive Service Association
PO Box 929
Bedford, TX 76095-0929
800-272-7467
asainfo@asashop.org
http://www.asashop.org

Automotive Service Excellence
101 Blue Seal Drive, Suite 101
Leesburg, VA 20175
877-273=8324
http://www.asecert.org

I-CAR
N127 South Park Drive
Appleton, WI 54914
800-832-4990
http://www.i-car.com

National Automobile Dealers Association
8400 Westpark Drive
McLean, VA 22102
703-821-7000
nada@nada.org
http://www.nada.org

National Automotive Technician Education Foundation
101 Blue Seal Drive, Suite 101
Leesburg, VA 20175
703-669-6650
http://www.natef.org

SkillsUSA-VICA
PO Box 3000
Leesburg, VA 20177-0300
703-777-8810
http://www.skillsusa.org

BIBLIOGRAPHY

The following is a sampling of materials relating to the professional concerns and development of automotive body repairers:

McShane, Clay. *The Automobile: A Chronology of Its Antecedents, Development, and Impact.* Chicago: Fitzroy Dearborn Publishers, 1997.

Richardson, Jim, and Tom Hovarth. *Pro Paint and Body: Includes the Latest Paint Technology & Body Repair Techniques Used by Today's Pros.* New York: Berkley Publishing, 2002.

Toboldt, William K., and Terry L. Richardson. *Auto Body: Repairing and Refinishing.* South Holland, IL: Goodheart-Willcox Company, 2000.

Weber, Robert M., Philip A. Perry, and Ronald H. Weiner. *Opportunities in Automotive Service Careers.* Lincolnwood, Ill.: VGM Career Horizons, 2001.

Witzel, Michael. *The American Gas Station.* Osceola, Fla.: Motorbooks International, 1998.

AVIONICS TECHNICIANS
||||||||||||||||||||||||||||||||||||||||||||||||||||||||||||||||||||||

The autopilot has been repaired and reinstalled, but a test flight is needed to make sure it is functioning correctly. An extension cable is attached to the autopilot control, and Craig Johnson sits with his head down in the cockpit, unable to see out of the plane but focused on making adjustments to the unit.

The pilot sits behind the wheel as they fly with the autopilot engaged. Craig notices that the plane seems to have picked up some speed, but he continues to work. The pilot asks, "Well, should I disconnect?" Craig finally looks up and sees the ground when he should be seeing the sky. He tells the pilot to disconnect the autopilot, and the plane lifts up.

"The autopilot was taking it someplace we didn't really want it to go," Craig says matter-of-factly, "and I didn't realize the plane was pointed in that direction because the way the autopilot put it there was so smooth I didn't notice it." Craig has plenty of similar stories, and the occasional unusual flight situation is not so unusual for an avionics technician.

What Does an Avionics Technician Do?

Pilots do a lot more than steer when they're flying a plane. They are responsible for navigating the plane, monitoring the instruments during the flight, communicating with air traffic controllers, and more. Pilots rely heavily on the electronic equipment that allows them to carry out these duties; without radios, navigational equipment, autopilots, flight recorders, and so on, pilots would be unable to fly safely. *Avionics technicians* make sure this equipment is in top working condition.

Avionics technicians use their knowledge of electronics to install, repair, test, and service electronic equipment used for navigation, communications, flight control, and other functions in aircraft and spacecraft. After installing new systems, avionics technicians test and calibrate the equipment to ensure that it meets specifications set by the manufacturer and the Federal Aviation Administration (FAA). They adjust the frequencies of radio units and other communications equipment by signaling ground stations and making

Definition
Avionics technicians install, repair, test, and service electronic equipment used in the aviation and aerospace industry.

Alternative Job Titles
Avionics engineering technicians
Avionics mechanics
Avionics repair specialists

High School Subjects
Mathematics
Physics
Technical/shop

Personal Skills
Mechanical/manipulative
Technical/scientific

Salary Range
$39,600 to $44,500 to $56,300+

Minimum Educational Level
Some postsecondary training

Certification or Licensing
Voluntary

Outlook
About as fast as the average

DOT
823

GOE
02.08.04

NOC
2244

O*NET-SOC
49-2091.00

adjustments until the desired frequency is set. Avionics technicians also perform preventive maintenance checks so equipment will perform effectively.

Technicians may be involved in the design and development of new electronic equipment. They must consider operating conditions, including weight limitations, resistance to physical shock, atmospheric conditions the device will have to withstand, magnetic field interference, and other crucial factors. Avionics technicians in research and development must anticipate potential problems and rigorously test the new components. For some projects, technicians may have to design and manufacture tools before they can begin to construct and test new electronic equipment.

Installation technicians are responsible for installing avionics equipment in aircraft. They must

An avionics technician works on a turbo prop aero engine. *(Peter Bowater / Photo Researchers Inc.)*

make sure the equipment works in conjunction with other components and test the equipment thoroughly. *Bench technicians* work in shops and repair and service defective units. They can specialize in communications equipment, which generally uses analog signals, or pulse equipment, such as radar. Bench technicians test, troubleshoot, and analyze faulty units to determine the problems. They may test down to the component level and replace defective components on the circuit board. Some technicians work down to the board level and replace entire boards instead of dealing with circuits. Most avionics technicians spend time on both installations and bench work, especially if they are employed in small repair shops.

Because the range of equipment in the avionics field is so broad, avionics technicians may specialize even further, especially if they are employed by large manufacturing companies or repair facilities. Technicians can focus on computerized guidance equipment, flight-control systems, or radio equipment, to name a few possibilities. New specialty areas arise frequently due to constant innovations in technology, and avionics technicians must keep informed by reading trade magazines, equipment manuals, and technical articles. Even if they do not plan to specialize

in these new areas, avionics technicians must learn about new equipment and have a good understanding of all innovations in the field.

What Is It Like to Be an Avionics Technician?

Craig Johnson works for the Avionics Shop Inc., a small, FAA-certified repair shop in Fresno, California, owned and operated by his family. Craig's workday generally alternates between installations and repairs, and some days he may be out in the field installing parts, while other days he is in the shop working on the bench. "To be a good overall technician," Craig says, "you need to have some experience in installation to understand how the equipment is installed and planned and what can fail. A lot of times, you'll have a failure in a unit on an airplane, but when you put it on the bench it works great. You need to have a good understanding of both installation and the bench."

One of the Avionics Shop's contracts is with a helicopter company. When a unit is squawked, or reported to be experiencing problems, Craig drives from the shop, which is located on the Fresno Air Terminal, to the other side of the airfield, where the helicopter company is located. The problem, for instance, may be a communication unit that doesn't transmit on one of the frequencies. Craig tests the unit in the aircraft using a portable service monitor to verify the problem and begins evaluating the cause. "The most important thing is to get a good description of the problem from the pilot or whoever squawked it," explains Craig. He checks the wires and connectors to make sure nothing is loose, and if the problem still exists, Craig removes all the suspected units and returns to the shop.

When Craig is back in the shop, he first tests the unit on the bench before disassembling it. He hooks the unit up to a test panel and re-verifies the problem, making sure the defect is in the unit itself. He then removes the cover and performs a visual check, looking for moisture, corrosion, or leaking parts. He then refers to the appropriate manual for descriptions of the circuits and a troubleshooting guide. Attaching oscilloscope probes to different points on the circuit board, Craig discovers the culprit—a bad integrated circuit in the control head. The shop has a spare in stock, so Craig replaces the circuit, makes sure everything is working, puts the unit back together, and tests it again. Craig cleans the unit, fills out the repair sheet and other paperwork, then heads back out across the field to install the unit back into the helicopter. Craig checks and tests the unit when it is reinstalled in the aircraft and makes entries in the aircraft's logbook.

Craig starts on a repair that has been sitting on the shelf when he returns to the shop, but he doesn't get very far when he receives a call to fix a radio on a helicopter used for medical emergencies. The radio is used to communicate with dispatch and all emergency units, including the police department and fire department, so its repair is urgent. Craig heads back across the field and verifies the squawk. He removes the unit and searches for a spare to insert temporarily. "Usually we'll take a spare unit and put it in there," Craig says, "and that puts them back on call again without much of a delay." None of the spares are in working order, so the helicopter must go off service while Craig repairs the radio. The problem turns out to be a loose solder connection, discovered by tapping on the unit and components to cause some vibration. Craig resolders the connection, checks the entire unit for other potential problems, cleans it, reassembles

Lingo to Learn

Altimeter A unit that measures the pressure outside an aircraft to determine the plane's altitude.

Cockpit The area in the front of the airplane where pilots sit. Flight controls and instruments are located in the cockpit.

Distance measuring equipment (DME) Equipment used to determine the plane's distance from a particular station.

Oscilloscope An instrument that displays variations in a fluctuating electrical quantity as wave forms on a monitor.

Radar A unit that consists of a radio transmitter and receiver that emits radio waves and processes the reflections.

Radar altimeter This unit measures the aircraft's distance above the ground by using radio signals that bounce off the ground and measure how high off the ground the aircraft is.

Squawk A complaint regarding a piece of equipment that is not functioning properly.

Transponder A unit on a plane that receives signals sent from airports and replies back with a code that identifies the aircraft.

Voltmeter An instrument that measures the differences, in volts, between various points of an electrical circuit.

it, completes the paperwork, then reinstalls the unit in the helicopter, checking and testing it again. Craig finally heads home at 9:00 P.M., the end of a long day. "It's supposed to be a 40-hour week," Craig admits, but it usually doesn't work out that way.

Do I Have What It Takes to Be an Avionics Technician?

Avionics technicians must have an aptitude for this type of work, so an interest in electronics and aviation, as well as mechanical skills, are crucial. You must have excellent analytical and problem-solving skills—you will be relying on those skills every day. Self-motivation, persistence, and the ability to follow through on projects are important as well, since many problems are elusive and you must continue to work to determine the causes.

People's lives may depend on whether the avionics equipment is working or not, so you must be thorough and detail oriented. There are many procedures that must be followed, such as checking the equipment in the aircraft, repairing all existing and potential problems on the bench, and completing all the paperwork. Units must be tested repeatedly in the aircraft and on the bench, so you need to be able to follow steps.

Craig has always been around electronics and avionics. "I think analytically and always want to figure out what makes things work," he explains, and this makes him suited for the avionics field. He admits to being a bit of a perfectionist, which assists him in his work because he will do whatever it takes to get to the root of a problem and solve it. Craig believes initiative and the desire to learn are important to be a successful avionics technician. "There's always something new coming out and something more to learn," Craig says.

> There's always something new coming out and something more to learn.

Craig finds himself working in all kinds of weather, and the hours can be quite long. "Everyone always wants everything done yesterday," Craig notes, and this can cause pressure. And because airplane cockpits aren't very spacious, equipment may be located in hard-to-reach spots. "You have to put yourself in pretty awkward positions," admits Craig. Being an avionics technician carries a lot of responsibility, but Craig willingly takes it on; he enjoys his work and finds the avionics industry exciting. "A lot of people are in this industry because they like being around planes and love aviation. That's a good motivator."

How Do I Become an Avionics Technician?

Craig's father started the Avionics Shop in the 1960s, and Craig grew up surrounded by airplanes and electronics. "I've been doing this since I was in high school," says Craig. "I've always been around electronics." Because Craig was exposed to electronics at a young age, he gained a solid fundamental understanding of electronics, which he has continued to build upon.

EDUCATION

High School

A solid educational background in mathematics and electronics is the most crucial element if you want to become an avionics technician. "Electronics is the most important if you want to go into this field," says Craig. Shop classes in electronics or related fields may be available at your school, and any class where you must use tools such as soldering irons or voltmeters will help you gain some manual skills and dexterity. As an avionics technician, you will read schematics and diagrams, so a blueprint reading or drawing class will come in handy. Science courses, especially physics, and English classes are also helpful. English is important for being able to write and read technical reports and to communicate clearly with others both verbally and in writing.

Opportunities to join clubs or organizations involved with electronics should be plentiful in high school. An amateur radio club will familiarize you with radio operation, frequencies, and some federal regulations. Many high schools often participate in science fairs or contests that require competitors to use their knowledge of electronics, problem-solving skills, and ability to build and fix things.

High school is an excellent time to learn about aviation as well. Many organizations offer programs designed to teach youths about flying. You may wish to contact a small regional airport to ask about any such opportunities. A class in ground school can teach you about avionics equipment and familiarize you with aviation terms, but the cost of such a class may be prohibitive. If you can land a part-time or summer job working in an airport or on an airfield, even if it is in the coffee shop, you will learn many of these terms as well.

Postsecondary Training

Some postsecondary training is necessary to obtain the basic skills you will need to be an avionics technician. Some community colleges and technical schools offer one- or two-year programs in avionics that can lead to associate's degrees or certificates of completion. Some of the FAA-certified trade schools may also have four-year programs in avionics or aviation technology. If an avionics program or course is not available in your area, you should take classes in electronics. "I would say that a community college course or associate's degree in electronics would be a very good step," Craig advises. Some large corporations, especially those in the aerospace industry, have their own schools and training facilities. The U.S. armed forces also provide training in avionics and electronics.

Along with some education in avionics and electronics, knowledge of aviation and the aviation field is important as well. Flying lessons may be a good idea, as you will gain more understanding of how planes function and how the equipment affects the planes. "If you're going to work in the industry," Craig says, "you have to understand the industry." Craig also indicates that flying lessons will demonstrate to a potential employer that you have initiative and an interest in the industry overall.

In an avionics program, some of the courses you may take include analog electronics, airframe, avionics line maintenance, radio fundamentals and FCC license preparation, digital circuits, and microprocessor fundamentals.

CERTIFICATION OR LICENSING

Two types of certification are available for avionics technicians, and generally speaking, neither is mandatory. Repair shops can be certified by the FAA as certified repair stations. These shops have a chief inspector who is authorized to sign off on other technicians' repairs and work. The individual technicians may receive FAA certification through their employer. For instance, Craig is the chief inspector at the Avionics Shop. If a technician were interested in obtaining certification as a repair person, Craig would write a letter of recommendation to the FAA indicating that the technician possesses the skills and qualifications necessary to work as an avionics technician for that particular shop. If the certified technician left the Avionics Shop to work for another employer, he or she would need to seek certification from the new employer.

Avionics technicians who work with radios, transmitters, or other communications equipment should obtain a license from the Federal Communications Commission (FCC). Applicants must pass a detailed written examination to obtain licensing. In recent years, the FCC has adjusted regulations in such a way that technicians who work for licensed avionics technicians do not need individual FCC licenses. It is a good idea, however, to seek licensing. As Craig notes, "It proves that you have the incentive to do this type of work."

SCHOLARSHIPS AND GRANTS

Technical schools and community colleges with avionics or electronics programs are good sources for scholarships. You should contact the financial aid office or your departmental advisor for information. Professional associations often provide scholarship opportunities as well. The Aircraft Electronics Association (AEA) awards 23 scholarships a year, ranging anywhere from $1,000 up to $22,000. Large manufacturers or companies in the aviation or aerospace industries may also provide financial awards. You should contact these companies directly or search for company home pages on the Internet. These companies may also list their scholarships with relevant associations such as the AEA.

INTERNSHIPS AND VOLUNTEERSHIPS

An internship may be required for students in avionics technology programs. The departmental advisor or student placement office will generally assist in locating internship opportunities and setting them up.

If you are not enrolled in school, however, internship opportunities may be a challenge to locate. Some large manufacturers or companies may have internship programs, and if they do not, you might want to contact them and inquire about volunteer possibilities. Small repair shops with fewer than 10 employees generally do not have the resources to offer internships. Usually these shops are operated by the owner and may employ only one or two other technicians. It never hurts, however, to ask about volunteer opportunities. As Craig has indicated, initiative is the key in the avionics field.

LABOR UNIONS

There is no union specifically designed to represent avionics technicians. Union membership will depend on the employer. Small repair shops are generally not unionized, but avionics technicians who work for

FYI

Visit http://www.avweb.com to read aviation news, reviews, training links, up-to-the-minute articles on new aircraft, and more.

major commercial airlines may be required to join a union, such as the International Association of Machinists and Aerospace Workers.

Who Will Hire Me?

Craig didn't have to look far for his first job in the avionics field. Although he worked for the family shop during his high school years, it wasn't until after college that he decided he wanted to pursue a career in avionics. "I went to college so I could do something else," he recalls, "but I came back to it."

The main employers of avionics technicians are commercial airlines, avionics equipment or aircraft manufacturers, and repair shops, both small, independent stations and large shops with several locations. The federal government may also have job opportunities.

Technicians who work for manufacturers will not only perform repairs and maintenance, but they will also be responsible for assembling units. If you have a particular fondness for autopilot equipment or transponders, for example, you may wish to narrow your job search to companies that specialize in producing or repairing these units. Because avionics is a highly specialized field, however, avionics technician jobs are not particularly plentiful, and you shouldn't narrow your search too severely.

If you are in school, the placement office should be able to help you locate prospective employers. Schools frequently host job fairs where students can meet prospective employers and undergo job interviews. If you cannot take advantage of a placement program, however, many repair stations and manufacturers have Web sites with job openings. The Internet is also an excellent tool for researching companies or airlines you may be interested in working for.

Craig believes that word of mouth is a good way to learn about job opportunities, since avionics is a close-knit industry. Maintaining membership in aviation clubs and professional organizations and attending meetings is one method for keeping in touch with others in the industry. You can also visit small shops to inquire about job opportunities.

"If you went to one shop and they didn't have a position, they'd probably tell you who did," Craig notes. He also suggests sending resumes to all the shops in the area where you live. You can look through the classified ads of newspapers, but Craig indicates that small shops generally don't advertise because most are always seeking qualified, experienced technicians. If you are just starting out, relocation may be unavoidable.

Professional associations usually publish magazines or newsletters with classified ads. "The best place to look is probably in the AEA magazine *Avionics News*," Craig says. "They have more job opportunities in there than any other publication I can think of." Associations representing the general aviation industry may also list avionics technician opportunities.

Where Can I Go from Here?

Craig plans to continue working in his family's repair shop, building the reputation of the shop. He hopes the Avionics Shop will someday be known as "the best shop in California." Craig is interested in doing some design work and looks forward to working with new, high-end equipment. "That's fun to work on because it's very complicated equipment," Craig says.

As avionics technicians gain experience and skills, they begin to work more independently, with only minimal supervision. Because most shops have fewer than 10 employees and may be operated by the owner, there aren't many opportunities for advancement. Technicians can advance to shop manager and supervise the staff of avionics technicians and oversee the daily operation of the shop. Shop managers usually act as the chief inspector and sign off on technicians' paperwork. Many technicians who reach this level may leave the shop to open their own avionics repair businesses.

Avionics technicians who work for manufacturing companies may move into supervision or administrative positions, such as regional manager. The regional manager may travel and visit customers, installing and servicing equipment and providing training sessions. They may also solicit new business or oversee a team of sales representatives.

With additional education, avionics technicians can become avionics engineers. This position generally requires a bachelor's degree in engineering or electrical engineering. Avionics engineers plan and design equipment and systems, figuring out how units will best work together.

What Are the Salary Ranges?

A 2005 salary survey published in the magazine *Aviation Today* indicates that avionics technicians working for regional airlines earned $44,500, and those employed by major airlines earned $56,300. Technicians employed by other facilities earned $39,600. Avionics managers working for corporate airlines earned $82,600. Managers working for regional or major airlines earned between $51,800 and $72,500.

According to the U.S. Department of Labor, the median annual earnings for avionics technicians were $43,580 in 2003. The highest paid 10 percent earned more than $56,490 annually, and the lowest paid 10 percent earned less than $30,780.

What Is the Job Outlook?

There will always be a need for skilled avionics technicians. Even though there are relatively few avionics jobs, Craig believes that if you are an experienced technician with plenty of initiative, you could walk into any repair shop in California and land a job. "It's hard to find somebody who is qualified," he indicates. Craig also feels this is a good time to become an avionics technician. Most of the skilled technicians are reaching retirement age, and there aren't enough younger avionics technicians to fill the void. "If someone got into this area," he believes, "they'd always have a job."

The *Occupational Outlook Handbook* reports that employment for avionics technicians is expected to grow about as fast as the average for all occupations through 2012. The job outlook is positive for avionics technicians and aircraft mechanics, but competition may be stiff for the highest paying airline positions. Opportunities are likely to be best at FAA-certified repair stations and smaller airlines. The commercial airline industry is usually affected by the state of the national economy. When the economy is strong, more people take advantage of air travel, both for business and pleasure. With more people flying, the demand for airplanes increases as well, creating job

ADVANCEMENT POSSIBILITIES

Shop managers oversee the work of avionics technicians and take care of the daily operation of the repair shop. They may also work as chief inspector and sign off on the work performed by the technicians.

Regional managers of manufacturing companies visit clients to install and service equipment. They may also train clients and solicit new business.

Avionics engineers apply engineering and electrical principles to design avionics equipment and systems.

opportunities for avionics technicians and other employees in the aviation industry.

Innovations and advances in technology will affect the avionics field positively as well. Avionics technicians are needed to assemble and test the new equipment, and they must also install and service these new units.

Many of the customers of small avionics repair shops are private citizens who own planes. Because flying is expensive, these customers generally have incomes that can support their flying activities. The avionics industry, therefore, is not as heavily tied to the national economy as other industries.

Furthermore, many businesses depend on airplanes and helicopters to perform their work. For example, firefighters often rely on helicopters to help put out forest fires; search and rescue teams must rely on aircraft to locate and rescue injured individuals; and the police department and highway patrol use aircraft to track suspected criminals. Employees of these businesses rely on avionics technicians to keep their electronic equipment in top working order so they can communicate with headquarters, navigate the aircraft, and fly safely and accurately.

How Do I Learn More?

PROFESSIONAL ORGANIZATIONS

The following organizations can provide information about the industry, including education, scholarships, and employment opportunities:

Aircraft Electronics Association (AEA)
4217 South Hocker
Independence, MO 64055
http://www.aea.net

Air Employment Assistance Corps
PO Box 260830
Littleton, CO 80163
info@avjobs.com
http://www.avjobs.com

Professional Aviation Maintenance
 Association
717 Princess Street
Alexandria, VA 22314
hq@pama.org
http://www.pama.org

BIBLIOGRAPHY

The following is a sampling of materials relating to the professional concerns and development of avionics technicians:

Helfrick, Albert D. *Modern Aviation Electronics*. 2d ed. Paramus, N.J.: Prentice Hall, 1997.

———. *Principles of Avionics*. 3d ed. Leesburg, Va.: Avionics Communications Inc., 2004.

Jones, Grady R. *How Airplanes Fly: A Flight Science Primer*. Dubuque, Iowa: Kendall Hunt Publishing Company, 1994.

Kayton, Myron, ed., and Walter Fried. *Avionics Navigation Systems*. 2d ed. New York: John Wiley & Sons, 1997.

Maher, Edward R. *Avionics Troubleshooting and Repair*. New York: McGraw-Hill, 2001.

BARBERS AND COSMETOLOGISTS

It was an awkward situation, to say the least. Colleen was visiting pleasantly with a client in her beauty salon when a second client arrived, and tension suddenly filled the room. "I had no idea they were both divorced from the same guy. And it wasn't like 20 years apart. It was like five years. That was kind of scary," she remembers with a rueful smile. "They both just sat there and got real quiet. I was almost done with one of them, and she got out of there, and the other one told me, 'Don't ever book us at the same time again.'"

One of the women was not angry about the encounter, although the other one was. Colleen kept her poise, handled the situation with tact, and managed to avoid losing either client. "I just talked about different things, like the weather," she recalls. "You have to be diplomatic and keep them both happy. In this business you have to be a doctor, divorce lawyer, counselor, psychologist."

Cosmetologists, like bartenders, are expected to be good conversationalists who can be trusted with confidences. "When one lady leaves," Colleen notes, "you don't want to talk about her to the next lady in the chair, or she'll think you'll talk about her. They told us in beauty school, don't talk about politics, religion, or the other customer."

What Does a Barber or Cosmetologist Do?

An attractive appearance increases a person's self-esteem and can contribute to professional success. In the United States beauty salons and barber shops are big business, comprising one of the largest personal service industries.

Barbers cut, trim, shape, wash, style, tint, and bleach hair, and they trim and style mustaches and beards. They also fit hairpieces, give scalp treatments, facials, facial massages, and shaves, but they seldom care for skin or nails. They offer grooming advice and information about cosmetic products. Barbers work with razors, razor sharpeners, scissors, clippers, brushes, combs, tweezers, and hot towels. Some barber shops feature shoe shine attendants, assistant barbers, and manicurists.

Definition
Barbers cut, shape, wash, color, and bleach hair, beards, and mustaches. Cosmetologists perform a wide range of personal services to improve the look of their clients' hair, skin, nails, and makeup.

Alternative Job Titles
Beauticians
Beauty operators
Hairstylists

High School Subjects
Business
Health

Personal Skills
Artistic
Mechanical/manipulative

Salary Range
$12,840 to $20,280 to $40,280+ (barbers)
$12,670 to $19,300 to $34,920+ (cosmetologists)

Minimum Educational Requirements
Some postsecondary training

Certification or Licensing
Required by all states

Outlook
About as fast as the average (barbers and cosmetologists)

DOT
330

GOE
11.04.01

NOC
6271

O*NET-SOC
39-5011.00

Cosmetologists are usually licensed to perform all the services provided by barbers, with the exception of shaving men, and they perform some services that barbers do not. They help improve the appearance of their clients' hair, skin, and nails. They wash, condition, cut, curl, straighten, color, and style hair. They also give manicures and pedicures, apply scalp and facial treatments, shape eyebrows and eyelashes, apply makeup, clean and style wigs, and offer body care and skin care services. Some cosmetologists give massages, analyze the most effective type of makeup for each client, and offer advice about what

Lingo to Learn

Booth A workstation in a beauty shop, usually consisting of a chair, countertop, mirror, small table, and access to hair dryers and a sink for shampooing.

Electrolysis The use of electricity to remove whiskers, scalp hair, body hair, moles, warts, and birthmarks.

First chair The chair nearest the door of a barber shop, a workstation usually reserved for barbers with the highest skills and seniority.

Pedicure A procedure having to do with the feet, such as filing and polishing the toenails.

Rods Special curlers, particularly those used to set a permanent wave.

Skin peel The application of a mild solution, such as acid from fruit juice, to remove dirt and dead skin cells and to encourage the growth of new, fresh skin cells.

products to use and how to apply them. Those who specialize as hairstylists may focus on an area such as permanent waving, cutting hair, or styling hair. Cosmetologists work with scissors, razors, brushes, combs, curlers, clippers, manicure equipment, hair dryers, reclining chairs, and cosmetic aids.

Some cosmetologists cut only children's hair, but usually their clientele includes people of all ages, both women and men. There are many areas of specialization within the field of cosmetology. *Nail technicians,* also known as *manicurists,* are experts in the care of nails on hands and feet. They trim cuticles, shape nails, apply polish, decorate nails, and attach artificial nails, sometimes using linen or silk wraps. *Estheticians* focus on skin care, body care, and makeup. An esthetician might help clear up acne, for example, by applying a mild acid solution, such as an alpha hydroxy product, to remove dead skin cells. Estheticians sometimes work with *dermatologists* and *plastic surgeons,* who perform cosmetic surgery and other advanced procedures.

Both cosmetologists and barbers must ensure that their tools and surroundings are clean; some items must be sterilized. In small shops they schedule appointments and clean equipment and their

work spaces. They also sell a variety of shampoos, conditioners, and other products designed to enhance a person's appearance. To improve their understanding of these products, they read trade magazines and other publications, and they attend trade shows, seminars, and other events where products are presented.

A large number of people in this profession are self-employed and must be proficient in business administration. That involves paying bills, keeping financial records, making sure equipment is in working order, purchasing supplies, and perhaps hiring, firing, and paying employees.

What Is It Like to Be a Barber or Cosmetologist?

Colleen Lyon has been in the cosmetology business for more than 34 years and now operates a beauty salon in her home in Missoula, Montana. Her work room is equipped with chairs that swivel and recline, hair dryers, curling irons, special sinks for washing hair, and an array of curlers, brushes, hair sprays, scissors, and other tools and products. Colleen performs a variety of services for men, women, and children, but hair care is her main focus. She applies conditioners and shampoos, and almost every day she colors someone's hair—a process that can involve anything from a total change of color to applying a "frost" or "streaking" to create the illusion of highlights. "I do a lot of haircuts. I like it when I have a lot of permanent waves," she says.

Colleen usually begins work by about 8:30 or 9:00 in the morning and tries to finish by 5:00 or 6:00 in the afternoon, but sometimes she's still working at 8:00 in the evening. "I try to work around the customer's schedule," she explains. She occasionally works on Saturdays but never on Sundays. Sometimes she performs her services for clients in their homes, most often for elderly women.

She has built up a loyal clientele over the years. Many of them come to the shop to have their hair done every week, and some have been coming for 20 years, following her each of the three times she has moved the business to a new location.

"In this business you never know from week to week what your income is going to be," she remarks. "You stagger [clients] so you're busy all the time. And you're trying to build your clientele. Word of mouth is the best way to get clients." It is important

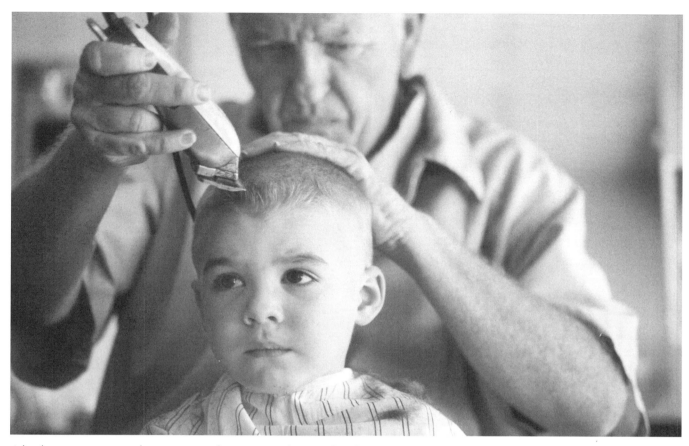

A barber gives a young boy a summer haircut. *(Mark Harmel / Photo Researchers Inc)*

for a beautician to build up a clientele; if you are self-employed, you need to know you can count on certain people to patronize the business, and if you are employed at a salon, you'll probably be receiving commissions as part of your pay."

Colleen was an employee in several salons before she opened her own business years ago. She enjoyed interacting with other beauticians but prefers working alone, because she is in charge here. She says, "The big reason I like running my own salon is you don't have the conflicts with other operators, the race to the telephone for appointments," and other disagreements.

"I spent a lot of years in the three salons I worked in," she recalls, adding that she was not very happy with her last employer. "The hours she made me work, and her attitude, were what made me get my own salon. I took some business schooling, and my sister owned a salon. We sat down one night and did some [financial planning] books. Most of it is common sense and treating the customer with respect."

Now that she has her own shop, Colleen keeps in touch with developments in her field by reading how-to books and magazines such as *American Salon* (http://www.americansalonmag.com) and *Modern Salon* (www.modernsalon.com). She says she learns tips on colors, cuts, and the latest trends through reading, but many of the styles in such magazines are not very helpful for her, since they are too unusual for Montana. She is not worried that she won't be able to style hair to suit her clients, though. "There's only so far they can go with hair," she comments, "so it seems like it makes a big revolution" from straight to curly, natural to wild, and back again every few years. A beautician who knows the basics, she says, can handle most trends as they become popular again.

Do I Have What It Takes to Be a Barber or Cosmetologist?

A cosmetologist or barber needs to be pleasant and friendly but able to maintain a professional demeanor. Creativity is important, since customers will rely on you to help them choose styles best suited to their

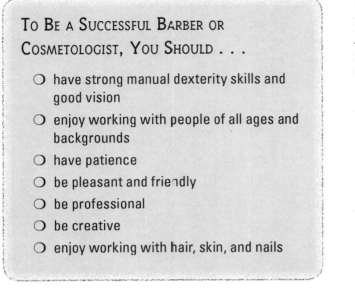

To Be a Successful Barber or Cosmetologist, You Should . . .

○ have strong manual dexterity skills and good vision
○ enjoy working with people of all ages and backgrounds
○ have patience
○ be pleasant and friendly
○ be professional
○ be creative
○ enjoy working with hair, skin, and nails

individual looks, and some will want new, trendy hair styles. You should enjoy working with hair, skin, and nails; this profession revolves around personal grooming services that require close contact with clients. The job requires patience, because customers can be difficult. "Sometimes I get tired of some of the people," Colleen says, "but I just try to overlook it. You have to be a person that likes people. If you're quiet and shy, you won't build up a clientele."

Since Colleen operates her own salon, she has been able to tailor much of the work to suit her personality. "I pretty much set my own hours," she notes. "When you get your own shop, you can do that." The downside is that she sometimes is tempted not to work diligently since she has no supervisor. "No matter what job you have, you have to have discipline," she remarks.

Another beautician in Missoula, Judy King, says that patience and communication skills are essential for a cosmetologist: "The biggest challenge is people who can't be satisfied. It's a challenge every day. You have to be real clear what they want. But it's fun," she is quick to add. Any cosmetologist has to communicate with customers to decide what tasks should be done. For example, it is important not to misunderstand how long a woman wants her hair to be. Once the hair is cut, an error cannot be remedied. The key, Judy says, is to discuss everything ahead of time and be sure you know what the customer is expecting.

Judy manages The Salon, a beauty shop within a large drugstore. The cosmetologists at The Salon stay busy throughout the day; they pierce ears, manicure nails, color and cut hair, sell retail products, and

offer many other services. "You do all those things in the same day. We just give 'em whatever they want," Judy says. Her typical day, she adds, is "Hectic! You get all types of people. Some of the clients have such a sense of humor. That's my favorite part."

> You get all types of people. Some of the clients have such a sense of humor. That's my favorite part.

How Do I Become a Barber or Cosmetologist?

Colleen recalls, "I fixed kids' hair all through high school and grade school. After I got out of school, I hated books, and I liked making people look good. I still do. Everybody said I have a natural knack for doing hair." Colleen wanted a career but did not want to go to college, so she attended Modern Beauty School in Missoula for about a year and a half to become a cosmetologist. "In Montana you have to go to school longer and learn more than in some other states. You get more practical experience and book learning," she notes.

Like Colleen, Judy King grew up in western Montana and earned her credentials in Missoula, but at Mr. Rich's Beauty College. She had raised two children and had been a seamstress, but when work began to damage her hands, she changed careers. "I was already trying to cut my kids' hair, and I was always interested in it. It was something I knew I'd enjoy going into, even though I knew I wouldn't make much money," she says. Judy has been a cosmetologist for over seven years and has worked at The Salon for about two years.

EDUCATION

High School

An eighth-grade education is a prerequisite for entry into most cosmetology schools, but a high school education is recommended and is required in some states. A high school education and, in many cases, a few more years of advanced schooling are required for advancement to some positions in the field. Some states require only a high school or even an eighth-grade education for barbers, but most require completion of barber school or an apprenticeship.

To prepare for a career in cosmetology or barbering, take science classes, particularly biology, physiology, and chemistry. These courses will help you understand how hair and nails grow, for example. Chemistry is important because you'll be working with permanent wave solutions and other chemical products. Business courses, including bookkeeping, accounting, and marketing, will prove helpful if you ever open your own beauty shop or manage a salon. To deal with the wide variety of customers, Colleen suggests that "a psychology class might be good."

Postsecondary Training

To practice cosmetology in any state or barbering in most states, you must complete special training. In some states separate schooling is required for estheticians, manicurists, and electrologists; this training usually takes much less time than barber or cosmetology school. Nationwide, there are about 400 private barber colleges and nearly 4,000 cosmetology schools. Training is also available through vocational training programs. Before enrolling in any school, be sure it meets the requirements of your state.

Programs at barber schools usually take nine months to a year and provide 1,000 to 1,800 hours of instruction. Course work often includes the use of tools and equipment, sanitation, skin and scalp diseases, the craft of barbering, business management, sales, advertising, ethics, and advanced hair coloring and styling.

Training for cosmetologists varies from state to state but is usually 1,000 to 2,000 hours of study that takes six months to about a year; in some states the program can take up to a year and a half. Some public training school programs last two to three years, because they also feature academic studies. Most programs include textbook studies in cosmetology and hands-on experience with mannequins, live models (including other students), or actual clients who receive reduced prices in exchange for allowing students to practice on them under close supervision.

Training for cosmetologists usually includes studies in the bone structure of the head, the nervous system, and other aspects of human anatomy. Students

FYI

- Relics found in Egyptian tombs such as combs, cosmetics, and razors, as well as written records, indicate that nobility and priests of ancient times were regular patrons of barbers. Among the skills of early practitioners of the "barbers' art" were shaving, haircutting and coloring, beard trimming, and applying facial makeup.

- In 296 B.C. Rome was well known for its baths and barber salons. At that time, all free men were clean shaved while all slaves wore beards.

- The word barber is derived from the Latin word *barba*, which means beard.

- By the early 9th century barbers had added surgery, such as blood-letting and teeth-pulling, and treating patrons with herbs and other medicines to their services. In about 1096 the first school of surgery for barbers was organized in France and for almost 1,000 years practitioners of the profession were known as barber-surgeons.

- By 1745, as the field of medicine grew, barbers were stripped of their roles as surgeons and the profession began to decline and lose respect.

- In 1857 the Journeyman Barbers International Union was created and, forty years later Minnesota passed the first barber license law, which established standards for the profession in that state, including sanitary practices and educational requirements. The *Standardized Textbook of Barbering* was published in 1931.

learn to cut, wash, color, and style hair; give facials, manicures, and pedicures; and apply makeup. They study skin care, body care, nail technology, chemistry, physiology, bacteriology, hygiene, sanitation, business, and applied electricity. Some knowledge of scientific subjects is necessary to understand how the skin, hair, nails, and other body systems function, but the training in these areas tends to cover only basic facts. "Most of the chemistry classes at beauty school were very simple," Colleen comments.

CERTIFICATION AND LICENSING

All states require that barbers and cosmetologists be licensed. Some require separate licenses for estheticians and manicurists. In some states applicants must pass an examination to become junior cosmetologists, then work in the field for one year and pass a second examination to become senior cosmetologists.

When Colleen graduated from beauty school, she received an operator's license that allowed her to work under the oversight of a licensed operator for one year. She now has a shop license, which is required for her to operate her own beauty salon, and a manager-operator license, which is required for her to practice cosmetology. When her shop was within the city limits, she also had a city business license.

If you are a practicing barber or cosmetologist and move to another state, you might need additional testing or a refresher course to obtain a new license, but some states recognize the licenses of cosmetologists and barbers from other states. In some states licenses must be renewed annually.

INTERNSHIPS AND VOLUNTEERSHIPS

In most states barbers must complete apprenticeships for a year or two before they can be licensed as journeyman barbers. Some cosmetology apprenticeships are also available, but few people enter the profession this way. Most cosmetology schools include hands-on experience, often in a beauty shop operated by the school. In some barber shops and beauty salons you can work a summer job, cleaning the shop and running errands; this would allow you to observe barbers and cosmetologists at work and decide whether the career interests you.

LABOR UNIONS

Cosmetologists and barbers sometimes belong to labor unions, most often the United Food and Commercial Workers International Union. Sometimes a union can help its members find employment.

Who Will Hire Me?

Colleen found her first job as a cosmetologist immediately after her graduation from beauty school. Her teachers put her in touch with a prospective employer, she was interviewed for the position, and at that time she was asked to cut a customer's hair as a test of her skills. The customer was surprised, and Colleen admits, "I was a little nervous, but I did a good job." She worked in that salon for four years.

Many barber colleges and cosmetology schools help their graduates find work. Local union offices sometimes also refer union members to employers. Newspaper advertisements, personal referrals, and state, city, or private employment services can also provide information about job openings. If you decide to approach shops directly by dropping off resumes, which is probably the most common way to find a job as a cosmetologist or barber, Colleen advises, "Don't call on the phone! Go in person and talk to different salons. Look nice. Ask if they have time to talk to you later and set up an appointment." Colleen says she finds it annoying when applicants call her salon and ask, "Are you hiring anybody right now?"

Barbers and cosmetologists may work in small shops with one or two operators or in large salons with perhaps a dozen employees. You might find a job in a combination barber-and-beauty shop, or you could work in a beauty shop in a hospital, retirement home, nursing home, department store, drugstore, resort, or hotel. Some cosmetologists demonstrate cosmetics and hair styles in retail stores, fashion centers, photographic centers, and television studios.

Where Can I Go from Here?

Colleen Lyon has achieved her goal of operating her own salon, and she has no plans to pursue other options. Opening your own shop requires experience, an understanding of business practices, startup money, and a clientele that will follow you to your new location. Highly successful entrepreneurs sometimes operate a chain of salons.

Judy King also worked her way up from an entry-level job as an employee in a salon, but instead of opening her own shop, she has become the manager of a salon with a number of employees. Whether you're working as an employee or renting a workstation in someone else's salon, she says, the key to success is

ADVANCEMENT POSSIBILITIES

Salon managers purchase and oversee the stock of supplies, make sure equipment is operating properly, set appointments, keep financial records, and ensure that the salon meets legal regulations.

Salon owners may employ other cosmetologists or perform all the work in the salon. The owner oversees the business, assuming a great deal of risk and responsibility but possibly making a sizeable profit.

Cosmetology or barber school instructors teach at cosmetology and barber schools and vocational training schools. These positions typically require experience in the profession, along with a general education that includes some college.

to build a clientele of loyal customers, a process that usually takes two to three years. A promotion into management will follow naturally if the salon's owners like your work. She adds, "If they know you've got the attitude and potential, it's easy to slide right in. When you have a good crew, it's not all that hard."

Since there are few management positions within small shops, cosmetologists and barbers with experience often move on to larger, more attractive shops with better equipment and more chances for promotion. They sometimes continue their education through graduate school and by attending functions sponsored by trade associations, such as professional fashion reviews. With knowledge from events of that type or from training programs offered through large cosmetic houses, you could be a demonstrator or sales professional in the cosmetic department of a large store. Cosmetologists with advanced skills can become beauty editors for magazines and newspapers or style hair and apply makeup for television personalities. Some beauticians specialize in cosmetology work for mortuaries. Some estheticians become makeup artists for motion picture studios or television studios.

"The one thing I've thought it would be fun to be is a beautician on a cruise ship. That's a type of thing that younger girls just going into the business might want to consider," Colleen suggests.

Judy says the best way to advance in this field is by branching out into related areas. "If you're working for someone else, you're pretty much at a standstill. The smart thing to do is to go into different avenues of the business. I encourage all of the people who do this for a living to take as many classes as they can."

Judy attends seminars and other events to learn about the latest styles and products, because she works in her spare time as a representative for companies that make cosmetics and personal care products. She says there are many opportunities to earn thousands of dollars on weekends and days off and still work full-time or part-time in a salon.

You could teach people about a company's products at educator shows. You could be a platform artist at hair shows, demonstrating on stage how to style hair in the latest fashions. You could be a company representative who sells products to beauty salons within a given territory. "But you've got to keep your license current," she warns, "or you don't qualify for anything."

What Are the Salary Ranges?

Earnings in this field vary widely, depending on the employer, the employee's skill and experience, economic status of the clientele, and whether the shop is in a rural or urban area. Workers in exclusive salons in cities often earn much more than the average, particularly if they are experts or specialists. Many workers in this profession receive no fringe benefits; those who work for nursing homes, department stores, beauty salon chains, and other large organizations are more apt to receive benefits such as health insurance and paid vacations. Some operators are paid only a percentage of the amount their clients pay the salon; others earn a base salary plus commission. Others are paid by the hour. Tips are an important and unpredictable source of income in this profession.

Judy King says she knows cosmetologists who are making almost $400 a day, but most start at minimum wage plus commission and gradually earn more as they gain experience. Being self-employed, she explains, is an important way to increase your earnings, but only if you have your own shop or branch out into related areas. Judy says cosmetologists who work in smaller salons in Montana are usually self-employed, paying weekly rent for a workstation, and making somewhere near the minimum wage.

Colleen Lyon points out that if you are self-employed, you keep 100 percent of what your clients pay, but you have to buy supplies and meet other expenses, including self-employment tax. "There is no retirement fund and benefits like that, unless you do it yourself. That's one of the drawbacks," she says. Colleen is an accomplished painter who helps make ends meet by using her salon as a gallery to display art for sale.

The U.S. Department of Labor reports that in 2003 cosmetologists made a median annual salary (not including tips) of approximately $19,300. The lowest paid 10 percent, which generally includes those beginning in the profession, made about $12,670. The highest paid 10 percent earned around $34,920. Again, both those salaries exclude tips. Tips can increase a person's earnings by thousands of dollars per year. (It is important to remember that many professionals in this field work only part-time, however.) Barbers had median earnings of $20,280 in 2003. The lowest paid 10 percent earned $12,840 annually, and the highest paid earned $40,280. According to the *Barber's Gazette*, a publication of the American Barber Institute, the average annual income for the hair styling industry was approximately $35,000.

What Is the Job Outlook?

Employment for barbers and cosmetologists is expected to grow about as fast as the average for all occupations through 2012. The demand for services will increase as the population grows, as more men patronize salons and as working women seek out cosmetic services more frequently. Opportunities for employment will be best for those licensed to offer a wide variety of services.

According to the U.S. Department of Labor, almost half of all barbers and cosmetologists are self-employed, but the current growth of nail salons and full-service day spas is expected to create new job opportunities. Colleen Lyon notes a new trend toward salons that offer a range of services, everything from manicures, pedicures, and body wraps for cellulite to tanning booths and even attached fitness centers: "I think the career itself is getting more into a healthy, total-body look instead of just hair and nails. It's changed that way in probably the last 12 years.

Facials and hair color seem to be the trends right now." She notes that the change is good for business, because it keeps customers interested and encourages them to visit salons more often.

How Do I Learn More?

PROFESSIONAL ORGANIZATIONS

The following organizations provide information on barbering and cosmetology careers, accredited schools and scholarships, and possible employment opportunities:

American Association of Cosmetology Schools
15825 North 71st Street, Suite 100
Scottsdale, AZ 85254-1521
800-831-1086
http://www.beautyschools.org

American Barber Institute
252 West 29th Street
New York, NY 10001
877-927-7337
http://www.americanbarberinstitute.com

National Accrediting Commission of Cosmetology Arts and Sciences
4401 Ford Avenue, Suite 1300
Alexandria, VA 22303
703-600-7600
http://www.naccas.org

National Association of Barber Boards of America
2703 Pine Street
Arkadelphia, AR 71923
501-682-2806
http://www.nationalbarberboards.com

National Cosmetology Association
401 North Michigan Avenue, 22nd Floor
Chicago, IL 60611
312-527-6765
http://www.ncacares.org

Professional Beauty Association
15825 North 71st Street
Scottsdale, AZ 85254
800-468-2274
http://www.americanbeautyassociation.org

BIBLIOGRAPHY

The following is a sampling of materials relating to the professional concerns and development of barbers and cosmetologists:

Aucoin, Kevyn. *The Art of Makeup.* New York: HarperCollins, 1996

Batson, Sallie. *Great Hair!: Your Complete Hair Care Guide and Styling Guide.* New York: Berkley Publishing, 1995.

Beatty, Deborah. *Milady's Standard Textbook of Professional Barber-Styling.* 3d ed. Albany, N.Y.: Milady Publishing, 1998.

Begoun, Paula. *The Beauty Bible: From Acne to Wrinkles and Everything in Between.* Seattle: Beginning Press, 1997.

Careers in Focus: Cosmetology, 3d ed. Chicago: Ferguson Publishing Company, 2003.

Lamb, Catherine. *Milady's Standard Textbook of Cosmetology.* Albany, N.Y.: Milady Publishing, 1999.

Rudiger, Margit, and Renate Von Samson. *388 Great Hairstyles.* New York: Sterling Publications, 1998.

BIOMEDICAL EQUIPMENT TECHNICIANS

||||||||||||||||||||||||||||||||||||||||||||||||||||||||||||||||||||||||||||||

Responding to a request for assistance, Brent Doyen walks into the operating room to find a roomful of medical professionals staring in his direction. He's steered toward the faulty equipment—an aortic balloon pump designed to assist the heart if it is not functioning correctly. Brent can't very well take the machine apart in the operating room, but he has diagnosed the problem. He exits the operating room, runs down two floors, grabs a new set of cables, and rushes back up. He plugs one end of the new cables into the machine, and it starts pumping as it should. He breathes a sigh of relief and leaves the operating room as the surgery team hurriedly resumes the operation. Brent heads back down to the equipment shop. Saving lives is all in a day's work for a biomedical equipment technician.

What Does a Biomedical Equipment Technician Do?

Biomedical equipment technicians (BMETs) are responsible for the maintenance, installation, calibration, and repair of biomedical equipment, electronic equipment designed to diagnose and treat medical conditions. This equipment may include anesthesiology machines, cardiac monitors, infusion pumps, defibrillators, radiology equipment, and ventilators and may range in size from a handheld unit to a machine that takes up an entire hospital room. BMETs, with their highly specialized training in electronics, are important links between technology and medicine.

Biomedical equipment technicians spend a considerable amount of time on preventive maintenance. All biomedical equipment must undergo regularly scheduled preventive maintenance checks to ensure that everything is in top working condition. Maintenance includes cleaning and calibrating, or adjusting the machine so it works in a standardized manner, and conducting operational verification tests to make sure the machine is operating as designed. Technicians may test circuits, clean and

Definition
Biomedical equipment technicians install, maintain, repair, and calibrate biomedical equipment used in hospitals, clinics, and other medical or laboratory facilities.

Alternative Job Titles
Biomedical electronics technicians
Biomedical engineering technicians
Biomedical instrumentation technicians
Clinical engineering technicians

High School Subjects
Chemistry
Mathematics
Physics

Personal Skills
Mechanical/manipulative
Technical/scientific

Salary Range
$25,000 to $36,380 to $40,000

Minimum Educational Level
Associate's degree

Certification or Licensing
Voluntary

Outlook
About as fast as the average

DOT
639

GOE
14.05.01

NOC
N/A

O*NET-SOC
49-9062.00, 51-9082.00

oil components, and replace worn parts. BMETs use tools such as voltmeters, oscilloscopes, spectrum analyzers, and computers to make sure equipment is functioning properly. Detailed records of all preventive maintenance checks must be kept by biomedical equipment technicians as well.

When equipment malfunctions, it's the job of the biomedical equipment technician to diagnose the problem and repair it. The BMET must determine whether the problem is due to operator error or whether the equipment is in need of actual repair. If the machine or instrument must be repaired, the BMET may refer to product manuals, test the equipment to try to pinpoint the problem, or speak with manufacturers about possible causes. The problem may be as elementary as a loose wire or as major as a defective motor. BMETs often take apart equipment and replace or repair parts, such as transistors, switches, or circuit boards.

Installing or upgrading equipment is also the responsibility of biomedical equipment technicians. BMETs follow manufacturer's guidelines to set up machinery, then inspect and test it to make sure it complies with safety standards.

Technicians often train those who will operate the equipment, such as nurses, doctors, and other health care personnel. They also answer questions regarding equipment usage.

Biomedical equipment technician I is a junior-level or entry-level technician. These technicians generally work under heavy supervision, and the majority of their work is maintenance-oriented. They are also capable of carrying out basic repairs on less-complicated equipment such as infusion pumps or defibrillators.

The *biomedical equipment technician II* is a senior-level technician and evenly splits time between preventive maintenance checks and repair work. These technicians work on equipment that is technically more demanding than the machinery entry-level technicians repair, including radiology equipment, laboratory analyzers, which involve robotics, pneumatics, and hydraulics, and anesthesiology equipment. Senior-level technicians may also oversee the installation of systems, such as nurse stations or heart monitor systems, while the junior-level technicians perform the physical tasks of installation. Technician IIs also evaluate new equipment and make purchasing recommendations.

The biomedical equipment technician who specializes in a particular area or type of equipment is known as a *biomedical equipment technician specialist*. Areas of specialization can include the catheter lab, pulmonary function machines, ultrasound, respiratory care, or X-ray equipment. Specialists must gain a solid foundation in biomedical equipment technology before focusing on a specialty. Many biomedical equipment technicians work in hospitals or clinics, taking care of all the equipment needs. Other BMETs work for third-party companies or manufacturers. Those working for manufacturers service and install equipment made by the manufacturing company. Frequent travel may be involved, and some technicians may be assigned a region covering several states.

Lingo to Learn

Biomechanics Explores the response of living matter to physical forces, such as how the knee of a jogger responds to repeated impact on the pavement.

Calibrate To adjust or set a device so that it records and measures accurately.

Defibrillator An electronic device that creates an electric shock designed to restore the rhythm of a fibrillating heart.

Fibrillation Irregular, rapid contractions of the heart muscles that cause the heartbeat and pulse to fall out of synchronism.

Heart-lung machine A machine used to divert blood from the heart during heart surgery and to keep it oxygenated and in circulation.

Metabolic imaging Noninvasive methods of seeing inside the body, such as positron emission tomography (PET), magnetic resonance imaging (MRI), X-ray computed tomography (CT or CAT scan), and ultrasound.

Pulmonary function machine A machine that examines and measures a patient's breathing efficiency and analyzes the gases throughout the lungs.

What Is It Like to Be a Biomedical Equipment Technician?

The first thing Brent Doyen, clinical engineering supervisor, does when he arrives at work at St. Joseph's Medical Center in Tacoma, Washington, is to check the work orders that have been generated over the course of the night.

The orders are prioritized according to type of equipment and urgency. For example, life support equipment will take precedence over a piece of equipment that is not in use or not being used to keep someone alive. Once the work orders are handed out, the biomedical equipment technicians disperse to take care of repairs and routine preventive maintenance checks. Smaller equipment may be brought back to the shop area, while the large machinery will stay where it is. Brent and the other technicians wear pagers and frequently respond to calls throughout the day. "You stay pretty darn busy," Brent admits.

At St. Joseph's, preventive maintenance checks are conducted on a monthly basis and require thoroughness and precision. When Brent checks a heart monitor, he first walks into the room and observes the overall condition of the monitor. Is the screen brightness at an acceptable level? Can he read everything clearly on the monitor? Is it in focus? If the monitor passes this initial check, Brent conducts an operational verification test. This entails hooking up a test device called a chicken heart to the machine. The test device simulates heart rate, blood pressure, temperature, and cardiac output and allows Brent to make sure the machine is functioning within specifications.

Brent then removes the heart monitor from the power source and prepares to examine the inside of the machine. He takes off the cover and cleans the inside, which attracts quite a bit of dust due to the heat of the components.

"That's one of your biggest enemies when it comes to electronics," explains Brent. "The dust and the dirt generate heat and cause components to overheat and burn out. So we keep them clean." Brent also checks the power supplies for proper voltage levels, examines the wires to make sure none are loose, and looks for any signs of wear, such as discoloration of components. If everything looks in order, Brent reassembles the unit and performs an electrical safety check, which tests for leakage of current, resistance, and line voltage using an electrical safety analyzer. "Any time we open up a piece of equipment," Brent says, "the last thing we do after it's all completed, before we give it back, is electrical safety." The entire preventive maintenance check can take anywhere from 30 minutes to an hour to complete.

If the equipment does not pass all of the tests and is determined to be faulty, Brent removes it from service and transports it to the shop. He troubleshoots and evaluates the unit to determine the cause of the problem. Brent tries to narrow down the problem to a specific circuit board or component and then must decide how to remedy the problem. "You have to constantly be thinking about what you're doing," says Brent. "Is it cost effective to put my time into this to try and repair this, or is it more cost effective to just buy a board? That's the big question: Which is the best way to go so it's cost effective?" As long as Brent considers the most economical approach to fixing problems and keeps the biomedical equipment in top working condition, his employer is happy.

Although Brent generally works a 40-hour workweek, he is on call on a rotational basis and may have to report to the hospital on weekends or holidays. He may also have to stay late on occasion to repair equipment that is needed for the following morning, but this doesn't happen very often, and Brent feels the hours balance out.

Do I Have What It Takes to Be a Biomedical Equipment Technician?

If you are interested in becoming a biomedical equipment technician, you should have technical aptitude for working on a variety of electronic equipment. You must also be detail oriented, enjoy working with your hands, and have excellent troubleshooting skills. Stamina and patience are also important, and you must be able to see projects through to the finish. There are times you may be stumped by a problem, but you need to persevere and follow through.

Although biomedical equipment technicians are trained to fix and service electronic equipment, they must also communicate and work with others, so people skills are crucial. You have to be adept at listening to others as they explain problems with machinery, and you need to be able to communicate clearly and tactfully when you are training people or correcting operator error.

"You shouldn't be in this job if you can't handle stress," Brent adds. "You're quite often the front line for life support. When the equipment fails, you're it." A person's life may depend on whether or not biomedical equipment is functioning properly, and occasionally you may be called upon to repair life-sustaining machinery on the spot, so you must be able to work under pressure. And if you have a weak stomach, you might want to consider another job. "You do see a lot of blood," Brent says. "There's equipment that has, shall we say, high-protein substance on it." You may also be exposed to hazardous substances, including chemicals and blood, so you must be careful and take precautions.

> You're quite often the front line for life support. When the equipment fails, you're it.

If you can handle the pressure and enjoy working with electronic equipment, however, biomedical technology can be very rewarding. One thing Brent particularly enjoys is the continuing education. "You're staying current with technology," explains Brent. "As technology advances, so does your education. You're always learning something new." He also enjoys the nationwide camaraderie with other biomedical equipment technicians and notes, "It's kind of like we're a big family."

How Do I Become a Biomedical Equipment Technician?

Brent was an electronics technician before he became a biomedical equipment technician. He worked on repairing and servicing amusement games and equipment, such as video games and jukeboxes. Brent had been working on a pinball machine in a bar one evening. "I came across a person who was having a beer watching me work on stuff, and he said, 'Hey, I do the same thing you do, but I get paid more.' It turns out he was a biomed tech," Brent recalls. The prospect of earning more money and being able to work indoors instead of moving pool tables in the snow appealed to Brent, and he looked into biomedical equipment technology.

EDUCATION

High School

If you're thinking about becoming a biomedical equipment technician, it's never too early to start preparing. In high school, you should take mathematics classes as well as science courses. Brent advises, "I would recommend taking any kind of electronics classes offered in high school, as well as

In-depth

Microshock

Biomedical technology began in the 1970s, when consumer advocate (and former presidential candidate) Ralph Nader publicized a document that suggested that people were being killed by microshock, the leakage of an electrical current whose level is below the sensation of feel and is therefore almost impossible to detect. The leakage can be caused by improper grounding, a loose wire inside the instrument, or leaking components. According to the document, microshock was occasionally causing patients' hearts to fibrillate, which is similar to a heart attack. The awareness of microshock and its potential hazards created a need for technicians who could test the electronic equipment to ensure proper grounding and minimal leakage of current.

math classes." He stresses that students shouldn't be scared off by the math; if math is not your forte, don't worry. Math can help your understanding of electronic processes and equipment, but it is not crucial to be a successful biomedical equipment technician. Shop classes can help you develop skills working with various tools, and if an electronics shop class is available, you should definitely enroll.

Computer science classes are helpful as well. As biomedical equipment becomes increasingly computerized, having an understanding of how computers function is important. Health science classes will acquaint you with medical terminology and basic anatomy, both very important in the realm of the BMET. Not only must you understand the electronic equipment, but you must also know how the equipment affects or works with the patient.

If there is an opportunity to join an electronics club in your school or community, you should. Many high schools also participate in statewide or nationwide technical or science fairs, which give students an opportunity to build various objects and compete against other schools. These fairs are an excellent opportunity for you to gain some experience seeing projects through to the end, working with hand tools, and troubleshooting.

Postsecondary Training

Although a college degree is not absolutely mandatory to become a biomedical equipment technician, it is highly recommended, and many employers list a degree as a hiring requirement. Brent believes, "You would definitely have to have an associate's degree in biomed to pursue a good job."

According to the Association for the Advancement of Medical Instrumentation (AAMI), there are currently 65 accredited two-year programs in biomedical technology offered in the United States. These two-year programs are available at both community colleges and technical schools. Training is also available through the armed forces.

A two-year degree in electronics is sometimes acceptable, but because biomedical technology is rather specialized, it is preferable to find a biomedical technology program. Brent already had an electronics degree when he decided to pursue biomedical technology. He thought he could waive some of the classes in the biomedical technology program at Spokane Community College in Spokane, Washington, but decided not to after speaking with the adviser. Brent is glad he decided to start from scratch when he entered the program, explaining, "Those classes are something you definitely have to be dedicated to. We started out with 24 students in the first year. By the time we finished the second year, there were only 10 of us left. The courses that he covers are very in-depth, and there's no time for monkeying around."

Courses in biomedical technology programs can include safety, including hospital and patient safety, medical terminology, medical instrumentation, physiology, circuits and devices, and digital electronics.

CERTIFICATION OR LICENSING

Certification is generally not required, but some institutions only hire certified biomedical equipment technicians. At Brent's workplace, you cannot become a senior technician without certification. Brent also believes that certified technicians command higher wages and that certification is important for the field.

"It's a way for the biomedical community to police themselves."

Operating under the direction of the International Certification Commission for Clinical Engineering and Biomedical Technology (ICC), the Board of Examiners for Biomedical Equipment Technicians, which is affiliated with AAMI, maintains the certification programs. Certification as a certified biomedical equipment technician (CBET) can be attained after passing a rigorous examination and meeting the education and experience requirements.

The candidate must have an associate's degree and/or proper work experience to meet the eligibility requirements. The examination tests the applicant's knowledge of anatomy and physiology, safety in the health care facility, electricity and electronics, medical equipment function and operation, and medical equipment problem solving. Two areas of specialization are also available: the certified radiology equipment specialist (CRES) and the certified clinical laboratory equipment specialist (CLES).

SCHOLARSHIPS AND GRANTS

Technical schools and community colleges with biomedical technology programs may have scholarship opportunities available. These schools may also have general scholarships open to the entire student population that you may wish to explore. Contact the financial aid office or your department adviser for further information.

Other avenues to investigate include professional associations involved in the biomedical or health care fields, manufacturing companies, or large health care organizations. Companies that manufacture medical instruments and equipment may offer scholarships to aspiring biomedical equipment technicians. Professional associations such as AAMI may either sponsor scholarships or provide lists of award opportunities to members. Large hospitals and health care organizations may also grant scholarships. Searching on the Internet and contacting organizations directly may lead you to some promising possibilities.

INTERNSHIPS AND VOLUNTEERSHIPS

Internships are an excellent way to gain experience, skills, and connections in the biomedical field. Internships are often required for students in associate's degree programs and can lead to job

> ### Advancement Possibilities
>
> **Biomedical engineers** design medical apparatus, including pacemakers, artificial organs, and ultrasonic imaging devices, by applying engineering principles.
>
> **Clinical engineers** design and evaluate biomedical systems and are involved with technology management.
>
> **Regional service managers** represent manufacturers or third-party companies. They supervise field offices and teams of technicians and may also develop customer relations and provide training to customers.
>
> **Customer service representatives** handle queries from customers about all aspects of the particular type of biomedical equipment their company sells.

opportunities after graduation. They are usually set up through the placement department and are without pay. "You're compensated slightly somehow," says Brent. "I know one facility that will give interns living quarters. Here you get a lunch every day." Compensation varies from facility to facility.

Volunteer opportunities in medical facilities are plentiful as well. Brent usually brings in an intern from one of the two biomedical technology programs in Washington, but, he recalls, "This last summer I had a high school student come to me and ask me if he could work with us, stay out of the way and just observe. And I said sure, and he turned out to be a real help." The student recently paid Brent a visit and told him that much of what he observed over the summer hadn't made sense to him, but now that he is taking chemistry and physics, things are starting to click. Volunteering can give you some exposure to the industry and to the health care field in general. Brent suggests, "Call and ask if you can volunteer a few hours a week."

Employers are fond of internships because it provides them a chance to teach aspiring technicians about the field. It is also a means to seek job candidates. Brent is involved with hiring personnel at St. Joseph's, and many of the former interns are now employees. "What I use it [internships] for is to look at potential employees in the future," Brent explains. "It's kind of like a three-month interview."

LABOR UNIONS

Union membership depends on the employer. Brent believes that there are currently more nonunion biomedical equipment technicians. There is no union specifically for biomedical equipment technicians, which means that technicians must usually join the union that represents the majority of the other health care workers in the facility. Some of the unions BMETs can join include the International Brotherhood of Electrical Workers, the International Union of Operating Engineers, and the Service Employees International Union.

Who Will Hire Me?

When Brent graduated from Spokane Community College's biomedical technology program, St. Joseph's Medical Center, where he had completed an internship, did not have a job opening. Brent sent out 100 resumes and found a job working for a third-party company that overhauled ventilators. He worked there for about a year when a position opened up at St. Joseph's. "Because of the internship," Brent feels, "they knew I would mix with the other employees there, so the internship did get me my job."

Many biomedical equipment technicians are employed by hospitals of all sizes. The federal government is another employer of BMETs, primarily through the Veterans' Administration Hospitals and medical centers on army bases. Technicians working for manufacturers often specialize in the repair of machinery. It is commonplace for manufacturing companies to provide maintenance agreements on new equipment, and biomedical equipment technicians are equipped to service the machinery. They may also install the equipment and train the operators or in-house technicians on its functions.

Independent service companies, or third-party companies, also service equipment. Hospitals that do not employ in-house biomedical equipment technicians may use the services of these third-party companies for repair, maintenance, and installation of equipment. Research and development departments within companies may also employ technicians to help test new equipment.

You may have to move a few times to find work as a biomedical equipment technician. "Basically, you probably won't find a job where you think you want to find a job," says Brent. Trade journal publications are an excellent source for job prospects. Magazines such as *Biomedical Instrumentation and Technology* and *Journal of Clinical Engineering* list job opportunities. Brent also suggests becoming involved with local biomedical associations and attending the meetings to find out about what is happening in the biomedical community and to develop some relationships and connections.

The Internet may provide some leads on job openings, and looking through the classified advertisements in the newspaper might be helpful as well. Many large hospitals, manufacturers, and health care organizations have job hotlines that announce new openings. These are often updated weekly. You might also send resumes and cover letters to all the facilities in the state you wish to live in to inquire about job possibilities.

Where Can I Go from Here?

Brent is content with his current job as a supervisor, but he thinks a regional position at some point in the future might be interesting. His employer is now part of a nationwide network of medical facilities, and if Brent's boss moves into a national position, there might be an opportunity for Brent to assume a regional administrative position. If there's one thing Brent is sure of, it's that he would like to stay with his current employer. "I really, really like working for the company I work for. They're very aggressive in their technologies and the business side of it, too. They're not asleep at the wheel. They're aware of what's happening within health care, and it's a real honor to work for them."

As biomedical equipment technicians gain more experience, they begin working more independently and on more technically demanding equipment. They may move into supervisory positions, training entry-level technicians and overseeing the daily operation of facilities. Experienced technicians may also choose to specialize in one type of equipment.

With a four-year degree in biomedical engineering, technicians may become biomedical or clinical engineers and assist in the research and design of new equipment and processes. Clinical engineers are engineers who assess and repair biomedical systems and may be involved in

technology management. They are more concerned with the big picture than with individual pieces of equipment. Biomedical engineers, on the other hand, design medical equipment and instruments by applying engineering principles.

Biomedical equipment technicians who enter the industry as field service technicians with manufacturers or third-party companies can move into regional service management positions. Regional service managers supervise biomedical equipment technicians and other staff and may oversee a number of field offices or service centers. Managers may also provide training to customers and solicit new clients.

What Are the Salary Ranges?

According to the Center for Health Careers in Pennsylvania, starting salaries for biomedical equipment technicians average about $25,000 annually. The *Occupational Outlook Handbook* reports that with certification and experience, technicians can expect to earn about $36,380, annually. Medical equipment specialists with several years' experience earn over $40,000 a year.

Biomedical equipment technicians generally receive generous benefits packages with medical benefits, pension plans, and more. Employers may also finance continuing education courses and seminars.

What Is the Job Outlook?

The *Occupational Outlook Handbook* indicates that jobs for biomedical equipment technicians will grow about as fast as the average. Technological advances will affect the health care industry, and qualified biomedical equipment technicians will be needed to install, maintain, and repair equipment, as well as train operators on proper usage and care. Equipment will rely more heavily on microprocessors and computers, which will also create a need for skilled technicians. New instruments and machines are developed and manufactured on a regular basis, and technicians are qualified to evaluate, test, and make recommendations from both the purchasing end and the design end.

The state of health care may influence the outlook for biomedical equipment technicians. As the trend toward health maintenance organizations (HMOs) increases, medical facilities will be persuaded to adopt cost-cutting measures. Biomedical equipment technicians will therefore be in demand to keep the existing equipment in top working condition.

Brent has noticed that many technicians who entered the field in the 1970s are nearing retirement, which means job openings will arise. And though he feels the biomedical community should have been more aggressive about presenting itself as a cost-saving option, he feels the future looks good. "Institutions like ours that realize there's a significant value in biomedical and clinical engineering are expanding the role there and developing it, so there are things on the horizon that will keep it going," Brent believes.

How Do I Learn More?

PROFESSIONAL ASSOCIATIONS

For information on health care engineering, contact
American Society for Healthcare Engineering
One North Franklin, 28th Floor
Chicago, IL 60606
312-422-3800
ashe@aha.org
http://www.ashe.org

To learn more about certification, contact
Association for the Advancement of Medical Instrumentation
1110 Glebe Road, Suite 220
Arlington, VA 22201-4795
certifications@aami.org
http://www.aami.org

To learn about careers in biomedical engineering, contact
Biomedical Engineering Society
8401 Corporate Drive, Suite 225
Landover, MD 20785-2224
301-459-1999
info@bmes.org
http://www.bmes.org

BIBLIOGRAPHY

Following is a sampling of materials relating to the professional concerns and development of biomedical equipment technicians:

Bronzino, Joseph D., ed. *The Biomedical Engineering Handbook.* 2d ed. Boca Raton, Fla.: CRC Press, 2000.

Careers in Focus: Medical Technicians. 4th ed. New York: Facts On File Inc., 2004.

Marshall, Jacquelyn. *Fundamental Skills for the Clinical Laboratory Professional.* Albany, N.Y.: Delmar Publishers, 1993.

BROADCAST ENGINEERS

How do you recreate a sound that no longer exists? That is what Chris Scarabosio is trying to figure out. He is working on a scene from a movie set in the past. A wooden lifeboat full of dozens of panic-stricken passengers is being lowered to the water. There are two crewmen on either side of the boat, clutching ropes and trying to ease the boat down as evenly as possible. The boat is heavy, and the rope is strained, putting pressure on the pulleys that are designed to help maintain the boat's balance on its descent. The pulleys squeak, and the rope makes stuttering noises as it jumps through the pulley, first on one side, then on the other. Chris must mimic the sound of the ropes and the pulleys. He edited together bits and pieces of sound samples, but the director didn't think the end result sounded realistic enough, so it was back to the drawing board.

One day, the sound designer, the person responsible for creating special sounds and effects, arrives looking rather dazed. He had been standing on an 18-foot-tall pole, holding a rope, trying to get the correct tension on the rope to create the sound, when he fell onto the ground. "I almost killed myself," he says, "but I think I got it." He plays back the sound, and sure enough, it works. Chris edits together the final sounds, and the director says it's perfect. "And that," concludes Chris, "is the lifeboat saga."

What Does a Broadcast Engineer Do?

Broadcast engineers, also known as *broadcast technicians*, set up, operate, and repair the electronic equipment used to record and transmit radio and television programs. They work with equipment such as television cameras, microphones, tape recorders, antennas, transmitters, computers, and more. Broadcast engineers generally work for television or radio stations in specific departments, such as the news, or for individual programs. They may work in controlled environments such as studios, or they may work from remote locations. Some broadcast engineers work for motion picture production studios developing sound tracks.

Definition
Broadcast engineers set up, operate, and maintain the electronic equipment used to record and transmit radio and television programs.

Alternative Job Titles
Audio engineers
Broadcast operators
Broadcast technicians
Maintenance technicians
Sound editors
Video technicians

High School Subjects
Computer science
Mathematics

Personal Skills
Communication/ideas
Technical/scientific

Salary Range
$14,960 to $28,170 to $61,440+

Minimum Educational Level
Some postsecondary training

Certification or Licensing
Voluntary

Outlook
About as fast as the average

DOT
194

GOE
01.08.01

NOC
5224

O*NET-SOC
27-4011.00, 27-4012.00, 27-4014.00

Transmitter operators or *transmitter technicians* operate and maintain the transmitters that broadcast television and radio programs. In other words, they beam the signals from the broadcasting station to the public. The operator must regulate and log the strength of outgoing signals and adjust the transmitters to the station's assigned frequency. Transmitter operators are also responsible for diagnosing and remedying transmitter problems.

The engineers who are primarily responsible for the installation, adjustment, and repair of the electronic equipment are *maintenance technicians*. They must make sure that every camera, microphone, transmitter, amplifier, and any cables used by the station are in proper working order.

Video technicians usually work in the control rooms of television stations and are responsible for adjusting the quality, brightness, and content of the visual images being recorded and broadcast. The video technicians who are primarily involved with broadcasting programs are known as *video control technicians*, or *video control engineers*. They monitor on-air programs, regulate the picture quality, and control individual studio cameras through a camera control unit in the control room. *Video recording technicians*, or *videotape engineers*, are more involved with videotaping programs than broadcasting them. They record performances on videotape using video cameras and sound recording equipment, then edit together separate scenes into finished programs or segments for replay during a live news broadcast.

It is often necessary to broadcast live or tape a story at a site outside the studio, which is what the *field technician* does. Field technicians are responsible for setting up and operating television and radio transmitting equipment from remote locations. They obtain a link to the station through telephone wires or microwave transmitters, then hook up microphones and amplifiers for the audio.

Technology advancements and the introduction of robotic cameras in television studios have created a new type of broadcast engineer known as the *video-robo technician*. Video-robo technicians direct the movements of the robotic cameras from a control room computer, using joy-sticks and a video panel to tilt and focus each camera. With robotic cameras, one person can perform the work of two or three camera operators.

Broadcast engineers who focus on the sound aspect of television and radio transmission are *audio engineers*. Audio engineers set up, operate, and maintain equipment that regulates the quality and relative level of sound. They set up microphones of all shapes and sizes to capture specific sounds and operate mixing consoles that switch between audio from microphones, studios, prerecorded music and sound effects, and remote broadcasting locations. Audio engineers take care of anything that has to do with sound, such as dialogue, music, narration, and sound effects. *Audio control engineers* control the strength and quality of sound being recorded through the use of amplifiers, microphones, and other audio equipment. Audio recording engineers operate the controls of the recording equipment in a recording studio, often under

Lingo to Learn

Amplifier An electronic device used to boost signals.

Analog A form of transmitting information.

Bandwidth A measure of spectrum (frequency) use or capacity.

Bit A single digital unit of information.

Broadcast quality May refer to both technical specifications and artistic quality.

Broadcasting Process of transmitting radio or television signals via an antenna to multiple receivers.

Channel A frequency band in which a broadcast signal is transmitted.

Circuit The connection of facilities that provides telecommunications service.

Digital Conversion of information into bits of data for transmission; allows simultaneous transmission of voice, data, and video.

Edit To assemble by cutting and rearranging.

Encryption To code or "scramble."

High definition television (HDTV) HDTV refers to the transmission of digital signals as opposed to analog. HDTV offers enhanced picture and sound quality.

Mixer An electronic unit used to control and blend sound sources.

MPEG-2 The name given to new international video compression standards.

Panning Rotating a camera horizontally.

Radio frequency Any of the electromagnetic wave frequencies, ranging from below 3 kilohertz up to 300 gigahertz, that includes the frequencies used for the transmission of radio and television.

Remote A broadcast being taped from outside a radio or television station's studio.

Tilting Moving a camera vertically.

Transmitter A device used to send radio or television signals.

the direction of a music producer. Audio engineers are sometimes responsible for manipulating and processing sound to produce special effects or to enhance existing sounds. These audio engineers are frequently called *sound editors* and usually work for motion picture production companies. *Sound mixers* also work in the motion picture industry, adjusting the volumes of the music, the dialogue, and the background sounds to produce the final sound track.

What Is It Like to Be a Broadcast Engineer?

Chris Scarabosio is a freelance sound editor in the motion picture industry. The majority of his work is for Skywalker Sound, a division of Lucas Digital Limited, in northern California. As a sound editor, Chris deals with creating and editing sound effects. "A lot of times we want to enhance the drama of a film," he explains, "and one way we do that is with sound effects."

Chris generally does not work a normal, 40-hour week. Film work is seasonal and sporadic, so he might work 10-hour days for three months, take a few weeks off, work on a two-week project, and so on. The days, however, are relatively standard—he edits. After collaborating with the sound supervisor and receiving direction, Chris sits down at his computer, ready to tackle and determine all the sounds, except for the dialogue and music, that should be included in the film.

At the computer, Chris watches a videotape of the film. The tape runs in synchronization with the

A broadcast engineer monitors the production of a science program. *(Mike Miller / Photo Researchers Inc.)*

computer, which allows him to match up the sound to the video image. When he needs a particular sound, like a distant tugboat, he searches through either the digital library database or sound network. Chris states that his work facility has "a pretty massive library," so almost any sound Chris needs is at his fingertips. Chris lays down numerous tracks, such as all the vehicle sounds on one set of tracks, all animal sounds on another set, and ambient, or atmospheric, noises on another. This allows flexibility when sounds need to be changed or removed.

Sound editing is a precise process and major undertaking. "You try and make it as realistic as possible in very subtle ways," Chris says. He must consider and add all possible background noises, from birds chirping (and they must be seasonally appropriate birds) to water lapping to cars honking off screen. "One of the keys is to not take away from the story but to enhance it," explains Chris. "We're trying to find the perfect sounds to make a sound track come alive so everything is adding to the drama, to the whole fantasy of the film, so when you're in there, you're really part of the film."

Dealing with reality rather than fantasy, Walt Ward is the chief engineer of the maintenance department at KSBY Television, the NBC affiliate in San Luis Obispo, California. KSBY has a maintenance engineering department and a separate operations department that handles the broadcasting tasks. Walt's crew is responsible for repairing equipment and performing preventive maintenance checks on everything from tape machines to cameras to satellite dishes. Walt says, "We're also responsible for handling the day-to-day brush fires, as we like to call them, which are immediate concerns, like if a piece of equipment is malfunctioning and they need it right away." Walt makes sure there are plenty of spare parts and backup equipment, since he must be prepared for anything. "Generally," Walt notes, "when maintenance is required, it's usually an emergency."

At the beginning of the day, Walt reviews reports filled out by operators and others in the news department regarding malfunctioning or faulty equipment. He prioritizes the jobs and spends the rest of the day fixing equipment, carrying out routine maintenance tasks, and making sure the work orders are executed effectively. He also checks transmitter readings, visits the transmitters to make sure they are functioning properly, and reviews the station logs, which are required for compliance with the Federal Communications Commission (FCC). As the news department begins preparing for the evening broadcasts, the tempo picks up in engineering because more equipment is in use. Engineers may also assist with live broadcasts out in the field, setting up shots, running the cables, and checking each piece of equipment.

Do I Have What It Takes to Be a Broadcast Engineer?

Anyone who wishes to become a broadcast engineer should be detail oriented, enjoy solving problems, and possess technical aptitude. Broadcasting, whether it is radio or television or audio or visual, does not leave much room for error, which is why you must be able to troubleshoot and diagnose problems and repair them quickly and efficiently. You must also have communication skills and work well with others. As Walt says, "People skills—I can't emphasize how important that is." Because the job of a broadcast engineer can often be stressful, with constant deadlines and harried coworkers, a calm temperament is essential.

If you want to focus on the visual aspect of broadcast engineering, it is important to have excellent vision and color perception, and if you are more interested in sound, it is crucial to have a keen ear and know what sounds will work. "It's not always about picking the sound that sounds the best," says Chris, "but it's picking the sound that you know will be heard." Chris stresses the importance of being computer literate as well. With technological advances and an increase in automation in broadcasting, more equipment will be controlled by computers.

> It's not always about picking the sound that sounds the best, but it's picking the sound that you know will be heard.

Although broadcast engineers generally work a 40-hour week, those hours may not be standard. Newscasts may air early in the morning or late at night, and most stations are on the air around the clock, regardless of holidays. Engineers may also work overtime in order to meet deadlines, whether it is for a television program or a motion picture. Chris finds that the long hours and deadlines can be stressful. "There are times when you get so inundated with a project that you're basically almost nonexistent. I think that's definitely the hardest part," Chris says. He notes, however, that he doesn't work long hours all the time, and that it all balances out in the end.

Broadcast engineering can be a rewarding job, and engineers are able to see or hear the fruits of their labors. "You see that your work is making the movie better," Chris says, "and that's a good feeling. It's the type of work where people can hear what you do. That's rewarding."

How Do I Become a Broadcast Engineer?

Chris has always been fascinated by sound, music, and how equipment works. As a child, he often took apart radios and tape recorders to find out what was inside and how they functioned. "I still think it's utterly incredible that you can have a blank tape, put it into a cassette player, hit record, and now you have that sound on that cassette."

EDUCATION

High School

Classes to take if you're interested in becoming a broadcast engineer include mathematics, the sciences (physics in particular), and computer science. If possible, you should take electrical or electronics shop courses. For audio engineering, music classes would be helpful, and if you're particularly interested in working in the motion picture industry, try to enroll in a film appreciation class.

Many high schools now offer video production classes, and some may have television or radio stations on campus. It would definitely be to your benefit to enroll in any of these classes or to join radio, television, or audiovisual clubs. You can also gain some skills by volunteering to be a stagehand for the drama club, where you can work with lighting, sound, and videotaping equipment. Becoming a member of an amateur radio club will give you experience working with electronics equipment and help you gain an understanding of frequencies and broadcast technology.

Part-time or summer jobs at local broadcasting stations may be available. Some television and radio stations have programs produced and written by high school students, which is an excellent way to gain experience and make some connections in the industry. Summer classes in broadcasting or filmmaking may be offered through extended education or recreational programs as well. If, however, you are unable to locate any opportunities, you can gain some skills on your own. If you have a video camera, you can practice filming and editing your own segments.

Postsecondary Training

Although a college degree is not mandatory for broadcast engineers, some postsecondary training is necessary in order to gain the requisite technical skills. Many technical schools and community colleges offer programs and classes in broadcast technology or electronics. The military is another source for training. Walt, who handles the hiring for his department, finds military graduates to be highly qualified. Walt says that vocational training or military schooling offers the best preparation for broadcast engineers. "I've interviewed a lot of people with college degrees who can't solder two wires together," Walt states matter-of-factly. "They can tell you why the two wires ought to be soldered together, but that's not what we need. We need people who can do it."

Some of the courses in a broadcast technology program include video technology, broadcast operations, electronic field production, physics, math, and audio technology and theory. Many programs offered by community colleges will lead to an associate's degree.

A college degree is not required for those working in the motion picture industry. Chris attended San Francisco State University and enrolled in broadcasting and audio recording classes, but he says it is difficult to find specialized training. "Our industry is more experience based," Chris explains, and on-the-job training is how he gained his skills.

CERTIFICATION OR LICENSING

Certification is not required for broadcast engineers. In fact, the FCC eliminated the licensing requirement for broadcast technicians in 1996. The Society of Broadcast Engineers (SBE), however, offers a certification program, and certification can sometimes lead to higher salaries and provide you with an advantage when seeking a job. Applicants must pass a written examination and provide proof of experience. There are four classes of certification: Broadcast Technologist, Broadcast Engineer, Audio or Video Engineer, and Senior Broadcast Engineer, each requiring more experience. Special endorsements in either television or AM/FM are available. Certification is valid for five years, after which renewal is necessary.

SCHOLARSHIPS AND GRANTS

Several organizations provide scholarships for students wishing to pursue careers in the broadcasting industry. Professional associations may also offer lists of scholarship or grant opportunities. The Broadcast Education Association, American Women in Radio and Television, National Association of Broadcasters, the Society of Broadcast Engineers, Inc., and Radio-Television News Directors Association are some associations to contact for information.

Technical schools and community colleges with programs in broadcast technology or broadcast engineering may award scholarships to students. Contact their financial aid offices or your departmental advisor for details. These schools may also offer general scholarships for which you may qualify.

INTERNSHIPS AND VOLUNTEERSHIPS

Internships are common in the broadcast technology field and are highly recommended. In fact, it is often difficult to find jobs without some internship

In-depth

Going Digital

High definition TV will offer approximately twice the vertical and horizontal resolution of your current television, which means the picture will be twice as clear. HDTV will also enhance the sound quality of programming. Also with HDTV, you'll have access to four times as many channels. Sounds too good to be true, doesn't it? It may be too early to tell, but going digital might have a few drawbacks. As television broadcasting switches from analog transmission to digital transmission, your analog television set is going to need an update. This will probably begin with analog-to-digital converter boxes, which may cost anywhere from fifty to several hundred dollars. Eventually, you will probably need to purchase a new television set that can accommodate HDTV. The first HDTV sets retailed in Japan for $28,000. The prices have since come down as low as $700, but top quality sets cost a few thousand.

Europe began offering two HD channels in 2004, and BBC plans to switch all of its production to HD by 2012. Germany launched HD on its pay channel in 2005 and the United Kingdom should begin using HDTV in 2006. China is planning to launch HD in conjunction with the 2008 Olympics in Beijing.

The Federal Communications Commission (FCC) was created in 1934 and is an independent agency of the U.S. government. It regulates radio, television, telephone, and telegraph systems, except those of the federal government. It licenses and regulates radio and television stations and assigns radio wavelengths and television channels.

experience. Chris participated in many internships and says, "If I hadn't done any internships, I don't know if I would have ever done this." Most internships are unpaid, but the experience you can gain is priceless.

If you are enrolled in a technical school or college, it is likely that participating in an internship is a graduation requirement. The school placement office or your advisor can assist you in locating appropriate internships. You may be able to earn college credit for your internship as well.

Many television and radio stations provide internship or volunteer programs of their own, so you should be able to find some opportunities even if you are not attending school. Don't discount the public-access cable television stations or the public radio stations, as they may welcome volunteers more readily than the network affiliates.

LABOR UNIONS

Union membership varies from station to station. KSBY, where Walt works, is in a small market, and union membership is not required. Stations in larger markets, however, are often unionized. The largest broadcasting union is the National Association of Broadcast Employees and Technicians. Union regulations often dictate what a broadcast engineer can or cannot do. For instance, because KSBY is not unionized, the maintenance engineers may occasionally fill in for operators, and job duties may overlap. This would generally not be allowed at a unionized station.

Union membership is not mandatory for sound editors in the motion picture industry, but most established editors belong to one union or another. Chris belongs to the International Alliance of Theatrical Stage Employees, but notes that sound editors in the Los Angeles area belong to a different union altogether. Membership is often determined by the employer and the region in which you work.

Who Will Hire Me?

Chris found his first job in the industry through an internship, which is why he considers internships so crucial. Even if you do not find a job through an internship, you can gain valuable contacts that may help you in your career. Chris was interning at a studio that had more work than it could handle, so he "volunteered" to take the job editing sound for an animated cartoon show. He believes he got the job because of his enthusiasm and his ability to get along with the other staff members. "Who you know is key, and that's why you have to be able to get along with others," he emphasizes.

The motion picture industry is an extremely difficult industry to enter, which is why Chris warns, "You've got to really want to do it." You should have a talent for it, as well as a passion for sound, because the field is highly competitive. Chris has won an Emmy award and worked on many Oscar-winning films, and yet, "There are absolutely zero guarantees that I will get hired," he states. "I have to make sure that I get hired. I'm on the phone, and I make my visits, and I try and maintain as many relationships as possible." Almost all sound editors are independent freelance editors, which means pounding the pavement is a normal part of the job.

Broadcast technology is also a difficult industry to break into. "To start out," Walt suggests, "the best thing to do would be to start sending resumes and contacting stations." Perseverance is key. Walt also advises reading the trade magazines, such as *Broadcast Engineering* (http://www.broadcastengineering.com). The back of the magazine lists job openings and also contains advertisements for employment agencies that specialize in broadcasting.

Walt also believes in maintaining good relationships with others in the industry. "Who you know is certainly the best," he states. "In fact, that's how I've done it my entire career. I've never, ever applied for a job. It's always been somebody calling me." But, he contends, it takes years of experience and time building a reputation before most will be in a similar position.

Professional organizations frequently provide lists of job opportunities as well, and most of them have Web sites with information. Some broadcasting jobs may be located in newspaper classified advertisements or on the Internet. Motion picture jobs, however, are usually not advertised.

The primary employers of broadcast engineers are television and radio broadcasting stations, cable and other pay television companies, and motion picture production companies. Entry-level broadcast engineers generally start in smaller markets, and the chances of finding this first job in your hometown are slim. This gives the engineer an opportunity to gain experience and decide on a field of specialization. After years of training, engineers can work their way up to larger stations in larger markets or cities.

Where Can I Go from Here?

As broadcast engineers move up the ranks and gain more experience, they can move to larger markets and bigger stations or assume supervisory positions. *Chief engineers* supervise the work of other broadcast engineers. They also assume management duties and are responsible for budgeting and planning radio or television broadcast activities. They may also prepare work schedules, take care of hiring and personnel issues, and make decisions about equipment purchases. A college degree in engineering is generally needed in order to become a chief engineer at a large TV station.

Broadcast engineers can also advance to the rank of *program director,* handling all aspects of the broadcast and directing and coordinating the activities of personnel engaged in the production of television or radio programs. This includes writing and rehearsing scripts. Like the chief engineer, program directors may also be responsible for personnel issues and monitoring department budgets. *Technical directors* coordinate the activities of radio or television staff to ensure the technical quality of picture and sound for programs originating in the studio or from remote field locations. *Producers* are responsible for the overall organization and planning of a program. They research ideas and develop scripts or working ideas. Producers may also coordinate the production schedule and make sure the program is within budgetary constraints.

For sound editors, there are a number of advancement possibilities. *Sound supervisors* oversee the work of sound editors. They meet with the director and picture editor for direction, then pass the information on to the sound editors. *Sound designers* create specialized sounds and conceptualize the overall sound environment for films. They may also work for theme parks, developing sound effects.

What Are the Salary Ranges?

According to the U.S. Department of Labor, median annual earnings for broadcast technicians were $28,170 in 2003. Those technicians in the middle 50 percent had earnings of between $19,340 and $43,290. Those in the lowest paid 10 percent earned less than $14,960, while those in the highest 10 percent earned more than $61,440. A 2005 review of salaries nationwide by Salary.com reports that

ADVANCEMENT POSSIBILITIES

Chief engineers supervise and assist broadcast engineers. They handle administrative duties such as the acquisition of broadcasting equipment, preparation of work schedules, and enforcement of station policies and procedures.

Producers are responsible for the overall planning, organization, and production of radio, television, and cable television programs.

Program directors coordinate the activities of all staff members involved in the actual production of television or radio programs.

Technical directors supervise personnel in radio and television studios to ensure the technical quality of picture and sound for programs.

Sound supervisors oversee a staff of sound editors. They collaborate with the motion picture's director and picture editor, receiving direction about the sounds they desire.

Sound designers design and create specialized sounds or sound effects. They may also contribute to creating a signature sound or sound environment for films.

the median earnings for broadcast technicians were $37,437. The lowest paid earned $28,077, and the highest paid earned $46,796.

What Is the Job Outlook?

The *Occupational Outlook Handbook* reports that employment for broadcast engineers is expected to grow about as fast as the average for all occupations through 2012. The U.S. Department of Labor Career InfoNet reports that there were 35,000 broadcast technicians holding jobs in 2002 and that number is expected to increase to about 39,400 in 2012.

Growth may be inhibited somewhat by the increasing automation of radio and television stations. Cameras, playback, program recording, and other procedures may soon become completely automated and controlled by computers.

As Walt explains, "Radio has been doing that for several years. You go into a radio station, and you'll be lucky if you find one person. Those things are running on autopilot. And TV is just starting to do that." Currently, stations such as KSBY record a large percentage of their programs from a satellite feed.

But Walt believes this is still a great time for broadcast engineers. "The job outlook for broadcast engineers in television is absolutely exceptional," he states emphatically. "Right now the industry is wide open, more than it has ever been. We can't get engineers fast enough."

Many engineers are reaching retirement age, and the television industry is going through a revolution. By the year 2006, every station in the United States must have switched from analog to high definition television (HDTV). "This is, hands down, much bigger than color was. It's going to completely revolutionize the industry," says Walt. He feels this digital revolution will open up unlimited job openings in broadcasting and with companies who supply equipment or services to the broadcasting industry.

Employment in the motion picture industry, according to the *Occupational Outlook Handbook*, is expected to grow rapidly; however, the competition for these jobs will be intense.

How Do I Learn More?

PROFESSIONAL ORGANIZATIONS

The following organizations can provide information about trends in the broadcasting industry including, educational and training programs, available scholarships and grant, career opportunities, and certification:

American Women in Radio and Television
8405 Greensboro Drive, Suite 800
McLean, VA 22102
703-506-3290
info@awrt.org
http://www.awrt.org

Audio Engineering Society
60 East 42nd Street
New York, NY 10165-2520
212-661-8528
http://www.aes.org

Broadcast Education Association
1771 N Street, NW
Washington, DC 20036-2891
202-429-5354
beainfo@beaweb.org
http://www.beaweb.org

National Academy of Recording Arts and
    Sciences
3402 Pico Boulevard
Santa Monica, CA 90405
310-392-3777
http://www.grammy.com

National Association of Broadcast Employees and
    Technicians
501 Third Street, NW, 6th Floor
Washington, DC 20001
202-434-1254
http://www.nabetcwa.org

National Association of Broadcasters
1771 N Street, NW
Washington, DC 20036
202-429-5300
nab@nab.org
http://www.nab.org

National Cable & Telecommunications
    Association
1724 Massachusetts Avenue, NW
Washington, DC 20036
202-775-3550
http://www.ncta.com

Radio-Television News Directors Association
1600 K Street, Suite 700
Washington, DC 20006-2838
202-659-6510
rtnda@rtnda.org
http://www.rtnda.org/rtnda

Society of Broadcast Engineers Inc.
9247 North Meridian Street, Suite 305
Indianapolis, IN 46240
317-846-9000
http://www.sbe.org

Society of Motion Picture and Television
    Engineers
595 West Hartsdale Avenue
White Plains, NY 10607
914-761-1100
http://www.smpte.org

BIBLIOGRAPHY

The following is a sampling of materials relating to the professional concerns and development of broadcast engineers:

Ellis, Elmo. *Opportunities in Broadcasting Careers.* Lincolnwood, Ill.: NTC/Contemporary Publishing Group, 1998.

Hartwig, Robert L. *Basic TV Technology: Digital and Analog.* 3d ed. Woburn, Mass.: Focal Press, 2000.

Jones, Graham. *A Broadcast Engineering Tutorial for Non-Engineers.* 3d ed. Woburn, Mass: Focal Press, 2005.

Whitaker, Jerry. *Standard Handbook of Broadcast Engineering.* New York: McGraw Hill, 2005.

Whitaker, Jerry, and Blair Benson. *Standard Handbook of Video and Television Engineering.* New York: McGraw Hill, 2000.

CABLE TELEVISION TECHNICIANS

Though cable TV may have its roots in reruns of old sitcoms, today's cable companies are bringing us hundreds of diverse channels, speedy Internet access, and even local phone service. Contemporary cable systems allow Web users to communicate with people around the world, to conduct business from their homes, and to enjoy digital programming.

Cable television technicians have been instrumental in helping companies replace copper cabling with fiber optic lines, allowing for a future of videoconferencing, renewing drivers' licenses online, taking long distance education courses, and a number of community applications.

What Does a Cable TV Technician Do?

Running along poles in rural and suburban areas and in tunnels under the ground in cities are miles upon miles of cables that help bring TV channels like MTV, VH-1, CNN, ESPN, and others to American households. Cable TV is a "closed path" system that eliminates the need to receive transmissions over the air. Signals from broadcast airwaves, microwave transmitters, or satellites are picked up by antennas at the local cable company's electronic control center plant, or head-end, and then sent through coaxial and/or fiber optic cables into people's homes. *Cable TV technicians* take care of these cable systems. Throughout the system, they make repairs, run tests to check for potential problems, replace worn-out components, add new technology to enhance reception, and perform other work to maintain and improve the system. They also bring the cable line into homes—the part of the technician's job that most people see—and may help to develop new cable systems.

In America, about 67 percent of homes with a television received cable service in 2005, or almost 74 million households, according to the National Cable Television Association (NCTA). The cable TV industry has grown from 25,000 employees in 1975 to approximately 131,000 employees in 1999. The industry is made up of three broad groups: the local cable systems, which provide cable service to

Definition
Cable television technicians install, maintain, and repair cable TV lines and equipment.

Alternative Job Titles
Bench technicians
Cable TV line technicians
Cable TV technicians
Installers
Trunk technicians

High School Subjects
Computer science
Mathematics
Technical/shop

Personal Skills
Leadership/management
Mechanical/manipulative

Salary Range
$22,690 to $41,020 to $59,020

Minimum Educational Level
High school diploma

Certification or Licensing
Voluntary

Outlook
About as fast as the average

DOT
821

GOE
05.02.01

NOC
7247

O*NET-SOC
49-9052.00

homes; the multiple system operators (MSOs), which are corporate groups of individual cable systems; and cable networks, which create the programming found on cable channels. The industry is expanding and changing as telephone companies and utilities provide access to cable television, and as cable companies offer services such as digital television and broadband Internet access.

Installers are the entry-level technicians. They get homes ready to receive cable by running a cable from a utility pole to the TV, installing a terminal device called a converter, or performing other work. After an installation, they may explain to customers how the system works and what options in programming and channels are available. Depending on their employer, installers also may upgrade or downgrade services, disconnect service when the customer has canceled his or her subscription, and take care of problems with feeder or drop lines. Feeder lines are the cable lines that run from the street to a group of homes. Drop lines are the direct lines to homes. Some installers also respond to customer calls about problems with service.

Trunk technicians fix electronic problems on the trunk line, which connects the feeder lines in the street to the head-end. The work includes fixing electronic failures in the feeder amplifiers. Amplifiers increase the strength of the electronic signal for clear reception to everyone and are spaced throughout the cable system.

Service technicians respond to problems with customers' cable reception. Their work takes them into customer homes as well as all over the cable system. They also electronically scan the system from time to time to find potential problems.

Bench technicians are electronics specialists who work in the cable system's repair facility. They examine and repair broken or malfunctioning equipment, such as cable converters.

Chief technicians are the most highly skilled technicians and head up the technical staff. Their main responsibility is to ensure good, clear delivery of signals to the head-end. This "nerve center" includes the antennas for receiving signals as well as the signal processing equipment. It is very sensitive to temperature and humidity and needs constant monitoring.

In addition, cable companies that have their own construction crew (for building a new system or expanding or upgrading an old one) may employ a technical specialist known as a *strand mapper*. The strand mapper surveys the geographic area, figures out how the cable can be laid out, and then draws diagrams showing the path for the cable and where amplifiers or other necessary system components should go.

What Is It Like to Be a Cable TV Technician?

John Manaro has worked as a cable TV technician for more than 20 years, in a variety of technical positions. He has worked as an installer, a service technician, a line technician, a maintenance technician, and a trunk technician. Currently, John

Lingo to Learn

Amplifiers Spaced throughout the cable system, these devices increase the strength of the electronic signal for clear reception to all customers.

Channel capacity The maximum number of channels that a cable system can carry at the same time.

Coaxial cable A transmission line for carrying television signals; the conducting material is copper or copper-coated wire that is insulated and encased with aluminum.

Converter A device that can increase the number of channels that can be received by the TV; sits on top of the set.

Drop lines Cable distribution lines that feed directly into customers' homes.

Feeder lines Cable distribution lines that connect the trunk line or cable to drop lines.

Fiber optics Transmission technology that uses a very fine, bendable tube of glass or plastic to carry frequencies.

Trunk line The main artery of a cable system; it is strung along main streets or highways of a city to the system's plant area.

works as a construction technician for Comcast Cablevision in Santa Ana, California. "That involves construction and activation of plant extensions," he explains, "which is where we go into areas that have not had cable before and build." His work also involves going into an area with existing service and moving the overhead cables underground. "My work also encompasses repairs to the physical plant, repairs of any damages that occur on the field through somebody else digging something up, breaking something, running into it." Because cable lines are not always buried deeply, they can be easily damaged; any cut in the line can result in loss of the signal and an interruption of service to subscribers. To get at the cables, John must trench through a variety of surfaces such as grass, concrete, and asphalt.

Most of John's time is spent in the field; very little of his work requires office time. While out in the field, John is usually involved in digging, excavating, and repairing damages that are underground. He has to push and pull cables and fiber, and perform splicings of cables. He also must take measurements with signal level meters and voltmeters to assure that signals pass properly through the cable. "You don't want to be afraid of heights," John says, "because you do have to climb in a lot of areas. You'll also have to be able to lift at least 100 pounds." John believes that construction is the most physically demanding area of technical work. "For the most part," John says, "a technician should be agile, with good coordination and motor skills."

Sometimes jobs are bigger than John's crew can support, so the company hires contractors. John provides quality control for the contract labor, while he oversees many aspects of a project. "I verify proper design protocol as applied to the system, making sure we're doing everything within spec. I make sure that when our designer predesigns a housing tract or a plant extension, that that's correct within design philosophy. I make sure everything's going to work out and proof okay." To "proof" a project upon completion, John takes physical measurements to assure that everything is operating correctly.

Unlike technicians in other industries, John doesn't need to provide his own tools. Trucks, ladders, pole-climbing gear, meters, and common hand tools are provided by the company. Those working as contractors, however, must often provide their own tools and vehicles.

The work can also require technicians to go into people's homes to discuss any cable problems with customers. But many of John's hours are spent right out in the elements. "You have to work in the rain, the sleet, the snow, whatever comes along," he says.

> You have to work in the rain,
> the sleet, the snow,
> whatever comes along.

In addition to a regular 40-hour workweek, John must also be on-call for one week every month. During this week, John must be available 24 hours a day to repair cable in the event of an interruption of service to subscribers. As cable companies expand, offering more services such as telephone and Internet to more subscribers, the on-call requirements may become even more demanding.

Overall, John appreciates the variety of the work. "If you're in the field," he says, "every day's a different adventure. Every day you're doing something new; you rarely do something exactly the same way twice. You're always running into a new situation, new people, and new problems and obstacles to overcome."

Do I Have What It Takes to Be a Cable TV Technician?

"You've got to be curious," John emphasizes. "You've got to enjoy learning." Because so much must be learned on the job, a technician must be prepared to ask questions, watch closely, and carefully explore the work at hand.

Strong interpersonal skills, physical agility, the ability to work at heights or in confined spaces, and the capacity to work as part of a team are all good personal traits for cable TV technicians. In addition, it is helpful to feel at ease with electrical equipment and electricians' tools.

Cable TV technicians who pay service calls on customer homes are acting as representatives of the cable TV system and company. They must be able to project a helpful, courteous, pleasant image. They may need to explain cable system operation and costs to customers, answer questions, and analyze descriptions of their problems so repairs or other work can be done. The ability to communicate with others is essential.

Technicians may climb utility poles to check a line, work in tunnels or underground cable passageways to inspect cables for evidence of damage or corrosion, or perform other work that demands physical agility and comfort in confined spaces. Some heavy lifting (50 to 100 pounds) may be required. Technicians must stay alert when working around the electrical conductors in order to avoid electrical shock. Those who work outdoors, such as trunk or service technicians, may have to do so in all kinds of weather. Bench technicians, who stay at the plant, must be able to concentrate for long periods of time.

How Do I Become a Cable TV Technician?

Most of John's training has been on the job or through seminars and classes. "Within the industry," John says, "your system will use several types of gear: amplifiers, power supply, etc. Occasionally these manufacturers come around and they offer seminars on their equipment." He has also taken correspondence courses through the National Cable Television Institute (NCTI) and is certified in a variety of areas.

EDUCATION

High School

Classes that give you experience with electrical/electronics systems and computers are helpful. Those considering the most highly technical positions, such as chief engineer, should get a good background in math and science. For all technicians, English and related classes are helpful for building strong communication skills.

Postsecondary Training

Some entry-level technicians just train on the job; others study cable television repair and maintenance in a one- or two-year program at a technical school or community college. Courses may include electrical wiring, electronics, broadcasting, blueprint

In-depth

Cable Choices

Television viewers now have a variety of sources for cable TV subscription. Telephone companies, direct broadcast services, utilities, and other alternatives to local cable operators served nearly 15.78 million consumers in 1999. According to the NCTA, the telephone company Ameritech provides more than 80 communities and 200,000 consumers with cable TV service in the Midwest. GTE and SBC/SNET have also expanded successfully into cable TV services. BellSouth offers digital services to more than 2 million homes and businesses in the South.

The NCTA reports that in 2004 the number of homes with cable subscriptions had reached 19.4 million, there were 24.3 million digital cable subscriptions, and 2.7 million cable telephone subscriptions. HDTV was available to 90 million U.S. households with TV.

and schematic diagram reading, and physics. Alternatively, some cable TV companies have their own special training schools for technicians.

Positions higher than entry level require more specialized training. For example, qualifications for trunk, service, and bench technicians include some electronics training. Chief technicians need an industrial background, electronics training, and lots of hands-on experience. A bachelor's or master's degree in electrical/electronic engineering may be needed for highly technical positions.

Technical training through self-study and correspondence courses is available from the National Cable Television Institute (NCTI). People in the industry, or those thinking about joining it, can enroll. One program includes five courses on technical training from installer to advanced technician.

ADVANCEMENT POSSIBILITIES

Bench technicians are electronics specialists who work in the cable system's repair facility, examining and repairing broken or malfunctioning equipment.

Chief engineers are responsible for all technical concepts of cable system design, equipment planning, layout for cable communications service, specification of standards for equipment and material, construction of facilities, equipment installation, and technical advice and counsel to staff and system operating managers.

Chief technicians are the highest-skilled technicians and head the technical staff.

General managers head the cable system office and are in charge of operations, company policies, and coordination of all functions of the cable system.

Service technicians respond to problems with customers' cable reception, may visit customer sites, and may work on the cable system to find and fix the problems.

Strand mappers survey the geographic area to be served by a cable system, determine necessary utility pole hookups, and diagram cable system layout, showing where amplifiers or line splitters should go.

Trunk technicians fix electronic problems on the trunk or main cable line, including problems with the system amplifiers.

CERTIFICATION OR LICENSING

Certification is voluntary, but technicians who drive a company vehicle must have a valid driver's license. The Society of Cable Telecommunications Engineers offers certification to installers, broadband communications technicians/engineers, and broadband service technicians. One professional cable association, Women in Cable and Telecommunications, has a joint program with the University of Denver that awards a Certificate of Cable Management for completion of courses in just about every area of the cable TV business.

SCHOLARSHIPS AND GRANTS

Fellowships of nine to 12 months are available from the Walter Kaitz Foundation for minorities with a college education who have at least three years of professional experience in an unrelated field. For more information, contact the Walter Kaitz Foundation, 1724 Massachusetts Avenue, NW, Washington, DC 20036, 202-775-3611, info@walterkaitz.org.

INTERNSHIPS AND VOLUNTEERSHIPS

You may be able to get an internship with your local cable TV system. Write or call to see if opportunities are available. For cable TV system companies, look in the phone book under "Television—Cable" or write to the NCTA for a free copy of *The Cable Development Book*, which lists all of the cable systems in the United States and Canada.

Who Will Hire Me?

John got his first job in the cable TV industry through a county job placement board. People who have completed a cable TV training program at a technical school or community college can get help from the school's placement division. Otherwise, a good option is to check local newspaper want ads or contact your local cable TV system directly. To find the name of local systems, look in the Yellow Pages or the *The Cable Development Book* published by NCTA.

Where Can I Go from Here?

"I answered calls about service problems," John says about his first job with a cable TV company, "and I dispatched technicians." He also ordered materials, stocked them, and issued them. "At some point, a technician went on vacation and they handed me a meter and some tools and said, 'Go do service calls.' I've been out in the field ever since." Now, John is hoping to further his technical knowledge and to move into a management or a supervisory position that would require less physically strenuous work.

With electronics training, technicians may advance into service, line, and trunk positions. Other possible advancements are bench technician or supervisor of other technicians. People with top technician and managerial skills plus good on-the-job experience may move into the role of chief technician. Beyond that, the highest position in the technical department is that of the chief engineer. This person is in charge of all technical aspects of cable system design, equipment planning, cable layout, standards for equipment and material, construction of facilities, equipment installation, and technical advice to the other personnel. Chief engineers typically are very important in the development of new services. A degree in electrical engineering or equivalent experience usually is required, says the NCTA. The construction crew's strand mapper should have knowledge of cable systems and utility construction. Other opportunities might be found with companies that supply equipment to cable TV system companies.

What Are the Salary Ranges?

According to the U.S. Department of Labor National Occupational and Wage Outlook, telecommunications line installers and repairers had median annual earnings of around $41,020 in 2003. The lowest paid 10 percent earned $22,690 a year, and those in the highest paid 10 percent earned $59,020. Salaries also vary by industry with those employed by wired telecommunication carriers earning average $48,840 annually; cable and other program distribution companies, $36,160; and cable and other subscription programming companies, $39,440. Companies offer a variety of benefit packages, which may include any of the following: paid holidays, vacations, and sick days; personal days; medical, dental, and life insurance; profit-sharing plans; 401(k) plans; retirement and pension plans; and educational assistance programs.

What Is the Job Outlook?

According to the U.S. Bureau of Labor Statistics, approximately 167,000 telecommunications line installers and repairers held jobs in 2002. The job outlook for telecommunications line installers and repairers is expected to about as fast as the average of all occupations through 2012. Cable companies will be closely involved in bringing advanced technologies into the homes of consumers. Cable companies are expanding into offering telephone service in addition to the cable channels, digital broadcast, and Internet access currently available in some areas. Demands for all these services are growing.

"It's a progressive industry," John says. "The industry is constantly evolving. Now we're getting into the hybrid fiber and coaxial technology, which is increasing the bandwidth by leaps and bounds. When I first went to work in cable, I started at a 12-channel system. Now I work in a system that offers 200 channels. We offer the high-speed-data Internet connection through the cable lines and all the pay-per-view and video on demand."

How Do I Learn More?

PROFESSIONAL ORGANIZATIONS

The following organizations can provide information about news and trends in the cable TV industry, including training and educational programs, scholarships and grants, and employment opportunities:

National Cable and Telecommunications Association
1724 Massachusetts Avenue, NW
Washington, DC 20036
202-775-3550
http://www.ncta.com

National Cable Television Institute
8022 Southpark Circle, Suite 100
Littleton, CO 80120-5658
303-797-9393
http://www.ncti.com

Society of Cable Telecommunications Engineers
140 Philips Road
Exton, PA 19341-1318
800-542-5040
scte@scte.org
http://www.scte.org

Women in Cable and Telecommunications
14555 Avion Parkway, Suite 250
Chantilly, VA 20151
703-234-9810
http://www.wict.org

BIBLIOGRAPHY

The following is a sampling of materials relating to the professional concerns and development of cable TV technicians:

Bartlett, Eugene R. *Cable Television Handbook*. New York: McGraw Hill, 1999.

Ellis, Elmo. *Opportunities in Broadcasting Careers*. New York: McGraw Hill, 2004.

Farmer, James, David Large, and Walter S. Ciciora. *Modern Cable Television Technology*. 2d ed. San Francisco: Morgan Kaufmann Publishers, 2003.

Hartwig, Robert L. *Basic TV Technology: Digital and Analog*. 3d ed. Woburn, Mass.: Focal Press, 2000.

CALIBRATION LABORATORY TECHNICIANS

||||||||||||||||||||||||||||||||||||||||||||||||||||||||||||||||||||||

In Boulder, Colorado, site of the National Institute of Standards Technology (NIST), there's a room where scientists establish the time standard for the entire country, maintaining a kind of "master clock" against which other clocks are set. By taking continuous readings from 20 to 30 special clocks, using complex mathematical formulas, and comparing the results to the international time standard and other sources, they tell the rest of us exactly what time it is to within an infinitesimal fraction of a second.

Consumers feel confident that a pound of butter in New Jersey will weigh exactly the same as a pound of butter in California. Why? Because in the United States, laws require commerce and industry to use standard weights and measurements. Every scale, for example, is supposed to be calibrated to the national standard, that is, checked against the "master scales" of NIST in Boulder and Washington, D.C. This way, the government makes sure all stores are measuring out the same weight, and customers know they're getting their money's worth.

Similarly, there are standards for many aspects of U.S. manufacturing. During the production process, for example, different instruments are used to test a part or equipment as it is being made. Then, from time to time, the instrument itself must be checked to be sure it is still producing an accurate reading. Just as there is a time standard by which to set clocks, and a weight standard by which to calibrate scales, there are standards by which instruments used in manufacturing can be checked.

What Does a Calibration Laboratory Technician Do?

This is where *calibration laboratory technicians* come in. People who develop the standards and check the instruments are called *metrologists*. Metrology is the science of measuring things. Calibration laboratory technicians are metrologists who work in calibration laboratories, running tests on various instruments. At higher levels, calibration laboratory technicians

Definition
Calibration laboratory technicians test, calibrate, and repair electrical, mechanical, electromechanical, electronic, and other instruments used to measure, record, and indicate voltage, heat, magnetic resonance, and numerous other factors.

Alternative Job Titles
Engineering laboratory technicians
Metrology technicians
Quality assurance calibrators
Standards laboratory technicians
Test equipment certification technicians

High School Subjects
Mathematics
Physics

Personal Skills
Following instructions
Technical/scientific

Salary Range
$31,220 to $36,509 to $51,264+

Minimum Educational Level
Some postsecondary training

Certification or Licensing
Voluntary

Outlook
About as fast as the average

DOT
003

GOE
02.08.04

NOC
2241

O*NET-SOC
17-3023.00, 17-3023.01

may help to develop new standards, such as for new instruments, and design the test procedures required to see if the instruments meet the standards.

U.S. manufacturers, however, are not required by law to check their instruments against NIST or other standards. To do so is generally voluntary. One exception to this involves drug manufacturing. But more and more U.S. manufacturers are working to standards, and using metrologists to help them achieve those standards, anyway. There are two important reasons for this.

First, meeting standards is a way of proving good quality control, and quality control is increasingly seen as a way to set yourself apart from the competition. If you can say, "We use quality control in our production process," you are more likely to stand out from other competitors for a job. If you can say, "Our quality control procedures include using trained metrologists to test our instruments," that is an added leg up on the competition.

In the global marketplace, ISO 9000 is further encouraging the use of metrology. This is a set of voluntary guidelines for helping to establish good quality control procedures and is recognized internationally. It is a mark of distinction to be able to say your company has received ISO certification and an important competitive edge in global business. One part of ISO 9000 specifies how to establish metrology labs and train metrology personnel.

Second, in some cases a manufacturer is required by a customer to meet specific manufacturing standards. If it does not, it loses the contract. The U.S. Department of Defense, for example, and some private businesses require their vendors to manufacture according to strict standards as a condition of winning the job. If the end product doesn't meet those standards, they can reject it and the manufacturer is out a lot of money.

A company may have its own internal standards. This is especially true when the manufacturing technology is so advanced that independent standards, like those from NIST, haven't been developed yet. More often, manufacturers work to standards designed by someone else, such as those developed by the military, NIST, or the International Standards Organization (ISO).

Metrologists help make sure manufacturers meet a given set of standards. For example, they might run a series of tests on oscilloscopes, which are used to measure electronic or electrical factors like voltage. The metrologist can put out a known quantity of voltage and see how close the oscilloscope comes to making the measurement. If it is close enough to conform to standards, it passes. If it is not, the metrologist tries to figure out if error sources are present and if these are affecting the results. He or she also may have to decide how to remove, report, or reduce those errors. If the instrument's readings do not conform to the standard, the instrument might be pulled and sent to another lab for repair.

About 50 percent of metrology work is in the area of electronics testing and calibration; about 40 percent is in the physical/dimensional area; and about 10 percent is in the mechanical. Specialized areas include laser, fiber optics, and microwave testing.

A lab for metrology or calibration may be part of a manufacturer's quality assurance department or the engineering, facilities, plant engineering, or manufacturing divisions. If the manufacturer doesn't have its own metrology lab, it may send its instruments to a specialized firm that does nothing but test other companies' instruments.

A calibration lab tends to be extremely clean and environmentally controlled. Factors such as temperature, humidity, vibration, and static are kept at constant levels to help make sure variances don't interfere with the accuracy of the tests.

Besides running tests and developing standards and testing procedures, calibration laboratory technicians also document and report on their findings.

What Is It Like to Be a Calibration Laboratory Technician?

Jerry Walker has worked as a metrology technician in both the military and in private industry. "In the military there was a lot of high frequency application," Jerry says in comparing the military with his work at Commonwealth Edison in Illinois. "Most of the stuff in the electric company is geared toward generating electricity, and that's very low frequency." At the electric company, Jerry has worked mostly with electronic equipment, calibrating oscilloscopes, digital multimeters, digital timers, and circuit breaker test sets.

Jerry works primarily in a laboratory setting, wearing safety glasses. "In the military we dealt with some more static-sensitive instruments, and we had a

Lingo to Learn

Accuracy The degree of closeness between a measured value and the true, or nominal, value.

Calibration Comparing a measuring device against an equal or better standard.

Environment The altitude, temperature, humidity, and other factors that may affect the performance of an instrument.

Measurement standard An object, instrument, system, or other thing that provides a physical quantity that serves as the basis for measurements of quantity.

Metrology The science of measurement.

Precision The degree of consistency and agreement among independent measurements of a quantity under the same conditions.

Quality control A system of actions that keeps the quality of goods or services at the level expected by users.

static-sensitive workstation which consisted of a mat that we put the equipment on that wouldn't generate static charges. And you'd have a strap that you'd put around your wrist that would be grounded. Then it would remove the charge that would develop from the body. Static electricity is very little current, but it's super-high voltage. It can be like 5,000 or 10,000 or 50,000 volts. So that high voltage with that little bit of current can zap static-sensitive components, certain microchips, and fry them."

Jerry does use some minor hand tools like screwdrivers to open the equipment for actual repair, but most of the work is based in electronics. "They teach you electronics theory," he says, "then they teach you troubleshooting techniques for when you have to do a repair. When you troubleshoot on a broken device, you start with the simplest elements and go to the most complicated. Before you decide a device doesn't work, you make sure it's plugged in, actually turned on. It actually starts at that simple of a level. Then you make sure the switch is in the right position. When you troubleshoot a problem, first you want to verify that it really is a problem, so that you don't go fixing something that wasn't broken."

Occasionally, Jerry may work in a soldering station. "If you're going to remove a component to replace it, there's a separate iron that removes solder. It's got a hollow tip and a tube and vacuum setting, and once the tool melts the solder, the vacuum actually sucks the solder off the connection."

There are other nonelectronics aspects of the work, as well. "There is some physical/dimensional metrology," he says. "If you were to have pressure gauges, you would want them to be accurate, so there's a service to calibrate those. Micrometers, those can be calibrated. In the Air Force, we did the personal weighing scales that they kept in the squadron. We calibrated those to make sure they measured within a pound or half a pound. Anything that measures something can be calibrated to measure accurately."

Do I Have What It Takes to Be a Calibration Laboratory Technician?

Patience, persistence, curiosity, integrity, a healthy sense of ethics, and the desire to be truly accurate—not just close—are all good traits for a calibration laboratory technician. "You have to have the desire to do the job right," Jerry says, "and not cut corners. That would defeat the purpose of calibrating the device. You're signing the paperwork that says this device measures accurately. The bulk of the time you're not being watched by a supervisor, so you need that personal integrity."

TO BE A SUCCESSFUL CALIBRATION LABORATORY TECHNICIAN, YOU SHOULD . . .

○ be patient, persistent, attentive to detail, and have a strong sense of ethics

○ enjoy problem-solving using mathematical concepts

○ have manual dexterity and good hand-eye coordination

○ be able to communicate well with others, both orally and in writing

In-depth

What Is ISO 9000?

ISO 9000 is part of a worldwide system of standards for measurements, products, and services. As more U.S. companies turn their attention to the global marketplace, they are increasingly interested in understanding and conforming to these standards as a way to gain a competitive edge.

International standards organizations fall into two basic types: those for physical standards (treaty organizations) and those for paper standards (nontreaty organizations).

Physical standards are specific references or artifacts for making measurements.

Countries that agree to trace their calibrations to these standards (chiefly, technologically advanced countries) have actually signed a treaty (the Treaty of the Meter) saying they'll do so. Thus, organizations that establish and maintain these international physical standards are called "treaty" organizations.

Paper standards are more like guidelines for quality control, suggesting "what to do and how to do it." For example, they might recommend that companies have a metrology lab and employ trained personnel to run them. Paper standards are more informal, and they're mostly voluntary; that is, no one signed a treaty agreeing to accept them. Hence, the organizations that establish and maintain these standards are known as "nontreaty" organizations.

The International Organization for Standardization (ISO) is one of several international, nontreaty organizations for paper standards. Some of its counterparts focus on specific disciplines, for example, there is an organization for electrical metrology and an organization for law enforcement-related metrology. But ISO writes standards for many different areas. ISO 9000 is just one of the sets of mainly voluntary, nontreaty, paper standards it issues (there also is an ISO 9001, 9002, and so on).

ISO 9000 is not concerned solely with metrology; it also describes manufacturing standards, contract standards, and so forth. "It's mainly about total quality management [TQM], of which calibration is a part," says Wilbur Anson of NCSL.

If ISO 9000 is voluntary, how come so many U.S. companies care so much about it? "It's not a requirement, but it is a 'pressure,'" Anson says. "More companies want to penetrate the European market or the world market; the world market involves ISO; those who want to sell abroad feel a 'pressure' to conform to these standards. Even at home, it's good to be able to put in a contract; it gives a company a competitive edge."

ISO and other international standards groups don't just make things up arbitrarily: They get input from all the national labs of different countries and then write the standard.

For the United States, the American National Standards Institute (ANSI) is the liaison between the U.S. technical community and ISO; it relays U.S. ideas about standards to the ISO. Once the ISO standard is established, ANSI supports and helps spread it in the United States.

In addition to technical prowess and problem-solving ability, the technician should have good interpersonal and communication skills, like the ability to admit mistakes and ask questions when you don't understand something and to work well with others. A strong aptitude in math and electronics, good decision-making skills, and the ability to communicate technical information in reports also help.

Good hand-eye coordination and manual dexterity are helpful physical traits in performing the work. Other helpful skills include having a good understanding of how to read specifications.

How Do I Become a Calibration Laboratory Technician?

Jerry trained for the work in the Air Force, calibrating instruments that were designed for avionics packages. "In this job," he says, "you'll find a lot of the people are from the military because of the official training."

EDUCATION

High School

You should take electronics courses whenever available, as well as physics and chemistry courses. English classes also help because of the amount of technical writing on the job. If working on a new instrument that has never been tested before, you may have to write a multiple-page procedure for it.

Postsecondary Training

Traditionally, postsecondary training for metrologists has been from the military or technical schools. These options are still viable, although military training programs have been cut back in recent years. "While it's still fairly simple or straight forward to enter the field," says Wilbur Anson, business manager for National Conference of Standards Laboratories (NCSL), "things are starting to change. Today's technicians really need a higher level of education. They should have the equivalent of college sophomore physics and know calculus concepts, trigonometry, and a smattering of statistics."

College degree programs in metrology typically are two years in length. "Metrology by itself could never be a four-year degree," Anson says. However, he adds, more four-year degree programs in engineering, physics, computer science and other areas are starting to incorporate metrology classes in the curriculum.

No matter where the technician is trained, experts say, it is very important to receive as broad an education in metrology as possible. Technicians should study all

FYI

The pyramids of ancient Egypt were built using "The Royal Egyptian Cubit," a measurement equal to the length of the forearm from the bent elbow to the tip of the extended middle finger plus the width of the hand's a palm. It is believed this unit of length was developed in about 3000 B.C. and is one of the earliest known records of precise measurement.

of the primary areas of the field, including electronic, physical/mechanical, and dimensional (including fiber optics). "You need the flexibility," Anson says. "That way, if your company downsizes and your particular lab is cut, or if your industry is hit by bad economic times, you'll still be employable. The day is gone when you can expect to start a career in one field and do the exact same thing for 30 years—or stay with the same company for 10 years. In order to survive, a calibration laboratory technician needs as good a basic knowledge as he or she can get, with an eye toward being flexible in the future.

"The calibration technician needs to have knowledge that can be used throughout the plant," Anson adds. "With today's distributed measurement, he or she must be able to go out into the plant, troubleshoot the systems, and prescribe a solution."

People in the field also make a point of getting ongoing training in order to keep up with new technology. Manufacturers like Hewlett Packard might offer one- or two-week training seminars in metrology practice or in new equipment. Associations, consultants, and colleges also provide ongoing training programs. NCSL's *Training Information Directory*, published annually, describes classes, self-study courses, videos, textbooks, and reference materials for ongoing education in the areas of metrication and metrology management, general metrology and digital technology, electrical metrology, physical metrology, and dimensional and optical metrology.

CERTIFICATION OR LICENSING

Currently, there is no industry-wide mandatory certification or licensing system for technicians.

NCSL and other groups are exploring the possibility of voluntary accreditation for laboratories, and the American Society for Quality (ASQ) began offering certification for calibration technicians in 2003.

Who Will Hire Me?

There is a drive in U.S. manufacturing to increase quality control, and that is boosting interest in metrology. Throughout a wide range of industries, manufacturers are finding that exacting standards can help them improve profitability: There are fewer rejected products and less wasted time and materials. Pressure to achieve rigorous standards also comes from external factors like increased competition, customer requests, FDA guidelines (for biomedical-pharmaceutical companies), the move toward ISO 9000 international certification, and so forth.

Therefore, calibration laboratory technicians are much more likely to be found in a wider range of manufacturing industries than their counterparts of a generation ago. Aerospace-defense and electronics manufacturers, the military, and the government are the traditional employers of metrologists and still use them today. However, technicians also are being used more and more by automotive, biomedical-pharmaceutical, chemical-process, nuclear energy, and other types of companies. They also are employed in university research and development facilities and by consultants.

A look at some of the industries participating in a recent NCSL conference illustrates the diversity of potential employers. They included chemical, automotive, optoelectronic, airline, health care, testing laboratory, wireless communication, and food and drug industries.

Associations like NCSL (whose members are companies, rather than individuals) are good sources of information about employers and employment opportunities. Trade magazines and newspapers also may have classified ads describing available positions.

Where Can I Go from Here?

As they develop skills and seniority, technicians may be able to advance into managerial positions. Employers may also pay for additional schooling, allowing technicians to pursue four-year degrees.

> ### ADVANCEMENT POSSIBILITIES
>
> **Metrology engineers,** or **metrologists,** develop and evaluate calibration systems that measure characteristics of objects, substances, or phenomena, such as length, mass, time, temperature, electric current, luminous intensity, and derived units of physical or chemical measure.
>
> **Quality control managers** plan, coordinate, and direct quality control programs designed to ensure continuous production of products consistent with established standards.
>
> **Standards engineers** establish engineering and technical limitations and applications for items, materials, processes, methods, designs, and engineering practices for use by designers of machines and equipment.

Professionals like engineers and physicists are more likely to design the standards and develop the testing procedures executed by the calibration laboratory technicians. This is not only more interesting to some people but also makes the technician more valuable to employers who need to develop their own internal standards.

"Today, companies like Lockheed, Hewlett Packard, and so forth will have engineers in their metrology department," Anson says. "There's pressure today for even more stringent standards than those provided by NIST. So there's a need for engineers who can extrapolate from NIST standards and help to develop and integrate these more stringent internal standards." Thus, technicians who go back to school and earn a four-year degree become more valuable to their employers.

What Are the Salary Ranges?

According to the U.S. Department of Labor Occupational Information Network, in 2003 the median earnings for calibration and instrumentation technicians (which is classified with electrical and electronic engineering technicians) were $45,400.

Those in the middle 50 percent salary range earned from $35,400 to $55,000. The lowest paid 10 percent earned $28,400, and the highest paid 10 percent earned $66,800.

A Salary.com 2005 review of salaries nationwide for calibration technicians showed that earnings, as with most professions, increased with years of experience. Entry level calibration technicians reported annual earnings between $31,220 and $41,085, with a median salary of $36,509. Those with two years experience earned between $38,855 and $51,264, with a median salary of $45,055. With four years of experience or more, earnings increased to a median $46,141. The lowest paid earned $41,316, and the highest paid earned $51,897.

What Is the Job Outlook?

The *Occupational Outlook Handbook* reports that in 2002 electrical and electronic engineering technicians held 204,000 jobs. Of those, 69,000 were with federal, state, and local governments. The remaining jobs were with manufacturing industries, primarily computer and electronic equipment companies; and with professional, scientific, and technical service industries. Overall, job growth in the profession is expected to increase about as fast as the average for all occupations through 2012.

Calibration laboratory technicians are becoming increasingly important as manufacturers work to achieve such quality standards as ISO 9000. Also, new technologies continue to emerge that require new standards and measurement techniques. However, somewhat offsetting this are cutbacks in areas of the defense industry and other traditional employers of calibration laboratory technicians as well as an increase in automation, which permits tests to be run faster and with fewer people.

"It's an up and coming technical career field," says Terrelle Wilson. "The number of jobs available is probably higher than ever before and continues to grow. This is partly because there aren't very many schools that are training calibration techs. It's not something you just walk into out of high school. You have to have some kind of technical or engineering background. You definitely have to have electronics. But I'm not sure there will ever be a need for 20 or 30 programs in different schools around the country." The entire curriculum of the CCA Metrology

Program is online, and Wilson suspects those courses will be used to supplement other programs across the country.

While some tests continue to be done manually, such as for certain dimensional standards, automation will continue to grow. One new development is the so-called "smart instruments" that can run tests on themselves and signal when they need to be calibrated.

Still, there are opportunities for calibration laboratory technicians. Much depends on the technician's breadth of education in the field and choice of industries. The biomedical-pharmaceutical industry promises some of the best prospects for growth. The industry as a whole is well paid, and FDA plans to enforce guidelines for these companies' research and development standards which will mean increased employment of metrologists.

Newer specialties like fiber-optics testing are also providing opportunities. Fiber optics are key in advanced communication systems. Lighter and faster than wire, fiber optics are attractive to a wide range of manufacturers, including NASA. The technology for it is still new enough that NIST and private companies are still developing the standards for testing and calibrating fiber optics communication test instruments. These include things like optical power meters, attenuators, tunable lasers, and other highly sophisticated measuring devices. Testing may involve such things as sending signals to test the breakdown point, seeing how it acts at different temperatures, and doing stress tests.

How Do I Learn More?

PROFESSIONAL ORGANIZATIONS

Information about the industry, careers in engineering, training and educational programs, scholarships, and professional development is available from the following organizations:

American Society for Quality
600 North Plankinton Avenue
Milwaukee, WI 53202
800-248-1946
http://www.asq.org

Institute of Electrical and Electronic Engineers
c/o IEEE College of Engineering
San Jose State University
One Washington Square

San Jose, CA 95192
sjsu_ieee@yahoo.com
http:///www.engr.sjsu.edu/ieee/contact.jsp

Instrumentation, Systems, and Automation Society
67 Alexander Drive
Research Triangle Park, NC 27709
919-549-8411
info@isa.org
http://www.isa.org

National Conference of Standards Laboratories
2995 Wilderness Place, Suite 107
Boulder, CO 80301-5404
303-440-3339
info@ncsli.org
http://www.ncsli.org

National Institute of Standards and Technology
100 Bureau Drive, Stop 1070
Gaithersburg, MD 20899-1070
301-975-6478
inquiries@nist.gov
http://www.nist.gov

BIBLIOGRAPHY

The following is a sampling of material relating to the professional concerns and development of calibration laboratory technicians:

Bucher, Jay L. *The Metrology Handbook*. Milwaukee: ASQ Quality Press, 2004.

Cable, Mike. *Calibration: A Technician's Guide*. Research Triangle Park, N.C.: The Instrumentation, Systems, and Automation Society, 2005.

Campbell, Paul. *An Introduction to Measuration and Calibration*. New York: Industrial Press, 1995.

Dotson, Connie et al. *Fundamentals of Dimensional Metrology*. Clifton Park, N.J.: Thomson Delmar Learning, 2002.

Fluke Corporation. *Calibration: Philosophy in Practice*. Everett, Wash.: Fluke Corporation, 1994.

CARDIOVASCULAR TECHNOLOGISTS

A major vessel in the patient's heart is blocked, potentially endangering the patient's life. He must undergo a special procedure that involves forcing a tube through the artery to unblock the obstruction. A team of health care professionals that specializes in diagnosis and treatment of heart ailments is assembled to carry out the procedure. On hand are a cardiologist (heart doctor), nurse, and various tech support people, including a highly trained cardiology technologist, which is a type of cardiovascular technologist.

After the patient is prepped, this special team begins its work. The physician begins by inserting a tube into the patient's leg. Slowly, carefully, the fine tube is woven up through the arteries and into the patient's heart. As she works, the physician watches a video monitor that shows an internal view of the tube making its way to the heart. The cardiology technologist is standing by, all senses alert, checking the view on the monitor, making adjustments to the camera as needed, entering information about the procedure into a computer, and providing other support. Afterward, she will process the film obtained from the camera for use by the doctor.

This procedure is not without risk; sometimes it doesn't work, and about 2 percent of patients—primarily older patients, weak patients, or those with very bad heart disease—may suffer from an infection, heart attack, or stroke while undergoing it. However, this patient is lucky: The obstruction is successfully cleared, and he is spared the need for open-heart surgery.

What Does a Cardiovascular Technologist Do?

Congenital heart disease. Acquired heart disease. Coronary artery disease. Peripheral vascular disease. Heart disease of all kinds is still the leading killer of men and women in this country, despite increased awareness in recent years of the ill effects on the heart of stress, poor diet, lack of exercise, smoking, and other unhealthy behaviors. As the

---

Definition
Cardiovascular technologists support physicians in the diagnosis and treatment of heart and related blood vessel ailments.

Alternative Job Titles
Cardiac monitor technicians
Cardiology technologists
Echocardiography technologists
Electrocardiograph (EKG) technicians and technologists
Holter monitor and stress test technologists
Vascular technologists

High School Subjects
Biology
Health

Personal Skills
Leadership/management
Technical/scientific

Salary Range
$21,500 to $37,800 to $57,660

Educational Requirements
Some postsecondary training

Certification or Licensing
Voluntary

Outlook
Faster than the average

---

baby boomer generation ages, health professionals are expecting to see the number of coronary patients increase.

Technologists who assist physicians in the diagnosis and treatment of heart disease are known as *cardiovascular technologists*. ("Cardio" means heart, "vascular" refers to the blood vessel/circulatory system.) They include *electrocardiograph (EKG) technologists, Holter monitor and stress test technologists, cardiology technologists, vascular technologists* and *echocardiographers* (both ultrasound technologists), *cardiac monitor technicians,* and others. As the services of EKG technologists may be required throughout the hospital, such as in cancer wards or emergency rooms, there may be a separate department for these EKG professionals. Increasingly, however, hospitals are centralizing cardiovascular services under one full cardiovascular "service line," all overseen by the same administrator. According to a spokesperson at the American Academy of Medical Administrators, "This is because cardiology services is the hottest area in health care today. At the present time, it is continuing to emerge, unfold, and expand."

In addition to cardiovascular technologists, the cardiovascular team at a hospital may include radiology (X-ray) technologists, nuclear medicine technologists, nurses, physician assistants, respiratory technologists, and respiratory therapists. For their part, the cardiovascular technologists contribute by performing one or more of a wide range of procedures in cardiovascular medicine, including invasive (enters a body cavity or interrupts normal body functions), noninvasive, peripheral vascular, or echocardiography (ultrasound) procedures. In most facilities they use equipment that's among the most advanced in the medical field; drug therapies also may be used as part of the diagnostic imaging procedures or in addition to them. Technologists' services may be required when the patient's condition is first being explored, before surgery, during surgery (cardiology technologists primarily), and/or during rehabilitation of the patient. Some of the work is performed on an outpatient basis.

Depending on their specific area of skill, some cardiovascular technologists are employed in nonhospital health care facilities. For example, EKG technologists may work for clinics, mobile medical services, or private doctor's offices. Their equipment can go just about anywhere. The same is true for the ultrasound technologists.

Some of the specific duties of cardiovascular technologists are described in the next sections. Exact titles of these technologists often vary between medical facilities because there is no standardized naming system.

ELECTROCARDIOGRAPH (EKG) TECHNOLOGISTS

Electrocardiograph (EKG) technologists use an electrocardiograph (EKG) machine to detect the electronic impulses that come from a patient's heart during and between a heartbeat. The EKG machine then records these signals on a paper graph called an electrocardiogram. The electronic impulses recorded by the EKG machine can tell the physician about the action of the heart during and between the individual heartbeats. This in turn reveals important information about the condition of the heart, including irregular heartbeats or the presence of blocked arteries, which the physician can use to diagnose heart disease,

monitor progress during treatment, or check the patient's condition after recovery.

To use an EKG machine, the technologist attaches electrodes (small, disk-like devices about the size of a silver dollar) to the patient's chest. There are wires attached to the electrodes that lead to the EKG machine. Up to 12 leads or more may be attached. To get a better reading from the electrodes, the technologist may first apply an adhesive gel to the patient's skin that helps to conduct the electrical impulses. The technologist then operates controls on the EKG machine or (more commonly) enters commands for the machine into a computer. The electrodes pick up the electronic signals from the heart and transmit them to the EKG machine. The machine registers and makes a printout of the signals, with a stylus (pen) recording their pattern on a long roll of graph paper.

During the test, the technologist may move the electrodes in order to get readings of electrical activity in different parts of the heart muscle. Since EKG equipment can be sensitive to electrical impulses from other sources, such as other parts of the patient's body or other equipment in the room, the technologist must watch for false readings.

After the test the EKG technologist takes the electrocardiogram off the machine, edits it or makes notes on it, and sends it to the physician (usually a cardiologist, or heart specialist). Physicians may use computers to help them use and interpret the electrocardiogram; special software is available to assist them with their diagnosis.

EKG technologists don't have to repair the EKG machine, but they do have to keep an eye on it and know when it's malfunctioning so they can call someone to fix it. They also may keep the machine stocked with paper.

HOLTER MONITOR TECHNOLOGISTS AND STRESS TEST TECHNOLOGISTS

Holter monitoring and stress testing may be performed by either Holter monitor technologists or stress test technologists, or may be additional duties of some EKG technologists. In Holter monitoring, electrodes are fastened to the patient's chest and a small, portable monitor is strapped to the patient's body, at the waist, for example. The small monitor contains a magnetic tape or cassette that records the heart during activity, as the patient moves, sits, stands,

Lingo to Learn

Angioplasty Procedure involving insertion into the heart of a catheter (tube) with a balloon at one end to widen a blocked blood vessel.

Cardiologist Physician who specializes in the heart. The prefix "cardio" means "heart."

Cardiology Of or relating to the heart.

Cardiopulmonary Of or relating to the heart or lungs.

Cardiovascular Having to do with the heart ("cardio") and the vessels around it ("vascular").

Catheter Small tube.

Catheterization Procedure involving insertion of a catheter (tube).

Congenital Condition or opportunity for condition that has existed since birth.

Diagnostic Disease—or condition—identifying (such as "diagnostic tests").

Echocardiography Procedure for studying the structure and motion of the heart using ultrasound technology.

Electrocardiogram The paper printout showing the results of the EKG test.

machine, attaching electrodes to the patient's arms, legs, and chest, and first obtains a reading of the patient's resting heart activity and blood pressure. Then, the patient is asked to walk on a treadmill for a certain period of time while the technologist and the physician monitor the heart. The speed of the treadmill is increased so that the technologist and physician can see what happens when the heart is put under higher levels of exertion.

CARDIOLOGY TECHNOLOGISTS

Cardiology technologists specialize in providing support for cardiac catheterization (tubing) procedures. These procedures are classified as invasive because they require the physician and attending technologists to enter a body cavity or interrupt normal body functions. In one cardiac catheterization procedure, an angiogram, a catheter (tube) is inserted into the heart (usually by way of an artery in the leg) in order to diagnose the condition of the heart blood vessels, such as whether there is a blockage. In another procedure, known as angioplasty, a catheter with a balloon at the end is inserted into an artery to widen it.

Unlike some of the other cardiovascular technologists, cardiology technologists actually participate in surgical procedures. They may assist in surgery by helping to secure the patient to the table, setting up a 35 millimeter video camera or other imaging device under the instructions of the physician (to produce images that assist the physician in guiding the catheter through the cardiovascular system), entering information about the surgical procedure (as it is taking place) into a computer, and providing other support. After the procedure, the tech may process the angiographic film for use by the physician. Cardiology technologists may also assist during open-heart surgery by preparing and monitoring the patient, and may participate in placement or monitoring of pacemakers.

VASCULAR TECHNOLOGISTS AND ECHOCARDIOGRAPHERS

These technologists are specialists in noninvasive cardiovascular procedures using ultrasound equipment to obtain and record information about the condition of the heart. Ultrasound equipment is used to send out sound waves to the part of the body being studied; when the sound waves hit the

sleeps, etc. The patient is required to wear the Holter monitor for 24 to 48 hours while he or she goes about normal daily activities. When the patient returns to the hospital, the technologist removes the magnetic tape or cassette from the monitor and puts it in a scanner to produce audio and visual representations of heart activity. (Hearing how the heart sounds during activity can help the physician diagnose a possible heart condition.) The technologist reviews and analyzes the information revealed in the tape. Finally, the technologist may print out the parts of the tape that show abnormal heart patterns or make a full tape for the physician.

Stress tests record the heart's activity during physical activity. In one type of stress test, the technologist hooks up the patient to the EKG part being studied, they send back an echo to the ultrasound machine. The echoes are read by the machine, which creates an image on a monitor, permitting the technologist to get an instant picture of the specific body part's condition.

Vascular technologists are specialists in the use of ultrasound equipment to study blood flow and circulation problems. Echocardiographers are specialists in the use of ultrasound equipment to evaluate the heart and its structures such as the valves. (Ultrasound also is used in other medical procedures, perhaps most familiarly in capturing images of a fetus to check its condition and learn what sex it is.)

CARDIAC MONITOR TECHNICIANS

Cardiac monitor technicians are similar to, and sometimes perform some of the same duties as, EKG technologists. Usually working in the intensive care unit (ICU) or cardio-care unit of the hospital, cardiac monitor technicians keep watch over all the screens that are monitoring the patients to detect any sign that a patient's heart is not beating as it should.

Cardiac monitor technicians begin their shift by reviewing patients' records to familiarize themselves with each patient's normal heart rhythms, the current pattern, and what types of problems have been observed. Throughout the shift, the cardiac monitor technician watches for heart rhythm irregularities that need prompt medical attention. Should there be any, he or she notifies a nurse or doctor immediately so that appropriate care can be given.

In addition to these positions, there may be other cardiovascular technologists, depending on the specific health care facility. For example, a *cardiopulmonary technologist* specializes in procedures for diagnosing problems with the heart and lungs. He or she may conduct electrocardiograph, phonocardiograph (sound recordings of the heart's valves and of the blood passing through them), echocardiograph, stress testing, and respiratory test procedures.

Cardiopulmonary technologists also may assist with cardiac catheterization procedures, measuring and recording information about the patient's cardiovascular and pulmonary system during the procedure and alerting the cardiac catheterization team of any problems.

Nuclear medicine technologists, who use radioactive isotopes in diagnosis, treatment, or studies, may participate in diagnosis or treatment

---

More Lingo to Learn

Electrocardiograph (EKG) machine Detects the electronic impulses that come from a patient's heart during or between a heartbeat, which may reveal heart abnormalities, and records that information in the form of a paper graph called an electrocardiogram.

Electrode Device that conducts electricity.

Holter monitor Cardiac-function monitoring device.

Invasive A medical procedure that penetrates into a body cavity or interrupts normal body functions; examples in cardiology include cardiac catheterization procedures.

Noninvasive A medical procedure that does not penetrate into a body cavity or interrupt body functions; examples in cardiology include ultrasound tests.

Phonocardiograph Sound recordings of the heart's valves and of the blood passing through them.

Radiographs X rays.

Vascular Relating to the blood vessels. Vascular technologists are concerned about the blood vessels around the heart.

---

of cardiology problems. *Radiology, respiratory,* and *exercise technicians* and *therapists* also may assist in patient diagnosis, treatment, and/or rehabilitation.

What Is It Like to Be a Cardiovascular Technologist?

Ted Christman has been working as a technologist for more than 15 years. As lead tech at a hospital in Fort Collins, Colorado, Ted did echocardiograms and vascular work. "Taking care of patients was number one in doing the ordered tests for the physicians," he says. He performed echocardiograms on a variety of patients, from children to adults. This involved using ultrasound instruments to record vascular information such as heart rate and blood pressure. The equipment transmits sound waves and records the resulting echoes on a computer screen. Ted also performed stress tests, which involved documenting a patient's vascular information while the patient was resting, then again while the patient was walking on a treadmill, in order to see the effect that the activity had on the body. Pharmacological stress tests involved injecting a chemical to increase the heart load.

"The echocardiographic technologist, or echo-tech, is the first filter," he says. "You go in and assess the patient, then perform the echo, and as you're doing the echocardiogram, you have to be able to look at it to determine what further parts of the echo need to be done. In other words, if a patient has a bad valve, then you need to know you have to do more Doppler, per se. You need to explore all the aspects you can about that valve."

When with a patient, Ted relied a great deal on his clinical knowledge. "You have to know when you're seeing something that's bad," he says. "If you go in there and the patient is at threat because of their disease state, then you have to be smart enough to tell somebody, 'You need to get in here and look at this right now.' That happens more often than you'd like to think. So the echo-tech is really the eyes and ears of the cardiologist at the first level." Ted says it is important for the echo-tech and the cardiologist to work as a team. The echo-tech does the study, then creates a preliminary report for the cardiologist. The tech then works alongside the cardiologist in interpreting the patient's situation to assure that everything is seen and done.

"The smart cardiologists respect their echo-techs because they help them quite a bit," Ted says. "A good tech can make a good doctor better. When I made a good call, when I saw something that was serious on a patient and let people know about it, I was rewarded with respect. It's a very responsible position."

A good tech can make a good doctor better.

In a hospital setting, the hours can be long and may also involve mobile service, requiring the tech to move from location to location. Ted adds that, for all the job's rewards, the work could also be frustrating because he was unable to see the patient's case all the way through. "I didn't get to sign off on reports," he says. "I wasn't the doctor."

Currently, Ted is using his experience as a technologist for a company called Agilent Technologies. Ted explains that, for a tech, industry work is often a natural next step in career advancement. "I'm implementing systems that read echocardiograms," he says. "A lot of techs do go into industry as people who know everything there is to know about a particular ultrasound machine. They're able to demonstrate all the features, plus train customers, techs, in the utilization of that instrument." This computer system works with the echo machine. "The images on the echo machine are recorded digitally," Ted explains, "and we download this into the system, and the system is able to read the images offline and actually create the tech's report and do the dictation without the tech ever having to pick up the phone. It's a digital echo lab."

Cardiovascular technologists usually work five-day, 40-hour weeks, but some may be on 24-hour emergency call, and almost all work occasional evenings or weekends. Cardiology departments may be closed or run only a skeleton crew on the weekends. Technologists whose tests usually are scheduled in advance—such as stress tests or Holter monitoring—usually don't face emergency work loads and the need for overtime. Some of the other types of cardiovascular technologists, such as the catheterization professionals, may work longer hours and evenings, and also be on call for emergencies.

Do I Have What It Takes to Be a Cardiovascular Technologist?

"It's a kind of position in which you need to be self-directed," Ted says. "There's a lot of work to be done during the day. Labs are not very often managed at the level where someone directs you. You pick up your own work, you pace yourself, you do the work that's scheduled."

Cardiovascular technologists need a combination of mechanical/technological, analytical, and people skills. They should be able to follow instructions and communicate what they know to others. Cardiovascular technologists should be detail oriented; test results are very important to accurate diagnoses. The ability to work under pressure, including during

> ## To Be a Cardiovascular Technologist, You Should . . .
>
> ○ have mechanical/technological aptitude and feel comfortable using computers
>
> ○ be able to empathize with others and project a calm and reassuring manner
>
> ○ have analytical and problem-solving skills; be able to measure, calculate, reason, evaluate, and synthesize information; and demonstrate good judgment
>
> ○ be detail-oriented
>
> ○ be flexible and adapt well to change
>
> ○ be able to work under pressure, if necessary

medical emergencies, also is helpful for some of these positions.

Mechanical/technological aptitude is helpful because the technologists in many of these positions use sophisticated diagnostic imaging equipment. Almost all of this equipment is computerized, so it helps to feel comfortable working with computers. Technologists also may have to calibrate or run tests on their equipment to make sure it is operating correctly.

All of the technologists need analytical skills. They have to be able to measure, calculate, reason, evaluate, and synthesize information. Problem-solving ability, flexibility, and good judgment are crucial. Technologists must be able to handle "out-of-the-ordinary" patients or problems (those that don't fit the "textbook case" mold) and use alternative methods when the regular ones won't work.

The ability to think spatially—that is, comprehend two-dimensional or three-dimensional relationships, for example, or visualize the relationships between the imaging equipment and the part of the body being studied—also is very useful for the imaging technologists.

At the same time, human skills—the ability to empathize with patients, calming their fears, explaining the procedure, and answering any questions—also are important for the technologist. Patience and a calm, reassuring, confident manner are helpful.

Finally, cardiovascular technologists should be able to adapt well to change. Every day brings different patients with different specific problems. Employers may tinker with positions or departments as they strive to find a good balance between services and cost-efficiency. Constant medical advances mean that the technologist has to be flexible and keep up with changes in equipment and procedures.

How Do I Become a Cardiovascular Technologist?

After completing a degree and working in a variety of jobs, Ted decided to take technical courses at a community college. "I thought I would go into medicine in some way or another," he says. "Maybe work as an OR tech, or something." A counselor at the college introduced him to echocardiography and to the many jobs available at the time.

"A person who has an interest in math, physics, medicine, and diagnoses," Ted says, "would do well in the job."

EDUCATION

In the past, EKG operators may have simply been trained on the job by an EKG supervisor. This still may be true for some EKG technician positions. However, increasingly, EKG technologists get postsecondary education before they are hired. Holter monitoring and stress testing may be part of the student's EKG training, or they may be learned through additional training. Ultrasound and cardiology technologists tend to have the most postsecondary schooling (up to a four-year bachelor's degree), and to have the most extensive education and experience requirements for credentialing purposes.

People can get into these positions without having had previous health care experience. However, it certainly doesn't hurt to have had some previous exposure to the business or even training in related areas. People with academic training or professional experience in nursing, radiology science, or respiratory science, for example, may be able to make the move into cardiology technology, if they wish.

High School

At a minimum, cardiovascular technologists need a high school diploma or equivalent to enter the field.

Although no specific high school classes will directly prepare you to be a technologist, learning problem-solving skills and getting a good grounding in basic high school subjects are important to all technologist positions.

During high school, take English, health, biology, and typing (data entry). Also consider courses in the social sciences to help you understand patients' social and psychological needs.

Postsecondary Training

As a rule of thumb, the medical profession values postsecondary schooling that gives real hands-on experience with patients, in addition to classroom training. At many schools that train cardiovascular technologists, you will be able to work with patients in a variety of health care settings and train on more than one brand of equipment. The Commission on Accreditation of Allied Health Education Programs (CAAHEP) provides a listing of accredited cardiovascular technology programs.

EKG. With some employers, EKG technicians are still simply trained on the job by a physician or EKG department manager. Length of time for this training varies, depending on the employer and the trainee's previous experience, if any; it is usually at least one month long and may be up to six months. The trainee learns how to operate the EKG machine and produce and edit the electrocardiogram, along with related tasks.

EKG/Holter/stress. Some vocational, technical, and junior colleges have one- or two-year training programs in EKG, Holter monitoring, or stress testing; otherwise, EKG technologists may obtain training in Holter and stress procedures after they've already started working, either on the job or through an additional six months or more of education. The formal academic programs provide more preparation in the subject than available with most on-the-job training and allow you to earn a certificate (one-year programs) or associate's degree (two-year programs). The American Medical Association's *Allied Health Education Directory* has listings of accredited EKG programs.

Cardiology technologists. These technologists tend to have the most stringent education requirements; for example, a four-year bachelor of science degree or two-year associate's degree or certificate of completion from a hospital, trade, or technical cardiovascular program

for training of varying length. A two-year program at a junior or community college might include one year of core classes (math, science, etc.) and one year of specialized classes in cardiology procedures.

Ultrasound (vascular and echocardiography). These technologists usually need a high school diploma or equivalent plus one, two, or four years of postsecondary schooling in a trade school, technical school, or community college. Vascular technologists also may be trained on the job. Again, a list of accredited programs can be found in the American Medical Association's *Allied Health Education Directory*. Also, a directory of training opportunities in sonography is available from the Society of Diagnostic Medical Sonographers (SDMS).

Cardiac monitor. These technicians need a high school diploma or equivalent, plus education similar to that of the EKG technician.

Cardiology is a cutting-edge area of medicine, with constant advancements, and medical equipment relating to the heart is always being updated. Therefore, keeping up with new developments is vital. Technologists who add to their qualifications through continuing education also tend to earn more money and have more opportunities. The major professional societies encourage and provide the opportunities for professionals to continue their education.

CERTIFICATION OR LICENSING

Currently certification or licensing for cardiovascular technologists is voluntary, but the move to state

> WHEN DOES A PHYSICIAN ORDER AN ECHOCARDIOGRAM?
>
> - In the event of a heart attack
> - When there is abnormality in the rhythm or the pumping action of the heart
> - When the patient shows symptoms such as shortness of breath or swelling of extremities
> - When the physician suspects that the heart may be enlarged
> - When there is a suspected infection or leaking of the heart valve

In-depth

EKG History

EKG machines are very high tech, and equipment manufacturers are constantly developing new improvements to these vital parts of cardiology care. However, electrocardiography can be traced back 300 years to the work of the Dutch anatomist and physiologist Jan Swammerdam, who in 1678 demonstrated that a frog's leg will contract when stimulated with an electrical current. It was not until 1856, however, that two German anatomists, Albert von Kolliker and Heinrich M. Mueller, showed that when a frog's heart contracted, it produced a small electrical current. In succeeding years, the electrical behavior of beating hearts was extensively studied, but always with the chest open and the heart exposed.

In 1887, Augustus Desire Waller discovered that the electrical current of the human heart could be measured with the chest closed. He was able to do this by placing one electrode on a person's chest and another on the person's back and connecting them to a monitoring device.

The first EKG was invented in 1902 by a Dutch physiologist, Willem Einthoven (1860–1927). Before that physicians had to rely mainly on their stethoscopes and their own perceptions. With the EKG, they now had a whole new insight into heart problems, especially irregular heartbeats and severe blockages.

The invention of the EKG came on the heels of the discovery of X rays just seven years earlier, in 1895. Together, they made detecting and diagnosing heart ailments much more of a science, with objective data to help in the process, and much less of a hit-and-miss proposition.

Even today EKGs can't spot everything. With women, for example, the breast tissue may make a reading more difficult, and a positron-emission tomography (PET) scan may be more useful. Also, EKGs still can't pick up subtle heart problems, although researchers are working on improving the EKG's ability to make more accurate and detailed readings of the heart. However, EKGs will continue to be in wide use in routine physicals, presurgical physicals, in diagnosing disease, and in monitoring the effects of surgery or drug therapy.

licensing is in the air. Many credentialing bodies for cardiovascular and pulmonary positions exist, including American Registry of Diagnostic Medical Sonographers (ARDMS), Cardiovascular Credentialing International (CCI), and others, and there are more than a dozen possible credentials for cardiovascular technologists. For example, sonographers can take an exam from the ARDMS to receive credentialing in sonography. Their credentials may be registered diagnostic medical sonographer, registered diagnostic cardiac sonographer, or registered vascular technologist. Especially at the level of cardiology technologist or ultrasound technologist, the credentialing requirements may include test-taking plus formal academic and on-the-job experience requirements. Professional experience or academic training in a related field—such as nursing, radiology science, respiratory science— may be acceptable as part of these formal academic/ professional requirements. As with continuing education, certification is a sign of interest and dedication to the field and is generally looked upon more favorably by potential employers.

INTERNSHIPS AND VOLUNTEERSHIPS

An internship as an EKG assistant is possible. Check local hospitals to learn of opportunities. Some employers prefer to hire a person who has already worked in the health care field, such as a nurse's aid. If you are interested in health care positions, consider being a volunteer at a hospital, which will give you exposure to patient-care activities. Or you might visit a hospital, clinic, or doctor's office where EKG or other cardiovascular procedures are used and ask to talk to a cardiovascular technologist.

Who Will Hire Me?

EKG technologists work in large and small hospitals, clinics, health maintenance organizations (HMOs), cardiac rehabilitation centers, cardiologists' or other physicians' offices, long-term care facilities, and nursing homes. Other types of cardiovascular technologists may work primarily in either community hospitals or teaching hospitals, in industry, for mobile medical service clinics, in academia, or in government hospitals (VA, armed forces, public health services, etc.). Another possibility is finding employment with a manufacturer of EKG or other equipment.

EKG technicians, by far, outnumber the other specialists in this field. There are fewer ultrasound technologists at this time, for example, because of the expertise required and the lower frequency of these tests. "Even in a large-size hospital where there may be a large radiology department with 15 rooms and a 20- to 30-person staff, the ultrasound department may have a staff of six and maybe two rooms," notes Dennis King, chairman of the diagnostic medical imaging program at Wilbur Wright College, Chicago. "However, sonography is a growing profession nationally, even if some areas are 'soft' for new hires, or oversaturated, from time to time."

Check the want ads (under "health care professionals" and related sections), contact national associations, and check with hospitals or other health care facilities in your area to learn of opportunities.

Where Can I Go from Here?

Rather than move into upper management, Ted chose to go into industry work. "I'm working with Agilent," he says, "which is providing the digital solution, and my clinical background makes me unique within the computer group." He hopes to expand his computer skills and go into consulting. As a consultant, Ted would go into a lab and evaluate workflow and the problems that could be solved by the technology company.

Opportunities for advancement are best for EKG technologists who learn to do or assist with more complex procedures, such as Holter monitoring, stress testing, echocardiography, and cardiac catheterization. With proper training and experience, they may become cardiology technologists or cardiopulmonary technologists, another type of heart-related technology specialist. Besides specialist positions, opportunities may be found in supervisory or teaching positions. At some hospitals there may be a *chief cardiopulmonary technologist,* for example, who coordinates the activities of technologists who perform diagnostic testing and treatment of patients with heart, lung, and blood vessel disorders. The *chief radiologic technologist* coordinates activities of the radiology or diagnostic imaging department in the hospital or other medical facility.

Besides those mentioned, areas of special experience for cardiovascular technologists may include infant pulmonary function testing, blood gas studies, sleep disorder studies, pacemaker procedures, and other related procedures. Nuclear medicine, which uses radioactive isotopes in diagnosis, treatment, or studies, also is applied to cardiology problems.

What Are the Salary Ranges?

According to the *Occupational Outlook Handbook,* the median annual salary for cardiovascular technologists and technicians was $37,800 in 2003. The lowest 10 percent earned less than $21,500 annually, and the highest 10 percent earned more than $57,660. The American Medical Association notes that in 2002 the average salary for cardiovascular technologists ranged from $36,000 to $40,000. The Society of Diagnostic Medical Sonographers (SDMS) reports that the starting salary for sonographers is $15 to $18 an hour. An SDMS survey released in 2000 reported that the median annual income for sonographers is between $40,000 and $50,000. According to the report, 75 percent of the sonographers responding to the survey earned between $30,000 and $65,000 annually.

Cardiovascular technologist positions are typically salaried, but overtime pay (or extra time off in lieu of overtime) may be available. Technologists in large hospitals may work one of three shifts and may receive a higher rate of pay for taking second- or third-shift work.

Hospital benefits generally are good, including health and hospitalization insurance, paid vacations, sick leave, and possibly educational assistance and pension benefits.

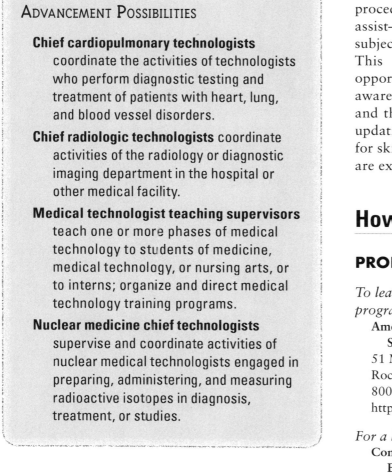

ADVANCEMENT POSSIBILITIES

Chief cardiopulmonary technologists
coordinate the activities of technologists
who perform diagnostic testing and
treatment of patients with heart, lung,
and blood vessel disorders.

Chief radiologic technologists coordinate
activities of the radiology or diagnostic
imaging department in the hospital or
other medical facility.

Medical technologist teaching supervisors
teach one or more phases of medical
technology to students of medicine,
medical technology, or nursing arts, or
to interns; organize and direct medical
technology training programs.

Nuclear medicine chief technologists
supervise and coordinate activities of
nuclear medical technologists engaged in
preparing, administering, and measuring
radioactive isotopes in diagnosis,
treatment, or studies.

What Is the Job Outlook?

The job outlook for cardiovascular technologists is quite good. According to the *Occupational Outlook Handbook*, employment of cardiovascular technologists and technicians is expected to grow faster than the the average for all occupations. Employment of EKG technologists is on the decline because the equipment and procedures have grown increasingly efficient and fewer technologists are required to do the work. Ultrasound technologists should see slow but steady growth into the next century. Some areas of the country currently have few openings for new hires, partly because of low turnover in the job, but in general this is a growing specialty.

Cardiology technologists should fare very well, however, due to the growing elderly population which will require increased staffing in almost every area of health care. Cardiology technologists will be in demand as more hospitals create cardiac catheterization units and as new procedures

and drug treatments are developed. Some of the procedures in which cardiology technologists assist—notably, angioplasties—are still the subject of some controversy and ongoing research. This shouldn't hurt cardiology technologists' opportunities for employment, but you should be aware that procedures are constantly changing and that what you study in school now may need updating in the near future. Because of the demand for skilled technologists, educational opportunities are expected to become more plentiful.

How Do I Learn More?

PROFESSIONAL ORGANIZATIONS

To learn about certification and accredited programs, contact
American Registry of Diagnostic Medical
    Sonographers
51 Monroe Street, Plaza East One
Rockville, MD 20850-2400
800-541-9754
http://www.ardms.org

For a list of accredited programs, contact
Commission on Accreditation of Allied Health
    Education Programs
35 East Wacker Drive, Suite 1970
Chicago, IL 60601
312-553-9355
caahep@caahep.org
http://www.caahep.org

For career and conference information and job listings, contact
Society of Vascular Ultrasound
4601 President's Drive, Suite 260
Lanham, MD 20706
301-459-7550
svuinfo@svunet.org
http://www.svunet.org

For information on credentials, contact
Cardiovascular Credentialing International
1500 Sunday Drive, Suite 102
Raleigh, NC 27607
800-326-0268
http://www.cci-online.org

For a career brochure, contact
Society of Diagnostic Medical Sonography
2745 Dallas Parkway, Suite 350

Plano, TX 75093-8730
800-229-9506
http://www.sdms.org

BIBLIOGRAPHY

The following is a sampling of materials relating to the professional concerns and development of cardiovascular technologists:

Careers in Focus: Medical Technicians. 4th ed. New York: Facts On File, 2004.

Lardo, Albert, Zahi Adel Fayad, Nicolas Chronos, and Valentin Fuster, eds. *Cardiovascular Magnetic Resonance: Established and Emerging Applications.* New York: Taylor and Francis, 2004.

Snook, Donald I., and Leo Paul D'Orazio. *Opportunities in Health and Medical Careers.* New York: McGraw-Hill, 2004.

CAREER INFORMATION SPECIALISTS

||||||||||||||||||||||||||||||||||||||||||||||||||||||||

Wouldn't it be nice to have someone devoted to making your dreams come true? That is partly what Rosemary Hill, a career information specialist, does for a living. Her job is to help people find jobs, and this can entail setting up interviews, tracking down potential employers, and offering interview and resume advice. "You know you're making a real positive difference in people's lives," Rosemary says, referring to the advice and guidance she offers the young engineers graduating from the College of Engineering at Ohio State University. "You're really helping them get their career off to a good start."

Now with the Internet, Rosemary is able to provide students with career information 24-hours a day, seven days a week. Despite the ease that the Web offers, Rosemary finds that it presents new challenges, as well. "The idea of these Web-based systems is to make things easy and efficient and convenient. Students can just do all their research at home at two in the morning in their bunny slippers. But at the same time, we want students to know that we're here to provide them with assistance and consultation—that there's a human face on the other side of that monitor, so to speak."

What Does a Career Information Specialist Do?

For many people just graduating from high school or college, choosing the right career can be a confusing and difficult task. Even if you already know what field interests you, you may be intimidated by the entire job hunting process. Where do you apply? What is the best company for you? Is your resume well written? How should you act during an interview? Since finding a job is a full-time job in itself, people often seek the expertise of career information specialists, trained and experienced professionals who help answer these types of questions.

Career information specialists, also called *career counselors* or *employment, recruitment, and placement specialists,* often work in the placement

Definition
Career information specialists help students and clients with career planning and job hunting.

Alternative Job Titles
Career/guidance counselors
Career services coordinators
Employment specialists
Labor relations specialists
Personnel recruiters
Placement coordinators
Recruitment specialists

High School Subjects
Business
Psychology

Personal Skills
Communication/ideas
Helping/teaching

Salary Range
$34,625 to $38,716 to $43,905+

Minimum Educational Level
Master's degree

Certification or Licensing
Required by certain states

Outlook
Faster than the average

DOT
094

GOE
12.02.02

NOC
4143, 4213

O*NET-SOC
13-1071.00, 13-1071.01, 21-1012.00

offices of universities, vocational schools, or high schools. They may also work in commercial employment agencies or career counseling centers. Job responsibilities vary according to the size and type of office in which they work.

Career information specialists work very closely with students, alumni, and clients. To help each person make a wise decision about a career, they may conduct interviews or give tests designed to evaluate the job hunter's education, work history, interests, skills, and personal traits. The results of the tests can suggest careers in which the clients may be happy and successful.

Career information specialists spend part of their time researching various companies and gathering resources in an informational library. The library offers a collection of printed and electronic resources and files to help clients and students research prospective employers and career paths. Career information specialists may also evaluate and make purchasing decisions regarding career services materials for the library, and they may spend time indexing and cataloging materials. They might also make a habit of scanning newspapers and trade magazines to be aware of the kinds of positions companies are trying to fill.

Clients often turn to career information specialists for guidance in developing job finding skills such as resume writing and interviewing techniques. The specialist may also be responsible for maintaining computer files on each client.

Career information specialists who work in commercial employment or personnel agencies have duties similar to those who work in academic environments. Their clients, however, are generally the hiring companies, though job seekers are also clients. The career information specialist's primary goal is to find job candidates for the client companies.

Career information specialists in employment agencies may administer skills tests to job seekers to assess computer aptitude, typing skills, or specific subject knowledge. They act as the liaison between hiring companies and job seekers, setting up interviews and making sure the hiring company receives the job seeker's resume and background information. In some cases, the career information specialist interviews the job candidate on behalf of the client company. Matching the job seeker's goals and skills to the appropriate job opening is an important duty of the specialist.

Career information specialists can also specialize in recruiting. They work very closely with companies to recruit interns and full-time employees in a particular field or specialty. *Recruiting coordinators,* or *personnel recruiters,* coordinate the hiring process for companies. They seek ideal candidates to fill employment openings for their client companies. Some large companies employ in-house recruiting coordinators to handle staffing needs.

Recruiters seeking candidates at schools post job profiles of the company's openings, request that qualified candidates send resumes, forward

FYI

The first funded employment office in the United States was established in San Francisco in 1886. The first program of vocational guidance, designed to help young people select and enter appropriate careers, was founded in Boston in 1908.

the information to the company, and help the company find potential matches. Since the number of interviews granted by one company is often very limited, recruiting coordinators establish priority lists and have some authority in final decisions regarding who receives an interview slot.

Recruiters may also actively search for qualified candidates. In some instances, this can entail luring a candidate away from a current employer. This is sometimes referred to as headhunting, although career information specialists prefer not to use the term because of negative connotations.

The work of recruiting coordinators is very detail oriented. They are in charge of setting up deadlines for both job seekers and companies. They are also responsible for keeping interview schedules. This task involves routinely sending confirmation letters or email to all concerned parties.

Although much of their work is performed over the telephone or on the computer, recruiting coordinators are often present for interviews. They may be in charge of making interviewers and interviewees feel welcome and comfortable.

A relatively new specialization for career information specialists is that of the *outplacement consultant.* Outplacement consultants help downsized or terminated employees find new jobs or career paths. They work on behalf of the companies that terminate employees. Outplacement is becoming a standard part of severance packages in the corporate world.

Outplacement consultants help people re-enter the workforce or find jobs through guidance sessions, interview training, resume assistance, and career assessment counseling. Outplacement consultants also contact potential employers. They sometimes provide adjustment counseling and management training for remaining employees.

Lingo to Learn

Career development The process of evaluating career goals and clarifying the means to achieve them.

Career planning and placement office An office whose function it is to help students find jobs.

Computer database A computer system that allows career planning and placement offices to store information about both students or clients and recruiting companies. It can also find matches between student profiles and company requirements.

Headhunter An employment specialist focused on recruiting personnel.

Human resources Refers to the division of a company that handles personnel issues.

Outplacement The process of assisting terminated employees in finding new jobs.

Recruiting An active search made by companies to hire highly qualified individuals for specific jobs.

Resume A summary of a job hunter's education, work experience, community activities, and interests.

What Is It Like to Be a Career Information Specialist?

Rosemary Hill is the director of Engineering Career Services at Ohio State University. "It's a really nice mixture of activities," Rosemary says of the work. "As the director of my department, I meet with the staff to resolve problems or determine policies and procedures. I spend time meeting with employers and talking with them over the phone or e-mailing them about recruiting on our campus and how to improve their recruiting strategies. I spend a fair amount of time with students who are looking for jobs, and I talk with them about their job search, or I review their resumes, or give suggestions. I also talk with faculty and academic advisors and with my colleagues in the administration within our college."

Being involved in so many different areas requires many hours every week. Rosemary typically arrives at work around 7:30 A.M. and is often busy until 6:00 P.M. or later if an evening program is planned. "About the only time I take a lunch hour is when I have a lunch meeting," she says. "Those going into this profession need to be prepared for that. They're going to have some fairly long hours and some weekend and/or evening involvement."

Though the job requires long hours, the constantly changing nature of the work keeps Rosemary from getting bored. "The student population changes," she says. "There are different generations of students with different value structures. You constantly have to change your approach so that it makes sense to them." Each individual student is different, as well, with different career needs. "If one size fit all," she says, "I could go home at five o'clock!"

Career services throughout a university can vary greatly in focus: A career counselor in a college of arts and sciences is going to have a different approach to the work than someone in education. "We have a pretty heavy and continuing demand for our candidates," Rosemary says of the engineering college. "So we have a high degree of on-campus recruiting activity, a very high amount of resume referral information. Last year, we had more than 2,200 requests from employers for us to refer candidate resumes. We had 1,500 individual job postings and over 650 interviews scheduled."

It is part of Rosemary's job to keep this employer interest high and to help both students and employers make job connections. Because she has regular interaction with employers, she is able to advise students on what employers are looking for. "Likewise, when I'm talking with employers, I can tell them, 'This is what students are thinking about when they're making a decision,' or 'This is what students have told me about why they didn't sign up for an interview with your company.' So it's a very beneficial relationship."

Rosemary's office also arranges a number of workshops and career-related events throughout the year. Recent workshops have focused on interviewing skills, careers in consulting, and resume writing.

Over the last few years, the Internet has had a large impact on Rosemary's work. "The Web has changed everything we do," she says. "Last year we went to a Web-based system for managing all our activities in our office. Students sign up for interviews online, and they don't have to come into our office to research through print materials. It's really quite remarkable."

Do I Have What It Takes to Be a Career Information Specialist?

"It's a very people-oriented job," explains Rosemary. As the director of the office, Rosemary must make certain to serve the needs of both the employers and the students. "Even though the demands are a little bit conflicting, you have to maintain a balance so that both groups of customers feel that their needs are met."

A great deal of organization is also required, along with the ability to keep students on schedule. A career information specialist should also be friendly and relaxed, despite the hectic work pace. Those seeking work are often nervous about job interviews and exploring the market; a career information specialist must be able to put them at ease.

How Do I Become a Career Information Specialist?

Rosemary has been in the profession off and on for more than 25 years. She holds a master's degree in career counseling in higher education. She recommends that job seekers consult the newsletter of the National Association of Colleges and Employers (NACE) and the *Chronicle of Higher Education* (http://chronicle.com) for listings. She also advises students to contact as many people in the profession as possible, starting with the career counselors at their own schools. "That way you can get a picture of how things are out in the field," she says. "There's variation. There are arts and sciences career services, business career services, education, law. There are specialty areas within our profession."

EDUCATION

High School

High school courses in English and business will give you a head start in developing the skills a career information specialist should have. Any course or project that requires you to be very organized

---

To Be a Successful Career Information Specialist, You Should . . .

○ be a people person, with genuine enthusiasm for the success of others

○ have friendly and professional telephone skills

○ be able to inspire trust and confidence in people with whom you interact

○ have the ability to organize large amounts of very detailed material

○ be able to work on deadlines and make sure others do the same

---

and work with many details also builds a strong foundation for success in this career.

Because the job of a career information specialist is so people-intensive, joining clubs and other organizations will give you the opportunity to work closely with others. Running for student government positions or assuming officer roles in clubs will teach you leadership skills and the art of negotiation and compromise.

Part-time or summer jobs in employment agencies, placement offices, or counseling centers can provide you with an in-depth look at the daily tasks of a career information specialist or counselor. Another method for gaining experience in guiding others and assessing their strengths and weaknesses is to volunteer in youth programs or community programs dedicated to helping others.

Postsecondary Training

Although a college degree is not required to work as an assistant in a university or vocational school placement office, most schools will not hire new employees who lack college degrees.

A bachelor's degree in a specific subject area can be helpful if you choose to specialize. For example, if you plan to work as a career placement specialist for the engineering department of a university, an engineering background or degree will provide you with the necessary tools for helping students and matching candidates with appropriate jobs. If you plan to work as a recruiter specializing in finance, an

In-depth

Hot Job

Technical recruiters find job candidates for executive positions in the ever-changing high-tech industry. Technical recruiters must possess strong sales skills and a background in the applicable subject area, whether it is networking, information systems, or relational databases. Technical recruiters work on a commission basis, and earnings can range from $100,000 to $450,000 a year.

Career information specialists are qualified to work in a number of full-time positions in career planning and placement offices. In addition, they can work in the human resources departments of government agencies and private businesses. With the proper education, they can work in career and psychological counseling centers, school guidance offices, and social service organizations. Also under this career classification are people who work as ergonomists, psychologists, demographers, sociologists, intelligence officers, anthropologists, and research assistants.

‖‖‖

accounting degree will help you understand the job requirements and the particular skills to look for in a candidate.

In order to advance in a career placement office, a career information specialist will need a college degree. Frequently a master's degree is required for top jobs. The American Counseling Association (ACA) offers lists of schools with accredited programs in career counseling.

Some career information specialists go to work in private industry. Private companies generally require new employees to have at least a bachelor's degree, but they tend to be flexible about the college major. For example, some career information specialists

hold degrees in such diverse disciplines as English, political science, education, psychology, human resource management, and business administration.

CERTIFICATION OR LICENSING

About 40 states require counselors to be licensed or certified in addition to holding a master's degree. The licensing and certification process varies from state to state, so you will need to check with your state's credentialing board for specific requirements.

Many career counselors also hold the voluntary certification National Certified Counselor (NCC) given by the National Board for Certified Counselors, Inc. (NBCC). Requirements include having a master's degree in counseling, at least two years of experience, and a passing score on the National Counselor Examination given by the NBCC. Some states accept NCC certification as a fulfillment of part or all of their licensing requirements. Counselors in most states must participate in special workshops and continuing education courses to maintain their certification.

Depending on where you want to work, you may also have to meet other requirements. If you want to work in a school, for example, you will need your state's school counseling certification. Many states also require that you have a teaching certificate and teaching experience. Again, you will need to check with your state's credentialing board for specific information.

Outplacement consultants can also seek voluntary certification. Outplacement consultants can be certified as Career Management Practitioners (CMP) by the International Board for Career Management Certification, which is a division of the International Association of Career Management Professionals (IACMP). This certification requires a bachelor's degree and work experience.

SCHOLARSHIPS AND GRANTS

If you plan to pursue a college degree, you should contact your school's financial aid office for a generalized list of scholarships and grants for which you may qualify.

INTERNSHIPS AND VOLUNTEERSHIPS

If you are a student, you might try to get your foot in the door by getting a job in a placement office at your school. If not, you might try to get a clerical job at a career counseling center or employment agency in order to gain experience and demonstrate your availability when job openings arise.

Internships in the human resources department of large companies may be available, as well as internships or work-study opportunities at your school's placement office.

Volunteering at agencies or organizations that provide guidance or counseling services to people will give you an idea of whether or not you enjoy working with others. You might also try to work as a temporary employee through an employment agency. Employment agencies often handle both direct placement and temporary positions. If you demonstrate your reliability and skills as a temporary employee and voice your interest in working as a career information specialist, chances are the agency will want to bring you on staff when a position becomes available.

Who Will Hire Me?

Many career information specialists work for career counseling and placement offices at universities and vocational schools. The number of such offices operating at one university depends on student enrollment. In large universities such as Ohio State and other Big Ten schools, every college or department has its own placement office, meaning there are between 15 and 25 offices at one university. Placement offices serving students with very specialized or technical degrees, such as law, pharmacy, and engineering, tend to need fewer employees with counseling certification. This is because those students often have a clearer vision of their career goals.

Other career information specialists work in commercial career counseling centers. Usually, however, these positions are reserved for individuals certified or educated as counselors. Consult your local telephone directory for a list of such businesses in your area. Employment or temporary agencies also provide a possible entry into the field; education and work experience requirements will vary depending on the company. Federal, state, and local government agencies may have some jobs in this field but may require training in social work or human services. Again, each agency has different regulations, so you should contact the ones in your area for specific information.

ADVANCEMENT POSSIBILITIES

Career counselors usually hold at least a master's degree in counseling or psychology and are licensed to work in private practice. They help clients choose careers well suited to their abilities, interests, and needs.

Career services assistant directors supervise a large section of a career placement office. They may organize and manage co-op or internship programs, recruit new companies to hire through their offices, or oversee computer automation of important office functions like interview scheduling and resume writing.

Career services directors manage all operations within the career placement office and have final say in decisions made by assistants and other employees. Typically, they hold at least a bachelor's degree and are qualified to meet with clients in one-on-one career counseling sessions.

Large businesses typically have a human resources department that may have related career services or recruiting positions available. Such businesses will most likely require a college degree, but it may be worthwhile to check with the major employers in your area.

NACE provides information on job opportunities and development in career services positions on its Web site. ACA also publishes several journals devoted to the concerns of individuals working in all areas of career services, including details about job opportunities. Many companies and professional organizations list job opportunities and helpful information on the Internet. You may also find job openings at one of the many Web sites devoted to job searches.

Where Can I Go from Here?

Advancement as a career information specialist normally requires an advanced degree and depends on the size and specialization of the office. Some placement offices employ several associate or assistant directors. In addition, those people who work for an organization that operates numerous placement offices have a greater chance of promotion because they can transfer to other offices when openings occur.

Career information specialists working for educational institutions may choose to move to private industry positions, where they could make more money as recruiters or human resource managers.

Other career information specialists go on to become directors of career service programs. These positions require at least a bachelor's degree and often a master's degree in counseling.

What Are the Salary Ranges?

According to the U.S. Department of Labor, employment, recruitment, and placement specialists had median annual earnings of $40,970 in 2003, with salaries for the middle 50 percent ranging between $31,590 and $56,090. Those in the lowest paid 10 percent earned $25,460, and those in the highest paid 10 percent earned $78,570.

A 2005 review of salaries nationwide for career counselors conducted by Salary.com reports that those working in college or university career offices had median earnings of $38,716. The lowest paid earned $34,625, and the highest paid earned $43,905. Counselors working in private industry earned higher salaries, ranging from $39,450 to $51,211. The median earnings for counselors in private industry were $44,584.

Most career information specialists and career services directors work for educational institutions or corporations, and their income is usually supplemented by a full benefits package including vacation, sick days, and insurance. Though university student schedules allow for long summer breaks and breaks between semesters, career service offices usually stay open year-round.

What Is the Job Outlook?

Overall employment of career services employees and counselors is expected to grow faster than the average for all occupations through 2012. The number of career information specialists needed in educational institutions depends in part on student enrollment, which has steadily increased in recent years.

More students, however, do not necessarily mean more job opportunities. When companies decide to put a hiring freeze in place, the need for career services employees is lower. During periods of economic hardship, the job duties of career information specialists may shift to include more research and marketing aimed at persuading more companies to interview students or clients.

When budget constraints become a problem in educational institutions, there may be little effort made to fill career services job openings or create new positions. Instead of hiring new people, employers tend to ask those already employed in career services to take on extra duties. However, career planning and placement offices are always considered an important part of the college because its reputation often depends on graduates' success at finding jobs. The reputation, in turn, affects student enrollment and tuition dollars, so universities like to keep placement offices well staffed.

Career information specialists working in the field of human resources in private industry can anticipate a positive job outlook. When the economy is strong, more jobs are created, and career information specialists and recruiters are needed to fill these positions. Along the same lines, some industries tend to be quite volatile, and there can be major layoff cycles, which increase the need for qualified outplacement consultants.

How Do I Learn More?

PROFESSIONAL ORGANIZATIONS

The following are organizations that provide information on career information specialists and other career services jobs, accredited schools, certification, and possible sources of employment:

American Counseling Association
5999 Stevenson Avenue
Alexandria, VA 22304
800-347-6647
http://www.counseling.org

Association of Career Firms International
204 E Street, NE
Washington, DC 20002
202-547-6344

acf@acfinternational.org
http://www.aocfi.org

Association of Career Professionals International
204 E Street, NE
Washington DC 20002
202-547-6377
info@acpinternational.org
http://www.iacmp.org

Career Planning and Adult Development Network
543 Vista Mar Avenue
Pacifica, CA 94044
650-359-6911
admin@careernetwork.org
http://www.careernetwork.org

National Association of Colleges and Employers
62 Highland Avenue
Bethlehem, PA 18017-9085
800-544-5272
http://www.jobweb.org

National Board for Certified Counselors
Three Terrace Way, Suite D

Greensboro, NC 27403-3660
336-547-0607
nbcc@nbcc.org
http://www.nbcc.org

BIBLIOGRAPHY

The following is a sampling of materials relating to the professional concerns and development of career information specialists:

Amundson, Norman E. *Essential Elements of Career Counseling: Processes and Techniques.* Upper Saddle River, N.J.: Prentice Hall, 2004.

Bolles, Richard Nelson, and Howard Figler. *The Career Counselor's Handbook.* Berkeley, Calif.: Ten Speed Press, 1999.

Brown, Duane, and Linda Brooks. *Career Choice and Development.* 4th ed. San Francisco: Jossey-Bass Publishers, 2002.

Savickas, Mark L., and W. Bruce Walsh. *Handbook of Career Counseling Theory and Practice.* Palo Alto, Calif.: Consulting Psychologists Press, 1996.

CHEMICAL TECHNICIANS

Imagine a chemical laboratory and most likely you conjure up visions of smoke, bubbling liquids, test tubes, beakers—what seems to be magic. Perhaps that is more of a movie maker's idea of a science lab.

Today's real-life laboratories do use test tubes and beakers, but they can also contain pumps, pipelines, tanks, valves, and computers or other electronic equipment, such as dilatometers, spectrometers, and X-ray diffraction devices. Modern laboratories are also clean, tightly controlled, and in compliance with very high standards of safety and health.

But the magic is still there.

The magic of chemistry is what appeals to Connie Murphy. "In high school, I didn't choose a career as a chemical technician and take chemistry to achieve that goal," she says. "I chose chemistry. I enjoyed the lab experience—watching things change and react right before my eyes."

It wasn't until many years later that Connie became a technician, but now she spends most of her workday in the lab making samples of new plastic packaging materials to be sent to another lab for testing. After more than 20 years of working on numerous projects for the same company, the laboratory still holds magic for Connie.

What Does a Chemical Technician Do?

Products you use every day—and their solid, liquid, and gas components—have been invented, tested, and manufactured in laboratories. Your food, drugs, fertilizers, plastics, paints, detergents, paper, petroleum, and cement, for example, are first studied in the laboratory to determine strength, stability, purity, chemical content, and other characteristics.

There are four general areas of chemistry a technician may work in: analytical, organic, inorganic, and physical. Analytical chemistry is involved with determining the composition of substances. Inorganic chemistry is concerned with the properties and reactions of compounds that do not contain carbon. Organic chemistry studies the compounds that do contain carbon. Physical chemistry is concerned with the role of energy transformations in reactions.

Definition
Chemical technicians conduct physical tests, chemical analyses, and instrumental analyses for research, product development, quality control, and establishing standards.

Alternative Job Titles
Analytical technicians
Associate chemists
Chemical engineering technicians
Chemical laboratory technicians
Chemical technologists

High School Subjects
Chemistry
Mathematics

Personal Skills
Mechanical/manipulative
Technical/scientific

Salary Range
$23,200 to $37,600 to $57,100+

Minimum Educational Level
Associate's degree

Certification or Licensing
None available

Outlook
More slowly than the average

DOT
022

GOE
02.05.01

NOC
2112

O*NET-SOC
19-4031.00

Chemical technicians work in research, new product development, quality control, or criminal investigation. Those in research and development often work in pairs or small groups with Ph.D. chemists and chemical engineers to develop chemicals, synthesize compounds, or develop new processes. Technicians who perform quality control tests often work together in groups under supervision. They make samples of new products or collect soil, water, or air samples. They study their compositions or test certain properties. Other technicians conduct physical tests on samples to determine such things as strength and flexibility, or they may characterize the physical properties of gases, liquids, and solids and describe their reactions to changes of temperature and pressure.

Usually, a chemist or chemical engineer plans and designs the experiment. Technicians help them conduct research, locate resources, create a statistical design, describe procedures in writing, or design and run computer simulations. Technicians obtain or make samples and make observations. They gather, clean, and calibrate all necessary glassware, reagents, chemicals, electrodes, and other equipment; choose, check, and calibrate test equipment; and perhaps fabricate or modify the test equipment for a particular use. Others analyze the samples and report the results.

Chemical technicians work in a wide variety of settings. They might test packaging for design, materials, and environmental acceptability. Others might test and develop new plastic compounds for use in the manufacture of small appliances, or develop a colorfast dye for fibers. Some collect and analyze samples of ores, minerals, gases, soil, air, water, and pollutants. Chemical technicians might manage the laboratories at a school, ordering equipment and maintaining supplies. Some work in the petroleum industry to ensure the quality of gasoline, furnace oil, and related products. And some chemical technicians help develop and test new drugs and medicines.

Exposure to hazardous conditions is common in laboratory work. There may be toxic or flammable chemicals or dangerous equipment like compression cylinders. Because of these hazards, technicians may be required to wear protective clothing, eye protection, or respirators. Following safety procedures is extremely important.

Chemical technicians usually work regular hours and spend most of their time in the laboratory, but they also are required to document the results of their tests and analyses. They compile data and keep accurate records, preparing charts, sketches, and diagrams, usually using a computer. Finally, technicians maintain the laboratory, its inventory, and equipment according to federal, state, and local safety and health regulations. They may be responsible for the transportation and disposal of materials and hazardous wastes in compliance with regulations.

Lingo to Learn

Differential scanning calorimetry (DSC)
Analytical method that measures the rate of heat release of absorption of a specimen during a programmed temperature change.

Differential thermal analysis (DTA)
Analytical method to compare thermal energy changes of a specimen and a standard control while they are both heated.

High-performance liquid chromatography (HPLC) Separation method for liquid samples.

Microscopy The use of a microscope; microscopic investigation.

Polymer A large molecule made by the linking of many smaller molecules, or monomers.

Reaction A change involving the rearrangement of the atoms, molecules, etc., of one or more substances and resulting in the formation of one or more additional substances that often have different properties.

Reagent A substance involved in a reaction, especially a substance used to detect the presence of other substances by the chemical reactions it causes.

What Is It Like to Be a Chemical Technician?

"My job responsibilities are pretty varied," says Connie Murphy, a senior research technologist for a major U.S. chemical manufacturer. "I do experimental work. Sometimes I perform analytical work on my own samples, but I also send samples out to our analytical facility or another testing facility for evaluation. I keep records in my data book, and give oral reports, written progress reports, and research reports."

Connie's primary function is as a research lab technician, and she does research in developing new polymeric materials for packaging applications. She works directly with a Ph.D. scientist, but has a lot of independence. She has been working over 20 years with the same organization in basic and applied research, and though she works in a number of different project areas, most of her work is related to polymer synthesis, processing, and evaluation.

"My current project is making samples to be evaluated for properties such as barrier to oxygen, tensile strength, glass transition temperature, and melting point. Most of my time is spent in the lab, but I also work at a desk. I describe in my data book how the samples are made and record all the information I need to track where the samples are sent. I sometimes synthesize new polymers, and sometimes make blends of existing polymers with other polymers or additives. The synthesis work involves setting up glassware, running the reactions, and recovering the polymer product. The polymer is then molded using a heated hydraulic press into samples that can be tested for properties. I analyze the samples with equipment, such as a differential scanning calorimeter."

"The data book is very important," Connie says. "We have regular staff meetings once a week for technicians and Ph.D.'s, and I am required to give an oral progress report once every six months." Connie also supervises and coordinates the work of a college co-op working in her group.

Mike Dineen is a research technologist at the same company as Connie, but in a different department. He works in research development and production of plastics using microscopy. "I use electron microscopes to study morphology [particle size, particle shape, and structure], and I correlate that with product performance: why it has a certain color, why it fractures or fails, why it does or doesn't take paint well. We work on everything from small appliances to automotive dashboards," he says.

Mike spends about 80 percent of his time in the laboratory, mostly running samples. Like Connie, he attends occasional group meetings and gives oral and written presentations. Unlike Connie, he does not work closely with his manager or the people he supports. He sets his own schedules and priorities. "I have both scheduled and crisis work. I generally have a backlog of two to six weeks worth of work and I do things chronologically or based on priority of the project. Then quite often there's a client who has a problem that must be solved immediately."

Another technician in the plastics division at this company is in charge of the research lab where quality assurance, product characterization, and testing take place. She maintains and calibrates all the equipment, which includes such thermal analysis equipment as differential scanning calorimeters to measure melting point, crystallization, and glass transition and a thermal mechanical analyzer for measuring melting point and heat distortion under

TO BE A SUCCESSFUL CHEMICAL TECHNICIAN, YOU SHOULD . . .

○ be detail oriented, precise, and meticulous

○ be able to communicate with a variety of people, both orally and in writing

○ be flexible and able to handle a number of tasks simultaneously

○ have analytical and problem-solving skills

○ be inventive and resourceful

loads. There is machinery for penetration, tensile, flex, and fatigue testing and rayometers for measuring flow rate of plastics. She researches new equipment, finds suppliers, handles the orders, installs new equipment, and keeps it running.

Debra McCombs is a technologist at AstraZeneca Pharmaceuticals. She sets up and conducts studies and works on research projects with her supervisor. "My job varies quite a bit, which is one of the reasons I really like it. I mostly work with high-performance liquid chromatography. We evaluate HPLC columns and look at different types of drugs on a particular column. We use biological matrices to troubleshoot separation problems in drugs, and then we research new and improved ways to handle those problems. We are also a support group for other departments in the company, providing them with drug metabolism information.

"It's exciting to be a part of research projects that are published and presented at national meetings," Debra says. Debra also belongs to a local group in Delaware called the Science Alliance. It is made up of volunteers from science industries who talk to elementary schoolchildren about a variety of science subjects. "The kids are really fascinated with science and it's worth the time you spend putting a presentation together."

Do I Have What It Takes to Be a Chemical Technician?

Chemical technicians spend anywhere from 50 to 80 percent of their time in the laboratory, but it is rare for them to work alone in a room full of test tubes and samples. "A chemical technician has to have excellent communication skills. That's probably number one," Connie says. "You have to be able to communicate the results of your work both orally and in writing."

Mike agrees. "Communication skills and people skills are important. I work with 40 to 60 customers a year whom I see routinely. You must be highly flexible to work with the company, customers, and coworkers from a variety of educational and cultural backgrounds." Technicians have to carefully follow directions from chemists or engineers and often work in teams with other technicians and scientists.

"Technicians are taking on more and more responsibilities, doing the things Ph.D.'s were doing 15 years ago. There's a lot more responsibility and accountability than ever before," Connie says, "so technicians who work in research in particular have to pay a lot of attention to detail. It's the small details that very often are the most crucial."

Debra's job requires her to be very organized, pay attention to detail, think analytically, and be able to troubleshoot. "The only difficult thing about my job," she says, "is being faced with a problem I can't figure out. But there's something new every day. It's not routine in any way."

Connie says she has experienced some monotony from time to time. "Sometimes you have to crank out samples or do repeated testing. I worked in adhesives for a while and a lot of that is making up samples and pulling them apart, but sometimes you just have to do the grunt work."

Mike finds it difficult sometimes to set priorities. "Writing reports is not a favorite part of my job, but at the same time it's good for you, sort of like cod liver oil. It's not always fun, but I know it's good for my career."

How Do I Become a Chemical Technician?

Chemical technicians usually have an associate's degree in chemical technology, laboratory science, or another science specialty. Some employers hire high school graduates and place them in their own training programs, but that practice is becoming rare.

Many industrial employers would rather hire a graduate from a two-year technical program than one with a bachelor's degree in chemistry. They believe four-year programs don't prepare students to work as technicians because they don't include enough laboratory practice. The bachelor's degree traditionally has more theoretical studies and is designed as preparatory work for graduate school.

"For many people, working as a chemical technician is a second-career choice," Connie says. "Many people entering the workforce as chemical technicians are older. I think the average age for the first level technologist in my company is 29. Personally, I went to college right out of high school, got married, divorced, worked in a factory for a while, and did all sorts of other things. But my interest had always been in chemistry. Then I found out about the two-year program." She says it is a good road for someone who needs to get a job quickly and start making money. Debra also waited until 10 or 15 years after she graduated from high school before she earned her associate's degree.

EDUCATION

High School

To prepare for a program in chemical technology, high school students should be interested in science and take courses in math, chemistry, physics, and computer science. Computers and computer-interfaced equipment are often used in research and development laboratories.

Students might find it valuable to participate in the extracurricular science clubs that many schools offer. Science contests are another fun way to apply principles learned in classes to a special project. You may work alone or in a team in competitions that are held within your own school, across the state, or even nationally.

Postsecondary Training

The American Chemical Society sponsors a Division of Chemical Technicians, which provides information about ACS-approved programs. On the Division's list of two-year chemical technology and related programs are about 40 colleges across the country. Some four-year bachelor's chemical technology programs have developed in recent years, as well.

"The two-year program can be very difficult," Connie says. "Many people drop out because it's very intensive in math, and there are difficult courses like organic chemistry. You spend a lot of time in the laboratory and studying many of the same chemistry courses you would in a four-year program. It's not easy."

Debra also found her two-year program very challenging. She has an associate's degree in biotechnology. Although chemistry is what she uses now, she also studied such subjects as microbiology and hematology.

Chemical technicians with two-year degrees are finding many opportunities, but Debra has found that the pharmaceutical industry is beginning to demand four-year degrees from new hires. "We're definitely not hiring people with two-year degrees," she says of AstraZeneca.

SCHOLARSHIPS AND GRANTS

Many technical schools offer scholarship programs and awards to their students. Connie received a couple of awards from Milwaukee Area Technical College. After her first year, she received the chemistry department award for being the outstanding chemistry student. After her second year, at graduation, she received an award from the chemical technology program for being the outstanding student. She thinks they were significant in helping her get her first job as a chemical technician.

INTERNSHIPS AND VOLUNTEERSHIPS

Mike took a different track. He studied electron microscopy at a community college and then participated in a government exchange program. He spent a year in Germany studying microscopy and working in a German company doing microscopy. "The real ace in the hole for me was my overseas experience: six months in a foreign university and six months in a company in my field was really what opened all the doors for me." He saw a notice on a bulletin board at the community college he was attending about the exchange program, Congress Bundestag, which accepts 50 U.S. students and 100 Germans. It is funded by the U.S. and German congresses. "The German company where I apprenticed was a world-renowned company in the field of microscopy. I think just the fact that an individual would take some risks and go to a foreign country to gain something helped me in my job search later," Mike says. "It wasn't an award or scholarship exactly, but considering that only 50 U.S. students were accepted, and adding the value of the foreign experience, I think of it as an award."

While working toward an associate's degree, some students work as co-ops or do summer work in their field. Co-ops are full-time students who work about 20 hours a week for a local company. Some co-op positions may be available to high school seniors.

Even after you earn your associate's degree and get a job as a chemical technician, there will always be more training on the job. Connie explains, "Most community college chemical technology programs give you a good background in basic laboratory skills, instrument skills, chemistry theory, inorganic chemistry, quantitative analysis, math, and physics. You have a good basic knowledge, but you're not ready to go into the lab and do things on your own. Much of what you do, you learn on the job. Most chemical technicians' jobs are so diverse, there has to be some on-the-job training."

LABOR UNIONS

Some chemical technicians belong to a union, but unionization varies widely across the country. In some cases, the plant is unionized but the laboratory is not. Many technicians have nonexempt status, meaning they are not exempt from federal wage and hour laws. Overall, the percentage of technicians who belong to a union is very small.

Who Will Hire Me?

Chemical technicians work for chemical companies, pharmaceutical companies, manufacturers, food processing companies, research and testing laboratories, schools and universities, petroleum refineries, biotechnology companies, agricultural organizations, and crime laboratories. Federal and state government agencies, particularly the federal departments of Defense, Agriculture, Interior, and Commerce, also hire chemical technicians.

Some companies that have ongoing needs for chemical technicians work with local community colleges and technical schools to develop two-year programs. This ensures them a supply of trained chemical technicians. Other companies have joined forces to establish local, independent, technician training programs.

Most employers recruit locally or regionally for technicians. They have found that trained technicians are not willing to relocate for a job. This is especially true if it is a second-career choice. By the time they earn their two-year degree, technicians may be settled with a family in a community they like. Because companies hire locally and work closely with technical schools, placement offices are usually successful in finding jobs for their graduates.

Connie has attended several recruiter panel discussions. "Employers say they prefer to hire people with associate's degrees, but there aren't enough people available. There's been basically a starvation mode for appropriately trained technicians for a number of years."

Some companies hire high school graduates and train them on the job, but it is not a common practice. Companies generally prefer a graduate of a two-year program in chemical technology or another science. When hiring, they consider your grades, but companies are also attracted by special awards or efforts. Connie's two awards, for example, helped her land a job, and Mike's overseas experience was impressive on his resume.

When he returned from Germany, Mike went through technical journals and geographically selected places of employment from companies mentioned in articles. "It may not be the best way to go," he says, "but I sent resumes to about 50 authors. Since authors don't usually have anything to do with hiring, I imagine many of those resumes got tossed." He did, however, receive 10 responses, interviewed with three firms, and was immediately hired by one of them. He has been with the same company for over 10 years.

Mike's company also hires co-ops to assist technicians and scientists. "Co-op work is highly regarded by employers," he says. "They can judge

technical competence from grades and scholastic achievements, but it's difficult for them to judge people skills at an interview." Co-ops have the opportunity to prove their social skills to employers, which gives them an edge.

Contracting is another option. There are local agencies that place technicians with companies for special projects or temporary assignments. Many technicians work as contractors, from one month to as much as a year or more, and then are hired as full-time employees.

"Be flexible about where you want to work and don't limit yourself to a specific area of chemistry," advises Debra. "Flexibility is a key. My degree was in biotechnology. I worked in a toxicology lab for a month and then got a job with a pharmaceutical company. I've been with the same company for over 19 years."

Where Can I Go from Here?

Connie, Mike, and Debra have all been working for their companies for over 10 years. And all three are happy. "I like what I do. The supervisors I work with have been very supportive, encouraging me to take on as much responsibility as I can handle," Connie says.

There are opportunities to work in the areas of technology development or technology management, with equal or comparable pay. Many companies offer the option to move to other departments, from research and development to manufacturing, for example. Technicians, however, can become specialists. Connie

FYI

Students interested in chemical technology may want to explore the career of chemical engineering technician. As a chemical engineering technician, you help to solve problems of productivity, environmental protection, and energy shortage. A typical two-year program consists of courses in principles of chemistry, general physics, technical computer applications, and engineering materials.

ADVANCEMENT POSSIBILITIES

Assayers test ores and minerals and analyze results to determine value and properties of components.

Chemical engineers design equipment and develop processes for manufacturing chemicals and related products.

Chemical research engineers conduct research on chemical processes and equipment.

Chemists conduct research, analysis, synthesis, and experimentation on substances.

Food chemists conduct research and analysis concerning chemistry of foods to develop and improve foods and beverages.

Chemical technicians also may shift to other science-related careers, such as in physics, geology, or biology. There are opportunities in the health care industry, including pharmacy and dentistry. People who work as chemical laboratory technicians may also move into work in the aircraft-aerospace industry, metallurgy, utilities, photo-optics, and spectroscopy.

explains, "They can become very good at a specific area of technology, so the higher up a technician is, the more difficult it is to move to another area, because they basically create their own job."

That is true in Mike's case. "I'm highly specialized, but I lack a higher degree for moving up the ladder. Fortunately I like what I'm doing and management allows me to do different things. My company would support continuing education if I were interested."

Some companies have the same career track for all lab technicians, whether they have an associate's degree, a bachelor's degree, or are highly experienced with no degree. Other companies have different promotion systems for technicians and chemists but will promote qualified technicians to the chemist level and allow them to progress along that track.

The associate's degree can be a stepping-stone toward a bachelor's degree in chemistry. Some technicians earn their two-year degree, get into the

workforce, and then return to school to work on their bachelor's degree. Many companies encourage employees to continue their education, and some help with tuition.

What Are the Salary Ranges?

The U.S. Department of Labor Occupational Information Network reports that the annual median earnings in 2003 for chemical technicians were $37,600. Those in the middle 50 percent earned between $29,400 and $47,300. The lowest paid 10 percent earned $23,200, and the highest paid 10 percent earned $57,100.

Most large companies that hire chemical technicians offer paid vacations, health insurance, and pension plans. Some employers also pay for continued education.

What Is the Job Outlook?

According to the *Occupational Outlook Handbook*, employment of science technicians is expected to increase more slowly than the average for all occupations through 2012. In 2002 chemical techncians held 69,000 jobs, and that is expected to increase by only about 5 percent to 72,300 in 2012. The best job opportunities are expected to be in the pharmaceutical and medical manufacturing industry.

While many interesting opportunities exist for chemical technicians, the chemical industry overall is expected to see some slowdown in employment. Many companies are cutting back on in-house training, preferring to hire those with degrees and proven skills, especially in the laboratory. Technicians are gaining more respect from employers. In the past they have been considered assistants to the "real" scientists, but their status is changing to one of valued, highly trained specialists who are indispensable in the workforce.

More and more companies are opting to hire contract employees as technicians for temporary assignments, but there is still a need for full-time, competent laboratory technicians. Connie, Mike, and Debra have proven they can have long-term careers in the same company. Technicians who have training in a variety of skills will find it easier to make lateral moves within a company as projects, programs, and reporting structures change.

Connie says, "The job outlook is very good to excellent. As the country becomes more technologically advanced, there will be a need for more training beyond high school." Most recent graduates of two-year programs in science are not likely to have difficulty finding jobs in the next decade. The Partnership for the Advancement of Chemical Technology (PACT) is a consortium of people within industry and academia devoted to revising chemical technician curricula and promoting careers in technology. PACT is in the process of establishing connections between students and teachers and making young people aware of chemical technology education and jobs within the industry.

How Do I Learn More?

PROFESSIONAL ORGANIZATIONS

The following organizations can provide information about careers in chemistry, educational and training programs, employment trends, and industry outlooks:

American Chemical Society (ACS)
1155 16th Street, NW
Washington, DC 20036
800-227-5558
help@acs.org
http://www.chemistry.org

American Institute of Chemical Engineers
Three Park Avenue
New York, NY 10016-5991
800-242-4363
http://www.aiche.org

Junior Engineering Technical Society
1420 King Street, Suite 405
Alexandria, VA 22314
703-548-5387
info@jets.org
http://www.jets.org

BIBLIOGRAPHY

The following is a sampling of materials relating to the professional concerns and development of chemical technicians:

Johnson, Catherine W. et al. *Essential Laboratory Mathematics: Concepts and Applications for the Chemical and Clinical Laboratory Technician.* 2d ed. Clifton Park, N.J.: Thomson Delmar Learning, 2003.

Kenkel, John. *Analytical Chemistry for Technicians.* 3d ed. Boca Raton, Fla.: CRC Press, 2002.

Rowh, Mark. *Great Jobs for Chemistry Majors.* Lincolnwood, Ill.: VGM Career Horizons, 1999.

Shugar, Gershon J. et al. *Chemical Technician's Ready Reference Handbook.* 4th ed. New York: McGraw Hill, 1996.

Woodburn, John H. *Opportunites in Chemistry Careers.* 2d ed. Lincolnwood, Ill.: VGM Career Horizons, 2002.

CIVIL ENGINEERING TECHNICIANS
||||||||||||||||||||||||||||||||||||||||||||||||||||||||||

Some of the most sought after work in civil engineering is the design of roller coasters. There are more than 300 million roller coasters in the United States, and new ones are being designed all the time. Engineers have the challenge of creating rides that feature new thrills with no spills; in other words, they must create the illusion of great danger, must frighten the rider, while assuring that every 200-foot drop and every 70 mile per hour loop is perfectly safe. When designing a coaster, engineers and technicians must keep in mind simple physics, making sure that fast cars have plenty of room in which to turn. With a proper turning radius, the g force of a superspeed coaster can be kept at 0 to 4. (People begin to pass out at 6 g.)

Engineers must also work to create tight spirals without increasing the potential for blackouts in riders. One way designers accomplish this is to keep the geometric center of the spirals near the rider's heart. No matter how wild the ride, how mammoth the structure, how deep the drops, roller coaster engineers are always restricted by something beyond their design capabilities: the limits of the human body.

What Does a Civil Engineering Technician Do?

If you have ever ridden on a train, driven along a highway, taken an elevator to the very top of a skyscraper, ridden a roller coaster, crossed a bridge, or gone for a stroll through a city park, you have relied on the expertise of a civil engineering technician. *Civil engineers and technicians* work together for the community, providing better, faster transportation; designing and developing highways, airports, and railroads; improving the environment; and constructing buildings, bridges, and space platforms. Civil engineering technicians get you to work or school on time, as well as take you around the world safely, quickly, and efficiently.

There are seven main civil engineering areas: structural, geotechnical, environmental, water resources, transportation, construction, and urban and community planning. The work is closely related, so a technician might work in one, or many, of these areas.

Structural engineering technicians assist in the design of the structures we use in our daily transportation, travel, work, and recreation. These technicians are involved in the planning of all kinds of structures: buildings, bridges, platforms, even amusement park rides. With their knowledge of building materials and the effects of weather and climate on these materials, they help design the best structure for the purpose. Structural engineering technicians calculate the size, number, and composition of beams and columns. Sometimes their work involves geotechnical engineering.

Definition
Civil engineering technicians work in the design, planning, and building of railroads, airports, highways, drainage systems, and many other structures and facilities.

Alternative Job Titles
Construction engineering technicians
Highway technicians
Water resources engineering technicians

High School Subjects
Mathematics
Physics
Technical/shop

Personal Skills
Artistic
Mechanical/manipulative

Salary Range
$23,900 to $38,200 to $66,587

Minimum Educational Level
Associate's degree

Certification or Licensing
Recommended

Outlook
About as fast as the average

DOT
005

GOE
02.08.04

NOC
2231

O*NET-SOC
17-3022.00

Geotechnical engineering technicians analyze the soil and rock that will be needed to support both underground and aboveground structures. The construction of tunnels, dams, embankments, and offshore platforms requires understanding of the soil and rock, so the structures will remain stable. If soil pressures from the weight of the structures will cause excessive settling or some other failure, technicians design special piers, rafts, pilings, or footings to prevent structural problems.

Environmental engineering involves removing pollutants and contaminates from the water and the air. *Environmental engineering technicians* also work with wastewater and solid waste management. With their understanding of biological processes, these technicians help to preserve our natural resources.

Water resources engineering technicians gather data and make computations and drawings for water projects such as pipelines, canals, and hydroelectric power facilities. A water resources technician helps with the control of water to prevent floods and to manage rivers.

Highways, airports, and railroads are designed and constructed by *transportation engineers* and

FYI

Geotechnical engineering was pushed to its technological limit in the 1926–28 construction of the St. Francis Dam. The dam was intended as an additional water supply for the city of Los Angeles, but structural errors resulted in catastrophe. When the dam failed after its first filling, more than 450 people died in the flood waters. At the time, the flood was second only to the San Francisco earthquake and fire of 1906 as the worst disaster in California history.

technicians. Transportation engineering technicians also work to improve traffic control and other systems that will allow for the faster, more efficient transportation of people and products. *Highway technicians* perform surveys and cost estimates as well as plan and supervise highway construction and maintenance. *Rail and waterway technicians* survey, make specifications and cost estimates, and help plan and construct railway and waterway facilities.

Construction engineering technicians help to bring a design project to the construction stages. They prepare specifications for materials and help schedule construction activities. They inspect work to assure that it conforms to blueprints and specifications. *Materials technicians* sample and run tests on rock, soil, cement, asphalt, wood, steel, concrete, and other materials. *Party chiefs* work for licensed land surveyors, survey land for boundary-line locations, and plan subdivisions and other large-area land developments.

Urban and community planning technicians work in the full development of a community. Technicians in this area coordinate the planning and construction of city streets, sewers, drainage systems, and refuse facilities, as well as identify recreation areas and areas for industry and residence.

Civil engineering technicians also may specialize in areas of sales and research. A *research engineering technician* tests and develops new products and equipment, while *sales engineering technicians* sell building materials, construction equipment, and engineering services.

Lingo to Learn

Cantilever beam A beam that projects beyond its support.

Catch basin A structure with a sump below the pipes for the purpose of causing sand and gravel to settle by slowing the velocity of the water.

Curvilinear A pattern of curved streets and tee intersections.

Development Improvement to the land for the benefit of the public.

Engineer's level The instrument most commonly used for determining elevations in the field.

Galvanizing Coating a pipe with zinc for protection against corrosion.

Grade The steepness of a slope.

Subdivision A parcel of land divided into more than one section.

What Is It Like to Be a Civil Engineering Technician?

Betsy McCullen is a senior drafting technician, working with computer-aided drafting, for the Geotechnical Engineering Bureau in Albany, New York. She works in the Structures Department. "For every bridge or structure they put up on any highway system, drillers go out and take soil samples, and they perform drill cores," she says. These drill cores, or borings, are cylindrical samples of earth strata. The drillers document the locations of the borings in log books, and Betsy works from these logs in translating information into the computer-aided drafting system and creating profiles. "I don't have to draw up the actual picture," she explains. "All I do is locate the borings, then I create a profile with all the soil types."

These soils profiles are then used by the Structures Design Department in the designing of footings for the bridge. "The Design Department can't design the structure without our profile," Betsy says, "as it tells the stability of the soil in which the footings will sit to support the bridge."

Betsy's job is performed entirely at the computer, using Microstation software. (According to a survey conducted by Civiljobs.com, the top programs used by technicians included AutoCAD 2000, SoftDesk, and Microstation.) She often works on several projects at a time. Though she spends most of her work hours in an office, she works closely with other members of the department in accessing information. "We all work as a unit," she says. "My boss works with the Automation Department and the Structures Design Department, collecting all the files we need." These files must include surveys conducted of the road before new work began. "We need the actual projected project and what they're going to do and how they're going to redo the project." Betsy works primarily from this file of information.

Sometimes this information is compiled by consultants, an increasing trend in civil engineering. "In another five years," Betsy says, "I don't think we'll even have our own drill crew, or our own soils labs. The governor is trying to turn everything over to consultants." This can create difficulties, because the consultants often work with a different kind of software. "We have problems getting them to give us the right information at the time we need it." Getting

> ### TO BE A SUCCESSFUL CIVIL ENGINEERING TECHNICIAN, YOU SHOULD . . .
>
> ○ be able to communicate and work well with others to solve problems
> ○ have an interest in building and planning
> ○ be curious about how things work
> ○ have an interest in the environment
> ○ have an understanding of math and the sciences

correct information can create the biggest challenges for Betsy.

Another challenge can involve creating large profiles within the computer-aided system. Albany is the main office for the entire New York State Department of Transportation, and Betsy is often required to work on projects based in New York City. "There you've got huge bridges, and huge amounts of drillings, borings, that I've got to log into my work. There are so many borings located around almost the same area so that they can get the structure to be solid. So that presents the most difficult thing for me: to get it all on paper." The "plan view" on the computer screen can often be dominated by borings, preventing Betsy from including the profile of the bridge itself. "We have to include all the borings that are needed. At that time, we have more information that we have room for."

Betsy works from 7:00 A.M. to 3:00 P.M. Monday through Friday. In emergency situations, such as a recent landslide as a result of soil failure, Betsy may be called on to work extra hours. Putting in overtime, however, is rarely required.

Do I Have What It Takes to Be a Civil Engineering Technician?

Civil engineering technicians are relied upon for solutions and must express their ideas clearly in speech and in writing. Good communication skills are important for a technician in the writing and presenting of reports and plans. These skills are also important for working alongside other technicians and professionals, people who are often from many different backgrounds and skilled in varying areas of engineering.

Betsy finds that her creativity, her artist's instinct, is important to her work in drafting. "I love to draw," she says. "I like the neatness of drawing on the computer. The way I place all my labeling is an art to me." She is also very meticulous in her work; she believes that good drafting requires a great deal of attention to detail.

How Do I Become a Civil Engineering Technician?

Betsy was with the U.S. Air Force before pursuing an education in civil engineering. Her eight years with the service helped her to prepare for the civil engineering technology program in Utica, New York. Betsy advises students to develop strong backgrounds in mathematics and the sciences, "And good writing skills help tremendously when writing reports."

EDUCATION

High School

Students interested in civil engineering technician work should take math and science courses, including at least two years of algebra, plane and solid geometry, and trigonometry. Courses in physics, chemistry, and biology can provide you with the necessary lab experience. Civil engineering technicians often make use of mechanical drawings to convey their ideas to others, and neat, well-executed drawings are important for accuracy. A shop class, or a class

A civil engineering technician with the California Department of Transportation reviews construction plans. *(Lawrence Migdale/Photo Researchers Inc.)*

in mechanical drawing, will prepare you for the drafting and designing requirements of the job.

Because computers have become essential for engineering technicians, a computer programming course can introduce you to the skills you will need. Also, develop your English and language skills; you will be working closely with engineers and their reports, as well as writing reports of your own.

Postsecondary Training

Technical schools, or junior and community colleges, offer basic math and science courses that prepare students for courses in surveying, materials, hydraulics, highway and bridge construction and design, railway and water systems, soils, heavy construction, steel and concrete construction, costs and estimates, and management and construction technology. In addition to the course work, laboratory and field experience is required for students in technical school programs. There are also some four-year bachelor's programs in civil engineering technology.

Civil engineering technicians may eventually want to enter an engineering program at a university. An engineering program requires courses in engineering science and analysis, engineering theory and design, as well as courses in the social sciences, the humanities, ethics, and communications. The Accreditation Board for Engineering and Technology (ABET) develops accreditation policies and criteria.

FYI

These are longest suspension bridges in the world, according to *Structural Steel Designer's Handbook* (McGraw-Hill, 1999):

Akashi Kaikyo in Japan, 6,066 feet

Great Belt Link in Denmark, 5,328 feet

Humber River in England, 4,626 feet

Verrazano Narrows in New York City, 4,260 feet

Golden Gate in San Francisco, 4,200 feet

CERTIFICATION OR LICENSING

Becoming a Certified Engineering Technician can help a technician advance in professional standing. An experienced technician may also take an examination for licensing as a Licensed Land Surveyor. With this licensing, technicians can operate their own surveying businesses.

Organizations that offer certification to engineering technicians include the American Society of Certified Engineering Technicians and the National Institute for Certification in Engineering Technologies.

SCHOLARSHIPS AND GRANTS

Scholarships and other financial aid should be available through the technical school or community college you choose to attend. For students pursuing an engineering degree, the American Society of Civil Engineers (ASCE) offers scholarships, fellowships, and grants.

INTERNSHIPS AND VOLUNTEERSHIPS

A local construction company may offer you the best opportunity for hands-on experience, either through part-time summer work or an internship. With a construction company, you can observe surveying teams, site supervisors, building inspectors, skilled craft workers, and civil engineering technicians.

Who Will Hire Me?

While Betsy was finishing her program in civil engineering technology, she had the opportunity to interview with the New York State Department of Transportation. "They wanted women then," she says, "and a military record didn't look so bad either, so they snapped me up." Within the department she has worked at a variety of jobs, including construction inspection and surveying.

State highway departments employ many civil engineering technicians, as do railroads and airports. Technicians can also find work for city and county transportation services. The Natural Resources Division of the United States Department of Agriculture (USDA) also employs civil engineering technicians for conservation and water management

In-depth

History

Engineering, both military and civil, is one of the world's oldest professions. The pyramids of ancient Egypt and the bridges, roads, and aqueducts of the Roman Empire (some of which are still in use) are examples of ancient engineering feats. It was not until the 18th century in France and England that civil engineers began to organize themselves into professional societies to exchange information or plan projects. At that time, most civil engineers were still self-taught, skilled craft workers. Thomas Telford, for instance, Britain's leading road builder and first president of the Institution of Civil Engineers, started his career as a stonemason. And John Rennie, the builder of the new London Bridge, began as a millwright's apprentice.

The first major educational programs intended for civil engineers were offered by the École Polytechnique, founded in Paris in 1794. Similar courses at the Bauakadamie, founded in Berlin in 1799, and at University College London, founded in 1826, soon followed. In the United States, the first courses in civil engineering were taught at Rensselaer Polytechnic Institute, founded in 1824.

From the beginning, civil engineers have required the help of skilled assistants to handle the many details that are part of all phases of civil engineering. Traditionally, these assistants have possessed a combination of basic knowledge and good manual skills. As construction techniques have become more sophisticated, however, there is an increased need for assistants to be technically trained in specialized fields relevant to civil engineering.

These technically trained assistants are today's civil engineering technicians. Just as separate educational programs and professional identity developed for the civil engineer in the 18th and 19th centuries, so it is for civil engineering technicians in this century. The civil engineering technician is a distinguished member of the civil engineering team.

projects. By contacting the USDA, transportation services, and other government agencies, you can receive information about job positions and opportunities. State and private employment services can also provide you with job listings and will sometimes arrange interviews.

Many schools have cooperative work-study programs with companies and government agencies. Students in these programs often move into permanent positions upon graduation. Also, by getting to know people who work in your chosen area, you'll learn about job and advancement opportunities.

A local college or university might sponsor an American Society of Civil Engineers (ASCE) Student Chapter, an organization that involves civil engineering students with engineering projects. Through the chapter, you can get to know the professionals in your area.

Where Can I Go from Here?

Betsy has become so familiar with working for the government that she feels very comfortable in her current job. Together with her employers, Betsy developed a 10-year career plan. In fewer than 13 years, she can retire from her job and receive retirement benefits.

Civil engineering technicians are constantly learning new things about the job as they gain more experience. They are required to learn new techniques and how to use the latest equipment. Some technicians move on to supervisory positions, while others go on to earn degrees in civil engineering.

Some civil engineering technicians go on to become associate *municipal designers*, a position in which they direct workers to prepare design drawings and feasibility studies for dams and municipal

ADVANCEMENT POSSIBILITIES

Civil drafters draft detailed construction drawings, topographical profiles, and related maps and specifications used in planning and construction of civil engineering projects.

Highway-administrative engineers administer statewide highway planning, design, construction, and maintenance programs.

Structural drafters draw plans and details for structures employing structural reinforcing steel, concrete, masonry, wood, and other materials.

Civil engineers, also known as structural engineers, are involved in the design and construction of the physical structures that make up our surroundings, such as roads, bridges, buildings, and harbors.

water and sewage plants. City or county building inspectors review and then approve or reject plans for construction of large buildings. *Project engineers* supervise numbers of projects and field parties for city, county, or state highway departments.

What Are the Salary Ranges?

According to the U.S. Department of Labor Occupational Information Network, the median annual earnings for civil engineering technicians in 2003 were $38,200. Those in the lowest paid 10 percent earned $23,900, and those in the highest paid 10 percent earned more than $57,300.

A salary survey conducted by Civiljobs.com found that engineering technicians had an average annual salary of $48,117. Those just starting out reported earnings of around $36,965, while those with 10 years of experience and more made between $54,036 and $66,587. Technicians working for the government often receive generous benefits, including health insurance and retirement plans.

Civil engineering technicians who operate their own construction, surveying, or equipment

businesses can make thousands of dollars more a year than technicians in salaried positions.

What Is the Job Outlook?

Civil engineering jobs are greatly affected by the economy; new building projects are usually only initiated in times of financial stability. But civil engineering technicians are always needed for improvements on highways, railways, and structures. Technological advances allowing for faster, safer modes of transportation also result in jobs.

According to the *Occupational Outlook Handbook*, employment of engineering technicians is expected to increase about as fast as the average for all occupations through 2012. Computer-aided design allows individual technicians to increase productivity, thereby limiting job growth. Those with training in sophisticated technologies and those with degrees in technology will have the best employment opportunities.

As more people and businesses become concerned with the preservation of natural resources, more civil engineering technicians will be employed in the treatment of water and air. Environmentally sound production systems and other advances and improvements will also lead to more opportunities for technicians.

How Do I Learn More?

PROFESSIONAL ORGANIZATIONS

For information about civil engineering technology, career guidance, accredited educational programs, fellowships, and certification, contact the following organizations:

Accreditation Board for Engineering and Technology
111 Market Place, Suite 1050
Baltimore, MD 21202
410-347-7700
http://www.abet.org

American Society for Engineering Education
1818 N Street, NW, Suite 600
Washington, DC 20036-2479
202-331-3500
http://www.asee.org

American Society of Certified Engineering Technicians
PO Box 1348
Flowery Branch, GA 30542-0023
770-967-9173
http://www.ascet.org

American Society of Civil Engineers
1801 Alexander Bell Drive
Reston, VA 20191-4400
800-548-2723
http://www.asce.org

BIBLIOGRAPHY

The following is a sampling of materials relating to the professional concerns and development of civil engineering technicians:

Chen, Wai-Fah. *The Civil Engineering Handbook.* 2d ed. Boca Raton, Fla.: CRC Press, 2002.

Chrimes, Mike. *Civil Engineering, 1839-1889: A Photographic History.* Wolfeboro Falls: Sutton Publishing, 1991.

Hagerty, Joseph D. *Opportunities in Civil Engineering Careers.* Lincolnwood, Ill.: VGM Career Horizons, 1996.

Randolph, Dennis. *Civil Engineering for the Community.* Reston, Va.: American Society of Civil Engineers, 1993.

Walesh, Stuart G. *Engineering Your Future: The Non-Technical Side of Professional Practice in Engineering and Other Technical Fields.* 2d ed. Reston, Va.: American Society of Civil Engineers, 2000.

Webster, L. F. *The Wiley Dictionary of Civil Engineering and Construction.* New York: John Wiley and Sons, 1997.

COMMUNICATIONS EQUIPMENT TECHNICIANS
||||||||||||||||||||||||||||||||||||||||||||||||||||||||||||||||||||

Gary Sanborn rolls out of bed. He is on call this week, and his beeper has just gone off. He glances at the clock beside his bed: 5:30 A.M. He groans and reaches over to telephone his company.

"Hey, Paul. This is Gary. What's the story?" he asks the dispatcher.

"It's Bowman and Bowman. They've got a problem with a bank of phones. They've just made a catalog drop and they're expecting a zillion calls today. We need these phones back on as soon as possible."

Several minutes later, now dressed, Gary climbs into the company van and heads for Bowman and Bowman, where he locates his contact person, Joe Lamb.

"Hey, Joe. Tell me about this problem and show me to the phones. We'll have them fixed in no time."

What Does a Communications Equipment Technician Do?

Throughout the world, radio and telecommunications systems are used to carry information over long distances via voice and data. When communication among many information sources is needed, the sources are connected within a network, and *communications equipment technicians* are employed to maintain this network. Also called *radio and telecommunications technicians,* these workers keep our phone systems and data communications systems in good working order.

To understand what communications equipment technicians do, you need to know the basics behind how a phone connection works. When a friend calls you on the telephone, that person's voice reaches your ear by making sound waves. These sound waves travel through the phone lines and are converted by a transmitter into electric waves that move through wires to a central switching office. Switching refers to equipment that allows any station in a telecommunications system to be connected with any other station. In other words, these automated

Definition
Communications equipment technicians install, repair, and maintain electronic communications equipment and systems, including telephone, telegraph, computer, radio, and data communications networks.

Alternative Job Titles
Communications equipment mechanics
Radio and telecommunications technicians

High School Subjects
Computer science
Mathematics
Technical/shop

Personal Skills
Following instructions
Mechanical/manipulative

Salary Range
$29,300 to $48,700 to $62,000

Educational Requirements
Some postsecondary training

Certification or Licensing
Required for certain positions

Outlook
Decline

DOT
822

GOE
05.02.01

NOC
7246

O*NET-SOC
49-2022.03

switching devices connect your friend's phone line to your line. When you pick up your telephone, your receiver converts the electric waves back into sound waves.

Today's telephone systems are part of larger interconnected telecommunications systems that can link phones with other equipment that sends information via microwave and television transmissions, fiber optics cables, undersea cables, and satellite signals. With the latest computerized switching equipment, telecommunications systems can handle millions of calls and other data signals simultaneously.

Gary Sanborn installs and repairs private branch exchange (PBX) equipment. PBXs are direct telephone lines, installed for businesses, that bypass regular phone company lines. PBX equipment can handle both voice and data communication and can provide specialized services such as voice mail and automatic routing of calls at the lowest possible cost. PBX technicians also work on mobile phones, microwave transmission devices, switching equipment, and data processing systems.

Central office installers and *central office repairers* are hired to work with the switching equipment at central offices of telephone companies. Installers set up, modify, and take down equipment for client businesses, while repairers do troubleshooting, conduct malfunction tests, resolve defects, and maintain the switching equipment, keeping it in working order.

Maintenance administrators figure out where and why malfunctions occur in customer phone lines. They use computers extensively in order to analyze circuits and determine how to resolve problems. *Trouble locators* have similar responsibilities. They work for cable television companies to ensure that subscribers receive the proper signal on their televisions.

Whereas telephone calls are transmitted by sound waves over wire or fiber optics, radiotelephony refers to sound that is transmitted by electromagnetic (radio) waves without the use of wire. *Radio repairers and mechanics* set up and repair stationary and mobile radio transmitting and receiving equipment. They can become certified as *radiotelephone operators* or *radiotelegraph operators*.

What Is It Like to Be a Communications Equipment Technician?

Gary has been employed as a PBX installer and repairer at Nortel Communications (Northern Telecom) Systems for several years. "This field is ever changing—never boring," he says. "Every few months there's a new product, a new media for communication, and we have to be trained on that new product right away. We're busy all the time."

Gary works 45 to 50 hours a week. That is an average of eight to 10 hours a day, and he is on call one week a month, which means he is readily available in case of any emergencies. "When we get a call, our customer usually wants the problem fixed right away. The goal is to keep the systems going no matter what it takes," says Gary.

Lingo to Learn

Local Area Network (LAN) A network of computers connected to one central computer.

Multiplexing Using an electronic transmission channel to carry two or more signals simultaneously.

Private branch exchange (PBX) system Direct telephone lines used by businesses. They bypass regular phone company lines and handle voice and data communication, as well as specialized services like voice mail and automatic call routing.

Radiotelephone A wireless device for carrying electronic signals by radio waves.

Switching Equipment and methods that allow stations in a telecommunications system to be connected with one another.

Transmission The passage of radio waves between transmitting and receiving stations.

After Gary checks in with his dispatcher in the morning, he may have to travel anywhere from 15 minutes to six hours to get to his work site. He may survey the site for future installation or he may install the data communications equipment that day. Nortel services all of its installations, so Gary is sometimes called in to troubleshoot a phone system or a data terminal problem.

Another telecommunications technician, Marty Burnette, installs data networking and communications equipment. Marty started his own business, Portland Technical Services, after retiring from Nynex in 1994. He installs voice equipment such as telephone systems, as well as computer networks such as LANs (local area networks) and MANs (metropolitan area networks).

In order to get his new business on its feet, Marty is willing to travel to wherever the work is. Most of his jobs are in New Hampshire and Massachusetts, two neighboring states. He leaves Portland, Maine, at 4:30 A.M. and may be gone for a day or a week, depending on the projects.

While he was at Nynex, Marty worked in several capacities, first in the central office, then as a maintenance administrator, and next as a cable splicer, splicing copper cable. Thanks to technological improvements, the copper wire that Marty worked with has been replaced by fiber optics. Most of the physical work that Marty performed during his tenure with the phone company is also a thing of the past. Efficient computerized devices have superseded electromechanical devices that needed frequent maintenance. As the field becomes less labor intensive, technicians are being required to have technical and computer training.

Do I Have What It Takes to Be a Communications Equipment Technician?

Communications equipment technicians need excellent mechanical and electrical skills, coupled with good manual dexterity. While the specific equipment used by each company varies, most technicians will need to have a working familiarity with electrical measuring and testing devices, hand tools, and computers. Technology improvements have made it important for technicians to adapt to a variety of tasks. You might splice fiber optic cable one day, program computerized switches the next, and install telephones the next. You should have the ability or educational background to study a new technical manual and grasp its contents. Gary takes pride in the fact that his company expects its technicians to stay on the cutting edge. "Incredible things have happened in this field," he says. "There's a new device to be learned every few months."

> Incredible things have happened in this field. There's a new device to be learned every few months.

It is also critical for technicians to have problem-solving abilities in order to work through a difficult installation or repair job without a lot of supervision. Good communication skills are important for all technicians, but particularly those who have contact with customers. Gary says that what he likes most about his job is leaving customers satisfied. However, some customers can be impatient and even rude, and it is important for technicians to keep their cool and remain courteous.

> ### TO BE A SUCCESSFUL COMMUNICATIONS EQUIPMENT TECHNICIAN, YOU SHOULD . . .
>
> - ○ have manual dexterity
> - ○ have electrical or mechanical aptitude
> - ○ adapt well to a variety of environments
> - ○ be a skilled communicator
> - ○ be willing to keep up with rapidly changing technologies

How Do I Become a Communications Equipment Technician?

Gary was working as a master electrician for a local hospital when the hospital decided to put in a PBX network with Nortel. They wanted someone on staff to have the knowledge to do repairs, so they sent Gary to Nortel for training. When Nortel advertised that they were hiring additional technicians, Gary applied and was hired.

EDUCATION

High School

In high school, shop classes in electronics, electricity, mechanics, and engineering are the most helpful. Gary says that students should also take as many computer classes as possible. Mathematics courses in algebra and geometry will come in handy as well.

As in many service occupations, English classes will prepare you to communicate well with customers, employers, and other workers. A background in English and composition will also be useful in reading technical manuals and writing reports.

Postsecondary Training

There are several ways you can enter the field of communications technology. Many telecommunications companies will hire and train entry-level technicians right out of high school. Applicants for these positions are usually tested for their general mechanical aptitude and manual dexterity before they are hired. Company programs include on-the-job training, as well as classroom work in electricity, electronics, and applied mathematics.

Some telecommunications companies prefer to hire technicians with some postsecondary training, which is available at community and junior colleges, trade and technical schools, and in the military. You should look into programs in a variety of subjects, including telecommunications technology, electronics, electrical or electromechanical technology, or even computer maintenance. Most of these programs last two years. While you are enrolled, you can focus on classes in electricity, electronics, computers, and fiber optics. Because military telecommunications play an important role in the nation's defense, the U.S. armed services (army, navy, air force, marines) runs its own telecommunications training program. Another way to train for the profession and to broaden your prospects for advancement is to pursue a bachelor's degree in telecommunications or computer science at a university.

CERTIFICATION OR LICENSING

Certification is required for certain specialties and by certain employers. Gary's company, like many others in the telecommunications field, offers its own certification process. At Nortel, employees are trained, tested, and certified in PBX installation, repair, and troubleshooting. Periodically, employees learn about new PBX equipment and practice installing it. In week-long classes, they may also learn electrical theory that applies to the installation. At Nortel, technicians are also certified according to experience level: Tech I, II, and III, with Tech I being the highest grade.

Other technicians and engineers who work with telecommunications equipment (such as radio devices and satellite or microwave systems) can be certified through the National Association of Radio and Telecommunications Engineers (NARTE). The Federal Communications Commission requires radio transmission technicians to obtain a Global Maritime Distress and Safety System (GMDSS) license.

NARTE's certification requirements are demanding, and they vary depending on the type and level of certification eligibility. The certification levels are Tech I, II, III, and IV, with Tech I being the highest level. For example, to apply for Tech IV level through NARTE, you must have completed a course of study or a training program in radio and/or telecommunications electronics offered either by an educational institution or through an internal company training course. You must also pass an exam, have less than two years of experience in telecommunications, and have one supervisory reference that supports your character and competence. NARTE offers its own study guides for the certification process. The tests are open-book exams, meaning that books, notes, and battery-operated calculators may be used during testing. As you move into other specialties, such as computer telecommunications, cable transmission systems, fiber optic splicing, international broadcast, frequency coordination, and education, there are additional certifications offered by NARTE. Many companies provide financial and educational support for employees going through the certification process.

SCHOLARSHIPS AND GRANTS

If you are planning to attend a university for a degree in telecommunications technology, check with the financial aid office to find out whether scholarships and grants are available. Many businesses in the telecommunications industry also offer scholarships to technicians interested in pursuing further education.

The Armed Forces Communications and Electronics Association (AFCEA) provides over $400,000 each year in scholarships, grants, and prizes to students in science, engineering, and telecommunications. Most local chapters of the AFCEA also sponsor high school and community college students.

LABOR UNIONS

Membership in a labor union, such as the International Brotherhood of Electrical Workers or the Communications Workers of America, often depends on one's employer. It is not mandatory to belong to a union, but you may wish to inquire about unions when you are considering a position with a company.

Who Will Hire Me?

The majority of communications equipment technicians work for telephone companies. Other employers include cable television companies, railroads, the aerospace industry, the federal government, and small electrical and communications companies.

Technicians with a breadth of experience can open their own businesses if they are willing to be responsible for their own schedules, insurance, and equipment. In addition, some qualified workers choose to work in educational settings as teachers, professors, and trainers.

Where Can I Go from Here?

Because of the changes in equipment and technology, technicians who hope to advance will need to keep their skills current by pursuing additional, ongoing training. Such training is offered by employers, technical schools, and professional organizations.

To become a *Class I telecommunication technician,* you need to have a minimum of eight years of experience in the field and at least one specialty certification, such as control systems or circuit design. Technicians who advance to a master endorsement have an even broader range of experience and are capable of working in many specialties.

After at least four years of engineering experience in telecommunications, technicians may become *radio and telecommunications engineers.* In order to get this promotion, it is advantageous to have a bachelor's degree in a relevant field. Engineers have a broad knowledge base, including principles of telecommunications, digital communications, data communications, opto-electronics, transmission line principles, and engineering economy.

Some technicians move into supervisory roles, such as *instrument repairer supervisor* or *central office repairer supervisor.* These individuals oversee other technicians, handle scheduling, and maintain quality control.

What Are the Salary Ranges?

In 2003 the U.S. Department of Labor reported that central office and PBX installers and repairers had median annual earnings of $48,700 with those in the middle 50 percent earning between $39,300 and $55,600. The lowest paid 10 percent earned $29,300, and the highest paid 10 percent earned $62,000.

Technicians generally receive overtime pay for hours worked in addition to their regular schedule and on weekends. Benefits vary, but usually include paid vacations and holidays, sick leave, health insurance, and some form of retirement plan.

Self-employed technicians like Marty determine their own work schedules, thus their earnings often reflect how much effort they put into marketing themselves and keeping a full schedule.

What Is the Job Outlook?

The U.S. Department of Labor projects employment for radio and telecommunications equipment installers to decline through 2012, in part because equipment is more reliable than in the past so fewer repairs are needed. In addition, higher-capacity equipment will reduce the amount of equipment required, and wireless technology will eliminate the need for companies to hire radio mechanics.

It will be difficult for new workers to gain employment as communications equipment technicians. Competition for existing positions will be keen and workers with the best qualifications stand the best chance of obtaining available jobs. Those with advanced electronics training and strong computer skills should have the best opportunity for employment in this field.

ADVANCEMENT POSSIBILITIES

Class I telecommunications technicians have a minimum of eight years of experience in the field and at least one specialty, such as in control systems or circuit design. Those with a master endorsement have an even broader range of experience and are capable of working in many specialties.

Instrument repairer supervisors and central office repairer supervisors oversee other technicians, do administrative work such as scheduling, and maintain quality control.

Radio and telecommunications engineers are skilled in digital communications, data communications, opto-electronics, and transmission line principles. They sometimes oversee the work of technicians.

How Do I Learn More?

PROFESSIONAL ORGANIZATIONS

Following are organizations that provide information on communications equipment technician careers, accredited schools, and possible employers.

Armed Forces Communications and Electronics
  Association
4400 Fair Lakes Court
Fairfax, VA 22033-3899
800-336-4583
edfoundation@afcea.org
http://www.afcea.org

Federal Communications Commission
445 12th Street, SW
Washington, DC 20554
888-225-5322
fccinfo@fcc.gov
http://www.fcc.gov

IEEE Communications Society
Three Park Avenue, 17th Floor
New York, NY 10016
212-705-8900
http://www.comsoc.org

National Association of Radio and
  Telecommunications Engineers Inc.

167 Village Street
Medway, MA 02053
508-533-8333
http://www.narte.org

BIBLIOGRAPHY

The following is a sampling of materials relating to the professional concerns and development of communications equipment technicians:

Bone, Jan. *Opportunities in Telecommunications Careers.* Lincolnwood, Ill.: NTC Publishing Group, 1995.

Dodd, Annabel Z. *The Essential Guide to Telecommunications.* 3d ed. Paramus, N.J.: Prentice Hall, 2001.

Gross, Lynne Schafer. *Telecommunications: An Introduction to Electronic Media,* 7th ed. Columbus, Ohio: McGraw Hill Higher Education, 1999.

Miller, Gary M. *Modern Electronic Communication,* 8th ed. Paramus, N.J.: Prentice Hall, 2004.

Newton, Harry, and Ray Horak. *Newton's Telecom Dictionary: Covering Telecommunications, Networking, Information Technology, the Internet, Fiber Optics, RFID, Wireless, and VoIP.* 21st ed. Gilroy, Calif.: CMP Books, 2005.

Paulson, Ed. *The Complete Communications Handbook,* 2d ed. Plano, Texas: Wordware Publishing, 1996.

COMPUTER-AIDED DESIGN (CAD) TECHNICIANS

"I do multiple-discipline drafting," says Gretchen Brough, a CAD drafter in Buffalo, New York. "I have to be able to work in all disciplines of drafting: electrical, structural, welding." Working in an office, sitting at a computer, Gretchen uses the program AutoCAD to draft an engineer's concept. This initial concept can find its way to Gretchen in various forms. "It can be anything from a very detailed sketch that he's drawn up on graph paper, to something he has sketched on a bar napkin."

Having worked as a drafter for several years, Gretchen has seen many changes in the work. She once used a drafting board, a parallel ruler, triangles, a compass, and other drafting tools, Gretchen now relies entirely on the computer. "I don't know of an engineering office that actually has drawing boards anymore," she says. "We have a few of them, but they're sitting in corners with a lot of paperwork piled on them."

What Does a CAD Technician Do?

Design and drafting are two steps needed to put engineering ideas on paper. The *designer* develops the concept; the *drafter* puts the concept into technical illustrations, which can be read by the people who actually make the product.

Until about 20 years ago, most designing and drafting were done by hand—with a pen or pencil and paper, on a drafting board. To make a circle, you used a compass. To draw straight lines and the correct angles, you used a straight-edge and triangle, or other tools. With every change required before a design was right, it was "back to the drawing board" to get out your eraser, sharpen up your pencil, and revise the drawing.

Everybody did it this way, whether the design was simple or complex: automobiles, hammers, printed circuit boards, utility piping, highways, buildings.

Some design and drafting work is still done by hand, but the days of the "pencil drafter" are pretty much over. Computer-aided design and drafting

Definition
Agricultural food and processing engineers design processes and systems for the efficient manufacturing and processing of food products.

Alternative Job Titles
CAD specialists
CADD technicians
Computer designer/drafters

High School Subjects
Art
Computer science
Mathematics

Personal Skills
Artistic
Mechanical/manipulative

Salary Range
$27,250 to $39,630 to $71,370+

Minimum Educational Level
Some postsecondary training

Certification or Licensing
Voluntary

Outlook
More slowly than the average

DOT
003

GOE
02.08.03

NOC
2253

O*NET-SOC
17-3011301, 17-3011.02, 17.3012, 17-3013.00

(CAD or CADD) systems are the tool of choice in industries that require detailed drawings, because they greatly speed and simplify the designer's and drafter's work. CAD systems do more than just let the operator "draw" the technical illustration on the screen. They add the speed and power of computer processing, plus software with technical information that eases the designer's or drafter's tasks. CAD systems make complex mathematical calculations, spot problems, offer advice, and provide a wide range of other assistance.

CAD technicians operate the CAD systems. They may do designing, or drafting, or both. The most basic CAD technician work is similar to data entry:

simply entering the drafting instructions given by the industrial designer or engineer. With more training and experience, the technician may also design. Exactly what the CAD technician does depends on the industry, the company, and the CAD technician's know-how. CAD technicians usually specialize in one industry, such as aeronautics or automobile manufacturing, or on one part of design, such as new product development, structural mechanics, or piping.

Like everything else in the computer world, CAD systems have evolved a lot over the last 20 years. The first ones were large, mainframe-based, and cost up to hundreds of thousands of dollars. Commands could only be entered at the keyboard.

Since then, lower-cost, PC-based CAD systems have been introduced, permitting more companies to afford the technology. Now, almost all CAD systems are PC-based. "Mac is used, too, but mainly for educational purposes," says John Jacobs, former coordinator of the drafting technology program at Belleville Area College (now Southwestern Illinois College), in Belleville, Illinois. "There's not much technical software for the Mac yet."

Most CAD systems look a lot like home or office computer systems. They may have bigger and better color displays, though, and more input devices, such as a light pen, which is touched to the screen to indicate a command, or a programmable "puck," which looks like a mouse. Output devices include printers and plotters that make oversized prints (up to six feet wide). CAD workstations also may be networked so drawings can be passed via computer among engineers, technicians, and supervisors.

As for software, different packages meet the needs of different industries and projects—from chemical, automotive, civil, structural, electrical, and other engineering to clothing and furniture design. The software may provide simple drawing aids all the way up to sophisticated modeling tools that turn flat drawings into three-dimensional images.

Increasingly, the CAD technician who does more than just input others' instructions is most valued by employers. "It's like the word processing pools of years ago," says Peter Marks of Design Insight, a California design consulting firm that counts Ford and other large companies among its customers. "Back then, it probably seemed like a good idea to get a two-year degree to be a Wang system secretary. But those jobs just don't exist anymore. In the same way, it's just not a good idea for a CAD technician to be someone who only knows how to sit there and input. The best combination today is a

Lingo to Learn

AutoCAD   Brand name of one of the most widely used software packages for CAD systems.

Digitizer   A device for inputting existing drawings or sketches into the CAD system; a mouse or other device is pulled over the drawing, and the CAD system "reads" the drawing and turns it into electronic data.

Entities   Basic drawing elements such as lines, points, and arcs.

Graphics card   An electronic circuit board that, linked with the display device, determines the display resolution, palette, and number of colors.

Layers   Typical structure for CAD software; it allows the user to work on just one element of the drawing at a time—such as the piping, or the electrical layout, or the HVAC (heating, venting, air-conditioning) system layout, etc.

Modeling   Creating a three-dimensional drawing from a flat drawing.

Plotter   An output device used for making a print from a CAD system.

Simulation   A test involving putting a product under specific conditions to test its performance or properties, such as durability.

blend of two things: some demonstrated aptitude on the CAD system and expertise gained over time in a specific area, like plastic molding. The CAD technician who can bring specific knowledge to the job is going to be the 'value added' employee."

What Is It Like to Be a CAD Technician?

Gretchen Brough uses CAD software to draft the concepts of a variety of different engineers and designers. "A structural engineer may bring in concept sketches for the foundations of a building," she says. "I usually get schematics from the electrical engineer." This kind of multidisciplinary work keeps Gretchen

> ## To Be a Successful CAD Technician, You Should . . .
>
> ○ be interested in the mechanical design or structure of things
> ○ like math, technical drawing, computer graphics, and engineering ideas
> ○ have an eye for detail and a passion for getting the "little things" right
> ○ like to work at the computer for long periods of time
> ○ enjoy sharing your work with others and discussing design points

from getting bored. "I took all the disciplines of drafting when I was in college," she says. "I decided that I would try to maintain ability, remain conversant with all the disciplines of drafting rather than specialize." To develop these multidisciplinary skills, Gretchen worked for many temporary services, filling in wherever needed. She also hired on with consulting engineers who took on different kinds of projects.

Gretchen works in an office and uses AutoCAD software for her work. "It's still probably the most popular CAD software package in the country," she says. "It has been for quite awhile. I think there are better CAD software packages, but AutoCAD has been around for so long and used by so many people, that it's still the most popular." The introduction of the computer to drafting work was the biggest change Gretchen has seen in the career over the last 20 years. "Starting from the mid- to late-1980s, there was a major migration in the small- to medium-sized businesses switching over from the drawing board to CAD. At this point, I would assume there are plenty of architects who still use a drawing board, but I can't imagine too many others still do." Though the program once required a digitizing pad, now the only peripheral equipment required is a mouse. "Everything's on screen, as a result of Windows."

To draw someone's design concept, Gretchen must realize spatial relationships and picture objects in her mind that she has never seen before. "When someone's design concept is only in their head, you have to pick the idea out of there and off the sheet of paper they gave you, and you have to draw it in such

a way that somebody can build it. You have to be able to picture something that doesn't exist." These plans could lead to anything from a crescent wrench to a battleship. "You have to be a little bit of a frustrated artist to enjoy drafting," she says.

You have to be a little bit of a frustrated artist to enjoy drafting.

Gretchen finds that the most demanding kind of drafting is that which involves some design as well. "I'm not an engineer, so design is difficult for me. I don't know the operating parameters, and the specifications necessary for those parameters. I always have to have an engineer check my work."

Richard Shenberger is a CAD technician at the MGM Grand Hotel and Casino in Las Vegas, Nevada. He draws floor plans that show the layout of conventions, meetings, and other events held at the hotel. These plans are then submitted to the fire marshal for approval by the county. "We begin with the drawing request form that's completed by the convention services manager," says Richard. "The manager is handling a particular group of people who want to come and have a convention in our conference center." From the form, Richard can tell which rooms and what types of seating are needed. "I draw a floor plan of the room showing where all those tables and chairs would be located, depicting aisles and dimensions for fire marshal approval purposes." Copies of the drawings are also submitted to the clients for their approval.

"Everything is drawn full scale in the computer," Richard says. "Our plots are such that typically what we submit to the fire marshal is 1/16 of an inch equals one foot." One thing Richard likes about the work is being able to see the concrete results of his efforts in the form of a final plan. But he also points out that CAD technicians are subject to eyestrain and carpal tunnel syndrome from the degree of computer work.

Do I Have What It Takes to Be a CAD Technician?

Technical drawings range from the simple to the extremely complex, but all must be exactly right.

Therefore, CAD technicians must be patient, methodical, and have a passion for getting the "little things" right. If you are fascinated by things like architectural blueprints, diagrams of machines or engines, even maps, this might be the line of work for you.

"The thing I've had the most trouble with over the years," Gretchen says, "is the fact that when you finish a drawing it's not done. It's never going to be done. There are always going to be revisions. You may revise a drawing six or seven times before it goes to construction. Even then, as-built is going to be different than construction drawing. You generate an original drawing, then for years there will be revisions to that drawing. Literally years."

With increasing responsibilities, CAD technicians must be good problem solvers, think logically and analytically, and help improve the designs they work on. Good communication skills are vital, because CAD technicians often interact with engineers or designers, fellow technicians, and supervisors. Though it's not necessary to be a programmer or other computer whiz, you clearly can't be computer-shy in this job.

How Do I Become a CAD Technician?

Gretchen became interested in drafting while in high school, where she took courses in mechanical and architectural drawing. She eventually worked with land surveyors, then completed an associate's degree program. Richard trained himself on an early version of AutoCAD back in 1982. Over the years he took classes periodically to build up his proficiency with the program. Richard recommends that high school students take mathematics courses and anything related to drafting. "It also certainly doesn't hurt to gain a good understanding of construction methods," he says, "so when you get down to talking about walls and ceilings, you can converse with some knowledge. So a shop course would be good."

EDUCATION

High School

Some jobs are still available for those with a high school diploma, but not as many as in the past. The positions also may be the most basic; additional

In-depth

CAM and CAE

Closely related to computer-aided design and drafting (CAD or CADD) are computer-aided manufacturing (CAM) and computer-assisted engineering (CAE). CAM uses computers to determine which manufacturing processes and equipment are needed to make the product. It also monitors and controls the automated manufacturing of the product, guiding the factory's robots, automated measuring machines, computer-controlled machine tools, and other automated systems. CAD and CAM are linked in some operations, with information flowing back and forth via the computers.

Computer assisted engineering (CAE) is another related field. It includes using computers to test and analyze various properties (such as weight, strength, durability, and other features) of a product or other design under specific conditions (simulation). Those doing CAE usually are engineers with four-year degrees.

Computer integrated manufacturing (CIM) can wrap everything—design, manufacturing, assembly, sales, and other steps—into one combined process.

training will help the CAD technician qualify to take on greater responsibilities.

Whatever route you choose, getting a good background in technical subjects in high school will pay off later. Algebra, geometry, and trigonometry, plus physics, are ideal. Other helpful classes include machine shop and electronics.

Postsecondary Training

One- and two-year programs in CAD design/drafting and technology are available at technical schools and community colleges. Southwestern Illinois College,

FYI

The following is a sample list of ADDA-certified drafting programs:

- architectural/CADD
- architectural drafting
- architectural engineering technology
- CADD
- computer-aided design drafting technology
- design drafter
- design and drafting technology
- drafter
- drafting/CAD technology
- drafting technology
- drafting technology industrial management
- electro-mechanical/CADD
- engineering designer
- engineering design technology
- engineering drafting technician
- mechanical design engineering technology
- mechanical design technology
- mechanical drafting
- mechanical drafting and design technology
- mechanical technology

a little exploring to find the program that best suits your interests. There can be classes in electronics, for example, for things like designing and drafting printed circuit boards. Some programs focus on specific areas, such as architectural engineering technology. A broader two-year program might include courses in drafting and basic engineering topics such as hydraulics, pneumatics, and electronics; courses in computer programming, systems, and equipment; product design; industrial and architectural drafting; and computer peripheral equipment and storage. Some may also require the student to complete courses in technical writing, communications, social sciences, and the humanities.

Good sources of information about programs are local technical schools and community colleges, as well as trade associations such as the Society of Manufacturing Engineers (SME). The American Design Drafting Association (ADDA) has developed a list of over 70 certified schools, available from the association, with design/drafting curricula that meet ADDA standards.

After a two-year associate's degree, any further degree will be in another field. "There is no four-year degree for drafting," John says. Four-year programs of interest might include engineering, marketing, computer programming, or other areas. "Another possible path is technical education," John says.

CERTIFICATION OR LICENSING

Certification for CAD technicians is voluntary. Certification in drafting is available from ADDA, which invites members and nonmembers regardless of formal training or experience to participate in its Drafter Certification Program. The certification process includes taking a 90-minute test of basic drafting skills.

Licensing requirements vary. According to Rachel Howard, former executive director of ADDA, licensing may be required for specific projects, such as in a construction project when the client (such as a hotel) requires it.

INTERNSHIPS AND VOLUNTEERSHIPS

Drafting-related jobs can sometimes be found through internships, and many future employers will look favorably on applicants with this kind of experience. Jobs relating to other engineering fields, such as electronics or mechanics, may be available, and they offer the student an opportunity to become

for example, offers a two-year associate's degree or a one-year certificate. "But 99 percent of our graduates opt for the associate's degree," says John Jacobs, "it gives them a competitive advantage." Though they will specialize once they're out of school, students who go through Southwestern's program get a background in CAD work in eight basic areas: basic drafting, machine drawing, architecture, civil drawing (with an emphasis on highways), process piping, electrical, electrical instrumentation, HVAC, and plumbing.

Different schools emphasize different things in their curricula, though, so it is a good idea to do familiar with the kind of workplace in which he or she may later be employed as a technician.

Who Will Hire Me?

Drafting is so prevalent in so many areas that it would be impossible to list all of the opportunities here. However, a basic list of industries in which CAD technicians might work include the electrical, electronics, automotive, aeronautic, civil, mechanical, oil and gas, furniture, and construction fields.

Specialties are plentiful and interesting. *Aeronautical drafting*, for example, involves technical drawings for airplanes, missiles, and related equipment like launch mechanisms. A *commercial drafter* might create the technical illustrations for a store layout. *Furniture detailers* create the drawings used for the manufacture of chairs, sofas, and other furniture. *Oil and gas drafters* prepare technical plans and drawings for layout, construction, and operation of oil fields, refineries, and pipeline systems. There are also *technical illustrators* for textbooks and other printed materials who create drawings to show things such as assembly, installation, operation, maintenance, and repair of machines, tools, and other equipment.

Types of firms that use CAD technicians include construction companies, architectural firms, machinery manufacturers, engineering firms, electronics firms, electrical manufacturers, transportation manufacturers, communications manufacturers, consultants, high-technology companies, utility companies, and government agencies.

Where Can I Go from Here?

The next step up from CAD technician might be designer, lead designer, or supervisor; opportunities will vary, depending on the company. Beyond designer/drafter positions, one possibility is to go back to school, earn a four-year degree, and become an engineer. You might choose to stay within the same field. If you were working as an electrical or electronics CAD technician, for example, you might go on to become an electrical engineer. Engineering programs sometimes require a class or two in CAD, but most engineers are not extensively trained in this technology.

"A lot of the industry is going toward 3D images and solid modeling," Gretchen says. "That's

ADVANCEMENT POSSIBILITIES

Chief design drafters (utilities) oversee architectural, electrical, and structural drafters in drawing designs of indoor and outdoor facilities and structures of electrical or gas power plants and substations.

Controls designers design and draft systems of electrical, hydraulic, and pneumatic controls for machines and equipment, such as arc welders, robots, conveyors, and programmable controllers.

Data processing managers oversee the gathering, storage, and retrieval of some type of computer data.

Electronics design engineers design and develop electronic components, equipment, systems, and products, applying knowledge of electronic theory, design, and engineering; may use CAE and CAD systems to formulate and test electronic designs.

Lead designers head CAD design/drafting departments or operations; responsible for supervising and training other CAD designers/drafters.

Integrated circuit layout designers design the layout for integrated circuits (IC) according to engineering specifications using CAD systems and utilizing knowledge of electronics, drafting, and IC design rules.

Printed circuit designers design and draft layout for printed circuit boards (PCBs) according to engineering specifications, utilizing knowledge of electronics, drafting, and PCB design.

something I'm going to have to go back and learn. You do have to keep up with upgrades in the software, and upgrades in the kinds of design-concept drawings the industry wants to see."

CAD technicians may first handle routine assignments, such as copying drawings or making minor revisions, and work up to helping to design and build equipment. Others get involved in concept and design right away. Titles for CAD technician positions include CAD specialist, computer designer, computer drafter, CAD designer, and CAD drafter.

Rather than becoming engineers, some technicians who continue their education and earn a bachelor's degree may become data processing managers or systems or manufacturing analysts. Other routes for advancement include becoming a sales representative for a design firm or for a company selling CAD, CAM, or CAE software, manufacturing services, or equipment. It also may be possible to become an independent contractor for companies using or manufacturing CAD or CAM equipment.

What Are the Salary Ranges?

According to the U.S. Department of Labor, in 2003 drafters had annual median earnings of between $39,630 and $46,120, depending on the type of drafting. The highest paid 10 percent of architectural and civil drafters earned $56,600 annually, while those in the lowest paid 10 percent earned $24,860. Electrical and electronic drafters in the highest paid 10 percent earned $71,370, and the lowest paid 10 percent earned $27,250.

A 2005 review of salaries nationwide by Salary. com found that entry-level CAD drafters earned between $31,158 and $41,148, with a median salary of $35,695. Those with four years or more experience had a salary range of $34,988 to $44,480 with a median of $39,405 annually.

Some technicians with special skills, extensive experience, or added responsibilities may earn more. Different industries also pay differently; a drafter working with motor vehicles may have a higher salary than a drafter working with fabricated structural metal products. Benefits usually include insurance, paid vacations, pension plans, and sometimes stock-purchase plans.

What Is the Job Outlook?

According to the *Occupational Outlook Handbook*, employment of drafters is expected to grow more slowly than the average for all occupations through 2012. CAD has made drafting more efficient,

requiring fewer technicians. Overall, demand is best for job applicants with a two-year associate's degree. As for specific jobs, opportunities are better in some industries than others; the healthier the industry, the healthier the prospects for the CAD technician.

In 2002 drafters held about 216,000 jobs. Of those positions, half were held by architectural and civil drafters, one third were held by mechanical drafters, and the remaining jobs were held by electrical and electronic drafters. Manufacturers tend to like CAD because it helps boost productivity. There also is continuing interest in computer-aided manufacturing (CAM), with which CAD can be linked.

While some say industrial designers and engineers will one day handle all design and drafting steps themselves, right now that does not seem too likely. Currently, most engineering programs have just basic CAD training, if any. For now, technicians can make themselves most valuable to their employers by developing as much expertise in their industry as possible and contributing ideas, in addition to keeping up their CAD operator skills.

According to John Jacobs, demand for Southwestern Illinois College graduates seems to be in the civil, electrical, and mechanical areas. "Civil includes a lot of different areas, but especially highways," John says. Demand for the latter is up right now in many parts of the country, including Illinois, that need to rebuild their aging infrastructure, he notes. "When the tax dollars are there, these kinds of projects get under way," John says.

In addition to following your interests, prospective CAD technicians should take a hard look at their market and see what types of local companies use CAD and are hiring. "A lot of students like architecture when they first start the program, but that profession is pretty full right now," John says. He notes that some areas, like Belleville, don't even require drafted plans for building new houses. "By the time they graduate, students know they have to go where the jobs are."

How Do I Learn More?

PROFESSIONAL ORGANIZATIONS

The following organizations can provide information about careers, certification, and educational programs:
American Design Drafting Association
105 East Main Street

Newbern, TN 38059
731-627-0802
http://www.adda.org

Institute of Electrical and Electronic Engineers
Three Park Avenue, 17th Floor
New York, NY 10016-5997
212-419-7900
http://www.ieee.org

Society of Manufacturing Engineers
One SME Drive
Dearborn, MI 48121
313-271-1500
http://www.sme.org

BIBLIOGRAPHY

The following is a sampling of materials relating to the professional concerns and development of CAD technicians:

Besterfield, Dale H., and Robert E. O'Hagan. *Technical Sketching With an Introduction to CAD: For Engineers, Technologists, and Technicians*. 2d ed. Paramus, N.J. Prentice Hall, 1997.

Chang, Tien-Chien. *Computer-Aided Manufacturing*. Paramus, NJ: Prentice Hall, 1997.

Goetsch, David L. *Structural, Civil, and Pipe Drafting for CAD Technicians*. Albany, N.Y.: Thomson Delmar Learning, 2002.

Jeffries, Alan and David Madsen. *Architectural Drafting and Design*. 4th ed. Albany, N.Y.: Thomson Delmar Learning, 2000.

Rehg, James A., and Henry W. Kraebber. *Computer Integrated Manufacturing*. 3d ed. Paramus, N.J.: Prentice Hall, 2004.

COMPUTER AND OFFICE MACHINE SERVICE TECHNICIANS

As a field technician for IBM, Leesa Hyde is on call 24 hours. Calls can come in the middle of the night and on weekends, and these can often be her most challenging assignments. She received a page one early Saturday morning: a server was shipped by a third party to an IBM customer. The company had promised one type of system but couldn't build it to specifications. So the machine was delivered not working, along with the parts needed to get it operating. Following a call, Leesa is required to be on site within four hours. She arrived with her laptop, ready to work with the server hardware, prepared for a fairly routine break-fix.

"I was faced with about 20 million parts," she says. To add to the difficulties, flaws in the written documentation didn't explain everything she needed. "It took me and another technician and our top gun in the area 15 hours on a Saturday to get that thing up and running. We could have built five other servers in that time."

What Does a Computer and Office Machine Service Technician Do?

Businesses make use of many different kinds of computers and machines in order to perform normal office tasks more efficiently and accurately. Like household appliances and cars, many of these machines require regular preventive maintenance. And, of course, like all machines, they develop problems or break down completely, often creating emergency situations in offices that depend entirely on their equipment running well. *Computer and office machine service technicians* are responsible for ensuring that machines are functioning properly at all times.

Most technicians, or *servicers* as they are sometimes called, basically perform the same duties: they install, calibrate, clean, maintain, troubleshoot,

and repair machines. The main differences among them lie in the particular machines they are qualified to work on and the nature and scope of the business they work for.

If they work in a specialized repair shop, technicians might be experts in fixing one or two types of machines, like manual and electric typewriters, for example. Or, they might know how to repair all types of basic office machines like calculators, adding machines, printers, and fax machines. Other repair specialties include *mail-processing equipment servicers* and *cash register servicers*.

As the use of computers in business continues to grow, an increasing number of technicians are discovering that they can make more money and

---

Definition
Computer and office machine service technicians install, test, calibrate, clean, adjust, and repair office machines and computer terminals and other computer-related machines.

Alternative Job Titles
Bench technicians/engineers
Computer and office machine servicers
Computer service technicians
Field service technicians/engineers

High School Subjects
Computer science
Technical/shop

Personal Skills
Mechanical/manipulative
Technical/scientific

Salary Range
$20,700 to $33,950 to $53,470

Minimum Educational Level
Some postsecondary training

Certification or Licensing
Recommended

Outlook
As fast as the average

DOT
633

GOE
05.02.01

NOC
2242

O*NET-SOC
49-2011.01, 49-2011.02, 49-2011.03

---

have more job security if they are well trained in the maintenance and repair of computers and computer peripherals. Many large computer companies provide a service contract with the purchase of their product.

Computer service technicians are employed by computer companies to fulfill the obligations of the service contract. They install and set up computer equipment when it first arrives at the client's business. They follow up installation with regular preventive maintenance visits, adjusting and cleaning mechanical pieces. In addition, one technician is always on call in case equipment fails. They know how to run diagnostic tests with specialized equipment in order to determine the nature and extent of the problem. They are usually trained in replacing semiconductor chips, circuit boards, and other hardware components. If they cannot fix the computer on site, they bring it back to their employer's service area.

Some technicians are employed in the maintenance department of large companies. They generally have a good working knowledge of mechanics and electronics and then are trained further by the company to work with the specific equipment the business uses most. In-house training is often provided by industrial and manufacturing companies as well as those corporations that depend on big machinery like mail sorters and check processors.

Employed either by a specialty repair shop, machine manufacturer, or product-specific service company, *field service representatives* are technicians who travel to the client's workplace to do maintenance and repairs. Their duties include following a predetermined schedule of routine maintenance. For example, they might change the toner, clean the optic parts, and make mechanical adjustments in photocopiers and printers. They also must make time each day to respond to incoming requests for emergency service. Even though supervisors are usually responsible for prioritizing maintenance and repair requests, juggling the variety and number of responsibilities can be hectic. In addition, technicians are required to keep detailed written explanations of all service provided so that future problems can be dealt with more effectively.

Sometimes machines need major repairs that are too complicated and messy to be handled in the office or workplace. These machines are taken to a repair shop or company service area to be worked on by *bench servicers,* that is, technicians who work at their employer's location.

Lingo to Learn

Bench servicer A repairer who works exclusively in his or her company's shop area and does not make house calls.

Calibrate To adjust precisely according to specifications.

Computer peripherals Any equipment linked to a computer hard drive such as magnetic tape drivers, disk drives, terminals or screens, printers, and modems.

Diagnostic tests Tests run on various mechanical and electronic machines to determine the nature and extent of a particular problem.

Field service representative A repairer who makes service calls at the client's business.

Troubleshoot To problem solve in a step-by-step fashion, checking first for the simplest causes and moving up to the more complex.

Some very experienced computer and office machine servicers open their own repair shops. Often, these entrepreneurs find it necessary to offer service for a wide range of equipment in order to be successful, particularly in areas where competition is tight. To further supplement their income, they might start selling certain products and offering service contracts on them. Business owners have the added responsibility of normal business duties, such as bookkeeping and advertising.

What Is It Like to Be a Computer and Office Machine Service Technician?

Joel Lutenberg is a personal computer (PC) and PC network technician at a government agency—the New York City Human Resources Administration. "I get calls from computer users throughout the main building," he says, "and I assist them with various hardware or software problems with their computers. That could be anything from someone not being able to access their e-mail to a hardware problem such as a power supply in a computer not working."

Joel is stationed in an office, where he reads manuals and studies software until a service call comes in. The number of calls per day ranges from four to 15. When he receives a call, he goes to the PC in question and diagnoses the problem. "A lot of people," Joel says, "when they're at their computers, they're so flustered and nervous, they don't know where to start. So you have to ask them, 'What exactly is the problem?' Once you've found out exactly what's wrong, you isolate the problem and try different methods of solving it. If one method doesn't solve it, you try another, and by using these different methods, you're eliminating possibilities."

To diagnose the problem, Joel relies on his own experience and knowledge of computers. In some situations, Joel may need to contact the technical support of the company that manufactures the PC or peripheral device (printer, scanner, etc.). The problem may lie in something as simple as the user not typing in the proper password, or there may be a major component in the computer that needs replacing. Joel doesn't make the replacements himself, because the agency doesn't have a supply of parts. In the event that the PC needs a new power supply, memory chip, or disk drive, Joel contacts the agency's private PC contractor. The contractor sends a technician to replace the part.

"Every computer technician should have a little tool set of screwdrivers and basic tools," Joel says, "because you're going to have to open up computers and printers and other peripherals. A can of compressed air helps clean out dust and debris that accumulates inside a printer or a computer."

One of Joel's favorite aspects of the work is the feeling of reward he gets when he is able to get a PC back into action. "You gain a lot of respect," he says, "people look to you as a knowledgeable person, and a skilled person." But sometimes Joel finds that people expect technicians to know PCs inside and out. "For example, they're going to think you know all there is to know about Microsoft Word and Excel and Access and the Internet. And they're going to come to you with all sorts of intricate questions about software. Of course, very few people know every single thing about every software package. Also, people expect you to know about all the electronic items, to know everything about phones and photocopiers." Overall, however, Joel appreciates the work environment. He works a regular 40-hour week with occasional overtime and receives excellent benefits by working for the city.

Leesa Hyde works out in the field as a technician for IBM. "Any machine that IBM builds is covered by a manufacturer's warranty," Leesa says. "Those are our contracts." Leesa covers several contracts, responding to service calls that come in over a pager. After receiving a page, she is required to contact the customer within one hour. "Most of the time we have to be on site within four hours. We have to have it fixed within eight." Leesa works exclusively with servers—the computers that run businesses. "A lot of times we replace systems boards or, depending on their contract, we build their software, or we load software. If they need to create adapter cards or need anything replaced, we'll go in and do that, and build configurations from their drives."

When out on an assignment, Leesa takes along a laptop provided by IBM. "With your laptop, you're able to access the IBM Web site which has every file or any update you need." Leesa is on call, which can mean making service calls in the middle of the night. The Gap stores, for example, use IBM servers to run all the cash registers. If a server is down, then the clerks cannot ring up purchases or run credit cards.

Leesa works about 55 hours a week, and considers the unusual hours to be a downside to the work. "Because these are servers," she explains, "most people don't want to shut them down during the 8-to-5 business hours."

Do I Have What It Takes to Be a Computer and Office Machine Service Technician?

Computer and office machine service technicians should have a solid grasp of the basics of mechanics, electronics, photography, and computers. This foundational knowledge is important for several reasons. First of all, it allows the technician to handle simple repairs easily. Second, it provides the background necessary for further training on more complicated machinery. A technician cannot learn the intricacies of a mail sorter, for example, if he or she does not already understand basic mechanics. Third, such knowledge adds to an individual's willingness to learn about new equipment and allows the individual to be flexible about the kinds of machines he or she can work on.

Technicians are often those who have long been interested in figuring out how things work and who have the manual dexterity to tinker around with gadgets, tools, and household machines. Computers and office machines often need repairs in spots that are hard to get to, where the parts and tools used are small, even tiny. "Like most teenagers, I grew up loving video games," Joel says. "This is a job for anyone who has an interest in electronics."

Joel emphasizes that a technician must be prepared to deal with an ever-changing field. "You've got to be reading the magazines that tell about new software and the tricks in software and hardware."

As is the case in most jobs, technicians should have solid communication skills. They should be able to explain technical problems to a wide variety of people, from people who have no understanding of how something works, to people who actually design certain machines. It can be a delicate issue and actually more important than one might think; companies that specialize in service lose customers if technicians make them feel stupid or do not take the time to carefully explain what is going on. "You'll do well if you're able to get along with all your customers," Leesa says. "I give my cell phone number out to a lot of customers instead of making them go through IBM. If people like you, they're not going to give you a bad time."

You'll do well if you're able to get along with all your customers.

How Do I Become a Computer and Office Machine Service Technician?

Leesa went to school and studied systems administration. Though she studied software, she now works primarily with hardware. She went to work for IBM upon graduating. Joel received a bachelor's degree in business then went to work at the agency as a caseworker. "While doing that," he says, "I went to a local city college and I took a certificate program that they offered in computer technology." Upon completing the program, he learned of the job opening in the computer systems division of the agency.

> **TO BE A SUCCESSFUL COMPUTER AND OFFICE MACHINE SERVICE TECHNICIAN, YOU SHOULD . . .**
>
> ○ have superior manual dexterity
> ○ be able to follow complex written instructions and diagrams
> ○ like to learn about new machines and technology
> ○ work well alone, without direct supervision
> ○ be able to communicate difficult technical ideas effectively to people with different levels of experience

EDUCATION

High School

A high school diploma is the minimum requirement for getting a job as a computer and office machine service technician. Traditional high school courses like mathematics, physics, and other laboratory-based sciences can provide a strong foundation for understanding basic mechanical and electronic principles. English and speech classes can help boost both written and verbal communication skills.

More specialized courses offered at the high school level, such as electronics, electricity, automotive/engine repair, or computer applications, are a very good source of practice in manual aptitude. Any other courses focusing on the use of flowcharts and schematic reading are also beneficial. In addition, any experience with audiovisual equipment is a plus. Opportunities for such experience might be found in school theatrical productions or any other kind of multimedia presentation.

Postsecondary Training

In smaller repair shops that do basic work on familiar machines, special training may not be required, given that the applicant has a good general knowledge of mechanics and electronics. For any more specialized positions, one or two years of courses in mechanics and electronics from a community college or vocational or technical school is recommended.

FYI

The Computing Technology Industry Association Workforce Study found a great shortage of skilled Information Technology service and support workers. The study estimates that 268,740 (10 percent) of IT service and support positions are unfulfilled, resulting in $4.5 billion a year in lost worker productivity.

Information Week reported that in 2004 one in every 50 jobs created in the United States were with companies offering computer systems design and other related services. IT services companies added about 49,000 positions.

For those individuals interested in specializing in computer and peripheral repair, courses designed around computer technology, like microelectronics and computer design, should be selected. Some technical schools already offer specialized degrees in computer technology. It is important to note that computer repair positions usually require the completion of at least an associate's degree, whereas office machine repair positions might only require some formal education in electronics. The additional education required of computer technicians includes courses in elementary computer programming and the physics of heat and light.

Even with a degree in hand, new employees will receive a heavy dose of on-the-job training. From the employer's point of view, the degree proves that the new employee has the ability to do the work, but he or she still needs to be trained specifically on the machines most used by the company. Training programs vary greatly in duration and intensity depending on the employer and the nature of the position. Training courses may be self-study or held in organized classrooms. Generally, they will include some degree of hands-on instruction.

Keeping up with technological advances is extremely important for technicians. In fact, anyone thinking about this career is advised to be prepared for the stress involved in working with such rapidly changing technology. Technicians are expected to participate in seminars and workshops offered at regular intervals by the employer, a machine manufacturer, or outside service companies.

Another way technicians keep up is by reading detailed brochures and service manuals on new equipment. They also read a variety of magazines and newsletters on electronics and mechanical devices.

CERTIFICATION OR LICENSING

Certification as a computer and office machine service technician is not mandatory to enter the field, but the International Society of Certified Electronics Technicians and the Electronics Technicians Association both offer a voluntary certification program. Individuals can take exams in order to be certified in fields such as computer, industrial, and commercial equipment, and audio and radar system repair. Those technicians with less than four years' experience can take an associate's test, while those with more can become Certified Electronics Technicians.

Other voluntary certification exists for individuals who are specialized computer technicians. The Computing Technology Industry Association offers a variety of certifications for those in the Information Technology industry, including "A+" certification for service technicians. The Institute for Certification of Computer Professionals (ICCP) offers certification to computer professionals under the titles of Certified Computing Professional (CCP) and Associate Computer Professional (ACP).

SCHOLARSHIPS AND GRANTS

There are no scholarships or grants offered uniquely to individuals wishing to pursue education for a career in computer and office machine service repair. However, vocational and technical schools have financial aid offices that disburse, among other types of aid, corporate scholarships to qualified students. Contact the financial aid office of prospective schools to find out about this type of opportunity. In addition, employers often have tuition reimbursement programs if educational courses benefit office operations. Check with the personnel or benefits office of current or prospective employers. Professional organizations often have information regarding scholarship programs as well.

In-depth

Office Machines over Time

The history of office machines can be traced as far back as ancient Babylonia and the invention of the abacus, a manual calculating device that is considered an ancestor of the computer.

Today's office machines stem from inventions of mechanical calculators in the 17th century, when French mathematician and philosopher Blaise Pascal developed the first such tool. Pascal's digital machine could perform addition and subtraction. American inventor William Burroughs developed the first truly practical adding machine in 1894.

The typewriter's history dates to the nineteenth century, although at this time many cumbersome typing machines were as big as pianos, and others resembled clocks. By the 1870s the Remington Company was producing much more practical machines. Thomas Edison invented the first electrically operated typewriter in 1872, and by the 1930s, such machines were being used in offices.

The computer is the most recently engineered office machine. The first experimental versions of modern computers were built during the 1940s. Some early computers used as many as 50,000 vacuum tubes, were very large, and required huge amounts of electricity.

Technical improvements made during the 1950s led to the first commercial computers. Their manufacturers leased them to users instead of selling them. By the late 1950s and early 1960s, the transistor was developed. It gradually took the place of vacuum tubes and helped make computers smaller, more reliable, and less expensive.

In the late 1960s the introduction of integrated circuitry made possible the development of minicomputers, which were smaller and cheaper but just as powerful as their predecessors.

The second phase of the computer revolution began in the early 1970s when the microprocessor became the heart of the modern computer. The discovery of how to store information on a tiny silicon chip (approximately .03 by .03 inches in size) rapidly caused new developments. The silicon chip opened up many new uses for computers. In addition, its development greatly reduced the computer's cost and increased the number of computer applications. This in turn increased the need for computer service technicians—a need that is still growing.

INTERNSHIPS AND VOLUNTEERSHIPS

As is true for someone trying to break into any field, initial entry may be difficult. If you are still in high school, you may wish to get a summer or weekend job in a local repair shop. This experience will give you a feel for the variety of activities that go on there. Technical schools often have internship programs for students, offering off-quarter employment in various companies. Many of these internships turn into full-time jobs after graduation.

Another way you can practice your skills is to offer repair services around the neighborhood, repairing VCRs, TVs, tape recorders, etc. In this way, you can begin to develop expertise at just those skills that will later make you an excellent computer and office machine service technician.

Who Will Hire Me?

Most vocational and technical schools manage job placement offices. Placement offices work very closely with local companies that regularly recruit at those schools and so are generally successful in placing graduates in a job. To get an idea of how successful a school's graduates are at getting jobs, ask an admissions counselor for the school's placement statistics.

Approximately three of every five computer and office machine service technicians work for wholesalers of computers and/or office machines and for independent repair shops. This includes service divisions of large computer companies that offer maintenance to the client with the purchase of a computer system; it also includes service companies that sell maintenance contracts to new equipment buyers or leasers.

Others work for large companies that have enough equipment to justify employing a full-time maintenance and repair staff. Corporations that typically have in-house repair departments are insurance companies, financial institutions (particularly those involved in any aspect of credit card processing), and banks. Large factories, whose production depends on large machinery, also have in-house technicians. Still other technicians work for retail companies. Different branches of the military, as well as federal, state, and local governments, provide opportunities for employment as well.

Most computer technicians work for computer manufacturers, often located in geographical clusters like California's Silicon Valley, or the "Valley up North" (that is, Washington State, where the headquarters of Microsoft, Inc. is located). Some computer repair specialists work for maintenance firms, and others work for corporations whose complex network of computers requires a full-time computer technician.

Office machine technician positions may be found everywhere but are concentrated in cities or suburban office complexes. Individuals may look in the classified ads of major metropolitan newspapers and related magazines for job opportunities. In addition, many professional organizations publish newsletters and magazines that include job lists.

Where Can I Go from Here?

In a government agency, such as where Joel works, the earning potential is not as great as it would be in a private company. Joel is happy with his current workplace but would like to move into the better paying private sector. Leesa is looking to go into

marketing. She believes her experience with the machines will allow her an edge in actually selling them. "As I get older," she says, "I can't be running around the field forever."

Most computer and office machine service technicians start working on relatively simple machines and gradually become familiar with more and more complex machines as their experience increases. When they are trained in most of the equipment, they may be promoted to maintenance supervisor. Then, with demonstrated leadership and business skills, technicians may be promoted to managerial positions. Promotion to management often requires further education in business or engineering, and the job often entails more office work than repair work.

Another advancement route a technician can take is to become a sales representative for the company whose product he or she has had the most experience with. Technicians develop expert hands-on knowledge of particular machines and are thus often in a better position than anyone to advise potential buyers about important purchasing decisions.

Some technicians might aspire to owning their own businesses, which is also an option for advancement. Entrepreneurship is always risky and the responsibilities are great, but so are the potential rewards. Unless they have already determined a market niche, technicians usually find it necessary to branch out when they open their own repair shop in order to service a wide range of computers and office machines.

What Are the Salary Ranges?

According to the *Occupational Outlook Handbook*, computer, automated teller, and office machine repairers had median earnings of $33,950 annually in 2003, with those in the middle 50 percent earning between $26,220 and $43,230. The lowest paid 10 percent earned $20,700, while the highest paid 10 percent earned $53,470.

In general, computer technicians make the highest salaries among service technicians, but the lowest in the Information Technology industry. According to a 2004 *InformationWeek* survey, salaries for IT help desk professionals and PC technicians declined 10 percent and 9.5 percent, respectively. The median earnings for help desk professionals were $33,600, and PC technicians had median earnings of $35,300. According to the survey, the salary decline is due in part to the technology slowdown of previous years. Salaries are expected to increase as technology demand rises and the supply of qualified employees tightens.

The rule of thumb about salaries for technicians is this: The more complicated a machine, the higher the salary. Self-employed technicians of even simple office machines do, however, have a potential for excellent earnings. In addition, some technicians may work for a company that pays commission for sales of machines and supplies and thus may be able to supplement their incomes in that way.

What Is the Job Outlook?

According to the U.S. Department of Labor, employment of computer, automated teller, and office machine repairers is expected to grow about as fast as the average for all occupations through 2012. The key for individuals interested in this career: Keep up with technology and be flexible.

There will be demand in large corporations with in-house repair departments for well-rounded technicians, those who can maintain and repair both computers and office machines. Many office machines, such as digital copiers, are part of an office's computer network. Computer companies and service contractors will look for people with strong computer backgrounds, whether in education or professional experience. Interested individuals should make a habit of keeping up to date with technological advances.

The computer industry has proven to be a very volatile market; when sales are up, so are the number of employees hired by computer companies. But when sales are down, layoffs are numerous. If technicians are planning specializations in computer repair, they should be qualified in several different kinds of equipment. For example, instead of becoming an expert in maintaining and repairing only laser printers, or a particular brand of laser printers, a technician might want to learn about terminal screens, color photocopiers, CD-ROMs, and modems as well. This flexibility will give technicians the edge when jobs in computer companies are difficult to find.

Many opportunities in computer repair will continue to open up as long as computer sales remain

ADVANCEMENT POSSIBILITIES

Maintenance supervisors assign repairers to handle specific jobs when repair requests come into the office. They are in charge of a group of employees, fulfilling such administrative duties as verifying that repair records are kept in good order by each repairer and keeping track of hours spent on different machines. They help other repairers troubleshoot problems and might also have expertise in working on more technologically complicated and expensive machines.

Maintenance managers perform many of the same duties as supervisors but are usually in charge of a greater number of employees. They might also be responsible for deciding when a machine should be replaced, which new machines should be purchased, and how the office should be laid out in order to ensure ease of repair. In addition, they perform normal managerial functions such as preparing departmental budgets, interviewing, and hiring.

Computer and/or office machine sales representatives may get their start in computer and office machine repair because such experience provides them with a very solid understanding of particular machines. Their knowledge, as well as experience in explaining technical problems in easy-to-understand terms, gives them a head start in the active "selling" of a product that salespeople must develop.

steady or increase. Many computer companies offer service contracts with new purchases, and they need technicians to fulfill these contractual obligations. Businesses are relying much more on computers and the Internet in order to conduct daily business. These systems need to be installed and properly maintained.

How Do I Learn More?

PROFESSIONAL ORGANIZATIONS

The following are organizations that provide information on computer and office machine service technician careers, accredited schools, and employers:

Computing Technology Industry Association
1815 South Meyers Road, Suite 300
Oakbrook Terrace, IL 60181-5228
630-678-8300
info@comptia.org
http://www.comptia.org

Electronic Industries Alliance
2500 Wilson Boulevard
Arlington, VA 22201
703-907-7500
http://www.eia.org

Electronics Technicians Association International
Five Depot Street
Greencastle, IN 46135
800-288-3824
eta@eta-i.org
http://www.eta-sda.com

International Society of Certified Electronics Technicians
3608 Pershing Avenue
Fort Worth, TX 76107-4527

800-946-0201
http://www.iscet.org

Institute for Certification of Computing Professionals
2350 East Devon Avenue, Suite 115
Des Plaines, IL 60018-4610
800-843-8227
office@iccp.org
http://www.iccp.org

BIBLIOGRAPHY

The following is a sampling of materials relating to the professional concerns and development of computer and office machine technicians:

Bigelow, Stephen J. *Troubleshooting, Maintaining, and Repairing PCs.* 5th ed. Columbus, Ohio: Computing McGraw-Hill, 2001.

Eberts, Marjorie, Margaret Gisler, and Maria Olson. *Careers for Computer Buffs & Other Technological Types.* Lincolnwood, Ill.: VGM Career Horizons, 1999.

Henderson, Harry. *Career Opportunities in Computers and Cyberspace.* 2d ed. New York: Facts on File, 2004.

Rosenthal, Morris. *Build Your Own PC.* Columbus, Ohio: McGraw-Hill Professional Publishing, 2000.

Vaughn, Joan. *Computer Technician Career Starter.* New York: Learning Express, 1998.

COMPUTER NETWORK SPECIALISTS

‖‖

Though Joseph Phair is a computer network specialist, he is not working for a large business connecting computers in order for employees to exchange files and memos; Joseph's job is to keep an elementary school wired. Whether installing software and hardware to the computers in the classrooms, or monitoring computer use to ensure that the software and Internet are not being used improperly, Joseph trains teachers and students, and he keeps the network flowing smoothly.

"Teachers can be very difficult students," Joseph says. "They do exactly what they don't want their students to do. They come to training late, don't listen, work ahead without listening to directions, and they won't admit they don't understand something." Joseph finds that solving problems within the network can be much easier than dealing with the computer users that the network is designed to link together.

What Does a Computer Network Specialist Do?

Businesses and organizations choose to network, or connect, their computers for many different reasons. One important reason is so that numerous computer users can simultaneously access the same hardware, software, and other computer equipment like printers, modems, and fax machines. By networking such equipment, the business avoids having to purchase individual products for each user. For example, if a small business has four different computer terminals, all terminals might be able to share a single printer instead of having four of them. In addition, if the company maintains a database that is accessed by multiple users, it has to set up the system in such a way as to make the database, with its constant changes, available to everyone.

These networks can range in size from two computer terminals to hundreds and can operate with one or more of several different network servers or none at all. Each network is different and tailored to the needs of the business or large corporate

Definition
Computer network specialists administer computer networks so that they operate smoothly and consistently for high efficiency and productivity.

Alternative Job Titles
Computer network administrators
Computer network security specialists
Data communications analysts
Data recovery operators
Network programmers
System administrators

High School Subjects
Computer science
Mathematics

Personal Skills
Helping/teaching
Leadership/management

Salary Range
$67,017 to $76,175 to $90,500

Minimum Educational Level
Associate's degree

Certification or Licensing
Voluntary

Outlook
Much faster than the average

DOT
031

GOE
02.06.01

NOC
0213

O*NET-SOC
15-1071.00, 15-1081.00

department. And each network is invariably messy—problems come up often, employees have difficulties learning the system, passwords and file names are regularly changed, software is updated, backup files must be made, communications lines are broken and must be reestablished—the list can go on and on. *Computer network specialists* must know the network well enough to be able to handle all of these situations.

The specific job duties of a computer network specialist vary greatly depending on the size and structure of the company or department and on the kinds of network systems used. For example, in larger

Lingo to Learn

Application A software program that allows users to perform certain tasks like word processing and record keeping.

Backup Copies of computer files stored in a place other than the main work site. Used in case of an emergency.

Hardware The physical equipment inside a computer that makes it operate.

LAN (Local Area Network) A network that exists at one location, typically an office.

Network Collection of computers connected by wires, radio waves, or optical fibers so that they can communicate to share hardware, software, and files.

Operating system Software designed to mediate between hardware and user applications.

Server The centralized computer in a network that stores all programs and other information required to make networks function properly.

WAN (Wide Area Network) A network that includes remote sites in different buildings, cities, states, or countries.

companies the positions may be extremely well defined; they may employ one person for computer securities, one for network administration, one for data recovery, etc. In smaller companies or those departments in which networks are just being introduced, however, employers may hire one or two people to do everything.

Computer network administrators are responsible for adding and deleting files to the network server. The server is a centralized computer that stores, among other things, software applications used on a daily or regular basis by the network users. The files updated might include those for database, electronic mail, or word processing applications. Network administrators also handle printing jobs. They must tell the server where the printer is located and establish a printing queue, or line, designating which print jobs have priority. They might also tell the server to hold or change certain files once they reach the printing queue.

Network administrators might also be responsible for setting up user access. Since highly confidential and personal information can be stored on the network server, employees generally have access to only certain applications and files; the network administrator assigns each user or group of users access to the appropriate files and often makes up passwords to be used by each employee. The passwords protect the system from both internal and external computer spying.

Network security specialists often work in companies that make extensive use of computer networks. They are responsible for regulating user access to various computer files, monitoring file use, and updating security files. If an employee forgets his or her password, the network security specialist changes it to grant access. Network security specialists ensure that security measures are running accurately by tracking nonauthorized entries, reporting unauthorized users to management, and modifying files to correct the errors. They maintain employee information in the security files. They add new employees to the list, delete former employees, and make official name changes.

Data recovery operators are responsible for developing, implementing, and testing off-site systems that will continue to work in case of emergencies at the main office, such as power outages, fires, or floods. This task is very important because many businesses cannot operate at all without their computer networks. Some businesses, like insurance companies and banks, depend even more on their computer systems during emergencies. Data recovery operators must determine which hardware and software should be stored at the emergency site, which applications receive operating priority in case of an emergency, where to locate the emergency site, and which employees would be needed to run emergency operations. After testing the system they develop, they report the results to supervisors and management. Like network security specialists, they work primarily in larger companies.

Network control operators are in charge of all network communications, which usually operate over telephone lines or fiber-optic cables. If a user cannot get the computer to send his or her file to the appropriate place, he or she calls the network control operator for help. The control operator then explains to the employee the step-by-step procedure he or she should have followed to send the file. If the error is not an employee mistake, the network control operator attempts to diagnose the problem by making sure information stored in computer files is accurate, verifying that modems are functioning properly, or running noise tests on the phone lines with special equipment. Sometimes, the control operator must ask for outside help from the company who sold or manufactured the malfunctioning system.

Network control operators also keep records of the daily number of communications transactions made, the number and type of problems arising, and the actions taken to solve them. They might also train staff to use the communications systems efficiently and help coordinate or install communication lines.

What Is It Like to Be a Computer Network Specialist?

Joseph Phair works for a public school serving grades kindergarten through 12 in Rapid City, South Dakota. He is the technology coordinator for the school, repairing computer hardware, administering the computer network, recommending software purchases, and training the staff. His day starts by checking the mail server and the other servers to make sure there were no problems in the night. Throughout the day, he takes calls from teachers and staff with computer problems, while also monitoring network traffic. "I check where e-mails are going to and from," he says, "and monitor IP destinations. I'm the network police. I makes sure people aren't accessing noneducational resources." He doesn't have to monitor the online activity of students, however; that is accomplished with firewall software.

Joseph also provides training on hardware and software to teachers and staff, and repairs and maintains that hardware. "I diagnose the problem," he says about making repairs, "swap out the bad parts, send in for repair if necessary. I reinstall software." Joseph has found that trial and error is important in problem solving. "You have to first rule out the things that *are* working," he says. "It tends to pinpoint the problem easier. You shouldn't focus on what's not working."

When training the teachers, he is teaching them to use the student administrative program. This program allows for electronic grading and keeping attendance, and provides Internet and e-mail access. "All the teachers have computers in their classrooms connected to the network."

> ### TO BE A SUCCESSFUL COMPUTER NETWORK SPECIALIST, YOU SHOULD . . .
>
> ○ be organized and possess logic skills
> ○ understand basic computer principles and be willing to learn more complex skills as technology advances
> ○ enjoy challenges and solving problems
> ○ be able to patiently communicate complicated material in simple terms
> ○ be able to work well under pressure

The school is on a dual platform, using both Macintosh and Windows. The software Joseph works with includes Microsoft Office, a network e-mail program called QuickMail Pro, a student administrative program called SASI, and a variety of educational programs used for different levels and subject areas.

Joseph always works more than 40 hours a week, though it is not really expected of him. "You've got to keep the people happy," he says, and this sometimes involves going beyond the call of duty. "When the network is down, no one is happy, and you have to react to emergencies in a timely manner and deal with them until they're solved." But Joseph enjoys having the time to spend with top-notch equipment and learning about new systems and programs. "You have access to a lot of expensive 'toys,'" he says.

Do I Have What It Takes to Be a Computer Network Specialist?

Computer network specialists work with a lot of detail; every type of computer, every software application, every network system has a particular set of codes that must be used to get things done. Since users contact them when they have problems, network specialists must have a running knowledge of all the codes, plus an understanding of how they all link together. This also requires strong logical thinking skills. To succeed as a network specialist, you must be very good at organizing and analyzing large amounts of detail at both the micro and macro levels. Often, network technicians are called on to solve multiple problems at once. "You have to have a concrete, sequential way of thinking," Joseph says. "But you also have to be willing to admit when you don't understand a problem so that you can seek the advice of others."

> ## You have to have a concrete, sequential way of thinking.

Working as a network specialist also involves a certain amount of pressure. When a system is down, you must be able to think things through thoroughly without panicking.

Effective communication skills are also important for network specialists, who must explain complex information to both technical experts and people who have little understanding of computers. Since the computer industry has generated a lot of jargon, it can be difficult to simplify explanations.

Computer network specialists usually start with a basic understanding of broad computer principles, although there is always room for improvement and training.

How Do I Become a Computer Network Specialist?

Joseph originally worked as a teacher at the school, then took over the network responsibilities because he had some understanding of computers. Since then, he has taken courses in a two-year program in computer specialist training.

EDUCATION

High School

A high school diploma is mandatory for getting started in the computer field. Formerly there were advancement possibilities for long-term employees without diplomas, but competition is so intense in the computer industry today that a diploma is considered the bare minimum requirement for new hires.

High school courses in computer science provide a solid understanding of basic computing principles. Math courses such as algebra and geometry help develop logical and analytical thinking skills, while those in psychology and English improve verbal and written communication skills. Any business courses will increase knowledge about the ways in which management decisions are made, often important for network administration and engineering choices. Joining computer clubs and using your home computer are important, too. The more experience you have, the better off you'll be. Summer jobs at local businesses that have computers can provide opportunities to learn about various network systems and issues.

Postsecondary Training

Although there is a way to advance in the computer industry without a college degree, it is important to give careful consideration to long-term career goals. More complex jobs like computer design, systems design and analysis, computer programming, and computer management are usually reserved for those with at least a bachelor's degree in some computer or engineering major. More specialized research and development positions may require an advanced degree.

College graduates tend to do the more theoretical part of computer networking, maybe developing hardware or software from scratch or deciding which systems to invest in. Importantly, they are usually the ones promoted to middle and upper management jobs.

Several major companies offer postsecondary training in network administration and engineering. Among them are Microsoft, IBM, and Novell. Certified administrators are trained to perform day-to-day network tasks, while engineers are trained more broadly to do system installation, configuration, and maintenance.

You can complete the required training courses either at a local licensed education center or on your own. Either method provides detailed explanations of course content, personalized feedback on homework assignments, and some hands-on experience.

CERTIFICATION OR LICENSING

There are a number of certification programs, and Microsoft and Novell are the most popular. If you are already employed, it is wise to become certified by a program designed to complement the system your company is already using, unless the goal is to branch off into a different career field. Novell's

In-depth

Terms of the Trade

Can't tell your WAN from your LAN or your intranet from your extranet? Join the club! With the high-tech industry changing by the minute, it's hard to keep up on the latest developments. Hey, it's hard enough just to figure out a basic word processing program, much less the differences between Microsoft NT and Novell NetWare. Let's try to clear up some of that fog so you can have a rudimentary grasp of some of the common terms.

LANs are local area networks and usually refer to networks that reside in one building. LANs usually connect workstations and personal computers so they can communicate and share peripherals, such as printers. LANs can transmit data much faster than data can be sent over a telephone line, but they are limited in distance and in the number of computers they can support.

LANs that are connected to one another via telephone lines or radio waves are called WANs, or wide area networks. The Internet is an example of a WAN, so you can imagine how wide-ranging the capabilities of WANs are.

Intranet refers to a company's internal Web server. Intranets are accessible only by authorized users within an organization or corporation and are used to share information, such as with a network. Intranets work with private network systems and are growing in popularity because they are economical to build and maintain. Think of an intranet as a company's own little Internet.

Extranets are intranets that allow some accessibility to authorized outsiders. They come in handy when, say, a business wishes to share information or provide access to outside clients or business partners. The outsiders must have valid usernames and passwords to access the extranet. Extranets, like intranets, are enjoying popularity, and many customer service-based businesses are taking advantage of them. For example, Federal Express Corporation allows clients to access its package tracking system through an extranet.

Firewalls protect private networks from unauthorized usage. They prevent hackers and other Internet users from breaking into intranets by evaluating messages and rejecting those that do not meet security criteria. Firewalls use a variety of techniques to filter out unwanted messages. Some employ security measures when an outside connection is made, while others check all incoming and outgoing messages.

CNA and CNE and Microsoft's MSLE certifications are granted when you successfully complete a series of tests which are administered separately from the training classes.

While certification may provide you with a competitive advantage over fellow job seekers, not all companies require certification. This is due in large part to the rapidly changing world of networking. You may receive certification one day and discover a new version of the operating system is being released the next. In addition, more and more systems will combine features from different companies and sources, so being strictly, say, a Microsoft NT specialist won't get you very far.

SCHOLARSHIPS AND GRANTS

If you choose to pursue commercial certification in networking, research tuition reimbursement plans are offered by many large employers. Eligibility for these plans varies with the companies and positions held. In small- and medium-sized companies, employers might

FYI

Despite an overwhelming shortage of IT professionals, minorities are still underrepresented in the IT workforce. Part of the reason is a lack of access for minorities to the latest technology. In 1999, the Department of Commerce released a report called *Falling Through the Net,* which found that African-American and Hispanic households are only 40 percent as likely as White households to be online. While about 46 percent of all Whites have computers, only about 21 percent of African Americans and only 23 percent of Hispanic Americans do. The IT industry is attempting to close this gap in a variety of ways, and to recruit more minority workers. These efforts include minority technology scholarships funded by Microsoft, mentorship programs in companies, and a number of publications devoted to minorities in IT. Publications include Minority Engineer, Workforce Diversity for Engineering and IT Professionals, and Diversity/Careers in Engineering and Information Technology.

be persuaded to pay tuition costs if certification will have a direct impact on the company's operations.

If you are pursuing a formal degree, contact your school's financial aid office for scholarship, grant, and student loan opportunities. In addition, many commercial businesses and professional organizations have fellowship programs for students with particular interests.

INTERNSHIPS AND VOLUNTEERSHIPS

Since many people complete commercial certifications while working full-time, there are not many internship opportunities available. Those people who would like to put their knowledge to work on a volunteer basis should contact local or national charities of interest. Most charity offices run on computers and such valuable help is often very sought after and appreciated.

College students should contact their college placement office for help identifying and applying to internship programs. Large companies may be persuaded to take you on, you just need to convince them of your value.

Who Will Hire Me?

Computer network specialists work in companies that rely on computer networks to do business. As insurance companies, banks, and other financial institutions automate more and more of their services, they will count more heavily on computer networking, creating many job opportunities for individuals trained in these areas.

Since most companies are moving toward networking, positions are multiplying, and demand for network specialists is currently very high. Some companies might decide to promote and train specialists from within, so employees wishing to work in networking should watch in-house job-opening lists. For these positions, individuals already certified are likely to be hired rather quickly, especially if they have experience and knowledge of multiple systems.

Federal and state governments are also a good place to look for jobs in computer networking. Since many governmental offices manage huge amounts of information on many different networks, their overall need for network specialists is high. In addition, these positions are often on the top of the list to be filled even during hiring slowdowns or freezes.

There are several professional newsletters and magazines offering job opening lists in the area of computer networking, most of which can be found on the Internet, another indispensable job search tool. Job openings are also listed in all major newspapers' classified sections and in the back of computer trade magazines like *PC World* (http://www.pcworld.com) and *Macworld* (http://www.macworld.com).

In addition, many professional associations, including the Association for Computing Machinery, the Network Professional Association, and the Association of Information Technology Professionals, provide job lists.

As with many areas of business, network specialists might find out about good job openings from their colleagues in the industry. As individuals work their way through education requirements for network certification, they might ask instructors and other education center personnel about where to apply.

College students should work through their college placement offices, since they have established recruiting programs with many employers. Other than companies specializing in the service industries like insurance companies and banks, graduates might look at Hewlett-Packard Co., Microsoft Corporation, and Novell Inc. Competition for jobs at these companies is very stiff, however.

Where Can I Go from Here?

Joseph keeps up with technology trends and attends conferences to make his job easier. "I have applied for other jobs outside of education," he says, "but because of where I am on the salary schedule, I would take a cut in pay to move."

Advancement for computer network specialists varies greatly, depending on education, experience,

ADVANCEMENT POSSIBILITIES

Computer network engineers set up computer networks, often from scratch. They interview employers and employees to determine their needs, analyze and prioritize those needs, select appropriate hardware and software, make any necessary changes, supervise installation and initial operations of the system, and sometimes provide training to network users.

Enterprise computer network engineers perform many of the same duties as a computer network engineer but at a higher level. For example, they may work on company-wide networks or systems instead of networks serving only one department or several departments in a large company.

Multimedia specialists design ways to make graphics, audio, and video work well together, producing multimedia games, presentations, and other types of programs.

and personal interest. If you begin as a network administrator, you might work toward becoming a network engineer. Then, you might progress to the level of enterprise network engineer, a position that includes responsibility of all computer systems within a single, medium- or large-sized company.

But a network specialist might wish to become more specialized and train as a network security specialist, data recovery planner, or data communications operator. Network specialists who want to get into computer programming or systems analysis and design will probably need to pursue a college degree in order to get the theoretical knowledge necessary.

Another possible career path to take is information systems management. Larger companies need someone in charge of all their computer systems and services. Specialists who have strong, effective communication skills, the ability to motivate and organize team projects, as well as technical expertise of the computer systems involved in their work, make exceptional candidates for such management positions. Network managers work closely with network specialists and systems analysts and are often responsible for selecting which computer equipment to buy.

What Are the Salary Ranges?

Because of the demand for well-trained workers in the computer technology field, starting salaries continue to grow for network specialists. *ComputerWorld* projects that network administrators will earn average salaries of between $63,750 and $90,500 annually in 2005. Those entering the field may also get sign-on bonuses. A *ComputerWorld* survey found that the highest salaries for network administrators were paid in the Pacific ($80,369) and the lowest were paid in the South Central ($67,017) regions. Salaries in other parts of the country ranged between $69,198 and $76,175.

Benefits and awards offered by companies include profit-sharing, health insurance, and 401(k) plans. Some employers also provide large sign-on bonuses, provide further education or training, and reimburse for college tuition.

What Is the Job Outlook?

Job opportunities for computer support specialists are expected to grow much faster than average through 2012. There are several reasons for this. Many companies that used to rely on very large-sized computers (mainframes) are now finding it better to develop a series of networks made of smaller computers that can communicate with each other and achieve the same results. The companies are already beginning and will continue to search for well-qualified people to help administer and engineer networking projects.

In addition, many service industries that used to rely more heavily on paperwork for record keeping now prefer to automate and keep records on computer databases. Insurance companies, for example, are looking to eliminate all paper forms from the insurance process. Instead, they want to have online forms that can be filled out by the client on the computer. This would allow them to avoid delays and expenses caused by the post office and paper processing. Computerized form procedures would be handled through a network that, in turn, would need administrators and engineers to run it. The economic and productive advantages of networking currently make it such that companies will continue to invest in network development, even in times of economic difficulty. This means that computer network jobs should be relatively easy to find for the next several years.

The growing trend toward networking is occurring particularly in insurance companies, banks, and other financial institutions, although any business with more than one computer may be heading toward networking. As you begin to prepare for careers in computer networking, you should pay attention to the current economic climate to ascertain which industries may be more financially stable.

The federal government is also very involved in the process of setting up networks among different offices and departments. This, combined with the fact that the government is handling ever-growing amounts of information and pays competitively in mid-level jobs, makes it a prime target in the future job hunting process.

If you develop expertise in a specific area, like computer security, you can look to larger companies and computer companies for jobs corresponding better to your exact qualifications. It is important to remain well trained in several areas, however, because companies may choose to hire one or two people to do everything instead of numerous specialists when business is down.

Many computer companies are shifting to a service-based paradigm, offering comprehensive service to clients. This means that big computer companies will be hiring more and more technical support staff who can help clients install their networks, train client staff, and answer client questions. Computer network specialists might be well qualified for some of these positions.

According to a 2005 *ComputerWorld* report, network security administrator is among the positions that will be in high demand in coming years. Other positions listed among the fastest growing in the industry are systems auditor, programmer/analyst, data security analyst, and disaster recovery specialist.

How Do I Learn More?

PROFESSIONAL ORGANIZATIONS

The following organizations provide information on computer network specialist careers, internships, scholarships, educational programs, and employers:

American Society for Information Science and Technology
1320 Fenwick Lane, Suite 510
Silver Spring, MD 20910
301-495-0900
asis@asis.org
http://www.asis.org

Association for Computing Machinery
1515 Broadway
New York, NY 10036
800-342-6626
http://www.acm.org

Association of Information Technology Professionals
401 North Michigan Avenue, Suite 2400
Chicago, IL 60611-4267
800-224-9371
http://www.aitp.org

IEEE Communications Society
Three Park Avenue, 17th Floor
New York, NY 10016
212-705-8900
http://www.comsoc.org

Network Professional Association
17 South High Street, Suite 200
Columbus, OH 43212
888-672-6726
http://www.npanet.org

BIBLIOGRAPHY

The following is a sampling of materials relating to the professional concerns and development of computer network technicians:

Bigelow, Stephen J. *Troubleshooting, Maintaining, and Repairing PCs.* 5th ed. Columbus, Ohio: Computing McGraw-Hill, 2001.

Eberts, Marjorie, Margaret Gisler, and Maria Olson. *Careers for Computer Buffs & Other Technological Types.* Lincolnwood, Ill.: VGM Career Horizons, 1999.

Henderson, Harry. *Career Opportunities in Computers and Cyberspace.* 2d ed. New York: Facts On File, 2004.

Peterson's Guides. *Peterson's Job Opportunities: Engineering and Computer Science.* Princeton, N.J.: Peterson's Guides Inc., 1999.

COMPUTER PROGRAMMERS

|||||||||||||||||||||||||||||||||||||||||||||||||||||||||||||||||||||||||||||

David Sheesley typically works alone on the variety of Web-based projects he handles for Information Management Services, a state agency, but sometimes he finds the need for an extra pair of eyes. After getting stuck, unable to unravel the problem in the programming language scrolling across his computer screen, David walks down to another cubicle in the office to snag a coworker.

"We then test step-by-step," he says, "so we can see the program running and can see the code go by, and we'll sit there and watch it. We'll try different things and make suggestions to each other. Sometimes the other person can see something the first person doesn't."

The development team consists of four programmers, and sometimes they all find themselves crammed into the same cubicle, hovering over the same computer. "We like to work together," he says. "When we have some success we can congratulate each other."

What Does a Computer Programmer Do?

Definition
Computer programmers write the instructions (also called programs or software) that tell computers what to do.

Alternative Job Title
Software engineers

High School Subjects
Business
Computer science
Mathematics

Personal Skills
Leadership/management
Technical/scientific

Salary Range
$35,900 to $61,700 to $97,900

Minimum Educational Level
Some postsecondary training

Certification or Licensing
Voluntary

Outlook
About as fast as the average

DOT
030

GOE
02.06.01

NOC
2174

O*NET-SOC
15-1021.00

Computer programmers work in a variety of business, industrial, professional, and governmental settings to create the detailed instructions that tell a computer what to do. These instructions are called programs, or software.

Because computers cannot think, computer programmers must know how to arrange instructions in an order and language that the computer can follow. The programmer's first step is to think about the task and how to instruct the computer to perform it. At this stage, programmers usually create a flowchart to illustrate each step the computer will have to follow to get the desired results. Programmers must then translate this flowchart into a coded language that computers can follow. There are many programming languages, including traditional languages such as COBOL, FORTRAN, and C; object-oriented languages such as Java, C++, and Visual Basic; fourth- and fifth-generation languages; graphic user interface (GUI); and more. Programmers put the coded steps of the language into the computer, thereby creating a program.

After the programmers have saved the program on disk, CD-ROM, or on the main computer, they must test it using sample data to see if it runs correctly. If the task is not being performed as intended, the programmers must examine the program and make changes in it until it provides the desired outcome. This process is called debugging.

Once a program is debugged and running as expected, the programmers may help write an instruction manual explaining how to operate the program. Because the end user may have limited technical knowledge, the programmer must be able to communicate in simple, clear language.

There are two main types of computer programmers: *applications programmers* and *systems programmers*. Applications programmers create or revise software for specific jobs or tasks, such as software to help a business office process payments or to help the navy monitor the course of submarines. As new tasks arise at an organization, applications programmers are asked to develop software that will perform the desired job. Applications programmers often specialize in one of two fields: business and commercial applications programming or engineering and scientific applications programming.

Business and commercial applications programmers write software to help a business run more smoothly. Often, their programs will involve accounting, billing, payroll, inventory, and database procedures. *Engineering and scientific applications programmers* create programs that are used for scientific or mathematical purposes. For example, their programs may instruct computers to analyze medical data or assist in air traffic control.

Systems programmers control and maintain the overall operation of the organization's computer system, including the central processing unit and peripheral equipment, such as printers, terminals, and disk drives. They instruct the computers on how to accept and store information and how to communicate with other equipment via cables, known as a network. Systems programmers often assist applications programmers with troubleshooting and problem solving because of their in-depth knowledge of the entire system.

Whether working in systems or applications, a computer programmer is the link between the computer needs of an organization and the capabilities of the machines.

What Is It Like to Be a Computer Programmer?

David Sheesley is a computer programmer working for a department called Information Management Services for the state of Nebraska. "I'm an Internet developer," David says. "I develop Web applications and I'm also involved with training and teaching." David is typically assigned a part of a project, sometimes working with a group of people. Essentially, he works to assure that the computer applications satisfy business requirements.

"The project I'm currently working on is a 'claim inquiry,'" he explains. "This is for organizations that provide services for the state of Nebraska. They submit claims for those services, then they get paid

> # Lingo to Learn
>
> **Alpha test** First test of newly developed hardware or software in a laboratory setting.
>
> **Beta test** Test of hardware or software performed by actual users under normal operating conditions.
>
> **Debug** To search for and correct errors in a program.
>
> **Documentation** Written instructions explaining how to operate the program.
>
> **Flowchart** A diagram that shows step-by-step progression through a procedure or system.
>
> **Hardware** The physical components of a computer.
>
> **Port** To adapt a program written for one type of hardware to another type of hardware.
>
> **Run book** Instructions written by programmers to explain to computer operators how to use a program.
>
> **Software** Programs, procedures, and related documentation associated with a computer system.

as a result of those claims. This is a Web-enabled system that will allow them to track their claims from their own computers." This new system will be an improvement over the current process that requires the organizations to contact a caseworker, who then accesses a closed system. "We're trying to create an open system that anyone can get to. In this case, we're taking an existing system, so we have some idea of how it's supposed to function, and we're rewriting that by using Java and Web pages."

To accomplish this, David relies on his understanding of the computer language, as well as a basic programming approach. "We fit applications into this basic paradigm, so we have an idea of what we need to do at all levels for the application and where we want to start plugging things in. It gives us a basic framework, which makes it easier for us to understand different applications because they'll have a similar look and feel."

Training other state departments in Web development is another of David's responsibilities. For example, the Department of Roads is starting its own Web team. "I'm going to help them set up their Web test environment," David says, "show them our programming model, show them how they plug applications into that. We're going to jump-start other teams."

Working for the state allows David to take advantage of flex time; instead of a five-day workweek, he put in all his hours in four days. He has his own cubicle and computer in a clean environment. David describes the workplace as fast-paced and dynamic. "We get to try new technologies," he says. "We try to implement them. You're always learning. There's a good chance you won't be stuck doing the same thing—it's always changing."

David also cites the good opportunities for advancement and high salaries offered by the career. "Organizations that are involved in computers are going to keep training you so that you're not just going to stay there and stagnate." A downside of the work can be the many hours. "It depends on the sort of organization you work for," David says, "but it can be pretty easy to overwork yourself. You could spend 60, 70 hours a week working. Some businesses demand a lot from their programmers, a lot of their time."

Mike Schaffert, a computer programmer for Farm Bureau Insurance, was also attracted to the number of job opportunities and the high salaries of computer programming. His employer is a leading provider of insurance to the farms and ranches of Nebraska, and Mike assists with the programs needed to manage the various policies and documentation.

"My supervisor gives me a project," Mike says, "that can be anything from going into an existing program to find a particular problem to creating a new system. I'm currently working on correcting a problem in the grading system of our automobile insurance." A project may take only a few weeks to complete, while others can take up to two years. He may have a number of projects going at one time. "I usually have one substantial, long-term project, along with a lot of smaller ones that require immediate attention."

Mike's work is very solitary; he rarely leaves the computer during the workday. He feels fortunate, however, to have his own office. "Most programmers I know work in cubicles," he says. Mike also enjoys a number of benefits through the job, such as a good 401(k) plan and health insurance that includes dental. Another appeal of the industry is how it is constantly improving. "The job is changing every month," Mike says.

Do I Have What It Takes to Be a Computer Programmer?

"The most important quality to have," David says, "is a 'can do' attitude, and a willingness to keep trying, to be able to handle setbacks and failures and to keep going forward. You're not always going to get it right the first time."

Computer programming requires a great deal of patience, persistence, and concentration. When creating software, programmers must focus on determining the correct steps and instructions for the computer to follow. This takes thought, planning, and immense creativity. Programmers must test and retest steps of the program, making sure they work before proceeding to the next steps. Programmers must have the patience and problem-solving skills to debug a program, going through the codes and carefully examining them for error, entering test data, and running the program again. For someone with little patience, this type of work might quickly become frustrating.

Being accurate and detail oriented is also essential to computer programming. Because computers only understand specific instruction codes, even the smallest error will make an entire program unusable. Finally, since computer programmers act as the link between the capabilities of the computers and the needs of the computer operators, programmers have

To BE A SUCCESSFUL COMPUTER PROGRAMMER, YOU SHOULD . . .

- ○ be able to think logically
- ○ be creative
- ○ be well organized, precise, and detail oriented
- ○ have a long attention span
- ○ like to work independently
- ○ enjoy solving problems

to be able to communicate with both people and machines. "You need to be able to listen well," David says, "to communicate succinctly and distinctly, to communicate what you mean." Programmers have to be able to listen to an abstract description of a potential computer project and turn this description into precise instruction code that the computer can follow.

"You need to be able to talk to people," Mike says, "to work alongside other people. You interact with the users all the time."

How Do I Become a Computer Programmer?

David was working as a custodian at a community college in order to take advantage of the lower tuition fees for staff members. Though he was uncertain about what courses he wanted to take, he found himself majoring in computer programming, because it was a program that allowed for part-time enrollment. He took a course called Intro to Microcomputers and enjoyed it, so he furthered his study and eventually earned an associate's degree. David does not currently hold any certification. "I don't feel that it's necessary," he says, though he does believe that it is a good addition to a resume. "I will probably pursue that as time permits, and as I get more experience and more comfortable with my knowledge."

Mike has also decided against certification for the time being. "Because there's such high demand for experienced programmers," Mike says, "certification doesn't provide that much of an edge." This high demand is what attracted Mike to pursue an associate's degree in computer technology after injuring himself as a construction worker. "Getting the degree was tough," he says, "but definitely worth it."

EDUCATION

High School

If you are interested in becoming a computer programmer, you must complete high school. You should take college-preparatory courses in mathematics, which is the basis for computer programming and will help you develop the logical sequencing abilities necessary in the field. High-level courses in physics will also help you.

FYI

Computer programmers may find work in a wide variety of settings, including medical laboratories, software companies, universities, banks, small businesses, large corporations, nonprofit organizations, research companies, robot manufacturers, commercial aviation companies, and the military.

If your high school offers courses in computers and has computer laboratories on campus, you should take as many of these courses as possible. In this way, you can become well acquainted with the functions of computers before entering college and the job market. High school courses in business are especially important if you are interested in becoming a business and commercial applications programmer or systems programmer for a business or corporation.

Postsecondary Training

As popularity and demand both skyrocket, most employers now require college degrees. In fact, according to the U.S. Depaprtment of Labor *Occupational Outlook Handbook,* 17 percent of computer programmers held a master's degree, 50 percent held a bachelor's degree, and 11 percent held an associate's degree in 2002. Only 7.7 percent had high school diplomas or less. Although it is possible for those with exceptional backgrounds and work experience but no college degree to find employment, your chances will be much stronger with a degree, and pursuing a college education is highly recommended.

Many junior colleges and technical colleges provide training in computer programming, operations, and data processing, providing a jumping-off point for transfer into a four-year college, job, or internship. Many employers do not specify a major field for college study for potential programmers. Currently, with the increase in the number of college and university computer science departments, people hired as programmers often have degrees in this field. However, this is not always the case. Programmers interested in business and commercial applications might major in business, finance, accounting, or marketing. Those interested in engineering and scientific programming could consider a major in engineering, mathematics, or physics.

Many employers also send new programmers to special training courses before the programmer is allowed to begin working with company computers. In this situation, expenses are usually paid by the employer, and training time can take anywhere from two weeks to two months. Some computer programming jobs do require graduate degrees.

CERTIFICATION OR LICENSING

Criteria and qualifications for being hired as a computer programmer vary between employers. Some employers may require work experience, others may require degrees from two- or four-year colleges, still others may look for a combination of the two. Most people who work as computer programmers are not certified in this field. It is possible, however, to become certified as a computer programmer, and certification could help in attracting the attention of potential employers. The Institute for Certification of Computing Professionals (ICCP) offers a series of exams that, once passed, will provide the programmer with certification at one of two levels: associate computing professional (ACP) or certified computing professional (CCP). The level at which programmers are certified depends upon the programmers' work and educational backgrounds and the exams taken. While ICCP certification is not required for most programming jobs, it may provide you with a competitive advantage over other job seekers.

INTERNSHIPS AND VOLUNTEERSHIPS

Today, most homes and even the smallest businesses have computers, providing ample opportunity for you to gain hands-on experience with computers and programming. At home, surf the Internet for information about computer-related careers, education, and scholarships. You may want to join a local or school computer club, and you should pick up some books or magazines about programming. You might be able to find summer or after-school jobs or internships working with a company computer, helping to input or process data and becoming familiar with the ways a computer is used in a business setting. You may be able to work at small shops, such as book and pet stores, helping to maintain inventory records on a computer, in a library using computerized library catalogs and loan information, or on a school or local newspaper that uses computers for writing, graphics, and production. Some young people's business organizations such as Junior Achievement may also offer high school students an opportunity to work with computers. While computer-oriented jobs for most high school students will not involve programming, these jobs will help you gain exposure to and experience with a variety of computer capabilities.

Who Will Hire Me?

Many programmers are hired right out of college, and most two-year colleges offer job placement services. These services help you set up interviews with local businesses even before you've finished the program. In most cases, programmers will have jobs, or at least job offers, by the time they have graduated.

The first step in finding a job in computer programming is to isolate the type of work you are interested in doing. Because computers are such a large part of today's world, programmers can find work at small or large businesses, in science, health, or the military, or even at a company that creates software to sell to other companies. You should think about whether you are interested in systems or applications programming and whether you are more interested in the business and commercial applications of computers or the engineering and scientific aspects of the field.

Once you have selected an area of interest, you may follow numerous approaches to job hunting. Often, the classified section in newspapers advertise job fairs and openings for computer programmers, but many employers now turn to the Internet for the job search. Thousands of companies and organizations advertise job opportunities on their Web sites, and there are many Web sites devoted specifically to helping you land a job. It is even possible to post a resume or apply for open positions directly online.

If you have a specific interest, such as flight simulation or medical technology, you might want to find companies in this field and contact them directly with a resume and cover letter. Systems programmers usually work for larger corporations or companies with extensive computer systems, and job-hunting efforts should be directed toward these companies.

In addition, some agencies specialize in placing computer professionals in both temporary and permanent positions. These agencies work to match programmers to companies needing computer assistance. Computer consulting and independent contracting is also a growing field. Rather than hiring computer programmers as permanent employees, many companies are turning to computer contractors who are hired to come into the company and perform computer work on an as-needed basis. These consulting firms are usually found on the Internet or in the Yellow Pages under "Computers-Consultants."

Where Can I Go from Here?

David wants to continue with his current responsibilities with the state, but would also like to take on a mentoring role. He'd like to become more active in training, and take a position of leadership. "We have a personal development process here," he says. "I have to initiate it, but I work with my supervisor to recognize opportunities and to create opportunities."

Though Mike frequently hears of higher paying positions with other companies, he anticipates staying in his current job for a while longer. He likes the work environment and gets along well with his employers. But with his daughter in college, the more lucrative salaries offered in bigger cities sound more and more appealing. "It's hard not to be tempted away," he says, "when the industry just keeps growing and growing, offering so many great opportunities."

Some companies offer a programmer with extensive programming background the job of *chief programmer.* This job entails overseeing the work of the programming staff, assigning projects, and consulting with management to determine deadlines and special needs and concerns. Programmers could also advance into the position of *systems analyst,* computer specialists employed by many large companies to examine the computer needs of the company and then create methods to improve the system.

Computer programmers may get involved in software or hardware sales, helping clients to select appropriate computer equipment and providing them

FYI

The following is a list of positions expected to be the fastest growing in the IT industry and the corresponding salary ranges as reported by *ComputerWorld* in 2005:

systems auditor
$63,250 to $81,750

programmer/analyst
$52,500 to $83,250

business systems analyst
$56,000 to $80,500

network security administrator
$63,750 to $90,500

Internet/intranet developer
$51,750 to $74,250

disaster recovery specialist
$60,500 to $93,000

pre-and post-sales consultants
$53,500 to $78,250

instructor/trainer
$43,250 to $65,500

with instructions on its proper use. They may open their own businesses to sell computer equipment or to offer consulting services to companies needing computer help. Computer programmers also work as computer science instructors at high school, community college, and university levels. With the prevalence of computers in today's society, skilled computer programmers have a wide variety of opportunities for advancement in their field.

What Are the Salary Ranges?

Because of the popularity of computer-related professions and the demand for workers in the Information Technology (IT) industry, a number of publications and organizations have conducted salary surveys in recent years. These surveys agree that although salaries declined for several years due to the technology downturn, they are on the rise again, as are the number of benefits.

According to the U.S. Department of Labor, the national median salary for programmers was $61,700 in 2003. The lowest paid 10 percent made $35,900, while the highest paid 10 percent made $97,900. A *ComputerWorld* study projected a 3.6 percent increase in salaries for programmers/analysts in 2005 to average annual salaries between $52,500 and $83,250. Geographically, in 2005 the highest average salary, $80,362, is projected to be in the Pacific region. Benefits typically include profit sharing, health insurance, and 401(k) plans. Some employers also provide large sign-on bonuses, provide further education or training, and reimburse for college tuition.

What Is the Job Outlook?

According to the *Occupational Outlook Handbook*, employment of programmers is expected to grow about as fast as the average for all occupations through 2012, but more slowly than other computer specialties. There were more than 498,000 computer programmers employed in the United States in 2002. Programmers are in high demand; the most talented workers are courted by many companies and offered great opportunities. Companies also offer lucrative rewards to their staffs in order to retain good workers. However, professionals and employers warn that workers must remain cautious. Programmers may price themselves out of the competition if their salary demands are too high.

As a result of the increased job opportunities, programmers are in the enviable position of looking beyond salaries. Programmers who have a background in the field in which they program will have an advantage in finding a job. For example, it would be advantageous for programmers interested in working for a bank to have banking knowledge and for civil engineering programmers to have worked or studied in the civil engineering field.

Computer programming fields that look exceptionally strong for the future include data processing firms, software companies such as Microsoft that create software to be sold to other companies and individuals, and companies that provide computer consulting or operation services to other organizations who do not employ their own computer personnel. The downside of the growth in consulting services is that many small companies are laying off their in-house computer programmers and opting for computer assistance from consultants on an as-needed basis. This enables these companies to cut costs by reducing employee salaries and benefits.

Because of the increasing use of computers in business, programmers with expertise in business and commercial application programming are expected to be in especially high demand, as are programmers who are able to work with multimedia systems. To maximize your chances of finding employment as a computer programmer, complete a college degree and get as much experience as possible in your field of interest before applying for a permanent position.

How Do I Learn More?

PROFESSIONAL ORGANIZATIONS

The following organizations provide information on computer programming careers, accredited schools and scholarships, and possible employers:

Association of Information Technology Professionals
401 North Michigan Avenue, Suite 2400
Chicago, IL 60611-4267
800-224-9371
http://www.aitp.org

IEEE Communications Society
Three Park Avenue
New York, NY 10016
http://www.comsoc.org

Institute for Certification of Computing
    Professionals
2350 East Devon Avenue, Suite 115
Des Plaines, IL 60018-4610
800-843-8227
http://www.iccp.org

BIBLIOGRAPHY

*The following is a sampling of materials relating
to the professional concerns and development of
computer programmers:*

Bryant, Randal E., and David R. O'Hallaron. *Computer Systems: A Programmer's Perspective*. Paramus, N.J.: Prentice Hall, 2002.

Eberts, Marjorie, Margaret Gisler, and Maria Olson. *Careers for Computer Buffs & Other Technological Types*. Lincolnwood, Ill.: VGM Career Horizons, 1999.

Henderson, Harry. *Career Opportunities in Computers and Cyberspace*. 2d ed. New York: Facts On File, 2004.

Lammers, Susan. *Programmers At Work: Interviews with 19 Programmers Who Shaped the Computer Industry*. Redmond, Wash.: Tempus Books, 1989.

COMPUTER SYSTEMS PROGRAMMER/ ANALYSTS

||||||||||||||||||||||||||||||||||||||||||||||||||||||||||||

Though Josh Everett's job as a programmer/analyst with a telemarketing company keeps him closely confined to his cubicle, he does more than just stare at the computer screen. The company contracts with several clients, and these clients rely on Josh to keep their computer programs running smoothly. They also rely on him for information and guidance.

"I'm at the computer all day," he says, "debugging programs, or working out the kinks." He develops programs, tests them, and modifies them, but he also often communicates with real, live human beings. "It's all teamwork," Josh says. "You're always involved with someone else." He not only works alongside others in the company's home office, but he is frequently on the phone to one of the many offices all over the world. "I talk to at least 10, 20 other people every day. I help them and they help me."

What Does a Computer Systems Programmer/Analyst Do?

In the rapidly expanding world of technology, definitions, titles, and job duties change almost daily. Traditional job descriptions may no longer apply to the current job market. There are no uniform job titles. Both *systems analysts* and *programmer analysts* have similar, often interchangeable roles.

Computer systems programmer/analysts define specific business, scientific, or engineering problems and design computer solutions for them. They may plan and create entirely new programs or find better ways to use existing systems. They also install, modify, and maintain functioning systems.

Companies depend on computer systems programmer/analysts to make work easier, more streamlined, and more efficient. Essentially, their job is to save the company money.

Analysts work a lot like detectives. When presented with a problem, they investigate. They analyze hardware and software and ask the people who actually use the system—the users—what they want the program to do. An analyst cannot create a good, workable program without the help of the people who need it. Because of this, good communication skills are important.

Once the needs of management and users are established and system goals determined, the analyst begins working on the program. Highly analytical and logical activities follow, and the analyst uses tools such as structural analysis, mathematics, data modeling, and cost accounting to determine which computers, hardware, software, and peripherals will be needed to reach the system goals. Analysts must carefully weigh the pros and cons of additional features and consider trade-offs between increased cost and extra efficiency.

Definition
Computer systems programmer/analysts plan and develop new computer systems or update existing systems to meet changing business needs.

Alternative Job Titles
Programmer analysts
Systems analysts

High School Subjects
Computer science
Mathematics

Personal Skills
Leadership/management
Technical/scientific

Salary Range
$40,650 to $65,050 to $95,860

Minimum Educational Level
Associate's degree

Certification or Licensing
Voluntary

Outlook
Much faster than the average

DOT
033

GOE
02.06.01

NOC
2162

O*NET-SOC
15-1051.00

Computer systems programmer/analysts then present reports and proposals to management. This is where attention to detail, organizational skills, and strong communication abilities come into play.

Once the system upgrades are approved, equipment is purchased and installed. This is where certain distinctions between a systems analyst and a programmer analyst arise. Traditionally, a systems analyst does everything up to the actual programming of the computer. The computer programmer then writes the code and plugs everything into the system.

More and more, however, programmer analysts combine both of these functions, rolling two jobs into one. As an increasing number of businesses use computer technology, the ability to program becomes an important part of the job. In addition, tools such as CASE (Computer Aided Software Engineering) make programming easier by providing scripts of common commands.

After the system is in place and the users trained, the analyst provides basic maintenance. Any problems or questions about the program? The analyst is once again called upon to clear this up. Often he or she must debug the system, cleaning up any mistakes or flaws in the program.

An analyst is also responsible for the security of the system, making sure that the data can't be accessed by anyone not authorized to use it. The analyst makes sure the system runs smoothly and accurately from start to finish.

What Is It Like to Be a Computer Systems Programmer/Analyst?

Josh Everett is a programmer/analyst for a tele-marketing company. The company contracts with American Express, and Josh works primarily on those projects. "We have employees who call all the people with American Express cards," Josh says, "and I write the programs they use. I maintain and update the programs." His primary responsibility is assuring client satisfaction. "We work with the client daily. We just have to keep them happy."

Josh's day starts at around 8:00 A.M. by checking phone messages and e-mail. He then tackles the problems that occurred overnight. "There could be multiple problems," Josh says. "Maybe some records errored because of an invalid date. Some days there aren't any problems at all, other days there are six or seven of them." After dealing with those problems, Josh focuses on the client's needs. This involves updating programs and making changes. "Sometimes I load records for the client. I'm busy all day." He is also at the computer all day, with the exception of a few trips to the fax and copy machines.

"First you analyze what the problem is," Josh says. "When you've determined that, you fix it based on your past work experience." Using Visual Basic and COBOL, Josh examines the code, looking for where the problem occurred in the program and what could be causing it. "We count every record that goes through. When we get to the end number and it doesn't match our back-end output from these programs, we begin to analyze for what went wrong." Some errors, such as spelling mistakes, can be identified simply with common sense; others require careful study of the computer code. Problems in programs crop up a few times a week. "The rest of my time is spent creating new programs or updating existing ones."

Lingo to Learn

ASCII (American Standard Code for Information Exchange) Numerical code used by personal computers.

Database A collection of information stored on the computer.

Debugging Identifying and correcting errors in software.

GUI (Graphical User Interface) A system that uses symbols (icons) seen on screen to represent available functions.

Network Several computers that are electronically connected to share data and programs.

LAN (Local Area Network) A network that exists at one location, typically an office.

Spreadsheet A program that performs mathematical operations; used mainly for accounting and other record keeping.

WAN (Wide Area Network) A network that includes remote sites in different buildings, cities, states, or countries.

Josh is very pleased with his choice of career. "With a two-year degree in programming," Josh says, "you can start out in a job making pretty good money." He also appreciates the support offered by the company for which he works. "The company is all about helping the people who work for them. I have a good, fast pace of advancement, because they send me out for further training." The company is also paying for his pursuit of a bachelor's degree in information systems management.

Loury C. Abella is a programmer/analyst in California who has also benefitted from the great demand for information technology (IT) professionals. She was brought to the United States from the Philippines by a company in Sacramento that sponsored her working visa. Loury says, "I'm currently waiting for my visa transfer to a company in south San Francisco where I'll be working as a system administrator for its BPCS [application software]." In addition to her primary responsibilities of coding, debugging, testing, and implementation, Loury also trains the computer users. Loury enjoys a fairly flexible schedule that allows her to start her day at 7:00 A.M. or at 9:00 A.M., depending on work priority. "Sometimes I'll log on at home," she says.

Spending many hours developing and testing computer programs can be a strain, though. Loury warns that thinking too much about codes can lead to a disconnection from the rest of the world. "Sometimes developers tend to forget the human factor of life even when not at work," she says. "They forget the human emotions."

Do I Have What It Takes to Be a Computer Systems Programmer/Analyst?

Analysts often work long hours and deal with a wide variety of people. They work both alone and in groups. Patience and attention to detail are important qualities, as well as logical thinking and an ability to translate highly technical and complex concepts into simple language. "One has to be an analytical and logical person," Loury says. "One should also be very patient and able to work under pressure."

If you prefer to sit at a computer by yourself all day, every day, computer systems/programmer

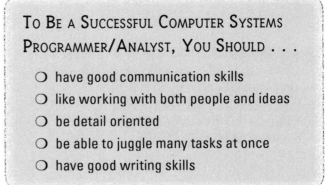

TO BE A SUCCESSFUL COMPUTER SYSTEMS PROGRAMMER/ANALYST, YOU SHOULD . . .

- ○ have good communication skills
- ○ like working with both people and ideas
- ○ be detail oriented
- ○ be able to juggle many tasks at once
- ○ have good writing skills

analyst is not the job for you. An outgoing personality, good communication and listening skills, and being able to work well with others are as much a part of the job as computer knowledge. An analyst must be able to talk easily to both technical personnel, such as programmers and management, as well as to staff who might not have any knowledge of computers.

Self-motivation and being able to juggle many different tasks at once are critical to the job. "You need problem-solving abilities," Josh says. "And you need to pay attention to minor details. You've also got to be willing to learn."

You need problem-solving abilities, and you need to pay attention to minor details. You've also got to be willing to learn.

How Do I Become a Computer Systems Programmer/Analyst?

Josh first became interested in computers while in high school and enrolled in every computer-related class available. He eventually went to a community college for an associate's degree in computer programming. "I wouldn't be where I am without the schooling," he says. "I'm happy with my choice of the associate's over the bachelor's because it allowed me to start working right away."

Loury holds a bachelor's degree in computer science. "I was working in a manufacturing firm and the MIS manager saw my skills and gave me additional training."

EDUCATION

High School

A high school diploma is necessary for a future as a computer systems/programmer analyst. A knowledge of IBM-compatible computer programs as well as Macintosh systems is very important. If possible, enroll in computer classes and labs to gain hands-on experience. Also join user groups or computer clubs to share information and make contacts.

High school courses in the sciences are necessary, since many computer systems/programmer analysts work in industries directly involved in the scientific fields. Math classes are good for understanding the programming languages taught in college. Mathematical ability is also useful when writing and developing computer programs, and a good math background helps develop skills in logical thinking.

Also useful for developing analytical thinking skills are strategy games such as chess. Play with friends or against a computer. And to make computer usage as natural as brushing your teeth, use your computer as frequently as possible—surf the Web, learn various software programs, and try to pick up some basic programming or networking skills.

Postsecondary Training

There is no universally accepted way of preparing for a job as a computer systems/programmer analyst, but having a four-year degree from an accredited college, university, or technical institute can be helpful. Because of the demand for knowledgeable computer programmers and analysts, graduates of two-year programs are also finding good paying jobs. However, many successful computer professionals hold not only an undergraduate degree but a master's or doctorate as well.

A degree in computer science was once mandatory, but employers are now looking for applicants with more varied backgrounds. A large company will usually want a computer systems/programmer analyst to have a background in business management or a related field for work in a business environment. A background in the physical sciences, applied mathematics, or engineering is preferred by

FYI

The IT industry has suffered from a critical shortage of skilled workers. One solution to this employment problem may lie in the hiring of people with mental disabilities. Those with neurological disorders such as autism have been excelling at IT work in data entry, programming, and Web design. IT projects require the talents possessed by many workers with mental disabilities: creativity, problem-solving abilities, and great concentration. The computer also allows these workers structure and allows them to somewhat avoid the prejudices against mental disabilities.

scientific organizations. Some analysts hold degrees in management information systems (MIS).

Regardless of college major, employers look for people who know programming languages and have a good knowledge of computer systems and technologies.

CERTIFICATION OR LICENSING

Getting certified as a computer professional is not a requirement for a job as a computer systems programmer/analyst, but might give you a competitive edge over other applicants.

The Institute for Certification of Computing Professionals offers the designation certified computing professional (CCP). Applicants must have at least four years of experience and pass a core examination. They then must pass exams in two specialty areas. The Quality Assurance Institute awards the titles of certified software quality analyst (CSQA), certified software tester (CSTE), and certified software project manager (CSPM) to those who meet education and experience requirements, pass an exam, and endorse a specific code of ethics.

SCHOLARSHIPS AND GRANTS

Following is a partial listing of the many organizations offering scholarships and grants for students pursuing a career in computer science. Some offer small amounts of money toward a degree, while others pay the full tuition and provide internships. Write early for information on eligibility, application requirements, and deadlines.

Microsoft National Minority Technical Scholarship
Microsoft National Women's Technical Scholarship
Microsoft Corporation
One Microsoft Way
Redmond, WA 98052
http://www.microsoft.com/College/default.mspxh

NAACP Willems Scholarship
The United Negro College Fund
Scholarships & Grants Administration
8260 Willow Oaks Corporate Drive
Fairfax, VA 22031
ATTN: Kimberly Hall
http://www.uncf.org

INTERNSHIPS AND VOLUNTEERSHIPS

An important, but not mandatory, part of preparing for a career as a computer systems programmer/analyst is participating in an internship program. Internships provide practical hands-on experience for students. Universities and technical institutes usually have programs that help arrange internships for their students.

Employers look for practical experience in job applicants. Most internships offer little or no pay for long hours and hard work, but the experience gained is priceless. Many students make valuable contacts this way, and some are hired as regular employees when the internship is finished.

Who Will Hire Me?

As more businesses, organizations, and federal agencies expand their computer systems, jobs for computer systems programmer/analysts open up in a variety of areas. The largest number of analysts is found in computer and data processing firms, but opportunities in many other fields exist as well.

Government agencies, manufacturers of computer-related equipment, insurance agencies, universities, banks, and private businesses all employ the skills of computer systems programmer/analysts.

Most analyst jobs are concentrated in or near larger cities. Many employers actively recruit

---

ADVANCEMENT POSSIBILITIES

Senior systems programmer/analysts, also known as lead programmer/analysts, are in charge of an entire project, coordinating and overseeing the work efforts of all the analysts working on a team.

Managers of information systems, also known as **project managers**, are overseers, operating as supervisors for all the projects the analysts are involved with.

Database design analysts work as liaisons between the computer systems programmer/analysts and the company. They evaluate project requests, their costs, and time limitations. They review and restructure the database to work with programs developed by the computer systems programmer/analyst.

---

applicants on college campuses, interviewing students while they're still in school. Most simply advertise in the want ads of big city newspapers.

Following a trend in the overall workforce, growing numbers of computer systems programmer/analysts are employed on a temporary basis as short-term consultants. A company that needs the services of an analyst to install or create a new computer program may not be able to justify hiring a full-time analyst but will turn to a computer consulting agency or contract a computer systems programmer/analyst to do the work. These contracts usually last for several months and sometimes up to two years.

Trade magazines often have job listings and are good sources for job seekers. They are also a great place to learn about changing technologies and trends in the industry. Reading several different publications may help to identify where the jobs are.

The Internet is an excellent tool for finding job opportunities. Most major companies post job openings, and many Web sites are dedicated solely to helping you land a position.

A computer systems programmer/analyst is not an entry-level job. Many analysts start in programming or data processing. Occasionally, some are promoted from another area altogether. For example, an auditor in an accounting department might become a systems analyst specializing in accounting systems development.

Where Can I Go from Here?

With the two-year degree, Josh was able to step quickly into a good paying job with a company that is also dedicated to staff improvement. His employer is currently paying for him to take night classes toward a bachelor's degree in information systems management. Upon completing the program, Josh anticipates even more great opportunities. "A bachelor's degree does help in the job market," he says, "but experience is probably more important." With both in hand, Josh hopes to move to a bigger city with more employment options.

As a greater diversity of businesses become dependent on computers, the need for consultants in the field grows. For example, a small bookstore chain may not have the need for a full-time systems analyst but will hire one as specific projects arise, such as creating an automated inventory and purchasing system.

The career path of a company computer systems programmer/analyst usually leads to management. After a few years' experience, those who show leadership ability, good communication skills, and diverse business and technical knowledge are promoted along these lines.

What Are the Salary Ranges?

According to the *Occupational Outlook Handbook,* the median annual salary for systems analysts was $65,050 in 2003. The lowest paid 10 percent earned $40,560, while the highest paid 10 percent earned $95,860. A salary survey conducted by *ComputerWorld* projects that in 2005 the average salary for programmer analysts is expected to increase 3.6 percent to between $52,500 and $83,250 annually. DataMasters' 2003 Computer Industry Salary Survey found that the highest median salaries for systems analyst programmers were in the Northeast, with $66,874 for staff positions, and the lowest median salaries were in the Southwest, paying $57,152 for staff positions.

Working for a large company or the federal government brings other nonsalaried benefits as

FYI

The following are regional salaries for programmer/analysts:

Southeast	$54,305 to $76,596
Northeast	$58,920 to $83,765
West coast	$54,796 to $76,203
Midwest	$57,840 to $76,498
Southwest	$46,743 to $66,481

well, such as health insurance, retirement plans, and paid vacations. Private consultants do not get these benefits and must provide their own; they also have the extra work of running their consulting business.

What Is the Job Outlook?

The job of computer systems programmer/analyst is one of the fastest growing occupations. According to the U.S. Department of Labor, demand for these skilled professionals is expected to increase much faster than average through 2012.

As smaller businesses utilize the efficiency of computers in the workplace, and technology becomes more affordable to private users, an even greater demand for systems programmer/analysts will arise.

There is an ever-increasing emphasis on personal computers. Businesses are moving away from the larger and extremely expensive mainframes that have traditionally been used by large companies. They are going toward a network of many smaller yet powerful computers that share the workload. As this trend continues, analysts will be indispensable in an office environment. Someone must program, organize, and link all these individual systems together.

As these intricate computer systems improve and grow, the analyst will be needed to continually upgrade and weed out errors in the programs. Maintenance and debugging will provide steady work as long as computers are part of our daily lives.

The role of computer systems programmer/analyst is an upwardly mobile one. Tens of thousands of jobs will be opening up as analysts move into managerial positions. Those who go into business for themselves or to private consulting firms will keep this field open for new analysts.

How Do I Learn More?

PROFESSIONAL ORGANIZATIONS

For information about careers in technology, certification, student membership, scholarships, and internships, contact the following organizations:

Association for Computing Machinery
1515 Broadway
New York, NY 10036
800-342-6626
http://www.acm.org

Association of Information Technology Professionals
401 North Michigan Avenue, Suite 2400
Chicago, IL 60611-4267
800-224-9371
http://www.aitp.org

IEEE Communications Society
Three Park Avenue, 17th Floor
New York, NY 10016-5997
212-419-7900
http://www.comsoc.org

Institute for Certification of Computing Professionals
2350 East Devon Avenue, Suite 115
Des Plaines, IL 60018-4610
800-843-8227
http://www.iccp.org

Quality Assurance Institute
7575 Dr. Phillips Boulevard, Suite 350
Orlando, FL 32819
407-363-1111
http://www.qaiusa.com

BIBLIOGRAPHY

The following is a sampling of materials relating to the professional concerns and development of computer systems programmer/analysts:

Eberts, Marjorie, Margaret Gisler, and Maria Olson. *Careers for Computer Buffs & Other Technological Types.* Lincolnwood, Ill.: VGM Career Horizons, 1999.

Henderson, Harry. *Career Opportunities in Computers and Cyberspace.* 2d ed. New York: Facts On File, 2004.

CONSERVATION TECHNICIANS

‖‖

The rug was old, valuable, and falling apart. Karen Clark focused on the task at hand, using thread to bind the pieces back together, but the job seemed to keep getting bigger as she worked. "For every row I stitched together, that area became stronger, so a nearby area would start to deteriorate very quickly," she recalls.

Then the problem was compounded as an adhesive on the back of the rug suddenly came through to the front. Karen spent hour after hour patiently scraping away the adhesive, restoring the old rug to its original beauty. As usual, the project was a learning experience and a test of her skills and creativity.

"Nothing comes in here quite the same. You may get five rugs, and they may be similar, but each one was made in a different way. They come from all over the world," she notes. The rug might have been brought back from a European vacation, or it might have been in the home of a local family for generations.

Like most of the items Karen helps stabilize and restore, the rug was unique, but she didn't allow herself to worry about damaging it as she worked. "Whatever you do is reversible," she kept reminding herself. "You can always fix it."

What Does a Conservation Technician Do?

Without proper care, vintage clothing, pottery, rare books, and other valuable items begin to deteriorate and could be lost forever. Many of the treasures in private collections and in institutions such as museums, art galleries, and libraries have been stabilized and repaired by *conservators* and the *conservation technicians* who assist them. A technician focuses primarily on stabilizing and restoring objects but might also construct part of a display for it, such as a backboard for a feather headdress or a frame for a painting.

Research, artistic skills, and scientific procedures all play a part in the conservation of artwork and objects of historical or cultural value. Conservation technicians gather information to learn how an item originally appeared. They sometimes conduct chemical and physical tests to determine its age and composition. Then they develop a plan for cleaning, stabilizing, and restoring the object.

Different types of items require different care. A textile might be dry-cleaned, but a suit of armor might be cleaned with chemical solvents. When making repairs, conservation technicians carefully sew, solder, or glue broken pieces back into place. They may also repaint objects, using materials of the same chemical composition and color as the original.

Conservation professionals frequently specialize in one type of object. *Armorer technicians* clean,

---

Definition

Conservation technicians restore artistic and historic objects, such as pottery, statuary, and tapestries, to their original or natural appearance.

Alternative Job Titles

Armorer technicians
Ceramic restorers
Lace and textiles restorers
Paintings restorers
Paper and prints restorers

High School Subjects

Art
Chemistry
History

Personal Skills

Artistic
Technical/scientific

Salary Range

$20,600 to $36,160 to $66,600

Minimum Educational Level

Bachelor's degree

Certification or Licensing

None

Outlook

About as fast as the average

DOT

102

GOE

12.03.04

NOC

5212

O*NET-SOC

25-4013.00

Lingo to Learn

Chain mail Flexible armor composed of many interlinked metal rings.

Controlled environment An area where relative humidity, light sources, and temperature are observed and regulated.

Cultural property Objects, structures, sites, or monuments of artistic, historic, scientific, religious, or social significance.

Etching The art of producing pictures or designs by printing from an etched metal plate.

Exhibition A presentation of objects and information.

Mount A bracket or support used to display objects safely in an exhibit.

Statuary The art of making statues.

Tapestry Heavy, handwoven, reversible textile used for hangings, curtains, and upholstery. Tapestries often depict complicated pictorial designs.

Titan hinge Until recently, a popular type of bookbinding.

repair, and determine the authenticity of medieval armor and arms. *Ceramic restorers* work with objects made of glass, porcelain, china, clay, or other ceramic materials. *Lace and textiles restorers* use their knowledge of weaving and sewing to clean and repair tapestries, clothing, lace, flags, and other fabric items. *Paintings restorers* clean, stabilize, and repair paintings. *Paper and prints restorers* work with paper objects of historical and artistic value, including books, documents, maps, and prints.

Conservation technicians usually work under the supervision of conservators. Other professionals in the field include *conservation scientists,* who develop varnishes and other materials used by conservators, *conservation educators,* who teach the principles, methods, and technical aspects of the profession; and *preparators,* who ensure that objects are displayed in a way that will protect them from deterioration.

What Is It Like to Be a Conservation Technician?

Karen Clark is learning to be a conservator through a sort of informal apprenticeship at Jessica Hack Textile Restorations, a privately owned studio in New Orleans, Louisiana. The business stabilizes and restores textiles and related items for museums and private clients.

Karen works with several other professionals, each bringing a specialization to the team: a master tailor, a master weaver, and an accomplished quilter. Karen is most interested in lace and wedding veils, but she has restored bridal gowns, vintage Mardi Gras costumes, antique flags, hats, shoes, and even decorated boxes from the 17th century. "We work on whatever comes in," she says.

Karen usually starts by vacuuming the object, and she might prepare it for washing or dry-cleaning. She performs any necessary repairs, which might require that thread or fabric be dyed to match the old fabric exactly. Then the item is pinned and sewed together; in some cases Karen uses an adhesive. She might cover a board with fabric to serve as a backing against which the item can be displayed, and if the object is an article of clothing, she might prepare a harness to hang it inside the display case.

She commonly spends several days on one project. Throughout the process, she documents her work with photographs and written reports for her own information and for the use of other conservators who might work with the object in the future.

Detailed reports are one of a conservation professional's primary duties, according to C. R. Jones, a curator-turned-conservator who has been in the profession since 1977. Another primary concern is monitoring the environment in which the object is stored or displayed to ensure that the temperature, humidity, and other conditions will not damage the item.

C. R. Jones is the conservator of the Farmers' Museum and the New York State Historical Association in Cooperstown, New York. He sometimes has help from volunteers, but usually he performs all the conservation duties for both organizations. His specialties are paintings, flat paper, and objects made of metal, wood, stone, or ceramics.

"One of the first things you have to do is figure out the anatomy of the object," he says. For that, he uses X rays, ultraviolet rays, infrared scanners, microscopes, and other equipment.

He might do a test to see if a certain cleaner would harm the object, or he might examine a painting's canvas to determine if it needs support. Then he takes photographs, writes a report, writes a treatment proposal, cleans the piece, and repairs it. He might apply varnish to protect a painting's surface or place it on a new stretcher to pull it flat, then frame it and hang it in the museum.

> One of the first things you have to do is figure out the anatomy of the object.

Another conservation technician who works with paper, Jim Boydstun, spends his days examining and repairing the seven million books in the library at the University of California–Berkeley. Jim works at a desk in a small alcove or at a workbench nearby, repairing books damaged by rough handling from library patrons or deterioration with age. Old, yellow, brittle paper and loose bindings are Jim's area of expertise. He is part of a team of workers who use scissors, shears, tweezers, erasers, glue, thread, and a special folder made of cattle bone to repair pages and bindings.

He repairs books with torn pages by gluing ripped edges back together or gluing a new corner on a page. Books that have become wet or whose pages are falling out of their bindings are more difficult to repair. Wet pages must be dried, and they may warp in the process and need further repair. Bad bindings must be torn out and sewed again. The job can be repetitive, but Jim remarks that with the large number of books in need of repair, "I'll never run out of work."

Do I Have What It Takes to Be a Conservation Technician?

Conservation technicians need manual dexterity to handle tools and complete exacting repairs, such as making stitches so tiny that they cannot be seen. Patience is essential for completing projects that often require hour after hour of intense concentration. Because the objects they handle are usually irreplaceable, technicians must exercise good judgment and refrain from making rash decisions that could further damage an item. The field requires

> **TO BE A SUCCESSFUL CONVERSATION TECHNICIAN, YOU SHOULD . . .**
>
> ○ be extremely patient
> ○ have an appreciation for art and history
> ○ have manual dexterity and good hand-eye coordination for using tools
> ○ be able to stand or sit for long periods of time

a sense of dedication to art, history, and culture, coupled with the ability to do research.

Karen says textile restoration is a job for "someone who likes fabrics, likes looking at things like rugs and historic dresses." She has always been fascinated with the clothing in movies about the 1800s, for example. She adds, "You have to have a good sense of color and know about the way fabric is woven."

A conservation technician cleans and restores a fragment of a sculpture. *(Mauro Fermariello / Photo Researchers Inc.)*

Many conservation technicians have training in art, which allows them to better understand how a book or art object was created. C. R. Jones says some talent with art materials is necessary to restore a painting, for instance, but since the goal is to repair someone else's work instead of producing a new painting, it is not necessary for the technician to be a creative artist. He enjoys the variety of his job and the opportunity to work with artifacts, but he dislikes working within a tight budget and having "too many things to work on and too little time to do it."

In contrast, Jim Boydstun likes his job because it does not put him under much pressure. "I really wanted to work in a stress-free environment," he says. "Mending books is a healthy occupation."

How Do I Become a Conservation Technician?

Karen became interested in conservation over four years ago, about 20 years after graduating from high school. She holds a college degree in special education, but so far she has taken no postsecondary courses to prepare for her new career in conservation. Instead, she is learning the old-fashioned way, by studying under a knowledgeable, established conservator.

Apprenticeship used to be the standard way to become a conservation professional, and it is still an accepted method of entry. Recently, however, graduate training, combined with on-the-job experience such as an internship, has become the preferred route.

EDUCATION

High School

To prepare for a career in textile conservation, Karen recommends a well-rounded education that includes creative, artistic courses and practical, scientific classes. "You'll be using both your creative mind and your analytical mind," she notes. She also advises taking some business courses, in case you end up freelancing or owning a studio. If she ever had to

In-depth

Painting Restoration

C. R. Jones recalls one of his early restoration projects, a watercolor painting of Elizabeth Cooper, mother of the novelist James Fenimore Cooper. In years past, someone had attempted to protect the painting by coating it with shellac. That was an ill-conceived idea. When C. R. began work, the painting was murky and yellowed.

C. R. decided to try removing the shellac with solvent, because he knew that older watercolors, unlike some of their modern counterparts, are not soluble in alcohol. (If a watercolor touches certain liquids, the pigment will run, and the painting will be ruined.) C. R. tested the solvent on a small part of the painting, then immersed the entire piece and watched it carefully for any sign that the procedure might be causing damage. The idea worked nicely, and the shellac soon disappeared.

Next, C. R. made a mold of the ornamental front of the painting's antique frame, from which several pieces had been chipped. He used rock-hard water putty, a substance similar to plaster of Paris, to cast the missing pieces in the mold. Then he repaired parts of the frame that were embellished with a layer of gold leaf, which can be applied as a liquid or as thin sheets that are dropped onto wet varnish.

With the painting and frame repaired, C. R. cut an acid-free mat, a sort of inner frame made from thick paper that resembles cardboard. A mat is placed on top of a painting to keep it from touching the glass in the frame and sticking to it. Finally, the painting, mat, glass, and frame were assembled and hung where museum visitors could see Elizabeth Cooper's likeness, professionally restored.

leave the studio and work on her own, she says, "That [business administration] would be the roughest part. I'd have to write estimates. I'd have to write reports."

Classes in art are important for conservation technicians in almost any area of specialization, because they help you understand how objects were created and give you some skills, such as painting, needed to repair them. A knowledge of science is also critical, because conservation professionals need to know, for instance, how chemical agents interact. A familiarity with history will help you research the times in which an object was made. Studies in archaeology and anthropology are also recommended.

Postsecondary Training

College programs in museum studies usually last from six months to two years and feature courses in art and the scientific procedures used to restore art objects. Classroom training is typically followed by an internship at a museum or library. It is possible to enter the trade via apprenticeship alone, but C. R. Jones says, "That would be difficult. You're going to have much better credentials if you have a college degree."

C. R. Jones prepared for his career by obtaining a bachelor's degree in science, then earning a master's degree in museum studies and, 10 years later, another master's degree in art conservation. "That's becoming pretty standard," he says. "If you want to break into the field [as a conservator or curator], you just about need a master's degree." He adds that some technicians hold only a bachelor's degree and may be able to work their way up from there, particularly if they are employed by the larger conservation laboratories.

CERTIFICATION

No certification or licensing is available for conservation professionals. Technicians are hired on the basis of their education and experience. Participation in professional organizations is not required, but it is taken into consideration during the hiring process.

SCHOLARSHIPS AND GRANTS

Some museums and other organizations, such as the Smithsonian Institution, offer scholarships and grants

for conservation technicians. Information is available through the American Institute for Conservation of Historic and Artistic Works and from colleges that offer training programs in the field.

INTERNSHIPS AND VOLUNTEERSHIPS

To gain crucial on-the-job experience, you can volunteer or complete an internship or apprenticeship at a museum, bookbindery, or other facility. An AIC survey revealed that nearly a third of conservation professionals learned the trade through some sort of apprenticeship, and about half had completed an internship or postgraduate fellowship, which usually lasted one to two years.

Here are two organizations that offer internships and volunteerships in conservation:

Smithsonian Center for Materials Research and Education
Museum Support Center
4210 Silver Hill Road
Suitland, MD 20746
301-238-1240
http://www.si.edu/scmre

Smithsonian American Art Museum
MRC 970, P.O. Box 37012
Washington, DC 20013-7012
202-275-1500
http://www.americanart.si.edu

Who Will Hire Me?

Karen first met her mentor, Jessica Hack, when she brought an item to her to be restored. The experience piqued her interest, and she began working on small projects with the professionals at the studio. "I just found myself gravitating in this direction," she remembers. "Most of what I'd done led up to it. I'd sewed my own clothes for a long time."

Jim Boydstun also entered the trade through happenstance, more than 15 years ago. "I kind of fell into it," he says. "A friend who owns a bookbindery needed some help. They taught me how to repair books, and I've been doing it ever since."

Most conservation technicians are employed by libraries, museums, historical societies, and state and federal agencies that have large, public collections of books, historical objects, or artwork. No matter where you hope to work in this field, networking

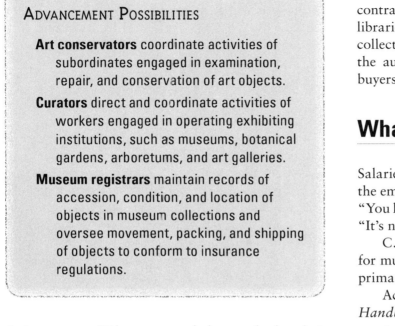

ADVANCEMENT POSSIBILITIES

Art conservators coordinate activities of subordinates engaged in examination, repair, and conservation of art objects.

Curators direct and coordinate activities of workers engaged in operating exhibiting institutions, such as museums, botanical gardens, arboretums, and art galleries.

Museum registrars maintain records of accession, condition, and location of objects in museum collections and oversee movement, packing, and shipping of objects to conform to insurance regulations.

is important. "I'd recommend that anybody who's interested should join a local historical society," says C. R. Jones. "You'll make good contacts, and you learn a lot, and it looks great on resumes." Joining a professional association is another good way to meet people in the field and learn of job openings, which are often published in the organization's newsletter. Some associations operate job banks that list openings and allow you to post your resume where it can be read by potential employers.

Where Can I Go from Here?

Karen is happy at the textile restoration studio and would like to remain there indefinitely. If circumstances forced her to move on, she could apply for a job in a museum or open her own studio.

Jim Boydstun would also like to remain in his current position, but his job depends on the amount of state and federal funding the university receives. If the government decides to reduce spending, Jim's position could be cut. If funding is adequate, he could be promoted.

Many conservation technicians advance through a series of grades as they gain the required years of experience. A conservation technician can advance to conservator and take on supervisory duties within several years. With further education, some conservation technicians become administrators in an institution's collections department. Those

with experience may also work as independent contractors, providing conservation services for libraries, museums, and individuals with private collections. Some appraise the value and determine the authenticity of art or artifacts for prospective buyers. Others become conservation educators.

What Are the Salary Ranges?

Salaries for conservation workers vary depending on the employer, geographic location, and other factors. "You have to really like this work," Karen comments. "It's not the world's best-paying job."

C. R. Jones says, "You will never get rich working for museums, so other considerations have to be the primary ones. In general, the salaries are adequate."

According to the *Occupational Outlook Handbook*, median annual earnings of archivists, curators, museum technicians, and conservators were $36,160 in 2003. The lowest paid 10 percent earned $20,600 annually, while the highest paid 10 percent earned $66,600.

Benefits typically include paid vacations, health and life insurance, a retirement plan, and a profit-sharing plan.

What Is the Job Outlook?

Thanks to the nation's strong interest in cultural materials, the field of conservation and preservation is growing. New areas of specialization are emerging as workers combine their skills in conservation, curating, and registration. The outlook is particularly good for private conservation companies that perform contract work. Museums and other institutions will probably rely on private contractors more as they cut their own staffs in response to a drop in government funding through tax dollars.

According to the U.S. Department of Labor *Occupational Outlook Handbook*, employment of archivists, curators, museum technicians, and conservators is expected to increase about as fast as the average for all occupations though 2012. Competition for these jobs will be stiff, however. Because such work is desirable to many people with interests in art, there are generally more people pursuing careers in conservation than there are jobs available. For the best opportunities, conservation technicians will want to pursue advanced degrees. The position of conservation technician is increasingly being seen as a stepping-stone to professional positions.

How Do I Learn More?

PROFESSIONAL ORGANIZATIONS

For information on education programs, conservation training programs, scholarships, professional development, workshops, seminars, and museum careers, contact the following organizations:

American Association of Museums
1575 Eye Street, NW, Suite 400
Washington, DC 20005
202-289-1818
http://www.aam-us.org

American Institute for Conservation of Historic and Artistic Works
1717 K Street, NW, Suite 200
Washington, DC 20006
202-452-9545
info@aic-faic.org
http://aic.stanford.edu

Costume Society of America
PO Box 73
Earleville, MD 21919
800-272-9447

national.office@costumesocietyamerica.com
http://www.costumesocietyamerica.com

Intermuseum Conservation Association
2915 Detroit Avenue
Cleveland, OH 44113
216-658-8700
http://www.ica-artconservation.org

Western Association for Art Conservation
PO Box 3755
San Diego, CA 92163-1755
619-236-9702
http://palimpsest.stanford.edu/waac

BIBLIOGRAPHY

The following is a sampling of materials relating to the professional concerns and development of conservation technicians:

Camenson, Blythe. *Opportunities in Museum Careers.* Lincolnwood, Ill.: VGM Career Horizons, 1996.

Careers in Museums: A Variety of Vocations. Washington, D.C.: American Association of Museums, 1994.

Glaser, Jane R. *Museums: A Place to Work: Planning Museum Careers.* New York: Routledge, 1996.

Oddy, Andrew, ed. *The Art of the Conservator.* Washington, D.C.: Smithsonian Institution Press, 1992.

Science for Conservators: Includes an Introduction to Materials, Cleanings, and Adhesives and Coatings. 3 volumes. London: Routledge, 1992.

CONSTRUCTION AND BUILDING INSPECTORS

A s a city building inspector, Tom Wolff noticed problems almost as soon as he stepped inside the poorly maintained apartment complex. A leaky roof had allowed water to saturate some of the building materials, weakening them, and as a result, the ceiling was starting to collapse.

"We found stairways that were in disrepair, handrails that weren't there. It was virtually a deathtrap," he recalls.

It was 5:30 in the afternoon, and the building's numerous tenants were not pleased when Tom gave the order for them to vacate the premises immediately. The families were housed temporarily in other rental units their landlord owned. Meanwhile, Tom was arranging for the Red Cross to provide services that would help the tenants cope, filling out paperwork to document the incident, and working with the landlord to make sure the building's problems were corrected. Within a few days improvements had been implemented, and the tenants were allowed to move back into their apartments.

"It was just something that had to be done," Tom says. "All in all, it went well. The complex ended up being taken care of better. There were about 48 families that were better off because of it."

What Does a Construction and Building Inspector Do?

If a house is built on a defective foundation, it can collapse. If electrical wiring is not installed correctly, it can cause a catastrophic fire. If the concrete in a dam is not properly reinforced, the dam can burst and flood communities downstream. If a bridge near a fault line is not somewhat flexible, it can tear apart during an earthquake.

It is the job of *construction and building inspectors* to ensure that these and other structures are built, altered, and repaired properly, in accordance with building codes, ordinances, contract specifications, and zoning regulations. Some inspectors specialize in one area of expertise, such as mechanical components

or plumbing, and others examine various aspects of homes and other structures.

Construction and building inspectors visit the site of new construction when work there is just beginning, make several additional visits as the project progresses, and perform an overall inspection after construction is complete. They also inspect older structures that are being altered or repaired, and sometimes they investigate reports of construction or renovation that is being done without the proper permits.

The job requires a thorough knowledge of building codes and other specifications, along with

---

Definition
Construction and building inspectors examine new and renovated buildings, roads, bridges, dams, sewer and water systems, and other structures to ensure compliance with zoning requirements, building codes and ordinances, and contract specifications.

Alternative Job Titles
Building officials
Code officials
Fire safety inspectors
Home inspectors
Public works inspectors

High School Subjects
Mathematics
Technical/shop

Personal Skills
Leadership/management
Technical/scientific

Salary Range
$27,100 to $43,100 to $66,760+

Minimum Educational Requirements
High school diploma

Certification or Licensing
Recommended

Outlook
About as fast as the average

DOT
182

GOE
02.08.02

NOC
2264

O*NET-SOC
47-4011.00

---

enough experience in construction to recognize potential problems before a disaster happens. Most inspections are visual, but the inspector sometimes tests the strength of concrete or uses metering equipment, survey instruments, tape measures, and other tools. Inspectors record their work in logs, document it with photographs, and compile reports. If necessary, they report violations or other causes of concern, which can stop work on the project until the problem is remedied.

Building inspectors watch for structural defects and safety problems in residential, commercial, and industrial buildings. Before construction begins, they examine the soil and footings where the foundation will be laid. Their inspections include an examination of fire sprinklers, smoke control systems, alarms, fire doors, and exits. Sometimes they calculate fire insurance rates, taking into consideration the type of building, its contents and fire protection system, and the types of buildings nearby.

Some building inspectors specialize in areas of expertise, such as reinforced concrete or structural steel. *Plan examiners* are specialists who study blueprints before the building is constructed; they ensure that the plans comply with building codes and that the building will be suitable for the site.

Plumbing inspectors check the building's water and sewer pipes, fixtures, traps, drains, vents, and other components.

Electrical inspectors ensure that lights, wiring, motors, generating equipment, sound and security systems, heaters, air-conditioners, and appliances are installed and functioning properly.

Mechanical inspectors check the installation of heaters, air-conditioners, commercial kitchen appliances, butane and gasoline tanks, natural gas and oil pipes, and other appliances. Some also inspect ventilation equipment and boilers.

Elevator inspectors examine elevators, escalators, lifts, hoists, ski lifts, moving sidewalks, inclined railways, and amusement rides.

Home inspectors examine houses that have just been built or that are up for sale; they are often hired by potential buyers to assess the home's condition. A home inspection includes almost every component of the building and its systems, from the foundation to the attic.

Public works inspectors examine structures built under the oversight of federal, state, and local governments, including dams, water and sewer systems, bridges, streets, and highways. They inspect the placement of forms for concrete; the pouring and mixing of concrete; asphalt paving; and projects that involve excavation, filling, or grading. Some specialize in reinforced concrete; structural steel; highways; ditches; or dredging for bridges, dams, or harbors. The job involves keeping records of materials used and the general progress of a project so contract payments can be calculated.

Lingo to Learn

Building code Regulations that specify which materials and techniques can be used in various types of construction. The code also regulates other factors to address safety concerns, aesthetic values, and other considerations. For example, a building code might require that a garage be placed at least three feet from a street or the edge of the property, or it might require that a retaining wall be strong enough to withstand a mudslide during a heavy rainfall.

Building permit Formal permission, granted by a regulatory agency, to build or demolish structures such as houses, patios, garages, attics, stairways, and new roofs. The permit is granted after a professional determines whether the proposed project will comply with building codes, zoning requirements, and other regulations.

Geotechnical review An inspection that assesses the soil and other geological factors at a building site. The review is intended to detect potential problems, such as an unstable hillside that might slide if a house were built there.

Occupancy classification The type of use for which a building has been approved by a regulatory organization. For example, a building classified as a residential rental property usually cannot be converted to an industrial use without a new inspection and new certificate of occupancy.

Zoning Regulations that designate the types of buildings and other structures, along with their uses, that will be allowed in particular areas of a community. Residential neighborhoods are usually separated from industrial areas and may also be separated from retail establishments.

Construction and building inspectors sometimes work with *architects* who design buildings and other structures, but more often they deal with trade foremen, construction superintendents, real estate salespeople, and people purchasing real estate. They also work with homeowners, who are required to obtain permits and schedule inspections for large projects and smaller undertakings.

What Is It Like to Be a Construction and Building Inspector?

Tom Wolff is a senior building inspector for the Clark County Building Department in Las Vegas, Nevada. He arrives for work at seven in the morning and spends about half an hour answering telephone inquiries, then begins planning his day. "We get requests the day before for inspections. We do as many as 15 or 20 stops in one day. We inspect, we compare, we advise, and we record," he says.

He looks at a building's structure, plumbing, electricity, heating, ventilation, and air-conditioning systems. He compares the building to minimum code standards or minimum design standards. If he finds anything unacceptable, he advises the builders to contact their architects to remedy the problems, or if he is dealing with homeowners, he has them propose a solution and then tells them whether the proposal would correct the defect. Tom has to choose his words carefully and avoid proposing a solution himself, since he could be sued if anything went wrong because of his advice. Throughout the inspection process, he keeps records of what he has seen, said, and done.

Tom says that one of the best things about his job is that it gives him opportunities to share his experience in construction. "Personally, I enjoy helping people. It's really hard for me to bring bad news. If you get a kick out of giving people bad news, you probably shouldn't be an inspector. You need empathy."

Inspectors are in a somewhat awkward position, trying to enforce the law without offending people in the construction industry, which is a vital aspect of any community's economy. "You're not a cop," Tom explains. "You're a public servant. Treat your job accordingly. The construction industry is very important to local government entities. The government wants to make sure the construction industry is happy."

The government entities that perform building inspections are divided into various jurisdictions in Las Vegas. In Tom's jurisdiction seven inspectors cover about 23 square miles. Some of the inspectors specialize in one area, such as plumbing, but Tom does combination inspections of residential homes. In a typical day he might inspect a swimming pool, the framing of a roof that is being remodeled, the general structure of a new home under construction, and assorted other projects.

To inspect all these sites, Tom drives 40 to 70 miles every day. He says he enjoys the variety of the work and being on the move instead of having to remain at a desk in an office all day: "I appreciate being outdoors, being on a different site from hour to hour."

Sometimes, though, Tom is frustrated by difficulties in communication, even though he is adept at technical writing. Talking to many people in many situations and writing clear, accurate reports is a major part of his job.

He also must continually read long, complex building codes, which can be a dull undertaking. There are four national codes, and inspectors must also be familiar with their jurisdiction's modifications to those codes, along with local zoning regulations. Tom says, however, that it is more important to know where to find the regulations than to attempt to memorize all of them.

Tom has to know his job well and keep accurate records, or he could be sued. Written records help maintain communication among the many people involved in construction and the county building department, and they can be used as evidence in case of a lawsuit. Although Tom has been to court only twice on civil matters, a construction and building inspector is always at risk of a lawsuit.

According to Gary Fuller, a home inspector who owns Building Tech, Inc., in Spokane, Washington, "There's a lot of liability. You have a chance of being sued every time you do an inspection." Gary carries liability insurance, but he says the key to avoiding lawsuits is to have enough experience in construction to recognize defects in a building. People who are about to purchase new or used homes hire him to check the buildings before they finalize their transactions, and they expect him to notice every flaw, from broken rafters to a leaky roof to a malfunctioning furnace. "You have to be like Superman with X-ray vision," he comments.

Usually, however, his clients appreciate the service he provides for them. As a member of the American

Society of Home Inspectors (ASHI), Gary examines components of each home as specified by ASHI. He reviews the building's general structure, foundation, basement, floors, walls, ceilings, windows, doors, attic, roof, visible insulation, plumbing, heating and air-conditioning systems, and electrical wiring.

He usually spends up to two hours on each inspection, taking notes as he works. Then he uses a computer to write a narrative report, but he says other inspectors merely make check marks on a printed list. Like most professionals in this trade, Gary has found that the ability to communicate and write clear, detailed reports is an important quality for an inspector.

Do I Have What It Takes to Be a Construction and Building Inspector?

A construction and building inspector should have experience in construction, have a good driving record, be in good physical shape, have good communication skills, be able to pay attention to details, and have a strong personality. Although there are no standard requirements to enter this occupation, an inspector should be a responsible individual with in-depth knowledge of the construction trades. Inexperience can lead to mistakes that can cost someone a staggering amount of money or even cause a person's death.

The trade is not considered hazardous, but most inspectors wear hard hats as a precaution. Inspectors might need to climb ladders and walk across rooftops or perhaps trudge up numerous flights of stairs at building projects where elevators are not yet installed. Or they might occasionally find themselves squirming through the dirty, narrow, spider-infested crawl space under a house to check a foundation or crawling across the joists in a cramped, dusty, unfinished attic, inhaling insulation fibers and pesticides.

After the inspection a construction inspector needs to explain his or her findings clearly in reports and should expect to spend many hours answering questions in person, by telephone, and in letters. Because they often deliver bad news, they also need the emotional strength to stand firm on their reports, even when someone calls them a liar or threatens to sue.

On the other hand, an inspector knows that their work is to protect people. For example, they help ensure that a couple's new house will not be

> ### To Be a Successful Construction and Building Inspector, You Should . . .
>
> - ○ have experience in construction
> - ○ be detail oriented
> - ○ have excellent communication skills
> - ○ be in good physical condition
> - ○ be organized and able to work independently
> - ○ enjoy helping people
> - ○ have self-confidence

apt to burn down from an electrical short, and they might point out less dangerous problems, such as a malfunctioning septic tank or a leaking roof, that could require expensive repairs.

How Do I Become a Construction and Building Inspector?

Gary Fuller was a building contractor for 20 years before he became a home inspector in 1989. Like Gary, most construction and building inspectors have some previous experience in carpentry, plumbing, electrical work, or some other related occupation.

"Typically," Tom Wolff says, "they're working in one of the trades for several years and have gone through an apprenticeship. I would say certification and experience are probably the key to getting hired." To enter this profession, you can complete an apprenticeship program, study the building codes independently, or complete some college-level studies, then obtain certification from one of the professional associations.

EDUCATION

High School

A construction and building inspector needs to have at least a high school diploma or GED. To prepare for a career in this field, you should take courses

In-depth

Projects That Typically Require a Building Permit

The number of construction projects regulated by most cities might surprise you. For example, in many communities it is illegal to replace a bathroom sink or toilet, install a lawn sprinkler system, finish an attic or basement, put up a fence more than six feet high, or cut an opening for a new door in your own home without having it inspected by an official from the building department. A permit is required to abandon a cesspool, erect a small shed, enlarge a porch or roofed patio, pave a driveway, or alter the exterior of a building in an area zoned for certain environmental or scenic qualities.

Minor repairs and maintenance, such as replacing a concrete walkway or installing shelves do not require permits or inspections. Usually a homeowner can also paint a building, build a small patio or deck, or clear small areas of vegetation without a permit. In many cases an inspection is not necessary for larger projects if the homeowner does the work, but if a professional, friend, neighbor, or relative performs any of the work, a permit and inspection may be required.

A new construction project may require inspections by many specialists, such as officials from a city's planning, transportation, fire, water, forestry, and environment departments.

Less complex projects, such as adding a roof over an existing outdoor deck, may require review by just one inspector from the building department.

such as basic mathematics, computers, typing, shop, drafting, art, electronics, architectural drawing, and law. "We're dealing with law every day," Tom notes.

In addition, a part-time or summer job in construction would give you valuable experience, help you decide whether this might be the best career for you, and put you in touch with people in the field. You might also consider becoming involved with a local chapter of one of the trade associations or the National Fire Protection Agency. "Students would be welcome to attend the meetings and to join," Tom says.

Postsecondary Training

You don't have to go to college to become a construction or building inspector, but courses in subjects such as construction technology, building inspection, blueprint reading, mathematics, and public administration would give you a solid background for this career. Studies at college or vocational school can sometimes be substituted for on-the-job experience, and they will help you prepare for the certification examinations. Many employers are now requiring that their inspectors hold two-year, four-year, or advanced degrees in addition to practical experience. Finally, your promotion at some time in the future might depend on your educational background.

Nevertheless, Tom emphasizes that no amount of theoretical study can take the place of hands-on work in the field. Advanced education is good, he says, but it is not as important as experience and certification.

To retain his certification, Tom must participate in continuing education courses. Training of this type is available through trade associations, community colleges and vocational schools, or employers. Gary Fuller also stays up to date by attending continuing education seminars seven to nine times a year. He says he enjoys these learning experiences, where he studies the latest trends in areas such as heating, electrical, and plumbing systems.

CERTIFICATION OR LICENSING

In general, a license or certification is highly recommended but not necessarily required. Certification and licensing requirements vary widely among the states and individual employers. Many employers hire only licensed or certified professionals.

Certification for construction and building inspectors is available through three model code associations: The Building Officials and Code Administrators International (BOCA), the International Conference of Building Officials (ICBO), and the Southern Building Code Congress International (SBCCI). These three associations offer three different certification programs, but all are nationally recognized. Certification is available in various categories, such as certified building official, building inspector, electrical inspector, mechanical inspector, and plumbing inspector.

Tom expects to see the development of a national, standardized building code within the next few years. He predicts that hiring standards will vary with the employer but certification will be standardized.

Home inspectors are certified through the American Society of Home Inspectors (ASHI). Gary Fuller is not required to hold such credentials in Washington State, but he voluntarily became certified.

INTERNSHIPS AND VOLUNTEERSHIPS

Experience is probably the most important qualification for a construction and building inspector. Any hands-on work will provide valuable preparation for a career in this field. You could volunteer to help build houses with a service organization, such as Habitat for Humanity. Some home inspectors, particularly those who belong to the American Society of Home Inspectors, would be willing to let you accompany them as an observer on a few inspections.

A few internships for construction and building inspectors are available in the private sector. Some are designed to help construction workers who are undergoing a career change after an injury on the job.

More commonly, prospective inspectors are graduates of apprenticeship programs that provide them with on-the-job training. Many apprenticeship programs in the construction trades are administered by local offices of labor unions, such as the United Brotherhood of Carpenters or the Associated Builders and Contractors. For other apprenticeship opportunities, inquire at any Job Service office.

LABOR UNIONS

Tom belongs to the Service Employees International Union (SEIU). Other building inspectors employed by government agencies belong to the American Federation of State, City, and Municipal Employees (AFSCME).

Who Will Hire Me?

Tom Wolff began his career as a building inspector in California in 1985. "I was working as a public works maintenance worker and was promoted from within," he recalls, adding that he was doing "everything from picking up trash in the park to trimming trees" before his promotion and subsequent three months of training.

Previously, the city had hired several inspectors, but they kept moving on when other opportunities arose. Tom was offered the position because he had shown loyalty by working for the city for some time; he stayed on as an inspector there for nine years. It was an unusual way to become an inspector. "I was in the right place at the right time," he says.

More commonly, candidates find openings in the public sector or government agencies by watching the classified advertisements in newspapers. Job openings are also listed in the classified advertising sections of Internet sites and newsletters of various trade organizations. Several magazines, including *Western City* (westerncity.com), *Jobs Available* (http://www.jobsavailableonline.com), and the *International Conference of Building Officials' Building Standards* (http://www.iccsafe.org), feature advertisements for positions as an inspector.

For information about openings with government organizations, contact state or local employment services. You can also leave an "interest card'" with a government agency that interests you, and you will be contacted when an opening arises.

Approximately 60 percent of the construction and building inspectors in this country work for local governments, most frequently for city or county building departments, which may employ large staffs of specialized inspectors. These jobs are concentrated in cities and rapidly growing suburbs. Other inspectors work for state and federal government organizations, including the U.S. Army Corps of Engineers, the General Services Administration, the Department of Agriculture, the Department of the Interior, and the Department of Housing and Urban Development.

Nearly 17 percent of construction and building inspectors are employed by firms that provide

In-depth

Becoming a Self-Employed Home Inspector

The American Society of Home Inspectors (ASHI) estimates that it takes at least $25,000 in working capital to launch an independent home inspection business. You would also need a dependable vehicle for driving to numerous job sites and a computer for writing reports and keeping track of clients and finances. Expect overhead costs (rent, utilities, and other expenses) to take about half your income. Instead of opening an independent business, you could buy a franchise from an established home inspection organization. A franchise is a semi-independent, branch operation of a larger company. It requires an investment of your money, but it also features training and other support, such as advertising, from the parent company. A franchise is particularly attractive for new inspectors who have little experience in construction and business. While preparing for a career as a home inspector, beware of inspection "schools" that can cost up to $10,000 but offer little real education. Some include classes that won't teach you much or that don't include the most important information a home inspector needs. Others waste most of your money on computer equipment and books that consist mainly of irrelevant material copied from other books. Before enrolling in such a training program, check with a local chapter of ASHI or discuss the program with a home inspector in your area.

||||||||||||||||||||||||||||||||||||||||||||||||||||||||||||||||

architectural and engineering inspections for a fee or on contract. Many home inspectors are self-employed, but others work for large franchises.

Where Can I Go from Here?

Tom stayed with his first inspector job for nine years, then moved to Nevada because there was more opportunity there. He might become the supervisor of a staff of inspectors in Las Vegas, but he says he does not expect to advance further than that.

With enough experience and perhaps more education, he could become a building official in charge of the entire building department. He could also become a *plan checker*, one of the people who reviews blueprints and other documents before a building is constructed.

With credentials, a license, and enough money, a building inspector could follow Gary Fuller's example and launch a home inspection service. Getting started, he says, is "probably the toughest part of the business." To succeed as a self-employed home inspector, you would need to promote your business through avenues such as advertising, cultivating referrals, and doing a professional job to build a good reputation.

Gary remembers that after his years as a building contractor, he expected less demanding duties as a home inspector: "I thought it would be like semi-retiring, but it wasn't." Even though he is self-employed, he finds that he must keep working full time, because clients expect him to be available when they need his services. Still, he enjoys his new line of work and expects to continue in it indefinitely.

What Are the Salary Ranges?

Tom estimates that construction and building inspectors in government jobs earn about $20,000 to $48,000 a year nationwide, and it is not unusual to start at $30,000 to $32,000. In Las Vegas a county building inspector is paid about $39,578 to $54,748 annually.

In addition to his salary, Tom receives paid vacation time, paid sick leave, and a pension plan. Like other government employees, he is exempt from paying Social Security taxes.

In contrast, a self-employed home inspector's earnings depend entirely on the individual. Expertise, professionalism, and the ability to attract a large number of clients are the deciding factors. Gary Fuller says, "I know inspectors who make $300,000 a year, down to $10,000 a year."

According to the U.S. Department of Labor, the median annual salary of construction and building inspectors was $43,100 in 2003. Those in the middle 50 percent of earnings had salaries between $34,070 and $54,410. The lowest paid 10 percent earned $27,100, and the highest paid 10 percent earned $66,760.

According to a review of 2005 salaries for construction and building inspectors nationwide by Salary.com, the median earnings were $45,684. Pay is generally higher in the West and lowest in the Southeast, and workers in large cities usually earn more than those in rural areas.

What Is the Job Outlook?

Tom expects to see standardized building codes and other changes within his profession during the next decade or so, but he says, "Building inspectors will be here forever. As long as they're building buildings, the career will be in demand."

The U.S. Department of Labor expects that the number of openings for construction and building inspectors will grow about as fast as the average for all occupations through 2012. More buildings and other structures are being inspected because of increasing concern for public safety and improvements in the quality of construction.

Although the field is expanding, most job openings will be created as inspectors transfer to other professions or leave the workforce. There is a relatively high turnover in this field, because most inspectors are older workers who have years of experience but are nearing retirement age.

Workers with the most experience and education will have the best opportunities. Some college education, training in architecture or engineering, or certification as an inspector or plan examiner will give you a competitive edge. The ability to read and assess plans and blueprints is essential. There will be opportunities to work for architectural, engineering, and management firms that provide inspection services for government agencies, particularly at the state and federal level, as those agencies cut costs by contracting with the private sector.

Rapid growth is expected in the field of home inspections because more real estate will be sold as the population expands. Home inspectors enjoy a degree of job stability even during recessions, since their services are required for maintenance and repair

ADVANCEMENT POSSIBILITIES

Building officials are the managers in charge of city and county building departments. They usually have a background in public administration or business administration.

Plan examiners, also known as plan reviewers or plan checkers, review architectural drawings and other documents that describe proposed structures, along with related specifications, structural design calculations, and soil reports. The examiner checks for compliance with building codes. Plan examiners typically work for government agencies, architectural and engineering firms, or private consulting companies.

Supervisors are experienced, knowledgeable inspectors who oversee the rest of an inspection staff. Frequently, they have completed studies in business management and personnel management.

projects, not just for new construction. According to Gary Fuller, the field of home inspections is "growing by leaps and bounds. More people are becoming aware of inspection and finding a value in it."

How Do I Learn More?

PROFESSIONAL ORGANIZATIONS

The following organizations provide information on construction and building inspector careers, accredited schools, and employers:

American Construction Inspectors Association
12995 6th Street, Suite 69
Yucaipa, CA 92399
888-867-2242
http://www.acia.com

American Society of Home Inspectors
932 Lee Street, Suite 101
Des Plaines, IL 60016
800-743-2744
http://www.ashi.com

Association of Construction Inspectors
1224 North Nokomis, NE
Alexandria, MN 56308
320-763-7525
http://iami.org/aci

International Code Council
5203 Leesburg Pike, Suite 600
Falls Church, VA 22041
703-931-4533
http://www.iccsafe.org

The following organizations consolidated and can be reached through the International Code Council:

Building Officials and Code Administrators International

International Conference of Building Officials

Southern Building Code Congress International

BIBLIOGRAPHY

The following is a sampling of materials relating to the professional concerns and development of construction and building inspectors:

Burgess, Russell W. *Real Estate Home Inspection: Mastering the Profession.* Chicago: Real Estate Education Company, 1998.

Careers in Focus: Construction. 3d ed. Chicago: Ferguson Publishing Company, 2001.

Domel, August W. *Basic Engineering Calculations for Contractors.* New York: McGraw-Hill, 1996.

Friedman, Donald. *The Investigation of Buildings: A Guide for Architects, Engineers, and Owners.* New York: W.W. Norton & Company, 2000.

Glover, P.V. *Building Surveys.* 3d ed. Woburn, Mass.: Butterworth-Heinemann, 1996.

O'Brien, James J. *Construction Inspection Handbook: Total Quality Management,* 4th ed. New York: Chapman & Hall, 1997.

Sumichrast, Michael. *Opportunities in Building Careers.* Lincolnwood, Ill.: VGM Career Horizons, 1999.

CYTOTECHNOLOGISTS

The room is quiet, the lights bright. Bill Crabtree positions a glass slide under the microscope lens and studies the collected cell sample. He's on the lookout for abnormal growth patterns. A cytotechnologist and director of the Indiana University School of Medicine's Cytotechnology Program, Bill spends the majority of his day at the bench, peering through the microscope and picking out cell samples that appear to be cancerous. "We're cell detectives," says Bill. "We really affect people's lives. What we do can be a matter of life or death."

Like good detectives, cytotechnologists are careful and precise. They are laboratory specialists who search cell specimens, seeking out abnormalities. Some forms of cancer, a tumor growing on someone's liver, for instance, can be seen with the naked eye, but other types of cancer are not so easily detected. Cytotechnologists are particularly effective at finding cancer of the cervix. Much of their work involves diagnosing Pap smears, cell samples that are taken during routine gynecological exams. Because of the detective skills cytotechnologists bring to their profession, the death rate from cancer of the cervix is 25 percent lower than what it was 40 years ago.

"Cytotechnology is a challenging field," says Bill, "but it's a good one if you like laboratory work. Plus it's a field where you can really make a difference."

What Does a Cytotechnologist Do?

Cytotechnologists perform the majority of their work by looking through a microscope at prepared slides. They study cell growth patterns and check to see whether the specimens under the lens have normal or abnormal patterns. Abnormal patterns can indicate the presence of disease. Cytotechnologists search for changes in cell color, shape, or size. A change in any one of these can be cause for concern. In any single slide there may be more than 100,000 cells, so cytotechnologists must be patient and thorough in order to make accurate evaluations.

Cytotechnologists do more than peer through microscopes. When they are away from the laboratory, they may work at patients' bedsides assisting doctors in the direct collection of cell samples. The respiratory system, urinary system, and gastrointestinal tract

Definition
Cytotechnologists study cells. They assist in the collection of body cells, prepare slides, and examine cells using microscopes. Cytotechnologists search for cell abnormalities in order to aid in the diagnosis of disease.

High School Subjects
Biology
Chemistry
Computer science

Personal Skills
Following instructions
Technical/scientific

Salary Range
$30,530 to $42,910 to $58,000

Minimum Educational Level
At least one year of professional instruction in cytotechnology after or included in a bachelor of science degree.

Certification or Licensing
Required by certain states

Outlook
About as fast as the average

DOT
078

GOE
14.05.01

NOC
3211

O*NET-SOC
29-2011.00

are some of the body sites from which cells may be gathered. Cytotechnologists also assist physicians with bronchoscopies and with needle aspirations, a process that uses very fine needles to suction cells from many locations within the body. Needle aspirations sometimes replace invasive surgeries as a means of gathering microscopic matter for disease detection. Once cells are collected, cytotechnologists may prepare the slides so that the cell samples can be examined under the microscope. In some laboratories, medical technicians prepare slides rather than cytotechnologists.

Another part of the cytotechnologist's day is spent keeping records, filing reports, and consulting with co-workers and pathologists on cases. Cytotechnologists can issue diagnoses on Pap smears if the diagnosis is normal. However, if cell examination indicates any abnormalities, Pap smear results as well as other cytological results are sent on to supervising cytotechnologists or to pathologists for review.

Most of the time cytotechnologists work independently. They may share lab space with other personnel, but the primary job of a cytotechnologist is to look through the microscope and search for evidence of disease. Most cytotechnologists work for private firms that are hired by physicians to evaluate medical tests, but many cytotechnologists also work for hospitals or university research institutions.

What Is It Like to Be a Cytotechnologist?

"Where I work," says Bill, "it's routine for cytotechnologists to spend 50 or 60 percent of their day at the microscope. Like all cytotechnologists, we see a lot of Pap smears, but at the Indiana University School of Medicine we also look at cell samples that are nongynecological, too. We look at material collected from any kind of solid tumor, at abdominal fluids, thoracic fluids, urine samples, sputum, brushes and washes of the lungs and bronchial passages, lesions from the gastrointestinal tract, scrapings from the mouth or skin, and spinal fluid. Occasionally we can identify microbiological infections, bacteria, fungus, and such, but principally we're diagnosing cancer or its precursors."

Cytotechnologists usually work a standard eight-hour day, five days a week. They also do a lot of work on computers. They enter and retrieve information using computers. Diagnostic results are entered into computers so that pathologists can directly access the information and make the results available to patients.

"Since I'm at a university medical school," says Bill, "part of my day is involved with the education program for cytotechnology students and part of my day is involved with research. Another part of my time is spent working on quality control and going through quality assurance procedures. I also file reports and keep records using the computer."

Susan Dingler also works at a teaching hospital. "Simply working in a laboratory can be repetitive," she says, "but here at the School of Cytotechnology at Henry Ford Hospital in Detroit, cytotechnologists rotate job duties. One week I might work in the

Lingo to Learn

Bronchoscopy The taking of tissue samples from the bronchi (in the lungs) with the use of a bronchoscope.

Cell The structural unit of which all body tissues are formed. The human body is composed of billions of cells differing in size and structure.

Cervix The hollow end of a woman's uterus that forms the passageway to the vaginal canal.

Gastrointestinal Relating to the digestive system.

Gynecology The branch of medicine that deals with the reproductive system of women.

Needle aspiration The taking of tissue with the use of a long, syringe needle.

Pathologist A doctor who specializes in the study of diseases.

Sputum Expectorated matter, usually from the lungs.

Tumor A swelling in or on a particular area of the body, usually created by the development of a mass of new tissue cells having no function. Tumors may be benign (noncancerous) or malignant (cancerous).

preparation area, extracting cells and preparing slides. We use various methods, depending on the source of the cells and the amount of sample available. Another week I might assist with needle aspirations. Or I could be working in the CAT scan room. Then again, I could be involved with coordinating our education program.

"Everybody's cells and every single tumor is different," says Susan. "There are similarities—otherwise we wouldn't be able to do our work—but because no two cells look exactly the same, I'm never bored when I'm looking through the microscope. Cytotechnology is an especially challenging field."

Bernadette Inclan works for a private company in Phoenix, Arizona. Unlike Bill and Susan, she does not teach students or perform research. She does not work for a university. As a quality insurance inspector, she oversees the work done in several private laboratories located across the Southwest and along the West Coast.

Because the diagnoses that cytotechnologists make can literally be matters of life and death, the profession is governed by a system of checks and balances. Bernadette and other supervisors help make sure that the medical tests cytotechnologists perform are accurate. For example, she does second screenings to assure quality control and to confirm test results on high-risk patients.

When specimens are hard to screen because the sample itself is very small or because the cells are obscured by too much blood, Bernadette is also called upon to give her expert opinion. In fact, any time any cytotechnologist in her company's laboratories marks a sample "Please Check" (meaning that the cytotechnologist is unable to make an unequivocal decision about the contents of the cell sample), Bernadette or one of the other supervisors double-checks the work. Bernadette is also involved in managing people. "It's an exciting time for us,"she says. "My firm is merging with another health lab and so that means a lot of changes. I'll do a lot of traveling between company sites and help make sure that the merger goes well for our cytotechnology team. I'll also make sure that the work continues successfully in the lab."

Cytotechnologists work more closely with physicians, especially with pathologists, than do most laboratory workers.

Teamwork is an important feature of cytotechnology. "Sure, we're behind individual microscopes a lot of the time," says Bill. "But really we're rather unique in the health care field. Cytotechnologists work more closely with physicians, especially with pathologists, than do most laboratory workers. Plus we work together as cytotechnologists, consulting with each other and with our supervisors on unusual cases."

Do I Have What It Takes to Be a Cytotechnologist?

"The person who gets straight A's does not necessarily make the best cytotechnologist. Our job involves more than learning facts and memorizing information. You need to know how to apply what you learn when you look through the microscope. You need a knack for detail," Bill says. "Cytotechnologists are very art-oriented really." He goes on to explain that cytotechnologists must be good observers. Like artists they search for subtleties in color, shape, and size. "Cytotechnology is an art as well as a science," Bill says.

"If you like to work jigsaw puzzles, cytotechnology just might be the career for you," suggests Susan. "Like jigsaw puzzle fans, cytotechnologists enjoy comparing the shapes and sizes of small objects, scanning a lot of similar objects as they try to detect subtle differences. Both puzzles and microscope work require hard concentration, patience, and observation of acute detail."

Bernadette adds, "You must be meticulous and able to make your own decisions. The supervisor is there to back you up, but a lot of your original work will be done at the bench, working alone at the microscope. Cytotechnologists use worksheets and must follow the printed orders exactly. In addition, you must be able to sit for long periods of time without moving from the bench. It's not like working with a computer keyboard. You can't shift positions and place the microscope on your lap."

"One big advantage of working in cytotechnology," says Bernadette, "is that you can come to work, do your job, and then go home. It is literally impossible to take your work home with you. Oh, you may go home and mull over an interesting case sometimes, but that's all you can do. Plus, if you're ever unsure about a diagnosis, there's always another set of eyes there to help you out. Still, cytotechnology can get monotonous at times, especially if you're working in a huge lab and doing nothing but processing Pap smears."

Cytotechnology is a good field for someone who is less people oriented but who still enjoys working in the medical field. "I wanted a job with stability and lots of opportunities," says Bill, "where I could make good money and work at an interesting job in a laboratory."

To Be a Successful Cytotechnologist, You Should . . .

- ○ be patient and precise
- ○ be detail oriented
- ○ be a problem solver
- ○ enjoy working at a microscope
- ○ be a responsible decision-maker
- ○ be willing to stay seated for long periods of time

"It's an especially challenging field," Susan says. "The best thing for me is that cytotechnologists are involved in patient diagnosis. We don't just handle specimens and pass on the results. We're the first to evaluate. We get to give our opinion. Cytotechnology appeals to people who want to be responsible and who want to be involved in something that will have a direct effect on patient care."

How Do I Become a Cytotechnologist?

Bill fell into the career of cytotechnology by accident. "I always enjoyed studying biology," he says. "I was interested in disease, but I knew that I didn't want to become a physician. Then I stumbled across a brochure that described laboratory careers, including cytotechnology. It sounded good." He attended school at the University of Tennessee and then had the chance to work on a large research project, the National Bladder Cancer Project. He's been in the field for more than 18 years and now directs a program to train new cytotechnologists.

Susan entered the field of cytotechnology after studying medical technology for two years. She'd taken seven chemistry classes already and didn't look forward to taking any more. She enjoyed studying the biological sciences, however, and began searching for a new course of study that could take her in that direction. Cytotechnology fit what she was looking for, and, more than 32 years later, she still enjoys her work as a cytotechnologist.

EDUCATION

High School

Biology, chemistry, and other science courses are necessary for students wishing to become cytotechnologists. Math, English, and computer literacy classes are also important. In addition, you should be sure to fulfill the entrance requirements of the college or university you plan to attend.

Postsecondary Training

There are two routes you may take to become a cytotechnologist. One route involves obtaining a bachelor's degree in biology, life sciences, or a related field. Following this, you can enter a one-year, postbaccalaureate certificate program sponsored by a hospital or university accredited by the Commission on Accreditation of Allied Health Education Programs (CAAHEP).

The second route involves transferring into a cytotechnology program during your junior or senior year of college and earning a bachelor of science degree in cytotechnology. In both cases, you earn a college degree and complete at least one year of training in cytotechnology.

General college course work includes biology, microbiology, parasitology, cell biology, physiology, anatomy, zoology, histology, embryology, genetics, chemistry, computer science, and mathematics. Additional courses include cytochemistry, cytophysiology, diagnostic cytology, endocrinology, medical terminology, the study of inflammatory diseases, and the history of cytology. You learn how to prepare slides, use microscopes, and follow safe laboratory procedures.

CERTIFICATION OR LICENSING

Cytotechnology graduates (from either degree programs or certificate programs) may register for the certification examination given by the Board of Registry of the American Society of Clinical Pathologists. Most states require cytotechnologists to be certified, and most employers insist that new employees be certified. Usually it is a requirement for advancement in the field.

Many continuing education programs exist for professionals working in the field of cytotechnology.

It is important that practicing cytotechnologists remain current with new ideas, techniques, and medical discoveries.

SCHOLARSHIPS AND GRANTS

Most colleges and universities offer general scholarships. Institutions with specific cytotechnology programs are most likely to have scholarships available for students interested in the field.

In exchange for a promise of two to three years of staff work at a private laboratory, some employers offer scholarships to students.

INTERNSHIPS AND VOLUNTEERSHIPS

Colleges and universities, along with professional organizations, are sources of information on work-study projects and student internships. For more information, contact the program director at individual teaching institutions. A list of accredited cytotechnology programs may be obtained through the American Society of Cytopathology (see "How Do I Learn More?").

Who Will Hire Me?

Like many veteran cytotechnologists, Susan now directs a teaching program. More than 50 hospitals and universities have CAAHEP-approved programs in cytotechnology. Other cytotechnologists are involved in research. Some cytotechnologists work for federal and state governments and some work in private industry, nursing homes, public health facilities, or businesses. The majority of cytotechnologists work for either hospitals or for private laboratories.

Demand for cytotechnologists is high, and recruiters often visit universities and teaching hospitals in the months prior to graduation. Professional journals also list advertisements for employment.

Where Can I Go from Here?

Cytotechnologists who work in larger labs may move up to supervisory positions. However, cytotechnologists seeking managerial or administrative positions

FYI

The field of cytotechnology is only a half century old. It began in the 1940s, more than 10 years after Dr. George N. Papanicolaou (1883–1962), a Greek-American physician, developed a procedure for early diagnosis of cancer of the uterus in 1928. Dr. Papanicolaou collected cell samples by scraping the cervixes of female patients. He placed these cell samples on glass slides. The slides were then stained so that individual cell differences and abnormalities could be studied more easily. Using microscopes, medical laboratory workers then compared cells known to be healthy against those known to be diseased. As the value of the "Pap smear" (the term used for the test Dr. Papanicolaou developed) became more widely accepted, demand for laboratory personnel trained to read Pap smears grew, and the career of cytotechnologist was born. Over time, the field of cytotechnology expanded to include examination of other cell specimens besides gynecological samples.

in smaller labs may find limited opportunities for advancement. Another career move might be to enter the teaching field and direct classes or oversee research.

Some cytotechnologists join forces with medical directors and open their own laboratories. One creative cytotechnologist opened his own business by concentrating on his expertise at staining cells. He developed his own line of chemicals and is now a leader in the staining industry.

What Are the Salary Ranges?

According to the American Society of Clinical Pathologists (ASCP), in 2003 the national average

Advancement Possibilities

Teaching supervisors in medical technology teach one or more phases of medical technology to students of medicine, medical technology, or nursing arts.

Chief medical technologists direct and coordinate activities of workers engaged in performing chemical, microscopic, and bacteriologic tests to obtain data for use in diagnosis and treatment of diseases.

Cytology supervisors supervise and coordinate activities of staff in cytology laboratories.

Pathologists are medical doctors who specialize in the study and diagnosis of diseases.

annual salary for cytotechnologists was $41,600. Supervisors averaged $50,960 annually. A 2002 wage survey of medical laboratories conducted by ASCP found that the median annual salary for those starting out as medical technologists was $40,186. The median top rate for these technologists was $45,760 annually. According to the *Occupational Outlook Handbook*, the median annual earnings of clinical laboratory technologists were $42,910 in 2002. The lowest paid 10 percent earned less than $30,530 annually, while the top 10 percent earned more than $58,000. Those employed by the federal government earn slightly less overall. Cytotechnologists working in private laboratories earn slightly more than those working in hospitals. Geographically, salaries are highest in the West.

What Is the Job Outlook?

The U.S. Department of Labor reports that employment of clinical laboratory workers is expected to grow about as fast as the average for all occupations. Competition to enter cytotechnology programs is keen and shortages still exist for qualified graduates. The demand for cytotechnologists is especially high in private industry. As more and more hospitals contract with private companies to perform

work formerly done inside hospitals, more jobs will open up. Additional governmental regulations now limit the number of slides cytotechnologists may work with each day and this adds to the shortage of qualified personnel.

In the future, the demand for cytotechnologists may be slowed somewhat by advances in laboratory automation, but for now demand remains very high.

Vacancy rates for cytotechnologists are highest in the southern United States and in the mountain states of the West. Vacancy rates are lowest in areas closest to universities or teaching hospitals with cytotechnology programs, but shortages in this field exist in every geographical area.

How Do I Learn More?

PROFESSIONAL ORGANIZATIONS

For information about training programs and educational materials, contact the following organizations:

American Society for Cytopathology
400 West 9th Street, Suite 201
Wilmington, DE 19801
302-429-8802
bjenkins@cytopathology.org
http://www.cytopathology.org

American Society for Cytotechnology
1500 Sunday Drive, Suite 102
Raleigh, NC 27607
800-948-3947
info@asct.com
http://www.asct.com

FYI

To prepare a slide, cells are spread, or "fixed," in the center of narrow glass rectangles. Following this, colored dye is added to emphasize cell structure and make disease detection easier. Finally, using a smaller piece of glass, the specimens are covered and sealed in order to preserve them.

Contact ASCP for information on educational courses and a career brochure about cytotechnology and other clinical technology careers:

American Society of Clinical Pathologists
2100 West Harrison Street
Chicago, IL 60612
info@ascp.org
312-738-1336
http://www.ascp.org

To learn about accredited cytotechnology programs, contact

Commission on Accreditation of Allied Health Education Programs
35 East Wacker Drive, Suite 1970
Chicago, IL 60601-2208
312-553-9355
anned@caahep.org
http://www.caahep.org

BIBLIOGRAPHY

The following is a sampling of materials relating to the professional concerns and development of cytotechnologists:

Bibbo, Marluce, ed. *Comprehensive Cytopathology.* 2d ed. Philadelphia: W. B. Saunders, 1997.

Geisinger, Kim R. et al. *Modern Cytopathology.* New York: Churchill Livingstone, 2003.

Gray, Winifred and Grace T. McKee. *Diagnostic Cytopathology.* New York: Churchill Livingstone, 2002.

Keebler, Catherine M. *The Manual of Cytotechnology.* 7th ed. Chicago: American Society of Clinical Pathologists, 1993.

DATABASE SPECIALISTS

As a database administrator for e2 Communications, a leading company in e-mail marketing, Henry Jackson works with the Microsoft SQL Server 7.0. "The marketing done by e2," Henry says, "differs from what is classically known as spam. All our customer base, anybody we send e-mail messages to has to be an active client of the company."

The company has been helping clients to better promote themselves and serve their customers through the inexpensive medium of e-mail, and a variety of data must be carefully managed. Henry sees his work as having two sides—the physical side of assuring that the database is performing as needed, and the logical side which consists of conceptualizing how the database can best serve the business.

"When you think about a database," he says, "think of a picture with a lot of entities. Say you have an order-centric business: You have the entity that's the customer, an entity that's the order, and each of those entities will have an attribute. A customer will have a first name, last name, address, personal information like date of birth, credit card number, etc. You'd have another entity that's the product, and then you marry an order with one or many products. It becomes a big puzzle that you put together, and if you do it correctly, the logical design should reflect how your business operates."

What Does a Database Specialist Do?

Because of the incredible strides in computer technology and the promise of continued advances, issues surrounding information management are at the forefront of the industry. What is the best way to store information in a computer? How should data be organized to allow easy access by multiple users? How can files be encoded so that only specified ones are retrieved by a given search? Everything from judicial court decisions to credit card customer accounts to professional organizations' mailing lists has to be stored in computers in an organized fashion so that the information can be accessed and updated easily, accurately, and efficiently.

Definition
Database specialists design, install, update, modify, and otherwise maintain computer databases and provide technical support and training.

Alternative Job Titles
Database design analysts
Database managers
Database programmers
Information systems managers

High School Subjects
Business
Computer science
Mathematics

Personal Skills
Leadership/management
Technical/scientific

Salary Range
$70,681 to $81,416 to $94,416+

Minimum Educational Level
Associate's degree

Certification or Licensing
Voluntary

Outlook
Much faster than the average

DOT
039

GOE
02.06.01

NOC
2172

O*NET-SOC
15-1061.00

The branch of computer science and technology that attempts most directly to answer these questions is database management. A database management system, also called a database engine, is the commercial software used to organize information. The word "database" refers to the actual collection of information stored by the database engine.

Database specialists design, install, update, modify, maintain, and repair computer databases. This range of duties involves numerous and varied tasks, usually too much work for one person to handle (unless he or she works for a small company). Typically, several individuals or a whole group of database engineers and technicians team up to make sure that all functions are covered.

Specific assignments for each position in database technology and management differ according to the nature and scope of the company or department, as well as the education and work experience of the end user. Although job titles are flexible, most database specialists perform some combination of the responsibilities described in this section.

Database administrators rely on their knowledge of database management in order to code, test, and install new databases. They also coordinate changes made to already existing ones. Many administrators work closely with other computer professionals in order to determine the most logical and efficient way to operate databases in a given situation. They might instead concentrate on reviewing descriptions of database changes and thinking through how those changes might affect the way information is stored, where it is stored, and the method used to access it.

For example, if the management of a bank decides to use a new system for the assignment of personal identification numbers for automated teller machines, the database administrator has to analyze, among other things, how those changes will be encoded in the database system at large, how such codes will be entered into each customer's account number, and how and by whom they will be accessed, since the information is highly confidential. They then execute all necessary programming changes, such as specifying who can get access to what files when, testing and correcting errors, selecting a utility program to monitor database performance, and advising programmers and analysts about the need for further improvements. They may also be involved in training users on new procedures.

Lingo to Learn

Application A complex software program that allows users to perform certain tasks such as word processing, record keeping, or page layout.

Backup Copies of computer files on disk or CD-ROM stored in a place other than the main work site. Used in emergency situations.

Data dictionary Information about data, including name, description, source of data item, and key words for categorizing and searching for data items.

Hardware The physical equipment inside a computer that makes it operate.

Physical database Location, space requirements, and access methods used to protect the system from unauthorized users and accidental destruction.

Software Computer programs that are designed to perform very specific functions, such as word processing programs and games.

Technical support Maintenance and repair performed by a computer technician on a computer, peripherals, or software applications. Also includes verbal support via telephone or Internet.

User support Online or live telephone assistance offered by a computer technician to a system user.

FYI

Database management systems (DBMS) include

- Oracle9i
- Sybase SQL (Structured Query Language)
- Microsoft SQL Server
- IBM DB2
- Informix Dynamic Server (IDS)

Database design analysts design databases and coordinate database development as part of a team. Database design includes very broad as well as very detailed work. First, design analysts review the database request, meeting at length with clients and colleagues. Next, they analyze the desired parameters of the database and decide whether or not existing database programs can be updated to include changes. Only very rarely do they design an entirely new database management system. Design analysts then present to clients or colleagues a time and cost estimate of the implementation of the proposal. If it is approved, design analysts use database manuals to figure out how changes should be made. They revise

In-depth

Databases in Everyday Life

Many people do not realize the extent to which they come into contact with computer databases in their daily lives. In fact, databases are used all around us in order to make everyday interactions more efficient and accurate. Think about some typical Saturday afternoon errands to understand just how much this is true.

The first stop might be to return the movies you rented the night before. Since the video store keeps a record of all its videos/DVDs and clientele on a computer database, the clerk logs the return into the computer, and the database automatically credits the account, tallies appropriate fees, and marks the movie as available for the next customer.

The second stop is the library. Here, you look up a book on the electronic card catalog, which itself is a huge database that might even be connected to even bigger library databases around the world. Some libraries have online access to databases offering information on about anything you can think of.

If you want to read reviews of current movies, see what is good on TV, or go through recent publications to do research for your English paper, you can find it quickly and easily, thanks to databases.

The next stop is the music store. If you want to know if a favorite old song is out on compact disc, the clerk checks either directly on the computer database or consults a printed book, the hard-copy product of the commercial music database.

Virtually any purchase made involves contact with a database. At the grocery store, the clerk uses a laser scanner that reads the product code on your box of cereal, which has the product name and price information stored on a database that is accessed with the input of the code. At the department store, the clerk uses a similar scanner to total up the cost of your new pair of jeans. Databases allow businesses to do much more than check out customers, however; they also make it easier for store managers to do inventory and ordering (that is one less pair of jeans, 25 are left, order more when the total reaches 15), and for owners and business executives to do better financial analysis and market studies (Jane Smith, aged 18, bought one pair of jeans on October 23; last purchase two T-shirts, October 21, send sale advertisement when jeans are on sale again).

Databases on a much larger scale also affect our lives every day. Social security numbers, and the employment, benefits, and tax information stored with them, are organized in databases. The U.S. Census Bureau keeps all of its data on databases as well. The bureau compiles statistics from these files, which store hundreds of millions of pieces of information. The Internal Revenue Service maintains databases similar in scope, as do welfare and Medicaid offices, and all other government agencies.

Have you or your parents ever received junk mail? Lists of names and addresses for political and commercial mailings are kept on databases. With the use of special codes, companies can keep track of regional or even individual consumer preferences.

These are only a few of the databases we come into contact with every day. A complete list would be so long and intricate, we would need another database to organize it!

the current data dictionary and write descriptions for programmers of how programs should access data. They also write descriptions of the logical and physical databases.

Those who specialize in adding, deleting, and modifying data items in data dictionaries are sometimes called *data dictionary administrators*.

What Is It Like to Be a Database Specialist?

Although e2 Communications has only been around for a few years, it is somewhat of a veteran in the world of Internet business and e-mail marketing. Henry Jackson, a database administrator, plays a key role in keeping the company's business practices directed toward its ultimate goals. "When they started the company," Henry says, "there was no such thing as e-mail marketing. Now it's as mature as it can be for the Internet world. My job is to determine where we are as a business, and where we're going, and try to model data storage so it reflects how our business operates."

To meet these goals, Henry finds himself working many hours a week, and must be on call. "My primary responsibilities," Henry says, "are to make sure the production database environment is alive and well, plan for disaster recovery, and develop database solutions for our company."

Henry explains that typically in a company there are two types of database administrators. "One is a *production support administrator*. They are mainly concerned with making sure the physical database environment is alive—which means everyone is able to access it, that it performs fast, that it can run queries fast. They work closely with network administrators.

The other type is the *database developer*. They work with application concerns—making sure the database runs in such a manner to work effectively with the application. I've been fortunate that I've been able to straddle the fence, so I've had a wide range of experience. But a large company, like a Fortune 500, will make clear delineations between the two. They have a staff for production support, and a staff for database development."

Henry's day begins much as the days of most computer professionals—he makes sure that no problems occurred during the night. "I have the

server pretty much automated, so that if problems occur, I'm automatically notified." Henry then deals with any pressing requests. "When we have new companies, we have to add new users to the database, or maybe make some security changes."

Once Henry determines that the "physical" environment is running as needed, he moves on to the "logical," design portion of the database. He says, "The majority of my time is spent in development of logical design of database objects and working closely with the application developers."

> The majority of my time is spent in development of logical design of database objects and working closely with the application developers.

Henry says that a database administrator should have quite a bit of downtime when everything is running efficiently. "So my focus becomes more of that of a database developer throughout the day." When he first comes onto a new project, he analyzes the existing database structure and looks for ways to improve it to better meet business needs. "Once I analyze, I come up with an optimal design, which usually isn't going to jive with what's currently there. It's not an easy transition, either. I have to develop a plan, to say, 'This is where we need to be and here are the incremental steps we can take so that we don't impact our business while we get going in the right direction.'"

In essence, Henry is modeling e2's business. "I compare the logical model with what is currently in place, and we try to take the best parts of the current system and also implement the parts we feel will move us in the direction we need to be in the company." After Henry has figured out that right direction, he must convince the company's decision makers of it. "That's usually not a hard sell," he says. "The hard part is sparking the proper amount of urgency to actually move in the direction we need to be. From the time you determine what the optimal, logical design is, to the time you implement any portion of it in the production environment, you're probably looking at nine to 12 months. It's not a very swift process."

To Be a Successful Database Specialist, You Should . . .

○ be detail oriented

○ have strong analytical and problem-solving skills

○ like to figure out creative solutions to challenging problems

○ be able to communicate effectively with people on all levels of technical understanding

○ be able to analyze a problem from several angles

Do I Have What It Takes to Be a Database Specialist?

Database specialists, whether involved with design, programming, or administration, must eventually be able to account for every bit of information used by the system. The ability to pay extremely close attention to detail is therefore an indispensable quality of a database specialist.

To be a successful database specialist, you must be a strong problem solver. You need good analytical thinking skills and a flair for intellectual creativity in order to be able to invent new ways of doing things.

For Henry, the challenges are the most rewarding aspects of his job. "What you do day to day changes," Henry says, "and when you meet those challenges, it's very satisfying."

Solid communication skills, both verbal and written, are essential if you want to be a database specialist. Technicians deal all the time with people who have little technical knowledge. A specialist has to be able to explain to users in nontechnical terms the nature of the situation.

Although database specialists are trained to develop the most efficient and logical solution to a problem, you should not become frustrated if time limitations or client preferences somehow impinge on that. You also must be prepared to put in many hours. "Some days you might work four hours," Henry says, "and some days you work 18. It's an inconsistent schedule."

How Do I Become a Database Specialist?

Henry developed his skills as a database specialist while training in other computer jobs. "I was exposed to many different relational databases," he says. "I worked with IBM DB2, with Oracle. Late in the game, I worked with an SQL Server." After working as a consultant, he decided he wanted to work as a database administrator, so he sought out jobs in which he could work under a mentor. "But my first position as a DBA [database administrator], and really wherever I've worked, I was the only DBA. There was no mentor, so it was a lot of trial by fire. I knew enough about database systems to stay afloat, and I've never been shy about reading additional reference materials."

EDUCATION

High School

A high school diploma is required for all database specialists. Among the traditional subjects, mathematics, including algebra and geometry, are particularly good at helping you develop strong analytical and problem-solving skills. Science classes, especially those like chemistry and physics that rely on investigative laboratory experiments, train you how to approach a problem and solve it by using precise scientific methods. English and speech classes help you develop solid communication skills which can be necessary in presenting proposals to clients.

High school courses in computers, whether in basics, business applications, programming, or computer science, give prospective database specialists an excellent background. Business classes like accounting or statistics can be important for technicians involved in the decision-making process that surrounds project selection, as well as giving an insight into the basic needs and operations of businesses (and future clients). Drafting and mechanical drawing classes allow you to practice skills that become important in flow-chart and schematic-drawing construction and analyzing.

Postsecondary Training

In many instances, companies pay long-time employees to acquire training in database management through self-study, vendor educational workshops, and technical school classes.

Self-study involves reading related trade books and magazines, investigating and learning about the computer products on the business and consumer market, talking with people in the field to find out what's out there, and practicing database design and programming.

Hardware and software vendor workshops provide employees of a client company with training on the systems purchased by their employers.

Depending on the scope and needs of the company and the prior experience of the employee, postsecondary training is not always necessary. Employees interested in pursuing database management who work in a company that could benefit from such on-staff expertise should investigate these types of opportunities. Employers may offer educational assistance or time off to facilitate study.

Newcomers to the work force, however, should be formally educated in some area of computer technology. Many technical schools offer courses in database management as part of an associate's degree in a business-related computer applications program. An associate's degree demonstrates to a prospective employer that the applicant has the intellectual ability, general computer knowledge, and professional drive to become an outstanding database specialist. Some employers look for applicants with bachelor's degrees.

CERTIFICATION OR LICENSING

There is no standard certification for database specialists, though Microsoft and Oracle offer certification in their products. By completing special programs offered in college technology programs, you can become a Microsoft Certified Database Administrator or an Oracle Certified Professional. Such certification is rarely required by employers, but it does demonstrate an applicant's understanding of the popular database systems.

SCHOLARSHIPS AND GRANTS

There are currently no scholarships or grants specifically designated for individuals who wish to pursue education in database management. As mentioned above, individuals already employed should speak with supervisors, managers, and the personnel office about opportunities for tuition reimbursement and scheduled time off for education.

If you are seeking formal education, work closely with your school's financial aid department to keep on top of the latest scholarships, grants, and federally subsidized student loans. Some professional associations geared toward the computer industry offer student scholarships and grants. The Association for Computing Machinery (ACM) maintains scholarship and grant information at its Web site.

INTERNSHIPS AND VOLUNTEERSHIPS

There are not many internships available for individuals interested in database management. This is due in part to the fact that so many people train themselves in the field while already employed full time. As demand for database specialists grows, however, companies may be open to internship possibilities. It may be to your benefit to convince them.

As in any computer specialty, hands-on experience is vitally important. One way to put database knowledge to work is to offer volunteer services to a local charity, church, or small business. These organizations have a lot of information to keep track of, such as membership and donor files, mailing lists, and monthly newsletters. Joining local or school computer clubs and learning database software programs at home will also be to your benefit.

Who Will Hire Me?

Henry worked through a series of computer-related jobs before deciding to pursue work as a database specialist. "My first real world experience was in customer support," he says. "I worked at one company, then switched companies in a support capacity. While I was with the second company, I was able to transition from support to integrator. As an integrator, you're basically a jack of all trades." In that role, Henry developed much firsthand experience with database systems.

Database specialists work in any business or company that relies on computer databases for part of its business operation. Retail stores, catalog companies, insurance companies, online database or communications services, financial institutions, hospitals, government agencies, universities, public

ADVANCEMENT POSSIBILITIES

Database programmers design database systems by converting commercial software programs to systems appropriate to the company's needs. They do much of the actual programming themselves, but often pass detail work on to junior programmers or technicians.

Information services managers oversee a large corporate or governmental department that specializes in the installation, maintenance, and repair of information systems such as databases.

Independent database consultants are hired by small and medium-sized companies that require temporary assistance in designing a customized database.

and private school systems, computer companies, and any service industry business are just a few of the types of organizations for whom database management is crucial.

In order to understand who typical employers of database specialists might be, just imagine a company like a mail- and phone-order catalog. A retail company such as this has hundreds of items for sale and all pertinent information about them is stored on the computer. Item prices, available stock, and general descriptions are readily accessible to both sales representatives and warehouse personnel. In addition, the status of an item changes frequently—prices change, stock is depleted, or the item is discontinued. Then, imagine the company's mailing lists; they may have customers numbering in the thousands and tens of thousands. Customers have identification and account numbers; their addresses change and they might only receive some, rather than all, catalog mailings. This is a lot of information to encode, store, and organize, and database specialists do it all. So, in any business where such a large quantity of information needs to be organized, there is a demand for database specialists.

If you are seeking a position in database management, you should consult local newspaper classified ads. You should also read the job lists in computer trade magazines, such as *PC World* (http://

www.pcworld.com), and *Macworld* (macworld.com), as well as check company and job search sites on the Internet. Many Web sites also list free job postings; ITcareers.com allows you to search for jobs in particular cities and nationwide, and features thousands of job postings.

The Association for Computing Machinery publishes a list of job openings in database management and maintains a resume file for prospective employers of member professionals seeking employment.

As with many areas of business, and especially the computer industry, database specialists might find out about good job openings from colleagues employed in the industry. Professional networking can also be done with vendors, workshop instructors, and online contacts. Students can find out about employment opportunities through their school's placement office.

Where Can I Go from Here?

Henry plans to eventually move back into work as a consultant. "One of the keys to keeping your options open," he says, "is to not become vendor-dependent. If you're in an environment where you only work with Microsoft SQL Server, or DB2, you'll want to try to transition into being platform independent. I'd like to have varied experience, so that if a project comes up, I can handle it."

In a large computer and information services (CIS) department, a database specialist who starts as a database administrator might next get into database design analysis and programming. These jobs require more extensive knowledge of the database programs being used. Design analysts and programmers have to have a solid understanding of the entire scope of the project and some idea of how the larger goals will translate into program specifications. Some design analysts and programmers might have technicians under them, who do the very detailed work of filling in the programming gaps. Further education, in any of the forms described above, is usually required for these positions.

Computer professionals generally have the option of advancing in one of two ways. The first, more technical route, includes working with computer projects of larger and larger scope. Instead of one department's small database, for example, a technician might go on to work on the overarching system of a company's databases.

The second route is to go into the managerial side of things, which requires at least some formal business education or demonstrated leadership ability.

Along the technical route, a programmer may be promoted to the position of systems analyst; along the managerial route, he or she may become a computer and information services manager. Another possibility for advancement is to become an independent database consultant. This option really combines both the technical and managerial paths since consultants operate as small business owners.

What Are the Salary Ranges?

Salaries for database specialists vary significantly depending on education level, experience, and specific job responsibilities of the employee. Salaries also depend greatly on the nature and size of the employer. As with other professionals in the Information Technology (IT) industry, database administrators are in high demand and have been receiving high starting salaries and bonuses.

According to Datamasters.com, in 2003 database administration managers had median earnings between $92,890 and $110,405. The Northeast region of the country reported the highest salaries with earnings between $95,448 and $126,936, while the Southwest region reported the lowest salaries, ranging from $82,558 to $117,391.

Despite a decline in salaries in the early 2000s due to the technology slowdown, *InformationWeek* reports that salaries are slowly rising again. In 2005, salaries for those in the IT industry increased by 3.6 percent in the Washington, D.C., area, 2.6 percent in Atlanta, and about 1 percent in Southern California. A 2005 review of database administration salaries nationwide by Salary.com found that the median earnings were $81,416. The lowest paid earned $70,681, and the highest paid earned $94,416. Benefits and awards typically include profit-sharing, health insurance, and 401(k) plans. Some employers also provide large sign-on bonuses, provide further education or training, and reimburse for college tuition.

What Is the Job Outlook?

According to the *Occupational Outlook Handbook*, database administration is expected to be among the

FYI

According to *Computerworld,* the fastest growing professions in the IT industry and 2005 entry-level salary ranges are:

systems auditors	$63,250 to $81,750
pre- and post-sales conslutants	$53,500 to $78,250
programmer/analyst	$52,500 to $83,250
instructor/trainer	$43,250 to $65,500
network security administrator	$63,750 to $90,500
data security analyst	$68,250 to $93,000
quality assurance/testing manager	$64,750 to $86,750
disaster recovery specialist	$60,500 to $90,750
Internet/intranet developer	$51,750 to $74,250
business systems analyst	$56,000 to $80,500

fastest growing occupations through 2012. The major reason is that businesses of the "Information Age" continue to generate more and more information that needs to be organized on computer databases. In addition, businesses that before kept their records in hard copy form, like doctors with their long shelves of patient files, are finding it more accurate and efficient to maintain computer-automated files. As always with technological advances, business demands will become more sophisticated as technology becomes more complex.

Prospective database specialists should watch the economic situation surrounding the largest employers of database specialists. Banks, insurance companies, and other major service corporations will need more database specialists; they promise to enjoy economic stability in the years to come. Even during periods of economic slump, computer automation projects such as database design, implementation, and maintenance will tend to have priority since they offer long-term financial savings and highly efficient productivity in return. Local, state, and particularly federal government agencies will also rely heavily on database technology in the years to come, since they are also primary players in the transition to file and record automation.

Database specialists might also find increasing opportunities as user or technical support staff for major database software manufacturers. They might also be employed as workshop instructors who teach customers how best to use the programs. The trend in the computer industry is toward offering this kind of training and troubleshooting service, so possibilities are expected to increase.

How Do I Learn More?

PROFESSIONAL ORGANIZATIONS

The following organizations provide information on database specialist careers, accredited schools, and employers:

American Society of Information Science and
    Technology
1320 Fenwick Lane, Suite 510
Silver Spring, MD 20910
301-495-0900
asis@asis.org
http://www.asis.org

Association for Computing Machinery
1515 Broadway
New York, NY 10036

800-342-6626
http://www.acm.org

Association of Information Technology
    Professionals
401 North Michigan Avenue, Suite 2400
Chicago, IL 60611-4267
800-224-9371
http://www.aitp.org

IEEE Communications Society
Three Park Avenue, 17th Floor
New York, NY 10016
212-705-8900
http://www.comsoc.org

BIBLIOGRAPHY

The following is a sampling of materials relating to the professional concerns and development of database specialists:

Careers in Focus: Computers. 4th ed. Chicago: Ferguson Publishing Company, 2004.

Connolly, Thomas, and Carolyn Begg. *Database Solutions: A Step-by-Step Guide to Building Databases.* Boston: Addison-Wesley Publishing Company, 1999.

————. *Database Systems: A Practical Approach to Design, Implementation, and Management.* Boston: Addison-Wesley Publishing Company, 2004.

Hernandez, Michael J. *Database Design for Mere Mortals: A Hands-On Guide to Relational Database Design.* 2d ed. Boston: Addison-Wesley Publishing Company, 2003.

Kimball, Ralph. *The Data Warehouse Toolkit: The Complete Guide to Dimensional Modeling.* New York: John Wiley & Sons, 2002.

DENTAL ASSISTANTS

The boy is screaming, his face red from the effort and streaked with tears. He hasn't even met the dentist, and he's already terrified of having his teeth examined. While his mother tries desperately to pull him out of the waiting room chair he's gripping with both hands, his older brother sits nearby, smiling smugly after having filled his brother's head with horror stories about the dentist.

Although the job of a dental assistant entails many duties such as cleaning and sterilizing the dental office and performing clerical tasks, a major part of the work is calming nervous patients. The assistant walks over to the boy and after a few soothing words and her promise that he can tour the office first and then decide whether or not to see the dentist, the little boy takes the assistant's hand and together they walk through the office. By the time he meets the dentist, his face is dry of tears and he's smiling as he waves a pack of sugar-free gum at his older brother.

Dental assisting requires a lot of attention to detail and repetition throughout the day. Dental assistants must clean up after each patient, making sure the dental operatory is clean and sterilized for the next, they must wear proper protective equipment, and must follow very specific industry guidelines for cleaning the dentist's instruments. Speed and efficiency are of utmost importance. The most valuable quality for patients who are often afraid to visit the dentist, however, is the dental assistant's ability to be personable.

What Does a Dental Assistant Do?

Looking forward to your next visit to the dentist? For many people, the very mention of a check-up brings to mind sharp, noisy equipment, pain, and lots of discomfort. But the talents of a good dental assistant can keep you from associating your dentist with pure misery. *Dental assistants* perform a variety of duties in the dental office, including helping the dentist examine and treat patients, performing office and laboratory duties, and making patients feel comfortable in the dentist's chair.

Definition
Dental assistants help dentists treat and examine patients. They clean, sterilize, and disinfect equipment and prepare dental instrument trays. They pass the proper instruments to the dentist, take and process X rays, prepare materials for making impressions and restorations, and instruct the patient in oral health care. They also make appointments, maintain patient records, and handle billing.

High School Subjects
Biology
Chemistry
Health

Personal Skills
Helping/teaching
Technical/scientific

Salary Range
$17,570 to $33,779 to $40,370

Minimum Educational Level
Some postsecondary training

Certification or Licensing
Required by certain states

Outlook
Much faster than the average

DOT
079

GOE
14.03.01

NOC
3411

O*NET-SOC
31-9091.00

Individual states regulate what assistants are allowed to do. Usually assistants are involved in the sterilization and preparation of equipment, and in preparing trays for individual procedures. They retrieve and update patient records, and prepare rooms. They help patients get comfortable before dental treatment, as well as explain the treatment to them. They may anesthetize patients and administer nitrous oxide (laughing gas). In such cases, the dental assistant will stay with the patient while waiting for the dentist. They may also place rubber dams in the mouth or on the teeth to protect the patient and to isolate areas for treatment. An assistant serves as an extra set of hands during treatment, helping the

Lingo to Learn

Amalgam An alloy containing silver, mercury, and other metals used as a dental filling material.

Gypsum Powdered material used to make models, dies, and denture molds that help the dentist diagnose patients and develop a treatment plan.

Operatory Patient treatment room which contains an electronically controlled reclining chair and a dental unit containing an overhead light, a small sink, a saliva ejector, an instrument tray, and air hoses.

Periapical films An X ray that helps detect those suspected diseases that show no physical symptoms.

Saliva ejector A small suction pump used to keep the patient's mouth dry and free of blood or saliva during treatment.

dentist by operating suction machinery that keeps the mouth clear of blood and saliva so the dentist can see himself or herself work. Dental assistants also take and develop X rays, ask medical history questions before an examination, and take each patient's blood pressure, pulse, and temperature. Following a procedure, an assistant will instruct the patient on oral care and how to take any medications required. Assistants also make appointments for patients with referred specialists such as orthodontists and oral surgeons. Assistants may also provide patients with floss, toothbrushes, and other dental care supplies, and instruct in their proper use.

Many dental assistants perform office duties, such as scheduling appointments, answering telephones, handling billing, and working with vendors to replenish office and clinical supplies. Dental laboratory duties may include making impressions of a patient's teeth so the dentist can use the models to study the patient's condition and monitor progress, or they may make temporary crowns. They may also process X-ray film.

A dental assistant's tasks can be divided into categories. An *administrative assistant* acts as a receptionist, handles appointments, manages patient records, and may be responsible for inventory control,

and handling correspondence and bookkeeping. A *chairside assistant* works directly with the dentist by seating patients, preparing the instrument tray, operating the suction devices while the dentist works, performing X rays, and educating patients. (The majority of dental assistants work chairside.) A *coordinating assistant* may work where needed, such as processing X-ray film and performing laboratory procedures. Dental assistants often act as business managers who perform all nonclinical responsibilities such as hiring auxiliary help, scheduling and terminating employees, and overseeing accounting, supply ordering, and records management.

An assistant may work for only one dentist, or may work in a group practice where he or she may assist two or more dentists. Some assistants work full time, while some either work part time or on a temporary, self-employed basis, filling in at more than one office over a period of time. Some assistants work in the offices of specialists. There are also opportunities outside of the dentist's office: Some assistants visit schools and community centers to instruct in proper dental care; they may teach in dental school clinics; and they may visit hospitals and nursing homes to assist dentists caring for bed-ridden patients.

Dental offices typically are clean, modern, quiet, and pleasant. They are also well lighted and well ventilated. In small offices, dental assistants may work solely with dentists, and in larger offices and clinics they may work with dentists, other assistants, dental hygienists, and laboratory technicians.

Although dental assistants may sit at desks to do office work, they spend a large part of the day beside the dentist's chair where they can reach instruments and materials. Taking X rays poses some physical danger if handled incorrectly because regular doses of radiation can be harmful. However, all dental offices must have lead shielding and safety procedures that minimize the risk of exposure to radioactivity.

What Is It Like to Be a Dental Assistant?

Dawn Ashcraft works in a two-doctor office, assisting both doctors as the need arises. Her responsibilities have expanded over the years as she has gained more experience and as the job has become more demanding. "Initially, dental assistants were referred to as 'spit suckers,' because that was basically all they did," she says. Now, in addition to seating patients and assisting with the four-handed passing of instruments, Dawn's responsibilities include restorative procedures, impressions, placing deposit fillings, making temporaries, assisting in crown and bridge procedures, and taking X rays.

The practice for which Dawn works follows a trend in dentistry: It is open only Monday through Thursday, with additional hours on Thursday night. She is usually the first one to the office in the morning, and she starts the work day by preparing the sterilization units. She also starts the X-ray machine. Dawn then goes through the patients' charts. "I make sure that what's on the schedule for the day goes along with the charts." At a start-up meeting with the other assistants and hygienists, Dawn discusses any problems or discrepancies between the schedule and the charts. She then begins to prepare trays and rooms. "Usually we'll set up basic trays for the whole morning's procedures."

In the case of root canals, for example, Dawn brings patients back, seats them, and helps them get comfortable. "As you know," she says, "most people don't like coming to the dentist. You have to try to soothe them and calm them." Dawn takes a starting film X ray, then prepares the patient for the procedure. "We use topical anesthetic before the doctor gets the patient numb with the injection. We put them on nitrous oxide, if necessary." After the doctor has made the injection and the mouth is numb, Dawn then places the rubber dam in the patient's mouth. During the procedure, Dawn and the doctor pass the instruments back and forth as needed. Following the procedure, Dawn takes a final X ray, then releases the patient.

In a crown and bridge procedure, Dawn places a temporary crown or cap over the top of the tooth. The crown may be made of acrylic materials, silver, or metal, and is fit with resin. "Sometimes we do a preliminary impression," she says, "so that we can put the material in the preliminary impression and place it back in the patient's mouth. Or we have to do a ball impression, which means making a big ball of acrylic material, placing it over the tooth, then forming it to look like a tooth."

Throughout any procedure, Dawn may be required to check on other things that need to be done as well. There may still be instruments that need sterilizing, or another patient who needs attention. "You have to know when the doctor's ready to start," she says, "and where he is at all times. So if you go

> ## TO BE A SUCCESSFUL DENTAL ASSISTANT, YOU SHOULD . . .
>
> - be cheerful; you're the patient's first impression of the dentist
> - have compassion and understanding for people with fears about dental procedures
> - be patient, calm, and flexible
> - be able to anticipate the dentist's needs
> - be able to sit still and remain alert for several hours through longer procedures

into central sterilization to help out there, you have to know when you're needed right back."

Dawn's office has three assistants and three to four hygienists at any given time. Though Dawn likes the stability of the job, working for two different dentists and managing their different personalities can be difficult. "I like the expanded duties of the work," she says, "because you're not doing the same thing every day."

Do I Have What It Takes to Be a Dental Assistant?

"Assistants should have an easiness about them," Dawn says, "so they can calm the patient." It's also important for assistants to be able to work well with all the other employees in their offices. "The number one thing doctors want is teamwork within their staff," Dawn says. Dawn is also expected to handle a variety of tasks at any given moment. Not only must you be able to learn quickly, but you must be capable of managing multiple duties. Assistants must remain alert, and must be able to recognize when they can move onto another task. "When I see help needed elsewhere, I go."

How Do I Become a Dental Assistant?

Part of Dawn's training involved a nine-month dental assisting course at a community college. Since then,

FYI

Dental implants are a new alternative to dentures. To meet the demand for more permanent and stable dental replacements, dentists are placing implants, which involves placing a metal screw into the jaw. A prosthetic tooth or set of teeth are attached to the screw. The specialty areas that offer implant surgery are prosthodontics, oral and maxillofacial surgery, and periodontics.

she has had to take continuing education courses in order to maintain certification. "If you get in with a good practice," Dawn says, "they'll be willing to teach you and train you." Dawn feels fortunate for having had the opportunity to work for doctors dedicated to their assistants. "I've worked for five different dentists through the years. Each one of them has been very helpful as far as my expanded duties are concerned. They've helped me grow."

EDUCATION

High School

If you are considering a career as a dental assistant, take science courses, such as biology and health, and obtain office skills such as typing and bookkeeping. With an increasing number of small businesses using computers, one or more computer courses are also recommended. In addition, some dental assisting programs require you to pass physical and dental examinations and have good high school grades.

Postsecondary Training

Students who attend two-year college programs receive associate's degrees, while those who attend trade and technical school programs earn a certificate or diploma after one year.

Graduating from an accredited school ensures that you learn all necessary information required to successfully practice dental hygiene. There are approximately 259 accredited programs in the United

States that are approved by the American Dental Association's Commission on Dental Accreditation (CDA). The commission is responsible for setting standards for dental assisting programs.

CERTIFICATION OR LICENSING

Some states require dental assistants to become licensed or registered, but even if you practice in states that don't require it, certification helps boost knowledge and earning power. Graduates from CDA-approved schools are automatically eligible to take examinations required to become certified. The certification process evaluates a dental assistant's knowledge. The Dental Assisting National Board (DANB), which offers a national certification, requires that an assistant have completed an accredited dental assisting program, or have completed two years of full-time work as a dental assistant. There are approximately 30,000 Certified Dental Assistants (CDAs) nationwide.

Who Will Hire Me?

Since the dental community is rather small in most cities and towns, many positions are learned about by word of mouth. High school and college guidance counselors, family dentists, dental schools, dental employment agencies, and dental associations are ways to learn about job openings. Also, many dental assisting training programs offer job placement assistance.

Dental assisting associations also help you gain a foothold into the field and help you cultivate knowledge and skills while developing a local and national network of friends and colleagues. The American Dental Assistants Association keeps assistants up to date on all aspects of their profession by offering home study courses, monitoring local and national legislation that affects dental assistants, and publishing a newsletter identifying clinical and practice trends in dental assisting.

Most dentists work in private practices, so that's where an aspiring dental assistant will most likely end up working. According to the U.S. Department of Labor, in 2002 there were 266,000 dental assistants holding jobs, most in dental offices. An office may have a single dentist or may be a group practice with several dentists, assistants, and hygienists. Other places to work include physician's offices, educational services, dental schools, hospitals, public health departments, and U.S. Veterans and Public Health Service hospitals.

Where Can I Go from Here?

Dental hygiene is a natural step for an assistant looking to advance in the dental field, but Dawn feels that the work of a hygienist is too repetitive. Dawn would prefer to go into teaching in a dental assisting program. She'd also like to go on the market as a temporary, filling in at offices in her area. "I think I'm capable of picking up on anything in any office," she says.

Becoming a dental hygienist requires taking more courses and taking state and national licensing exams designed for hygienists.

Dental assistants advance in their careers by moving to larger dental practices where they can take on more responsibility. An assistant's ability to command higher pay is tied to the prestige of the dentist for whom the assistant works. By upgrading skills, continuing education, and achieving national certification, dental assistants may achieve higher pay in small offices.

Specialists in the dental field, who typically earn higher salaries than general dentists because of their specialized knowledge, often offer higher salaries to their assistants. DANB lists several specialized dental fields with opportunities for dental assistants, including periodontic, oral surgery, orthodontic, and prosthodontic.

Dental assistants also may use their dental knowledge to obtain sales jobs at dental product companies or work for placement services or insurance companies.

What Are the Salary Ranges?

Although wages for assistants have not kept up with inflation, salaries naturally increase with experience. Working for a specialist, such as a pediatric dentist or orthodontist, often results in higher pay. According to the U.S. Department of Labor *Occupational Outlook Handbook,* dental assistants working full time earned a median salary of $27,248 in 2002. Those in the lowest paid 10 percent earned less than

ADVANCEMENT POSSIBILITIES

Dental hygienists perform many of the same skills as dental assistants, but they also take more courses and certification exams in order to assume some of the responsibilities of a dentist.

Assistants to specialists study the procedures of a dental specialist, such as an orthodontist or pediatric dentist, to assist in complicated or specialized techniques or oral surgeries.

Dental office managers schedule appointments, maintain business records, and depending on the size of the dental office and its staff, manage staff schedules. In addition, they are responsible for maintaining and ordering the proper clerical and dental supplies.

$17,570, while those in the highest 10 percent earned more than $40,370. DANB reports that in 2002 the national median salary for certified dental assistants was $32,198 annually. According to the American Medical Association, in 2004 the median annual salary for dental assistants was $33,779.

Benefits may include health and disability insurance, dues for membership in professional organizations, paid vacations, and provision of uniforms. Assistants may have to work more than 30 hours per week to be eligible for these benefits.

What Is the Job Outlook?

The employment outlook for dental assistants looks bright. Employment for dental assistants is expected to grow much faster than the average for all occupations, according to the U.S. Department of Labor. As the median age of the U.S. population rises, and people become more aware that they can keep all of their teeth and be healthy, more people will seek dental services for preventive care and cosmetic improvements. Moreover, younger dentists who earned their dental degrees in the 1970s and '80s are more likely than other dentists to hire one or more assistants. As dentists increase their clinical knowledge of innovative techniques, such as implantology and periodontal therapy, they will delegate more routine tasks to assistants so they can make the best use of their time and increase profits. Job openings also will be created through attrition as older assistants retire and others assume family responsibilities, return to school, or transfer to other occupations.

How Do I Learn More?

PROFESSIONAL ORGANIZATIONS

The following organizations provide information on dental assisting careers, accredited schools and scholarships, and possible employers:

American Dental Association
211 East Chicago Avenue
Chicago, IL 60611-2678
312-440-2500
http://www.ada.org

American Dental Education Association
1400 K Street NW, Suite 1100
Washington, DC 20005
202-289-7201
adea@adea.org
http://www.adea.org

American Dental Assistants Association
35 E. Wacker Drive, Suite 1736
Chicago, IL 60601-2211
312-541-1550
adaa1@aol.com
http://www.dentalassistant.org

For information about certification, contact
Dental Assisting National Board
676 North Saint Clair, Suite 1880
Chicago, IL 60611
312-642-3368
danbmail@danb.org
http://www.danb.org

BIBLIOGRAPHY

The following is a sampling of materials relating to the professional concerns and development of dental assistants:

Anderson, Pauline C., and Alice Pendleton. *The Dental Assistant*. Albany, N.Y.: Delmar, 2000.

Bird, Doni. *Torres and Ehrlich Modern Dental Assisting*. 7th ed. Philadelphia: W. B. Saunders, 2002.

Dietz-Bourguignon, Ellen. *Materials and Procedures for Today's Dental Assistant*. Clifton Park, N.Y.: Delmar, 2005.

Ehrlich, Ann B., and Hazel O. Torres. *Essentials of Dental Assisting*. 2d ed. Philadelphia: W. B. Saunders, 1996.

DENTAL HYGIENISTS

Hectic isn't the word for Mary Hafner Myers' morning—it is more like controlled chaos. After getting her kids dressed and dropping them off at the babysitter's, she has to dash off to the office to be in time for a 9:00 A.M. appointment.

Fortunately, Mary is an organized woman. She won't have to set up her dental instrument trays this morning because she normally does that at the end of each day, after she has cleaned and sterilized all of the instruments required to clean and scale debris from her patients' teeth. Once in the office, she takes off her jogging pants and walking shoes and slips into freshly laundered "scrubs," her uniform as a dental hygienist, and then pulls on rubber-soled shoes comfortable enough to stand in all day. Mary's daily goal in a fast-paced environment of seeing eight or nine patients a day is to be relaxed enough to put patients at ease and spend enough time educating them about proper oral care and good nutrition.

After getting dressed, Mary glances down at her watch and smiles. She still has 10 minutes to spare before her appointment with Mr. Vincenzo. She washes her hands and dons rubber gloves for her and her patients' protection. She slips a clear plastic shield over her head to block any saliva or blood that may splatter while peering inside her patients' mouths. She is ready for her first patient.

What Does a Dental Hygienist Do?

Dental hygienists perform clinical tasks, serve as oral health educators in private dental offices, work in public health agencies, and promote good oral health by educating adults and children.

In clinical settings, hygienists help prevent gum diseases and cavities by removing deposits from teeth and applying sealants and fluoride to prevent tooth decay. They remove tartar, stains, and plaque from teeth, take X rays and perform other diagnostic tests, place and remove temporary fillings, take health histories, remove sutures, polish amalgam restorations, and examine the head, neck, and oral regions of patients for disease.

Definition
Dental hygienists provide preventive dental care by performing clinical tasks such as cleaning and scaling teeth to remove tartar and plaque, instructing patients in proper oral care, taking X rays, administering anesthesia, and assisting dentists.

High School Subjects
Biology
Chemistry
Mathematics

Personal Skills
Helping/teaching
Technical/scientific

Salary Range
$36,000 to $55,300 to $81,000

Minimum Educational Level
Associate's degree

Certification or Licensing
Required by all states

Outlook
Much faster than the average

DOT
078

GOE
14.03.01

NOC
3222

O*NET-SOC
29-2021.00

Hygienists' main responsibility is to perform "oral prophylaxis," a process of cleaning teeth by using sharp dental instruments, such as scalers and prophy angles. With these special instruments they remove stains and calcium deposits, polish teeth, and massage gums. They teach patients proper home dental care, such as choosing the right toothbrush or how to use dental floss. Their instruments include hand and rotary instruments to clean teeth, syringes with needles to administer local anesthetic (such as Novocaine), teeth models to explain home care procedures, and X-ray machines to take pictures of the oral cavity that the dentist uses to detect signs of decay or oral disease.

A hygienist also provides nutritional counseling and screens patients for oral cancer and high blood pressure. More extensive dental procedures are

Lingo to Learn

Calculus The hard deposit of mineralized plaque that forms on the crown or root of the tooth.

Curette A spoon-shaped blade on a long handle used for extensive tartar removal on teeth and below the gum line.

Mouth mirror A small round mirror on a long handle that allows the hygienist to see hard-to-reach areas of a patient's mouth.

Probe A tapered, rodlike blade on a long handle. The probe is inserted under the gum line to measure gum depth, an indicator of gum disease.

Scaler A sickle, chiseled, or hoe-shaped blade instrument on a long handle used to remove "tartar" from the tooth surface. A scaler is also used to smooth the tooth surface so it will resist reaccumulation of deposits that cling to rough surfaces.

Sealant A composite material used to seal the decay-prone pits, fissures, and grooves of children's teeth.

done by dentists. In some states, a dental assistant is permitted to perform some of the same tasks as a dental hygienist, such as taking X rays, but a hygienist has more extensive training and has received a license to perform the job.

Like all dental professionals, hygienists must be aware of federal, state, and local laws that govern hygiene practice. In particular, hygienists must know the types of infection control and protective gear that, by law, must be worn in the dental office to protect workers from infection. For example, dental hygienists must wear gloves, protective eyewear, and a mask during examinations. As with most health care workers, hygienists must be immunized against contagious diseases, such as hepatitis.

Dental hygienists also are required by their state and encouraged by professional associations to continue learning about trends in dental care, procedures, and regulations by taking continuing education courses. These courses may be held at large dental society meetings, colleges and universities, or in a more intimate setting such as a nearby dental office. These

meetings also foster comradery among fellow dental professionals, which is important in a field where the majority of people work in offices with small staffs.

In some private dental offices, a dental hygienist may perform office duties, such as answering phones, ordering dental supplies, keeping patient records, scheduling appointments, and processing dental insurance claims. Hygienists also visit local schools to perform oral prophylaxis on students and to teach them how to properly brush and floss their teeth. While most hygienists in clinical practice work in private dental offices, others may work in hospitals, correctional facilities, health maintenance organizations, and school systems.

Hygienists also carry out administrative, educational, and research responsibilities in private and public settings. They hold administrative positions in education, public health, hospitals, and professional associations. They sell dental products and supplies and evaluate dental insurance claims as consultants to insurance companies. Dental hygienists may teach in dental hygiene schools, present seminars, conduct clinical research, write grant proposals, and publish scientific papers.

What Is It Like to Be a Dental Hygienist?

Mary Hafner Myers, a registered dental hygienist with a bachelor of science degree (R.D.H., B.S.), works full-time, about 30 hours in a four-day workweek. On average, she sees five or six patients in the morning, and she takes an hour lunch. During the remaining three hours, she sees the rest of her patients.

Most patients are on a regular recall schedule, such as every six months, to get a checkup, cleaning, and to have their health history updated. "I clean their teeth and go over special areas they need to pay attention to, such as plaque or tartar accumulating in certain areas," Mary says. "I spend a lot more time with new patients, and I show kids their X rays. They're always excited about that."

Most hygienists work in private dental offices. Dental hygienists must be flexible to accommodate varying patient schedules, which includes working evenings or Saturdays. Approximately 50 percent of all hygienists work full time, about 35 to 40 hours a week. Full timers and part timers may work in more than one office because dentists typically only hire hygienists to work two or three days a week. Many piece together part-time positions at several different dental offices and substitute for fellow hygienists who take days off.

> ## I spend a lot more time with new patients, and I show kids their X rays. They're always excited about that.

FYI

Dental hygienists clean teeth of plaque and calculus deposits to prevent gum damage, or periodontal disease. Untreated teeth cause gums to become inflamed and infection to spread to the roots of the teeth. Regular cleanings help prevent the disease.

Flexibility is key for hygienists. Before Mary got married, she worked in many dental offices as a substitute for the staff hygienist. Fortunate to have an annual eight-week vacation at her present job, Mary can easily fill up her schedule subbing at nearby dental offices whenever she wants the extra work and money. Usually, she prefers to enjoy her vacation. "If I didn't want to take a week off, there are at least four dentists I could call to fill a schedule for me," Mary says. "I can make good money doing that because as a sub they aren't paying my benefits, so the hourly rate is a little higher."

Work conditions for the dental hygienist in a private office, school, or government facility are pleasant with well-lit, modern, and adequately equipped facilities. The hygienist usually sits while working. State and federal regulations require that hygienists wear masks, protective eyewear, and gloves as well as follow proper sterilizing techniques on equipment and instruments to guard against passing infection or disease, such as hepatitis or AIDS.

Mary wears scrubs in the dental office because they are designed to protect her from transmitting or getting an infection from patients, particularly those who have infectious diseases. She doesn't wear any jewelry, such as earrings or her wedding band. She used to launder her work clothes at home, but new government infection control procedures for health care workers require her to change into her street clothes and leave her work clothes at work. Some dentists have a washer and dryer on site to launder clothes according to government guidelines. Mary's dentist pays a laundry service to pick up all his employees' uniforms and launder them. "I used to wear short sleeves, but now I'm covered from head to toe," Mary says.

As a licensed health care worker, Mary knows all the laws governing infection control, and she knows how to properly clean and sterilize her instruments. The dentist pays for all of her instruments and the machinery necessary to keep them clean and safe. He buys all the barrier items, such as plastic to cover chairs and trays. Whenever Mary needs a new instrument, she just asks her employer and he orders it because he wants her to do the best job she can.

Government hygienists work hours regulated by the particular agency. For a salaried dental hygienist in a private office, a paid two- or three-week vacation is common. Part-time or commissioned dental hygienists in private offices usually have no paid vacation. Benefits will vary, however, according to the hygienist's agreement with the employer.

When Mary was pregnant with her two children, the dentist accommodated her schedule and always understands when family emergencies arise. "My dentist was super with both of my pregnancies. I could take off as much time as I needed," she says. "I also like that he's very much for continuing education, and I have full-time benefits, health insurance, and pretty much everything that I need."

Do I Have What It Takes to Be a Dental Hygienist?

"There's a lot of blood in dentistry, but it's not the life-and-death kind that you find in medical careers," Mary says. Dental hygienists operate in a more controlled atmosphere, and that appeals to her.

However, being a hygienist requires grace under pressure, Mary says. Although patient schedules are often full with one patient after another, hygienists must possess the manual dexterity to properly clean and scale below the patients' gum lines, answer the patients' questions, and make them feel so relaxed

To Be a Successful Dental Hygienist, You Should . . .

- ○ enjoy working with people of all ages
- ○ be patient, flexible, and calm in stressful situations
- ○ be articulate and organized
- ○ work well as part of a team
- ○ be willing to follow strict safety and health guidelines

that they feel they are all that matters. Fortunately, Mary has a dental assistant who helps her in the afternoons to usher in patients, clean up after every appointment, adjust the chair, and make patients feel comfortable.

"Hygienists must have patience to work on really tight schedules, be organized, and able to work on a team," Mary says. Dental hygiene school prepared her for real practice because in that strict atmosphere, she learned discipline. Mary had to find her own patients and learn to talk to strangers. Skipping a class was unheard of. "You have to really feel bad not to go to work," Mary says. "Patients will be there waiting for you and they depend on you. School definitely prepared me for that."

As an oral care educator, hygienists must be capable of communicating with patients because if they don't understand, they won't come back, Mary says. She also tells patients what she's doing and what instrument she's using because if they haven't been to the dentist in a while, sharp instruments can startle them if they don't understand their purpose.

How Do I Become a Dental Hygienist?

Mary was naturally drawn to college prep courses in high school because challenging herself provided personal satisfaction. She knew she wanted to do something related to health and education, and the comradery among dental workers at her family dentist's office convinced her to seek a career in dental hygiene.

EDUCATION

High School

Dental hygiene programs vary, but all require you to have a high school diploma or general educational development (GED), also known as general equivalency degree. Recommended high school courses include mathematics, chemistry, biology, and English. College entrance test scores are needed, and some dental hygiene programs require prerequisite college courses in chemistry, English, speech, psychology, and sociology.

Math and science courses proved to be most helpful as Mary first worked to earn an associate's degree in dental hygiene science and later a bachelor's degree in public health, which gave her teaching experience on top of her clinical skills.

Postsecondary Training

Dental hygiene education takes a minimum of two years in an accredited two-year program that offers a certificate or associate's degree, or an accredited four-year program offering a bachelor's degree. A master's degree may be an option for those seeking opportunities in education, research, or administration. Thirty percent of hygienists have a bachelor's or master's degree. The Commission on Dental Accreditation lists 265 accredited programs in dental hygiene.

The dental hygiene curriculum generally consists of approximately 1,000 hours of instruction, including more than 600 hours of clinical experience that involves working on patients. Courses include chemistry, anatomy, physiology, biochemistry, dental anatomy, radiology, pain control, dental materials, and pharmacology. Dental hygiene science courses include oral health education and preventive counseling, patient management, clinical dental hygiene, and ethics.

Mary earned an associate's degree and immediately went to work for a private dental office almost 50 miles from her home. She completed her studies toward a bachelor's degree in dental hygiene so she could teach and increase her earning power.

"Dental hygiene school was tough because I worked full time to pay for school," Mary says. "The instructors are very strict, and you have to be very attentive and disciplined. There is so much responsibility because you have to set up your own schedule, find your own patients."

In-depth

Endodontists

Dental hygienists work in every dentist's office, from the orthodontist to the endodontist.

Endodontists treat diseased inner tooth structures, such as the nerve, pulp, and root canal. Every tooth has the same basic structure. The outer covering of the tooth exposed above the gum line is called the enamel, the hardest substance in the human body. Beneath the enamel is another layer of hard material, dentin, that forms the bulk of the tooth. Cementum, a bonelike substance, covers the root of the tooth. Finally, a generous space within the dentin contains the pulp, which extends from just beneath the crown, or top of the tooth, to down through the root. The pulp contains blood vessels that supply the tooth and the lymphatic system.

Not so long ago, if a tooth was diseased, that was it; yank—no more tooth. Things have changed. Modern preventive endodontic techniques now make it possible to save many teeth that would have been extracted once decay spread into the pulp canal. These specialized procedures include root canal therapy, pulp capping, and pulpotomy.

In root canal therapy, the endodontist first examines the pulp to determine the extent of infection. Using rotary drills and other instruments, the pulp is removed and the empty canal surrounding the root is sterilized and filled with gutta-percha (a tough plastic substance) or silver, or a combination of the two.

Pulp capping consists of building a cap over the exposed pulp with layers of calcium hydroxide paste and zinc oxide. These layers are then topped with a firm dental cement.

Pulpotomy involves removing the pulp within the crown while leaving intact the pulp within the root canal. A pulp-capping procedure is used to seal and restore the crown of the tooth.

CERTIFICATION OR LICENSING

A state or clinical examination is required for licensing, as is a written national dental examination that is required by all states and the District of Columbia. Upon passing required exams, a dental hygienist becomes a Registered Dental Hygienist (R.D.H.). Other designations include Licensed Dental Hygienist (L.D.H.), and Graduate of Dental Hygiene (G.D.H.). If a hygienist moves to another state, he or she must pass that state's licensing exam and requirements. In Alabama, for example, hygienists may forego college and obtain on-the-job training in a dentist office that has been approved by the state. This is called preceptorship.

Mary's dentist supports her need to update her education and pays for her continuing education courses. To maintain her license, she must take a certain number of continuing education courses. She takes others to keep up to date and because she finds them quite interesting.

Who Will Hire Me?

Once hygienists pass national board exams and licensing exams for their particular state, they must decide where to work, such as a private dental office, a school system, or a public health agency. Hospitals, industry, and the armed forces also employ a small number of dental hygienists. Graduating students have little difficulty finding a satisfactory position. Most dental hygiene schools maintain placement services, and dentists make announcements at local dental hygiene meetings. Often, temporary services match hygienists with dentists.

Upon earning an associate's degree, Mary had no trouble finding a job. As a matter of fact, the job found her. A dentist from a small community 50 miles from her home asked her school for a list of new graduates, and she was invited for an interview. She was hired to work three days a week, and the dentist paid her an extra dollar for each hour worked to compensate for travel expenses.

"I liked it because it was a small office and it just seemed like a real homey atmosphere," Mary says. "I thought even if I just worked there one year, it would be fun to get out of my general area and meet new people. Who would have thought I'd end up living there?"

Where Can I Go from Here?

Opportunities for advancement, other than salary increases and benefits that accompany experience in the field, usually require postgraduate study and training. Educational advancement may lead to a position as an administrator, teacher, or director in a dental health program or in a more advanced field of practice. Only

a small number of dental hygienists have continued their education to become practicing dentists.

With her bachelor's degree, Mary is qualified to teach college-level dental hygiene courses, which she has done. She plans to earn a master's degree in a different field, although she hasn't quite figured out what field that will be. "I'll probably branch out more into teaching," Mary says.

What Are the Salary Ranges?

A dental hygienist's income is influenced by such factors as education, experience, geography, and type of employer. Most dental hygienists who work in private dental offices are salaried employees, though some are paid a commission for work performed, or a combination thereof.

According to the *Occupational Outlook Handbook*, the median hourly earnings of dental hygienists were $26.59 in 2002 (or approximately $55,300 annually). Those in the lowest paid 10 percent earned less than $17.34 an hour (around $36,000 annually); those in the highest 10 percent earned more than $39.24 an hour (over $81,000 annually).

Dental hygienists working in research, education, or administration may earn higher salaries. Another factor affecting earning power is the hygienist's level of responsibility. In addition, an increased demand for dental care and higher wages has provided incentives for hygienists to work in the field longer or to return to the field.

What Is the Job Outlook?

The *Occupational Outlook Handbook* reports that employment for dental hygienists is expected to grow much faster than the average for all occupations. The demand for dental hygienists is expected to grow as younger generations who grew up receiving better dental care, keep their teeth longer. For example, 59.9 percent of solo dentists employed a hygienist in 1997 compared to 66.9 percent in 2001, according to the American Dental Association. In 2002, dental hygientists held about 148,000 jobs nationwide.

Older dentists, who are less likely to hire one hygienist, let alone more than one, will retire, and younger dentists will hire one or more hygienists to perform preventive care so they can have more time to perform more profitable, medically complex procedures. Population growth, increased public awareness of proper oral home care, and the availability of dental insurance should result in more dental hygiene jobs. Moreover, as the population ages, there will be a special demand for hygienists to work with older people, especially those who live in nursing homes.

Because of increased awareness about caring for animals in captivity, hygienists are also among a small number of dental professionals who volunteer to help care for animals' teeth and perform annual examinations. Dental professionals are not licensed to treat animals, though, and must work under the supervision of veterinarians.

How Do I Learn More?

PROFESSIONAL ORGANIZATIONS

The following organizations provide information on dental hygienist careers, accredited schools and scholarships, and possible employment:

American Dental Hygienists' Association
444 North Michigan Avenue, Suite 3400
Chicago, IL 60611
312-440-8900
mail@adha.net
http://www.adha.org

American Association of Dental Examiners
211 East Chicago Avenue, Suite 760
Chicago, IL 60611
312-440-7464

info@aadexam.org
http://www.aadexam.org

American Dental Education Association
1400 K Street NW, Suite 1100
Washington, DC 20005
adea@adea.org
http://www.adea.org

American Dental Association
211 East Chicago Avenue
Chicago, IL 60611-2678
312-440-2500
http://www.ada.org

BIBLIOGRAPHY

The following is a sampling of materials relating to the professional concerns and development of dental hygienists:

Alvarez, Kathleen H. *Williams & Wilkins' Dental Hygiene Handbook.* New York: Lippincott Williams & Wilkins, 1998.

Kendall, Bonnie L. *Opportunities in Dental Care Careers.* Chicago: VGM Career Horizons, 2001.

Nathe, Christine Nielsen. *Dental Public Health: Contemporary Practice for the Dental Hygienist.* 2nd ed. Upper Saddle River, N.J.: Pearson Prentice Hall, 2005.

Requa-Clark, Barbara S. *Applied Pharmacology for the Dental Hygienist.* 4th ed. St. Louis, Mo.: Mosby, 2000.

Wilkins, Esther M. *Clinical Practice of the Dental Hygienist.* 8th ed. Philadelphia: Lippincott Williams & Wilkins, 1999.

DESKTOP PUBLISHING SPECIALISTS

Kathy Richardson stared down at the hand-drawn sketch on butcher paper spread out before her. The colors, the lines, the details—all were perfectly rendered. But too flat. The sketch somehow had to end up on a paper cup for instant hot cereal, and Kathy needed to get the drawing into her computer and manipulate it to produce a file ready to print. She was stumped. She needed to maintain the integrity of her client's artwork while also getting the design to wrap around the cup without becoming distorted. Kathy looked for ideas on the Internet, spoke with printers, and consulted members of professional organizations, but she came up empty-handed. Kathy finally found a product promoted as a 3-D special effects tool for Web designers. Although her project had nothing to do with special effects or the World Wide Web, she used some ingenuity and applied it to the design. After working closely with the new program, the product took shape before her eyes, all of the artist's design vivid and perfectly translated.

What Does a Desktop Publishing Specialist Do?

Desktop publishing specialists work on computers, converting and preparing files for printing presses or other media. Much of desktop publishing fits into the prepress category, and desktop publishing specialists typeset, or arrange and transform, text and graphics into finished products or products ready to be printed. Typesetting and page layout work entails selecting font types and sizes, arranging column widths, checking for proper spacing between letters, words, and columns, placing graphics and pictures, and more. Desktop publishing specialists also deal with the technical issues of files, such as resolution problems, colors that need to be corrected, and software difficulties.

Desktop publishing specialists who work for service bureaus handle the technical issues of graphic designers and provide prepress services, including film output. Graphic designers use their creativity and artistic skills to create designs, often from scratch.

Definition
Desktop publishing specialists use computers to prepare files for printing. They take files that others have created and manipulate the images and text so they will print properly.

Alternative Job Titles
Digital prepress operators
Digital production operators
Electronic prepress operators
Imagesetters
Preflight technicians
Prepress workers

High School Subjects
Art
Computer science

Personal Skills
Artistic
Communication/ideas

Salary Range
$18,670 to $31,410 to $52,270

Minimum Educational Level
Some postsecondary training

Certification or Licensing
Voluntary

Outlook
Faster than the average

DOT
979

GOE
01.07.01

NOC
1423

O*NET-SOC
43-9031.00

Some may use computer software programs, while others draw with pencil and paper. They provide the desktop publishing specialists with their designs, and the desktop publishing specialists must convert these designs to the format requested by the designers. A designer may come in with a hand-drawn sketch, a printout of a design, or a file on a diskette, and he or she may want the design to be ready for publication on the World Wide Web, in a high-quality brochure, or in a newspaper. Each format presents different issues, and the desktop publishing specialist must be familiar with the processes and solutions for each. Service bureaus also provide services such as scanning, laminating, image manipulation, or poster production.

Desktop publishing specialists at commercial printing houses generally focus less on the technical issues of designs and more on the printing end and prepress operations, although many commercial printers now have in-house service bureaus. Desktop publishing specialists take disks from customers, check the files for problems, then print the files to film or directly onto printing plates. The process of converting files on disks to film or printing plates is known as digital imaging. The job of the desktop publishing specialist is to ensure that the images on the film or plates will print perfectly and accurately.

One specialization within desktop publishing at the commercial printing house is the *preflight technician.* After a customer brings in a disk, the preflight technician performs an initial check of the files to make sure the files are ready to go into production. This can entail checking the disk contents against a hard copy or printout supplied by the customer and making sure the fonts, colors, resolutions, and all other details are satisfactory. Once the check is complete, the process of printing the files to film can begin.

Desktop publishing specialists can also specialize in scanning. *Scanner operators* focus on color correction, color separation, and image manipulation. They use computerized equipment to output the film that will be used to print the final product. The computer handles the color separation process, which involves producing four-color separation negatives from a print. In printing, photographs must be printed from images consisting of millions of tiny dots. In order to create an accurate reproduction of an original color print, it is necessary to produce separation negatives that will be combined during the printing process. Each scan produces an image of the tiny dots representing one of four colors: cyan, yellow, magenta, and black. Separate printing plates are made for each of these scans and, using transparent color inks, they are printed one at a time. The final result combines all the colors and produces a replica of the original print or photograph. The scanner operator corrects color errors and enhances color where necessary. For instance, the original print may have uneven color or fading problems.

What Is It Like to Be a Desktop Publishing Specialist?

Kathy Richardson spends most of her day sitting at a Macintosh computer, troubleshooting and manipulating her designer clients' files so she can provide them with the end results they want. "Basically," says Kathy, "what you would say my

Lingo to Learn

Air White space in a layout.

Bitmap A representation of a graphical image made up of a series of dot patterns.

Bleed Type, pictures, or graphic elements that extend beyond the trim marks on a page.

Body The main text of a work, not including headlines.

Cutout A halftone (photograph) in which the background has been removed to produce a silhouette.

Digital imaging Taking computer files and converting them directly into printing plates.

Display type Larger type used for headings and banners; usually 18 points or larger.

File format A format for storing or encoding information in a file.

Gutter The blank space between left and right pages.

Imposition The arrangement of pages on a printed sheet for printing. When the sheet is printed on both sides, folded and trimmed, the pages fall in their correct order.

Phototypesetting Assembling images into page format and photographing the images to create film negatives. The negatives are then used to make printing plates.

Pixels Tiny elements that together create or constitute an image.

Preflight To perform a cursory check of a file to ensure its integrity and readiness for production.

Raster graphics An image created by using a series of dot patterns.

Resolution Refers to the sharpness and clarity of an image.

Vector graphics An image created by using a series of lines.

position is is a problem solver for the graphic designer." Kathy works at Direct Imaging, a computer imaging service bureau in San Luis Obispo, California.

Kathy works primarily with five software packages: QuarkXPress, Adobe PageMaker, Macromedia FreeHand, Adobe Illustrator, and Adobe Photoshop. These are the basic tools used by desktop publishing specialists who work with Macintosh computers, and Kathy may use all of them on one project. Kathy understands the strengths and weaknesses of each program, which enables her to provide software solutions to her clients. Part of her job is also to respect clients' designs. "What they end up getting is what delivers without compromising their design," Kathy states. "They want someone like me who respects their design, who doesn't trash it, who doesn't start redesigning it."

Because Kathy finds she is more productive after the shop is closed, she usually arrives at work around 10:00 A.M. Direct Imaging has clients all over the world, so the first part of Kathy's day is spent checking messages and making East Coast and international calls. The bulk of Kathy's day, however, is spent on projects. Some may take one day to complete, while others may take a week or longer. She may ready a logo for letterhead, prepare a catalog for the printer, or work on a file that will be published on the World Wide Web.

Kathy works with two deadlines every day. "Everything revolves around FedEx and UPS," she asserts. The latter part of each afternoon is devoted to getting projects completed and ready for either Federal Express or United Parcel Service. This can sometimes cause problems, especially when there are rush jobs. "I would say that practically all the jobs that are rush jobs are the jobs with the most problems."

Scott Gordon, president and prepress manager of Haagen Printing in Santa Barbara, California, spends much of his time at a Macintosh computer as well. His situation, however, is unique. "I wear the hat as prepress manager as well as the president," he explains, "so one minute I might be color correcting an image, and the next minute I might be in a meeting with a banker or a lawyer." Although a fair amount of prepress work is done on IBM-compatible PCs, Scott finds, "Out of 1,000 jobs, a handful are PCs. Ninety-nine percent of our production is done on a Macintosh."

Haagen Printing is a commercial printing firm that specializes in high-quality printed material, such as annual reports, custom printing jobs, and eight-color brochures. The prepress department must take the customers' files and ready them for the printing presses. This may include preflighting the files, troubleshooting certain types of problems or files, and color correcting and scanning. Each desktop publishing specialist in the prepress department has a propensity for one niche of the business, but "the ultimate goal is to get what's in the computer out onto a piece of film or out onto a plate or whatever you're trying to print to," Scott says.

Kathy enjoys the flexibility and variety her job offers her. Because new software is released on a constant basis, Kathy is always learning something new and discovering new solutions, which she finds fun. She also likes working with graphic designers and teaching them about the capabilities of the software, although this can sometimes work against her. "I try to educate them," Kathy says, "and in some cases I've ended up shooting myself in the foot because I've taught myself out of a job."

Scott also enjoys the variety and creativity of desktop publishing. "I get to make something new every day," he declares. "You're making film, and you're making proofs, and you're making pictures, and they're all different."

Do I Have What It Takes to Be a Desktop Publishing Specialist?

If you want to be a desktop publishing specialist, you must be detail oriented, possess problem-solving skills, and have a sense of design or some artistic skills. A good eye and patience are critical, as well as endurance to see projects through to the finish. As Scott relates, "I often call our prepress department the emergency room. Every day new patients come in, and we open them up and fix them. All jobs are basically just problems we solve. They don't print themselves, and it takes a lot of work to get them out right."

A design background is helpful so you can comprehend the designer's approach. "You have to be technically inclined," Kathy states, "but you also have to have some kind of creative background to understand where these designs are coming from." This background can also assist you in troubleshooting problem files. "You're trying to get things to output," explains Scott, "and when you run into problems, you have to get inside the mind of the designer and understand how he built the file, or what he did there."

> ## All jobs are basically just problems we solve. They don't print themselves, and it takes a lot of work to get them out right.

A calm temperament comes in handy for desktop publishing specialists. You have to be able to work under pressure and constant deadlines. Sometimes Kathy finds herself caught in the middle between graphic designers and printing firms, which can be difficult. The designers may blame Kathy for a problem with the design, and printers may blame her for issues with the output. Kathy takes this all in stride and strives to find solutions rather than dwelling on who is to blame.

How Do I Become a Desktop Publishing Specialist?

Both Kathy and Scott entered the desktop publishing industry from the design side. Kathy's father was a printer, so she grew up in print shops. She studied graphic design in college but realized her strength lay in working with computers and software tools rather than creating art from scratch.

TO BE A SUCCESSFUL DESKTOP PUBLISHING SPECIALIST, YOU SHOULD . . .

- ○ have a good eye and design sense
- ○ possess strong problem-solving skills and analytical thinking skills
- ○ be creative and curious
- ○ enjoy working with computers and software tools
- ○ have endurance to see things through to completion

Scott worked as a commercial photographer and provided design services as well. "It just so happened that that was the era that desktop publishing was invented," he recalls. "It was the early eighties, and in 1984 the Macintosh hit the streets." Scott naturally developed prepress skills because he used the Macintosh as a tool for his photography and design business. Scott followed along as improvements to the Macintosh were made and new software tools were created.

EDUCATION

High School

Classes that will help you develop desktop publishing skills include computer classes and design or art classes. Computer classes should include both hardware and software, since understanding how computers function will help you with troubleshooting and knowing the computers' limits. In photography classes you can learn about composition, color, and design elements. Typing, drafting, and print shop classes, if available, will also provide you with the opportunity to gain some indispensable skills.

Kathy also suggests enrolling in a chemistry class. "I learned how to follow a recipe and do what it said in real life. I learned how to apply what's in a manual to doing something. There aren't that many classes where you can do that." Laboratory experiments taught Kathy how to follow instructions and pay attention to detail.

Working on the school newspaper or yearbook will train you on desktop publishing skills as well, including page layout, typesetting, composition, and working under a deadline. Learn the software as quickly and as well as you can, and others will turn to you for help and advice, Kathy says.

Endurance sports, such as cross-country running or long-distance swimming, will teach you the discipline to see projects through to the finish. Kathy emphasizes, "You have to have endurance development, and you don't develop that on a computer," which is why she advises participating in activities "that help you go for the long haul."

Joining computer clubs or volunteering at small organizations to produce newsletters or flyers are other activities that will be to your benefit. If you have a computer at home, use it and experiment with it. You may also be able to find part-time or summer employment with printing shops or companies that have in-house publishing or printing departments.

Postsecondary Training

Although both Kathy and Scott graduated from four-year colleges, a college degree is not required for desktop publishing work. Kathy had planned to become a graphic designer and studied in the graphic communications department at California Polytechnic State University in San Luis Obispo, California. She ended up switching from the design emphasis to the management concentration halfway through her schooling when she realized she preferred to help designers rather than be one herself.

Kathy stresses that experience is the key to becoming a good desktop publishing specialist, and she gained experience by working in the field while attending school. It took her 10 years to graduate, but, she says, "I was able to apply what I was learning while I was learning it. I don't think you should learn in a vacuum for this kind of field, because it changes so quickly that you can't expect to earn a living just by what you learn on campus."

Some two-year colleges and technical institutes offer programs in desktop publishing or related fields. A growing number of schools offer programs in technical and visual communications, which may include classes in desktop publishing, layout and design, and computer graphics. Four-year colleges also offer courses in technical communications and graphic design. There are many opportunities to take classes related to desktop publishing through extended education programs offered through universities and colleges. These classes can range from basic desktop publishing techniques to advanced courses in Adobe Photoshop or QuarkXPress and are often taught by professionals working in the industry.

CERTIFICATION OR LICENSING

Certification is not mandatory, and currently there is only one certification program offered in desktop publishing. The Association of Graphic Communications has an Electronic Publishing Certificate designed to set industry standards and measure the competency levels of desktop publishing specialists. The examination is divided into a written portion and a hands-on portion. During the practical portion of the examination, candidates receive files on a disk and must manipulate images and text, make color corrections, and perform whatever tasks are necessary to create the final product. Applicants are expected to be knowledgeable in print production, color separation, typography and font management, computer hardware and software, image manipulation, page layout, scanning and color correcting, prepress and preflighting, and output device capabilities.

The Printing Industries of America, Inc. (PIA) is in the process of developing industry standards in the prepress and press industries. PIA may eventually design a certification program in desktop publishing or electronic prepress operation.

SCHOLARSHIPS AND GRANTS

A number of professional organizations and schools offer scholarship and grant opportunities. The Graphic Arts Education and Research Foundation (GAERF) and the Education Council of the Graphic Arts Industry, Inc., both divisions of the Association for Suppliers of Printing and Publishing Technologies (NPES), can provide information on scholarship opportunities and research grants. Other organizations that offer financial awards and information on scholarship opportunities include the Society for Technical Communication, the International Prepress Association, PIA, and the Graphic Arts Technical Foundation, which offers scholarships in graphic communications through the National Scholarship Trust Fund.

Colleges and universities that offer programs in desktop publishing and related fields may also grant scholarships. Contact your advisor or financial aid office for additional information and resources.

INTERNSHIPS AND VOLUNTEERSHIPS

Internships and cooperative work experiences are common and highly recommended in the desktop publishing industry. Many major newspapers offer internship and apprenticeship opportunities in the pressroom. Most internships in the publishing or printing industry are nonpaid or do not pay well, but the experience and connections you gain will pay off in the long run. When Kathy was in college, *USA Today* had an internship program in desktop publishing and prepress operations that was highly coveted by students. Landing a well-respected internship will facilitate your career and provide you with credibility.

A good place to look for internship opportunities is through your school counselor or adviser, whether

In-depth

Tools of the Trade

Desktop publishing specialists who work with Macintosh computers use the following software programs extensively. PC users can also use these programs, as well as Corel Draw and Adobe FrameMaker. Macromedia FreeHand specializes in vector-based drawings and images. Vector-based images are more flexible than bitmap or raster graphics when it comes to sizing. FreeHand provides a large variety of tools for the desktop publishing specialist, including 3-D capabilities, Web publishing functions, and the ability to work with different page sizes in the same document.

- Adobe Illustrator also specializes in vector-based drawings and images and has been the industry standard for years. If you can use Illustrator, you should have no problem learning FreeHand. Illustrator can be used to create graphic images that are then transferred to PageMaker or QuarkXPress.
- Adobe PageMaker is a desktop publishing program that is ideal for documents such as newsletters, letterhead, business cards, advertisements, and envelopes. PageMaker is often the preferred format for a file before delivery to the printer.
- Adobe Photoshop specializes in bitmap-based images and is the preferred tool for editing photographs and converting images. Photoshop provides versatility for Web design as well. Bitmaps offer more flexibility than vectors when it comes to creating images.
- QuarkXPress is another desktop publishing program and is ideal for longer documents such as books, catalogs, newspapers, and pamphlets. QuarkXPress is a bit harder to master than Adobe PageMaker but offers more flexibility and features once you've gotten the hang of it. QuarkXPress is the preferred format for the fully composed document before delivery to the printing shop.
- Adobe InDesign is considered an alternative to Quark, and integrates fully with the other Adobe products mentioned above. The program allows for sophisticated design and high-end, multicolor layout.
- Corel Draw is a vector- and bitmap-based program that has 3-D capabilities and powerful functions and tools for desktop publishing.
- Adobe FrameMaker is ideal for book and textbook publishing because of its capabilities for managing large amounts of text. FrameMaker can also be used for Web publishing and preparing documents in multiple languages.

---

you are in high school or college. Professional associations often have information regarding internships, and you may wish to contact major newspapers, magazines, or publishing houses as well.

If you are unable to find an internship, there are plenty of organizations that would be happy to have volunteers adept at desktop publishing. Many small businesses and nonprofit organizations need help producing newsletters, brochures, letterhead, flyers, catalogs, and more. Volunteering is an excellent way to try new software and techniques and to gain experience troubleshooting and creating final products.

Who Will Hire Me?

Kathy found her first job in the field through connections and says, "Most people find jobs by networking." Kathy worked primarily as an administrative assistant to the art director at a company that manufactures fitness attire. Her duties included clerical tasks as well as desktop publishing projects using PageMaker. Kathy discovered that her co-workers were not very skilled at using the software tools, so she was able to help them and demonstrate her value as an employee.

Scott was involved with desktop publishing before the term was even coined. "I just sort of grew up with it," he states. Scott developed prepress skills because he worked as a commercial photographer, media coordinator, and art director, and desktop publishing and design are natural extensions of those jobs. Scott had been a customer at Haagen Printing for years, and when the shop decided to switch to digital prepress operations, it contacted him and asked if he would help with the transition. He has been employed with Haagen ever since.

The primary employers of desktop publishing specialists are printing shops, service bureaus, newspaper plants, and large companies with in-house graphics or design staffs. Basically, any organization with a printing department will have a need for desktop publishing specialists. Printing shops handle both commercial and business printing. Commercial printing involves catalogs, brochures, and reports, while business printing encompasses products used by businesses, such as sales receipts or forms.

Jobs with the federal government are another option for desktop publishing specialists. The Government Accounting Office (GAO) and the Government Printing Office (GPO) publish a large amount of documents. The GPO even has a Digital Information Technology Support Group (DITS Group) that provides desktop and electronic publishing services to federal agencies.

Kathy suggests looking for a position as a production artist if you are just starting out. Production artists take the work of graphic designers and work on layout. Kathy explains that production artists are not designers or technical experts. "You're just a grunt," she says bluntly, "but you can learn, and if you know your stuff, you can help them when something goes wrong." Printing houses and design agencies are places to check for production artist opportunities.

Both Scott and Kathy agree that networking is the best way to find a job, so it might be a good idea to keep up on your membership dues for appropriate professional organizations and clubs. Most professional organizations offer career services and job listings to members. If you enroll in classes or school, talk to your instructors about job openings they have heard about.

The Internet is another job search tool that can come in handy, especially, says Scott, if you're willing to relocate. Newspaper classified advertisements and trade magazines are also sources for job leads.

Where Can I Go from Here?

Kathy enjoys working with computers and pushing software tools to their limits, which is why she is interested in working as a software developer for a software publisher at some point in her career. She thinks it would be exciting to be on the cutting edge of technology, helping programmers develop software innovations. Kathy is also interested in moving into management. "I would like to work for a publishing house, to be the head of a department and make purchasing decisions." Kathy would also like to get more involved in teaching. Currently, she teaches about one software class per session through extended education programs.

Scott became a co-owner of Haagen Printing in June of 1997, so his future goals revolve around building the business and making it the best printing shop possible. Providing the highest quality and the best service are goals for Scott, and after that, maybe he will retire and go sailing.

Desktop publishing specialists can move into middle management or sales positions within a printing firm. Prepress managers oversee prepress departments and supervise staff members. Prepress managers may be responsible for scheduling, staffing, and purchasing of equipment, including computer hardware and software. Sales representatives work for printing firms or publishing houses. Their job is to find new customers and expand business.

Scott and Kathy entered the desktop publishing realm with design backgrounds, and both feel it is important to have an understanding of design to be a successful desktop publishing specialist. It is possible, however, to transition into graphic design from prepress if the desktop publishing specialist has an aptitude for it. Graphic designers are artists, and not everyone possesses these skills.

What Are the Salary Ranges?

According to the U.S. Department of Labor National Occupational Employment and Wage Estimates, the median annual earnings for desktop publishing specialists were $31,410 in 2003. Those in the lowest paid 10 percent earned $18,670 annually, and the highest paid 10 percent earned $52,270. The middle 50 percent had salaries between $23,810 and $41,210.

Graphic Arts Monthly's 2003 salary survey found that an art/design specialist working as a department foreman had a median annual salary of $35,492. Earnings ranged from a low $11,700 to a high $60,000.

A 2005 Salary.com review of earnings nationwide for desktop publishing operators reported entry level salaries of between $33,427 and $43,279 annually. Those with four years of experience or more had annual earnings between $37,467 and $48,034.

What Is the Job Outlook?

According to the *Occupational Outlook Handbook,* employment of desktop publishing specialists is expected to grow faster than the average through 2012. As technology advances, the ability to create and publish documents will become easier and faster, thus influencing more businesses to produce printed materials. Desktop publishing specialists will be needed to satisfy typesetting, page layout, and design demands. With new equipment, commercial printing shops will be able to shorten the turnaround time on projects and in turn can increase business and accept more jobs. For instance, digital printing presses allow printing shops to print directly to the digital press rather than printing to a piece of film, and then printing from the film to the press. Digital printing presses eliminate an entire step and should appeal to companies who need jobs completed quickly.

Prepress machine operators may notice a decline in employment opportunities as their work becomes more automated. Printing plants may also lose jobs to large companies with in-house printing and preparation capabilities. Desktop publishing

Advancement Possibilities

Prepress managers supervise prepress departments and delegate work to prepress operators or desktop publishing specialists. Managers also make purchasing decisions for the department.

Printing sales representatives work for printing firms and solicit work from clients and companies.

Graphic designers create designs and artwork based on clients' requests and needs.

Software developers work in research and development for software publishing firms. They design and test software.

specialists are best suited to fill these positions because of their skills with computers and electronic prepress operations.

Both Kathy and Scott concur that the job outlook is positive. Scott says, "It's looking good for the next five years." He feels computers will increasingly mechanize printing processes, and the prepress operator's job will become easier. Kathy also feels this is a good time to be in desktop publishing. "It's growing so much," she asserts. She acknowledges that many prepress jobs are being phased out because many are learning to do their own layout and design on computers, but she says, "There will still always be the need."

How Do I Learn More?

PROFESSIONAL ORGANIZATIONS

For information about trends in the graphics arts and the printing industry, scholarships and grants, certification and education, and employment opportunities, contact the following organizations:

Association of Graphic Communications
330 Seventh Avenue, 9th Floor
New York, NY 10001-5010
212-279-2100
info@agcomm.org
http://www.agcomm.org

Association for Suppliers of Printing and Publishing Technologies
Education Council of the Graphic Arts Industry, Inc.
Graphic Arts Education and Research Foundation
1899 Preston White Drive
Reston, VA 20191-4367
703-264-7200
npes@npes.org
http://www.npes.org

National Association for Printing Leadership
75 West Century Road
Paramus, NJ 07652
800-642-6275
info@napl.org
http://public.napl.org

Society for Technical Communication
901 North Stuart Street, Suite 904
Arlington, VA 22203
703-522-4114
stc@stcc.org
http://www.stc.org

BIBLIOGRAPHY

The following is a sampling of materials relating to the professional concerns and development of desktop publishing specialists:

Devall, Sandra Lentz. *Desktop Publishing StyleGuide.* Clifton Park, N.Y.: Thomson Delmar Learning, 1998.

Giambruno, Mark. *3D Graphics and Animation.* 2d ed. Indianapolis: New Riders Publishing, 2002.

Litwiller, Dan, and Patrice-Anne Rutledge. *The Essential Publisher 97 Book: The Get-It-Done Tutorial.* Rocklin, Calif.: Prima Publishing, 1997.

Studer, Linda, and Marvin Jacobs. *Graphic Design for 21st Century Desktop Publishers.* North Olmsted, Ohio: Words & Pictures Publishing, 2002.

Toor, Marcelle Lapow. *The Desktop Designer's Illustration Handbook.* New York: John Wiley & Sons, 1997.

Wempen, Faith. *10 Minute Guide to Office Pro 97 for Windows 95: Access, Excel, Powerpoint and Word.* Indianapolis: Que Education & Training, 1997.

DIAGNOSTIC MEDICAL SONOGRAPHERS

The young expectant mother waits on an examination table, her forehead creased with lines. It seems like weeks since she last felt the sharp kick of her baby from within her body. She is worried that something has gone wrong with the development of her child.

Carol Seguin maintains a steady dialogue with the frightened woman in order to distract her from her anxiety; she calms her patient with gentle humor as she coats her stomach with ultrasound gel. She then explains the procedure and positions the woman in order to assure optimum scanning.

Using a device called a transducer, Carol directs high-frequency sound waves toward the unborn baby. These waves will reflect off the body tissue to form a two-dimensional, real-time image on a video monitor. She is careful to observe the screen as she moves the transducer, aware of the need for a high-quality ultrasound image.

An image of a baby, a healthy, breathing boy, appears. Carol quickly points to the baby's beating heart on the monitor. She also points out the baby's head and other body parts; and the mother is overwhelmed with happiness and relief.

Carol is extremely happy for the young woman, yet also knows there is a job to complete. She finishes recording the images of the baby and prepares the film to be taken to a physician for further analysis. This high degree of professionalism, combined with compassion, allows diagnostic medical sonographers like Carol to be prepared and able to do their jobs in the event of good news, as with the young mother, or bad news. The image of another young mother whose baby girl did not survive still lingers in her memory.

Carol wishes the young woman well and readies her equipment for the next patient. In the course of her day she will complete procedures that test for cysts, abdominal tumors, and impeded function of blood vessels and heart valves.

What Does a Diagnostic Medical Sonographer Do?

Diagnostic medical sonographers (DMSs), sometimes known as *ultrasound technologists,* or simply

Definition
Diagnostic medical sonographers use advanced technology, in the form of high-frequency sound waves, to produce images of the internal body for analysis by radiologists and other physicians.

Alternative Job Title
Ultrasound technologists

High School Subjects
Biology
Chemistry

Personal Skills
Helping/teaching
Technical/scientific

Salary Range
$35,800 to $48,660 to $66,680

Minimum Educational Level
Associate's degree, hospital certificate program, or bachelor's degree

Certification or Licensing
Required

Outlook
Faster than the average

DOT
078

GOE
14.05.01

NOC
3216

O*NET-SOC
29-2032.00

sonographers, use high-frequency sound waves, which are an offshoot of World War II SONAR technology, to produce images of the internal body. A picture is obtained when these sound waves bounce off internal structures, becoming echoes that are then displayed as two-dimensional gray images on a video screen. The recorded images are used by a physician in diagnosing disease and in studying the malfunction of organs.

Diagnostic medical sonographers, working under the supervision of a qualified physician, are responsible for the selection and the setup of the proper ultrasound equipment for each specific examination. They also explain the procedure to the patient, record any additional information that may help in the diagnosis, and help the patient into the proper physical position so the test may begin.

Lingo to Learn

Doppler A stethoscope-like instrument that is used to measure blood flow velocity.

Megahertz The degree of strength for a sound wave in an ultrasound procedure.

M mode A reading that determines the fetal heart rate.

Sonography A diagnostic procedure that uses sound waves, instead of radiation, to create an image of the human body.

Transducer A technologist-controlled device that directs high-frequency sound waves to a specific body part in order to create a two-dimensional moving image for analysis.

When the patient is properly aligned, the sonographer applies ultrasound gel to the specific test area. He or she is responsible for selecting the transducer and adjusting controls in relation to the depth of field, organ or structure examined, and other factors. The sonographer physically moves the transducer, a microphone-shaped device that sends high-frequency sound waves into the area to be imaged. At the same time, the sonographer watches the video monitor to be sure that a quality ultrasonic image is being produced. The sonographer must also be aware of subtle differences between healthy and diseased areas in order to be able to record the correct image.

Once the target area is located and a quality image appears consistently on screen, the sonographer then activates the equipment that begins to record images on magnetic tape, a computer disc, strip printout, film, or videotape. The sonographer is responsible for filming individual views or sequences of real-time images in affected areas. When a procedure is completed, the sonographer removes the film and prepares it for analysis by a specially trained physician. The sonographer may also be asked to discuss the test with a supervisor or attending physician.

In addition to diagnostic procedures, DMSs must also maintain patient data relating to each test, and check and adjust their equipment to ensure that readings are accurate. They may also, after considerable experience, have a role in preparing

work schedules and evaluating potential equipment purchases.

What Is It Like to Be a Diagnostic Medical Sonographer?

Diagnostic medical sonographers work in a variety of settings such as hospitals, imaging centers, health maintenance organizations (HMOs), physicians' offices, mobile imaging clinics, industry, and clinical research labs. They may also work in departments of cardiology, radiology, obstetrics, and vascular surgery.

Carol has been a diagnostic medical sonographer since 1971. She received her training at Rush-Presbyterian-St. Luke's Medical Center, which is a teaching hospital in Chicago. In addition to X-ray techniques, she also learned magnetic resonance imaging (MRI), CT scan, and ultrasound, which became her career choice.

Carol's day begins at 8:00 A.M. and ends at 5:00 P.M. There is no overtime for DMSs at Meyer Medical, her current employer. She sees 20 to 25 patients in the course of those nine hours and describes her day as, "Busy, busy, busy." There is no typical day for DMSs like Carol, in that they complete a wide variety of sonographic examinations. Among the most frequent exams done are fetal ultrasounds, gynecological (e.g., uterus, ovaries) and abdominal (e.g., gallbladder, liver, and kidney) tests.

Carol has a lot of expertise in dealing with patients, many of whom are frightened. "We have to exercise a lot of patience and understanding," she explains. "We have to talk to the patients, explain the procedure . . . reassure them so we can successfully complete the examination."

Carol's secondary duties include setting up her work area for each new patient and checking her equipment for malfunction, although she is quick to declare, "We have excellent equipment. Our machines are never down." Actual maintenance and monthly preventive programs are taken care of by an outside firm. Carol does little paperwork except what is done during actual tests. "We leave that to our receptionist-helper," she says, "so we can concentrate on our patients." She is also required in her off-hours to maintain her certification by completing 30 hours of continuing education over a three-year period.

Carol is a member of the Society of Diagnostic Medical Sonographers (SDMS), whose main goal is to organize seminars for continuing education and keep members updated about new technology and the ultrasound field throughout the country and the world. Carol reads trade magazines such as the *Journal of Diagnostic Medical Sonographers,* which she receives as a member of SDMS. "A trade magazine like JDMS is beneficial," she explains, "because it keeps us aware of any new ideas that may be out there, as well as updates on the latest technology."

Aspiring DMSs should take to heart Carol's comment that, "There are many highs and lows in this job." The good parts of being a DMS may include the opportunity to help people. Carol likes the idea that when she goes home at night she feels that she has helped both patient and physician with her imaging expertise. The most exciting or rewarding part of Carol's job is her opportunity to work with pregnant women. "We get to show couples, especially first-time parents, their healthy babies. We get to share in their excitement."

On the other hand, there are significant downsides to her job. Her work may reveal cancer, untreatable disease, even fetal death. "If you want to work in this field," Carol counsels, "you'll have to learn how to handle tragedy and the devastating effects of disease on patients." It is important for prospective DMSs to acquire a professional demeanor to be able to confront tragedy and still do their jobs.

Carol cautions students to be aware of the repetitive nature of the job, the long hours on one's feet, and the patience and good nature one must possess to succeed in the field. "This is hard, grueling work. It's not easy," Carol warns. Students should be aware of the physical and mental energy that this job requires, and also keep in mind the amount of outside work, in the form of continuing education, that they will be responsible for.

Royceanne Faggins works as an echocardiographer in the Veterans Administration Medical Center in Stillwater, Oklahoma, focusing exclusively on the heart. She has been with the center for several years, before which she worked in an outpatient clinic and in a private hospital. "I didn't really like the clinic," she admits. "There's a wider variety of cases in a hospital." Royceanne had done some vascular work in the past, primarily general circulatory system tests.

She prefers working on the heart. "It just clicked with me," she says. "At the time I was getting into echocardiography, it seemed to be the area that was changing the fastest." Many labs do not differentiate between echocardiography and vascular sonography, she adds, but the lab at the Veterans Administration Hospital works just on hearts.

The work for the day is arranged with the most serious cases first. "Once the schedule is set, you just move from case to case," says Royceanne. Doctors order a standard series of tests, called a protocol. The protocol has been established by the American Society of Echocardiography.

"You have a series of views you have to give, but to be good, you have to go beyond that to give the doctor the best possible information," Royceanne says. The full heart series takes about an hour, so Royceanne sees about seven or eight patients a day. Other kinds of sonographers may handle up to 25 patients a day.

Working with patients means talking—explaining procedures, telling them when and how to move, etc.—but it also means listening. "Sometimes patients will tell you things they haven't even told their doctors," she says. She will pass that information to the doctor along with the test results. The results are recorded on VHS tape. Still pictures are available, but the beating heart requires a moving record.

Do I Have What It Takes to Be a Diagnostic Medical Sonographer?

DMSs should be technically adept and possess a thorough knowledge of medical terminology. They must have a superior understanding of human physiology, combined with an artistic approach in order to visualize human anatomy. Kathy Radcliffe, Carol's supervisor, comments, "You have to see the body and conceptualize the image-taking."

DMSs must also have good communication skills in order to understand and implement physicians' orders, and also to instruct and guide patients into the proper position. They must also learn how to respectfully deflect any questions that they are unauthorized to answer. Carol explains, "Most bad news must be handled by the doctor, so that he or she can answer the many questions the patient might have." Like other members of the diagnostic field, DMSs must learn to be objective and unemotional in order to accomplish their duties. DMSs must also possess good people skills such as compassion, patience, kindness, and empathy in order to help very ill, scared, young, or very old patients understand and complete a procedure.

Although diagnostic sonography does not involve harmful radiation, DMSs should be aware that they will be exposed to sick people who might carry communicable diseases. Universal standards do exist to ensure safety for both patient and technologist. The only hazardous material that sonographers are exposed to is waste from invasive procedures. "We wear gloves and dispose of the waste in special containers to maintain safety," Carol explains.

DMSs can assure continuing safety by keeping updated on current hazardous waste disposal methods and being diligent in applying universal safety standards to every procedure.

How Do I Become a Diagnostic Medical Sonographer?

After completing her two-year hospital certificate Carol "lucked out," as she puts it, in terms of finding a job. On the first day of her job search she found employment at the second of three hospitals at which she applied, Little Company of Mary. She clearly had the educational and practical experience to qualify for immediate employment.

Royceanne was a high school senior when she first discovered sonography. "I was headed for radiology [X-ray technician]," she says. "My school counselor got me thinking about ultrasound. I was able to observe a sonography lab at a local medical center, and that convinced me."

EDUCATION

High School

Students intent on a career in diagnostic medical sonography should take courses in chemistry, biology, physics, anatomy and physiology, mathematics, speech, and technical writing. Carol counsels students still in high school to take four years of science, when possible, especially chemistry, since it is a main component of the state boards which grant licensure.

Postsecondary Training

Instruction in diagnostic medical sonography is offered at technical schools, colleges, and universities

FYI

The following are different types of sonography:

Abdominal Evaluation of all the soft tissue structures in the abdomen and retro-peritoneal space (liver, spleen, kidneys, pancreas, aorta, vena cava).

Echocardiography Evaluation of the heart and its structures such as the valves.

Neurosonology Examination of the contour and inner structures of the brain.

Obstetrics/Gynecology Evaluation of the pregnant and non-pregnant female pelvis.

Ophthalmology Examination of the eye, including orbital structures and muscles.

Vascular Sonography Evaluation of the peripheral vascular structures including Doppler.

either as four-year bachelor's degree programs or two-year associate's degree programs, in teaching hospitals in the form of a two-year hospital certificate, and also in the armed forces.

Carol characterizes the training she received as excellent, yet harder than she expected. "We were on call at any time, after an eight-hour work/school day." Carol's curriculum included instruction in medical technology and procedures, patient care and medical ethics, general and cross-sectional anatomy and physiology, principles and techniques of diagnostic soundwave imaging, and others. Carol encourages prospective students to thoroughly check school accreditation before investing time and money. A list of accredited programs can be obtained through the Society of Diagnostic Medical Sonographers (see "How Do I Learn More?").

CERTIFICATION OR LICENSING

All medical employers of DMSs require certification by the American Registry of Diagnostic Medical

Sonographers (ARDMS). After completion of educational requirements, DMSs must register with ARDMS and take and pass the National Boards to obtain their license. Carol is certified in radiology by the American Registry of Radiologic Technologists (ARRT), and in ultrasound technology by the ARDMS, which certifies technologists in the United States and Canada. ARDMS administers examinations and awards credentials in the areas of diagnostic medical sonography, diagnostic cardiac sonography, vascular technology, and ophthalmic biometry. Licensing requirements may exist at the state level also, although requirements vary from state to state. The Department of Health and the Food and Drug Administration also have a role in regulating the sonographic industry.

In addition to standard licensing, Carol must also complete 30 hours of continuing education in three years to keep her certification current. Carol comments, "Many hospitals and ultrasound equipment companies sponsor continuing-education programs so we can earn our credits. If we don't keep updated, we could possibly lose our license."

SCHOLARSHIPS AND GRANTS

Information regarding scholarships and grants can be accessed through national and regional trade organizations, trade periodicals such as the *Journal of Diagnostic Medical Sonography,* local lending institutions, government programs, and technical, university, and hospital programs that offer training in diagnostic sonography.

To Be a Successful Diagnostic Medical Sonographer, You Should . . .

- ○ have good communication skills, oral and written
- ○ have patience for sometimes monotonous or repetitive procedures
- ○ enjoy helping and working with people as part of a team
- ○ be technically adept and detail-oriented
- ○ have a compassionate nature

INTERNSHIPS AND VOLUNTEERSHIPS

Although no one except a licensed DMS may actually work in the field, experience and insight may be gained from dialogue with a DMS, visiting a job site, or for those still in high school, arranging informational exchanges between student groups and a local employer of diagnostic medical sonographers. Another possibility for experience is to speak with a teacher at an accredited ultrasound program. Carol gained valuable internship experience and enjoyed informative interaction with professionals during her practical student hours at Rush-Presbyterian.

Who Will Hire Me?

Some may not find a job as quickly as Carol did. Certified technologists should seek out the publications of professional organizations, such as the SDMS which maintains a list of job openings. Other avenues include employment agencies specializing in the health care field, "headhunters," or direct application to the personnel officers of potential health care employers.

Hospitals are the main employers of diagnostic medical sonographers. Career opportunities also exist in HMOs, private physicians' offices, imaging centers, research labs, educational institutions, and industry.

Rural areas and small towns may offer the best employment opportunities for those willing to relocate and accept lower wages and compensation as compared to jobs in larger cities.

Where Can I Go from Here?

There are many avenues of advancement open to experienced DMSs, yet technologists and prospective students should be aware that advancement can only occur through further education. Those with a bachelor's degree stand the best chance for promotion or advancement. Advanced education can be obtained through technical programs, colleges and universities, teaching hospitals, and sometimes through in-house retraining. Further education will allow DMSs to become certified in nuclear medicine technology, radiation therapy, magnetic resonance imaging, CT scan, computer tomography, or special procedures.

In-depth

Ultrasonics

Ultrasonics is the branch of physics and engineering dealing with high-frequency sound waves. The waves are produced by objects vibrating more than 20,000 times a second, creating sound that is beyond the range of human hearing—ultrasound.

Ultrasonic vibrations may be created electronically, by passing alternating current through a quartz or ceramic crystal; mechanically, with special sirens; or magnetically, by the action of an alternating magnetic field on a hollow metal rod.

Pierre Curie discovered how to produce ultrasonic vibrations in 1890. By World War II their first practical application—the detection of submarines underwater—had been developed (i.e., sonar).

Today ultrasonic waves have many important applications. In addition to the medical imaging uses discussed in this chapter, ultrasonic energy is also used in medicine to heat deep tissues. The method has been used to treat arthritis, bursitis, muscular dystrophy, and other diseases. High-energy ultrasonic waves can also be focused into a pinpoint "scalpel" for bloodless brain surgery.

In dentistry ultrasonic devices are sometimes used to remove calcium deposits from the surface of teeth.

Ultrasonic vibrations in a liquid cause millions of bubbles to form and collapse thousands of times a second. This process, called cavitation, blasts clean the surface of objects immersed in the liquid. Applications of this process include sterilization of surgical instruments and the scouring of precision metal parts. Diamonds, tungsten carbide, and tool steel are readily carved and drilled by ultrasonic techniques. The material to be machined is fixed in place and the cutting tool is lowered until it is in contact with the surface. Then a liquid abrasive is poured over the material in a steady stream. The tool vibrates at an ultrasonic frequency and drives tiny particles of the abrasive against the material with tremendous impact. This bombardment, together with cavitation, grinds an exact counterpart of the tool face into the material being machined. Odd-shaped cuts not possible with other methods can be made.

Sound waves beamed into solid materials will not readily cross air barriers such as cracks. When a crack or other defect is encountered, the sound waves are reflected to a measuring instrument. This form of inspection has replaced the use of X rays in many industries.

Ultrasound is used in some types of burglar alarms and remote-control television tuners. It is also sometimes used in welding and soldering metals, mixing liquids, and dyeing and bleaching textiles.

With considerable experience, DMSs can rise to teaching positions in sonography education programs, or train other technologists in-house or at another location. Other DMSs may become involved in the sales and marketing aspect of their profession, working as equipment demonstrators and instructors for the medical industry. In a hospital setting, DMSs with advanced degrees can become clinical supervisors, administrators, or assume other managerial positions.

Carol, while aware of the vast assortment of advancement opportunities open to her, plans to stay for now in her position at Meyer. She enjoys the diagnostic part of her job and her chance to help physicians and patients alike.

What Are the Salary Ranges?

According to the U.S. Department of Labor, diagnostic medical sonographers earned a median annual income of $48,660 in 2002. The lowest paid 10 percent of this group, which included those just beginning in the field, earned less than $35,800. The highest paid 10 percent, which included those with experience and managerial duties, earned more than $66,680 annually.

Hospital DMSs earned on average $47,390 while those employed by private physicians' offices earned on average $50,390. The American Medical Association reports that the national average salary for all diagnostic medical sonographers in 2002 was $48,000. As always, pay scales and compensation vary based on education level, experience and responsibilities, and location of employers, with urban employers offering more financial compensation than rural or small town employers. The American Society of Radiologic Technologists reports that the most financially lucrative areas for sonography in the United States are the Northeast and Pacific regions. Beyond base salaries, sonographers can expect to enjoy many fringe benefits, including paid vacation, sick and personal days, and health and dental insurance.

What Is the Job Outlook?

Although not as big as the radiology field, diagnostic sonography offers excellent prospects. Ultrasound technology will enjoy even more widespread use, especially in the expanding fields of obstetrics/gynecology and cardiology. Demand for qualified DMSs exceeds the supply in some areas of the country, especially in rural areas and small towns. Those who are flexible about pay scales and compensation will find ready employment in these areas. Increased employment opportunities also exist in California and the Southeast region of the United States.

Those interested in the diagnostic field should be aware of potential roadblocks to future employment. The health care industry currently is in a state of great potential change as the government and public debate future health care policy and the role of third-party payers in the system. Some procedures may not be readily used due to their cost to insurance

---

ADVANCEMENT POSSIBILITIES

Chief technologists and **administrators** are sonographers who, as a result of advanced education and experience, have risen to supervisory positions in hospitals and other medical settings.

Sonography instructors teach in technical programs, teaching hospitals, and university settings.

Sales representatives for ultrasonic equipment sell electronic devices that clean, test, or process materials by means of high-frequency sound waves, such as disintegrators for cleaning surgical instruments, electronic guns for bonding plastics, and sonic devices for detecting flaws in metals, cutting steel and diamonds, and separating fossils from rocks.

---

companies and the government. Job opportunities and growth may be limited as a result.

Hospitals will also continue to downsize, causing some procedures to be done on weekends, nights, or on an outpatient basis. Future DMSs should be aware of the growth of imaging centers, HMOs, and physicians' offices as significant employers of their profession. These employers will compete with hospitals for the most qualified DMSs.

According to the U.S. Department of Labor, employment of diagnostic medical sonographers should grow faster than the average. One reason for this growth is that sonography is a safe, nonradioactive imaging process. In addition, sonography has proved successful in detecting life-threatening diseases and in analyzing previously nonimageable internal organs. Sonography will play an increasing role in the fields of obstetrics/gynecology and cardiology. "It's a good field," Carol says. "Nothing is becoming obsolete. All of our specialty fields are growing." She sees CT scan and magnetic resonance imaging as areas with great growth potential.

Prospective sonographers need to be aware that stiff competition exists for good jobs. Those with advanced education, experience, and certification in other specialized areas such as CT scan, mammography, radiation therapy, nuclear medicine technology, and other fields stand to prosper in future job markets.

How Do I Learn More?

PROFESSIONAL ORGANIZATIONS

The following are organizations that provide information on careers, accredited schools, and employers:

American Institute of Ultrasound in Medicine
14750 Sweitzer Lane, Suite 100
Laurel, MD 20707-5906
301-498-4100
http://www.aium.org

American Medical Association
515 North State Street
Chicago, IL 60610
800-621-8335
http://www.ama-assn.org

American Registry for Diagnostic Medical Sonographers

51 Monroe Street, Plaza East One
Rockville, MD 20850-2400
800-541-9754
http://www.ardms.org

Society of Diagnostic Medical Sonography
2745 Dallas Parkway, Suite 350
Plano, TX 75093-8730
800-229-9506
http://www.sdms.org

BIBLIOGRAPHY

The following is a sampling of materials relating to the professional concerns and development of diagnostic medical sonographers:

Fleischer, Arthur C., and Donna M. Kepple. *Diagnostic Sonography: Principles and Clinical Applications.* 2d ed. Philadelphia: W. B. Saunders, 1995.

Kremkau, Frederick. *Diagnostic Ultrasound: Principles and Instruments.* 6th ed. Philadelphia: W. B. Saunders, 2002.

Sanders, Roger C. *Clinical Sonography: A Practical Guide.* 3d ed. Philadelphia: Lippincott-Raven, 1998.

DIALYSIS TECHNICIANS

|||||||||||||||||||||||||||||||||||||||||||||||||||||||||||||||||||

After setting up the dialysis machine, technician Robert Kinnecom prepares for his first patient of the day. Two weeks ago, this patient had arrived at the dialysis unit having put off care too long. She'd stopped eating because of a loss of appetite, but her extremities had swollen. "A few weeks ago," he reminds his patient, "if I were to push my finger in your arm and pull it away, the indentation would have stayed for a minute or two." She had also had to rely on a walker, which she has left at home today.

"I'm eating again too," she tells Robert, smiling. "I have more energy. I feel better." Though she doesn't express it, she clearly credits Robert with helping her to get her health back. Robert attaches the blood pressure cuff, reminded of why he finds the work so inspiring. He feels that he has helped this patient find some hope.

What Does a Dialysis Technician Do?

The kidneys are vital organs; they remove the waste products of daily living that accumulate in the bloodstream and are normally eliminated from the body as urine. Many people, particularly those who are diabetic or suffer from undetected high blood pressure, develop a condition known as chronic renal failure (CRF) in which their kidneys no longer function properly. Before artificial kidney machines were developed in the 1940s, such patients would die of uremic poisoning as toxic products built up in their bloodstream.

The use of artificial kidney machines is called hemodialysis. In the process of hemodialysis, blood is pumped from the body through a dialyzer, where it passes through tubes constructed of artificial membranes. The outer surfaces of these membranes are bathed with a solution called the dialysate; body waste chemicals pass from the blood through the membrane into the dialysate, but blood cells and other vital proteins do not. The cleansed blood is returned to the patient's body without the harmful waste products. The rate of waste removal depends on the extent of the patient's kidney failure, the

Definition

Dialysis technicians set up and operate hemodialysis (artificial kidney) machines. These machines filter the blood of patients whose kidneys no longer function. Dialysis technicians also maintain and repair this equipment.

Alternative Job Titles

Hemodialysis technicians
Nephrology technicians
Renal dialysis technicians

High School Subjects

Biology
Chemistry
Mathematics

Personal Skills

Helping/teaching
Technical/scientific

Salary Range

$24,977 to $31,280 to $42,910

Minimum Educational Level

High school diploma

Certification or Licensing

Required by certain states

Outlook

About as fast as the average

DOT

078

GOE

N/A

NOC

3212

O*NET-SOC

N/A

concentration of waste products in the blood, and the nature and strength of the dialysate.

The National Association of Nephrology Technicians/Technologists recognizes three types of *dialysis technician*, although in some hospitals and dialysis centers the responsibilities may overlap. These are the patient-care technician, the biomedical equipment technician, and the dialyzer reprocessing (reuse) technician. Dialysis technicians always work under the supervision of medical personnel, usually nurses.

Patient-care technicians are responsible for setting up the dialysis machine and connecting it to the patient's body, for measuring the patient's

Lingo to Learn

Anticoagulant A chemical substance that prevents blood from clotting.

Artificial kidney A dialysis machine used to filter impurities and waste products from the blood of patients whose kidneys do not function properly.

Chronic renal failure (CRF) Long-term kidney disease.

Continuous ambulatory peritoneal dialysis (CAPD) A form of dialysis that takes place within the patient's body.

Dialysate A solution used in artificial kidney machines; impurities and waste products pass from the patient's blood to the dialysate through a semipermeable membrane.

Dialysis The process of removing waste products from the blood.

Dialyzer The part of a kidney dialysis machine in which impurities and waste products are removed from the patient's blood.

End stage renal disease (ESRD) Kidney disease so severe that the patient can only be kept alive by dialysis or a kidney transplant.

Hemodialysis The process of removing waste products from the blood using an artificial kidney machine.

vital signs (including weight, pulse, blood pressure, and temperature), and for monitoring the process of dialysis. They must be able to administer cardiopulmonary resuscitation (CPR) or other life-saving techniques if an emergency occurs during a dialysis session. In some states, including Illinois, technicians are not permitted to administer drugs to patients; this can only be done by nurses.

Biomedical equipment technicians are responsible for maintaining and repairing the dialysis machines (see chapter "Biomedical Equipment Technicians"). *Reuse technicians* care for the dialyzers—the apparatus through which the blood is filtered. Each one must be cleaned and

bleached after use, then sterilized by filling it with formaldehyde overnight so that it is ready to be used again for the next patient's treatment. To prevent contamination, a dialyzer may only be reused with the same patient, so accurate records must be kept. Some dialysis units reuse plastic tubing as well; this too must be carefully sterilized.

The spread of hepatitis and the growing risk of HIV infection have necessitated extra precautions in the field of hemodialysis, as in all fields whose procedures involve possible contact with human blood. All patient-care personnel must observe universal precautions, which include the wearing of a protective apron, foot covers, gloves, and a full face shield.

While most hemodialysis takes place in a hospital or a free-standing dialysis center, the use of dialysis in the patient's home is becoming more common. In this case, technicians may travel to patients' homes to carry out the dialysis procedures or to instruct family members in assisting with the process.

Another form of dialysis is continuous ambulatory peritoneal dialysis (CAPD). In CAPD, the membrane used is the peritoneum (the lining of the abdomen), and the dialysis process takes place within, rather than outside, the patient's body. Dialysis technicians are not needed for this form of treatment.

What Is It Like to Be a Dialysis Technician?

Robert Kinnecom works as a dialysis technician in two different settings: in a U.S. Navy facility and at the University of California at San Diego. In the Navy setting, Robert performs a number of procedures that include removing one component of the blood, such as platelets or plasma; suctioning someone's blood from his or her own body and "cleaning" it with saline and reinstilling the blood; and dialysis using the abdomen, in which fluid is put into the abdomen, allowing the body to perform the exchange through diffusion. "Any of these modalities may be activated on a daily basis here [in the Navy unit] because we're an acute unit," Robert says. "We only do patients in the hospital and some patients from our clinic. So, day to day it can be very different here, versus UCSD where it's more mass productive." At UCSD, Robert is assigned three to four outpatients a day. He checks a patient's vital signs, puts them on the machine, monitors them during treatment, then prepares for the next patient. With the Navy unit, Robert functions more as a nurse, with more responsibilities. "We work directly with the doctors," he says. "We can go to the intensive care unit. We can do all kinds of things that we wouldn't be able to do in the civilian world, as far as giving heart medications, transfusing blood, responding to our patients in ways to continue the treatment in the other modes, and respond to low blood pressure or high blood pressure."

In the Navy setting, the dialysis unit consists of seven machines, while the UCSD unit consists of 17 machines. Most units have many more machines. "If you can picture 30 to 50 machines in a big room," Robert says, "even though it's clean with white floors, it's still like a factory setting." When the patient arrives, Robert takes the patient's weight. When the kidneys fail, a patient tends to gain fluid; Robert checks the patient's current weight against the "dry weight," or the weight at which the patient would be without the excess fluids. Robert enters the figures into a palm pilot which calculates how much time will be needed for gradual fluid removal. Robert then takes the patient's blood pressure. "We take a standing and sitting blood pressure because this tells us the fluid balance inside the body," he says. "Often if your fluid is imbalanced, and you're dehydrated, your fluid pressures will be 20 to 30 degrees different in standing to sitting. Then we take a temperature, because that way if they have a fever at the end of treatment, we know it's isolated to whatever they come into contact with during dialysis."

Typically, a patient will have a surgically placed access, usually in the arm—either a graft, which is a piece of surgical rubber connecting a vein to an artery, or a fistula, which is a surgical connection between a vein and artery without using a foreign object. "That's for the purpose of having arterial blood flow and not grabbing and returning to the same line. So, if we pull from the artery and return to the vein, then we've effectively opened up the system circulatory." Robert inserts two needles into the patient's access, one connected to an outflow tube and the other to an intake tube. "The bigger the needle, the better the blood flow," Robert says. Because of poor blood vessels, some patients are unable to have these accesses. In such cases, the patient has a catheter in the jugular or another major vein in order to circulate the blood system. "It has two tubes in it," Robert explains. "One of the tubes is further downstream than the other, so we pull from the tube closest to us and we return further downstream so that we don't reclean the same blood over and over again."

FYI

The 2002 Data Report of the United States Renal Data System found that:

- There were over 4,100 dialysis facilities in the United States.
- The estimated annual cost of treating end stage renal disease (ESRD) in the United States was more than $25.2 billion.
- There were over 431,000 patients treated for ESRD.
- The estimated growth of new ESRD has steadily decreased since 1990 to 2.5 percent per year.
- There has been a progressive improvement in first-year survival among dialysis patients, credited to the changes in dialysis therapy over the previous 10 years.

Once the tubes have been connected to the patient, the cleansing process starts. "We start the bloodflow, and their blood is cleansed through the machine through what looks like any other filter, but is of course a sterile filter built for dialysis. After three to four hours, we rinse all their blood back to them. We pull needles out and hold pressure for 10 minutes." Robert again takes the patient's blood pressure to assure that the machine didn't remove too much fluid. He also takes the patient's temperature again to rule out an infection that may have occurred during the run, and he also weighs the patient to determine if the patient is now at the desired weight.

The work is extremely dangerous, which is of concern to Robert. "The biggest concern to anyone in the medical field is hepatitis," he says. "Hepatitis can survive on a droplet of dried blood for one to two weeks and still infect someone." But such dangers don't prevent Robert from appreciating the rewards of helping patients. "You have such an impact on a life," he says. "I literally see people start dialysis hesitantly where they are in wheelchairs because they've let themselves get so symptomatic, where they didn't have any energy, or they had so much

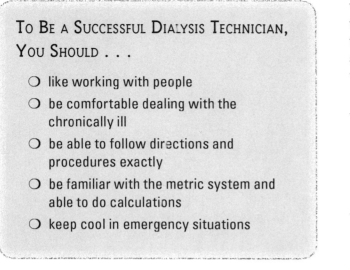

To Be a Successful Dialysis Technician, You Should . . .

○ like working with people

○ be comfortable dealing with the chronically ill

○ be able to follow directions and procedures exactly

○ be familiar with the metric system and able to do calculations

○ keep cool in emergency situations

fluid around their lungs that they couldn't breathe. Within a two week period, you can see their whole lives turn around."

Do I Have What It Takes to Be a Dialysis Technician?

The ability to talk easily with patients and their families is essential. Kidney patients, especially those who are just beginning dialysis, are confronting a major—and permanent—life change. The technician must be able to help them deal with the emotional as well as the physical effects of their condition. Good interpersonal skills are crucial not only in the technician-patient relationship but in working with other team members. "You have to be a people person to an extreme extent," Robert says. At the same time, a good technician can't afford to get so involved with a patient or patients that he or she loses objectivity. "You have to care about people's feelings and be able to put your own aside. You can't be too timid. Some people have problems with needles, or doing any kind of medical care that could cause harm to someone if it's done wrong. If you draw blood, even if it's done right, it still causes pain. So if you don't have the type of personality that can relax your patient and reassure them and give them confidence in you, it could give them a negative experience."

A good head for mathematics and familiarity with the metric system are required. Technicians must be able to calibrate machines and calculate the correct amounts and proportions of solutions to be used, as well as quickly determine any necessary changes if there are indications that a patient is not responding to the treatment appropriately. Technicians keep logs and fill out daily reports; their signature on the log verifies the accuracy of its content.

> You have to care about people's feelings and be able to put your own aside. You can't be too timid.

How Do I Become a Dialysis Technician?

After graduating from high school, Robert enlisted in the Navy where he studied dialysis. Robert's six month training in the Navy was in-depth, preparing him for a number of aspects of dialysis treatment. "Our training is more extensive in theory, response, medication, and knowledge," he says. During his training, he worked in intensive care and in the emergency room. "That was very exciting compared to working on the ward where you're doing basically routine things every day." To prepare for the career, Robert recommends courses in mathematics and science. "You should take the same basic things you would take if you were interested in becoming a doctor."

EDUCATION

High School

Interested high school students should study general science, chemistry, biology, mathematics, and communication. Volunteering in a hospital, nursing home, or other patient-care facility can give you a taste of what it's like to interact with patients in a health care setting.

Postsecondary Training

If you are interested in the requirements for becoming a dialysis technician, you can obtain job descriptions from the National Association of Nephrology Technicians/Technologists (NANT). If you are interested in nursing, contact the American Nephrology Nurses Association (ANNA). Until there are a greater number of organized and accredited training programs, those who are interested in this career must seek information about educational opportunities from local sources such as high school guidance centers, public libraries, and occupational counselors at technical or community colleges. Specific information is best obtained from dialysis centers, dialysis units of local hospitals, home health care agencies, medical societies, schools of nursing, or individual nephrologists (physicians who specialize in treating kidney disease).

Other ways to enter this field are through schools of nurse assisting, practical nursing, or nursing and programs for emergency medical technicians. In these programs you learn basic health care and elementary nursing. After that, you must gain the specific knowledge, skills, and experience required to become a dialysis technician. The length of time required to progress through the dialysis training program and advance to higher levels of responsibility should be shorter if you first complete a related training program.

CERTIFICATION OR LICENSING

The Board of Nephrology Examiners—Nursing and Technology (BONENT) offers a voluntary program of certification for nurses and technicians. The purposes of the program are to identify safe, competent practitioners, to promote excellence in the quality of care of kidney patients, and to encourage study and advance the science of nursing and technological fields in nephrology. You must be a high school graduate to become certified. You must either have at least one year of experience and currently be working in a hemodialysis facility or have completed an accredited dialysis course.

The certification examination contains questions related to anatomy and physiology, principles of dialysis, treatment and technology related to the care of patients with end stage renal disease, and general medical knowledge. Certified technicians use the title CHT (certified hemodialysis technician) after their names (See "How Do I Learn More?").

Recertification is required every four years. To be recertified, you must continue working in the field and present evidence of having completed career-related continuing education units.

States have their own regulations for certification of dialysis technicians. Some states require that you take a training program through the state's health department, that you be certified by BONENT, or that you graduate from the training program of an accredited college.

Who Will Hire Me?

Dialysis technicians are employed by most major hospitals and by free-standing dialysis units. Many of these are listed under "Clinics" in the local Yellow Pages. Health care chains that provide home dialysis, either independently or in conjunction with a clinic, also employ larger numbers of technicians.

Where Can I Go from Here?

Dialysis technicians who have gained knowledge, skills, and experience advance to positions of greater responsibility within their units and can work more independently. The NANT guidelines encourage a distinction between technicians and technologists, with the latter having additional training and broader responsibilities. Not all dialysis units make this distinction.

"At one point," Robert says, "I did want to be a physician, but I have a family and I really feel I would dedicate more time to the hospital than to

---

ADVANCEMENT POSSIBILITIES

Biomedical equipment technicians repair, calibrate, and maintain medical equipment and instrumentation used in health care.

Counseling psychologists provide individual and group counseling services in universities, schools, clinics, rehabilitation centers, Veterans Administration hospitals, and industry to assist individuals in achieving more effective personal, social, educational, and vocational development and adjustment.

Registered nurses provide general medical care and treatment to patients in medical facilities, under the direction of physicians.

my family." Though he's not sure he wants to stay in dialysis because of the standardization that is occurring, he does want to continue to work with patients. "Anything where I can get this feeling," he says. "It's addicting once you're able to help people on this personal level. It's hard to feel the same gratification and impact doing anything else."

A technician looking for career advancement in the patient-care sector may elect to enter nurses' training; many states require that supervisory personnel in this field be registered nurses. Social, psychological, and counseling services may appeal to others who find their greatest satisfaction in interacting with patients and their families.

Someone interested in advancement in the area of machine technology may elect to return to college and become a biomedical engineer. Technical support and equipment maintenance is of major importance, and biomedical equipment technicians may go on to become management personnel in this field.

What Are the Salary Ranges?

According to the *Occupational Outlook Handbook,* clinical laboratory technologists and technicians had median earnings of $42,910 in 2002. The lowest 10 percent earned less than $30,530, while the highest 10 percent earned more than $58,000. The median salary in 2005 for renal dialysis technicians reported on Salary.com was $27,565. The lowest 10 percent earned $24,977 while dialysis technicians in the highest 10 percent earned $31,280. Whereas experienced technicians could once make upwards of $30 an hour, standardization in the field has resulted in lower wages.

Technicians receive the customary benefits of vacation, sick leave or personal time, and health insurance. Many hospitals or health care centers not only offer in-service training but pay tuition and other education costs as an incentive to further self-development.

What Is the Job Outlook?

According to the *Occupational Outlook Handbook,* employment of clinical laboratory workers is expected to grow about as fast as the average for all occupations. The need for dialysis in particular is growing at a rate of about 2.5 percent per year. The average wait for a kidney transplant is two to three years. In 1998, there were 12,166 transplants according to the National Kidney Foundation; as of 2000, there were 44,350 registrants on the waiting list. More than 2,000 new patients are added to the waiting list each month. For those waiting for a transplant, dialysis is necessary. Technicians make up the largest proportion of the dialysis team, since they can care for only a limited number of patients at a time (the ratio of patient-care technicians to nurses is generally about four to one). In addition, there is a shortage of trained dialysis technicians in most locales and a high turnover rate in the field.

As medical technology advances, dialysis becomes more standardized and refined. As a result, the work of a dialysis technician is becoming more routine. Hourly wages have decreased in recent years as the work has become less demanding of technicians. Increasingly, the manufacturers of the dialysis machines are investing in dialysis units and staffing them.

How Do I Learn More?

PROFESSIONAL ORGANIZATIONS

To learn about nephrology nursing, scholarship opportunities, publications, and educational programs, contact
American Nephrology Nurses' Association
East Holly Avenue, Box 56
Pitman, NJ 08071-0056
888-600-2662
http://anna.inurse.com

To learn about certification, contact
Board of Nephrology Examiners—Nursing and Technology
PO Box 15945-282
Lenexa, KS 66285
913-541-9077
http://www.goamp.com/bonet/

For career information, contact
National Association of Nephrology Technicians Technologists
PO Box 2307
Dayton, OH 45401-2307
877-607-6268
nant@nant.meinet.com
http://www.dialysistech.org

BIBLIOGRAPHY

The following is a sampling of books relating to the professional concerns and development of dialysis technicians:

Daugirdas, John T. *Handbook of Dialysis.* New York: Lippincott Williams & Wilkins, 1994.

Gutch, C. F., Martha H. Stoner, and Anna L. Corea. *Review of Hemodialysis for Nurses and Dialysis Personnel.* 6th ed. St. Louis, Mo.: Mosby 1999.

Henrich, William L. *Principles and Practice of Dialysis.* 3d ed. New York: Lippincott Williams & Wilkins, 2004.

Levy, Jeremy. *Oxford Handbook of Dialysis.* 2d ed. New York: Oxford University Press, 2004.

Nissenson, Allen R., and Richard N. Fine. *Clinical Dialysis.* 4th ed. New York: McGraw-Hill Medical Publishing, 2005.

DIETETIC TECHNICIANS

Karen Lucas stops in front of Room 203 in the Cardiovascular Services wing and taps lightly on the door, glancing down at the chart in her hand. After pausing a moment, she pushes the door open and smiles broadly at the elderly woman in the bed nearest her. "Good afternoon, Mrs. Breeden. How are you feeling today?" She pulls a chair nearer the bed and sits down. "Oh, pretty good, honey," the woman responds weakly. "It looks like you get to go home tomorrow, right?" Karen asks, as she organizes the papers on her lap. Mrs. Breeden's face brightens. "Dr. Whiting says I do. I'll be glad to sleep in my own bed."

Smiling, Karen nods. "Now, Mrs. Breeden, you know Dr. Whiting has put you on a salt-restricted diet for your heart. We don't want you to end up in here again." Mrs. Breeden tells Karen, "I always watch my salt, honey."

Continuing to smile, Karen says, "Good! Good for you. You're a step ahead, then. I'm just going to give you this list of foods that are high in sodium to take home." Karen pauses to hand Mrs. Breeden a printed sheet. "The doctor says you should be getting no more than four grams a day. Now, what that means is . . ."

What Does a Dietetic Technician Do?

Definition
Dietetic technicians usually work under the supervision of a dietitian on a food service or health care team. Their responsibilities include taking dietary histories, planning menus, supervising food production, monitoring food quality, and offering dietary counseling and education.

High School Subjects
Biology
Chemistry
Family and consumer science

Personal Skills
Leadership/management
Technical/scientific

Salary Range
$24,000 to $31,000 to $41,100

Minimum Education Level
Associate's degree

Certification or Licensing
Voluntary

Outlook
About as fast as the average

DOT
077

GOE
14.08.01

NOC
3132

O*NET-SOC
29-2051.00

Dietetic technicians work in a variety of different settings, such as hospitals, nursing homes, community programs and wellness centers, public health agencies, weight management clinics, schools, day care centers, correctional facilities, and food companies. They may work independently, or in partnership with a dietician, depending on their employer and what they do.

Dietetic technicians work in food service administration and clinical nutrition, which is the nutritional care of individuals. Technicians in smaller facilities may be involved in both areas of work, while in a larger facility they will probably have more specific duties in one area or the other.

Dietetic technicians working in food service administration will probably be involved in the management of other food service employees. They develop job descriptions, plan work schedules, and help train staff members in methods of food production and equipment operation. They may also work directly in the kitchen, supervising actual food preparation, or in the cafeteria, supervising the workers who assemble and serve the food. In some cases, dietetic technicians are responsible for meeting standards in sanitation, housekeeping, and safety.

Another area of responsibility for the technician in food service administration can be diet and menu planning. Technicians may help modify existing recipes, or create new menus to meet the particular needs of individuals or institutions. They may also be in charge of monitoring the quality of the food and service. Finally, some dietetic technicians are involved in purchasing supplies and equipment, keeping track of the inventory, supervising food storage, and budgeting for cost control measures.

Dietetic technicians working in clinical nutrition at hospitals and nursing homes observe and interview patients to obtain diet histories and food preferences. Using this information, they work with a dietician to determine each patient's nutritional status and dietary needs, and to develop diets that meet these needs. They also counsel and educate the patients and their families on good nutrition, food selection and preparation, and healthy eating habits. Some dietetic technicians make follow-up contacts with these patients to monitor their progress and offer them further help.

Technicians employed by a community program, such as a public health department, clinic, youth center, or home health agency, have many of the same counseling duties as the technicians in patient-care facilities. They provide health screenings and dietary education for low-income families, elderly persons, parents of small children, or any groups of people who might have special questions about nutrition and health care. In some cases, they make follow-up visits to their clients' homes to check on their progress, or make permanent arrangements for continuing care for the needy, such as hot meals for the housebound, or school lunch programs for children.

Dietetic technicians in a community program may also be in charge of developing and coordinating community education efforts. Technicians may help create brochures and teaching materials, or plan classes in nutrition, weight loss, and other health-related topics. Some diet techs teach or co-teach the classes. They may also work with other community groups, corporations, or schools to promote an interest in health and nutrition.

What Is It Like to Be a Dietetic Technician?

Karen Lucas and Joan Shaw are both dietetic technicians working in the area of clinical nutrition at the same hospital, and their duties are almost exactly the same. Because one of them must be there every day, during the hours meals are served, they do not work together.

"We have 10-hour days," Joan says, "and we alternate weekends. It works out so that we work eight days and have six days off in a two-week period." Although this particular schedule is not the most common for dietetic technicians, the 40-hour workweek is standard.

Lingo to Learn

Diet history A background of eating habits, diet restrictions, appetite fluctuations, and weight gain or loss that is used to help assess nutritional status and prescribe diet changes.

Four-gram sodium diet Usually called a "no added salt" diet, restricts patients from adding salt to already prepared foods and from eating such high-sodium foods as bacon and ham.

Health screening A battery of tests, including blood pressure, cholesterol, weight-appropriateness, and body fat percentage, used to detect any potential health concerns.

Low-fat diet A diet that restricts fat intake to between 30 and 40 grams per day.

Practicum A period of supervised practice experience in various health care and food service facilities, and community programs.

Two-gram sodium diet A stricter diet than the four-gram, allows patients only 2,000 milligrams of sodium daily.

Wellness From a dietetic standpoint, a lifestyle that promotes good health in terms of diet and exercise.

For Karen and Joan, the typical day at work begins at 6:30 A.M. "The first thing that must be done is to check the breakfast tray line for completeness and accuracy, because at 6:45, the first wave of breakfast trays goes upstairs to the patients." According to Joan, it usually takes about an hour to check all the trays.

The diet tech on duty then has the responsibility of collecting all of the patient menus for the next day. Each day, the patients are given menus that contain all of their food options, and they are instructed to mark their choices on the menu form. Every morning, Karen or Joan goes to each floor to collect all menus that have already been completed. After taking the completed forms back to the department to be processed, she checks a computer printout to see which patients still need to make up menus.

"We try to get everyone to fill out a menu," Karen says, "so we go to each patient's room. If they haven't already done it, we try to help them make the choices." Because patients may be sleeping, out of the room, being bathed, or receiving doctors' visits, seeing every one of these patients may take a number of trips, and often lasts until nearly lunch time.

Afternoons are mostly reserved for nutrition assessment and education, according to Karen and Joan. After conferring with one of the three dietitians to determine which patients need attention, and receiving diet orders for these patients, the dietetic technician checks each individual's chart to find out if he or she needs nutrition education. Not everyone on a special diet needs the training. "Sometimes they already know what they're supposed to be eating," Joan says. "Maybe they've had the counseling before, or have been on the diet for a long time already."

If the patient does need dietary counseling, Joan or Karen makes a personal visit to explain the prescribed diet and to go over the restricted foods. "We talk through it with them," Karen says, "and we have printed material, also, for them to take home."

There are different diets that the technicians must understand and be able to explain, such as two- and four-gram sodium, bland, low-fat, low-residue or low-fiber, and no sugar. "We don't usually see the diabetic patients," Karen says. According to her, the dietitians do the counseling for those patients, because the education is much more extensive and time consuming. Many of the patients Joan and Karen see are on low-salt and low-fat diets because of heart problems.

Although most of the days follow the same routine, Karen's duties do vary slightly on one day each week. On these days, she works for the Wellness Center, which is an offshoot of the hospital. "I do on-site health screenings for corporations and organizations," she says. The Wellness Center also offers on-site classes in better nutrition, stopping smoking, weight loss, and other health-related issues. Karen helps teach some of these classes. "It is a part of the hospital," she says, "but it serves the whole community." She enjoys her time at Wellness, as she calls it, because it adds variety to her job.

Do I Have What It Takes to Be a Dietetic Technician?

The duties of individual dietetic technicians vary widely from person to person, depending both on

workplace and area of service. Likewise, the personal qualities necessary to excel depend somewhat on the responsibilities of the particular job.

Karen and Joan agree that one of the most important skills is being able to communicate and deal well with people. "You have to really like people," Joan says. "We have to deal with patients all the time. A large part of our day is spent with them." Although the majority of patients she sees are very friendly and cooperative, she acknowledges that some of them are difficult to communicate with. "Sometimes, you walk into a room and the patient won't talk to you," she says. "Sometimes it's because of medication, or they're groggy, or they're depressed. Occasionally, but not often, they are unpleasant and argumentative." Because the technician has to deal with all sorts of people in all different circumstances, compassion and a desire to serve others are important. "The personal interaction can be a positive point about the job," Karen says. "You really feel like you're helping, and that's very satisfying."

> The personal interaction can be a positive point about the job. You really feel like you're helping, and that's very satisfying.

Interpersonal skills are significant for the dietetic technicians who work in food service administration, as well as for those who, like Karen and Joan, work in nutrition and counseling. Food service administration may involve managing, scheduling, training, and evaluating other employees. Communication skills and an aptitude for dealing with people are essential for this area.

For the dietetic technicians who work in food service administration, it is also extremely important to be well organized, efficient, and able to deal with stress. Both Karen and Joan worked previously in food service supervision, and they say it's very different than the jobs they now perform. "Supervising is stress times ten," Karen says. "I was always swamped with work. Staffing the department, making sure the employees are there, and finding replacements for the ones who cancel at the last minute can be especially taxing." On the other hand, she says, she did enjoy the challenge of the job, and the duties she now performs, while much less stressful, can sometimes be a bit too routine.

Finally, the dietetic technicians say that an interest in nutrition and health care is important to being a success in this job. Joan has a long-time interest in cooking and home economics, while Karen has always been interested in health and fitness. "I think you need to be interested in some aspect of nutrition," Joan says. "I don't think you'd be in this field if you weren't."

How Do I Become a Dietetic Technician?

Karen and Joan took different paths to becoming dietetic technicians. Joan has a four-year bachelor of science degree in home economics, and was a high school teacher before deciding to move into dietetics. Karen, on the other hand, enrolled in the two-year dietetic technician program at her college, after learning that such a degree was offered. "I'd always been interested in nutrition and wellness, and I wanted a two-year degree, so it seemed like a natural choice," she says.

EDUCATION

High School

To become a dietetic technician, you need at least a two-year college degree. The American Dietetic Association (ADA) suggests that students who are considering a technician career should emphasize science courses in their high school studies. Biology, anatomy, and chemistry will provide a very important background for success both in college classes and in the course of a career. High school math and business courses will also be good training, since the college requirements for this degree include some accounting and purchasing classes. Finally, the ADA recommends sociology and psychology classes, to broaden the student's understanding of people, as well as English to improve communication skills.

You might also want to check in your area to see if there are summer or part-time jobs, or volunteer opportunities available in the field of dietetics. Actually working in the field can provide valuable

> ### To Be a Successful Dietetic Technician, You Should . . .
>
> ○ have a desire to serve people
> ○ be a good communicator
> ○ have an interest in health care and nutrition
> ○ be able to follow instructions well
> ○ be a good planner and organizer

experience, as well as insight into what the jobs are like.

Postsecondary Training

In order to become a dietetic technician, you must enroll in one of the 69 colleges offering the ADA's approved program. The program is a combination of classroom training and at least 450 hours of supervised practical experience, usually called a practicum. The classes generally include a number of science courses, such as biology, anatomy, and chemistry, and some business and administrative courses, such as accounting and institutional administration. General education classes, such as English and psychology, are also part of the curriculum. The technical, specialized dietetic training may include classes in food preparation, therapeutic diets, meal management, community nutrition, quantity food purchasing, and nutritional management of disease.

Over the two-year period, you also get a certain amount of supervised practical experience in various health care and food service facilities. The type of field experience a student dietetic technician might receive includes practicums in clinical nutrition; food service planning, purchasing, equipment use, sanitation, and training; and management. You may be assigned to a patient care facility for practicum, where you help prepare schedules, order food, cook, or instruct patients. If you are assigned to a community agency, you might go on home visits with a nutritionist, help teach individuals, or assist in demonstrations and classes.

Karen especially enjoyed the practicums. "You really get a feel for what the job is like in practicum," she says. She doesn't remember the classes being extremely difficult, although she did have to study.

Overall, she felt like her college program left her well prepared to enter the dietetics field.

CERTIFICATION OR LICENSING

After successfully completing a dietetic technician program approved by the ADA, you are eligible to take the ADA's registration examination for dietetic technicians. The exam is given in October each year and consists of 240 multiple choice questions broken down into four subject areas.

Technicians who have passed the registration exam are known as Dietetic Technicians, Registered, and are allowed to use the initials DTR after their names. They are also eligible to become members of the American Dietetic Association.

It is not a requirement that dietetic technicians be licensed or certified. However, many do choose certification. As a newly graduated dietetic technician, it is a good credential to have, since it indicates that you have met a certain standard of competence. While it may not be necessary to be registered in order to get a job, it might provide a competitive edge in some cases.

Registered dietetic technicians are required to earn 50 hours of continuing education every five years to maintain the credential. You can do this by attending hospital programs, symposiums, or college classes. You can also perform approved self-studies or self-assessment modules for credit.

SCHOLARSHIPS AND GRANTS

Students in the dietetics field have a number of possibilities for financial aid to help pay for schooling. In addition to federal grants, the ADA also offers aid, in the form of scholarships, to encourage eligible students to enter the field. Students in the first year of a dietetic technician program may apply (see "How Do I Learn More?").

Finally, qualified students might be able to obtain a grant or scholarship from corporations, community or civic groups, religious organizations, or directly from the college or university they plan to attend.

Who Will Hire Me?

When Karen graduated from college, she sent her resume out to several hospitals, nursing homes, and food service companies. Her first dietetics job was as manager of a corporate cafeteria for a vending and food service company. After four years in that position, she decided she'd like to work in a clinical setting, because of her interest in therapeutic nutrition. She applied at a hospital near her home, and was hired as the assistant director of the food service department.

The majority of dietetic technicians are employed by hospitals. Technicians who work in long-term patient care facilities, such as nursing homes, make up the second largest group. A smaller percentage of dietetic technicians work in community health care programs or outpatient clinics. Finally, some dietetic technicians work in settings that are not directly related to health care, such as schools, colleges, hotels, or, as in Karen's case, employee cafeterias.

Graduates of a dietetic technician program who are looking for a first job should check the placement office of their school. Also, since they have spent a considerable amount of time in various dietetic workplaces to complete practicums, they may have excellent contacts in the field, which can serve as job leads. Applying directly to the personnel offices of all area hospitals, nursing homes, and public health programs is another possible route to finding a position. Finally, the classified ads of local newspapers, private and public employment agencies, and job listings in health care journals are all potential employment sources.

In some locations, the labor market for dietetic technicians may be flooded, particularly in areas near schools that offer the training program. In such cases, you might have more luck by broadening your search to include less competitive areas, and by looking for creative job opportunities. Karen advises that the dietetic technician who is looking for a job should keep an open mind about the possibilities. "Anywhere a dietician is, a dietetic technician could investigate," she says. Joan agrees. "Look for situations where there's too much work for one dietician, but not enough for two," she counsels.

Where Can I Go from Here?

Karen is currently in the process of finishing her bachelor's degree in business administration. She hopes that the extra schooling in administration, combined with her training and experience in dietetics, will help her obtain a managerial position. "I'd like to get more into the Wellness Center type of work," she says. "I'd like a supervisory job in something like that."

Beginning technician positions are usually closely supervised, but after spending some time on the job, the dietetic technician may be able to take on more responsibilities. Many technicians, after proving their abilities, are allowed to perform some of the same functions as entry-level dietitians, such as diagnosing nutrition problems, prescribing diets, helping develop educational materials, and being involved in the financial management of the department. With the expanded range of duties, technicians may then earn higher pay, while either keeping the same title, or officially changing positions. For example, a dietetic technician could be promoted to kitchen manager.

A very common means of advancement in the field of dietetics involves further schooling. The dietetic technician who wants to attain a higher position, such as dietician, may decide to pursue a bachelor's degree. A major in dietetics, nutrition, food science, or food service systems management, plus a year of internship, are the requirements for becoming a dietician. Although earnings vary widely with employer and amount of experience, the salary range for dietitians is $28,000 to $45,000 annually.

Further advancement possibilities for experienced dietitians include assistant, associate, or director of a dietetic department. With a graduate degree, the dietician could move into research or an advanced clinical position.

What Are the Salary Ranges?

According to the ADA, in 2002 dietetic technicians earned between $24,000 and $30,000 annually. Those with more experience reported incomes of between $30,000 and $40,000 annually. The American Medical Association lists a median salary of $31,000 in 2002 for dietetic technicians. The lowest paid 10 percent earned $24,000 and the highest 10 percent earned up to $41,100.

Most technicians are offered a benefits package by their employers, usually including health insurance, paid vacations and holidays, and meals during working hours.

What Is the Job Outlook?

Although the *Occupational Outlook Handbook* indicates that the outlook for dietitians is expected to be average, it appears as though opportunities for dietetic technicians may be better than average. Because the position is a fairly new one, dating back only to the early 1970s, the demand for technicians has previously been unsteady and patchy. Now, however, as employers are becoming more aware of the advantages of hiring dietetic technicians, the need is increasing yearly and is expected to continue to expand.

One major reason for the positive job forecast is that hiring dietetic technicians is cost-effective for employers. Many functions that dietitians used to perform can be done easily by dietetic technicians, leaving the dietitians free to concentrate on the work that only they can do. Since dietitians are expensive to hire, it makes sense for employers to supplement their nutrition or food service team with technicians who can do many of the same tasks but do not earn as high a wage. This method of reducing expenses may become even more popular, with the increasing public and governmental concern over health care costs.

ADVANCEMENT POSSIBILITIES

Clinical dietitians, also known as **therapeutic dietitians,** plan menus and oversee preparation of meals for patients in hospitals or nursing homes, consult with doctors to determine diet needs and restrictions, and instruct patients and families in nutrition and diet planning.

Community dietitians coordinate food services for public health care organizations, evaluate nutritional care, instruct individuals and families in diet and food selection and provide follow-up, and conduct community dietary studies.

Administrative dietitians, also known as **dietetic department directors,** or **chief dietitians,** direct food service and nutritional care departments of institutions, establish policies and procedures, hire and supervise staff members, and are responsible for menu planning, meal preparation, purchasing, sanitation, and finances.

The emphasis on nutrition and health in today's society is another reason for the positive outlook for dietetic technicians. In future years, more health services, some of them involving nutrition, diet training, and monitoring, will be used. The population is growing, and with it, the percentage of older people who have the greatest health care demands. The increasing need for health care services translates into an increasing need for workers.

How Do I Learn More?

PROFESSIONAL ORGANIZATIONS

The following organization provides information on dietetic technician careers, accredited schools and scholarships, and possible employers:

The American Dietetic Association
ADA Student Operations
120 South Riverside Plaza, Suite 2000
Chicago, IL 60606-6995
800-877-1600, ext. 5400
education@eatright.org
http://www.eatright.org/careers.html

To learn about advancement opportunities in nutrition, contact

American Society for Nutritional Sciences
9650 Rockville Pike, Suite 4500
Bethesda, MD 20814
301-634-7050
sec@asns.org
http://www.asns.org

BIBLIOGRAPHY

The following is a sampling of materials relating to the professional concerns and development of dietetic technicians:

Caldwell, Carol Coles. *Opportunities in Nutrition Careers.* Rev. ed. New York: McGraw-Hill, 2005.

Careers in Focus: Medical Technicians. 4th ed. New York: Facts On File, 2004.

Kane, Michael T., ed. *Role Delineation for Registered Dietitians and Entry-Level Dietetic Technicians.* Chicago: American Dietetic Association, 1990.

DISPENSING OPTICIANS

||||||||||||||||||||||||||||||||||||||||||||||||||||||||||

By 3:30 on a Tuesday afternoon, Carla Hawkins has been at work for several hours. She's had to send back a young man's contact lenses because he couldn't adjust to them. She spent an hour helping an elderly woman who didn't want glasses in the first place to find a pair of frames she liked, and that was no easy task. A shipment of new display frames arrived damaged, and one of her coworkers called in sick. Carla hopes that the rest of her day will be easy. Instead she sees a little girl, around eight years old, nearly dragged in by her mother.

"We need glasses," the mother says when Carla approaches them with a smile. She hands Carla a prescription. The little girl is pouting.

"Not too excited to get glasses, huh?" Carla says, leaning down. The little girl doesn't answer. "Come over here with me," Carla says, and leads her to a stool where she can sit. Carla and the mother sit, too.

"You might feel like the only one," she says, "but I see kids your age and much younger every day who come in here and don't want glasses, feel mad or disappointed, or just that they're not going to look good, and I've had nearly everyone leave pretty happy with what they've chosen." The little girl is starting to show some interest.

"Maybe you're afraid you can't play ball as well with glasses or that you're going to stick out, but I will show you some frames you'll like. We can even make you some sunglasses."

"None of my friends have glasses," the little girl says finally.

"They will sometime," Carla says. "I promise you, it's going to feel good to see properly. Tell me about what you do after school."

A little while later they've found some frames the little girl likes, and she and Carla are looking for a chain for them to hang from around her neck. "I think it was the idea of the chain that won her over," her mother says to Carla as her daughter tries one on in the mirror.

What Does a Dispensing Optician Do?

With 70 percent of the workforce needing corrective eyewear, *dispensing opticians* are in demand. Carla

---

Definition
Dispensing opticians are health professionals who fit eyeglasses and contact lenses using prescriptions written by eye doctors.

High School Subjects
Biology
Mathematics
Physics

Personal Skills
Helping/teaching
Mechanical/manipulative

Salary Range
$16,310 to $25,600 to $43,490

Minimum Educational Level
Apprenticeship

Certification or Licensing
Required by certain states

Outlook
As fast as the average

DOT
299

GOE
14.04.01

NOC
3231

O*NET-SOC
29-2081.00

---

is one of many people throughout this country as well as throughout the world, who help customers find glasses or contact lenses that fit their needs and their lifestyles. Customers count on dispensing opticians to guide them through their eyewear process, and even the most experienced customers need to be sure that their glasses or contacts fit and correct their vision.

Glasses were widely used in the 1500s when printed matter for reading first became readily available, and the use of corrective lenses continued over the next several hundred years. From the start, dispensing opticians have been necessary to ensure the accuracy of the corrective eyewear prescribed. The optician needs to be sure that eyeglasses or contacts are made according to the optometrist's prescription specifications. They need to be certain of the placement of the lenses in relation to the pupils of the eyes. Dispensing opticians are valuable in helping customers select lenses or frames appropriate

Lingo to Learn

Astigmatism A vision problem caused by an irregularly shaped cornea.

Diopter Measurer of visual deficiency.

Hyperopia Scientific term for farsightedness, or inability to see close up.

Myopia Scientific term for nearsightedness, or inability to see far away.

Presbyopia Latin for "old eyes"; the process of vision deterioration that occurs in most people once they pass the age of 40.

Refractometry The process by which visual accuity is measured.

Visual accuity The measurement of how well an individual is able to see.

for their lifestyle. They also prepare work orders for the optical laboratory workers.

Dispensing opticians work around people all day long. Once a customer has obtained a prescription from the optometrist or ophthalmologist, he or she gives the prescription to an optician and begins the selection process. The optician asks the customer about what he or she does. Will the glasses be for everything? Just for reading? Will they be needed while playing sports or engaging in hobbies? What types of jobs does the customer have? What kinds of hobbies? The optician can tell from the prescription whether the customer will require thick or thin lenses in the glasses, and can therefore advise certain frames. They offer suggestions as needed to the customer regarding the style and color of the frames.

Dispensing opticians are responsible for making certain that glasses fit the customer's face once the glasses have returned from the lab. While the process of finding and fitting glasses used to take some time, it has been turned into a one- or two-hour process thanks to the optical superstores with in-store labs.

Regardless of the time period, however, the optician fits the glasses for the customer when they return from the lab. They use small tools and instruments to make minor adjustments to the frames.

When fitting contact lenses, opticians must be precise and skilled. The optician measures the curvature of the cornea and prepares very specific directions for the optical mechanic who will make the lenses. They must be very careful and patient when placing the lenses on the customer's eyes and when teaching the customer to insert and remove the lenses.

What Is It Like to Be a Dispensing Optician?

Carla Hawkins has been a dispensing optician for more than five years. "I started because I needed a job I'd be interested in," she says. "I'd just decided that I'd had enough of community college and wanted to take a break because without knowing what I wanted to do, I was wasting time." Carla found a job with Lenscrafters, an optical superstore where customers can have their glasses made for them, on-site, in less than an hour. She started at minimum wage. "The funny thing is that I mainly needed to earn money," she says. "I learned more about the work and liked it a lot. I ended up deciding to go back to school for opticianry."

Like most dispensing opticians who work in retail stores, Carla works a mix of shifts. She is in school so she doesn't work full time, but dispensing opticians who work a full-time schedule generally put in a 40-hour week, and often evening and weekend shifts are worked into that schedule. Salaried employees are sometimes asked to work overtime, but not regularly. Dispensing opticians who are paid by the hour get paid time-and-a-half for overtime work. Retail opticians are usually expected to work some holidays.

Dispensing opticians work in pleasant surroundings—clean, well-lit areas, whether in retail stores or in doctors' offices. They spend their time alternately sitting and standing. To aid customers in finding suitable frames, the dispensing optician generally points out several frames in different parts of the store. Customer information and medical history is generally taken sitting down. Fitting glasses and contacts involves sitting.

Carla works with a variety of people all day every day. Her job is to make sure the customers who walk into her store feel that they've received the best possible service and care. "People like to feel taken care of," Carla says. "For many people, buying glasses is a new experience. It's not just any purchase—people have to feel comfortable with their choice of frames because

In-depth

History of Lenses

The early history of lenses is unknown. In 1845 an archeologist uncovered in what is now Iraq an ancient rock crystal ground to form a small convex lens, but there is no evidence that lenses were widely known or used in ancient times.

An early investigation of the principles of lenses was made in the 11th century by Alhazen, a Persian physician. Spectacles with convex lenses were in common use both in Europe and in China as early as the thirteenth century.

Zacharias Janssen, a Dutch optician, is credited with combining lenses to make a compound microscope about 1590. Another Dutchman, Hans Lippershey, built the first telescope in 1608. The art of designing and manufacturing lenses has progressed steadily since that time.

With certain exceptions, the lenses in conventional eyeglasses sold in the United States are required by federal law to be either plastic or specially treated impact-resistant glass. Frames are generally plastic or metal.

Eyeglasses are used primarily to correct refractive errors of vision. Defects in the size and shape of the eye cause various kinds of vision problems because they interfere with the normal refraction, or bending, of light rays passing through the various parts of the eye and coming to a focus on the retina. Two common disorders of refraction for which corrective eyeglasses are needed are nearsightedness (myopia) and farsightedness (hyperopia).

Contact lenses, which are worn directly on the eyeball, are usually more expensive than ordinary eyeglasses, and they must be removed from time to time to prevent irritation to the eye. Contact lenses are used primarily for correcting nearsightedness.

---

they're going to wear them. I know from experience that the customer is very grateful if they feel you've spent a lot of time with them, getting to know them a bit so that you can make suggestions. People feel vulnerable when it comes to glasses."

The work Carla does requires a lot of patience because of the different people she encounters every day, but the work is not physically difficult. Before the store opens in the morning, she makes sure that the store is neat and attractive, that new merchandise has been registered on the computer, and that the customer records are up to date. There is behind-the-scenes work that allows the dispensing optician to devote her full attention to the customer when the customer is there.

Once the initial duties have been taken care of and the store is open, Carla's day revolves around the people she serves. "Some days it's all people who have never worn a pair of glasses before," she says.

"This happens a lot with older people who need corrective eyewear as they age. Some days it might be all older people and little kids. Other days I get people who have all been wearing glasses for years. It's easier to help people who know what it's like to wear them, but I like to help people get over the hump of adjusting to themselves in glasses."

Carla finds out about each customer's lifestyle: what type of work they do, what type of hobbies, whether or not they play sports. "Unless they're getting two pairs of glasses or glasses and contacts, you need to do your best to make the glasses fit their lifestyle. For someone really active and involved in contact sports, you can't suggest some small delicate frame. It'll never survive." Carla works to make the customer at ease. Once she knows a bit about what they're looking for, she is ready to suggest some frame options. She goes through the store selection, suggesting frames she thinks suit the customer's needs and appearance. "It's important to find a style that's flattering to the face of the person," she says.

Some dispensing opticians spend time on the phone talking with the labs that make their glasses and contacts, but at Lenscrafters where Carla works, the lab is on-site. "I know a lot of places call you up when your glasses are ready and you go in for a fitting or a lesson in how to wear contacts," she says, "and sometimes people come back for their glasses here, but mostly I deal with same-day service since we can make most prescriptions in an hour."

Like every dispensing optician, Carla is meticulous about the prescription she gets for glasses or contact lenses. Lenscrafters has an on-site optometrist, the doctor who prescribes the strength of corrective eyewear, but just as many people come with prescriptions from their own doctors. Because of the importance of the accuracy of prescriptions, Carla tests the customer's eyes before sending the prescription to the lab, and then later fits the customer with the glasses or contacts and has them do a reading test. "You have to be certain that they can see," she says. "After all, this is the reason they've come in the first place." She laughs.

Do I Have What It Takes to Be a Dispensing Optician?

"Dispensing opticians have to like people," says Carla. "All day long you are interacting with people, and you can't get upset or impatient if things get frustrating. You need to be able to adjust yourself to get along with anyone." Children can be the most frustrating to deal with, but also the most rewarding, she says. "Kids come in here dragging their feet and it's not like we transform them into great fans of glasses every time," she says, "but it is very rewarding to watch their faces when they put their glasses on and you know they can really see. It's the best part of the job."

Opticians need to have steady hands and good hand-eye coordination for the tiny, tedious tightening and adjustment jobs that need to be done to glasses. They need to be patient and meticulous when it comes to measuring the cornea for contact lenses or making sure by checking their lens machine that someone's prescription is exactly right. A soothing and confident manner is beneficial for an optician. "People are very sensitive when it comes to their eyes,"

Carla says. "When you're asking someone to sit still for a few minutes so you can check the accuracy of their prescription through the lensometer, they feel more at ease with a quiet voice. I've been told that." Opticians touch their customers, when checking the fit of frames, when checking their eyes, when adjusting the finished glasses, or inserting someone's contacts for them initially. A fine sense of touch is an attribute of a good dispensing optician.

You need to be able to adjust yourself to get along with anyone.

Since dispensing opticians very often play a large role in a customer's frame selection, it is important that the optician has a good sense of color and feels comfortable advising the customer. Taking hair and skin color as well as face shape into account is what helps the optician to point out flattering and practical frames for the customer. "You wouldn't believe how many people want your opinion on the frames they choose," says Carla. "Some people have very strong ideas, but there are just as many who almost want you to choose for them. I guess they figure that since you work with eyewear, you must know best."

There are many qualities important to a dispensing optician, but perhaps the most important of all is good communication skills. To be able to obtain the information needed to help customers through the eyewear process, to make them feel at ease and in a friendly environment, to have a nonthreatening and efficient manner: These are the crucial skills.

How Do I Become a Dispensing Optician?

EDUCATION

High School

A high school diploma is preferred but not absolutely mandatory in the field of opticianry. While it is necessary to have completed high school to go on to a program offered by a community college, it is not impossible to work as an apprentice without a high school diploma. Students interested in entering

In-depth

Transforming Light Energy into Vision

If you could lock through the opening in the front of your eye (the pupil), and see to the very back surface, you would see your retina. On your retina are all the sense receptor cells that enable us to see. There are none anywhere else in the body.

On the paper-thin retina are two distinct sense receptors (nerve endings) called rods and cones. The cones are concentrated at a tiny spot on the retina called the fovea. If the focusing machinery of the eye (cornea, lens, etc.) is working just right, light rays from the outside have their sharpest focus on the fovea. Surrounding the fovea is a yellowish area called the macula lutea. Together, the fovea and macula lutea make a circle not much bigger than the head of a pin.

The cones are responsible for all color vision and fine detail vision, such as for reading. Beyond the circumference of the macula lutea, there are fewer and fewer cones, and rods become the dominant structures on the retina. It is estimated that there are roughly 10,000,000 cones on each retina, but more than 10 times as many rods. The rods are responsible for vision in dim light and peripheral vision. Because the rods are not sensitive to colors, our night vision is almost completely in black and white.

The momentary interval after the cones stop working but before the rods begin to function is explained by a curious pigment in the eye called visual purple. This substance is manufactured constantly by the rods, and must be present for them to respond to dim light, but it is destroyed when exposed to bright light. Thus, after entering a darkened room, it takes a few moments for visual purple to build up in the retina. One of the principal constituents of visual purple is vitamin A, which is why this vitamin is said to increase our capacity to see in the dark.

Every nerve ending is part of a larger unit, a neuron or nerve cell, and the rods and cones are no exception. Like all nerve cells, each rod and cone sports a long nerve fiber leading away from the site of reception. In each eye, the fibers converge at a certain spot just behind the retina, forming the optic nerve. There are no rods or cones at the point where the optic nerve exits from behind the retina at the back of the eyeball. That is why everybody has a "blind spot" at that point. An image passing through that spot completely disappears.

From the retina, each eye's optic nerve goes almost directly to the middle of the brain, and the two converge a short distance behind the eyes. The optic nerve trunk then proceeds toward the rear of the head where the occipital lobes, the brain's "centers for seeing," are located. Just before reaching the occipital lobes, the optic nerve splits again into thousands of smaller nerve bundles that disappear into the visual cortex or "outer bark" of the occipital lobes. Only at this point are the bits of light energy that have stimulated our rods and cones transformed into images that our brain can "see."

---

the field will find it much easier having earned their diploma, simply because employers tend to attribute a higher level of knowledge and competency to students who have successfully completed their high school studies.

Courses such as algebra, geometry, and physics will help the aspiring optician later, as well as any course work in mechanical drawing. Communications classes are also valuable, because opticians need to be able to relate to a variety of people on all different levels.

Postsecondary Training

There are two ways of entering the field of opticianry. One is through a two-year associate's degree in optical dispensing from a community college. The Commission on Opticianry Accreditation lists 22 accredited programs that award two-year associate's degrees. The other is by serving a supervised multi-year apprenticeship with an optician or optical association. Once you finish a program, you can sit for licensing (that is, if you live in one of the 21 states that require licensing to practice opticianry). If there is no licensing requirement, you take an exam with the American Board of Opticianry.

Community colleges and trade schools concentrate on mechanical and geometric optics, ophthalmic dispensing procedures, contact lens practices, business concepts, communications, and mathematics, as well as lab work in grinding and polishing lenses.

Opticians who work as apprentices learn all aspects of the business by following in the footsteps of another optician and gradually working up to taking on tasks and responsibilities individually. The apprenticeship process tends to take longer than the community college or technical school training; however, apprentices are paid while they learn, while students of opticianry must pay for the training they receive.

CERTIFICATION OR LICENSING

Currently, 21 states require dispensing opticians to have a state license. The requirements for these licenses vary from state to state, but all require passing a written examination. Opticians who work in doctors' offices are not required to have state licensing.

Regardless of the requirements of the states in which they live, many opticians choose to be certified at the national level by either the American Board of Opticianry (ABO) or the National Contact Lens Examiners (NCLE). Certification is achieved after successful completion of examinations and is maintained by attending continuing education classes that meet with the approval of the associations. Opticians are expected to renew their certification every three years. Examinees are not required to have had formal training or experience to sit for these examinations, but some experience or education improves your chances of passing. According to the ABO-NCLE, well over half of the estimated number of dispensers in the United States are certified by the organizations. ABO certifies approximately 30,000 opticians, and NCLE certifies about 8,000 contact lens dispensers. A survey by the ABO-NCLE found that 28 percent of employers required certification of their opticians, and 75 percent preferred to hire certified applicants.

Many opticians choose to become members of professional organizations, such as the Opticians Association of America. These organizations offer the dispensing optician good resources for professional networking, continuing education, and career enhancement, as well as possible sources of employment (see "How Do I Learn More?").

Who Will Hire Me?

The U.S. Department of Labor reports that in 2002 dispensing opticians held 63,000 jobs. More than half of the dispensing opticians in the United States work in the offices of optometrists and ophthalmologists, and in hospitals and eye clinics. Others work in small retail optical stores, in optical departments of department stores and large discount chains, and in optical superstores that have laboratories on-site and offer to make the customer's glasses in an hour.

In urban areas, employment opportunities are particularly good because of the number of eyewear stores and departments in the area. There are also more hospitals and more doctors' offices in larger urban areas than in smaller towns or rural areas.

Community colleges and technical schools with programs in opticianry generally have good career placement centers to help their graduates find work. Apprenticeships often turn into full-time, well-paying jobs for the certified optician. The Opticians Association of America and other professional organizations also help opticians find work in their field.

Where Can I Go from Here?

When Carla began working at Lenscrafters, she was taking a break from community college. Once she realized that she loved what she was doing, she went back to school full time and graduated with a bachelor's degree in health sciences. She is presently enrolled in graduate school for optometry. "It's a

ADVANCEMENT POSSIBILITIES

Managers of eyewear stores perform the duties of a dispensing optician as well as the day-to-day duties of any manager in charge of running a retail store.

Ophthalmologists, or **oculists,** are medical doctors who diagnose and treat diseases and injuries of eyes.

Optometrists examine eyes to determine the nature and degree of vision problems or eye diseases and prescribe corrective lenses or procedures.

four-year degree," she says. "It's been great working at Lenscrafters. I started knowing nothing. They are good about promoting you. I've been promoted as I've been going to school. I'm a day manager now, while I'm becoming an optometrist."

Why did she decide to go into optometry? "I became very interested in the field and realized that I could go a lot further as a doctor," she says. "I guess I always knew I'd finish school, but I didn't know I'd go this far. It's been incredible." Carla's schedule is anything but easy. She works 25 hours a week at Lenscrafters, attends school full time, studies, and works on campus at the eye clinic. "Working at an eye clinic is interesting," she says, "but since it's on campus, nothing we see is very serious. People who are working in the inner city or in poor areas of the country get a lot of exposure to serious eye problems."

Will she stay on at Lenscrafters once she has her degree? "I don't know," Carla says. "If there's an opening here for an optician, I may stay for a while. I'm most interested in going into private practice. That's when you have the most freedom and make the most money." She laughs. "I have to get some patients first, though. Right now I don't have any patients. It'll probably be slow going for the first few years."

What Are the Salary Ranges?

According to the *Occupational Outlook Handbook,* the median annual earnings of dispensing opticians were $25,600 in 2002. Those opticians in the lowest 10 percent earned less than $16,310 annually, while those in the highest 10 percent earned more than $43,490. As with other professions, where dispensing opticians practice usually affects their wages. Dispensing opticians working in physicians' offices earn a median salary of $28,250; in health and personal care stores, $25,860; and in other health care practices, $24,900. A survey by ABO-NCLE found that 75 percent of employers offered higher beginning salaries to certified applicants. The survey also found that, after 10 years of experience, certified opticians can earn about $6,000 more per year than noncertified opticians. Full-time employees may receive health and retirement benefits.

What Is the Job Outlook?

According to the *Occupational Outlook Handbook,* job opportunities for dispensing opticians are expected to increase as fast as the average for all occupations. As the population grows older due to advances in medical technology, and as baby boomers move into their 50s and 60s, there are more people around who need glasses. One out of every four children aged five to 12 requires corrective eyewear. Many employers across the nation are adding eyecare allowances to their benefits packages offered to employees. Also, with the increased use of computers in the workplace, more workers are complaining of eye strain and blurred vision. Special prescriptive eyewear for use by those who spend many hours staring at a computer screen has also been developed, and may be covered by employer insurance plans.

The optics industry will also grow because of the influence of fashion. With a wider selection of colors and styles and materials of frames to choose from than ever before, people are interested in owning more than one pair of glasses. The optical superstores repeatedly offer specials encouraging people to buy two pairs of glasses, or contacts and glasses, for a price barely higher than the price of one pair.

Demand in the industry will also increase because of innovative ideas along the lines of special lens treatments and new lens and protective materials, as well as innovations relating to contact lenses, such as extended wear and disposable lenses.

To be competitive for the future of opticianry, students are encouraged to follow a course of study through a community college or tech school, and to become certified. The future holds good jobs for dedicated dispensing opticians.

How Do I Learn More?

PROFESSIONAL ORGANIZATIONS

For information about certification, contact
    American Board of Opticianry/National Contact Lens Examiners
    6506 Loisdale Road, Suite 209
    Springfield, VA 22105
    800-296-1379
    mail@abo-ncle.org
    http://www.abo-ncle.org

For information about accredited opticianry programs, contact
    Commission of Opticianry Accreditation
    PO Box 3073
    Merrifield, VA 22116-3073
    703-940-9134
    coa@coaccreditation.com
    http://www.coaccreditation.com

For information about education, training, and career preparation, contact the following organizations:
    National Academy of Opticianry
    8401 Corporate Drive, Suite 605
    Landover, MD 20785
    800-229-4828
    info@nao.org
    http://www.nao.org

    Opticians Association of America
    441 Carlisle Drive
    Herndon, VA 20170
    800-433-8997
    oaa@oaa.org
    http://www.opticians.org

BIBLIOGRAPHY

The following is a sampling of materials relating to the professional concerns and development of dispensing opticians:

Belikoff, Kathleen M. *Opportunities in Eye Care Careers.* Rev. ed. Chicago: VGM Career Horizons, 2004.

Trobe, Jonathon D. *The Physician's Guide to Eye Care.* 2d ed. San Francisco: American Academy of Ophthalmology, 2001.

DIVERS

Although diving can be incredibly difficult, strenuous, and dangerous work, commercial diver Mark Rhodes always found time to appreciate his unique surroundings when on a dive. "Picture the North Sea," he says, "where you have a sand bottom and good visibility. With diving saturation, you work out of an excursion bell, a chamber you live in that is pressurized to the depth where you work, whether it is topside on the deck of the barge or at the bottom. That's where you live. Two of you, usually two-man bell chains, lock-out into your excursion in a bell to the bottom. When you're at the bottom, you have visibility. These bells have big floodlights."

With these lights, and the barge slowly rocking above, Mark often felt like he was in a scene from *Close Encounters of the Third Kind*. He says, "The barge is hovering or levitating above you, and you're running around in this hot-water suit and 'space helmet' doing things by yourself out there in a complete alien world. It's phenomenal at its best."

What Does a Diver Do?

Most job opportunities for divers are with commercial diving contractors. The work is frequently dirty, exhausting, and dangerous, and the duties vary greatly. Some common underwater jobs include inspecting structures or equipment using visual, photographic, or videotape methods; operating hand or power tools in mechanical construction or repair; cleaning marine growth from structures; welding or cutting in salvage, repair, or construction functions; and surveying for geological or biological research teams.

Divers do not always work below the water. Sometimes they work at the surface as experts in the life-support system for divers and in the management of the equipment. They work with the controls that supply the proper mixture of gases for the diver to breathe, maintain the correct pressures in the hoses leading to the underwater worker, and act as the communicator and life-support partner of the diver. They also monitor water depth, conditions inside diving bells and chambers, and decompression schedules for divers. This is a highly skilled position involving many responsibilities, and it is vital to the success of all deepwater diving operations.

Definition
Divers perform a wide variety of underwater jobs, both in oceans and in fresh water, using special underwater breathing equipment. The jobs include offshore oil well piping, building and repair of foundations and other underwater construction, salvage work, and ship repair and service. Many divers also work as recreation specialists, teaching diving classes to the general public and supervising diving activities for resorts and cruise ships.

High School Subjects
Physical education
Technical/shop

Personal Skills
Leadership/management
Mechanical/manipulative

Salary Range
$23,200 to $34,100 to $59,100+

Minimum Education Level
Some postsecondary training

Certification or Licensing
Voluntary

Outlook
About as fast as the average

DOT
899

GOE
02.02.03

NOC
7382

O*NET-SOC
49-9092.00

It is possible in the future that the scientific and technological demands made on the life-support team may cause the development of a group of specialists who do not dive. However, the usual practice now is for divers to work both underwater and on deck.

Other important areas of employment for divers are in oceanographic research and underwater military engineering. While the total number of technicians engaged in these activities is relatively small, it may increase as it becomes more desirable to extract minerals from the ocean floor. Even during peacetime, military diving crews are needed in rescue and reclamation.

Divers also work as recreation specialists. They may be employed by dive resorts, dive charter boats, municipal recreation departments, dive stores, or

Lingo to Learn

Bailout A small cylinder used by divers for breathing in emergency situations.

Bathysphere This round vessel is tethered to the surface ship and can be lowered to great ocean depths.

Dry suit A suit worn by divers to keep the body warm in cold waters; provides insulation with a layer of gas.

Hypothermia A condition that results from a drop in body temperature. Severe problems occur when body temperature drops below 95 degrees Fahrenheit.

Nitrox A gas mixture of oxygen and nitrogen contained in tanks and used by divers for breathing underwater.

ROV Remotely operated vehicle, used in deepwater oil and gas production.

Saturation diving Diving after nitrogen has dissolved fully in the blood.

postsecondary institutions. The work performed varies depending on the employer's specific business, but it frequently includes teaching the general public about recreational diving, supervising and coordinating recreational dives at resorts and on cruise ships, teaching diving lessons, selling equipment at a retail dive store, and repairing equipment for customers of a dive store.

Newly hired divers are normally assigned to organize the shop and care for and maintain all types of company equipment. Soon, they will be assigned a similar job on a diving boat or platform. When on a diving operation, diver's tenders help maintain a safe and efficient operation by providing topside or surface support for the divers: They assist them with equipment, supply hoses, communications, necessary tools, and lines. They may monitor and control diving descent and ascent rates, breathing gas supplies, and decompression schedules. They must also be able to assist in an emergency and help treat a diver injured in an accident or suffering from the bends.

As divers gain experience in company procedures and jobs, they are given more responsibility. Divers usually can start underwater work within a few

months to two years after being hired, depending on the technician's skills and the company's needs.

Divers' first dives are shallow and relatively easy; subsequent dives match their ability and competence. With time and experience, they may advance to work deep-dive bell and saturation diving systems. Saturation divers are gradually compressed in an on-deck chamber, as they would be when diving, then transferred to and from the work site inside a pressurized bell. These divers stay in a pressure-controlled environment for extended periods.

All of the personnel on a diving crew should know how to care for and use a wide variety of equipment. Some of the commonly used diving equipment includes air compressors, decompression chambers, high-pressure breathing-gas storage tanks, pressure regulators and gas regulating systems, hoses and fittings for handling air and gas, and communications equipment.

A diver's personal equipment ranges from simple scuba, now seldom used, to full face masks; lightweight and heavy helmets for both air and helium/oxygen use; diving bells; and diving suits, from wet suits to the heavy dry suits that can be bolted to a breastplate to which the heavy helmet is attached. For cold water and deep or long-duration dives, a hot-water suit may be used. This allows a flow of warm water supplied from the surface to be passed through a loose-fitting wet suit on the diver's body, protecting the diver from body heat loss.

Commercial diving crews use simple hand tools, including hammers, crescent wrenches, screwdrivers, and pliers. Items such as wire cutters and volt/ohm meters are often needed. Divers may also be expected to use many types of power tools, as well as sophisticated and often delicate instruments, such as video and camera equipment, measuring instruments, ultrasonic probes, and metal detection devices. Knowledge of arc welding equipment and underwater arc or other metal-cutting equipment is very important for many kinds of work, such as salvage, construction, or repair and modification of underwater structures. These needs are often associated with underwater petroleum explorations, well-drilling, or management of piping systems.

What Is It Like to Be a Diver?

John Williams is the owner/manager of Southern Marine Maintenance, an inland-based commercial

Divers cover sea floor that has been invaded by an alien species of green algae (Caulerpa taxifolia) with a tarpaulin, as part of measures to control spread of the algae. *(Alexis Rosenfeld / Photo Researchers Inc.)*

dive company in Florida. "We do power plant, steel mill, paper plant, industrial-type underwater maintenance and services," John says. Work includes cleaning, pump removal, and water screen installations. "It's really underwater mechanical work." John himself dives about five times a week, and he manages four full-time dive crews.

"A power plant operates on water intake," John explains. "Without water coming into a plant, you can't make steam. If you can't make steam you can't make power. Power plants use a lot of divers. We can go in if something breaks and fix it right away." Normally, a diver working for John will make two three-hour dives a day.

"All our diving is surface supplied, from the air compressor to an umbilical to a dive helmet that a diver wears. Everything runs from the surface down through a hose to the diver." Before going underwater, a dive plan is made up to detail the depths, the length of time, the breathing medium (such as air or mixed gas), and other details.

"Most of our work," he says, "is done by touch. There's very limited sight. It takes a while to get used to working underwater. If you're going to drive a pin underwater with a hammer, it's harder to swing a hammer underwater than it is on the surface. You constantly have to work against the resistance of the water. But if you're moving pins, the water makes everything a little bit lighter. You don't get sweaty, but you do get cold. Something all divers have to fight is hypothermia. If you're down working three to four hours on the bottom, you'll slowly get chilled." The amount of time needed in the water depends on the nature of the job. "We do a lot of inland work in the power plants, so we'll work a regular three hours on the bottom. Out in the oil fields, it may be an hour, or if you're doing saturation diving, it might be all day."

Because of the heavy workload, John sometimes has trouble finding the divers he needs. "They can be gone for up to two months at a time," he says. "Everybody normally averages a 60-hour week. You get tired. You get burned out." Travel is often required, and may involve going to foreign countries.

The job can also be dangerous, though safety regulations keep improving. "I've had too many friends who have lost fingers or lost a hand or been killed because of poor procedures. When you're working underwater, under pressure, zero visibility, you have to think." But John's business follows safety regulations closely, resulting in little lost-time injury. And for divers, power plant work can be safer for them than for other technicians. "Nuclear plants, on a refueling shutdown, use a lot of divers. Because the water is a natural protection, and your rubber suit is a protection, we get much less radiation dosages than somebody working in a dry area."

John says a downside of the job is being frequently "dirty and cold and wet," but he finds the work challenging and much more satisfying than working in an office every day. "It's mostly a younger guy's job. I'm 55 years old, but I own the company, so I have a vested interest."

Mark Rhodes has worked as a military diver and as a commercial diver in oil field construction, until a recent on-the-job injury that has kept him out of the water. "There were a lot of variations in what we did," Mark says. "Diving was just a vehicle to get you to the job site. We didn't work 8 to 5, because you're diving and you have time against you from your exposure at depth. We worked in rotation." His work schedule was basically on-call. "They called you when they needed you, kept you as long as they wanted."

Mark was involved in all phases of oil field construction, including setting the platform on the well heads, and working with clamps and flanges. "One of the trickier things of working out there was having to work by feel, with no visibility whatsoever. Adding to the difficulty level, whenever you're aligning things such as pipeline flanges, they're suspended by the construction barge up above, and with the sea not being very stable, the barge is rolling around. So you have no visibility and you have these things jumping all over on the bottom, and you're trying to put them together blind."

Mark found the work exciting, and he loves the water; but the work obviously is not for everyone. "A career in commercial diving can be totally disastrous for some. For me, it was just a dream come true. It gave me a lot of opportunity to travel around the world. I've encountered amazing marine life. At its best, it's like working for NASA without leaving the planet."

Do I Have What It Takes to Be a Diver?

Commercial divers must possess numerous technical job skills. Working conditions may vary tremendously depending upon the nature of the work, the duration of the job, and the geographic location. Recreation specialists are frequently responsible for the welfare of inexperienced divers. Although they may work in a resort, under seemingly idyllic conditions, satisfying the needs of a group of diverse individuals may sometimes be stressful.

Working hours or shifts offshore may only require the diving crew to be available if needed, as is common on drilling vessels. More often, however, as in construction work or jobs that are continuous and predictable in nature, the dive crew will work up to 12 hours a day, seven days a week. As might be expected, the more rigorous work provides greater pay.

Divers are taught to be conscious of appropriate clothing and safety practices and to follow these guidelines as they work in the potentially dangerous conditions encountered in deepwater diving.

Offshore work, especially construction diving, is rigorous and often physically demanding. You must be physically fit to enter this field. Companies commonly

---

To Be a Successful Diver,
You Should . . .

- ○ be able to work independently as well as on a team
- ○ be in excellent physical condition
- ○ have initiative and be willing to take risks
- ○ be able to solve problems without panic or confusion
- ○ be able to tolerate being away from family and friends for long periods of time

place a maximum age limit, usually 30 to 32 years, for entry-level employees seeking to become divers. Although many divers work well into their 40s or 50s or older, long-duration deep diving is considered a young person's work. "You have to be physically strong," John says, "because of the equipment you wear. A dive helmet is 54 pounds. You have close to 150 pounds of gear on when you're working."

> You have to be physically strong because of the equipment you wear. A dive helmet is 54 pounds.

Travel, excitement, and some amount of risk are a part of the diver's life. While on the job, divers should be self-starters, showing initiative and the ability to work independently as well as on a team.

If you choose a career in diving, you should be ready to adapt to a lifestyle that seldom offers stable home and family life. You must be able to follow the work and expect occasional changes in job locations. There is also the reality of an uncertain work schedule, where a job might last for months or where the only available work may be on a short-term basis. Offshore work tends to run in a "feast or famine" pattern.

Divers must be confident of their own ability to cope with the uncertainties and risks of deepwater diving. They must be able to analyze and solve problems without panic or confusion. For most divers, there is real satisfaction in confidently and successfully performing tasks in an unconventional setting.

How Do I Become a Diver?

John got started in the job through the U.S. Navy, working with an underwater demolition team, and he recommends this route as the best way for young people looking to become divers. "You should join the military and go into the military diving program to get the hands-on experience. Someone coming out of the military has already been seasoned a little bit and knows what's up. He is in much more demand than a 19-year-old coming out of dive school."

Mark also gained his training in the military, but had been interested in the work since he was a

FYI

Diveweb.com is a valuable online resource for information about diving. The site features up to date articles about the commercial diving, ROV, marine technology, offshore/telecommunications, and inland/coastal underwater industries. It also features an archive of articles published in *Underwater,* the trade publication of the Association of Diving Contractors.

kid. "I was always heavy into the water, swim team, the ocean. I guess I started snorkeling when I was on vacation with my folks, when we'd go to south Florida. I started scuba diving when I was about 15."

EDUCATION

High School

Typical basic requirements for enrollment are a high school diploma or its equivalent, ability to read and understand what is read, demonstrated capability to study college-level scientific subjects, completion of three to four years of language and communications subjects, at least one year of algebra, and one year of physics or chemistry with laboratory work.

Postsecondary Training

The best way to train for this career is through the military, or to attend one of the postsecondary schools and colleges that offer an organized diving program, usually two years in length. Depending on the program, you receive a basic theoretical and practical background in science. Mastery of several construction-type work skills is also necessary. A typical postsecondary program in marine diving technology is designed to develop the skills and knowledge required of a commercial diver, an understanding of the marine environment, and an ability to communicate well.

The Diver's Institute of Technology in Seattle, a leading school in the field, offers a seven-month program with courses in diving medicine, diving physics, chamber operations, nondestructive testing of materials, underwater welding, underwater cutting, salvage operations, underwater tool packages, hot water systems, and hazardous materials handling both on the surface and in diving. "Any continuing education is done on the job," says John Paul Johnston, director of the Institute. "Divers are constantly learning, doing job safety analysis, and learning new techniques."

Programs for prospective recreation specialists focus on understanding the marine environment and developing communications skills, but instead of welding, drafting, and other technical classes, these programs require the development of basic business skills. Courses in small business management, marketing, organizational behavior, computer science, and business law are usually offered. Schools that provide programs for these technicians often have special admission requirements relating to swimming ability and skills.

The Association of Commercial Diving Educators (ACDE) lists five schools in the United States that meet its training requirements: College of Oceaneering, San Diego; Divers Academy International, Camden, New Jersey; Divers Institute of Technology, Seattle; Oceaneering Corporation, Houston; and Santa Barbara City College, Santa Barbara.

When you seek employment, you will usually find that many employers require completion of a recognized training program or documentation of comparable experience. Additionally, an emergency medical technician certificate is valuable and may be required by some companies.

CERTIFICATION OR LICENSING

There are no special requirements for licenses at the entry level in the United States. However, the United Kingdom and some of the North Sea countries do have specific requirements for divers, which can be met only by training in their countries.

Certification is required for recreational diving instructors and is available through such organizations as Professional Association of Diving Instructors, National Association of Underwater Instructors, and the YMCA. Certification for commercial divers is not required, but is available through the Association of Diving Contractors.

For specific work beyond entry level, a welding certificate may be required. Also, a certification in nondestructive testing (NDT) may enhance the

technician's opportunities. Both of these certificates are specific and beyond entry level. The employer will be able to specify the method of obtaining the special certificates desired.

Who Will Hire Me?

Schools with commercial diver programs usually have three or more staff members with professional commercial diving experience. These instructors keep abreast of the diving industry through occasional summer work, consultation, and professional and personal contacts. These contacts enable them to assess industry needs and to offer job placement help.

Major offshore contractors and other potential employers may visit schools with diving programs each year before graduation to interview prospective employees. Some employers offer summer work to students who have completed one year of a two-year program.

The major employers of diving technicians are companies that search for petroleum and natural gas from undersea oil fields. Hydroelectric power generating plants, dams, heavy industry, and sanitation plants that have cooling water lines or water discharges are also a source of work for divers and surface crews.

"I have more jobs than I have divers," John Paul Johnston of the Diver's Institute says. "They're going to go work for international diving companies that provide support to the oil and gas industry. They're going to go to inland diving industries which take care of all the underwater infrastructure in the United States, and some overseas work."

Certain ship repairs, usually of an emergency nature, require divers who can repair the trouble at sea or in dock, without placing the ship in dry dock to correct the problem.

While some work is being done in aquaculture, marine culture, and ocean mining, these areas are currently relatively undeveloped. While the potential for these fields is great and the possibilities for divers exciting, the total employment in these areas is presently small.

Where Can I Go from Here?

A well-trained, highly motivated diver can expect to advance steadily, depending on personal competence and the employer's needs. Over a three- to five-year period a diver may be a shop hand, a tender (tending equipment and maintaining gear), a combination diver/tender, a diver, lead diver, and possibly supervisor of a diving crew. Or a diver may advance from surface support duties to supervisor of surface support or supervisor of a diving crew, possibly within three to five years. The nondiving life-support career, however, is much more limited in terms of employment opportunities than the combined diving and support career. Management opportunities within the company are also a possibility for qualified divers. Those who want greater opportunities for earnings, independence, and growth may start their own business as a contractor or consultant.

What Are the Salary Ranges?

Earnings in this career vary widely and depend on factors such as location, nature of the job, and the diver's skills or experience. A commercial diver might work almost anyplace in the oceans, rivers, and lakes of the world, although in the United States there is much work to be found in the Gulf of Mexico and in the Louisiana coastline, areas close to offshore wells. Some types of work pay the employee on an hourly or daily basis.

Underwater Technology Systems, based in Cincinnati, Ohio, reported periodic job offerings paying experienced divers the industry's "prevailing wage" of $33 to $41 per hour; however other companies reported paying divers with five years experience or more about $19 per hour.

Recently, some industry articles have been critical of diving schools that promote the career as very high paying with many job opportunities. An article in *Underwater* magazine quoted managers and diving school admissions directors, reporting that annual earnings for divers in their first or second years range from $25,000 to $35,000. More experienced divers can expect to earn between $40,000 and $70,000, with skilled veterans earning even more. In the Gulf, however, tenders may make only $8 an hour with little opportunity for advancement. "Commercial diving has one of the toughest apprenticeships of any career," the *Underwater* article says. "The dive school graduate must often endure months or even years of tending and low-end, low-paying work before he is allowed to enter the water as a breakout diver."

ADVANCEMENT POSSIBILITIES

Diver supervisors oversee dive crews and create dive plans.

Commercial diving managers operate diving businesses, working with clients and organizing dive crews.

Pay can be good for experienced recreational diving instructors. The Professional Association of Diving Instructors reports that 62 percent of divers have an average annual income above $50,000.

The U.S. Department of Labor reports that in 2003 the median annual earning for commercial divers were $34,100, with the middle 50 percent earning between $27,900 and $42,800. The lowest paid 10 percent earned $23,200 annually, and the highest paid 10 percent earned $59,100. Employees of diving contractors typically receive life and health insurance benefits. Some companies also provide paid vacation time.

What Is the Job Outlook?

The world is increasingly turning to the sea to supply mineral resources, new and additional sources of food and medicine, transportation, and national defense alternatives. This growth in marine activity has resulted in a continuing demand for qualified diving technicians. The U.S. Department of Labor projects job growth to be about as fast as the average for all occupations through 2012.

In the past few decades, the greatest demand for skilled diving technicians has been related to the search for more petroleum and natural gas from undersea oil fields. With the production of oil and gas from the oceans, there was a virtual explosion in the amount of work and the numbers of people employed. Whether this activity will be a source of new jobs in the future is uncertain. Employment will depend on levels of drilling activity, which, in turn, will depend on world oil prices. Traditionally, divers have been able to find jobs even during tough economic times, although it will take longer before a newcomer gets "wet" on an assignment. Diving technicians also have the flexibility to switch into the commercial diving areas in order to take advantage of job openings.

"I've seen a lot of changes in relation to safety and procedures," John says. "There's better equipment, and the industry is much more safety-conscious." In 1998, the Centers for Disease Control, a government agency that studies injury and mortality, reported that fatalities related to commercial diving are 40 times higher than in any other industry. The industry will continue to work to improve safety and training, but in times of corporate downsizing, crews may work with too few tenders and divers. In any event, injury prevention is at the forefront of the industry's concerns.

John has also watched as diving schools have promoted the career heavily. "There are a lot more people doing it now, a lot more people coming out of school. The schools make a big push, advertising that you can make $100,000. Divers who get on with a full-time company will make that kind of money. Divers who do freelance, work here and there, they don't." Despite the large numbers of divers graduating from schools and entering the workforce, a small percentage of those divers actually stays with the job. Because of the hard work required, and the long apprenticeship with low pay, diving companies find themselves with a high turnover rate.

How Do I Learn More?

PROFESSIONAL ORGANIZATIONS

The following organizations can provide information about a career in diving, training and educational programs, scholarships, certification, and job opportunities:

    Association of Commercial Diving Educators
    Santa Barbara City College
    721 Cliff Drive
    805-560-6059
    http://www.acde.us

Association of Diving Contractors
    International
5206 FM 1960 West, Suite 202
Houston, TX 77068
281-893-8388
http://www.adc-usa.org

National Association of Underwater Instructors
PO Box 89789
Tampa, FL 33689-0413
800-553-6284
nauihq@nauiww.org
http://www.naui.org

Professional Association of Diving Instructors
30151 Tomas Street
Rancho Santa Margarita, CA 92688-2125
800-729-7234
http://www.padi.com

BIBLIOGRAPHY

The following is a sampling of materials relating to the professional concerns and development of divers:

Barsky, Steven M., and Robert W. Christensen. *The Simple Guide to Commercial Diving.* Ventura, Calif.: Hammerhead Press, 2004.

Jackson, Jack, ed. *Diving: The World's Best Sites.* New York: Rizzoli, 1997.

Maas, Peter. *The Terrible Hours: The Man Behind the Greatest Submarine Rescue in History.* New York: HarperCollins, 2000.

Parker, Torrance R., and William B. Lee. *20,000 Jobs Under the Sea: A History of Diving and Underwater Engineering.* Palos Verdes Pennins, Calif.: Sub-Sea Archives, 1997.

DRAFTERS

||||||||||||||||||||||||||||||||||||||||||||||||||||

What do you do when a 20-story commercial building is under construction, with the first floor nearly complete, and the owner's wife decides she wants the elevators moved? "You move the elevators," says Ken Young, a drafter in Pueblo, Colorado.

Ken says the building under construction was a bank and its design included a large entry area where the elevators were located, with the offices situated around the perimeter. "The owner's wife came in and she didn't like that [entry area]. She wanted a hallway, so we had to move everything, the elevators, plumbing, electrical . . ."

If the project's drafters had drawn the building plans the traditional way, using paper and pencil, "We would have had to start over," Ken says, which would have delayed the project for months and added thousands of dollars to the cost.

Technological advancements in drafting saved the day. "We had done all the work in CAD so we were able to redesign the building in about a week and we saved the owner about a half million dollars," Ken says.

What Does a Drafter Do?

Drafters take the ideas, notes, and rough sketches created by scientists, engineers, architects, and designers and use the information to prepare accurate, exact, detailed specification drawings of the object, product, or building to be constructed. The drawings generally include information about the quality of materials to be used, the processes to be followed, and the cost of doing the project.

In the past when drafters developed the drawings, tools such as protractors, compasses, triangles, squares, drawing pens, and pencils were used. While those tools are still occasionally used for drafting projects, today most drafters leave the old instruments in a desk drawer and turn to their computers and computer-aided design and drafting (CADD) software to get the job done.

Some drafters choose to specialize in particular areas of drafting such as mechanical, electrical, electronic, structural, aeronautical, or architectural. The work of drafters is similar regardless of the field of specialization, but the objects they deal with vary greatly.

Commercial drafters create plans for building sites, layouts of offices and factories, and drawings of charts,

Definition
Drafters prepare working plans and detailed drawings of products or structures based on rough sketches, specifications, and calculations provided by engineers, architects, and designers.

Alternative Job Titles
Aeronautical drafter
Architectural drafter
Automotive design drafter
Cartographic drafter
Civil drafter
Commercial drafter
Computer-assisted drafter
Electrical drafter
Geological drafter
Landscape drafter
Mechanical drafter
Topographical drafter

High School Subjects
Art
Mathematics

Personal Skills
Artistic
Technical/scientific

Salary Range
$30,820 to $40,566 to $65,985

Educational Requirements
Some postsecondary training

Certification or Licensing
Recommended

Outlook
More slowly than the average

DOT
017

GOE
02.08.03

NOC
2253

O*NET-SOC
17-3011.00, 17-3011.01, 17-3011.02, 17-3012.00, 17-3012.01 17-3012.02, 17-3013.00

forms, and records. *Computer-assisted drafters* in this specialty use computers to make drawings and layouts for aeronautics, architecture, or electronics.

Civil drafters develop drawings for civil engineering projects such as roads and highways, river and harbor improvements, flood control, and drainage. In this same field, *structural drafters* draw

Lingo to Learn

CAD Computer-aided design. Computer software programs used by drafters.

CADD Computer-aided design and drafting. Computer software programs used by drafters to create made-to-scale drawings of an object to be built rather than doing the work by hand using pencils, drawing pens, compasses, protractors, and other instruments.

Checkers Drafters who carefully check drawings for errors in computing or in recording dimensions and specifications.

Detailers Drafters who complete drawings by providing dimensions, materials, and other information needed for each part shown on a layout.

Formal perception The ability to compare and discriminate between the shapes, lines, forms, and shadings of an object.

Layouts Assembly drawings that provide several different views of a specific object, product or building. The drawings must be exact, accurate, and contain enough detail so they can be used to construct the object, product, or building.

Orthographic projection The basis for the branch of mathematics known as descriptive geometry. It is a way of seeing the relation between the parts of an object.

Spatial perception The ability to visualize objects in two or three dimension.

Tracers Entry-level drafters who make corrections and prepare drawings to be reproduced by tracing them onto transparent cloth, paper, or plastic film.

plans for bridge and roof trusses, plate girders, trestle bridges, and other structures that require materials like reinforcing steel, concrete, and masonry.

Cartographic drafters prepare maps of geographic areas that show natural and manmade features, political boundaries, and more. Additional jobs in this specialty are *topographical drafters*, who draft and correct maps from original maps, surveying notes, and aerial photographs; *architectural drafters* draw

building plans that include artistic and structural features; and *landscape drafters* make detailed drawing from sketches provided by landscape architects.

Mechanical drafters make working drawings of machinery, automobiles, power plants, and other mechanical devices. Also in this field are *plumbing drafters*, who draw diagrams for the installation of plumbing equipment; *casting drafters* prepare detailed drawings of castings (objects formed in a mold); *heating and ventilating drafters* create plans for heating, air-conditioning, ventilating, and occasionally refrigeration equipment; *tool design drafters* create manufacturing plans for tools; and *patent drafters* make drawings of mechanical devices, which lawyers then use to obtain patent rights for their clients.

Electrical drafters create schematics and wiring diagrams used by construction crews working on the equipment and wiring in power plants, communications centers, buildings, or electrical distribution systems; and *electronics drafters* draw schematics and wiring diagrams for television cameras and television sets, radio transmitters and receivers, computers, radiation detectors, and other electronic equipment.

Electromechanisms design drafters make designs of electromechanical equipment like aircraft engines, data processing systems, gyroscopes, automatic materials handling and processing machinery, or biomedical equipment. Also in this specialty are *electromechanical drafters*, who draw wiring diagrams, layouts, and mechanical details for the electrical components and systems of a mechanical process or device.

Aeronautical drafters prepare engineering drawings for planes, missiles, and spacecraft. Others in this field are *automotive design drafters* and *automotive design layout drafters*, who create working layouts and master drawings of components, assemblies, and systems of automobiles and other vehicles. In addition, design drafters make original designs from specifications, while layout drafters make drawings based on earlier layouts and sketches. *Marine drafters* draft the structural and mechanical features of nuclear submarines, ships, docks, petroleum drilling platforms, and marine buildings and equipment.

Geological drafters make diagrams and maps of geological formations and the locations of mineral, oil, and gas deposits; *geophysical drafters* draw maps and diagrams based on information gathered by petroleum prospecting instruments such as seismographs, gravity meters, and magnetometers; *directional survey drafters* plot bore holes for oil and gas wells; and *oil and gas drafters* create plans for the construction and operation of oil fields, refineries, and pipeline systems.

What Is It Like to Be a Drafter?

Ken says he has been a drafter for about 20 years, and in the early 1980s when he was in school earning his degree computers were not the mainstay of the profession like they are today. But Ken has learned the technology and stays up-to-date with changes.

"I spend most of my time in front of the computer producing drawings. I prepare detailed drawings per design specifications, and most of my contact with clients is by e-mail," he says. Ken also does most of his work in his office with only an occasional visit to a job site.

Because he owns his own company, Young Technology Group, Ken is responsible for a variety of activities necessary to run his business, from maintaining his office, which he describes as "small with a nice atmosphere," to marketing and advertising his services, keeping supplies on hand and equipment operational, paying bills, invoicing clients, and more.

Do I Have What It Takes to Be a Drafter?

According to Ken, to be a successful drafter you should have an ability to concentrate and be someone who pays close attention to details. You also should enjoy activities like drawing, woodworking, building models, and repairing or remodeling projects. A strong sense of spatial perception and formal perception are important as are good eye-hand coordination, which are necessary for the fine detail work used in drafting.

How Do I Become a Drafter?

"I have a bachelor of science degree in civil engineering technology," Ken says. "Unfortunately I was not trained on the computer in college. I would recommend that anyone in school now take CAD related courses. Take as many CAD classes as you can because all of the work is done on the computer now."

FYI

- French mathematician Gaspard Monge's book *Géométrie Descriptive*, published in 1798, is recognized as the first written explanation of descriptive geometry and the formalization of orthographic projection. The application of Monge's concepts led to the growth and development of the drafting profession.

- In the 1960s the first drafting programs for use on the computer were developed to aide in the composition of graphic images on screen, to retain and retrieve the data in the computer's memory, and to drive plotting devices that could transfer the various levels of detail to paper. Today, computer-aided design and drafting (CADD) software is the industry norm and is used by drafters in all fields.

EDUCATION

High School

You should begin preparing for a career in drafting while you are in high school. Take all the mathematics classes offered, particularly algebra, geometry, and trigonometry. Also important are mechanical drawing and art classes. Shop classes will be beneficial so take wood, metal, or electric shop, depending on the area of drafting you are considering as a specialty. Geography and earth science may be helpful, and because most of drafting is done using CAD, you should take computer classes.

Postsecondary Training

Most employers now prefer to hire drafters with some postsecondary training in drafting, and as the work becomes more technologically advanced,

TO BE A SUCCESSFUL DRAFTER, YOU SHOULD . . .

- ○ have good spatial and formal perception
- ○ have good eye-hand coordination
- ○ be able to concentrate
- ○ have good attention to detail

additional educational training, especially using CADD programs, will be beneficial when looking for a job or career advancement.

Training is available through technical institutes, community colleges, and four-year universities. The quality of educational programs varies, so be sure to choose a school that meets your needs. In most cases, two-year community college programs lead to an associate's degree and provide a more comprehensive education than may be available through a technical school. Also, four-year universities typically do not offer specific drafting programs, but courses in areas such as engineering, architecture, and mathematics are available. Upon successful completion of most four-year programs a bachelor's degree is awarded.

The American Design Drafting Association International (ADDA) lists schools with certified drafting programs, and information about accredited schools with drafting programs is available from the Accrediting Commission of Career Schools and Colleges of Technology.

CERTIFICATION OR LICENSING

Certification is not currently required for drafters, but it is recommended since many employers are now looking for drafters whose skills have been industry approved by a reliable source. The ADDA offers certification in drafting that requires passing an examination that demonstrates the candidate's level of expertise. It tests areas of knowledge such as geometric construction, working drawings, and architectural standards and terms. Recertification is required every five years.

SCHOLARSHIPS AND GRANTS

Many colleges and universities offer scholarships and grants. For information contact the financial aid office of the school you plan to attend. Professional organizations, including the International Federation of Professional and Technical Engineers (IFPTE) also offer scholarships. The IFPTE awards three $1,500 scholarships each year to qualified students who are the children or grandchildren of IFPTE members. Scholarship and grant information is available on the Internet at several sites, including http://www.findtuition.com, http://www.allscholar.com, and http://www.fedmoney.org.

INTERNSHIPS AND VOLUNTEERSHIPS

Internships are not required, but may lead to a job with the company where the internship is completed. Contacting companies in your field of interest may lead to a part-time summer job or volunteer position, giving you an opportunity to learn more about the profession. Ken says he completed a two-year internship with the Bureau of Land Management working in Alaska.

Who Will Hire Me?

Entry-level drafters often start with companies as tracers, but those with postsecondary training may qualify for positions as junior drafters. About half of all drafters are employed by architectural, engineering, and related service firms that design construction projects. More than one-fourth of drafting jobs are in manufacturing industries, and most of the remaining positions are in construction, government, and utilities.

Many colleges and technical schools offer job placement services for graduates, and the American Design Drafting Association International includes a

PLACES WHERE DRAFTERS WORK

- ○ architectural firms
- ○ construction companies
- ○ engineering companies
- ○ federal, state, and local agencies
- ○ heavy equipment manufacturers
- ○ utility companies

career resource center on its Web site where jobs are listed and applicants may post their resumes.

Ken says waiting for job openings to appear listed in newspaper classified ads is not the best way to find a job. "When you are ready for a job, beat the bush," he says, "don't wait for them [job listings] to come out in the paper because everyone is looking at the same ads and you'll be there with 40 others with the same credentials wanting the same job." He suggests looking in the yellow pages for surveyors, engineers, and architects and "then go to an employer and ask for a job."

Where Can I Go from Here?

Drafters generally advance in their careers by gaining additional experience and improving their skills to become checkers, detailers, design drafters, or senior drafters. Because each business modifies work assignments to meet its specific needs, a drafter may move between positions. Other related jobs that drafters may advance into are technical report writers, sales engineers, engineering assistants, production foremen, and installation technicians. Some experienced drafters start their own companies. Ken says that opportunities are "excellent if you are willing to progress in the technology."

What Are the Salary Ranges?

Earnings in this profession vary and are usually determined by a number of factors, including skills and experience, the area of specialty, the level of responsibility, and the location of employer. For example, the U.S. Department of Labor reports the median annual earnings in 2003 for architectural and civil drafters were $38,200, mechanical drafters earned $42,400, and electrical and electronics drafters earned $42,600.

A 2005 review of drafter salaries nationwide by Salary.com listed annual earnings of between $31,749 and $38,642 for entry-level mechanical drafters, while those with four or more years of experience earned between $40,566 and $57,144. Entry-level architectural drafters reported salaries between $30,820 and $46,692. With four or more years of experience, earnings ranged from $40,178 to $65,985.

ADVANCEMENT POSSIBILITIES

Chief drafters or senior drafters use the preliminary information and ideas provided by engineers and architects to make design layouts. They also assign work to and supervise other drafters.

Chief design drafters head design teams of architectural, electrical, and mechanical drafters working on electrical or gas power plants and substations.

What Is the Job Outlook?

According to the U.S. Department of Labor, employment opportunities for drafters are expected to increase more slowly than the average of all occupations through 2012 due in part to the growing use of CAD technology, which will limit the need for less skilled drafters. In 2002 drafters held about 216,000 jobs and that is expected to increase less than 3 percent to 222,000 in 2012. New job openings will be created as drafters leave the profession to pursue other careers or to retire. In addition, positions may become available for experienced drafters who increasingly do the work traditionally performed by engineers and architects. Employment opportunities will be best for candidates with at least two years of postsecondary training in drafting and for those with experience and strong skills using CADD systems.

How Do I Learn More?

PROFESSIONAL ORGANIZATIONS

For information about the career of drafting, accredited or certified educational programs, professional certification, and employment opportunities contact the following organizations:

Accrediting Commission of Career Schools and Colleges of Technology
2101 Wilson Boulevard, Suite 302
Arlington, VA 22201
703-247-4214
http://www.accsct.org

American Design Drafting Association International
105 East Main Street
Newbern, TN 38059
731-627-0802
corporate@adda.org
http://www.adda.org

**International Federation of Professional and
    Technical Engineers**
8630 Fenton Street, Suite 400
Silver Spring, MD 20910
301-565-9016
http://www.ifpte.org

BIBLIOGRAPHY

*The following is a list of materials relevant to the
profession of drafting:*

Jefferis, Alan. *Commercial Drafting and Detailing.*
    Albany, N.Y.: Thomson Delmar Learning, 2001.

Madsen, David, and Alan Jefferis. *Architectural Drafting
    and Design.* 4th ed. Albany, N.Y.: Thomson Delmar
    Learning, 2001.

Shumaker, Terence M., and David A. Madsen. *Civil
    Drafting Technology.* 5th ed. Paramus, N.J.: Prentice
    Hall, 2003.

Wallach, Paul Ross. *Fundamentals of Modern Drafting.*
    Albany, N.Y.: Thomson Delmar Learning, 2002.

ELECTRONEURO-DIAGNOSTIC TECHNOLOGISTS

Although the neurodiagnostics department at St. Vincent's Health Center has been computerized for more than 10 years, Darlene Albrecht, R. EEG T., still works closely with patients. "That hasn't changed," she says. Darlene brings in the patient and offers a general explanation of the procedure, then asks about the patient's history. "We find out why they're being tested, what kind of medical problems they may have, medications, right-handedness, left-handedness, family history." Darlene then begins to prepare the patient for the procedure. "It takes probably a good 20 minutes to prepare and place the electrodes for monitoring."

The test is a 30-minute recording of the brain's electrical activity. "We do awake, drowsy, asleep, depending on what the physician is looking for. For instance, if someone comes in for a seizure disorder evaluation, we try to get as many states of consciousness as possible." But the technicians don't have a step-by-step process they follow; they must often rely on their instincts and understanding of the procedure. "I'd say that 95 percent of what we do, how we handle the recording, is at the tech's discretion."

What Does an END Technologist Do?

Electroneurodiagnostic (END) technology is the branch of medicine that deals with using tracings (graphic recordings) of the brain's electrical waves in order to diagnose and determine the effects on the body of certain diseases and injuries, including brain tumors and accidental injuries, strokes, Alzheimer's, epilepsy, and various infectious diseases. By interpreting END test results, physicians are able to prescribe needed medicines or surgeries in the attempt to cure or relieve the suffering of a patient.

Electroneurodiagnostic (END) technologists are responsible for obtaining accurate tracings of the brain's electrical activity so that a doctor can use them in diagnosing patients. END technologists conduct a variety of electroneurological tests. Electrocardiograms (ECGs) are tracings of electrical

---

Definition
Electroneurodiagnostic technologists obtain recordings of the electrical activity in various body parts. They run tests like electroencephalograms (EEGs), electromyograms (EMGs), and electrocardiographs (ECGs). They prepare patients for tests, monitor equipment, note irregularities, and ensure the reliability of results.

Alternative Job Titles
END technicians
Electroencephalographic (EEG) technologists

High School Subjects
Biology
Chemistry
Physics

Personal Skills
Mechanical/manipulative
Technical/scientific

Salary Range
$34,726 to $44,621 to $46,000

Minimum Educational Level
Some postsecondary training

Certification or Licensing
Recommended

Outlook
Little change or more slowly than the average

DOT
078

GOE
14.05.01

NOC
3218

O*NET-SOC
N/A

---

activity associated with the heart ("cardio" refers to the heart). Electrooculograms are similar but have to do with the eyes, and electromyograms (EMGs) have to do with the muscles. The most common ones, electroencephalograms (EEGs), are tracings of the brain's electrical activity. END technologists generally perform some or all of these tests.

END technologists also administer newly developed tests like the Evoked Potential (EP), which records the electrical reaction from the brain, spinal nerves, and/or sensory perceptors in response to external stimuli. They might conduct the polysomnogram

(PSG), an electroneurodiagnostic procedure that combines an EEG with other physiologic measures like heart rate, eye movements, and blood oxygen levels, in order to diagnose and treat sleep disorders.

All of these tests must be administered methodically and with close attention to detail. END technologists start by preparing a patient for a test. They write down the patient's medical history, listening carefully for family or personal illness that might influence either testing procedures or tracing interpretation and diagnosis. Next, they explain each step of the procedure to the patient so that he or she can remain calm throughout the test. Making the patient comfortable in this way is very important since his or her relaxation level can directly affect test results. Technologists must practice good "bedside manner," develop compassion for the patient's concerns, and learn to answer respectfully any questions the patient might have.

Next, the more technical part of the test begins. Technologists fasten electrodes to the patient's head or to other prescribed locations and connect them to the monitor. They make educated decisions about exact placement of electrodes and combination of machine settings, which they note in the patient's file. Once the machine is activated, it begins collecting data, which is amplified and recorded on moving strips of paper or on optical disks. The resulting graph is the "tracing" of the brain's electrical activity.

During the test or "study," technologists must keep an attentive eye on both the patient and the machines, taking notes about the patient's reactions and making any necessary adjustments to the equipment. They may keep track of vital signs like heart rate, blood pressure, and breathing, to make sure the patient stays out of danger. They are trained in basic emergency care in case something does go wrong with the patient during the test. If drugs have been prescribed, they are frequently responsible for administering them.

At the conclusion of the test, some technologists simply pass results on to the prescribing physician, while others evaluate them and note whether they are normal or abnormal. Still others might participate in the diagnostic process with the doctor by writing up a report summary. A technologist's degree of involvement in the interpretative process depends on the doctor who ordered the test originally and the education and experience of the technologist.

Although technologists do not necessarily interpret tracings, they are responsible for identifying abnormal brain activity and any extraneous readings collected by the machine during the test. In order to do so properly, they consider how an individual should perform on the test based on his or her medical history and current illness.

Technologists can also detect mechanical malfunction or human error in faulty recordings. They can fix some mechanical problems themselves but may have to call on the assistance of a supervisor or equipment technician.

Lingo to Learn

Brainwaves Patterns of wavy lines recorded by electroencephalographs (EEG machines) that result from electrical activity in the brain.

Cerebral Of or having to do with the brain.

Electrocardiograms Recordings of activity related to the heart.

Electroencephalograms (EEGs): Recordings of the electrical activity in the brain.

Evoked potentials Recordings of the peripheral nervous system.

Neurologists Physicians who specialize in the study of the brain and diagnosis and treatment of diseases in or relating to the brain.

Polysomnograms Recordings of sleep processes.

Vascular Of or having to do with the circulatory system.

What Is It Like to Be an END Technologist?

At the St. Vincent's Health Center in Pennsylvania, the neurodiagnostics department is a center for EEGs and other tests, such as all modalities of Evoked Potentials. The sleep lab, where tests for sleep disorders are performed, is shared between the neurodiagnostic department and the respiratory therapy department. Darlene Albrecht, an EEG tech with St. Vincent's, has been in the career for more than 20 years. In her years of work, she has been involved in the conversion from paper and ink systems to digital, computerized EEG.

"We've all worked together for a long time," Darlene says of the techs at St. Vincent's, "and they're all pretty good at what they do, so they have the flexibility to run a test as to how they see fit. It's based on the individual patient."

Darlene's center administers sleep tests in addition to the EEG and Evoked Potentials. "We have a clinical polysomnographer who's the medical director, and we deal with all possible sleep disorders." A third shift comes in at 8:00 P.M. to work with patients. Hooking up the patient for a sleep test is similar to that for an EEG. "Everything's glued on the body," Darlene explains, "and the patient basically sleeps in one of our bedrooms overnight. We do EEG monitoring during that time; there are eye monitors, sub-mental EMG; there are respiratory belts put across the chest and abdomen. We watch oxygen saturation throughout the night. It's pretty all-encompassing."

Though Darlene works closely with patients, she does spend a fair amount of time in a dark room administering the tests. "There are days when we all feel like moles," she says, "because even though we're responsible for our daily load of patients, we have to work independently."

That independence, however, is something Darlene often appreciates about the work. "You do have the independence to do the best for any given patient on an individual basis," she says. She also appreciates the variety. "We do infants, we do elderly. The variety of patients is incredible. Plus, we don't just do EEGs. Within the END field, we're doing Evoked Potentials. Some days I'm down in the OR." But Darlene hopes for the field to get more recognition within the health care industry. "I don't think it commands the respect that other disciplines do, because we've only been

emerging. It's still considered an infant career. The whole organization nationwide has made strides, but it doesn't have the recognition that other areas, such as respiratory therapy and cardiology, have."

Ken Ashby has been an EEG technologist for over 23 years, and currently works at the University of Utah. Ken's work is similar to Darlene's, and he works with about four or five patients a day. "The time we spend with patients varies," Ken says. "The minimum amount of time spent is probably about an hour." Preparing a patient for a test involves measuring the head, then applying the electrodes and ensuring they have good contact. "When something arises during a test," Ken says, "our job is to make sure that's really brain-wave activity and not something else. Our position is not to interpret the recording; that's up to the neurologist."

> When something arises during a test, our job is to make sure that's really brain-wave activity and not something else.

When present in the operating room, Ken helps the surgeon by watching for signs of problems. "It's an early warning system," he says. "If they're working on the spinal cord and they damage an artery that supplies blood to the spinal cord, we'll see the signal from that." Because of this, a relationship with the others in the OR is important. "You have to build a rapport with the surgeon," he says.

Ken also witnessed the change from paper-generating machines to computers. "An EEG record would be about an inch thick," he says. "Now we archive all our EEGs to CD-ROM."

Do I Have What It Takes to Be an END Technologist?

"You have to be very people-oriented," says Darlene. "That's the whole way to make it work: How you can establish a rapport with the patients." The ability to communicate effectively with people should be accompanied by quick thinking skills since technologists often have to change tasks abruptly. For example, if an emergency request is made for an EEG on a 30-year-old, a technologist might have to interrupt his or her work on a 65-year-old woman to do it. The technologist must then make rapid mental adjustments to accommodate physical differences and test expectations of the new patient.

The best END technologists generally have strong manual dexterity, coupled with an aptitude for working with computers, good vision, and good abstract thinking skills. Technologists should have an eagerness to learn and the ability to learn quickly.

Technologists generally write observations, comments, and summaries in a report composed primarily of very technical language. Writing skills are thus very important for this job. Verbal communication skills are equally essential.

Working in a hospital or clinical laboratory can prove to be quite stressful, especially in the larger and busier ones. Just like their TV counterparts, doctors, nurses, and technologists of all specialties go in a million different directions and the effect can ruin concentration. Therefore, technologists should be good stress managers and should be able to perform well under pressure.

How Do I Become an END Technologist?

Darlene trained on the job, under the guidance of a trained EEG tech. On-the-job training has continued at St. Vincent's in the years since. "There are so few formal schools out there," Darlene points out. "There are none in our area. Unfortunately, when you're in a working situation and learning at the same time, it becomes a little demanding."

Ken holds an associate's degree in general studies, and studied on his own for registration. "There are a lot of good techs who aren't registered," Ken mentions, "and there are probably a lot of techs who are registered who aren't very good."

EDUCATION

High School

A high school diploma is required of all prospective END technologists. Science classes, especially biology, chemistry, physics, and anatomy, are particularly useful for helping students to build a solid foundation in scientific knowledge, methods, and reasoning. Mathematics courses should include at least algebra and are equally important since they encourage you to develop strong analytical and abstract thinking skills. Three or more years of both science and math are recommended.

English and speech courses provide good opportunities to enhance verbal and written communication skills. Social science classes, like psychology and sociology, help students begin to think about the affective, or emotional, needs of patients. This understanding leads prospective END technologists to develop a good "bedside manner."

In some high schools, vocational or technical courses dealing with mechanical and electrical equipment are offered. These courses can provide students with a head start on understanding END equipment and teach them how to approach and solve a technically oriented problem.

Postsecondary Training

There are two types of postsecondary training for prospective END technologists. The first is on-the-job training, and the other is formal classroom training at either a hospital, medical center, technical school, college, or four-year university. Often, intellectual ability is proven through completion of a postsecondary degree; it can also be proven through work and volunteering experience. As technology continues to change, however, it is generally considered preferable to pursue formal education. The American Society of Electroneurodiagnostic Technologists now requires that all END technologists have a two-year associate's degree or higher and successfully complete a program reviewed by the Joint Review Committee on Education in Electroneurodiagnostic Technology and accredited by the Commission on Accreditation of Allied Health Education Programs.

On-the-job training usually lasts anywhere between three months and one year, depending on the nature and scope of the employer. During on-the-job training, END technologists learn firsthand how to operate the equipment and carry out specific testing, maintenance, and repair procedures. They receive instruction from doctors and senior END technologists. They may be required to do some reading at home.

Formal training in electroneurodiagnostic technology consists of both academic course work and clinical practice. The length of formal programs varies between one and several years and results in either a certificate or an associate's degree. At the university level, curricula for a bachelor's degree in END technology is being developed in some areas, but degrees are already available in many related health professions. ASET offers a nationally comprehensive list of formal educational programs in END technology.

Academic instruction is usually concentrated on basic medical subjects, like human anatomy, physiology, neuroanatomy, clinical neurology, neuropsychiatry, clinical and internal medicine, and psychology. Courses specific to END technology include normal and abnormal pattern recognition, patient preparation, recording techniques, and electronics and instrumentation. The clinical practice incorporates what is taught in on-the-job training programs, but may do some of it in staged, not authentic, situations.

CERTIFICATION OR LICENSING

Certification of END technologists is regulated at the state level and so varies from state to state. Past attempts at national certification programs have not been entirely successful, so now most END technologists are encouraged to obtain official registration instead. Individuals who have completed one year of on-the-job training or have graduated from a formal training program and been in the field for at least one year and completed a required number of recordings may apply for registration with the American Board of Registration of EEG and Evoked Potential Technologists Inc. (ABRET).

After application, the individual takes a two-part examination. The first part is written and the second oral. Only students who pass the written part may take the oral. Both sections comprehensively cover subjects related to the work of an END technologist.

ABRET offers two registrations: R.EEG T., or registered electroencephalographic technologist, and R.EP T., or registered evoked potentials technologist. Though not required for employment, registration is official acknowledgement of a technologist's expertise. It also makes advancement and financial promotion easier.

ASET recommends that within two years of graduation from an accredited END program technologists also pass a nationally recognized exam for professional credentials in one of the electroneurodiagnostic specialty areas.

FYI

Sometimes, other more specialized diagnostic tests are needed to help a physician visualize the structure of the patient's brain and spinal cord. The CT scanner (for computed tomography) takes computer-generated X rays of different "slices," or areas, of the brain. For information on careers in this area of diagnostic testing, see the chapter "Special Procedures Technologists."

SCHOLARSHIPS AND GRANTS

END technologists who receive on-the-job training are usually paid regular salaries, so tuition is not an obstacle. Those who pursue formal education in hospitals and medical centers should contact them directly about costs and financial aid opportunities. Technical school or university students should seek financial aid from their school's financial office. These offices usually maintain a complete list of available awards, as well as a profile of requirements. They should be contacted directly.

The American Society of Electroneurodiagnostic Technologists (ASET) sponsors conferences and continuing education courses; it offers some scholarships to ASET members for these courses.

If you are currently employed in a health- or medical-related business and want to pursue a degree in END technology, you may be eligible for tuition reimbursement programs offered by your employer. You should contact the company's personnel or benefits office.

INTERNSHIPS AND VOLUNTEERSHIPS

It is extremely difficult to find internships or part-time jobs in the field of electroneurodiagnostic technology since most clinics and labs are staffed by fully trained, full-time professionals. Prospective END technologists have to rely on the clinical practice that is part of both formal education and on-the-job training for in-depth exposure to daily routines. In some formal education programs, however, there may be some paid internships or co-op work (apart from regular clinical practice) organized by the school or clinic as part of the curriculum. Information about these kinds of opportunities can be obtained through the program administration.

Volunteerships are readily available at local hospitals, clinics, and medical centers. Experience of this type may be helpful for several reasons. First, as a hospital volunteer, you witness the everyday trials of hospital work and discover firsthand if a medical profession is right for you. Second, you may be allowed to specify that you would like to work in an electroneurodiagnostic area, which would provide a sort of direct, advanced training. Third, hospital volunteerships show employers and education program administrators that you are serious, interested, and enthusiastic about the health professions. Contact local hospitals and clinics for more information. ABRET and ASET may also have lists of specialized END labs across the country.

LABOR UNIONS

There are no labor unions designated specifically for electroneurodiagnostic technologists. In some areas or certain hospitals and clinics, an allied health union may operate. If you are employed in such an area, you may be required to join the union.

Who Will Hire Me?

Darlene began working as a medical assistant in the cardiology department of St. Vincent's. At the time, the EEG department was part of the cardiology department, and Darlene learned a bit about the testing. When an EEG tech left, Darlene was invited to step into the position. Ken also began in another area of health care, working as a nursing assistant. He learned other forms of therapy, and eventually began working as an EEG tech.

Electroneurodiagnostic technologists work in any doctor's office, clinic, group medical center, health maintenance organization, urgent care center, emergency center, psychiatric facility, lab, or hospital that has the equipment necessary to perform END tests. Most END technologists, however, hold full-time positions in hospitals.

On-the-job trainees usually have no problem finding a job after training, since their employer/trainer hires them directly. END technologists who complete formal education in this field work closely with the placement office of the medical center, technical school, or university where they study. Such offices have long-standing working relationships with area employers and are often successful at placing graduates in full-time jobs.

For all END technologists, whether trained on-the-job or through formal education, newspaper and magazine classified ads are a good place to look for job openings in the area. You can also contact the personnel offices of the various medical facilities directly.

ASET sponsors a service called "Employment Exchange" which regularly provides subscribers with job listings. Membership in ASET provides the occasion to become part of a close-knit network of employed professionals, who may also be able to pass on information about job openings. Membership is beneficial in several ways, not the least of which is networking for employment opportunities. ABRET may also have job lists and job hunting ideas.

Where Can I Go from Here?

After registration and several years' experience, an electroneurodiagnostic technologist is eligible for promotion to a supervisory position. Supervisors generally perform the more complex tests or the regular tests on potentially problematic patients. They might also be called upon to conduct tests in emergency situations. Depending on the size of the lab, some supervisors may be involved with training new employees and have some administrative duties like job assignment, patient and employee scheduling, and supply ordering.

Supervisory positions may be followed by promotion to chief electroneurodiagnostic technologist. The chief technologist or lab director has much more immediate contact with doctors and hospital administration than do technologists; they may consult on the diagnosis of a case, offer input into the establishment of hospital regulations and policies, and manage the lab's budget. Although they still work with patients, they are in effect lab or departmental managers, with managerial and fiscal responsibilities.

Years of experience and a solid educational foundation put certain END technologists in a prime position to move into education. Some technologists may go to work for a manufacturing company, training their customers (medical END labs) in the proper use of END equipment. Others might teach in the on-the-job or formal training programs offered at medical centers and hospitals. People with advanced degrees might go to work in technical schools and universities.

What Are the Salary Ranges?

According to the American Medical Association, END technologists had median annual earnings of $44,621 in 2003. Those in the lowest paid 10 percent earned $34,726 a year, while those in the highest paid 10 percent earned more than $46,000.

END technologists working in hospitals generally receive full benefits packages that may include health insurance, paid vacations, and sick leave. In some locations, benefits may also include educational assistance, pension plans, and uniform allowances. Technologists working outside the hospital setting usually receive benefits as well, though they vary in content with different employers.

What Is the Job Outlook?

The U.S. Department of Labor estimates that the number of positions in electroneurodiagnostic technology will grow more slowly than the average for all other occupations. Increasingly sophisticated equipment requires fewer technicians to operate it. Also, technicians in other areas of care will be trained to work with END technology.

One area of growth will be in surgical units. Surgical teams find it more and more useful to have an END technologist prepared to do an EEG in the operating room for the duration of certain surgeries. END testing is proving to be an effective way to monitor the patient's condition and reactions to various surgical procedures.

Private neurologists' offices and neurological clinics were formerly predicted to be the area of greatest increase in demand for END technologists. However, this will certainly not be the case. The initial prediction was based on a trend in the medical community of doctors buying or leasing their own END equipment. This meant that if a doctor ordered an EEG, the patient would be able to have the test performed on the doctor's premises instead of going to the hospital or a specialized lab.

ADVANCEMENT POSSIBILITIES

Electroneurodiagnostic technologist supervisors administer the more difficult or specialized lab tests and supervise other END technologists. They might also be involved in training new employees on testing techniques specific to the lab. They may share some administrative duties with the chief END technologist.

Chief electroneurodiagnostic technologists usually work directly under the direction of a neurologist, neurosurgeon, or other physician. They supervise or manage the END laboratory, establish lab procedures, make work and appointment schedules, keep records, and order supplies. They are also involved in teaching and training new employees from END technology education programs.

Electroneurodiagnostic technology educators or researchers teach in academic programs focused on END technology or in on-the-job training programs in hospitals and clinics. Researchers may work on improving, developing, and inventing electroneurodiagnostic procedures.

Recent legislation in Congress makes this process of self-referral illegal. The concern was that since the END tests are so expensive to the patient and insurance companies and profitable to the doctors, the latter might tend to order tests when they were not really needed. Prospective END technologists should pay attention to health-related legislation at both the federal and state levels, since it can have an enormous impact on employment growth and outlook.

How Do I Learn More?

PROFESSIONAL ORGANIZATIONS

For information on registration, contact
American Board of Registration of EEG and
EP Technologists

1904 Croydon Drive
Springfield, IL 62703
217-553-3758
abreteo@aol.com
http://www.abret.org

For a career brochure and information about scholarships and educational opportunities, contact
American Society of Electroneurodiagnostic Technologists
426 West 42nd Street
Kansas City, MO 64111
816-931-1120
info@aset.org
http://www.aset.org

American Association of Electrodiagnostic Technologists
28 Sabins Lane
North Chatham, MA 02650
508-945-2781
aaet@aaet.info
http://www.aaet.info

For information on accredited training programs, contact
Joint Review Committee on Electroneurodiagnostic Technology
Route 1, Box 63A
Genoa, WI 54632

BIBLIOGRAPHY

The following is a sampling of materials relating to the professional concerns and development of electroneurodiagnostic technologists and technicians:

Careers in Focus: Medical Technicians. 4th Edition. New York: Facts On File, 2004.

Rumack, Carol M. *Diagnostic Ultrasound.* 2nd Edition. St. Louis, Mo.: Mosby-Year Book, 1998.

Sherry, Clifford J., and Robert S. Ledley. *Opportunities in Medical Imaging Careers.* Lincolnwood, IL: VGM Career Horizons, 2000.

ELECTRONICS TECHNICIANS

"People don't realize how much electronics play a part in their lives until the day when something breaks down," says Fred Smith, a long-time certified electronics technician. "Then they call up in a panic because their TV, VCR, or CD player went out." As a part-time freelance electronics technician, Fred receives several calls a week. "One time a woman called me at 10:00 A.M. She had to have her television set fixed by the time her favorite show came on at 1:00 P.M. She really couldn't understand why it might take any longer than that. When men call, it's usually so they can have their TVs fixed before a big game or movie. They rely on electronics just as much as anybody else," explains Fred.

As a full-time electronics teacher, Fred always tells his students they should be trained and ready for anything. As high-tech machines and gadgets originally introduced as luxury items become more and more standard in American homes, keeping up with technology is a very challenging endeavor for electronics technicians.

Maybe that's why Jacob Straw, who owns two electronics businesses, went back to school to earn an associate's degree in electronics technology. "I was already in the business, a sort of self-taught electronics tech, but I wanted the schooling," says Jacob—or Jay as he's called by friends. "I wanted to learn the mathematics of electronics, because that's what it is. A voltage is a number, you know, and I was committed to understanding the technology of what I was doing."

What Does an Electronics Technician Do?

Electronic devices play a part in practically every business and even many leisure activities found around the globe. Such diverse activities as NASA space missions, sophisticated medical testing procedures, and car and airplane travel would be impossible without the use of electronic equipment. So would a rock concert. *Electronics technicians* help develop, assemble, install, manufacture, maintain, and service industrial and consumer electronics, including sonar,

Definition
Electronics technicians work individually or with engineers to help design, produce, improve, maintain, test, and repair a wide range of electronic equipment. Equipment varies from consumer goods like televisions, computers, and home entertainment components, to industrial, military, and medical goods, such as radar and laser equipment.

High School Subjects
Chemistry
Mathematics
Technical/Shop

Personal Skills
Mechanical/manipulative
Technical/scientific

Salary Range
$17,430 to $41,683 to $58,614+

Work Environment
Indoors and outdoors
One location with some travel

Minimum Educational Level
Some postsecondary training

Certification or Licensing
Recommended

Outlook
More slowly than the average

DOT
828

GOE
05.02.01

NOC
2242

O*NET-SOC
49-2094.00, 49-2097.00

radar, computers, radios, televisions, stereos, and calculators.

The products made by the electronics industry can be divided into four basic categories. The first one, government products, represents a high percentage of sales in the industry. Missile and space guidance systems, communications systems, medical technology, and traffic control devices are just a few of the products in this area.

The second area comprises industrial products, which include large-scale computers, radio and television broadcasting equipment, telecommunications equipment, and electronic office equipment.

The third area, consumer products, is the most commonly known and includes such things as televisions, VCRs, and radios.

The fourth category comprises the smaller pieces that all electronics are made of—components. Capacitors, switches, transistors, relays, and amplifiers are among the well-known components.

Electronics technicians are needed to work in various capacities on all of these kinds of products; the nature of the work done on a specific product generally falls into one of three areas—product development, manufacturing and production, and service and maintenance.

Electronics development technicians generally work with an engineer or as part of a research team. *Engineers* draw up blueprints for a new product; technicians build a prototype, or an original model, according to specifications. This job involves using hand tools and small machines to construct complex parts or components. In some cases, technicians are encouraged to offer suggestions for improvement and modifications of the design of the product.

After the prototype is finished, technicians work with engineers in testing the product for performance in various stressful conditions, analyzing how a component reacts, for example, in extreme heat and cold. Tests are run using complicated equipment and detailed, accurate records of every aspect of the test must be kept. Technicians in development may also have to construct, install, modify, or repair laboratory test equipment.

Electronics drafters do work closely related to that of development technicians. They are responsible for converting rough sketches as well as written and verbal communications, all provided by engineers, into easily understandable diagrams to be used in manufacturing the product. They prepare lists of all parts and components needed in the production of various products.

Cost-estimating technicians work in an area closely related to development. They are responsible for reviewing new product proposals in order to determine the approximate total cost of production for that product, including labor, materials, and equipment costs. Other people in the company, like sales representatives, then use these figures to decide whether or not production is economically feasible.

Electronics manufacturing and production technicians deal with any problems arising from

Lingo to Learn

Alternating current (AC) An electric current that reverses its direction, usually at regular intervals of time.

Amplification The process of strengthening an electrical signal.

Direct current (DC) An electric current that does not change direction.

Electrode A conductor through which a charge enters or leaves an electrical device.

Frequency The number of times a signal repeats itself identically per unit of time. It is measured in hertz.

Oscilloscope An instrument used by electronics technicians that allows them to "see" the variations in a fluctuating electrical quantity by producing wave forms on a screen.

Signal generator An instrument that provides electricity of a desired frequency and amplitude to machines being tested by electronics technicians.

Transistor A semiconductor (solid-state) device with three terminals used to amplify electrical signals or to act as a switch in electronic circuits.

Voltmeter An instrument that measures in volts the differences in potential between two points of an electrical circuit.

the production process. They install, maintain, and repair assembly or test line machinery. In quality control, they inspect and test products at various stages in the production process. When a problem is discovered, they are involved in determining what the problem is and in suggesting solutions.

Electronics service and maintenance technicians diagnose and repair malfunctions in a variety of electronics products from all four categories described above. Generally, the same procedure is followed regardless of the product in question. First, the technician gathers information from the consumer or user about the nature of the problem. Using these details, the technician investigates and fixes minor problems on the spot. If the problems are too complicated, the machine must be taken back to the electronics laboratory, where test equipment like voltmeters, oscilloscopes, and signal generators attempt to locate the difficulty.

What Is It Like to Be an Electronics Technician?

You might say that Jay Straw dabbles a little in all the different areas electronics technicians could work. Jay's career as an electronics tech started out when he was a musician buying electronic amplifiers and expensive sound equipment. "Out of necessity, I learned how it worked and how to fix it if it broke down," says Jay. "As I got better at using the equipment, the technology that went into it got more and more complicated. That's one reason I had to go back to school."

Jay's musical ambitions led him into the business of setting up for bands and live musical shows. "I provide the sound and lighting equipment and all the people who set it up and run it." Major performers such as the band Blue Oyster Cult and singer Joan Baez have employed Jay's Hi Tech Audio and Lighting company. He also sets up for orchestras and musical productions. "Sometimes I go on tour with them," Jay says, "but it's usually cheaper for shows to hire people in the area. . . ."

Jay runs another business, Hi Tech Electronics. "If my equipment breaks down, I can bring it into the shop, analyze the problem, and solve it." Hi Tech Electronics does some installation of public address (PA) and sound systems in schools and hospitals. "But mainly," says Jay, "we do repairs on musical instruments for shops in town." Jay spends a lot of time rewiring guitars and replacing tubes on power amplifiers.

He's also in the process of designing an original device to stop the feedback on guitars. "When guitars are plugged in, they feed a constant high or low frequency hum back through the speakers," says Jay. "I'm developing what's called a notch filter so the guitar won't feed back, and it's almost perfected." Once complete, Jay plans to market his creation.

Fred Smith's been in electronics a long time. As he looks back over his career, he can safely say he's held as many different positions as an electronics technician can have. Fred's an electronics teacher and CET (certified electronics technician) test administrator

in San Luis Obispo, California. He also does some freelance electronics service work on the side.

Fred's first job was at a Sears Service Center, where he initially did field work. "I would go to the office in the morning, pick up my service calls, and start out on the road." It was hard to estimate the amount of time each stop would take, since Fred really didn't know the extent of the problem. "Electronics technicians have a bad reputation for not showing up when they say they are going to, but the thing is, no matter how well you try to schedule things, something always puts you behind," Fred explains.

Most all of Fred's service calls were handled in a similar manner. He would talk to the customer about the problem and the performance history of the machine. It's important to know, for example, if a television set has been repaired for the same problem in the past. Then, he would inspect the machine on the premises. If some wiring was loose or a simple circuit needed to be replaced, he could usually finish the repair there. If the problem was more complicated, he would load the machine in his van to take back for more tests and further repair in the service center.

Fred had to keep detailed records of everything he did—which tests he ran, which parts he used, time spent on each call—and hand them in to his supervisor at the end of every day. Fred's next job was as a *bench work technician*. With this job, he no longer went on calls outside the lab but worked instead on machines brought back to the lab for further inspection. The electronic problems he encountered there were more difficult to solve. He would inspect the machine, run tests on it if needed, estimate the cost of repair, including labor and parts, and call the customer back with the information.

Fred had to offer honest advice about whether or not he thought the repair was worth the cost or if the client should just replace the machine. "Customers tend to be distrustful of servicing technicians, thinking we are all out to rip them off. I always tried to put them at ease by explaining exactly what the problem was and how I was going to fix it."

Fred's current job is less hands-on. Much of his day is spent teaching classes on electronics. The program he works for lasts three years and the curriculum includes basic math, science, and electronics classes as well as more complex circuit-design and electrical machinery classes. He has a fair amount of equipment in his laboratory, which provides his students with hands-on experience.

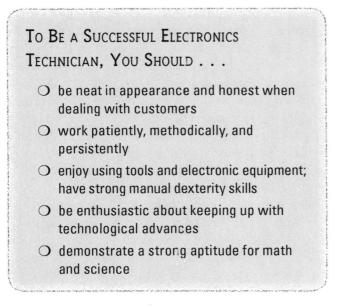

TO BE A SUCCESSFUL ELECTRONICS
TECHNICIAN, YOU SHOULD . . .

- ○ be neat in appearance and honest when dealing with customers
- ○ work patiently, methodically, and persistently
- ○ enjoy using tools and electronic equipment; have strong manual dexterity skills
- ○ be enthusiastic about keeping up with technological advances
- ○ demonstrate a strong aptitude for math and science

Electronics technicians usually work 40-hour weeks, and hourly-wage earners are paid extra for overtime. Depending on the company, technicians employed in manufacturing and production may have to work any of the shifts during which production runs.

Most electronics laboratories are clean, well lighted, and well equipped. A technician may have his or her own office or may occupy one desk among several in a larger room or lab. Technicians who work extensively with assembly lines may spend part of their time in damp, greasy, or noisy surroundings. Service technicians spend a great deal of time on the road.

Do I Have What It Takes to Be an Electronics Technician?

"With the constant advances and changes in technology, you just have to have a solid foundation in the basics of electronics and the ability and desire to learn quickly," explains Fred. Jay would agree. "Electronics is very complex stuff. Circuit design is complicated, and it's changing all the time," he says. Electronics technicians have to keep their skills up-to-date, and the ability to learn quickly and a naturally inquisitive mind are good qualities to have in this field. An aptitude for math and science is also important, as is the capacity to understand technical writing and drawing.

Keeping up with technological advances can be difficult. "It's the most frustrating part of my job,"

says Fred, "I know I am outdated, but I just don't have the time to keep up." Electronics technicians have to learn to deal with this frustration effectively; if not, it can become a great source of stress. "I'm supposed to get educational leave from my employer, but with budget cuts, I never see it. I just do as much as I can and stay satisfied with that."

Many tasks assigned to electronics technicians require patience and methodical, persistent work. Good electronics technicians work well with their hands, paying close attention to every detail of a project. Some technicians are bored by the repetitiveness of some tasks, while others enjoy the routine.

Since many technicians in industry work as part of an engineering team or directly for an engineer, they must also be good team players.

Individuals planning to advance beyond the technician's level should be willing to and capable of pursuing some form of higher education.

How Do I Become an Electronics Technician?

Once Jay realized he needed more and better knowledge of electronics, he applied to a two-year program at the University of Montana in Missoula, where he lives. "I went to school eight hours a day for two years, working my audio and lighting business at the same time." In the summer, Jay did concerts. The rest of the year, he hit the books. "I put in a lot of late-night studying and long hours," says Jay. "My social life was nothing for two years, but it was worth it." Jay graduated with an associate's degree in electronics technology.

After working as an electronics technician in the military for many years, Fred earned his associate-level CET certification just before being discharged. "The military let me take the CET exam to make sure I was qualified for a job when I got out." Later he went on to successfully complete several other exams and credentials.

EDUCATION

High School

A high school diploma is necessary for anyone wishing to build a career as an electronics technician. You should focus on mathematics and science courses.

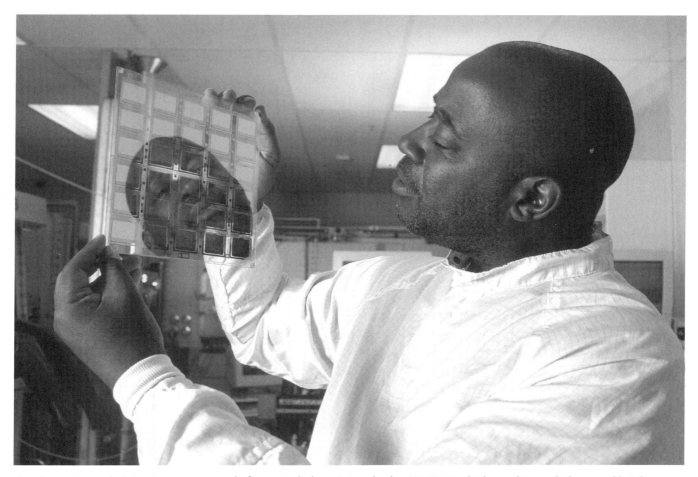

An electronics technician inspects a panel of organic light emitting diodes (OLEDs), which are thinner, lighter, and brighter than traditional liquid crystal displays. *(Volker Steger / Photo Researchers Inc.)*

Algebra and geometry are both important skill builders, as are chemistry and physics, particularly in their coverage of electron theory and properties of electricity. Courses offered in electronics or electricity are obviously pertinent to the field as well. Participation in electronics, math, or science clubs in high school might boost your understanding of these very crucial, yet basic, subject areas.

English and speech courses provide invaluable experience in improving verbal and written communication skills. Since some technicians go on to become technical writers or teachers, and since all of them need to be able to explain technical matter clearly and concisely, communication skills are important.

Any shop classes that emphasize electronics or other technical principles in laboratory work allow you to get a head start in understanding the field. Since electronics technicians work with technical drawings all the time, mechanical drawing courses are also helpful.

Postsecondary Training

While some current electronics technicians enter the field without prior academic training, it is increasingly difficult to do so. The demand for technicians with education and knowledge of the most sophisticated electronics products and systems is only going to increase. To stay competitive, you need to graduate from a two-year electronics technology program and then continue to gain more advanced training in the field. In addition to two-year technical programs offered at schools, you might also explore opportunities offered by the military. Some major companies, particularly utilities like phone companies, hire people straight out of high school and train them through in-house programs. Others promote people to technicians' positions from lower-level jobs, provided they attend educational workshops and classes sponsored by the company.

Most electronics technicians complete a two-year degree in electronics technology at a community college or a technical school. Though programs do vary, a typical first-year curriculum includes courses in physics for electronics, technical mathematics, electronic devices, communications, AC/DC circuit analysis, electronic amplifiers, transistors, and instruments and measurements. The second year of study may include courses in communications circuits and systems, introductory digital electronics, technical reporting, control circuits and systems, electronic design and fabrication, new electronic devices, and industrial organizations and institutions.

As a certified educator, Fred teaches many of these courses to his students. "The more advanced classes build directly on previous ones. That's just one more good reason to have a solid foundation in the basics, to make all future learning easier." Without a good grasp of basic electronics taught in the first year of technical school, the second year can be difficult. "If you keep up with your studies and follow the logical progression of things, you'll do fine," says Fred.

There are many reputable education programs in electronics technology. Consult the local telephone directory, electronics technicians employed in the area, or one of the professional organizations listed at the end of this article for more information.

Some electronics technicians decide to pursue advancement in their field by becoming an engineer or branching off into research and development. These higher-level and higher-paid positions usually require the completion of at least a bachelor's degree in electronics or another engineering or technology discipline. Technicians with significant experience can sometimes finish such degrees through correspondence school, while others attend night or weekend classes.

CERTIFICATION OR LICENSING

Certification as an electronics technician is generally not mandatory, although for some specific subfields such as radio and television transmission, it is strongly recommended. Though voluntary, certification as a certified electronics technician (CET) at any level is proof of professional dedication, determination, and know-how. "I'm convinced I got my first job at the Sears Service Center only because I had my associate-level CET," says Fred. "If it comes down to two applicants, one a CET and the other not, the employer is going to hire the first one," he says.

CET certification is awarded to those who successfully complete a written, multiple-choice examination. The associate-level CET test is designed

for technicians with less than four years of experience. It is composed of the basic electronics portion of the advanced test and must be passed with a score of 75 percent or better.

After four years of education or experience, a technician can take another CET exam in order to earn a journeyman-level CET certification. This test contains the same basic electronics portion, plus one or more of several specialty options. The specialty option tests evaluate a technician's knowledge of advanced theoretical material applicable to that specialty. Some specialty options include consumer, industrial, communications, computer, audio, medical, radar, and video.

For more information, including a catalog of CET exam study guides and a list of test sites and test administrators in every state, interested individuals should contact either the ISCET or the ETA, who both offer CET certification.

SCHOLARSHIPS AND GRANTS

There are no outstanding scholarships or grant awards earmarked for those wishing to pursue education in electronics technology. Community college and technical school students should contact the financial aid office of their school to obtain information about financial aid options, including scholarships offered by companies directly through schools and federally subsidized and commercial educational loans.

If you're currently employed and plan to pursue an education in electronics technology, you should contact your personnel or benefits office for information about any tuition reimbursement programs available.

INTERNSHIPS AND VOLUNTEERSHIPS

Community college and technical school students may be able to secure off-quarter or part-time internships with local employers through their college placement office. Internships for people not in school are difficult to find. You should look in the help wanted sections of local newspapers and magazines in search of opportunities. You might also contact the personnel department of industrial employers and governmental agencies for information. Some internship opportunities may be included in job lists published by ISCLET, ETA, and other professional organizations.

LABOR UNIONS

There are no unions organized exclusively for electronics technicians. However, those working in electronics product development and manufacturing companies are often required to join the union operating within the company. The principal unions involved are the International Union of Electrical, Radio, and Machine Workers; International Brotherhood of Electrical Workers; International Association of Machinists and Aerospace Workers; and the United Electrical, Radio, and Machine Workers of America.

Employers in other areas may have unions as well. Many local, state, and federal governmental agencies operate with unions, and technicians employed by them are required to become members.

Who Will Hire Me?

Fred got his first electronics technician job doing bench work repair with Sears Service Center by answering an advertisement in the local newspaper. "They hired me even though I had no experience outside the military. The CET certification was key, but I also agreed to take a course on electronic consumer products at DeVry," says Fred.

Electronics technicians are employed in one of three broad areas of electronics: product development, manufacturing and production, and service and maintenance. Manufacturers of electronic equipment employ the most electronics technicians, and these manufacturers are highly clustered in eight states—California, New York, Illinois, Massachusetts, Pennsylvania, Indiana, New Jersey, and Texas.

There are a wide range of electronics companies that make equally diverse products, such as consumer, aircraft, or broadcast electronics; hospital and/or medical equipment; satellites; computers; marine navigation, audio/visual, test, quality control, or telecommunications equipment; commercial radar; office equipment; and farm machinery. Companies that specialize in the development and servicing of such products also hire electronics technicians.

Utilities companies nationwide hire a large number of electronics technicians, especially telephone, telegraph, electric light and power, and nuclear energy companies. Local, state, and federal governments, as well as all branches of the active and reserve military, are big employers of electronics technicians. Federal agencies such as the U.S. Department of Defense, the

FYI

The most rapid expansion of electronics technology occurred during World War II, when the need for long-distance communications equipment and missile-guidance systems increased greatly.

National Aeronautics and Space Administration, and the National Institutes of Health hire a particularly high number of electronics technicians.

Going into business for yourself, as Jay did, is another option. The electronics field is vast and growing, and opportunities to offer a service, like High Tech Audio and Lighting does, or to service and repair consumer products, such as TVs, stereos, and computers, are there for the entrepreneurial individual.

Many community college and technical school students find their first full-time position through their school's placement office. These offices tend to develop good working relationships with area employers and therefore offer you excellent interviewing opportunities. Such offices provide resume writing and interviewing seminars and advice on how and where to pursue job searches.

ISCET provides information about job openings around the country on its Web site. "ISCET really does a good job of keeping you informed about what's going on. Their job list seems to be pretty comprehensive and reliable," says Fred. Other associations listed also compile such lists. Trade magazines about electronics, particularly those about computer-related technologies, generally publish lists of job opportunities in the back of each issue.

Where Can I Go from Here?

As an electronics technology educator and CET test administrator, Fred has advanced about as far as he can go in his career. "After over 30 years in the business, I'm looking forward to retirement," he says. To get where he is today, Fred has worked hard and continued his education, obtaining several journeyman CET specialties, as well as credentials in related technical areas.

Starting at Sears as a field work electronics technician, Fred was promoted to bench work after several years. Then, he went into private industry as a senior electronics technician. His next promotion was to the calibration lab, where he was a technician and later senior supervisor/manager. Having done some teaching in the military, he eventually decided to get back into it.

Fred's career path illustrates a typical one for electronics technicians. After obtaining the journeyman CET certification, technicians may become eligible for supervisory positions. The particular duties associated with these jobs vary according to the nature of the employer. In general, however, electronics technician supervisors work on more complex projects than technicians. They also have some degree of administrative responsibility; they may make the employee work schedule, assign laboratory projects to various technicians, oversee the training progress of new employees, and keep the work place clean, organized, and well stocked. Electronics technician supervisors, moreover, tend to have more direct contact with project engineers or managers.

Some electronics technician supervisors may decide to further their education in order to become *engineering technicians* or engineers. Electronics engineering is concerned with the research and development of new products and the improvement and revision of old ones. It also focuses on methods of ensuring production efficiency and quality control.

Electronics technicians might also look for advancement in production testing or quality control.

Production test supervisors make detailed analyses of production assembly lines in order to determine where production tests should be placed along the line and the nature and goal of the test.

Quality control supervisors determine what kinds of quality control tests should be conducted after the completion of production in order to ensure that only high-quality products go out.

With further education in business, some electronics technicians take the management route, moving further and further away from hands-on technical work each time they are promoted.

What Are the Salary Ranges?

According to the *Occupational Outlook Handbook*, electronics repairers of commercial and industrial equipment had median hourly wages of $20.04 an hour, or $41,683 annually for full-time workers. Those in the lowest 10 percent earned less than $12.24 an hour ($25,460 a year), while those in the highest 10 percent earned over $28.18 ($58,614 a year). Electronic home entertainment equipment repairers had median hourly earnings of $13.36, or $27,788 annually. Those in the lowest 10 percent earned less than $8.38 an hour ($17,430 a year), while those in the highest 10 percent earned more than $21.53 ($44,782 a year).

Most electronics technicians receive a full benefits package, including paid vacation, higher compensation for overtime, health insurance, and pension plans. Some employers may offer educational reimbursement incentives, as well as paid time off for special training workshops and academic classes.

What Is the Job Outlook?

The U.S. Department of Labor estimates that overall employment of electronics technicians will grow at a rate that is slower than the average over the next 10 years, but the outlook varies a bit by specialty. For example, installers of commercial and industrial equipment are expected to experience an average rate of job growth as companies invest in more sophisticated machinery for automation. Electronics technicians will be needed both to install and repair such machinery. Job opportunities for home electronics installers and repairers is expected to grow more slowly than the average due to the an overall decline in repair services for these items. As electronics become more affordable, it is often just as easy to replace malfunctioning personal electronics than it is to have these items repaired. Thus, the demand for electronics technicians that specialize in this area will be limited.

All electronics technician positions, whether in industry, consumer goods, or the military, depend on a variety of factors. Foreign competition, general economic conditions, and government spending all have an impact on the field. Prospective electronics technicians should begin paying attention to certain factors that might affect the area they are thinking about working in. For example, if you are planning to work for the military or for a military contractor or subcontractor in radar technology, keep an eye on federal legislation concerning military spending cuts or increases.

The key to success for an electronics technician is to stay up-to-date with technology and to be professionally versatile. Building a career on a solid academic and hands-on foundation in basic electronics enables you to remain competitive in the job market.

How Do I Learn More?

PROFESSIONAL ORGANIZATIONS

For certification information, contact
The Electronics Technician Association International
5 Depot Street
Greencastle, IN 46135
800-288-3824
eta@eta-i.org
http://www.eta-i.org

For industry information, contact
Electronic Industries Association
2500 Wilson Boulevard
Arlington, VA 22201
703-907-7500
http://www.eia.org

To learn about certification and student chapters within the professional society, contact
International Society of Certified Electronic
Technicians
3608 Pershing Avenue
Fort Worth, TX 76107-4527
800-946-0201

ADVANCEMENT POSSIBILITIES

Electronics technician supervisors are responsible for bigger or more complicated projects than technicians. They have some administrative duties, such as scheduling, ordering supplies, and overseeing lab procedures. They supervise other technicians and may train new employees.

Engineering technicians work with teams of engineers and other technicians on developing new products or improving current ones. Their knowledge and experience are wider in scope than that of electronics technicians; their education may include exposure to the theories of electronics and engineering to complement hands-on experience.

Production test supervisors analyze a factory assembly line production process and determine what tests should be run on the emerging products and where. They may also be in charge of designing the equipment set-up used in production testing.

info@iscet.org
http://www.iscet.org

For information about JETS, a program that introduces students to careers and education in technology and engineering, contact
Junior Engineering Technical Society (JETS)
1420 King Street, Suite 405
Alexandria, VA 22314
703-548-5387
http://www.jets.org

BIBLIOGRAPHY

Following is a sampling of materials relating to the professional concerns and development of electronics technicians:

Buchla, David. *Experiments in Electronics Fundamentals and Electric Circuits Fundamentals.* Upper Saddle River, N.J.: Prentice Hall, 2000.

Faissler, William L. *An Introduction to Modern Electronics*. New York: John Wiley and Sons, 1991.

Floyd, Thomas L. *Electronics Fundamentals: Circuits, Devices, and Applications*, 6th ed. Upper Saddle River, N.J.: Prentice Hall, 2003.

Matt, Stephen R. *Electricity and Basic Electronics*. Tinley Park, Ill.: Goodheart Wilcox Company, 1998.

Reis, Ronald A. *Becoming an Electronics Technician: Securing Your High-Tech Future*, 4th ed. Upper Saddle River, N.J.: Prentice Hall, 2004.

EMBALMERS

||||||||||||||||||||||||||||||||||||||||||||||||||||||||

"The family is grieving and struggling with the loss of their loved one," says Tom Elliott. "Those of us working in funeral service make a very difficult situation as easy as possible on families given the circumstances." Elliott is an embalmer and funeral director at Elliott Mortuary in Hutchinson, Kansas.

"Since most embalmers are also funeral directors, our job doesn't end in the preparation room. We're involved in all aspects of the service," Tom says. "A lot of people think that all embalmers do is prepare bodies. Others think that we only wear suits and drive limousines all day. But our job is much more involved than that, especially in a mid-sized firm like this one. Today, for instance, I started by sweeping the driveway of the funeral home and vacuuming the front hall. Then, because it rained, I helped rewash our vehicles before the afternoon service began. Later on I'll do a bit of bookkeeping and visit with another family to consult about tomorrow's funeral. Sure, I do embalming too, but that's not all I do."

What Does an Embalmer Do?

Embalmers prepare the human body for funeral services and for burial. First the body is washed with an antibacterial soap and dried. Next a tube is inserted into an artery and blood is evacuated from the body while embalming fluid is pumped into the body. Fluids and wastes are removed from body organs. All incisions are closed using sutures. Embalming fluid, a scientifically-formulated mixture, slows down decomposition, prevents the spread of disease, and maintains body firmness for cosmetic purposes.

Embalmers also repair body parts that have been disfigured due to illness or injury. This is called restoration. Depending on the nature of the repair, a number of materials may be involved in restoration. These include clay, cotton, mortuary putty, plastics, plaster, wire, and wax.

After restoration, the deceased person's hair is shampooed and styled. Cosmetics are applied in order to give the person as natural an appearance as possible. The deceased are dressed appropriately, their bodies are positioned, and they are placed in caskets.

Definition

Embalmers prepare the dead for burial. They wash the body and replace blood with embalming fluid to preserve it. When necessary, they reconstruct diseased or disfigured bodies. They dress the body and transfer it to a casket. Many embalmers also direct funerals or assist in other aspects of funeral service.

Alternative Job Titles

Funeral directors
Morticians

High School Subjects

Biology
Business

Personal Skills

Leadership/management
Technical/scientific

Salary range

$19,200 to $34,500 to $55,100+

Minimum educational level

Some postsecondary training

Certification or licensing

Required by all states

Outlook

More slowly than the average

DOT

359

GOE

11.08.01

NOC

6272

O*NET-SOC

39-4011.00

During the embalming process, records are kept of chemical usages. Safety measures are scrupulously followed in order to comply with OSHA (Occupational Safety and Health Administration) regulations. To protect themselves from disease and prevent the spread of infection, embalmers wear protective clothing, which may include surgical-type masks, gloves, face shields, goggles, and shoe covers. Following the process, the preparation room is cleaned, equipment and clothing is sanitized, and all waste is disposed of according to government standards.

Since many embalmers also work as *funeral directors*, their other job duties may include greeting

Lingo to Learn

Cosmetology The use and application of cosmetics.

Funeral director A professional responsible for caring for the deceased, including arranging and conducting such services as embalming, funerals, administrative work, and counseling for bereaved families. Funeral directors are sometimes called morticians or undertakers.

Funeral home The place where the deceased are cared for and where funeral services may be held. Sometimes known as a mortuary.

Interment The act of burial.

Preparation room The area within the funeral home where embalming takes place.

Restoration In preparation for a funeral, the technical repair of bodies damaged by illness or injury.

Thanatology The study of death, in particular the medical, psychological, and social aspects associated with death.

family members and friends of the deceased, arranging and conducting funeral services, writing obituary notices, serving as or organizing pallbearers, arranging with cemeteries to open and close graves, preparing grave sites for outdoor services, transporting the deceased in hearses, driving family members to and from funerals, transporting floral arrangements, handling various forms of paperwork, doing administrative tasks, and looking out for basic building maintenance at the funeral home.

What Is It Like to Be an Embalmer?

Millions of people die each year in the United States, at every hour of the day and night. As a result, embalmers and funeral directors are on call 24 hours a day, seven days a week. They often work long, irregular hours, including weekends and evenings. Today, on a Sunday in spring when most people are enjoying a day off and relaxing with their families, Tom Elliott is at work, speaking with families who request his firm's embalming and funeral services. There are already three funerals scheduled for Monday at his funeral home, four scheduled for Tuesday, and two for Wednesday.

"Very few embalmers," Tom explains, "spend eight hours a day in the preparation room. Those who do usually work for very large firms where each job is extremely specific and you're hired to do only that one task. But here, as in most firms, you get a little bit of everything. That's good, of course, because no one gets bored and you get to follow the family and help them through the entire process.

"There's no typical day at a funeral home," Tom adds. "My day might begin with picking up a body and bringing it here for embalming. Or I might assist the coroner during an autopsy and then complete the embalming process and clean the preparation room. Later on, I might discuss music for a funeral with a family or explain to them how to claim veterans' and social security benefits. Sometimes I'm arranging floral sprays in the chapel or transporting bouquets to gravesides prior to services there.

"Sometimes I'm doing government paperwork or basic bookkeeping. Or I might be on the telephone with casket manufacturers, checking on availability. Or I could be outside shoveling snow or raking leaves from the driveway."

He leans back in his chair and sighs. "Of course, a big part of my job is basic listening. Listening is tremendously important. So many times there's not much you can say really. The spoken word can do so little. Mostly families simply need to tell their stories." He adds, "At times of stress, families aren't likely to remember everything you say so follow-up is an important part of our service. A week or two after the funeral we contact the family and help them with insurance, legal odds and ends, government benefits, and such. We also have a family services coordinator on staff who helps with grief counseling and offers a support group to families who request that service."

Elliott explains that the actual embalming process is highly regulated. "All employees go through hazardous materials training, including basic handling and safe disposal techniques."

"Years ago, embalmers didn't even wear gloves, and exposure to chemicals was a real problem for them. Now we have a ventilation system, emergency showers, and an eyewash station, all in order to keep ourselves safe and comply with governmental regulations."

Working in the embalming room requires a mixture of art, aptitude, and practice. "You can learn the basics of embalming from a textbook or in a college class, but applying what you've learned to a human body is something else again," Elliott says. "You start with a basic knowledge of anatomy, and then you need to be skillful with your hands. Embalmers aren't in the same league as artists, but over time, you learn to be good at what you do."

He continues, "But every body is different. How we deal with the body of an 80-year-old man who's been ill and living in a nursing home for many years is quite different from how we deal with the body of a 37-year-old man who burned to death in a fire. Sometimes there's only so much restoration that you can do, and that's hard to explain to a family."

One of the things Elliott appreciates about his profession is that through his work as an embalmer, he has been able to become a licensed eye enucleator. When directed to do so, he recovers the corneas from deceased people, packs them in refrigerated containers, and ships them to hospitals where they are used for cornea transplants. Other embalmers may become involved in other types of tissue or organ recovery.

Do I Have What It Takes to Be an Embalmer?

Good embalmers are good listeners. They pay attention when families describe how their loved ones looked while alive and make every effort to honor that memory throughout the entire embalming and restoration process. They are genuinely respectful when handling the dead, treating each deceased person as if he or she were a cherished parent or sister or brother.

But such attention to the needs of others can take its toll. "You are what you feel," says Tom. "You have to be truly compassionate. It can't just be a hat that you put on when you arrive at work. Still, it's important that you be able to separate yourself a bit from what's going on. You need to accept that what you're doing is a way to assist families and that by doing a good job, you help them through a difficult time."

Embalming is also a physically demanding job, requiring strength and endurance. Exposure to hazardous chemicals and disease is another occupational concern. The AIDS virus, for instance,

TO BE A SUCCESSFUL EMBALMER, YOU SHOULD . . .
○ be a good listener
○ enjoy working with people
○ be tactful in difficult circumstances
○ have a genuine respect for the dead
○ have compassion for the feelings of others
○ be respectful of different religious beliefs and cultural practices
○ have good manual dexterity
○ be physically fit and able to lift heavy objects

continues to live for an unknown amount of time after death within an infected individual's body. Even after death, many body fluids, including tears, saliva, urine, and blood, can carry disease.

Embalmers need to be well trained, use common sense, and maintain basic sanitary standards. However, embalming and its associated field, funeral directing, can be very rewarding. It is a good job for someone who is outgoing and enjoys working with people, especially someone who is sensitive to the unique needs of others during times of grief. Embalmers and funeral directors perform a function that is very basic to society. Their work and the ceremonies surrounding death help make the loss of loved ones more bearable for the living.

Embalming is also a good job for someone who likes challenging work and who is easily bored by repetitive types of labor. No two embalming jobs are ever the same. Each body brought into the preparation room presents a unique challenge.

Job security is also a big factor to consider. Funeral homes exist in every area of the country and qualified embalmers are always in demand. The armed forces and the federal government also have staff embalmers.

How Do I Become an Embalmer?

Tom Elliott grew up in the funeral business. His grandfather started the firm in 1935, and his father,

In-depth

History of Embalming

Every civilization must deal with the death of its individual members. Some societies burn their dead, while others bury them in caves, place them high in trees or in rock niches, or sink them beneath the ocean.

Egyptians were the first to develop embalming techniques. Around 4,000 B.C. embalmer-priests held respected positions within their society. They soaked bodies in chemical solutions, rubbed them with oils and spices, and wrapped them in linen shrouds before burial. Following the decline of Egyptian culture, other societies continued to anoint their dead with essences of cypress, frankincense, rosewater, or musk, but few practiced full-scale embalming.

In the United States, embalming was not practiced widely until during the Civil War. Then it became necessary to transport deceased soldiers over long distances in order that they might be buried on their home ground. Standardized chemical solutions and the discovery of formaldehyde in 1867, combined with the large number of battle casualties resulting from the Civil War, greatly accelerated the acceptance of embalming practices in the United States.

Throughout the early part of this century, embalming was often done in the homes of the deceased, using portable embalming tables. Now the procedure is conducted in specially designed preparation rooms, immaculately clean facilities that are equipped with many types of special equipment and are used only for this purpose.

uncle, and brother continued the tradition. Tom did not set out to study embalming or to become a funeral director, however. Nevertheless, during his junior year of college while studying for a degree in history, he decided that embalming was the career for him after all. He finished his bachelor's degree and then entered a two-year mortuary science program. "I'm lucky," Tom says. "Some people enter mortuary school and they've never even seen the inside of a funeral home, but I already had a lot of background. Still, I learned so much at school and even more during my apprenticeship."

EDUCATION

High School

Receiving a high school diploma is the first step toward a career in embalming. Students should take as many laboratory science classes as possible in high school, including chemistry, biology, and physics. English, public speaking, math, and business courses are also helpful, as are computer science and typing classes. In addition, students should be sure to fulfill the entrance requirements of the college, university, or mortuary science program they plan to attend.

Postsecondary Training

Currently there are 55 schools offering funeral service education and/or mortuary science degrees. Each program is accredited by the American Board of Funeral Service Education. Some embalming programs are associated with mortuary colleges, and some are associated with community colleges or universities. Some programs offer certificate-level credentials, while others grant associate's or bachelor's degrees.

The amount of postsecondary education necessary to become an embalmer varies from state to state. States require either one or two years of college plus one or two years at a mortuary college; or an associate's degree in mortuary science; or a high school diploma plus one year of mortuary college.

General course work includes classes in anatomy, biology, chemistry, business, mathematics, computer science, and English.

Students also learn about pathology, microbiology, public health, embalming theory, restorative art, cosmetology, mortuary chemistry, funeral service counseling, grief psychology, mortuary law, funeral service merchandising, and mortuary management.

State board examinations follow completion of postsecondary course work. After successfully passing the examination, all embalmers must serve an apprenticeship under the guidance of a licensed embalmer. Apprenticeships are determined by state regulation and last from one to three years.

CERTIFICATION OR LICENSING

Licensing for embalmers varies according to the state of residence. Most states require graduation from an accredited mortuary science program, one to three years' apprenticeship, and successful completion of the state or national examination. Contact your state's Board of Funeral Directors and Embalmers or Bureau of Professional Licensure for more information.

SCHOLARSHIPS AND GRANTS

Most colleges and universities offer general scholarships. Institutions teaching mortuary science also set aside monies to be used exclusively for students entering this field. In addition, individual state and national funeral directors associations provide scholarships for future embalmers. Information on scholarships available to students in funeral service or mortuary science is available through the American Board of Funeral Service Education.

INTERNSHIPS AND VOLUNTEERSHIPS

"The greatest experience for any student is to work at a funeral home," Tom says. "You can learn only so much in the classroom. As with any trade, there's no substitute for on-the-job training. Even though I came from a funeral business background, it was good to see how a different firm operated. Any experience someone can gain before committing full-time to the profession is invaluable. Take a part time job cutting the grass at your local mortuary. Or wash the limousines. If you don't have some idea about what the job entails before you enter it, you're not likely to have a long tenure as an embalmer."

Who Will Hire Me?

Tom has been an embalmer for over a decade. Before he joined his family's firm, he served an apprenticeship with an established funeral home near Kansas City

FYI

Hoping your funeral will be a lively tribute to your tastes and interests, rather than a traditionally somber event? A company called WhiteLight (www.artcaskets.com) is capitalizing on a new trend in the funeral industry—more individualized services for those bored with the idea of wreaths, mahogany caskets, and funeral dirges. WhiteLight, which calls itself a "custom casket design group," is contributing to more colorful, perhaps more memorable, memorial services with its line of unique coffins decorated with photographs and painting. The company's brochure allows you to choose from caskets covered with religious-theme artwork (inspired by the stained glass window of a cathedral, or featuring Our Lady of Guadalupe); nature scenes (a sunset or a mountain lake); popular places (Manhattan's cityscape or images of Texas, including The Alamo); and favorite pastimes (golf or auto racing). For those putting their funny-bones to rest, there's the humorous "Return to Sender" model, which looks like a wrapped, plain-paper parcel with cancellation stamps and marked "Express Delivery."

Community College where he studied mortuary science. "You can pick your place of employment from coast to coast," Tom says, "because practically every city has a funeral home. Job description varies to some degree, but it's basically the same no matter where you are."

The average funeral home has been in its community for over 40 years. Often funeral homes are multigenerational businesses, passed down from parent to child, but you need not be part of a family business in order to start a successful career as an embalmer. Only five of the 60 students Elliott attended mortuary science school with had any sort of funeral business background. Nationwide only about one-third of all funeral service students have any connection to family businesses. With or without family connections, building a career as an embalmer starts with successful completion of a mortuary science program, passage of state exams, and serving of an apprenticeship at an established funeral home under the guidance of a practicing embalmer.

> You can pick your place of employment from coast to coast, because practically every city has a funeral home.

Women are entering the profession in increasing numbers. In the recent past women had been discouraged from entering funeral service in general and from becoming embalmers in particular. However, about 51 percent of the funeral service graduates in 2003 were women. At Tom's funeral home, two of the six directors are women.

Most schools provide placement services for their graduates. Sometimes students find full-time work at the same firms where they served their apprenticeships. *The Director* magazine, a publication of the National Funeral Directors Association, offers classified ads for prospective employees and employers.

ADVANCEMENT POSSIBILITIES

Funeral directors arrange and direct funeral services.

Funeral home owners are usually licensed funeral directors and embalmers who perform those functions in addition to those of running a business.

Mortician investigators inspect mortuaries for sanitary conditions, equipment, and procedures, and competence of personnel. They examine the registration credentials of trainees and licenses of funeral directors to ensure compliance with state licensing requirements. They investigate complaints and recommend license revocation or other action.

Where Can I Go from Here?

Without a license, embalmers cannot independently practice their trade. Every state except Colorado requires a license. However, according to the Colorado Funeral Directors Association, although the state's legislative assembly eliminated Colorado's funeral service licensing system in 1982 as "overly bureaucratic, expensive, ineffective, and not relevant to current business practices," the funeral industry is regulated by other state laws and agencies. Entry-level technicians (apprentices gaining work experience prior to official licensing) remain under the supervision of certified embalmers until they complete their apprenticeships and successfully pass required exams. Without a license, technicians will remain on the lowest rung of funeral service.

Most embalmers eventually become licensed funeral directors, too. Funeral directors oversee and participate in all aspects of funerals. Embalmers must have some amount of college and/or mortuary science education. Funeral directors are regulated by individual state boards and must pass an examination to qualify for licensing. The goal of many embalmers is to become an owner/operator of a funeral home. This opportunity is most available to those people who have credentials as both an embalmer and a funeral director, have several years of experience in the funeral business, and have developed a reputation for friendliness, professional courtesy, and respect.

What Are the Salary Ranges?

Experience, employer, and location determine the salary range for embalmers. In general, salaries are higher in metropolitan areas and lower in rural areas. The American Board of Funeral Service Education estimates salaries for newly licensed funeral directors to be $25,000 to $29,000 annually, estimates which are echoed by the School of Funeral Services of Miami-Dade Community College. The school advises students that they can make up to $35,000 their first year, once fully licensed.

According to the *Occupational Outlook Handbook*, in 2003 embalmers had median annual earnings of $34,500 with the middle 50 percent earning between $25,300 and $43,600. Those in the lowest paid 10 percent earned $19,200 annually, and the highest paid 10 percent earned $55,100.

Embalmers who also work as funeral directors had median annual earnings of $46,100 in 2003. Those in the lowest paid 10 percent earned $26,600 a year, while those in the top paid 10 percent earned $91,900. Embalmers who work as funeral directors and who also own their own funeral homes can earn considerably higher salaries.

What Is the Job Outlook?

The U.S. Department of Labor projects that employment prospects for embalmers are expected to increase more slowly than the average through 2012. Some professionals predict that funeral service work will require a four-year degree in the future.

However, as the average age of the general population rises and as diseases such as AIDS take their toll, demand for services provided by embalmers may grow. Because of the growing age of the baby boomer population, the number of funerals from 2010 onward is expected to be higher than in recent decades. In 1990, there were 8.6 deaths per 1,000 population according to The National Funeral Directors Association, projections reveal that the number of deaths per 1,000 population will reach over 13 by 2080.

With the industry's growth, a number of mergers and acquisitions have occurred in recent years. "That has changed funeral service completely," Tom says, "and it certainly hasn't been for the benefit of funeral service." Tom predicts that corporate ownership will continue to increase, and the number of family-owned funeral homes will decrease. With major companies buying up funeral homes and focusing on profits, the quality of service can be negatively affected.

Tom mentions another change in the industry: an increase in the number of cremations. According to the Cremation Association of North America, this number is increasing because of environmental concerns, diminishing religious restrictions, and the lesser expense of preparation. The association predicts that by 2010 the rate of cremation will reach 42 percent of all deaths, compared to 23.6 percent in 1997.

"In certain parts of the country," Tom says, "that percentage varies greatly. Our percentage here in the Midwest is about 10 to 12 percent. The higher cremation rates are on the East and West coasts, some areas having as high as 50 to 60 percent in larger, metropolitan areas." These percentages are lower in smaller communities and regions such as the Midwest and the South where there is more emphasis on tradition.

Increased cremation is not expected to have a large impact on the career of funeral directors, as licensed individuals must be involved in the transporting of the body, and also assist with the planning and the traditional memorial services. Though embalming is not necessarily required with cremation, it is still often used because of health, time, and legal issues. As cremations increase, more funeral homes may extend their businesses to include crematories.

How Do I Learn More?

PROFESSIONAL ORGANIZATIONS

The following are organizations that provide information on embalming careers, accredited schools, scholarships, and employers:

American Board of Funeral Service Education
38 Florida Avenue
Portland, ME 04103
207-878-6530
http://www.abfse.org

Federated Funeral Directors of America
1622 South MacArthur Boulevard
PO Box 19224
Springfield, IL 62794-9244
217-525-1712
info@ffda.com
http://www.ffda.com

National Funeral Directors and Morticians Association
3951 Snapfinger Parkway, Suite 570
Decatur, GA 30035
800-434-0958
info@nfdma.com
http://www.nfdma.com

National Funeral Directors Association
13625 Bishop's Drive
Brookfield, WI 53005
262-789-1880
nfda@nfda.org
http://www.nfda.org

National Selected Morticians
500 Lake Cook Road, Suite 205
Deerfield, IL 60015
800-323-4219
http://www.nsm.org

BIBLIOGRAPHY

The following is a sampling of materials relating to the professional concerns and development of embalmers:

Dorn, James M. *Thanatochemistry: A Survey of General, Organic, and Biochemistry for Funeral Service Professionals*. Paramus, N.J.: Prentice-Hall, 1997.

Mayer, Robert G. *Embalming: History, Theory, and Practice*. 3rd ed. New York: McGraw-Hill, 2000.

Sacks, Terence J. *Opportunities in Funeral Services Careers*. New York: McGraw-Hill, 1997.

Szabo, John F. *Mortuary Science: A Sourcebook*. Lanham, Md.: Scarecrow Press, 2003.

EMERGENCY MEDICAL TECHNICIANS

A t 6:45 A.M. Kelly Richey clocks in, says hello to the EMTs going off duty, and goes to the soda machine for her first Diet Coke of the day. It is half gone when the first call comes in, and 15 minutes later she is inside a crumpled black Camaro, placing an oxygen mask on a critically injured teenager.

"Are you still in school?" she asks him as she works over him. "What grade? Senior?" She is trying to determine his level of consciousness, and she has to speak in a near-shout because the fire department is cutting the roof off the car while she works. As soon as the roof comes off, she and her co-worker must work quickly to get the patient out of the car and on the way to the hospital. He has injuries to the chest and both legs and is losing blood quickly. If he doesn't reach surgery within an hour, his chances for survival are greatly diminished.

In the ambulance, Kelly continues to talk to the young man, taking his vital signs every four to five minutes. She calls in to the hospital emergency room to notify them that they have a serious trauma patient coming in. "We have a 17-year-old patient, conscious and alert," she begins. "Involved in a single-vehicle accident. Patient has chest wounds and injuries to both legs. Vital signs are stable. We have an ETA of five minutes."

At the hospital, Kelly and her partner unload the patient, deliver him to the emergency staff, and give a brief report to the doctor who will be on his case.

Kelly gets a blank "run report," and her second Diet Coke, and starts to document the first run of her day.

What Does an Emergency Medical Technician Do?

If you are sick or hurt, you usually go to a doctor; if you are very sick or hurt you may go to the emergency room of a local hospital. But what if you are alone and unable to drive, or you are too badly injured to travel without receiving medical treatment first? It

---

Definition
Emergency medical technicians give immediate first aid treatment to sick or injured persons both at the scene and en route to the hospital or other medical facility. They also make sure that the emergency vehicle is stocked with the necessary supplies and is in good operating condition.

Alternative Job Title
Paramedics

High School Subjects
Biology
Health

Personal Skills
Helping/teaching
Technical/scientific

Salary Range
$15,530 to $24,030 to $41,980

Minimum Educational Level
Some postsecondary training

Certification or Licensing
Required

Outlook
Faster than the average

DOT
079

GOE
04.04.01

NOC
3234

O*NET-SOC
29-2041.00

---

often happens that an accident or injury victim needs on-the-spot help and safe, rapid transportation to the hospital. *Emergency medical technicians* are the ones who fill this need.

Emergency medical technicians, or EMTs, respond to emergency situations to give immediate attention to people who need it. Whether employed by a hospital, police department, fire department, or private ambulance company, the EMT crew functions as a traveling arm of the emergency room. While on duty, an EMT could be called out for car accidents, heart attacks, work-related injuries, or drug overdoses. He or she might help deliver a baby, treat the victim of a gunshot wound, or revive a child who has nearly drowned. In short, EMTs may find

Lingo to Learn

Amkus cutter A handheld rescue device, similar to scissors, used to free trapped victims by cutting through metal.

Amkus rams A handheld rescue device used to free trapped victims by pushing or pulling obstructions, such as dashboard and seats, away from the victim.

Amkus spreader A handheld rescue device used to free trapped victims by pulling crumpled metal apart.

Backboard A long, flat, hard surface used to immobilize the spine in the case of neck or spinal injury.

Cardiac arrest The complete stoppage of the heartbeat.

Defibrillator An apparatus consisting of alternating currents of electricity, with electrodes to apply the currents to heart muscles in order to shock the muscles into operation. Requires the operator to interpret the heart rhythms and apply the shock at the proper time.

Endotracheal intubation The insertion of a tube into the trachea, or windpipe, to provide a passage for the air, in case of obstruction.

IV or intravenous Administered by an injection into the vein.

themselves in almost any circumstance that could be called a medical crisis.

Usually working in teams of two, they receive their instructions from the emergency medical dispatcher, who has taken the initial call for help, and drive to the scene in an ambulance. The dispatcher remains in contact with the EMT crew through a two-way radio link. This allows the EMTs to relay important information about the emergency scene and the victims and to receive any further instructions, either from the dispatcher or from a medical staff member. Since they are usually the first trained medical help on the scene, it is very important that they be able to evaluate the situation and make good, logical judgements about what should be done in what order,

as well as what should not be done at all. By observing the victim's injuries or symptoms, looking for medic alert tags, and asking the necessary questions, the EMTs determine what action to take and begin first aid treatment. Some more complicated procedures may require the EMT to be in radio contact with hospital staff who can give step-by-step directions.

The types of treatments EMTs can give depend mostly on the level of training and certification they have completed. The first and most common designation is *EMT-Basic* or *EMT-Ambulance*. A basic EMT can perform CPR, control bleeding, treat shock victims, apply bandages, splint fractures, and perform automatic defibrillation, which requires no interpretation of EKGs. They are also trained to deal with emotionally disturbed patients and heart attack, poisoning, and burn victims. The *EMT-Intermediate*, who has finished the second level of training, can start an IV, if needed, or use a manual defibrillator to apply electrical shocks to the heart in the case of a cardiac arrest. A growing number of EMTs are choosing to train for the highest level of certification—the *EMT-Paramedic*. With this certification, EMTs are permitted to perform more intensive treatment procedures. Often working in close radio contact with a doctor, they may give drugs intravenously or orally, interpret EKGs, perform endotracheal intubation, and use more complex life-support equipment.

In the case where a victim or victims are trapped, EMTs first give any medical treatment, and then remove the victim, using special equipment such as the Amkus Power Unit. They may need to work closely with the police or the fire department in the rescue attempt.

If patients must be taken from the emergency scene to the hospital, the EMTs may place them on a backboard or stretcher, then carry and lift them into the ambulance. One EMT drives to the hospital, while the other monitors the passenger's vital signs and provides any further care. One of them must notify the hospital emergency room, either directly or through the dispatcher, of how many people are coming in and the type of injuries they have. They also may record the blood pressure, pulse, present condition, and any medical history they know, to assist the hospital.

Once at the hospital, the EMTs help the staff bring in the patient or patients, and assist with any necessary first steps of in-hospital treatment. They then provide their observations to the hospital staff, as well as information about the treatment they have given at the scene and on the way to the hospital.

Finally, each run must also be documented by the EMTs for the records of the provider. Once the run is over, the EMTs are responsible for restocking the ambulance, having equipment sterilized, replacing dirty linens, and making sure that everything is in order for the next run. For the EMT crews to function efficiently and quickly, they must make certain that they have all the equipment and supplies they need, and that the ambulance itself is clean, properly maintained, and filled with gas.

What Is It Like to Be an Emergency Medical Technician?

Kelly Richey is a calm, soft-spoken woman who may save a life as a routine part of a day's work. Kelly works for the hospital in an average-sized Indiana city as an EMT. Although her father had been an EMT for years, Kelly had no intention of working in Emergency Medical Services when she first took the training course. "I just took the course for knowledge," she says. "I didn't really plan to do it as a job." However, during the training course clinicals, when she got the opportunity to actually go on runs, she changed her mind. "I just kind of got the fever," she says, laughing. "I decided it was something I wanted to do. I decided it was something I could do, and I thought if I can do this and I can save a life, I should maybe make this my profession."

Kelly's unit gives its EMTs the option of working two 24-hour shifts or one eight-hour and two 16-hour shifts each week. Kelly has done both, but prefers the shorter hours, which she currently works. This number of hours is fairly common for employees of ambulance firms and hospitals. EMTs who work for fire and police departments may be scheduled for as many as 56 hours per week.

EMT work can be physically demanding. EMTs often work outside, in any type of weather, and most of their time on a run is spent standing, kneeling, bending, and lifting. It is also stressful and often emotionally draining. "I'm pretty tired at the end of a shift," Kelly says. The sort of shift an EMT has depends almost entirely on how many and what type of calls come in. Some shifts are incredibly busy—up to 15 runs, according to Kelly, although not all of those are emergency runs. Her ambulance is

frequently dispatched to carry nursing home patients to and from the hospital for treatment, as well as to transport stable patients from the local hospital to the larger medical complex an hour away for scheduled surgeries. Other shifts are considerably slower, with maybe only seven runs in the entire 16 hours.

At Kelly's hospital, the average length of a run is an hour and a half from dispatch until return to ready status. The location of the emergency and its seriousness greatly affect that time frame, however. There is a perception among many people that most calls involve life-or-death situations. That is not really the case, in Kelly's experience.

"On a monthly basis, only about 10 to 15 percent of my runs are actually life-threatening," she says. Other calls run the gamut from serious injury to cut fingers. "You wouldn't believe the stuff I've been called out for," Kelly says. "I've gotten calls for things you could put a Band-Aid on and go right about your business."

No matter what the call, the EMTs must respond. Each team of two is assigned to a certain area of the city, but any team will take any call if the designated team for that area is already out. Kelly's hospital employs approximately 70 EMTs and paramedics, including several who work on a part-time schedule, and it staffs up to five ambulances during the busiest parts of the day.

All the EMTs in Kelly's unit are required to take a driver training program when they are hired, so they are all qualified to drive. Kelly says that she usually drives on every other run, alternating turns with her partner. The team schedule is set up in such a way that the same partners always work together. That way, they get used to working as a team and communicating with each other. Also, they are able to become accustomed to each others' techniques and work habits and are able to function more efficiently.

Not every emergency requires that a patient be taken to the hospital. If it isn't necessary, or if the patient refuses to go, the EMTs give treatment on-site and return to await the next call. If a patient does need further attention, he or she is transported to the emergency room and unloaded by Kelly and her partner. The attending doctor is briefed on the case and the treatment. Whether a patient is transported or not, each run must be documented on a state-issued form called a run report.

Between calls, Kelly and her co-workers wait in the crewhouse. Complete with a kitchen, living room with TV, and two sleeping rooms, it has a comfortable, homey atmosphere. The ambulances are kept in an adjoining garage, and during each shift, if time allows, the crew is responsible for washing its vehicle and making sure it is fully stocked and ready to go. "Some people like to restock after every run," Kelly says. She and her partner prefer to take stock at the end of their shift and make sure everything is replaced. "That way you know you're leaving it in good shape for the shift coming on."

Ree Braham is an EMT in Texas and, like Kelly, she feels particularly close to the work. "I believe the work is something that's in your blood," Ree says. "It's an addictive job. When I was seven years old, I just decided I wanted to work on an ambulance." Ree thrives on the gratification she gets from coming to the rescue. "Don't expect any thank-yous," she says, "you're not going to get them. You don't make money, and you can't pay your bills. You're away from your family for 24 hours at a stretch. You do this for the love of helping people. If you want to help somebody, and you've got a compassionate heart, you get gratification."

It's an addictive job.

Ree's work schedule consists of 24 hours on the job and 48 hours off, answering anywhere from two to 24 calls a shift. "Idiot permitting," Ree says, meaning that many of her calls are the result of careless accidents, drinking, and other avoidable mishaps. "It depends on the moon," she says. "On a full moon, you can pretty much count on running around a lot."

Following a particular format, Ree prepares the injured patient for the ambulance ride. "We do everything that an emergency room does, but we're on wheels." The ambulance is stocked with drugs, splinting, bandaging, a defibrillator, oxygen, trauma gear, and other first aid. "A lot of what you do is common sense. If it's bleeding, make it stop. If it's broken, splint it. You can't fix what's broken, but hopefully you can eliminate some of the pain." But Ree is quick to point out that every case is different. "There are no textbook cases. You're going by your wits. It's a lot of improvising, a lot of hair pulling. Meanwhile, you've got family members crying on your shoulder, or they're mad at you because they swear up and down that you've done something wrong."

The TV series *ER* offers a good representation of the work, Ree says. "You see the EMTs bringing the patients in, and you hear them giving the report to the nurses and doctors. You're wheeling in and, depending on how critical your patient is, you're talking while you're wheeling and you're giving compressions and bagging the patient. If they're bleeding out, you've got IVs going, and you're holding pressure." Ree has seen many dramatic situations over the years, and recalls a particularly frightening car accident that involved an infant, icy roads, and drunk driving. "The mother was dead and the baby had been ejected from the car seat out of the vehicle. We found the car seat upside down out in a field, probably 100 feet from the car. When we finally got up to it, there was no noise. We flipped the seat over. The baby was sleeping. We worked the baby up from head to toe and transported, and the hospital released him. There was nothing wrong with him." Fortunately, not every day is filled beginning to end with drama. "You have 23 hours, 15 minutes of total boredom," Ree says, "and 45 minutes of uncontrollable excitement."

Do I Have What It Takes to Be an Emergency Medical Technician?

EMTs regularly encounter situations that many people would find upsetting. Because they are faced with unpleasant scenes, crises, and even death, they need a certain emotional capability for coping. They must have stable personalities and be able to keep their heads in circumstances of extreme stress.

The stress level is the hardest thing about the job for Kelly. She also warns that the potential EMT must be able to deal with death. "There have been times when the family members have hung out in the E.D. [Emergency Department] after we brought patients in and that really gets to me," she says. "I feel like they're looking at me and saying 'Why didn't you do more?' when I know I've done everything I could do." At Kelly's hospital, the staff has initiated a debriefing process to help EMTs work through a bad experience on a run. It's important that the EMT be able to cope with such bad experiences without suffering lasting negative results. The stress and the emotional strain can take its toll; there is a high turnover rate in the Emergency Medical Services field.

"You're holding people's lives in your hands," Ree says. "You've got to have a strong mind-set because some of your patients are going to die. You can't save everyone. We're the first on the scene, we make all the decisions. When we're the only ones there, we're the difference between life and death."

Such responsibilities can often be difficult to handle. "You can get burned out," Ree says. "They used to say the average longevity for someone in the job was seven years. I'm on year eight." Ree relies on the camaraderie of her co-workers in tough times. "The people you work with are a very tight-knit family," she says, "which can be hard on your own family members, because you start confiding more in your co-workers. A lot of marriages break up in this career field. Families don't always understand why at 3:00 A.M. you're willing to dart out of your bed to go help someone else."

How Do I Become an Emergency Medical Technician?

All states offer EMT training programs consisting of 100 to 120 hours of training, usually followed by 10 hours of internship in a hospital emergency room. To be admitted into a training program, you must be 18 years old, be a high school graduate, and hold a valid driver's license. Exact requirements vary slightly in different states and in different courses.

Ree has been through a Basic-EMT course and an Intermediate-EMT course, as well as a semester of paramedic school. The course work and registry has proven extremely important to Ree. "You've got to be able to handle anything that comes your way," she says. "The classes are very compact for what we do. You've got to pay attention."

EDUCATION

High School

A high school diploma, or its equivalent, is required for admission into the EMT training program. While most high school studies will not yield experience with emergency medical care, health classes may

---

TO BE A SUCCESSFUL EMERGENCY MEDICAL TECHNICIAN, YOU SHOULD . . .

- ❍ have a desire to serve people
- ❍ be emotionally stable and clearheaded
- ❍ have good manual dexterity and agility
- ❍ have strong written and oral communication skills
- ❍ be able to lift and carry up to 125 pounds
- ❍ have good eyesight and color vision

---

offer a good introduction to some of the concepts and terms used by EMTs. It may also be possible to take courses in first aid or CPR through the local Red Cross or other organizations. This sort of training can be a valuable background, giving you advance preparation for the actual EMT program. Some science classes, such as biology, can also be useful in helping you become familiar with the human body and its various systems.

Driver's education is recommended as well for anyone who is interested in a career as an EMT. The ability to drive safely and sensibly in all different types of road conditions, and a firm knowledge of traffic laws is essential to the driver of an ambulance. English is a desirable subject for the potential EMT, since it is important to have good communication skills, both written and verbal, along with the capacity to read and interpret well. Finally, depending on what area of the country you might work in, it might be very helpful to have a background in a foreign language, such as Spanish, to assist in dealing with patients who speak little or no English.

Postsecondary Training

For the high school graduate with a strong interest in Emergency Medical Services, the next step is formal training. The standard training course was designed by the Department of Transportation and is often offered by police, fire, and health departments. It may also be offered by hospitals or as a nondegree course in colleges, particularly community colleges.

The program teaches you how to deal with many common emergencies. You learn how to deal with bleeding, cardiac arrest, childbirth, broken bones, and choking. You will also become familiar with the specialized equipment used in many emergency situations, such as backboards, stretchers, fracture kits, splints, and oxygen systems.

If you live in an area that offers several different courses, it might be a good idea to research all the options, since certain courses may emphasize different aspects of the job. After completing the basic course, there are training sessions available to teach more specialized skills, such as removing trapped victims, driving an ambulance, or dispatching.

EMTs who have graduated from the basic program may later decide to work toward reaching a higher level of training in the EMS field. For example, the EMT-Intermediate course provides 35 to 55 hours of additional instruction to allow the EMT to give more extensive treatment, and the EMT-Paramedic course offers an additional 750 to 2,000 hours of education and experience.

CERTIFICATION OR LICENSING

After you have successfully completed the training program, you have the opportunity to work toward becoming certified or registered with the National Registry of Emergency Medical Technicians (NREMT). All states have some sort of certification requirement of their own, but 39 states accept registration in NREMT, in place of their own certification. Applicants should check the specific regulations and requirements for their state.

Whether registering with the NREMT or being certified through a state program, the applicant for an EMT-Basic title will be required to take and pass a written examination, as well as a practical demonstration of skills. The written segment will usually be a multiple-choice exam of roughly 150 questions. After passing the exam, EMTs usually work on a basic support vehicle for six months before certification is awarded.

While it is not always required in every state that EMTs become certified or registered, certification, at least, is a common requirement for employment in most states. It certainly is recommended, as it will open up many more job possibilities. The higher the level of training an EMT has reached, the more valuable he or she will become as an employee.

EMTs who are registered at the Basic level may choose to work on fulfilling the requirements for an EMT-Intermediate certification. After the mandatory 35 to 55 hours of classroom training, as well as further clinical and field experience, you must take and pass another examination. To earn paramedic status, you must already be registered as at least an EMT-Basic. You must complete a training program that lasts approximately nine months, as well as hospital and field internships, pass a written and practical examination, and work as a paramedic for six months before receiving actual certification.

All EMTs must renew their registration every one to two years, depending upon the state's requirement. In order to do so, you must be working at that time as an EMT, and meet the continuing education requirement, which is usually 20 to 25 hours of lecture and practical skills training.

LABOR UNIONS

Some EMTs may have the opportunity to join a union when they become employed. The unionization of this industry has been fairly recent and is not yet widespread. Therefore, membership in a union will not likely be a requirement for employment, and may not even be offered as an option. However, the EMT unions are growing rapidly, particularly in the public sector.

One of the principal unions of EMTs and paramedics is the International Association of EMTs and Paramedics, which is a division of the National Association of Government Employees, AFL-CIO. The other is the National Emergency Employee Organization Network.

EMTs with membership in a union pay weekly or monthly dues, and receive in return a package of services designed to improve working conditions, which include collective bargaining for pay and benefits, governmental lobbying, and legal representation.

Who Will Hire Me?

Kelly was lucky when she started to look for a job as an EMT. "I just went to the hospital and filled out their application," she says. "They called me in for an interview and I got the job. I didn't even have to apply anywhere else." Not everyone will be lucky enough to get a job on the first try, but currently the statistics are in the favor of EMTs. The demand exceeds the number of persons trained to do the work.

After serving in the U.S. Air Force, Ree went to work on a county ambulance in Idaho. "In Idaho," she says, "you could be a driver for an ambulance if all you had was CPR certification. But you couldn't do anything more than drive." Meanwhile, she enrolled in school and took the courses required for EMT work.

Nearly one-half of EMTs work in private ambulance services. An estimated one-third are in municipal fire, police, or rescue departments, and one-fifth work in hospitals or medical centers. Also, there are many who volunteer, particularly in more rural areas, where there often are no paid EMTs at all.

Because new graduates will be in heavy competition for full-time employment, it may be easier to break into the field on a part-time or volunteer basis. By beginning as a volunteer or part timer, the new EMT can gain hours of valuable experience, which can be useful in landing a paid, full-time position later. The competition is also stiffer for beginning EMTs in the public sector, such as police and fire departments. Beginners may have more success in finding a position in a private ambulance company. There are also some opportunities for work that lie somewhat off the more beaten path. For example, many industrial plants have EMTs in their safety departments, and security companies sometimes prefer to hire EMTs for their staff. Most amusement parks and other public attractions employ EMTs in their first aid stations, and in many cities there are private companies that hire EMTs to provide medical coverage for rock concerts, fairs, sporting events, and other gatherings.

One good source of employment leads for an EMT graduate is the school or agency that provided his or her training. Job openings may sometimes be listed in the newspaper classifieds under "Emergency

Medical Technician," "EMT," "Emergency Medical Services," "Ambulance Technician," "Rescue Squad," or "Health Care." Many professional journals, and national and state EMS newsletters list openings. Finally, the National Association of Emergency Medical Technicians (NAEMT) provides members with a professional placement service and a bimonthly newsletter featuring employment information.

It is also a good idea to apply directly to any local ambulance services, hospitals, fire departments, and police departments. The best approach is usually to send a current resume, complete with references, and a letter of inquiry. The letter should consist of a brief description of your situation and interests, and a request for an application. Most agencies have specific applications and employment procedures, so the resume and cover letter alone is not necessarily adequate. It is important to remember that most employers will accept applications to keep on file even if there is no specific job open at the time.

Where Can I Go from Here?

Kelly decided that she wanted to pursue more advanced levels of training shortly after she started working as an EMT. At present, she has already passed the paramedic training course and is getting ready to test for her certification. Eventually, she says, she might like to get into EMS education and train EMTs to do the job she does now.

Moving into the field of education and training is only one of several possible career options. For an EMT who is interested in advancement, usually the first move is to become certified as a paramedic. Once at that level, there are further opportunities in the area of administration. Moving into an administrative position usually means leaving fieldwork and patient care for a more routine office job. An EMT-Paramedic can pursue such positions as supervisor, operations manager, administrative director, or executive director of emergency services. Or, like Kelly, he or she may be interested in a career in education and training. Also, several new areas of specialization in EMS have recently received more emphasis. Quality control, safety and risk management, communications, and flight operations are some examples of these up-and-coming administrative areas.

Some EMTs move out of health care entirely and into sales and marketing of emergency medical

ADVANCEMENT POSSIBILITIES

Training directors plan and oversee continuing education for rescue personnel, design and implement quality assurance programs, and develop and direct specialized training courses or sessions for rescue personnel.

Emergency medical services coordinators direct medical emergency service programs, coordinate emergency staff, maintain records, develop and participate in training programs for rescue personnel, cooperate with community organizations to promote knowledge of and provide training in first aid, and work with emergency services in other areas to coordinate activities and area plans.

Physician assistants work under the direction and responsibility of physicians to provide health care to patients: They examine patients; perform or order diagnostic tests; give necessary injections, immunizations, suturing, and wound care; develop patient management plans; and counsel patients in following prescribed medical regimens.

equipment. Often, their experience and familiarity with the field make them effective and valuable salespersons. Finally, some EMTs decide to go back to school and become registered nurses, physicians, or other types of health workers. Kelly has seen EMTs take many different paths. "One woman who was a paramedic when I started at the hospital is a doctor now," she says, "so you can see how far you can go with it."

What Are the Salary Ranges?

According to the *Occupational Outlook Handbook,* median annual earnings for EMTs were $24,030 in 2002. Those in the lowest paid 10 percent made less than $15,530, while those in the highest paid 10 percent earned more than $41,980. A review of wages nationwide for EMTs in 2005 reported by Salary.com listed the median earnings as $23,881. The lowest paid 10 percent earned $21,018; the highest paid 10 percent earned $26,007. The median salary for paramedic-EMTs is $31,105. The lowest 10 percent earned $27,626 and the highest 10 percent earned $35,238.

The most significant factor in determining salary is whether the EMT is employed in the private or the public sector. Private ambulance companies and hospitals traditionally offer the lowest pay, while fire departments pay better. In 2002 EMTs working for fire departments earned on average $27,440; in hospitals, $24,760; and in other health care services, $22,180. Benefits may include life insurance, major medical insurance, uniform allowance, retirement or pension plans, and paid seminars and conferences.

What Is the Job Outlook?

Employment opportunities for EMTs are expected to grow faster than average for all occupations, according to the *Occupational Outlook Handbook.* One of the reasons for the overall growth is simply that the population is growing, thus producing the need for more medical personnel. Another factor is that the proportion of elderly people, who are the biggest users of emergency medical services, is growing in many communities. Finally, many jobs will become available because, as noted earlier, the EMT profession does have a high turnover rate.

The job opportunities for EMTs will depend partly upon the community where you wish to work. In the larger, more metropolitan areas, where the majority of paid EMT positions are found, the opportunities will probably be best. In many smaller communities, financial difficulties are causing many not-for-profit hospitals and municipal police, fire, and rescue squads to cut back on staff. Because of this, there are likely to be fewer job possibilities in the public sector. However, since many of the organizations suffering cutbacks opt to contract with a private ambulance company for service to their community, opportunities with these private companies may increase.

The trend toward private ambulance companies, which have historically paid less, is an important one, since it is likely to influence where the jobs will be found, as well as what the average pay is. One reason for the growth of the private ambulance industry is the growth of managed-care systems. The reason this affects the EMT profession is that medical transportation is one of the major services typically contracted for by managed-care providers. As managed care gains popularity, there is a greater need for the private ambulance contractors.

Because of America's growing concern with health care costs, the person considering a career as an EMT should be aware of the fact that health care reforms may affect all medical professions to some extent. Also, as mentioned before, the increase and growth of private ambulance services will almost definitely change the face of the emergency services field. In looking at a future as an emergency medical technician, both of these factors are worth keeping in mind.

How Do I Learn More?

PROFESSIONAL ORGANIZATIONS

For a list of accredited educational programs and general information on the health care industry, contact
    American Medical Association
    Division of Allied Health Education and
      Accreditation
    515 North State Street
    Chicago, IL 60610
    800-621-8335
    http://www.ama-assn.org

To learn about union membership, contact
    International Association of EMTs and Paramedics
    159 Burgin Parkway
    Quincy, MA 02169
    617-376-0220

info@iaep.org
http://www.iaep.org

For information about educational programs, contact
    National Association of Emergency Medical
      Technicians
    PO Box 1400
    Clinton, MS 39060-1400
    800-346-2368
    info@naemt.org
    http://www.naemt.org

To learn about national registration, contact
    National Registry of Emergency Medical
      Technicians
    Box 29233
    6610 Busch Boulevard
    Columbus, OH 43229
    614-888-4484
    http://www.nremt.org

BIBLIOGRAPHY

The following is a sampling of materials relating to the professional concerns and development of emergency medical technicians.

Aehlert, Barbara, and Garret Olson. *Aehlert's EMT Basic Study Guide.* Baltimore: Lippincott Williams & Wilkins, 1998.

Copass, Michael K. *EMT Manual.* 3d ed. Kent, U.K.: W. B. Saunders, 1998.

Mistovich, Joseph J. *Prentice Hall Health Review Manual for the First Responder.* Upper Saddle River, N.J.: Prentice-Hall, 2005.

Sanders, Mick J. *Mosby's Paramedic Textbook.* 2d ed. St. Louis: Mosby, Inc., 2001.

Sheehy, Susan Budassi, and Gail Pisarcik Lenehan. *Manual of Emergency Care.* 5th ed. St. Louis: Mosby-Year Book, 1999.

ENERGY CONSERVATION TECHNICIANS

Working for a nonprofit organization that relies on state funding, John Maggs has seen more than a few projects bound up in government bureaucracy. Not only is he involved in the actual testing of furnaces and homes for drafts, carbon monoxide levels, temperatures, and other heating concerns, but he must also follow funding restrictions and budgets. "We just did a house here," he says, referring to the home of an elderly woman, "where we were allowed to replace the furnace under state guidelines, but we weren't allowed to touch the asbestos that was in the pipes. But we couldn't do one without the other."

Because he works for a large nonprofit organization that houses many different agencies under one roof, John was able to just go down the hall to the Office of Aging. "They had a pool of money that could deal with asbestos. So we called in a contractor who removed the asbestos from the pipes, then we went in and disconnected, and we got our new furnace." One of the most gratifying aspects of John's job is being able to help the elderly with their energy bills. "We're looking at cutting her fuel bill 30 or 40 percent."

What Does an Energy Conservation Technician Do?

Energy conservation technicians work in a wide variety of settings. They may inspect homes, businesses, and industrial buildings to identify conditions that cause energy waste; recommend ways to reduce the waste; and help install reduction measures. They may be employed in power plants, research laboratories, construction firms, industrial facilities, government agencies, or companies that sell and service equipment.

There are four general areas of energy activity: research and development, production, use, and conservation. In the area of research and development, technicians usually work in laboratories testing mechanical, electrical, chemical, pneumatic, hydraulic, thermal, or optical scientific principles.

Such laboratories are found in institutions, private industry, government, and the military. Technicians in laboratories assist engineers, physicists, or chemists with experiments. They help record data and analyze it using computers, and they may also be responsible for maintaining and repairing equipment.

Companies that are involved with energy production include manufacturers, installers, and users of solar energy equipment; power plants; and process plants that use high-temperature heat, steam, or hot water. In these settings, energy conservation technicians work with engineers and managers to develop, install, operate, maintain, modify, and

---

repair systems and devices that convert fuels or other resources into useful energy.

In the field of energy use, energy technicians might work in an industrial facility to improve efficiency in engineering and production-line equipment. They also maintain equipment and buildings for hospitals, schools, and multifamily housing.

In the area of energy conservation, manufacturing companies, consulting engineers, energy-audit firms, and energy-audit departments of public utility companies use energy technicians to determine building specifications, modify equipment and structures, audit energy use and efficiency of machines and systems, then recommend modifications to save energy. These types of energy technicians work for municipal governments; hotels; architects; private builders; and heating, ventilating, and air-conditioning equipment manufacturers.

More and more utility companies are providing services, called demandside management (DSM) programs, that help customers reduce the amount of their electric bill. DSM programs use energy conservation technicians to visit customers' homes and interview them about household energy use, such as type of heating system, number of persons home during the day, furnace temperature setting, and prior heating costs.

Whether a technician works for a utility, a nonprofit agency, or a private company, the energy audit process is similar. In addition to the client interview, technicians draw a sketch of the house, measure its perimeter, windows, and doors, and record dimensions on the sketch. They inspect attics, crawl spaces, and basements and note any loose-fitting windows, uninsulated pipes, and deficient insulation. Technicians read hot-water tank labels to find the heat-loss rating and determine the need for a tank insulation blanket. They examine furnace air filters and heat exchangers to detect dirt in filters and soot buildup in exchangers that might affect furnace operation.

Energy conservation technicians then discuss problems with the home owner and recommend actions to reduce energy waste, such as weatherstripping, reducing hot water temperature settings, adding insulation, and installing storm windows. They may also suggest new lighting systems, such as compact fluorescent lamps, fixtures that reflect more light onto work surfaces, electronic ballasts, or sensors that detect daylight and occupancy, and control lighting accordingly.

Lingo to Learn

Asbestos A mineral fiber once used to insulate and fireproof buildings. Asbestos use was discontinued by the EPA in 1970 after studies linked it to major health problems, including cancer.

DSM (Demandside Management) Services provided by utility companies that help customers reduce the amount of their utility bills.

Energy audit An inspection of a home or business by an energy conservation technician. The audit involves checking the furnace, hot water heater, airflow, crawl spaces, windows and doors, and other areas of the structure to determine energy loss.

Lead A home hazard that usually appears in the form of paint. As an ingredient of some paints manufactured before 1978, and lead water pipes, lead poses a threat primarily to young children, who can be poisoned by ingesting it.

Minimum ventilation guideline (MVG) The minimum amount of airflow necessary to keep a house or office "healthy."

Radon A colorless, odorless radioactive gas that seeps into homes through the crevices or spaces in the material on which homes are built. Exposure is linked to serious health problems, specifically lung cancer.

Technicians give customers literature describing energy conservation improvements and sources of loans. They record the results of their audit on a computer and use software programs to calculate heat-loss estimates. A printout of the data is usually mailed to the customer. Some companies conduct one-visit residential programs, in which the technician conducts an energy audit; installs energy-saving measures, such as low-flow showerheads, insulation wrapped around a water heater, caulking, and weatherstripping; and then inspects the installation. Some companies have technicians that only conduct audits, while others employ one team of technicians to do audits and another team to do installations.

What Is It Like to Be an Energy Conservation Technician?

John Maggs is an energy auditor for Step, Inc., a large nonprofit agency that does weatherization for low-income housing. He starts out the week by planning and scheduling audits, which he conducts Monday through Wednesday. "In one day, my round trip is up to 100 to 125 miles around the two counties our agency covers. I do a complete audit on each home, including a furnace test and a blower door test. I return to the office and start writing up estimates on the computer." Though a few years ago he was performing two or three audits a day, he can now only do one a day. "It's a lot more intense," he says about the testing. "It's gotten more technical. We're using a lot more electrical testing."

John spends Thursday and Friday writing up and finalizing the week's activities, so he can hand in reports. "I always leave a half day for any questions or problems that might come up," he says, "and there's always something."

The U.S. Departments of Energy, and Health and Human Services fund Weatherization Assistance Programs in many states. Training courses are offered for individuals employed by local governments and nonprofit agencies, like Step, Inc., that administer home energy conservation assistance to low-income clientele.

"I do a preassessment on a house and furnace, and identify areas where we can save energy. I am also qualified to do asbestos and lead tests. I give the client information, including pamphlets, brochures, and advice on how to conserve energy. I communicate the problems to other technicians who do the repairs and then I inspect their work."

John uses an electronic furnace analyzer, which gives carbon monoxide levels, and a draft gauge, which shows how the furnace is drafting. He also uses a blower door, which depressurizes the house and tells where the leaks are. A smoke stick helps him locate chaseways and leaky spots. Indoor and outdoor pressures are entered into a computer, which gives a leakage rate in cubic feet per minute (CFM). "Since a home needs a certain amount of air moving through it to make it safe, we also set up a minimum ventilation guideline," John explains. "We take into account the number of smokers, pets, space heaters, and fireplaces and adjust the MVG accordingly." After

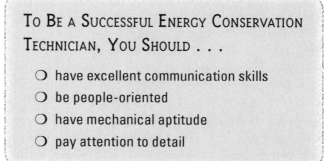

To Be a Successful Energy Conservation Technician, You Should . . .

- ○ have excellent communication skills
- ○ be people-oriented
- ○ have mechanical aptitude
- ○ pay attention to detail

weatherization measures are installed, he takes a post-weatherization CFM measurement. "That's how we justify our expenses and see how well we've done our audits."

John mentions some equipment used in residential audits. Energy conservation technicians may use other technologically complex machinery that may contain electric motors, heaters, lamps, electronic controls, mechanical drives and linkages, thermal systems, lubricants, optical systems, microwave systems, pneumatic and hydraulic drives, pneumatic controls, and in some instances, even radioactive samples and counters.

Rhode Islanders Saving Energy has seven technicians who serve about 1,000 home owners. They use state-of-the-art equipment, such as infrared scans, polaroid equipment, and Bacharach testing equipment. All technicians use computers and portable printers on-site.

Great Lakes Controlled Energy Corporation in Elk Grove Village, Illinois, specializes in building automation and control systems, energy management systems, lighting control systems, and energy audits for commercial properties. The company employs energy technicians who travel to sites coast to coast. Some are engineers who do surveys and audits, and some are installers.

Bonnie Esposito of the Center for Energy and Environment in Minneapolis, Minnesota, says, "Technicians range along a whole continuum of skills. Half of our technical staff do research and testing, and also sometimes do audits. Some are engineers who don't do audits, but some do audits on commercial properties. I also have technicians who are full-time auditors. We use different technicians for each project, depending on the service we need to provide for that particular job."

Although many energy technicians have normal daytime work schedules, they may also have to work in shifts, especially in energy-production or energy-use plants. Many technicians have to travel to customer locations and work indoors and out. Sites are often dirty and noisy, and technicians must pay attention to safety measures, including protective clothing and equipment.

Do I Have What It Takes to Be an Energy Conservation Technician?

Energy conservation technicians must have an interest in machines—how they are made, how the parts fit and work together, and how they operate. But what's the most important skill for a technician? "Communication," says John Maggs. "You have to be able to talk to people of all kinds. I can talk to anybody of any race or creed. Our clients are mainly low-income, but since I've become more specialized in asbestos and lead testing, I also deal with higher-income people. It doesn't matter. We've been very well trained, are knowledgeable, and can speak confidently about weatherization."

John Clune, of Eastern Utilities Association Citizens Conservation, has also done residential audits on multifamily units. He says, "You move around a lot and meet a lot of people in residential work. You need good personal skills. Some homeowners are going to be drunk or nasty. But some will treat you really well. You may see three or four customers per day, all unique. In addition to mechanical skills, you must have good verbal and communication skills to relate to clients."

> In addition to mechanical skills, you must have good verbal and communication skills to relate to clients.

David Fenton, manager of program marketing for Rhode Islanders Saving Energy, agrees. "Communication skills are definitely important in dealing with the public—equally as important as knowledge of the industry."

Problem solving is one of the most challenging aspects of the work energy conservation technicians do. They often have to respond to urgent calls and crisis situations involving unexpected breakdowns of equipment. They have to interrupt other duties to fix machinery that is not working properly.

Maggs sometimes finds it cumbersome to comply with the state guidelines that regulate government agencies. "Politics often get in the way. Sometimes you have to shut down a job or just say it's beyond our scope, instead of attempting to do something to make it better."

How Do I Become an Energy Conservation Technician?

Energy conservation technicians must understand the physical sciences and have mathematical aptitude. They must be able to understand operation and maintenance manuals, schematic drawings, blueprints, and formulas. They must be able to communicate with clients, and also make themselves clear in scientific and engineering terms.

Energy technicians have a wide range of educational backgrounds, from high school to a four-year engineering degree. At least two years of formal technical education beyond high school is recommended.

EDUCATION

High School

It is recommended that high school students take at least one year of algebra and geometry, physics, chemistry, and ecology, including laboratory work. Computer science and mechanical or architectural drafting are practical and necessary for those who want to pursue an engineering degree.

Students should look for opportunities to participate in special projects on solar equipment, energy audits, or energy-efficient equipment.

Postsecondary Training

Bill Van der Meer, director of the Weatherization Training Center at Pennsylvania College of Technology in Williamsport, says, "Energy technicians often come up through the ranks without college education. There is a wide variety of positions, from crew-technician level through auditor positions to selling energy-efficiency products.

"We train people under a federal grant to work for nonprofit organizations that provide weatherization for low-income housing. We teach a variety of skills, including carpentry, installation of insulation, and air sealing to reduce infiltration. We teach them to use diagnostic equipment and tools, such as blower doors. They must understand the house as a system and know potential interactions that go on."

Training is both theoretical and practical hands-on instruction. After students fulfill competency requirements and pass examinations and laboratory exercises, they are awarded certificates. Courses may include weatherization tactics, diagnostics, residential heating systems, combustion analysis and retrofit, home-energy auditing, blower-door tests, duct-leakage tests, and installation of energy conservation materials.

Some regions have youth corps. The South Bronx in New York City has a Youth Energy Corps, a weatherization agency that does air sealing, replaces windows, and blows high-density cellulose insulation. The workers are all high school dropouts who alternate one week of work with one week of school for one year. Youth Energy Corps teaches them weatherization skills and helps them earn a General Equivalency Diploma (GED), get a job, or both.

Maggs speaks highly of state-funded weatherization training programs. "Weatherization training centers are funded very well. Trainers go to all the conferences and are on top of new technologies."

Although many employers do not require energy technicians to have a degree, further education definitely expands career options. A degree from a technical institute, community college, or other specialized two-year program, can lead to a higher-paying position with a private firm. A technical degree includes courses in physics, chemistry, mathematics, the fundamentals of energy technology, energy-production systems, fundamentals of electricity and electromechanical devices, heating systems, air conditioning, and microcomputer operations.

Additional courses might include mechanical and fluid systems; electrical power and illumination systems; electronic devices; blueprint reading; energy conservation; codes and regulations; technical communications; instrumentation and controls; and energy economics and audits.

FYI

U.S. Department of Energy (DOE) studies have found that low-income families pay an average of 14 percent of their annual income for energy. Other households pay only 3.5 percent. Since its inception in 1976, DOE's Weatherization Assistance Program has weatherized about 5.3 million low-income homes with $5.8 billion in funding for the projects provided by the federal government. In 2005 the DOE's goal is to weatherize 92,500 homes, and the federal government has allocated $228 million to help fund the effort.

Many technical colleges, community colleges, and technical institutes provide two-year programs specifically in energy conservation and energy-use technology, or energy-management technology. There are related programs in solar power, electric power, building maintenance, equipment maintenance, and general engineering technology. Graduates with associate's degrees in energy conservation and use, instrumentation, electronics, or electromechanical technology will normally enter the work force at a higher level, with more responsibility and higher pay. Jobs in energy research and development almost always require an associate's degree.

Dick Walsh of Great Lakes Controlled Energy Corporation says, "We don't require that anyone be a graduate of a trade school or any kind of an apprenticeship program. But our employees have a great deal of experience. We have a journeyman pipe fitter who has an in-depth understanding of HVAC and mechanical equipment, so it's easy for him to do audits. Electrical installers have learned enough on the job about mechanical equipment to do audits as well, and we also have auditors with four-year engineering degrees who have studied mechanical or electrical engineering.

"Some of our installers are field laborers who pull wire and bend conduit, but we also have an ongoing training program on the crew, so if workers are capable of learning and progressing, they can."

David Fenton prefers that technicians have a background in building or home construction, any type of heating including home heating and solar heat, plumbing, or insulation.

Bonnie Esposito says, "Field experience is more important than technical training. I can teach employees calculations, computer skills, and the latest technologies with electronic ballasts, but to have real field experience to deal with owners, contractors, vendors, to know buildings, to know businesses—that's invaluable."

Bonnie believes the future trend will be to hire more graduates with four-year degrees. "There will always be lower-level technical jobs," she says, "but with a four-year degree you have a lot more options."

CERTIFICATION OR LICENSING

Certification is not required in every state, but many states approve certain training programs and award certificates to students who complete classes and tests in residential, commercial, or multifamily audits and installations. A certificate from the National Institute for Certification in Engineering Technologies or a degree or certificate of graduation from an accredited technical program, are highly regarded credentials, although not required by most employers. Some employers require technicians to undergo security clearances and psychological tests.

INTERNSHIPS AND VOLUNTEERSHIPS

Part-time or summer work is available to technicians in large hospitals, major office buildings, hotel chains, universities, and large manufacturing plants.

Summer youth programs are offered in some regions and communities. John Maggs worked on a crew for about three months and then got placed in a weatherization program. There are many opportunities for on-the-job training in energy conservation.

LABOR UNIONS

Jobs offered to high school graduates in electrical power production are represented by employee unions such as the International Brotherhood of Electrical Workers or the International Association of Machinists and Aerospace Workers. Workers often start as apprentices with a planned program of work and study for three to four years.

Union membership is not usually required for government-agency workers, research and development technicians, and conservation technicians.

Who Will Hire Me?

Institutions, private industry, government, and the military employ research and development technicians. Energy-production technicians are employed by solar-energy equipment manufacturers, installers, and users; power plants; and process plants that use high-temperature heat, steam, or hot water.

Energy-use technicians work in hospitals, schools, and apartments. Energy conservation technicians are hired by manufacturing companies, consulting engineers, energy-audit firms, and energy-audit departments of public utility companies. Technicians are also hired by municipal governments, hotels, architects, private builders, and heating, ventilating, and air-conditioning equipment manufacturers.

Technicians who were trained or employed in the military can find opportunities in building or equipment maintenance. Former U.S. Navy technicians are particularly sought after in the field of energy production.

Power companies need technicians to perform energy audits. Technicians in these firms assist energy-use auditors and energy-application analysts while they make audits or analyses in businesses or homes of their customers.

Industrial facilities hire energy technicians to manage machinery and equipment, including its planning, selection, installation, modification, and maintenance.

There are also sales and customer-service opportunities with manufacturers of energy-efficient or energy conservation equipment.

John Clune says, "Nonprofit organizations have different requirements than profit companies, and there is a wide spectrum of opportunities available for technicians, trained and untrained. But more and more companies are hiring people with engineering degrees. I got involved in the mid-1970s after the energy crisis. I am not an engineer, but because of my 20 years of experience, I now have about the same knowledge as a licensed professional engineer."

Where Can I Go from Here?

Technicians with experience and money to invest may start their own businesses, selling energy-saving products or providing audits, weatherizations, or energy-efficient renovations. Though John once considered starting his own business because of the few advancement opportunities in government-funded, nonprofit agencies, he has seen more cooperation between agencies in the last few years. As organizations have pooled resources, practices have become more cost-effective, and John has begun to receive a better wage.

Technicians in private companies can move into supervisory and management positions. Some become trainers or add training responsibilities to their job duties. Hotels, restaurants, and stores hire experienced technicians to manage energy consumption and then provide training in energy-saving procedures.

Experienced technicians can also move into sales or customer service as representatives for producers of power, energy, special control systems, or equipment designed to improve energy efficiency.

What Are the Salary Ranges?

According to the U.S. Department of Labor, engineering technicians and technologists had median annual earnings of $38,180 in 2003. Those in the lowest paid 10 percent made $23,700, and those in the highest paid 10 percent made $62,460. Environmental science and protection technicians had median earnings in 2003 of $35,800. The lowest paid 10 percent earned $21,500 annually, and the highest paid 10 percent earned $56,500.

What Is the Job Outlook?

The economy and prices of oil and other energy sources will affect the availability of jobs for energy technicians. Since energy use constitutes a major expense for industry, commerce, government, institutions, and private citizens, the demand for technicians trained in energy conservation is likely to remain strong. In addition, the United States is still dependent on foreign fuel supplies of petroleum, so energy conservation will continue to be an issue for all energy consumers. "This is a big industry getting bigger every day," says John Maggs. "It's proportionate with the oil prices. They're going through the roof, so we'll get more money to serve the client base we have now."

Bill Van der Meer of Pennsylvania College of Technology's Weatherization Training Center comments, "I'd say that the outlook in employment in energy retrofit situations is going to be driven by a market that perceives energy to be an issue once again," he predicts. "Definitely a pocketbook issue. Heating and oil prices, natural gas prices, and electric are going way up, so that may trigger a private sector response. But it may also trigger a public sector response in terms of pressure being put on legislators to introduce more money for low income and elderly people vulnerable to surging energy prices."

Utility companies are moving toward deregulation, opening new avenues for energy-service companies. Utilities have begun to work with manufacturers and government agencies to establish energy-efficiency standards, for example, to produce energy-efficient appliances. The Consortium for Energy Efficiency, a collaborative effort involving a group of electric and gas utilities, government energy agencies and environmental groups, is developing programs for commercial air-conditioning equipment, clothes washers, lighting, geothermal heat pumps, and industrial motor systems. These efforts will create job opportunities for technicians.

Utility DSM programs, which have traditionally concentrated on the residential sector, are now focusing more attention on commercial and industrial facilities. They are expanding to work with contractors, builders, retailers, distributors, and manufacturers with the goal of realizing larger energy savings, lower costs, and more permanent energy-efficient changes.

Another factor affecting the field of energy conservation is the growing awareness of environmental and global warming issues. The financial costs of purchasing natural resources will always be a major concern, but now we have the added reality of the physical costs of depleting those resources.

How Do I Learn More?

PROFESSIONAL ORGANIZATIONS

The following are organizations that provide information on energy conservation technician careers, accredited schools, and employers:

American Society of Heating, Refrigerating, & Air Conditioning Engineers Inc.
1791 Tullie Circle, NE
Atlanta, GA 30329-2305
404-636-8400
http://www.ashrae.org

Energy Efficiency and Renewable Energy Clearinghouse
PO Box 3048
Merrifield, VA 22116
800-363-3732
http://www.eere.energy.gov

National Institute for Certification in Engineering Technologies
1420 King Street
Alexandria, VA 22314-2794
888-476-4238
http://www.nicet.org

Weatherization Training Center
Pennsylvania College of Technology
One College Avenue
Williamsport, PA 17701
570-327-4768
bvvanderm@pct.edu
http://www.pct.edu/wtc

BIBLIOGRAPHY

The following is a sampling of materials relating to the professional concerns and development of energy conservation technicians:

Capehart, Barney L. et al. Guide to *Energy Management.* 4th ed. Lilburn, Ga.: Fairmont Press, 2002.

Thumann, Albert et al. *Handbook of Energy Engineering.* 5th ed. Lilburn, Ga.: Fairmont Press, 2002.

Turner, Wayne C. *Energy Management Handbook.* 5th ed. Lilburn, Ga.: Fairmont Press, 2004.

FIBER OPTICS TECHNICIANS
||||||||||||||||||||||||||||||||||||||||||||||||||||||||||||||||||||

Chad Tietje works as a fiber optics technician for MCI Worldcom in Texas. "The machines we work on deal with a lot of traffic," Chad says, referring to the amount of data transmitted by the company's fiber optic lines. "On one of our systems, a technician could knock out half a city. If you don't know what you're doing, you could knock down 911 calls, and people can be without 911 in the city for four or five hours." This is why fiber optics technicians need to be well trained and have a good solid education before taking responsibilities out in the field.

When talking about fiber optics, technicians may be referring to the long lines of cable that connect telephone networks and cable TV systems, cable that may contain over 200 glass fibers that may be buried underground or hung from poles, and may stretch for hundreds of miles. Or they may be talking about "premises" cable that links buildings of a college campus, for example, or even shorter lines connecting personal computers in an office, and that contain fewer than 50 fibers.

What Does a Fiber Optics Technician Do?

Fiber optics technicians prepare, install, and test fiber optics transmission systems. These systems are composed of fiber optic cables and allow for data communication between computers, phones, and faxes. The fibers in the cable are made of glass, and they carry light. Today, the career of fiber optics technician is one of the fastest growing, as telecommunications companies recognize the importance of fiber optics in the future of high-speed, high-definition service. Most phone connections made today are over fiber optic cables. The Internet is also transmitted by fiber optics.

Some fiber optics technicians are responsible for preventing the severing of buried fiber optics cables, and for the repair of the fibers when severed. This can involve supervising digs and construction, and locating the cables and marking where they run beneath ground. To repair a cable, a backhoe will dig the cable from the ground for the technician. In the event of a low signal, a technician will test fiber optic

Definition
Fiber optics technicians work with the optical fibers and cables used in transmitting communications data. Depending on the area of employment, technicians splice fibers, fuse fibers together, and install fiber cables beneath ground and in buildings. These technicians work for telephone and cable companies, and other businesses involved in telecommunications.

High School Subjects
Mathematics
Technical/Shop

Personal Skills
Mechanical/manipulative
Technical/scientific

Salary Range
$35,155 to $40,204 to $46,748+

Minimum Educational Level
High school diploma

Certification or Licensing
Voluntary

Outlook
About as fast as the average

DOT
N/A

GOE
05.02.01

NOC
7246

O*NET-SOC
49-9052.00

lines by using special tools to transmit light. Some technicians have their own tools, but some equipment is very expensive and is typically provided by the employer. Tools may include a FOtracer (flashlights to check that a fiber transmits light), a fiber optic power meter (measures how much light is coming out of the end of the fiber optic cable), and splice bushings (used to mate two cables that have connectors).

When working for a telecommunications company, technicians are often required to install lines for local area networks (LAN)—these data networks serve small areas of linked computers, such as in an office. These networks have become increasingly important in businesses, and allow for the easy transmission of files, e-mail, documents, and other data.

The telecommunications company for which a technician works contracts with a company to create a communications system. A salesman evaluates the customer's need, then orders the materials for the installation. Fiber optics technicians take these materials to the job site. Each job site may be very different. First, fiber optics technicians need to get a sense of the area. They walk through with the client, evaluating the areas where they'll be installing fiber optic cable. Newer buildings are usually readily equipped for installation; in some older buildings, it may be more difficult to get behind ceiling tiles and in the walls.

After they prepare the area for cable, fiber optics technicians run the cable from the computer's main frame to individual work stations. They then test the cable, using power meters and other devices, by running a laser through it. Fiber optics technicians use equipment that measures the amount of time it takes for the laser to go through, determining any signal loss or faults in the fiber link.

Technicians may also fuse fibers together. This involves cleaning the fiber and cutting it with a special diamond-headed cleaver. After they have prepared both ends, they place them into a fusion splicer. At the press of a button, the splicer fuses the two fibers together. When working with fibers, technicians must keep the work area very clean and free from any dirt and particles. Dirt on the cable can impair the transmission of the signal. Technicians must also be careful when cutting the fiber, as tiny pieces of glass can get on the skin.

Fiber optics technicians may work as *assemblers,* for which they work at a bench cutting and measuring fiber, or *installers,* for which they lay the cable and make repairs on site.

What Is It Like to Be a Fiber Optics Technician?

Chad Tietje is in the field most of the time, and he works from systems designed by engineers. The engineers map out the specifications for MUXes, or multiplexers, that convert electrical signals into light and allow data to be transmitted over fiber optic cables. These signals may come into a building through copper cables, while the building itself contains fiber optic cables. The conversion of the signal to light enables data to be transmitted farther, secures communications, and reduces interference.

Lingo to Learn

Bandwidth The frequencies at which fiber optic terminal devices can transmit data. (Clear, fast exchange of data requires a high bandwidth.)

CATV Community antenna television, refers typically to cable TV.

Cleave Controlled cutting of a glass fiber to create a flat, smooth, fiber end.

Demultiplexer A piece of equipment that separates signals that have been combined by a multiplexer.

LAN Local area network, linking the communication sources in a small area, such as an office building or short distances between buildings.

Multiplexer Modules that convert electrical signals into light and allow data to be transmitted over fiber optic cabling.

Optical fiber A fiber made of glass or plastic, capable of guiding light along its axis, and used in fiber optic cabling.

The technicians take the engineers' plans and put them to work. "There is at least one MUX in about every big building there is," Chad says. "A big building has a lot of data, and a lot of networks, going through it. It takes a fiber MUX to actually hold all this information and transport it. So that means many lines that we have to map out and put in place and MUX into light."

Chad is essentially ensuring the transport of information. "I turn a signal into light, and I transport it to where it needs to go on that line, then de-MUX it back into a signal. Then it goes through the equipment back into copper. LANs, home telephones, data lines, any aspect of communications is done on our MUX, then we transport it."

Following an engineer's plans is not always easy; the designs sometimes have mistakes, and it is up to the technician to find these mistakes and correct them. "We don't like to go back to the contractor to have them recharge us to do something they did wrong," Chad says. "If they've switched the fibers, with the receive going to transmit and the transmit going to

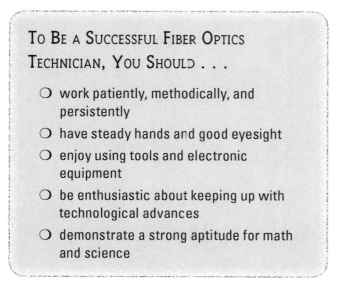

TO BE A SUCCESSFUL FIBER OPTICS TECHNICIAN, YOU SHOULD . . .

○ work patiently, methodically, and persistently

○ have steady hands and good eyesight

○ enjoy using tools and electronic equipment

○ be enthusiastic about keeping up with technological advances

○ demonstrate a strong aptitude for math and science

receive, you'll get an AIS [alarm indication signal]. You can get AIS from any number of things. It's a tedious process. You have to narrow down your problem, basically. You have to isolate it. You figure out one thing, it's not that, you go to another section."

Chad works Monday through Friday with a lot of overtime. Extra hours and weekends are not required by Chad's employer, but he finds that it is expected of the technicians in order to fulfill quotas. Despite the many hours of work, Chad is glad to have the training and experience in fiber optics. "If you know the job and know it well," he says, "you'll always have a job. Nothing moves faster than light, so they're always going to need fiber optics for communication."

Do I Have What It Takes to Be a Fiber Optics Technician?

"You have to have the initiative to learn," Chad says. "It's a very fast-paced job. But you also need to have patience. Some problems will take five minutes to solve, while some will take a week to solve. You can't just throw your hands up and say 'I quit, I'm giving it to somebody else.' That's not what they want to see. They want you to get the job done, no matter how long it takes you."

Because of the fine nature of the fibers, you should have a steady hand and good eyesight in assembling fiber optic cables. You also need good math skills for working with detailed plans and designs. Some companies may require you to have your own special fiber optic tools. Fiber optics technicians who work as assemblers spend most of their time sitting at a bench.

Technicians who work as installers usually work out in the field installing fiber beneath the ground. There is little physical exertion required because machinery is used to dig the trenches. Fiber optics technicians spend part of their time outside repairing fiber, and part of their time in a van preparing the fibers for installation. They may also install fiber cables in buildings; this requires some climbing of ladders and working beneath floor boards.

How Do I Become a Fiber Optics Technician?

Chad received his training on the job. "The work isn't hard," Chad says, "if you have the initiative to go out and do it. If you go into it wanting to learn, you're going to learn."

EDUCATION

High School

There aren't really any specific high school courses that will prepare you for work as a fiber optics technician, but shop classes will give you experience

A technician monitors optical fibers being wound onto a spool. *(Maximilian Stock Ltd. / Photo Researchers Inc.)*

In-depth

History

A need to convey messages quickly led to experimentation in the use of light to communicate. Before the introduction of the electric telegraph in the mid-1800s, a series of semaphores atop towers allowed for communication between tower operators. Ships also used light signals to communicate with each other. But the reliability of wires to carry electricity, and the invention of the electric telegraph and the telephone, put the further development of optical communications on hold.

Studies in the field of medicine led to the discovery that rods of glass or plastic could carry light. In the 1950s, these developments helped such engineers as Alec Reeves of Great Britain in the experimentation of fiber optics for telecommunications. High television and telephone use demanded more transmission bandwidth, and the invention of the laser in 1960 made optical communications a reality. Technical barriers remained, however, and experimentation continued for many years, leading to the first telephone field trials in 1977.

working with tools to complete a variety of projects. In these classes, you may also be working with electrical plans and blueprints. Speech and writing classes will help you develop your communication skills.

Postsecondary Training

A college degree is not required, but can give you an edge when looking for work as a fiber optics technician. A number of community colleges across the country offer programs in fiber optics technology or broadband networks technology. These programs offer such courses as cable construction, fiber optic installation techniques, singlemode and multimode systems, and wavelength and bandwidth. They also may include lab and certification components. Short-term training opportunities, lasting only a few days, may also be available at some schools. Programs generally last six months, but some programs designed for people starting their own fiber optics installation businesses may last longer. The Fiber Optic Association approves 120 training programs worldwide, and features a list of these programs on its Web site (http://www.thefoa.org).

CERTIFICATION OR LICENSING

Certification is not required of fiber optics technicians, but may be available from local community colleges and training programs. The Fiber Optic Association (FOA) offers different levels of national certification; there are currently over 13,000 fiber optics technicians (CFOT) certified by FOA, and the number is rapidly growing. Some technicians are certified by the National Association of Communications Contractors (NACC) in Fiber Optics.

LABOR UNIONS

Some fiber optics technicians are members of the International Brotherhood of Electrical Workers. The IBEW works with members and employers to negotiate wages, benefits, job training, safety controls, and other aspects of the job.

Who Will Hire Me?

Fiber optics technicians work for telephone companies, cable companies, and computer networking businesses. They may also work freelance, hiring on with companies on special installation projects. Technicians may work as fiber splicer technicians, fiber cable assemblers, and fiber testers and installers.

There are a great many sources of information about developments in fiber optics and the telecommunications industry, including Fiber Optic Technology (http://www.fiberoptictechnology.net), which features employment opportunities. The Fiber Optic Association also posts job openings, and can direct you to trade shows and conferences. When

ADVANCEMENT POSSIBILITIES

Fiber optics consultants advise companies on data transmission problems.

Fiber optics engineers design telecommunications systems, map out data, and give instructions and plans to technicians for installation.

Telecommunications salespeople evaluate customers' needs and orders the necessary materials for installation.

you complete a fiber optics technology program, your school will be able to direct you to local job opportunities.

Where Can I Go from Here?

Even without special fiber optics training, fiber optics technicians may be able to enter the job market in an entry-level position with a telecommunications company. The company may have its own training program, or offer tuition reimbursement for outside seminars in fiber optics technology. After gaining experience working with fiber optic cable, fiber optics technicians may be able to move into a management or executive position. They may also become consultants, advising companies on data transmission problems.

Chad plans on going to school. "I want to be an engineer," he says, "the one who actually maps the stuff out, and figures out what needs to go where, how it works, what it does."

What Are the Salary Ranges?

According to the U.S. Department of Labor, median annual earnings for line installers and repairers were $41,000 in 2003. Those in the lowest paid 10 percent made $22,700 while those in the highest paid 10 percent earned $59,000.

A 2005 review by Salary.com of earnings nationwide for telecommunications technicians reported an annual median salary for entry level technicians of $40,204, with the lowest paid earning $35,155 and the highest

paid earning $46,748. With two or more years of experience, technicians earned between $43,499 to $58,387 with a median of $50,958.

Companies offer a variety of benefit packages, which can include any of the following: paid holidays, vacations, and sick days; personal days; medical, dental, and life insurance; profit-sharing plans; 401(k) plans; retirement and pension plans; and educational assistance programs.

What Is the Job Outlook?

The U.S. Department of Labor expects employment of line installers and repairers to grow about as fast as the average through 2012. Digital transmissions will soon be the norm for telecommunications—not only do modern offices require data communications systems, but cable companies are investing in fiber optics to offer digital TV, as well as quality phone service. Also, the cost of fiber is dropping, which means more companies will invest in fiber optics. Corning, which manufactures about one-half of the world's supply of fiber, reports that optical fiber consumption in 2004 was 55 million kilometers. North America accounts for 30 percent of the demand, followed by China at 25 percent. Western Europe and Japan each account for 15 percent of the optical fiber demand.

How Do I Learn More?

PROFESSIONAL ORGANIZATIONS

The following are organizations that provide information on fiber optics careers, accredited schools and scholarships, certification, and possible employers:

The Fiber Optic Association
1119 South Mission Road, Suite 3551
Fallbrook, CA 92028
760-451-3655
info@thefoa.org
http://www.thefoa.org

Optical Society of America
2010 Massachusetts Avenue, NW
Washington, DC 20036-1023
202-223-8130
info@osa.org
http://www.osa.org

Women in Cable & Telecommunications
14555 Avion Parkway, Suite 250
Chantilly, VA 20151
703-234-9810
information@wict.org
http://www.wict.org

BIBLIOGRAPHY

The following is a sampling of materials relating to the professional concerns and development of fiber optics technicians:

Chomycz, Bob. *Fiber Optic Installers Field Manual.* New York: McGraw Hill, 2000.

Crisp, John. *Introduction to Fiber Optics.* Boston: Butterworth Heinemann, 1997.

Hayes, Jim. *Fiber Optics Technician's Manual.* Albany, N.Y.: Delmar, 2000.

Hecht, Jeff. *Understanding Fiber Optics.* 4th ed. Paramus, N.J.: Prentice Hall, 2001.

Sterling, Donald. *Technician's Guide to Fiber Optics.* 4th ed. Albany, N.Y.: Thomson Delmar Learning, 2003.

FIRE PROTECTION ENGINEERING TECHNICIANS

Richard Rowell walks through the office building ensuring that his design plans are being properly installed. In his years as a fire protection technician, he has worked on a variety of projects, ranging from government designs of very obscure systems, such as clean agent systems protecting computer rooms, to private designs for homes of the wealthy requiring state of the art fire alarms.

His current job involves working within code requirements to design fire alarm and sprinkler systems. Richard has seen the project through from the planning stages of budget and assigning personnel, the design stages of preparing reports and drawings, and the administration stage of meeting with clients, contractors, and local authorities.

"The work has a goal," Richard says about the appeal of the work, "an ending. Unlike sales or people-specific lines of work, I have a feel for what I'm going to be doing and when I will be finished. There's a sense of accomplishment when a project is closed out and you go to see your system at work."

What Does a Fire Protection Engineering Technician Do?

Each year, fire causes billions of dollars of damage to property and claims many thousands of lives. Helping to prevent fires and to reduce the destruction they cause is the chief concern of the fire protection engineering technician.

Fire protection engineering technicians help design fire alarm and sprinkler systems to protect commercial, residential, and industrial buildings from the hazards of fire. They are employed by local fire departments, fire insurance companies, government agencies, and businesses that design, fabricate, install, or sell fire protection devices and equipment.

The primary role of the fire protection engineering technician is to draft plans for the installation of fire protection systems for buildings and other structures. They must create plans that adhere to strict fire protection and building codes, design systems that

Definition
Fire protection engineering technicians design and draft plans for the installation of fire protection systems. They also estimate the cost and oversee the installation of their fire protection plans.

Alternative Job Titles
Fire alarm superintendents
Fire inspectors
Fire insurance adjusters
Fire safety technicians

High School Subjects
Chemistry
Mathematics

Personal Skills
Following instructions
Mechanical/manipulative

Salary Range
$28,160 to $45,810 to $71,330

Minimum Educational Level
High school diploma

Certification or Licensing
Required by certain states

Outlook
About as fast as the average

DOT
373

GOE
02.07.02

NOC
6262

O*NET-SOC
17-2111.02

will perform as designed in the event of a fire, and provide cost-effective solutions for the property owner.

Fire protection engineering technicians often take their cues from engineers and architects who develop specifications, plans, and design standards. Once the design decisions have been determined, the technician creates working plans and layout drawings. The technician analyzes the blueprints and specifications to select the appropriate type and size of fire protection system.

Fire protection engineering technicians also assist in the installation of fire protection systems to ensure that the working plans are being followed.

It is not unusual for technicians to specialize in one kind of fire protection system, such as foam, water, dry chemicals, or gas.

Fire protection engineering technicians work in the larger field of fire prevention. Within the field, there are many specialists, scientists, and others who work together to minimize the risk of fire.

Fire protection engineers have completed a higher level of education than fire protection engineering technicians. They evaluate information to determine the extent of fire and explosion potential. Fire protection engineers may also conduct studies on fabric flammability, fire safety in high-rise buildings, or evaluate the damage caused to property by fire.

Insurance companies employ a number of fire protection professionals. *Fire insurance inspectors* work for insurance companies. They inspect buildings to determine the risk of fire and make recommendations for improving fire safety. *Fire insurance adjusters* investigate claims for loss due to fire, compute rates for adjustment, and settle the claims.

Fire inspectors check firefighting equipment and report any potential fire hazards. They recommend changes in equipment, practice, materials, or methods to reduce fire hazards.

Plant protection inspectors inspect industrial properties to assess the potential for fire and report their findings and make recommendations to eliminate any fire hazards.

Fire alarm superintendents inspect fire suppression systems and fire alarms in public, private, and government buildings.

Sprinkler layout technicians plan how sprinklers and piping should be installed in buildings. They work with blueprints and building plans designed by engineers and architects and must make sure their working plans conform to the standards and specifications indicated.

What Is It Like to Be a Fire Protection Engineering Technician?

Richard Rowell says his responsibilities as a fire protection technician center on providing a client with a system that meets that client's individual needs. "This is broken down into steps," he says. "I design, according to code requirements and the client's

Lingo to Learn

Fire door A door treated with a flame retardant to block or slow the passage of flame or dangerous smoke.

Flame-retardant Chemical or substance that resists burning.

Flammable A material that ignites easily or is capable of burning.

Hydrostatic testing A pressure test to determine the safety of a fire extinguisher.

Water pressure The degree of force at which water is channeled through pipes.

requirements, a fire alarm design, sprinkler design, life safety design and/or code consulting services. I manage the project which includes scheduling, task hours, invoicing, and dealing with any problems that might arise to ensure that the project doesn't go over either the company's or the client's budgets."

To prepare for a job, Richard reviews the project extensively, studying criteria, background, budget, and the scope of the project. He also assigns personnel to the job. He then visits the site to determine the existing conditions and to meet with the client. When it is time to design the project, he prepares reports, drawings, specifications, and any necessary calculations, such as hydraulic, cost estimating, and life safety calculations (occupant load, travel distance, etc.). Construction administration involves reviewing the contractor's intent, hardware, and experience. He then visits the site during construction.

"Sometimes there isn't enough time in a day to complete the work," Richard says. "Sometimes my work load is really light. An eight-hour day usually cuts it, but sometimes you have to sit there for 10, 12, 14 hours to get something done. In one extreme case, I worked 28 hours straight." Despite the occasional extra hours he works, Richard does not find the work stressful, and he does not take the work home with him. He appreciates the variety of the work projects, which keeps his job from becoming mundane. "Sometimes you come across something so new and different, your brain gets overloaded from figuring out where to begin." Richard also enjoys the travel that the work demands from time to time. He has been sent to California, New York, Europe, and other places.

Frank Ballante's work as a fire protection technician involves servicing existing fire protection systems, mostly in restaurants. "The kitchens have special fire systems," he says. "They have to be serviced every month. I also service fire extinguishers and some sprinkler systems inside companies." Servicing involves testing the systems to assure they work properly, and replacing parts when necessary. Because different sprinkler systems exist, Frank has to be familiar with a variety of ways to disarm and "dry fire," or trip, the systems. Following a successful test, Frank certifies the system for when the fire inspector visits the restaurant. "A lot of this involves climbing," Frank says. "It's pretty physical work." Frank also checks fire extinguishers to ensure that they have the proper amount of pressure and chemical.

Frank spends most of his time out in the field, seeing to the approximately 1,000 accounts that are his responsibility. "You're your own boss, pretty much," he says. "You're always in different companies, seeing different things, meeting different people."

Larry Rosen also works with restaurant fire protection. He designs and installs the restaurant hood systems in the kitchens. "I take an exhaust hood in a kitchen," Larry says, "and protect the cooking equipment with nozzles that spray wet chemical. I have to do pipe fitting for that." Designing the system involves working within manufacturers' requirements in order to create a hood with the proper number of nozzles at the correct height.

Though Larry does not feel that the work is very dangerous, he does have to be careful of certain hazards when installing a system. He says, "There's quite a bit of drilling and hole making in stainless steel for the various penetrations into the hood. I also use a pipe cutter and threading machine for the pipe work." But Larry likes working with his hands, and is happy to be out in the field, for the most part. "If things are going well, I'm not in the office much. I work in the whole county so each city has its own fire department and own set of rules." Having to deal with authorities and the varying regulations of different cities can be difficult, but the rules of the fire departments are mostly consistent throughout the county.

Do I Have What It Takes to Be a Fire Protection Engineering Technician?

Fire protection engineering technicians provide a service that can save lives and protect property in the event of a fire. Because their work is so important, fire protection engineering technicians must be competent in the skills that the career requires.

If you want to be a successful fire protection engineering technician, you should have basic drafting skills and be able to understand and grasp spatial relationships. Communication skills are important as well—if you cannot convey your ideas or plans clearly or accurately, your fire protection plans are not going to go far. You must be mechanically inclined and computer savvy. "Attention to details," Richard says, "organization, and ability to schedule are critical, as well as flexibility and the ability to learn."

Another challenge is being able to work with complex equations and calculations. The size and width of the pipe, the amount of pipe required, and the spray area of the sprinkler head are all variables that you must consider when designing a fire sprinkler system. While many of the calculations are performed using computer programs specifically designed for the field, much of the work must still be done by hand. "Problem solving is very important," Larry says. "No two jobs are the same. Basic math skills are helpful, not just for the design, but for calculating what a system has or needs."

If working out in the field, you should be prepared for some climbing and stooping, along with carrying equipment. "It's strenuous," says Frank, "physically demanding, so you have to be in pretty good shape."

How Do I Become a Fire Protection Engineering Technician?

Richard holds an associate's degree, but has learned mostly on the job. Larry and Frank have also received their training at work. Larry is required to be certified by the manufacturer of the systems on which he works. "We go through a day or two of training," he says, "take the test, and get our certificate." Frank also holds certification from manufacturers, and he stresses that students should learn as much as they can about electrical systems.

EDUCATION

High School

A high school diploma is mandatory for anyone considering a career as a fire protection engineering technician. High school courses can provide the basic skills that fire protection engineering technicians use each day on the job, such as science and mathematics.

High school courses in physics, mathematics, algebra, calculus, and geometry are important to learn the basic principles involved in making calculations and measurements. Courses in computer science and computer-aided design (CAD) are also recommended, since drafting is such an essential skill for some fire protection engineering technicians, and most all of them work with computers.

Do not think, however, that you can forget about English and focus on math and science. Written and verbal communication skills are crucial for fire protection engineering technicians.

Summer or part-time jobs with fire alarm installation companies or sprinkler system service companies will expose you to the daily rigors of fire protection engineering technicians. Insurance companies may also have job openings in their fire insurance divisions.

Postsecondary Training

The most common way of becoming a fire protection engineering technician is through on-the-job training. As one's knowledge and skills develop, it is then

FYI

The following are statistics from the National Fire Protection Association report "Overview of 2003 U.S. Fire Experience":

- Fire departments attended 1,584,500 fires in 2003, which was a decrease of 6.1 percent from 2002.
- Of all fire deaths, 3,145 occurred in homes, an increase of 17.8 percent, or back to the levels of 2001–2002.
- In 2003, fires caused an estimated $12.3 billion in property damage.
- An estimated 37,500 structure fires in 2003 resulted from arson or suspected arson, a decrease of 15.7 percent from 2002.
- In 2003, more people died in highway vehicle fires (455 deaths) than in apartment fires (410 deaths).

possible to find better-paying and more interesting work with companies that design and install fire extinguishing systems.

Some colleges and training schools, such as Delaware Technical and Community College and Northeast Wisconsin Technical College, offer two-year programs in fire protection engineering technology. In addition to learning skills in such courses as drafting and computer science, students may also find work-study opportunities that will make it easier to find employment after graduation.

The curriculum in an associate's degree program in fire protection engineering technology includes classes in industrial fire hazards, chemistry, codes and standards, water supply analysis, and fire protection design, just to name a few. Associate's degrees in fire science or mechanical engineering technology are also applicable in fire protection engineering technology.

If you aspire to become a fire protection engineer, you'll need a bachelor's degree from a four-year college. Check with your school counselor for additional information or contact the Society of Fire Protection Engineers or the National Fire Protection Association.

CERTIFICATION OR LICENSING

Licensing requirements for fire protection engineering technicians vary from state to state. Certification is conducted by the National Institute for Certification in Engineering Technologies (NICET), a division of the National Society of Professional Engineers (NSPE). Fire protection engineering technicians must pass written examinations and accumulate five years of work experience or related education to become Certified Engineering Technicians (CET) in Fire Protection Engineering Technology. Subfields in automatic sprinkler system layout, special hazards systems, and fire alarm systems are also available for those who wish to specialize. A CET in automatic sprinkler system layout, for example, is qualified to independently prepare working plans and layouts from an engineer or architect's designs. While the CET certification is not always required, it can give you a competitive edge in the job market.

SCHOLARSHIPS OR GRANTS

Scholarship and grant opportunities are often available from colleges with fire science or fire protection engineering programs. Contact your advisor for further details. You may also find scholarships through professional organizations or large manufacturers of fire equipment.

INTERNSHIPS AND VOLUNTEERSHIPS

Internships or cooperative work-study programs where students study part time and work part time may be available through college programs. Large insurance companies or manufacturers may also sponsor internships. It would be a good idea to check with your departmental advisor or the school's placement office.

If you are interested in the hands-on firefighting end of fire protection, it may be possible to join a group of volunteer firefighters. This may be a good way to work your way into the field, gain some experience and firsthand knowledge of the cause and prevention of fires, and determine which specialization may be right for you.

Who Will Hire Me?

Richard began as a CAD operator with his current employer, then trained in the fire protection division of the company. Larry started as a fire extinguisher

FYI

In 1874, American Henry S. Parmalee invented sprinklers to protect his piano factory. While the pianos remained safe, human beings sometimes did not. Sprinklers were used primarily to protect buildings, such as factories and warehouses, until the 1940s and 1950s, when some large fires took many lives. In Boston in 1942, a fire in the Coconut Grove Nightclub killed 492 individuals. In 1946, a fire in the LaSalle Hotel in Chicago left 61 people dead, and a fire in the Winecoff Hotel in Atlanta took the lives of 119 individuals. Since then, fire sprinkler systems have become as important for protecting lives as for safeguarding buildings and material wares.

technician, before gaining more training to become a fire safety technician.

The most common employers of fire protection engineering technicians are private companies that design and install fire extinguishing systems. These companies work as subcontractors, members of the construction team that build or renovate commercial, industrial, or residential property. The size of these companies varies—it may be a "one-man shop" or a large business that employs 50 or more fire protection engineering technicians. These companies may also specialize in fire sprinkler systems, fire alarm systems, restaurant systems, and more.

Fire protection engineering technicians may also work for private consulting firms or insurance agencies. At these companies, the role of the fire protection engineering technician is to assist in the evaluation of a structure's fire hazards and suggest ways to correct them.

Where Can I Go from Here?

All the fire protection technicians featured here are happy with their jobs, and do not anticipate any major changes. Richard hopes to follow the line of promotion at his company, but Frank prefers to stick with the field work. "I like being on the road," he says. "I don't know if I'd want to move up into management. They're inside all day and have a lot more responsibilities."

Some fire protection technicians find employment with state or local fire regulatory agencies and inspect fire alarms and fire sprinkler systems in buildings.

With further education, some technicians choose to become fire protection engineers. Fire protection engineers have typically completed a four-year course of study in fire science or industrial engineering. Fire protection engineers are more deeply involved in identifying fire hazards and often conduct experiments to determine a material's flammability. They also strive to improve or develop new methods of fire suppression.

What Are the Salary Ranges?

Salaries for fire protection engineering technicians are comparable to those of other engineering technicians. According to the *Occupational Outlook Handbook*, median annual earnings of engineering technicians were $38,180 in 2003. Those technicians in the lowest paid 10 percent earned $23,700, while those in the highest paid 10 percent earned $62,460. The U.S. Department of Labor reports that in 2003 fire inspectors and investigators had median annual earnings of $45,810, with the lowest paid 10 percent earning $28,160 and the highest paid 10 percent earning $71,330.

According to the National Fire Sprinkler Association, Inc. (NFSA), which offers four levels of certification, fire protection engineering technicians with CET certification in the fire sprinkler field earn $30,000 to $50,000 a year. Entry level certified technicians, as expected, earn less than those who have reached Level IV, or senior engineering technician.

Fire protection engineering technicians generally receive full benefits packages from their employers.

What Is the Job Outlook?

The *Occupational Outlook Handbook* reports that job growth for all fire fighting jobs, including fire investigators and fire prevention and code inspectors is expected to be about as fast as the average through 2012. The outlook for a career as a fire protection engineering technician should be good in the years ahead. Since the 1960s, the field of fire prevention

and fire safety has been growing. Many businesses and industries realize that it is more cost efficient to invest in fire prevention systems, such as sprinklers and alarms, than it is to replace a building or property destroyed by fire.

To some extent, the amount of work available for fire protection engineering technicians will depend upon the construction industry. When construction is booming, the demand for the services that a fire protection engineering technician provides will also increase. But because older buildings also need fire suppression systems or have systems that need upgrading, fire protection engineering technicians should be able to find work throughout the year.

A fire protection technician's job will also be affected by changing regulations. New safety precautions and government restrictions can result in companies needing to hire more technicians in order to meet the demands of fire codes.

How Do I Learn More?

PROFESSIONAL ORGANIZATIONS

To learn about certification, educational programs, professional development, technical information about sprinkler systems, and careers in fire protection, contact the following organizations:

ADVANCEMENT POSSIBILITIES

Fire protection engineers, or fire loss prevention engineers, advise and assist private and public organizations and military services in safeguarding life and property against fire, explosion, and related hazards.

Fire prevention research engineers conduct research to determine causes and methods of preventing fires and prepare educational materials concerning fire prevention for insurance companies.

Fire insurance claim examiners analyze fire insurance claims to determine the extent of an insurance carrier's liability and settle claims with claimants in accordance with policy provisions.

National Fire Protection Association
1 Batterymarch Park
Quincy, MA 02269
617-770-3000
http://www.nfpa.org

National Fire Sprinkler Association
PO Box 1000
Patterson, NY 12563
845-878-4200
info@nfsa.org
http://www.nfsa.org

National Institute for Certification in Engineering
    Technologies
1420 King Street
Alexandria, VA 22314
888-476-4238
http://www.nicet.org

Society of Fire Protection Engineers
7315 Wisconsin Avenue, Suite 620E

Bethesda, MD 20814
301-718-2910
sfpehqtrs@sfpe.org
http://www.sfpe.org

BIBLIOGRAPHY

The following is a sampling of materials relating to the professional concerns and development of fire protection engineering technicians:

Cassidy, Kevin A. *Fire Safety and Loss Prevention.* Boston: Butterworth-Heinemann, 1992.

Drysdale, Dougal. *Introduction to Fire Dynamics.* 2d ed. New York: John Wiley & Sons, 1998.

Nolan, Dennis. *Encyclopedia of Fire Protection.* Albany, N.Y.: Thomson Delmar Learning, 2000.

Traister, John E. *Security/Fire-Alarm Systems: Design, Installation, Maintenance.* New York: McGraw-Hill Text, 1995.

FLUID POWER MECHANICS

||||||||||||||||||||||||||||||||||||||||||||||||||||||||

"Looks like a hydraulic fluid leak," Stan Durnal, a fluid power mechanic, says as he examines a huge orange and green combine in the repair shop of Claas. The combine, although new, had been left outside an equipment dealership through a harsh Iowa winter and was sent back to Claas's North American headquarters for repair. The greasy liquid that should be inside the hydraulic cylinder covers Stan's hands. "We'll fix it up, and it'll be good as new," he says, wiping his hands with a soft cloth.

The warehouse/repair room is filled with farm equipment of all shapes and sizes, most of which uses fluid power to move, lift, or pull. Even the forklift used to stock the warehouse shelves uses fluid power.

What Does a Fluid Power Mechanic Do?

From agriculture and construction to industry and recreation, fluid power is used to make life easier and industry more efficient. Anywhere there is moving equipment, fluid power is most likely part of that equipment and helps to push, pull, rotate, regulate, or drive.

There are two types of fluid power machines. Hydraulic machines use water, oil, or another liquid in a closed system to transmit the energy to do needed work. Pneumatic machines use air or another gas instead of a liquid. *Fluid power mechanics* may work with either or both of these types of machines. They operate, maintain, repair, and test fluid power equipment or components.

Fluid power mechanics who are responsible for testing fluid power systems typically work with a team or group that includes other mechanics, engineers, or scientists. The mechanic is responsible for setting up fluid power equipment as well as testing that equipment under operating conditions. This is accomplished by connecting the equipment to testing units that measure fluid pressure, flow rates, and power loss from friction or wear. Once the equipment is established and working, the mechanic gathers data for development and quality control and may recommend changes to the system.

Definition
Fluid power mechanics manufacture, assemble, install, test, maintain, and service fluid power systems, which utilize the pressure of a liquid or gas to transmit or control power.

Alternative Job Titles
Fluid power technicians
Hydraulic technicians
Machinists
Pneumatic technicians

High School Subjects
Mathematics
Technical/shop

Personal Skills
Following instructions
Mechanical/manipulative

Salary Range
$24,710 to $37,170 to $53,720

Minimum Educational Level
Some postsecondary training

Certification or licensing
Voluntary

Outlook
More slowly than the average

DOT
864

GOE
N/A

NOC
2132

O*NET-SOC
N/A

Many times, fluid power mechanics are involved in the maintenance and repair of fluid power systems. They are the official troubleshooters, and when a machine breaks down or needs adjusting, the mechanic is called to detect and fix the problem. Knowledge of hydraulics, pneumatics, electric motors, control systems, and mechanical devices is necessary for the fluid power mechanic to properly diagnose and repair problems.

Fluid power mechanics often work in plants or factories where fluid power systems are used in manufacturing processes. For example, pneumatically controlled machines that might bolt together products on an automated assembly line may be in need of repair or service, a job for the fluid power mechanic.

Lingo to Learn

Actuator A mechanical device designed to move or control something.

Flow rates The rate of flow in a fluid power system—measured in GPM (gallons per minute).

Fluid mechanics A branch of mechanics that deals with the properties of liquids and gases.

Fluid power The technology of transmitting energy through pressurized fluid or air.

Hydraulic cylinders Devices that accept hydraulic pressure and use it to create motion to do work.

Hydraulic energy The use of water, oil, or another liquid in a closed system to transmit the energy used to do work.

Machine tool A machine designed for shaping solid work. The machines often rely on fluid power to function.

Pneumatic energy The use of air or another gas in a closed system to transmit the energy used to do work.

Research and development teams also need the help of fluid power mechanics to find better ways to develop and use fluid power systems. Mechanics may help set up and test equipment under operating conditions.

Fluid power mechanics can also work in sales and services for companies that make and sell fluid power equipment to industrial plants. With their knowledge and background, mechanics are ideal sales and service representatives and can travel to plants, providing customers with specialized information and assistance with their equipment needs.

Fluid power mechanics analyze blueprints, drawings, and specifications, as well as communicate with the rest of the team both verbally and with written technical reports.

Fluid power mechanics use many types of equipment and machinery, including milling, shaping, grinding, and drilling machines to make precision parts for fluid power equipment. They also use sensitive measuring instruments to measure parts and hand and power tools to assemble the components in the fluid power system.

What Is It Like to Be a Fluid Power Mechanic?

Stan is a fluid power mechanic and service manager at Claas's North American headquarters in Columbus, Indiana. Claas is the world's largest manufacturer of harvesting equipment, and, as is common throughout the agriculture industry, fluid power is used in almost every aspect of Claas's equipment.

Stan's primary duties as a fluid power mechanic involve the maintenance and repair of fluid power farm machinery. Components and machines from all over North America are sent to Stan's repair shop to be fixed and sent back to the owner or retailer or are sold as used farm equipment at the headquarters facility.

Stan must be familiar with many types of fluid power systems—mostly hydraulic—from the largest combine to the smallest handheld equipment.

"Fluid power is the thing that makes our machinery move," Stan says. "Our machines operate on a stop/go basis, which means if everything's okay then the machine is moving, and if one thing is wrong, it's not. When the machine's not moving, the operator is obviously not happy."

Keeping that operator (and customer) happy is Stan's job, so efficiently analyzing and fixing fluid system problems are essential. With many years of experience, Stan is familiar with the basic problems that arise in hydraulic farm equipment systems. "Bad fluid, a faulty seal, or a leak are mostly the causes of breakdown. Because the hydraulic cylinder moves so many times during operation, it is bound to be where problems occur," Stan says. "We basically do whatever we have to do to get the machine running. The good news is that fluid power systems are very fixable. Finding the problem is usually the hard part."

Stan also coordinates on-site training at Claas. In the training room and on the repair shop floor, Stan must communicate with other employees, teaching them how to repair and analyze the machines.

Although Stan's work involves mostly repair, technicians and mechanics in other industries and facilities may work with manufacturing, testing, or developing fluid power equipment.

Stan's repair shop is very large and includes huge garage doors to accommodate the immense size of the agricultural equipment. The different work areas are often dotted with grease and other fluids that have leaked out during hydraulic repair.

Many fluid power mechanics work in industrial settings. Some mechanics work as fluid power field mechanics. Field mechanics travel to different customer locations to repair equipment for a manufacturer, and others may work in a laboratory or test facility to develop new ways to use fluid power.

Grady Coggins performs field service work in Georgia, and operates his own business. When he receives a call from a client, he goes to the site and tests the equipment, orders or purchases any necessary parts, then returns to the site to repair or replace them. Testing includes checking flows, pressures, and electrical circuits. "About 80 percent of the hydraulic calls I go on are electrical problems," Grady says, "not hydraulic problems." To locate the problem, Grady uses a process of elimination. "You've got certain places that you start, then you work out. If you know one thing works perfectly, then you go from there and test everything else."

Grady uses electrical meters, test units that detect flows and pressures, and digital and analog test equipment, among other tools. "It takes about $20,000 worth of equipment to test a system out." Grady has built up his collection of tools over his more than 20 years of doing field service work.

"Everything hydraulic is logical," he says. "You cannot repair two things at one time on one machine. Everybody wants to get up there and turn this knob, and it doesn't do anything. Well, turn it back to where it was and go on to the next step. If you don't turn it back, then you've got two problems. You've created a problem, and you're looking for another one." Usually such poor efforts of repair are what lead to a client's service call to Grady. "Every piece of equipment I go to is different from the last one. You start at the pump, and you make sure you've got a good pump. Test the pump first, test your valves, test your filters, and test your cylinders. That's before you even need the schematic." The schematic is a diagram which details the flows, pressures, and electrical circuits. Grady uses a computer program which assists him with creating a schematic, if the original schematic for the machine is unavailable. "You can look at a valve, but the valve doesn't tell you what it does. The number tells you, but you've got to know what that number means. If you've got a schematic, you can

look at it and know what that valve does. The valves all look alike, they just do different things."

Do I Have What It Takes to Be a Fluid Power Mechanic?

Fluid power mechanics must be good at understanding and analyzing mechanical systems. Because of the troubleshooting nature of the job, the ability to meet a challenge is also extremely important.

Henry Math, a technical services manager for a fluid power distributor, says, "Mechanical aptitude is probably the most important quality." He says mechanics also must be able to accept changes as they come along. "The people I send out to do work must be creative," he says. "A lot of times, we'll get to a job site and what we're told was to be there isn't always what is there. So we have to be able to take a step back and evaluate."

The work of a fluid power technician is interesting, challenging, and not at all repetitive. "I really like the challenge of the job," Stan says. "You always have to be flexible and look at each repair individually." The ability to work well with others is important as well, since fluid power mechanics often work on teams.

"You can't be afraid to get your hands dirty," adds Stan, explaining that, for some people, the potential grimy nature of fluid power work might not be appealing. Also, the physical strength required to work on some of the larger machines and systems might be considered a drawback.

"I enjoy fixing things and finding out what's wrong with them," Stan says. "I think a natural curiosity and talent for understanding complicated systems are most important to this job."

TO BE A SUCCESSFUL FLUID POWER MECHANIC, YOU SHOULD . . .

○ have excellent mechanical aptitude

○ have an inquisitive and analytical mind

○ be able to work well and communicate with others

○ enjoy challenges and troubleshooting problems

How Do I Become a Fluid Power Mechanic?

Many older fluid power mechanics like Stan were hired by companies on the basis of some technical expertise and were then trained in fluid power technology. Currently, however, postsecondary training is extremely beneficial if you want to become a fluid power mechanic. "Attend a technical school in fluid power," Henry advises. "I work with people who have four-year university degrees in fluid power, and in my opinion they haven't learned as much as the people who went through the two-year programs."

Grady stresses the importance of an apprenticeship. "You've got to learn the trade," he says. "It's a complicated trade, and many trades in one. You've got to know how to work a lathe, a milling machine, a grinder, a welder, torches. You've got to know metallurgy." Grady recommends vocational school, and to learn how to read schematics and blueprints. "You have to pay your dues in the industry. If you don't know what you're doing, you can get seriously hurt."

EDUCATION

High School

High school subjects that provide a good background for fluid power mechanics include computer science, mathematics, physics, shop, English, and drafting. With the movement toward integrating fluid power and electronics, an electronics class would also be helpful. Joining organizations where you can gain skills working on fluid power equipment or any type of machinery would be beneficial. Working on automobiles or farm machinery will give you experience working with your hands and learning how to solve mechanical problems.

Postsecondary Training

Although a college diploma is not mandatory in order to become a fluid power mechanic, most employers prefer to hire those who have had at least two years of postsecondary training. Postsecondary training may be pursued at vocational or community colleges or may be provided by employers at their own training facilities or at outside educational facilities. Classes may include fluid power fundamentals and components, calculations (the application of math concepts), hydraulic components, accessories and circuits, electricity/electro-mechanical control, basic computers, systems analysis, and labs. There are only about 30 technical training programs that focus specifically on fluid power technology, but many provide related courses in mechanical or electronics technology, for example. These programs may lead to diplomas, certificates, or associate's degrees, depending on the school and the program.

Stan teaches in a company-sponsored training program that focuses on hands-on activities as well as classroom work. Taking up an entire wall of Stan's training room is a complete hydraulic system from a combine. This model can simulate real problems and allows trainees to actually see the system in progress. "We really try to present realistic problems so that the mechanics can learn in a nonthreatening classroom situation what may work when they're on the floor," Stan says.

CERTIFICATION OR LICENSING

Certification for fluid power mechanics is not mandatory but is available through the Fluid Power Certification Board, a division of the Fluid Power Society.

Certification consists of an optional educational review session followed by both a written and practical examination. The Fluid Power Society offers certification for fluid power mechanics and also fluid power engineers, specialists, and technicians. Technologies included in the certification programs include hydraulics, pneumatics, electronic control, and vacuum. Certifications are valid for five years and then the mechanic must be recertified based on career achievement over those past five years.

Though certification may be beneficial to experienced fluid power mechanics, hands-on education or apprenticeship is of much more importance to beginners. "Customers expect the certified fluid power specialist they hire to know more than 120 answers," Grady says, referring to the certification exam. "They expect him to have experience in the field." Grady believes that the certification process is too easy. Because of the dangers involved, those who work with fluid power must have first-hand understanding of the equipment.

SCHOLARSHIPS AND GRANTS

Information regarding scholarship opportunities may be available from professional associations. One source is the Fluid Power Educational Foundation, a division of the National Fluid Power Association.

Training facilities or colleges may also offer scholarships and financial awards, and can also

In-depth

Then and Now

Machinery that operates on fluid power has been used for thousands of years. Have you seen rotating paddle wheels with water flowing through? In Roman times, they were used to produce power necessary for milling.Today, however, fluid power systems are much more sophisticated. They are also more pervasive. You may not be aware of this, but fluid power plays a major role in our daily lives. Automatic door closers, bicycle pumps, brakes on your car, and spray guns all use fluid power systems to operate. Hydraulic-powered machines make plastic containers for milk, shampoo, and motor oil.

Fluid power systems are faster and less costly to operate than manual power, which means the cost savings can be passed on to the consumer.

direct students to scholarships offered by individual companies. Contact the financial aid offices or your advisor for additional details.

INTERNSHIPS AND VOLUNTEERSHIPS

Internship opportunities may be available at large manufacturing plants or through colleges. Consult your advisor or career placement office for information and possible leads.

A few employers may offer on-the-job training programs, although most prefer to hire candidates with some previous experience or training. It may be to your benefit to contact large companies you are interested in working for and inquire about internship opportunities.

LABOR UNIONS

Many mechanics working in industry and manufacturing may belong to labor unions. For example, the United Auto Workers of America would be the union for any technician or mechanic working in the automotive field. Union membership and dues vary from industry to industry. There is no specific union for fluid power mechanics.

Who Will Hire Me?

Fluid power is used in practically every branch of industry. Machine tools, cars, farm machinery, airplanes, boats, and kitchen appliances all use fluid power. It is one of the most versatile means of transmitting power and creating movement. This versatility also means that fluid power mechanics work in every facet of American industry, including aerospace, agriculture, construction, distribution, government, machine tools, manufacturing, marine, mining, packaging, plastics, and more.

Fluid power has always been used in farm equipment to provide the horsepower and speed needed for crop cultivation and harvesting. Energy is another area that utilizes fluid power in offshore oil drilling and other energy applications.

Mechanics in automation and industry help keep the integrated manufacturing systems working smoothly. In the area of construction, machines that dig, crush, level, and move earth and rock rely on fluid power equipment. In fact, the construction industry is one of the largest users of fluid power.

ADVANCEMENT POSSIBILITIES

Fluid power instructors teach the basics of fluid power, including hydraulic and pneumatic systems.

Field service representatives advise, repair, and work with the equipment of a manufacturer at the customer's location.

Sales/marketing personnel market and sell fluid power systems and components.

Application engineers design fluid power systems to accomplish required tasks.

Fluid power consultants work with different companies to analyze, design, or improve fluid power systems.

Stan started working at Claas because of a basic interest in agriculture that later developed into more specified training in fluid power. Most mechanics today will obtain their jobs through schools and placement offices.

Organizations such as the Fluid Power Society and the Fluid Power Educational Foundation have lists of their corporate members that can be used for job location.

Where Can I Go from Here?

Stan has already realized a few of his advancement goals since he is now the service manager at Claas and also plays a part in training other mechanics. Another area that he has an interest in is field service. Very similar to the job he currently holds, *field service representatives* travel to different areas of the country to solve problems with Claas equipment that is not shipped to the headquarters facility. Fluid power mechanics may also wish to move into sales or marketing positions. Although sales jobs are more administrative than mechanical, the representative will be able to use his or her knowledge of fluid power systems to help customers make appropriate purchasing decisions.

Henry is in the process of moving into the management of a division of his company. "That's one of the interesting things about the industry," he says. "If you get into it, and you know what you're doing, you can make things happen. Your growth potential is fairly unlimited. Most companies in the fluid power industry are real open. If you've got a better way of doing something, and you can prove your ideas are valid, you can kind of do things your own way."

Fluid power mechanics with additional education such as a bachelor's degree can advance into positions as application engineers or fluid power consultants. *Application engineers* apply engineering principles to design fluid power systems. *Fluid power consultants* are called upon by various companies to assist in analyzing, designing, or improving fluid power systems.

What Are the Salary Ranges?

Salaries can vary greatly depending on the type of work, the employer, and the geographical location. Most people in the industry agree, however, that salaries are increasing, and that hard working, experienced mechanics can find good financial reward. Those who don't graduate from a fluid power program may have to start at about $10 an hour until they gain the necessary experience that is attractive to employers; once the mechanic has learned the trade, the opportunities increase. The FPEF job placement survey found that graduates of key fluid power programs have starting annual salaries in the mid- to upper-$30,000 range. These starting salaries have increased by about $2,000 a year since 1997. Some schools reported seeing their students get salary offers of $50,000. Some companies are even offering substantial sign-on bonuses.

"If somebody wants to get out there and apply themselves," Grady says, "and they don't mind reading the books and getting dirty, they can make $100,000 to $150,000 a year. Everyone I know who owns a shop is trying to find mechanics."

The U.S. Department of Labor reports annual median earnings in 2003 for heavy vehicle and mobile equipment service technicians and mechanics of $37,170. The lowest paid 10 percent earned $24,710, and the highest paid 10 percent earned $53,720.

Because of the high demand for knowledgeable employees, fluid power mechanics are receiving good benefits along with the wage increases; benefits may include health and life insurance and retirement plans.

What Is the Job Outlook?

The U.S. Department of Labor projects slower than the average growth for this occupation through 2012. Employment opportunities will be best for those who have completed postsecondary training programs. Most companies across the country have been disappointed by the few numbers of graduates of fluid power programs. The demand definitely exceeds the supply, and this will likely continue in the years to come. Those graduates with hands-on experience who are willing to relocate will have the best opportunities and salary offers. Foreign fluid power companies are also looking for graduates who speak more than one language.

The job itself is also changing, requiring fluid power mechanics to stay on top of technological developments. Electronics and computers are playing more substantial roles in the controlling of hydraulics and pneumatics. The Internet is also allowing fluid power companies to expand by providing customers with 24-hour access to information and to reach global customers.

Environmental legislation may also continue to affect the industry and the job of the technician. Mechanics may have to do additional documentation to meet government regulations. Also, fluid power professionals expect there may be a move away from hydraulics toward pneumatics because of environmental and noise control issues.

How Do I Learn More?

PROFESSIONAL ORGANIZATIONS

For information on the fluid power industry, educational programs and scholarships, career opportunities, and certification, contact the following organizations:

Fluid Power Distributors Association
PO Box 1420
Cherry Hill, NJ 08034-0054
856-424-8998
http://www.fpda.org

National Fluid Power Association
3333 North Mayfair Road, Suite 211
Milwaukee, WI 53222-3219
414-778-3344
nfpa@nfpa.com
http://www.nfpa.com

Fluid Power Educational Foundation
3333 North Mayfair Road, Suite 211
Milwaukee, WI 53222
414-778-3364
info@fpef.org
http://www.fpef.org

Fluid Power Society
PO Box 1420
Cherry Hill, NJ 08034
800-303-8520
info@ifps.org
http://www.ifps.org

BIBLIOGRAPHY

The following is a sampling of materials relating to the professional concerns and development of fluid power mechanics:

Johnson, James. *Introduction to Fluid Power.* Albany, N.Y. Thomson Delmar Learning, 2001.

Kissell, Thomas E. *Electricity, Fluid Power, and Mechanical Systems for Industrial Maintenance.* Paramus, N.J.: Prentice Hall, 1998.

Kokernak, Robert P. *Fluid Power Technology.* Paramus, N.J.: Prentice Hall, 1999.

Sullivan, James A. *Fluid Power: Theory and Applications.* Paramus, N.J.: Prentice Hall, 1997.

Taylor, Robert P., and K. Hodge. *Analysis and Design of Energy Systems.* Paramus, N.J.: Prentice Hall, 1998.

Wright, Terry. *Fluid Machinery: Performance, Analysis, and Design.* Boca Raton, Fla.: CRC Press, 1999.

FOOD TECHNOLOGISTS

What happens to food after farmers grow it and before it hits the shelves at your neighborhood store? Who develops new brands of soup or cake mix, or things like freeze-dried coffee, powdered soup, and breakfast cereal? Who discovers new ways to use things like soybeans or tofu?

And who helps make sure things like fruit and vegetables do not spoil before they get to the store? Who determines the shelf life of a can of soup? Who helps develop the chemicals that control things like mold or rancidity? Who is responsible for all those labels on food? Finally, who develops the packaging that keeps food fresh, preserves it for as long as possible, helps it hold up during shipment, and makes it attractive to consumers?

Most of us take the food we eat for granted, rarely thinking about the complexities of its production. But the fact is, behind almost every food we buy is a history of research, development, testing, refining, and packaging. This is the world of the food technologist.

What Does a Food Technologist Do?

Food technologists help to ensure the safety and nutrition of processed foods. They develop new products, production methods, preserving techniques, and food distribution methods. They also create new packaging to improve the shelf life and preserve the nutritional value or other qualities of food. In addition, they develop food standards, nutrition labeling, safety and sanitary regulations, and waste management and water supply specifications.

Americans' constant appetite for new foods is part of what drives the profession of food technologist. But another important influence is advancing scientific knowledge. Food technologists help to apply advances in science and engineering to all phases of food development and production, improving the quality of the food we eat. This includes everything from developing ways to retain more nutrients in product processing to formulating low-fat and low-salt products, for example.

Definition
Food technologists use knowledge of the physical, microbiological, and chemical makeup of food to develop new or improved food products; devise new or improved food production, packaging, storage, and distribution technology; and test foods for compliance with industry and government specifications and regulations.

Alternative Job Title
Food scientists

High School Subjects
Biology
Chemistry
Family and consumer science

Personal Skills
Leadership/management
Technical/scientific

Salary Range
$29,250 to $49,610 to $86,930

Minimum Educational Level
Bachelor's degree

Certification or Licensing
Voluntary

Outlook
More slowly than the average

DOT
311

GOE
02.03.04

NOC
N/A

O*NET-SOC
19-1012.00, 19-4011.02

As the Institute of Food Technologists (IFT), a major trade group, points out, food technologists also come up with ways to feed an exploding population. For example, they explore ways to use inexpensive food sources like soybeans, cereal grains, and fish meal to feed hungry people in developing countries.

A food technologist generally specializes in one area, such as basic research, quality control, product development, processing, packaging, labeling, technical sales, market research, production, technical management, or standards, laws, and safety. Other areas include technical writing, teaching, or consulting. A food technologist also may focus on a specific category of food, such as cereal grains, meat and poultry, fats and oils, seafood, animal foods, beverages, dairy products, flavors, sugars and starches, stabilizers, preservatives, colors, and nutritional additives. In addition, there are many different types of companies to work for—food processing, agricultural science, chemical and biochemical, canning/preserving, bakery and confectionery, dairy, pasta, and more.

Increasingly, this is an industry of scientists—even in positions formerly held by people with degrees in business or marketing. "More and more of the industry is being run by food scientists, people in research and development [R&D], rather than business people," says IFT's Dean Duxbury. "I used to work for a big company years ago and the salespeople weren't trained in science. If there was a

Lingo to Learn

Biotechnology As applied to food production, the science of plant breeding, gene splicing, microbial fermentation, plant cell tissue culturing, and other activities to produce enhanced raw products for processing.

Emulsify To turn into an emulsion, or liquid.

FDA The Food and Drug Administration, a government agency that regulates food safety, nutrition, and labeling for all foods except meat and poultry.

Pasteurize To sterilize a food or beverage (cheese, milk, wine) by exposing it to high temperatures that destroy microbes or germs.

Preservative A chemical substance or preparation used to slow down the decomposition of food.

Rancidity A condition that some foods reach when the fat reacts with oxygen and breaks down into component parts like hydroxy acids, causing the "stale" smell and taste of spoiled food.

Stabilizer A substance added to food during processing to prevent or stop unwanted chemical changes in the food.

Test kitchen A facility for testing new food formulations.

Two food technologists evaluate apples after an antimicrobial wash treatment. *(Peggy Greb / U.S. Department of Agriculture)*

question or problem, they'd bring an R&D person in. That's changed now. At one major supplier I know of, all of the sales reps are degreed scientists."

Duxbury also observes that fast R&D and marketing is the rule today. "In the past, individual processing companies had top secret R&D; they did it all themselves," he says. "Now, with cutbacks and other economic concerns, processors and suppliers are working together to develop the formulas; it's a joint effort. It's much quicker and cheaper to do it this way, and much more efficient. When I was in the field, development time for a new product might be five years. Now it might be five months."

Conditions of work vary depending on the specific position and industry. You might work out in the plant overseeing food production, and it might be bustling and noisy. On the other hand, you may work in a quality control or research lab that is clean, quiet, and temperature-controlled.

What Is It Like to Be a Food Technologist?

Food technologist Bob Benson of Vanee Foods in Berkeley, Illinois, agrees that the length of time to develop a new product has dropped dramatically. "Maybe some of the big companies can still take two or three years," he says. "But here, it's more like three to four months."

Unlike many U.S. food producers, Vanee Foods is a family-owned company of about 225 employees. Here, #10-sized (large) cans of sauces, gravies, beef stew, chili, corn beef hash, and other foods are produced, along with paste-like concentrated soup bases. Vanee is a customizer of food, which means it works with the customer to develop specific formulas to meet the customer's needs. Although it sells some food directly to end-users, Vanee primarily sells to other food producers, such as Kraft and A&W. "Almost all of what we produce is private-label," Bob says.

As Vanee's director of research and development, Bob has his fingers in a lot of pies. "It's a small company, so we all wear many hats," he notes. "But my primary job here is to come up with, develop, and modify new food ideas." Bob spends most of his time in Vanee's research and development lab, but if there's a problem on the production line, he'll go out to the plant floor to troubleshoot a machine or otherwise help out.

"I started out here as a one-man department, but now I have two assistants doing R&D with me," Bob says. Other food technicians and technologists who work at Vanee include about 10 to 15 quality assurance (QA) and quality control (QC) people.

Vanee's R&D lab is a simple, efficient one with a scale, a stove, and various instruments for checking things like salt, pH, and other factors. Here, says Bob, "we may come up with 40 new-product formulations a year, although only 10 may come to fruition." On a typical day, "I'll look over various formula modifications, maybe get the marketing people in on it, and decide what changes should be made."

"People sometimes lose sight of it, but food is basically nothing but chemicals," Bob says. "In development, we're working with an understanding of what's going on at the chemical level. So when you're combining foods, for example, you must understand the chemical reactions that can take place—what will happen when these two foods are put together. There's also an art to it; you have to be a bit of a chef: Do the flavors interact well together? Does it taste and smell good? You can be a good technician, but if you're missing the art of it, you're not going to produce good food.

> There's also an art to it; you have to be a bit of a chef: Do the flavors interact well together? Does it taste and smell good?

"Say we're making a new cream sauce," he says. "Just like a cook, you'll get your flour, starch, and other ingredients together, all of them with the right properties. Sometimes you'll have an ingredient modified by the supplier, such as a preservative to retard spoilage. Then you test to see which combinations provide the cream sauce you want. When the proteins and the sugars in the starches and flours combine, for example, you don't want the sauce to turn brown; it's got to stay a light color. Here's where chemistry comes in: You have to understand how the products interact in order to avoid that brown color.

"A lot of this is trial and error," he acknowledges. "In time, you might know something won't work from past experience. But a lot of it is simply trying something, checking it, and then modifying it and trying again."

Throughout both the R&D and production phases, Vanee Foods tests for quality, safety, shelf life, and numerous other factors. "Probably the single biggest test is to make sure it looks the same as it did before," Bob says. "There's a great need for consistency. That's because ultimately the consumer is not going to be doing the sophisticated tests we do; he or she just wants it to taste and look the same as before."

Vanee Foods' products primarily are thermo-processed, and part of Bob's job is to make sure the food is properly sterilized for staying on shelves for extended periods of time. The testing process includes

> ## TO BE A SUCCESSFUL FOOD TECHNOLOGIST, YOU SHOULD . . .
>
> ○ like food and cooking
> ○ be innovative and inquisitive
> ○ enjoy trying to recreate precise chemical reactions
> ○ excel in science, especially chemistry
> ○ be methodical, detail-oriented, observant, and patient

detecting the temperature of the thermal lining inside the can. The USDA and FDA require food producers to run such tests, and Bob has developed something of a side specialty in it.

"Also, when a new product is finished, part of my responsibility is to help develop the labeling, which the quality assurance manager then submits to the USDA and FDA," Bob says. He also works closely with customers and may be involved with meetings or presentations at customer sites.

Do I Have What It Takes to Be a Food Technologist?

"First, a food technologist is usually someone with an interest in science—chemistry, biology, the life sciences," Dean Duxbury says. "You really need that in this field; it's really all science. Second, the person usually has an interest in the preparation and the formulation of food—they like cooking food and especially coming up with their own recipes."

Bob agrees with this assessment. "First and foremost, you have to have a scientific approach to things—an inquisitive mind, the desire to know how things work," he says. "And almost always, people who get into this field have had some interest in food, at least at some point in their life. For example, the quality control manager here grew up on a farm; I'm from a small town, and growing up we had a garden where we raised fresh vegetables. I still have a vegetable garden today. I don't think of myself as a chef but I do like to cook, grow fresh foods, and so forth. There are exceptions to this—some people at the very technical end may not have that interest—but most of us do."

Others have an interest in the government end of things, says Dean, such as regulation or inspection. Dean himself got into the field while in the army, when for a time he considered being a meat inspector.

The IFT says that good traits for a food technologist are similar to those for any type of scientific and research environment: curiosity, analytical thought, detail-orientation, tact, and self-confidence. Food technologists also need to be able to communicate verbally or in writing. Good business and marketing sense can help those who seek growth in the field.

How Do I Become a Food Technologist?

"I'm not sure exactly how people decide to join the industry, but they find it," Dean says. "One of the major reasons why is opportunity—people will switch into it from other degree programs or fields because of all the opportunity. After all, food is the world's biggest industry. "

Bob is a good example of someone who happened onto the field. "I started out as a chemistry major in college," he says. "Sophomore year, I was having some problems in one chemistry course, putting in 40 hours a week in the lab. I went to my adviser and said, 'I like chemistry, but not the dull, dry aspects of it.' He said, 'Have you ever considered applying chemistry or microbiology to food? Imagine applying science to ketchup. . .' I interviewed the head of the food science department and switched over. I'd never heard of food science before that; I've always been grateful that adviser steered me in this direction."

EDUCATION

The educational requirements for being a food technologist are fairly stringent. Generally, you need at least a bachelor of science degree, usually in food science, although some food technologists have some other type of science degree. The quality control manager at Vanee Foods, for example, has a chemistry degree. In addition, according to IFT, more than half of all food scientists also have an advanced degree.

Those who are interested in the field but are not sure they want to earn a four-year degree can enter as a food technician, which generally requires only a high school diploma. "The usual breakdown is

In-depth

Read the Label

Before the Nutrition Labeling and Education Act, food producers were disclosing the nutritional value of their products in a wide variety of formats, if at all. They could put them in any order. They could leave things out. Or they could just not say how much protein, fat, carbohydrates, or other components you were eating.

Now there are very strict, very uniform guidelines for nutrition labeling. How do food companies feel about having to conform to this law? The National Food Processors Association, which has 500 member companies and among other things helps to represent the food processing industry in Washington, D.C., worked with Congress in the development of the act. "The food industry was very supportive of it," says Tim Willard, a spokesperson for NFPA. "We made comments and suggestions on it."

Will the act provide more opportunities for food technicians and technologists? "Absolutely," Tim says. "It was a big project to get existing foods labeled. And now, for every new food coming on the market, there's a need for full nutrition analysis. People with that kind of technical knowledge will certainly be in demand."

‖‖‖

that the technologist has supervisory and decision-making responsibilities, and the technician doesn't," Duxbury says.

High School

If you are considering a career in food technology, take a wide variety of science courses while in high school, especially chemistry. "Chemistry is extremely important," Bob says. "It provides the broad base for understanding everything that goes on with food.

"As a food technologist, you've also got to be able to communicate well, so English classes are very important," he adds. "You must be able to write reports and communicate technical information to your peers. Also, you'll need to be able to say it in a nontechnical way" for communicating with marketing people or customers who aren't scientists themselves.

The Institute of Food Technologists' recommended high school courses include English, biology, physics, chemistry, social science, math, and—partly because of the expanding opportunities for food technologists in the global market—a foreign language.

Postsecondary Training

As mentioned above, food technologists earn a four-year degree in food science or a related area such as chemistry, microbiology, or even engineering. "There's actually a food engineering degree now that allows you to focus your studies in that area," Bob says.

According to IFT, undergraduates should take physics, biology, chemistry, nutrition, microbiology, mathematics and statistics, food chemistry and analysis, food microbiology, and food processing operations and engineering. A list of 50 colleges in the United States and Canada offering training in food technology is available from IFT.

With a bachelor's degree in science, technologists may work in research and development, quality control and assurance, technical sales, marketing, or other positions. Those who go on to earn an advanced degree increase their opportunities and may become managers, supervisors, company executives, researchers, and professors. Common advanced degrees in the field include M.S., Ph.D., and M.B.A. degrees.

In a 2003 IFT membership survey, most respondents named food science and technology as the field of their highest degree, followed by business/marketing, chemistry, and biological sciences.

Bob attends workshops to keep up with new developments in product development and production technology, and he is a member of IFT and the Institute for Thermoprocessing Specialists. He also reads trade magazines like Food Engineering, Food Technology, and Food Processing, to keep up with ongoing change in the field. "There's always something new to learn," he says. "New regulations, new technologies. Just when you think you've got the rules down, they change."

SCHOLARSHIPS AND GRANTS

Contact individual colleges and universities for school-specific loans and scholarships. Nationally, a good source for undergraduate and graduate-level scholarships is IFT's Scholarship/ Fellowship Program, available to students who attend a university with a food science/technology department or program approved by IFT. In 2004, IFT offered 111 undergraduate scholarships and 33 graduate fellowships, with awards totaling over $130,000. A brochure about the Scholarship/Fellowship Program is available from IFT.

Who Will Hire Me?

Bob's first job was with a now-defunct company called Continental Coffee, where he worked in research and development and had three promotions during his tenure. He first learned of Vanee Foods, his present employer, when he came to the Vanee plant to do a test for Continental Coffee.

Food technologists are part of the food processing industry, which is one of the largest employers in the country. The IFT says most of all U.S. food scientists work for private companies. Others work for federal government agencies like the FDA, USDA, Department of Health and Human Services, Defense Department, State Department, and Commerce Department; state and local government agencies; and international agencies like the World Health Organization of the United Nations. Those who work for the government may become involved with such things as developing and testing standards and regulations for producing, labeling, and distributing food; inspection; or research.

Food technologists typically specialize in one area. For example, they may focus on research or applied research; quality control or production; processing or engineering; sales and marketing; or management. They may concentrate on one kind of food or beverage or develop a specialty like nutritional labeling or sensory testing. Some food scientists may be employed by suppliers or processors. Teaching, consulting, and writing also are possibilities.

FYI

Basic versus Applied Food Research

Food technologists in basic research study food's structure and composition by observing changes that take place during storage or processing. What they learn enables them to develop new sources of proteins, determine the effects of processing on microorganisms, or isolate factors that affect the flavor, appearance, or texture of foods. Technologists in applied R&D have the task of creating new food products and developing new food methods. They also continue to work with existing foods to make them more nutritious or flavorful, or to improve their color or texture.

"There are many independent consultants," says Dean. "They're usually former researchers, hired because of their expertise in a specific area. They may be hired by the hour, day, week, project, or other basis. They can help food companies meet their goal of faster R&D."

In private industry, employers may include:

- Processing plants. This is where foods and beverages are produced—converted from raw agricultural and other materials into the finished consumer goods we buy at the store. There are different kinds of processing plants for different foods, such as those for cereal; chips and other snack foods; meat, fish, or game; soft drinks and other beverages; fruits and vegetables; and so on.

- Food ingredients plants. Ingredients plants are where the various things added to foods (or that you can buy to put on or in them) are made—vitamins, preservatives, salt and pepper, spices, flavorings, and more.

- Food manufacturing plants. This is where new foods are created out of unexpected raw materials. Cheese made from soy products,

FYI

According to information provided by the FPA, innovative methods of food preservation developed by two men— Nicolas Appert and Clarence Birdseye— helped create today's most commonly used food processing techniques: canning and freezing.

In the 1700s Nicolas Appert, a little-known candy maker, brewer, and baker, had a theory that fresh foods sealed in airtight containers and heated would not spoil. To test his theory he packed foods in bottles, sealed the bottles with corks, then heated the bottles in boiling water. The technique worked and laid the foundation for today's canned foods.

Almost 100 years after Appert's development of canned foods, Clarence Birdseye, while on an expedition in Labrador, noticed that meat quickly frozen by the area's frigid Arctic air retained its fresh flavor and quality for months. Knowing that slowly freezing foods by traditional methods would not preserve its quality, Birdseye came to the conclusion that to retain quality and flavor freezing foods had to be done rapidly. Following his return home he developed a "Multiplate Quick Freeze" machine and made his first product: frozen fish sticks. His technique for fast-freezing foods worked and today frozen foods are now a key part of most American's diets.

tofu pizza, nondairy creamers, and other foods are manufactured in these types of plants.

After many years of being "the industry that people stumble into," the food science industry now is actively recruiting young people to join their ranks. Although white males still dominate the field, the percentage of women is increasing. Positions in the industry are well suited or can be adapted for people with disabilities.

Where Can I Go from Here?

Steps up for the food technologist may include heading up a department, such as quality control or production; leading R&D teams; getting into product management; moving into regulatory work; or becoming involved with the sales end of the business. Increasingly, food sales and management positions are held by those with education and training in food science.

Food technology is an area in which it definitely pays to receive a master's or doctoral degree, and about half of the people in the industry do so. Food chemistry and technology are quite sophisticated, and there is a need for advanced knowledge to help propel new research and development, manufacturing techniques, and distribution methods.

There are good opportunities for those who have developed expertise in a specialized area. Specialists include people like sensory evaluation experts, who measure consumers' response to the look, smell, and taste of food. Nutrition labeling is another specialty that currently is in high demand. Another possibility is to become a food marketing specialist, who might help a U.S. food company understand and penetrate international markets. Consulting is another option, and gives the food technologist the opportunity to apply his or her knowledge to problem solving for a wide range of companies.

What Are the Salary Ranges?

According to the Occupational Employment Statistics, the median annual earnings of agricultural and food scientists and technologists were $49,610 in 2003. Those in the lowest paid 10 percent earned $29,250 annually, and those in the highest paid 10 percent earned $86,930.

The IFT's 2003 membership salary survey found that the overall median salary was $73,150, a 12.5 percent increase from the previous survey. Men had median annual earnings of $83,000, while women had median earnings of $64,500. This pay difference may be because many of the men responding have been in their jobs longer than the women have, and more men than women in the field have advanced degrees.

The average starting salary for those who hold bachelor's degrees was around $40,000. Technologists with more years of experience and/or higher degrees had higher earnings. The highest averages were reported for the Middle Atlantic and California regions, the lowest average salaries were in the Mountain region. The survey also found that the vast majority of employers provide health, life, and dental insurance, vacation, sick leave, and 401(k) plans.

What Is the Job Outlook?

According to the U.S. Department of Labor Occupational Outlook Handbook, job growth for food scientist and technologist is projected to be slower than the average through 2012; however the food nutrition labeling laws now in place opened up a number of opportunities for food technicians and technologists, as companies scrambled to get into compliance with the law. Even now nutrition analysis will be needed for each new food that comes onto the market.

Hazard analysis critical control point, or HACCP (pronounced "hay'-cep"), is a food safety system that is beginning to have a big impact on food technology. HACCP prevents the contamination of food by identifying at the microbiological level the critical point at which the food begins to break down. The FDA recently established HACCP for meat and poultry processing plants and the seafood industry, and is developing regulations for HACCP to become the food safety standard.

Everyone eats; there is always going to be a demand for food. But the fortunes of specific food-related companies rise and fall depending on changing consumer tastes, competition, and other factors. In recent years, sources of growth have included a rising population and global market to sell to, improved production technology, and the demand for healthier foods (low-fat, low-salt, or cholesterol-free, for example). These factors have provided significant opportunities for food technologists.

There can be a lot of competition among food companies for market share, though. (Think about the number of breakfast cereals on the market today.) Also, generic brands, house brands, and specialty foods have cut into the profits of some standard-brand companies. Still, food technologists can be valued weapons in food manufacturers' arsenal, speeding R&D time and helping to improve production and marketing. Product management and sales-related areas like marketing and advertising are cited by

---

ADVANCEMENT POSSIBILITIES

Directors of research and development plan, oversee, and direct activities for creating and testing new products or production methods or improving existing ones.

Food marketing specialists apply knowledge of sales and marketing to help food companies gain new consumers for their products, such as overseas markets.

Nutrition labeling specialists plan and direct tests to document food nutrition content and direct labeling activities to comply with the U.S. nutrition labeling law.

Quality assurance or quality control managers ensure company compliance with standards for safety, cleanliness, consistency, and other factors as established by state, federal, and other law; company policy; and/or customer requirements.

Sensory evaluation experts measure consumer response to food qualities, such as appearance, texture, taste, flavor, and smell.

---

some experts as good growth areas. International opportunities with U.S. food producers opening branches abroad also may be a growth area.

How Do I Learn More?

PROFESSIONAL ORGANIZATIONS

For information about food sciences career opportunities, educational programs, and scholarships contact the following organizations:

Food Processors Association
1350 I Street NW, Suite 300
Washington, DC 20005
202-639-5900
http://www.nfpa-food.org

Institute of Food Technologists
525 West Van Buren, Suite 1000
Chicago, IL 60607
312-782-8424

info@ift.org
http://www.ift.org

BIBLIOGRAPHY

The following is a sampling of materials relating to the professional concerns and development of food technologists:

Jones, Julie Miller. *Food Safety.* St. Paul, Minn.: Eagan Press, 1992.

Lund, Barbara M., ed. et al. *The Microbiological Safety and Quality of Food.* San Diego: Aspen Publishers, Inc., 2000.

McSwane, David et al. *Essentials of Food Safety and Sanitation.* 4th ed. Paramus, N.J.: Prentice Hall, 2004.

Sims-Bell, Barbara. *Career Opportunities in the Food and Beverage Industry.* 2d ed. New York: Checkmark Books, 2001.

FORENSIC TECHNICIANS

〡〡

Following an explosion in a garage where a group of men had built a drug lab, senior forensic technician Peter Williams does some lab work on pieces of skin found at the crime scene. "The guy was on fire," Peter says, "and his hands were melting, so he put them in his mouth. The chemicals that were on his hands melted his skin off, basically. He spit the skin out right next to his swimming pool." The crime scene investigators found the skin of the man's fingertips, which conveniently feature his fingerprints.

"We softened the fingertips up by soaking them in solution," Peter says. "Then I took the fingerprints and we're going to compare them against those of the known suspect. We know whose fingers they probably are, but we just want to confirm."

What Does a Forensic Technician Do?

Forensic technicians work in many different areas of crime scene investigation and forensic science. One technician may work only with cadavers in a morgue, another may work only in a lab analyzing evidence, another may investigate and photograph crime scenes, and another may analyze fingerprints. Some forensics technicians assist in a number of different areas of investigation, including crime scene and lab work. Some technicians assist criminalists, and use instruments of science and engineering to examine physical evidence. They use spectroscopes, microscopes, gas chromatographs, infrared and ultraviolet light, microphotography, and other lab measuring and testing equipment to analyze fibers, fabric, dust, soils, paint chips, glass fragments, fire accelerants, paper and ink, and other substances in order to identify their composition and origin. They analyze poisons, drugs, and other substances found in bodies by examining tissue samples, stomach contents, and blood samples. They analyze and classify blood, blood alcohol, semen, hair, fingernails, teeth, human and animal bones and tissue, and other biological specimens. Using samples of the genetic material DNA, they can match a person with

a sample of body tissue. They study documents to determine whether they are forged or genuine. They also examine the physical properties of firearms, bullets, and explosives.

At the scene of a crime (whether actual or suspected), forensic technicians collect and label evidence. This painstaking task may involve searching for spent bullets or bits of an exploded bomb and other objects scattered by an explosion. They might look for footprints, fingerprints, and tire tracks that must be recorded or preserved by plaster casting before they are wiped out. Since crime scenes must eventually be cleaned up, forensic technicians take

---

Definition

Forensic technicians assist medical examiners, criminalists, and forensic scientists to analyze, identify, and classify physical evidence relating to criminal cases. They may work in laboratories or they may travel to crime scenes to collect evidence.

Alternative Job Titles

Crime scene technicians
Forensic autopsy technicians
Forensic evidence technicians
Forensic science technicians
Identification technicians

High School Subjects

Biology
Chemistry

Personal Skills

Following instructions
Technical/scientific

Salary Range

$26,500 to $43,200 to $70,800

Minimum Educational Level

High school diploma

Certification or Licensing

Voluntary

Outlook

About as fast as the average

DOT

188

GOE

04.03.02

NOC

N/A

O*NET-SOC

19-4092.00

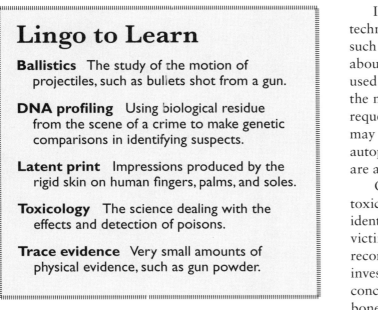

Lingo to Learn

Ballistics The study of the motion of projectiles, such as bullets shot from a gun.

DNA profiling Using biological residue from the scene of a crime to make genetic comparisons in identifying suspects.

Latent print Impressions produced by the rigid skin on human fingers, palms, and soles.

Toxicology The science dealing with the effects and detection of poisons.

Trace evidence Very small amounts of physical evidence, such as gun powder.

notes and photographs to preserve the arrangement of objects, bodies, and debris. They are sometimes called on later to reconstruct the scene of a crime by making a floor plan or map that shows the exact location of bodies, weapons, and furniture.

One important discipline within forensic science is identification. *Fingerprint classifiers* catalog and compare fingerprints of suspected criminals with records to determine if the people who left the fingerprints at the scene of a crime were involved in previous crimes. They often try to match the fingerprints of unknown corpses with fingerprint records to establish their identities. They work in laboratories and offices, as well as travel to other areas such as crime scenes. Retrieving fingerprints outside may be difficult and may require specialized processes, such as dusting glassware, windows, or walls with a fine powder. This powder contrasts with many different surfaces and will highlight any fingerprints that remain. Another method of retrieving fingerprints is to lift them off with a flexible tape, which can be brought back to the laboratory for further evaluation and matching.

Fingerprint classifiers compare new prints against those found after the commission of similar crimes. The classifier documents this information and transfers it to the main record-keeping system, often a large mainframe computer system. In the last decade or so, computers have greatly enhanced the possibility of matching new fingerprints to those already on file. A fingerprint classifier may keep individual files on current crimes and note any similarities between them.

In addition to handling fingerprint records, technicians also work with other kinds of records, such as police reports and eyewitness information about crimes and accidents. They operate equipment used to microfilm police records, as well as store the microfilm and retrieve or copy records upon the request of police or other public officials. Technicians may assist forensics pathologists who perform autopsies to determine the cause of death; autopsies are almost always performed on victims of crime.

Other areas of forensic science include forensic toxicology, which is concerned with detecting and identifying the presence of poisons or drugs in a victim's body, forensic odontology, which uses dental records and evidence to identify crime victims and to investigate bite marks, forensic anthropology, which concentrates on the examination and identification of bones and skeletal remains, and forensic psychiatry, which is used to analyze criminal behavior.

What Is It Like to Be a Forensic Technician?

As a senior forensic technician for the Riverside County Sheriff in California, Peter Williams supervises other forensic technicians, writes evaluations, and reviews reports. "When there's a major crime, something out of the ordinary like an officer shooting or a high-profile-type homicide case, we go out on those. We may process the scenes ourselves, or we direct people to process the scene." This processing involves collecting evidence, fingerprinting, photographing, and making crime scene diagrams.

Because forensic technicians are needed around the clock, Peter works a 5:00 P.M. to 2:00 A.M. shift. His shift begins with reviewing reports and fingerprints, then sending them over to the fingerprint lab. In some cases, he will go out to a crime scene. "In my office, we're classified employees, or nonsworn employees, so we don't carry a gun or a badge. But we do drive marked units."

The technicians drive a van to a crime scene. "Each technician is assigned a 35 millimeter camera, and in the vans we have different films, flashlights, a blood kit which has evidence collecting tools such as tweezers, scalpel, swabs, glassines to collect blood samples in, envelopes, bags. We have a generator and we carry two 500-watt lights, a ladder, shovel, sifters. Sometimes we have to go out and dig up a body. We have something called an electrostatic dust collector where we can lift dusty shoeprints." The technicians can also make composite sketches with a laptop computer and a software program from Smith and Wesson.

"We also have numbers and letters we can put out next to the evidence items we collect. We have dowels so we can do trajectories, like a bullet going through a wall. We have some kits we use for gunshot residue testing. If someone has fired a handgun, we can collect the residue off the hands, and then send it to the lab and get an analysis done on it. In our lab, we don't do any comparisons of bullets or blood or anything like that. We basically collect the items and send them to the state lab."

Peter has noticed an increased interest in the career ever since the O.J. Simpson trial in 1994. "Before that," he says, "people didn't really understand what forensics was. But I think a lot of people interested in the job think they're going to be able to go out there and snap a few photographs. On one case I took over 400 photographs." The work can also demand many irregular hours. "I have worked a case for three days straight," he says. "The first day was about 18 hours, the second day about 15, and the third about nine hours. We did work one case almost 36 hours straight. They're very long hours, and you don't know when it's going to happen."

As a forensic technician in Palm Beach County, Florida, Ralph Saccone Jr. has a somewhat more regular work schedule and spends most of his time in the county morgue. When a body is brought in, Ralph will undress it, clean it, and prepare documents. "We'll take the identification photo," he says, "and record wounds, lacerations, abrasions, scars, tattoos. Then we'll fingerprint. A copy stays in our file, and a copy goes to the Florida Department of Law Enforcement, so if the person had a criminal record, they can take them out of the system."

The forensic pathologist then leads the autopsy and directs the technicians. "We'll roll the bodies when needed, or open the eyelids, open the mouth. We'll do a Y-incision during the autopsy, retract the skin, open the ribs, take toxicology of the liver, bile, brain." The tools Ralph uses include forceps, scissors, and scalpels. "We use dura [the liner between the brain and the skull] strippers to see if there are any skull fractures underneath the liner. We open the ribs with hedge clippers we got at Sears. You can also use a saw, but it's faster.

"We take blood, we take the bile, we take the urine, then the organs just come out one by one. We

> **TO BE A SUCCESSFUL FORENSIC TECHNICIAN, YOU SHOULD . . .**
>
> ○ have an aptitude for scientific investigation
> ○ have an inquiring and logical mind
> ○ be able to make precise measurements and observations
> ○ be patient and persistent
> ○ have a good memory

weigh them, dissect them, we take micros for the histologist. We take tissue that stays a year in case the doctor has to go back, then we sew them up and we don't see them again."

Do I Have What It Takes to Be a Forensic Technician?

Forensic technicians usually perform the analysis portion of their work in clean, quiet, air-conditioned laboratories, but they are frequently required to travel to crime scenes to collect evidence or study the site to understand more fully the evidence collected by detectives. When gathering evidence and analyzing it, forensic technicians need to be able to concentrate, sometimes in crowded, noisy situations. For this reason, forensic technicians must be adaptable and able to work in a variety of environments, including dangerous or unpleasant places. "Ninety-eight percent of the time," Peter says, "you deal with the worst citizens in your area. You deal with people who are mad, and their houses have been broken into, and they think it's your fault that it was broken into. You have to be an even-keeled person and just listen to people."

Many crime scenes are grisly and may be extremely distressing for beginning workers and even for more seasoned professionals. "You have to be strong enough to deal with death on a constant basis," Peter says. "Not only do you have older people, but you have someone your own age, or you have a young child."

In addition, forensic technicians who work with human remains will regularly view corpses, and more often than not these corpses will have been mutilated in some way or be in varying degrees of

FYI

In Scotland during the late 1780s, a man was convicted of murder when the soles of his boots matched a plaster cast of footprints taken from the scene of the crime. This is one of the earliest recorded cases of the use of physical evidence to link a suspected criminal with the crime.

In the late 19th century, scientists learned to analyze and classify poisons so their presence could be traced in a body. At about the same time, a controversy arose over the different methods being used to identify individuals positively. Fingerprinting emerged in the early 20th century as the most reliable method of personal identification. With the advent of X-ray technology, experts could rely on dental records to substitute for fingerprint analysis when a corpse was in advanced stages of decomposition and the condition of the skin had deteriorated.

Forensic pathology (medical examination of suspicious or unexplained deaths) also came into prominence at this time, as did ballistics, which is the study of projectiles and how they are shot from firearms. The study of ballistics was aided by the invention of the comparison microscope, which enabled an investigator to look at bullets side by side and compare their individual markings. Since individual gun barrels "scar" bullets in a unique pattern, similar markings found on different bullets may prove that they were fired from the same weapon.

decomposition. Individuals interested in this field need to develop the detachment and objectivity necessary to view corpses and extract specimens for testing and analysis. Ralph also emphasizes the need for safety precautions in the morgue. "We gown up, wear a mask and goggles," he says. "I wear two gloves, boot covers. You have to treat everyone as if

they have a disease. You could catch something if you don't take precautions."

How Do I Become a Forensic Technician?

As a supervisor, Peter sends technicians through on-the-job training with specialized schools. "We go to a two-week school that's put on by Cal State, Long Beach," he says. "It basically emphasizes methods of collection of physical evidence, whether it's photographs, shoe or tire impressions, doing different types and methods of fingerprint collecting and developing, proper techniques of collecting blood by scraping and swabbing. Then we send the people to fingerprint schools. We have a basic pattern-recognition course, a print technique course, and a comparison course. We also have a new class on palm prints. It's all individualized training that's really geared for law-enforcement technicians that do the work. It's really hard for the general public to get into those courses."

EDUCATION

High School

In high school, you can begin to prepare for this field by taking a heavy concentration of science courses, including chemistry, biology, physiology, and physics. Computer skills are also important, especially for fingerprint classifiers, and to prepare for the technological developments in the field. A basic grounding in spoken and written communications will be useful because forensic technicians must write very detailed reports and are sometimes called on to present their findings in court.

Postsecondary Training

Forensic technicians typically need to have experience as law enforcement officers before being considered for the on-the-job training offered by most counties. "Probably two-thirds of the law enforcement agencies in the country require that you be a sworn police officer," says Joseph Polski of the International Association for Identification (IAI). Courses may be offered through community colleges but are generally designed only for those in law enforcement. Courses may include training

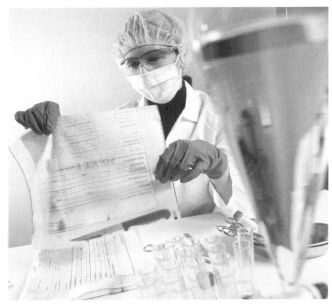

A forensic technician prepares to examine a knife from a crime scene. The knife will be inspected for fingerprints and other evidence, such as hair samples. (*TEK Image/Photo Researchers Inc.*)

in crime scene photography, fingerprint processing, blood splatter analysis, criminal profiling, and forensic biology. Annual retraining may be required. Some community colleges offer programs in crime scene technology that are open to the general public but do not necessarily lead to work in crime scene investigation. Forensic autopsy technicians may be required to have training as an embalmer or funeral director.

CERTIFICATION OR LICENSING

Technicians usually must be certified through a special training program designated by the county, but it depends on the job and the state. A number of special certifications are offered by the IAI, including latent print certification, crime scene certification, and forensic photography certification.

Who Will Hire Me?

Peter started working with the sheriff's department right out of high school. "I wanted to be a deputy," he says, "but I was too young. In California, you have to be 21 to carry a gun." So he worked as a sheriff's aid, taking care of the cars, booking, dispatching, and maintaining the evidence locker, among other

In-depth

Forensic Entomology

According to the American Board of Forensic entomology, forensic entomology, or medicocriminal entomology, is the science of using insect evidence to provide facts for law cases, including crimes. Forensic entomologists can determine the time of death, for example, using insect evidence gathered from and around a corpse.

The maggots and other insects crawling in the eyes, nose, and wounds on dead bodies were long considered a disgusting part of the decay process. Investigators concentrated on fingerprints, gunpowder residue, ballistics, and blood splatters. Through the years, a few scientists have researched the clues insects provide and in the last 10 years, entomology has become an important part of forensic science.

Forensic entomology includes uncovering a broad spectrum of evidence for a variety of legal issues. The brand related to violent crimes is sometimes called forensic medical entomology or medicocriminal entomology. It is used to

- determine the time or site of a human death
- provide evidence in cases involving possible sudden death
- investigate traffic accidents with no immediately obvious cause
- uncover possible criminal misuse of insects

duties. He did that for over three years before being placed in a position as an identification technician.

"You should contact a law enforcement agency in the area you want to live," Joseph Polski, chief operations officer of IAI, recommends. "Go to a fairly large police department, sheriff's department, or state crime laboratory and talk to the people who do the work. Ask them how they got to be where they are. The field's pretty big. Look at the options."

Forensic technicians are typically employed by large police departments or state or law enforcement agencies nationwide. They may also work in the private sector in large corporations, small firms, or government agencies. They may be employed by the military, medical examiner's offices, states attorney offices, and law firms.

Where Can I Go from Here?

If sworn police officers, technicians may move up through the ranks. In a large crime laboratory, forensic technicians usually advance from an assistant's position to working independently at one or more special types of analysis. From there they may advance to a position as project leader or being in charge of all aspects of one particular investigation. In smaller labs, one technician may have to fill many roles. With experience, such a technician may progress to more responsible work but receive no advancement in title. Fingerprint classifiers who work for police departments may pursue advancement with a different government agency or apply for positions with the FBI.

What Are the Salary Ranges?

The U.S. Department of Labor Occupational Information Network reports the median annual earnings in 2003 for forensic technicians were $43,200.

Those in the lowest paid 10 percent earned $26,500, and the highest paid 10 percent earned $70,800.

A survey conducted in 2004 by the International City/County Management Association (ICMA) found that the average minimum annual base salary paid to sworn full-time police officers was $36,347. The average maximum annual base salary was $50,793. Seven years of service are generally required for personnel to receive the maximum base salary. According to the survey, police corporals had minimum salaries of $41,793 and maximum of $51,661. Police captains had minimum salaries of $60,908 and maximum $75,497. Civilian technicians generally have lower beginning salaries.

Full-time technicians in law enforcement can expect to be provided with health, hospital, disability, and life insurance benefits.

What Is the Job Outlook?

Because of a lack of government support, forensic labs have more cases than they can handle in a timely matter. Other areas of criminal justice have benefited from federal assistance, but the expense of forensic science has resulted in a shortage of resources and a backlog of cases. Legislation is under way that could help to change that; in the meantime, labs may be limited as to how many technicians they can keep on staff.

The rapid development of high-tech crime scene tools and instruments will also change forensics. Technicians with training in new crime scene technology should find increasing job opportunities. "You should become technology literate," Joseph Polski says. "If you have a good understanding of personal computers, of Windows, then you can take that knowledge and learn the kind of system that you would use on the job. You're not going to find any uniformity. If you go to Miami, they're going to be doing things different than if you go to New York City. You just need a basis of understanding."

The year 2000 marked the introduction of FRENZY, the Forensic Sciences and Crime Scene Technology Conference and Exposition. FRENZY highlighted such new technologies as photogrammetry. With CAD software, a technician can use photogrammetry to take precise measurements based on a photographic image, allowing for careful analysis of a crime scene even after evidence has been moved or destroyed. This process may also be used with autopsy photos, to analyze a wound when the cadaver is no longer available.

Another new technology is a compact instrument that allows for the on-site analyzing of suspected illicit substances, eliminating the long wait for getting lab results back. Computer software is also assisting with the enhancement of video images and audio recordings.

Those trained in computer forensics will also find increased opportunities. According to a panel discussion at FRENZY, there were 120 million personal computers in use in the United States at the beginning of 2000. Only about 1 percent of all computer crimes are even detected, and only 7 percent of that 1 percent are reported to the law. Ultimately, only 3 percent of that 7 percent result in jail time. Therefore, computer crimes are increasing by 75 percent every year. Computer forensic technicians will need to know the number of software programs that are developing to assist in the investigation of computer crimes and to effectively find evidence hidden on a computer hard drive.

How Do I Learn More?

PROFESSIONAL ORGANIZATIONS

For information about careers in forensics, educational programs, and certification contact the following organizations:

American Academy of Forensic Sciences
Forensic Sciences Foundation

PO Box 669
Colorado Springs, CO 80901-0669
719-636-1100
http://www.aafs.org

American Society of Questioned Document Examiners
PO Box 18298
Long Beach, CA 90807
562-901-3376
http://www.asqde.org

International Association for Identification
2535 Pilot Knob Road, Suite 117
Mendota Heights, MN 55120-1120
651-681-8566
http://www.theiai.org

BIBLIOGRAPHY

The following is a sampling of materials relating to the the professional concerns and development of forensic technicians:

Carper, Kenneth, ed. *Forensic Engineering.* 2d ed. Boca Raton, FL: CRC Press, 2001.

Fridell, Ron. *Solving Crimes: Pioneers of Forensic Science.* New York: Franklin Watts Inc., 2000.

Michael, James et al. *Forensic Interpretation of Glass Evidence.* Boca Raton, Fla.: CRC Press, 2000.

Morrison, Robert D. *Environmental Forensics.* Boca Raton, Fla.: CRC Press, 1999.

Platt, Richard. *Crime Scene: The Ultimate Guide to Forensic Science.* New York: DK Publishing, 2003.

Saferstein, Richard. *Criminalistics: An Introduction to Forensic Science.* 8th ed. Paramus, N.J.: Prentice Hall, 2003.

FORESTRY TECHNICIANS

⁜⁜

It has been a long day, and at 9:00 P.M. forestry technician Jim Ets Hokin is ready to hit the hay. That is when his radio crackles to life. It is the dispatcher from the National Forest Service, and she is calling to report a possible forest fire in the Coronado National Forest in southern Arizona where Jim is stationed. Pulling on his boots, Jim hops into his truck and drives up one of the old rutted forest service roads until he comes to the coordinates where the dispatcher said the fire had been spotted.

Sure enough, as he approaches the coordinates Jim can see the distinctive glow in the distance of flames scorching the brush and timbers. It is a small fire, only two-tenths of an acre in size, nothing like the monsters that burned the previous summer in the nearby Rincon Mountains, consuming more than 28,000 acres of forest. Still, the wind is gusting on this night, and Jim knows that even a small fire can quickly turn dangerous. He radios to one of his fire crews for assistance, and using chain saws and a tool called a pulaski (a combination hoe and ax), the two clear a fire lane, removing most of the brush and timbers that fuel the fire. Then they wait for the fire to burn itself out.

In the morning, a fire engine will come to the site and spray the area with water, ending this fire's threat to the forest. But that won't mean Jim can rest easy. It is only the beginning of spring. In a few months, the forest will be dry from lack of rain. That is when it becomes a real powder keg. A lightning strike, a careless campfire, and Jim and his crew will be back in action again.

What Does a Forestry Technician Do?

Hundreds of years ago, much of America was covered with dense, majestic forests. These natural woodlands gave shelter and sustenance to the peoples and wildlife indigenous to the continent. With the arrival of European settlers, the forests were cleared for farming, and timber was cut to build houses and boats, furniture and tools. With the clearing of the forests, coupled with natural forces such as fire and

Definition
Forestry technicians help plan, supervise, and conduct operations necessary to maintain and protect the country's forests. They also manage forests and wildlife areas, control fires, insects, and disease and limit the depletion of forest resources.

Alternative Job Titles
Biological aides
Survey assistants
Technical research assistants
Wildlife technicians

High School Subjects
Biology
Geology

Personal Skills
Following instructions
Technical/scientific

Salary Range
$21,800 to $32,000 to $48,600

Minimum Educational Level
Some postsecondary training

Certification or Licensing
None available

Outlook
More slowly than the average

DOT
452

GOE
03.03.02

NOC
2223

O*NET-SOC
19-4093.00

disease, the forests began to be depleted faster than they could grow.

To diminish the loss of the forests and help in their restoration, the United States government enacted a series of conservation measures in the early 1900s. Among those measures was training and establishing a corps of forestry workers to protect and replenish the nation's fragile forestry reserves.

Forestry technicians work as members of a forest management team, which includes professional foresters and forestry scientists. Some also work for private companies in the forest industry.

The day-to-day duties of a forestry technician are based on a range of activities for managing and harvesting the nation's forest resources. They plant trees to replenish forest reserves that have become depleted through harvesting, fire, or disease. They care for maturing trees by spraying them with pesticides (if disease infested), by thinning to ensure the best growth of the forest, and by protecting them from fire and other dangers. They inventory (or scale) trees to determine the amount of lumber to be gained through harvesting. They then harvest forests and assist in the marketing of the lumber. And finally, they recondition the harvested forest and plant new trees, beginning the cycle anew.

Forestry technicians work under the supervision of professional foresters and managers who are responsible for developing an overall plan to manage a forest area. Each forest area is managed with a particular objective, and this affects the duties of the forestry technician. For example, a forest area might be tended for producing large sawlogs, in which case the planting, thinning, and care of the forest is different than it would be if the management plan called for producing timber as a habitat for wildlife.

Because the management plan and the care cycle of each forest area differs, forestry technicians often must perform various duties that require different skills. And while many forestry technicians are employed by the federal government, some also work for private companies such as lumber yards and sawmills.

Forestry technicians work under a variety of titles. *Biological aides* work in insect and disease control. They run experiments, analyze data, and map damage to forests caused by parasites. *Buyers for sawmills* purchase high-grade lumber for milling and furniture manufacture. *Information and education technicians* prepare media releases and serve as public relations specialists in nature centers. *Lumber inspectors* grade and determine the quantity of hardwood and softwood lumber at mills. *Pulp buyers* work at paper mills and purchase pulp wood for use in paper products. *Survey assistants* determine and mark boundary lines. They may also assist in the clearing of forests and in the construction of roads for logging operations. They consult aerial photographs and prepare maps of surveys, and assist in land appraisal and acquisition for federal, state, and private employers. *Technical research assistants* gather and analyze field data to help researchers understand problems that relate to timber, watershed, and wildlife management. *Tree-nursery management assistants* assist in the operation of tree nurseries. They run seed tests and assist in planting, and in

Lingo to Learn

Bucker A worker on a logging operation who trims off the tops of trees and bucks (cuts) the resulting logs into specified lengths.

Cruise timber To determine the volume of standing trees.

Deciduous Trees with broad leaves that are shed at the end of a season.

Dendrology The study of trees.

Mensuration The measuring of forests to determine lumber and timber volumes.

Prescribed burn An intentionally set and carefully controlled forest fire.

Pulaski A hand implement used by fire control technicians to clear brush and logs away from a forest fire.

Scale To determine the lumber content of a tree.

Silviculture A branch of forestry dealing with the development and care of forests.

the supervision of personnel. *Wildlife technicians* conduct field work for the nation's various fish and game commissions. They track and tag animals for census making, and help to implement animal control policies.

What Is It Like to Be a Forestry Technician?

Jim Ets Hokin has been a forestry technician since 1976. "I've always liked the outdoors," he says. So when he returned from a stint in the U.S. Army, he looked into careers with the National Forest Service, the government agency that oversees the country's 154 national forests.

Each of the national forests is divided into districts, the number of which depends upon the size of the forest. Jim works in the Palisades Administrative District of the Coronado National Forest, located near

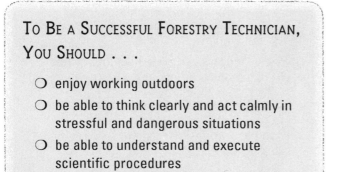

Tucson, Arizona. He lives in the forest, in quarters furnished by the federal government. Typically, he works from 9:00 A.M. to 6:00 P.M., but those hours can change when there are emergencies to tend to, such as a fire or a lost hiker.

For Jim, the most exciting part of his job as a forestry technician is when he and his crew have to fight a forest fire. "It can be dangerous work," he says. "But if you remember your training and pay attention to all the factors that you've been trained to pay attention to, you can stay out of trouble."

When mistakes happen, people can die. In 1994, for example, 14 forest fire fighters died fighting a blaze in Colorado. Because the work can be so dangerous, forestry technicians who work in fire-fighting functions have to be alert to conditions that can cause forest fires, and understand how fires spread.

"There are three basic factors you have to consider (when fighting a forest fire)," Jim says. "You have to understand the weather, how the wind can make a fire spread, and the natural topography of the area (where the fire is burning)."

The last factor includes the types of fuel feeding the fire. "A fire in a ponderosa pine forest will behave differently than a desert fire," Jim says.

While the work is not too physically demanding, Jim says, there are times when the job takes its toll on the human body. "When there's a desert fire it might be 105 degrees outside, and on the fire line it might be more like 180 degrees. You almost have to be a little nuts to do this type of work," he says with a laugh.

After a fire has been successfully extinguished, Jim returns to the district office. There he must complete a report detailing how the fire was treated and assess the damage that occurred to the forest. These reports help Jim's supervisors evaluate fire-fighting procedures and determine whether changes in those procedures should be made.

Sometimes, Jim sets fires as part of a carefully developed forest management plan to ensure the forest's long-term health. These fires, or "prescribed burns," are set to thin out sections of the forest, thereby eliminating a fuel source from which an accidental fire could escalate into a large-scale forest fire. And since fires return vital nutrients to the soil, some prescribed burns are set to enrich the soil so it will continue to sustain the forest.

Summers are the busiest season for Jim because of the number of fires that occur, and also because more people visit the forest during the spring and summer months. During the winter, the work load drops off significantly, although Jim keeps busy by doing trail maintenance, by holding training sessions for fire crew members, and by catching up on paperwork and reports that will ensure the fire crew has the necessary material supplies and personnel for the coming fire season.

Jim likes the diversity that being a forestry technician offers. He also says that by working for the federal government, he receives an excellent benefits package. And while each district office is run by a district forester, Jim says he works independently much of the time. This means he has to show initiative to see that the district's forest management plan is followed, and that he fulfills his job's obligations.

Do I Have What It Takes to Be a Forestry Technician?

Being a forestry technician can be dangerous work. When Jim and his fire crew head out to battle a blaze, each carries along a portable fire shelter, a specially designed pup tent built to withstand extreme heat. Each crew member carries a fire shelter in case he should suddenly find himself trapped by an approaching fire. "It's your last resort," Jim says. "Luckily, I've never had to use one."

Because of the dangerous nature of the fire-fighting duties, a forestry technician has to be able to think clearly in stressful situations. A rushed decision at a crucial moment could endanger the lives of the forestry technician and his or her crew.

Not all forestry technicians fight fires like Jim. Depending upon the forest management plan that has been enacted for the forest in which they work, forestry technicians may perform more research and data-gathering duties. While the chance for bodily harm is less, these forestry technicians must have a firm grasp of scientific procedures. They must also be skilled in recognizing insects and other diseases that might harm the forest.

Forestry technicians who work in national forests work under the supervision of a district manager. They must be able to follow direction and adhere to a carefully designed forest management plan that dictates how their forest will be managed. In some cases, a forestry technician might supervise a staff, too. During fire season, Jim supervises a crew of 20 fire fighters who work on a seasonal basis.

Ultimately, forestry technicians have to care for one of the planet's most important natural resources. Trees absorb carbon dioxide and release oxygen, playing an important role in providing the planet with the air we breathe. They provide shelter for birds and small animals, beneficial insects, and some reptiles. Trees are also used to provide wood and lumber so that we may have shelter ourselves, and tools and other implements. Forestry technicians are committed to ensuring that our country's forest areas serve all these functions.

How Do I Become a Forestry Technician?

For Jim, the decision to become a forestry technician was an easy one. He loved working in the outdoors, and when he returned to the United States after serving in the army, he looked for a job that would let him follow his passion. He worked for a summer in a national park in Colorado, and decided that he would like to pursue a career as a forestry technician.

EDUCATION

High School

To be a forestry technician, most employers require candidates to have completed a two-year postsecondary training program. These programs require applicants to have a high school diploma.

To prepare yourself for a career as a forestry technician, take high school courses in mathematics,

FYI

A personal friend of President Theodore Roosevelt, Gifford Pinchot, was one of the first people to advocate planned conservation of natural resources. Under his influence the U.S. Department of Agriculture established the U.S. Forest Service in 1905. President Roosevelt appointed Pinchot the first professional forester in the U.S. in 1910. After leaving the forest service Pinchot was elected governor of Pennsylvania.

computer science, chemistry, botany, zoology, ecology, and the social sciences. Good writing and communication skills are also needed to advance in the field.

Postsecondary Training

After high school, you will need to attend and graduate from a forest technology program. Most of these programs offer an associate's degree in forest technology. The Society of American Foresters (SAF) currently recognizes 25 educational programs (22 in the United States; three in Canada) that offer a two-year associate's degree in forest technology. The SAF also recognizes 48 educational institutions and more than 100 accredited bachelor's degree options in professional forestry.

While in a forest technology program, students receive instruction in mathematics, communications, botany, engineering, surveying, dendrology (tree identification), forest soils, computer applications, elementary business principles, timber harvesting, map drafting, outdoor recreation and environmental control, wildlife ecology, insect and disease control, forest measurement, and aerial photographic interpretation.

CERTIFICATION OR LICENSING

Forestry technicians who work with chemicals may need to be certified or licensed in some states. Technicians who do surveying work usually need a license to survey property for public records.

In-depth

National Parks and Forests

The first national park in the world, and the largest national park in the United States, is Yellowstone National Park, situated mainly in northwest Wyoming. It contains more than 3,450 square miles and was designated a national park by Theodore Roosevelt in 1872.

According to the U.S. Forest Service, in 1902 the San Isabel National Forest in southern Colorado west of Pueblo became the first forest in the world where large-scale public recreation and developments were planned and systematically built.

Landscape architect Arthur Carhart was hired in 1919 to develop and implement a recreation plan for the San Isabel National Forest. He created the Squirrel Creek Canyon, which became the nation's first forest area developed for public recreation. It included a campground, picnic area, public latrines, and trash cans.

In the 1920s San Isabel Lodge was built and during the Great Depression of the 1930s a 40-acre recreational reservoir, now known as Lake Isabel, was developed. Civilian Conservation Corps members built roads for access to the recreation area and completed landscaping.

San Isabel Lodge and Lake Isabel are still popular recreation sites used by visitors to the forest today.

INTERNSHIPS AND VOLUNTEERSHIPS

In addition to course work, nearly all forestry technician programs require students to get first-hand experience in the field. Students may work in nearby forests for the summer or during part of the school semester. They might also work at a sawmill or lumber mill.

High school students can get a sense of what it is like to work in a forest by participating in the Youth Conservation Corps, a summer employment and training program for students aged 15 to 18. Students spend approximately six weeks in a national park, forest, or wildlife refuge where they perform such duties as trail maintenance and building, tree pruning, campsite clearing and maintenance, and watershed maintenance. Students receive room and board and a small stipend. For more information, contact

United States Department of Agriculture
Forest Service
Youth Conservation Corps
PO Box 96090
Washington, DC 20090
202-205-8333
http://www.fs.fed.us

Who Will Hire Me?

About half of all forestry technicians work for government agencies. These include the Forest Service and the Natural Resources Conservation Service of the U.S. Department of Agriculture. They also work for the Bureau of Land Management, the Bureau of Indian Affairs, the National Park Service, and the Fish and Wildlife Service of the U.S. Department of the Interior. States also have forest areas where forestry technicians are employed.

Other forestry technicians work in the private sector. They are employed by logging, lumber, plywood, and paper companies. Others do reforestation work for mining, oil, and utility companies.

The Society of American Foresters can direct you to resource guides to jobs in forestry. They can also provide you with employment statistics and information on forestry training programs.

Where Can I Go from Here?

"I have to say I'm happy where I am," Jim says. "I really don't want to move again." Jim's plan is to remain in the Coronado National Forest working as a forestry technician until he is 55 and able to retire with full benefits.

A forestry technician's advancement often means having to move from one forest district or even national forest to another. As federal employees, forestry technicians are placed in ranks or grades. Workers advance to a higher grade after attaining a certain number of years' experience in their current grade. Advancement often means that the forestry technician assumes more administrative duties, which can keep him or her from working in the field as much as the lower grades do.

One advancement option is for a forestry technician to become a forester. This requires additional education—foresters complete a four-year course of study at an accredited university. *Foresters* are most often those responsible for developing the forest management plans that the forestry technicians help to implement.

What Are the Salary Ranges?

Forestry technicians who work for the federal government receive a salary determined by the current grade they hold. Typically, entry-level forestry technicians who work for the federal government earn slightly less than those working in the private sector, but their salaries generally become comparable after a few years on the job.

According to the *Occupational Outlook Handbook,* in 2003 forest and conservation technicians earn annual median salaries of $32,000. Those in the lowest paid 10 percent earned $21,800, and the highest paid 10 percent earned $48,600. Salary. com lists average annual earnings for forest aides as between $19,659 and $22,144.

In addition to their annual salary, forestry technicians who work for the government also receive numerous benefits. These include paid vacations, medical insurance and sick days, and retirement plan benefits. Some also receive financial assistance for further education and training so that they may keep abreast of changes occurring in the field.

What Is the Job Outlook?

Employment in forestry-related occupations is expected to grow slower than the average through the year 2012, according to the U.S. Department of Labor. This means competition for jobs as a forestry technician will be high. There are only 154 national forests in the United States, and while each is divided into districts,

ADVANCEMENT POSSIBILITIES

Foresters manage and develop forest lands and resources for economic and recreational purposes.

Fire wardens administer fire prevention programs and enforce governmental fire regulations throughout specific forest and logging areas.

Silviculturists establish and care for forest stands.

Smoke jumper supervisors supervise and coordinate activities of airborne firefighting crews engaged in extinguishing forest fires.

all of which employ forestry technicians, the number of available openings at any time is limited.

Because jobs as a forestry technician can be difficult to come by, many interested in the career work on a seasonal basis in order to gain experience in the field, making them more attractive candidates when openings do occur. Typically, the demand for seasonal workers occurs during the late spring and summer. This means that these individuals usually must have other jobs during the winter months in order to support themselves year round.

On the bright side, more people are enjoying our national forests than ever before. As recreational use increases, so will a need for forestry technicians skilled in managing forest resources. In addition, as demand for wood products continues to grow, so too will the need for a steady supply of timber. A forestry technician's forest management skills will play an important role in ensuring that this demand is met. Their knowledge of planting and forest care will create opportunities for forestry technicians in the years to come.

How Do I Learn More?

PROFESSIONAL ORGANIZATIONS

The following organizations provide information on forestry technician careers, accredited schools, and employers:

The Society of American Foresters
5400 Grosvenor Lane
Bethesda, MD 20814-2198
301-897-8720
http://www.safnet.org

United States Department of Agriculture
Natural Resources and Environment
1400 Independence Avenue, SW
Washington, DC 20250
202-720-7173
http://www.usda.gov

United States Department of the Interior
Bureau of Indian Affairs
1849 C Street, NW
Washington, DC 20240
202-208-3710
http://www.doi.gov/bureau-indian-affairs.html

United States Department of the Interior
Bureau of Land Management
1849 C Street, Room 406 LS
Washington, DC 20240
202-452-5125
http://www.blm.gov

United States Department of the Interior
Fish and Wildlife Service

1849 C Street, NW
Washington, DC 20242
800-344-9453
http://www.fws.gov

United States Department of the Interior
National Parks Service
1849 C Street, NW
Washington, DC 20242
202-208-4621
http://www.nps.gov

BIBLIOGRAPHY

The following is a sampling of materials relating to the professional concerns and development of forestry technicians:

Davis, Lawrence S. et al. *Forest Managaement.* New York: McGraw-Hill, 2000.

Helms, John A. *The Dictionary of Forestry.* Bethesda, Md.: Society of American Foresters, 1998.

Muir, John. *A Thousand-Mile Walk to the Gulf.* New York: Sierra Club Books, 1992.

World Commission on Forests and Sustainable Development. *Our Forests, Our Future.* Cambridge, U.K.: Cambridge University Press, 1999.

GEOLOGICAL TECHNICIANS

||||||||||||||||||||||||||||||||||||||||||||||||||||||||||||

Laura Burnett Blass looks through the morning's scout cards as if she is checking the winning lottery numbers. A few days earlier, an oil crew began drilling for oil in an area north of Houston. They picked that site to drill because research gathered by Laura indicated there might be pockets of crude oil located there. The crew may drill as many as 13,000 feet down into the earth searching for oil, which takes a considerable amount of time and money. Laura is anxious to see what the scout card, a report of the crew's findings, will show, since her work directly affected the crew's choice of drill site. As she scans the preliminary data, her eyes light up. The crew struck oil, and Laura can feel proud for a job well done.

What Does a Geological Technician Do?

Geological technicians work in the field of the geosciences. Geosciences are the sciences dealing with the earth, including geology, geophysics, and geochemistry. Usually, they work under the supervision of a geologist or geoscientist who is trained to study the earth's physical makeup and history. Often, geoscientists specialize in one area of study. Among these specialties are environmental geology, the study of how pollution, waste, and hazardous material affect the earth and its features; geophysics, the study of the earth's interior and magnetic, electric, and gravitational fields; hydrology, the investigation of the movement and quality of surface water; petroleum geology, the exploration and production of crude oil and natural gas; and seismology, the study of earthquakes and the forces that cause them.

Petroleum technicians most commonly work with petroleum geologists to determine where deposits of oil and natural gas may lay buried beneath the earth's surface. Since petroleum and natural gas play such a significant role in our daily lives, it is important that we find new deposits of these fossil fuels. There are small companies and large multinational corporations that search all over the world for deposits of oil and gas. They send teams of geologists and drill operators to scour farms, deserts, even beneath the ocean floor for new deposits of oil.

Definition
Geological technicians assist geologists and engineers by gathering, plotting, and storing samples and technical data.

Alternative Job Titles
Environmental technicians
Geological aides
Hydrologic technicians
Petroleum technicians
Seismic technicians

High School Subjects
Chemistry
Earth science
Mathematics

Personal Skills
Following instructions
Technical/scientific

Salary Range
$22,000 to $40,800 to $67,700+

Minimum Educational Level
Associate's degree

Certification or Licensing
None available

Outlook
Little or no growth

DOT
024

GOE
02.05.01

NOC
2212

O*NET-SOC
19-4041.00, 19-4041.01, 19-4041.02

Using data gathered from workers in the field, the geological technician drafts maps displaying where drilling operations are taking place and creates reports that geologists use to determine where an oil deposit might be located.

When drafting maps, petroleum technicians pinpoint the exact location where a drilling crew has dug a well. The map may also indicate the depth of the well and whether oil was found or, if not, that it was a "dry well." Once this information is included on a map, geologists are better able to determine the size of the oil deposit that lies buried beneath the surface of the earth.

When creating reports, petroleum technicians must analyze several types of raw data. Often,

383

Lingo to Learn

Dry well A well that has produced no oil or natural gas deposits.

Fossil fuel A nonrenewable energy source, such as oil or gas, derived from organic remains of past life.

Groundwater The water within the earth.

Hydrology The science of the properties, distribution, and circulation of water in the atmosphere and on and below the earth's surface.

Natural gas A combustible mixture of methane and hydrocarbons used chiefly as a fuel.

Petroleum An oily black substance that is found beneath the earth's surface and can be processed for use as gasoline, grease, and plastic. Also called crude oil.

Scout card A preliminary report from an oil drilling crew.

Seismic Of or relating to an earth vibration caused by an earthquake, a planned explosion, or an impact.

Seismograph An instrument designed to measure the severity and intensity of earthquakes. It records the seismic waves generated by earthquakes.

and landfills, can affect the geological landscape. The information they gather is used in environmental impact statements that are then used by developers, government officials, and private landowners to minimize damage to the environment.

Environmental technicians also study how pollution and other materials affect the earth by gathering and testing samples of soil, water, or other substances. For instance, environmental technicians monitor wells and sample groundwater, checking for contamination. If the water is contaminated, environmental technicians then assist with site remediation or cleanup.

Hydrologic technicians are concerned with weather patterns, precipitation, and water supply. They study the properties, distribution, and circulation of waters on or beneath the earth's surface as well as in the atmosphere. Hydrologic technicians also assist hydrologists in the study of precipitation, including the form, intensity, and rate at which it penetrates the soil. They also research how precipitation moves through the earth and returns to the ocean and atmosphere. Hydrologic technicians collect, analyze, and interpret hydrologic data to assess the availability and quality of water, including lakes, streams, groundwater supply, and more.

Seismic technicians help seismologists gather data so they can better understand and predict earthquakes and other vibrations of the earth. Seismic technicians use seismographs and other geophysical instruments to collect and analyze data.

What Is It Like to Be a Geological Technician?

Laura Burnett Blass has been a geological technician for over 15 years. For most of those years she has worked for gas and oil companies in central Texas. Today, she works at the Geotechnology Research Institute, a research facility that helps petroleum companies develop better and more efficient methods of finding and retrieving fossil fuels.

While some geological technicians frequently go out into the field where drilling operations are taking place, Laura's days are spent indoors at the institute's offices in The Woodlands, Texas. Typically she works an eight-hour day, five days a week, but when several projects are under way she must often put in overtime.

crews detonate carefully planned explosions that send shock and sound waves deep into the earth. These waves are recorded by microphones, and by studying the patterns of the waves, it is possible to determine the composition of the rock beneath the surface. Geological technicians take these patterns and remove any background noise (even an airplane flying overhead can create a sound wave that will be picked up by the receiving microphones) and then write a report that summarizes what the sound patterns indicate.

Some geological technicians work in the field of environmental engineering and are often known as *environmental technicians*. They assist geologists in studying how man-made structures, such as roads and commercial, residential, and industrial development

Each day she has certain specific duties she must perform. She first gathers the results of the previous day's seismic tests and enters the data into a database on her computer. Depending upon how active the seismic crews were the day before, this task can take anywhere from 10 minutes to four hours.

She also examines the drilling crews' scout cards. The scout cards are preliminary reports that reveal several types of information. They tell how deep into the earth the crew drilled, what type of rock was found at which depths, and whether oil was or was not found. Laura takes this information and places it on a map, which is called "spotting a well."

Often, she must draw her own maps on a drafting table in her office, but with advances in computer software technology, much of her work can now be performed on her computer.

Once she has compiled and written reports based on the various data she has gathered from the drilling and research crews, Laura gives the reports to a petroleum geologist. The geologist then analyzes her findings and may also ask Laura for maps showing all of the wells currently being drilled in a specific region. With the information Laura has compiled, the geologist then recommends where future drilling operations should take place.

Mark Meeks works as an environmental technician for Earth Systems Consultants in San Luis Obispo, California. He focuses on groundwater contamination and has two main duties: He monitors wells and collects groundwater samples, and he helps with site remediation when necessary. When a site is suspected to be contaminating the ground, such as leaking gas tanks, Mark's company is sent out to dig wells in various spots surrounding the area. The wells are monitored regularly and the groundwater tested to determine how far the contamination has spread, known as the plume, and the severity of the pollution.

On a typical day, Mark may visit up to 15 wells. Sometimes he works with a partner, depending on the size of the project and the number of wells. When he arrives at the well site, Mark opens the well cover, drops down an instrument designed to measure the distance down to the groundwater, which is usually four feet to 25 feet beneath the surface, then bails out the old water, which can entail bailing out buckets of stagnant water by hand. Mark then lets the wells recharge up to 80 percent, fills up three to four jars, then delivers the jars to a laboratory to test for contaminants, such as crude oil, benzene, or lead.

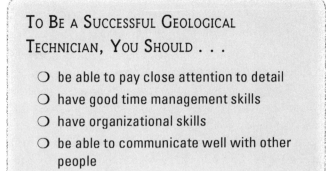

To Be a Successful Geological Technician, You Should . . .

❍ be able to pay close attention to detail

❍ have good time management skills

❍ have organizational skills

❍ be able to communicate well with other people

Sites are visited at different times; some are checked weekly, while others are visited semiannually. They are also located in many different areas. "If you do a gas station site," says Mark, "you have to cone off, and you have to watch for people trying to run you over. And then when I do the tank farm, which is semiannual, you have to put all your equipment in a backpack and hike out to the wells because they're inaccessible to traffic."

Mark also assists with site remediation, or cleanup, once the extent of the contamination is determined. "Once we know how big the plume is," Mark explains, "and how deep and how badly it's contaminated, then we put in vapor extraction systems or pump and treat systems." Vapor extraction systems clean the soil by sucking the fumes from the water and running them through a system that burns off the contamination. This process usually takes a year or two. With a pump and treat system, the water is run through carbon filters to clean it.

Do I Have What It Takes to Be a Geological Technician?

Geological technicians working in the petroleum industry are an important link in a company's search to find hidden pockets of fossil fuels. They take the data that field crews gather from seismic tests and other measures and process that information into a report that helps the company narrow its search. Because drilling for oil can be a costly and time-consuming venture, geological technicians must be competent in their ability to correctly interpret data.

Laura admits that working with such a weighty responsibility can sometimes be intimidating. Yet this responsibility can also be one of the most satisfying aspects of the job. "You actually get to see what happens to your work," Laura says. "They dig a well based on information you've provided. I know that my efforts make a contribution. And it's a good feeling knowing that they depend on you and trust your judgment."

To be a successful geological technician requires an ability to pay attention to detail since mistakes can cost time and money. "You also need to have very good time management and organizational skills," says Laura. "I wasn't a very organized person before I started working as a geological technician. But this job made me into one." Geological technicians working in environmental geology should be mathematically inclined, says Mark, since you are constantly dealing with calculations and volumes and distances. Mark also emphasizes the importance of being physically fit; there is a lot of lifting and outdoor activity involved in the job of an environmental technician.

> I wasn't a very organized person before I started working as a geological technician. But this job made me into one.

How Do I Become a Geological Technician?

Laura began her career as a geological technician in 1981 when an opening became available at the oil company she was working for in Woodlawns, Texas. Because she had no formal training in geology, she had to acquire her skills on the job.

Over the years, she has learned all about map reading and mapmaking, data evaluation, and performing complex calculations, all the skills that a geological technician must use each day on the job. Because of recent technical innovations, she is now learning how to make three-dimensional representations of oil fields and oil wells on a computer.

"It's fascinating," she says. "There's always new technology coming out, which means you're always learning something new."

EDUCATION

High School

A high school diploma is mandatory for anyone considering a career as a geological technician. High school courses in geology, geography, and math, including algebra, trigonometry, and statistics, are all recommended. The science courses will provide you with an understanding of the earth and the forces that affect it, while the math courses are important to learn how to perform complex calculations and statistical analysis. In addition, drafting courses can teach the skills used in mapmaking, and since many companies now design maps using computer software, courses in computer science are also recommended. Because the geological technician serves in many respects as a liaison between the field crews and the geologists, courses that develop communication skills are also beneficial.

Part-time or summer employment may be available with large oil and gas companies, environmental engineering firms, or other companies that employ those in the geological field. Summer camps with an educational focus may also expose you to various facets of geology and the environment.

You might also consider joining a club or organization concerned with rock collecting or the environment. Local amateur geological groups may

FYI

Scottish geologist James Hutton's (1726–97) concept of the formation of the earth's crust and surface features made him a founder of modern geology. He showed that granite was formed by solidification from a molten state, and that the earth was much older than scientists and theologians believed. Hutton originated the doctrine of uniformitarianism, which holds that the formation of the surface of the earth is due to various processes of erosion and land building that are at work even today. He summarized his finding in the statement that "the present is the key to the past."

sponsor events or activities such as local hikes or trips to sites of geological interest.

Postsecondary Training

While a college degree is not required for anyone considering a career as a geological technician, it is highly recommended, and many companies will not hire technicians who lack a degree. Mark does not possess a college degree, but he advises, "If you want to become a full-blown geological technician, you need to have a college degree in geology or soils engineering or something."

Some two-year colleges offer associate's degrees in geological technician programs, but most offer basic geology programs with credits that are transferable to four-year schools. Bachelor's degree programs in geology and the geosciences are readily available at most colleges and universities.

CERTIFICATION OR LICENSING

There is no certification specifically for geological technicians. Some environmental technicians, however, may need to acquire certification for handling and sampling hazardous materials such as crude oil. Certification requires attending a 40-hour class, with an eight-hour refresher course every year thereafter. Mark has found that most employers will finance the training.

SCHOLARSHIPS AND GRANTS

For those planning to attend college, there are plenty of scholarship opportunities. You may wish to contact your financial aid office or advisor for information on scholarships. There may be general school scholarships or department awards.

Professional organizations such as the Geological Society of America or the American Geological Institute offer scholarships and lists of scholarship opportunities.

INTERNSHIPS AND VOLUNTEERSHIPS

Some large corporations offer internship programs, and professional associations are excellent resources for information on internship opportunities. Contacting companies or organizations directly and inquiring about internships would be a good idea.

Students in two-year or four-year programs may find it easy to locate summer or part-time internship opportunities through the school placement program or departmental advisor. Completing an internship assures employers that you have hands-on experience and will make you a more desirable candidate.

Volunteer opportunities are plentiful, especially if you are interested in environmental issues. Many nonprofit groups sponsor activities and field trips, and volunteers are frequently needed to help geologists or geoscientists working in the field. The U.S. Geological Survey also offers volunteer opportunities. Volunteers must be 18 years of age or older.

Who Will Hire Me?

When Laura landed her first job as a geological technician, she was working as a secretary at a small, independent oil company in central Texas. "They needed someone to be a geological technician," she says, "and I was willing to give it a try."

Today, such stories are rare, she says. "It's really very tough right now [to find a geological technician position]," Laura says. But that does not mean jobs as a geological technician are not out there, and there are some resources available to help find those positions.

A good place to begin looking for a position as a geological technician is with the major oil and gas companies. Because of their size (most are multinational corporations), they are more likely to have several geological technicians on staff. Chevron, Arco, Shell, Texaco, and Exxon are some of the largest gas and oil companies in the United States, and each may have overseas departments where geological technicians work as well

The federal and state government agencies employ geologists, geoscientists, and geological technicians. The U.S. Geological Survey, a division of the Department of the Interior, the Department of Energy, the Forest Service, the Department of Agriculture, the U.S. Army Corps of Engineers, and state geological surveys are just some of the departments that may have job opportunities for geological technicians. Because the competition for federal and state jobs is fierce, most agencies require that applicants possess a bachelor's degree.

Many environmental engineering companies and environmental consulting firms also hire geological

ADVANCEMENT POSSIBILITIES

Geologists study the composition, structure, and history of the earth's crust.

Soil engineers study and analyze surface and subsurface soils to determine characteristics for construction, development, or land planning.

Environmental geologists study the effects of human activity, the atmosphere, the geosphere, and the hydrosphere on the earth to provide solutions to problems such as pollution, erosion, and waste management.

Petroleum geologists are involved with exploring for oil and natural gas resources.

technicians. With these firms, geological technicians assist in creating environmental impact studies and monitoring environmental resources. These companies can be found under the Environmental Engineering or Engineering headings in most cities' Yellow Pages.

There are several professional associations that may be able to provide further information about employment opportunities. Most of these professional organizations, as well as large corporations and governmental agencies, have Web sites that provide information on job openings.

Where Can I Go from Here?

"I'd really like to train or teach others to be geological technicians," Laura says.

Supervisory positions are available to those geological technicians who have several years of on-the-job experience. Typically, these geological technicians train new staff in proper procedures and methods, as well as check their work for accuracy before sending it to the geologist.

A geological technician's advancement depends partly on the size of the company he or she works for. At smaller companies and consulting firms, geological technicians may be called upon to perform some tasks that geologists might do, as well as perform some clerical duties. At larger companies, they might specialize in performing one set task, such as well spotting, or they might supervise a staff of several geological technicians.

With additional years of schooling, geological technicians can go on to become engineers or scientists, such as geologists, environmental geologists, soil engineers, or petroleum geologists. A master's degree and/or doctorate are generally needed for these positions. *Geologists* are concerned with the physical nature of the earth, while *soil engineers* study surface and subsurface soils. The work of soil engineers is especially helpful for land planning, construction, and land development. *Environmental geologists* focus on solving problems such as pollution, waste management, flooding, erosion, and urbanization. They accomplish this by studying and analyzing the interaction between human activities and the atmosphere, geosphere, and hydrosphere. *Petroleum geologists* work for companies in the petroleum and gas industry and are involved with the exploration for natural gas and oil resources. They also assist with the production of oil.

What Are the Salary Ranges?

According to the *Occupational Outlook Handbook*, geological and petroleum technicians earned a median annual income of $40,800 in 2003. The lowest paid 10 percent earned $22,000 annually, and the highest paid 10 percent earning $67,700.

Those with bachelor's degrees in geology and geological sciences can earn considerably more. According to a 2004 salary survey conducted by the American Association of Petroleum Geologists (AAPG), those geologists with four-year degrees and less than two years of experience had average annual salaries of $65,600. Those with three to five years of experience earned $67,700. Geologists with 15 to 20 years of experience reported incomes of well over $100,000. The survey notes that these salaries reflect no increase over the previous year, however.

What Is the Job Outlook?

The *Occupational Outlook Handbook* indicates that job opportunities for geological and petroleum technicians are expected to show little or no growth through 2012. This estimate is based on an overall slowdown in employment in the chemical industry. The AAPG 2004 survey reported no new hires in the field among those with only bachelor's degrees and less than 10 years of experience. The survey resuslts indicate not only a lack of hiring, but downsizing of staff by some of the industry's larger companies.

Despite this slower growth, well-trained technicians with degrees should find good job opportunities. With increasing concern about the environment, technicians will be needed for collecting soil, water, and air samples and assisting with the cleanup of contaminated sites. Employment can also be affected by industry. In recent years, the petroleum industry has seen a number of large mergers, which can freeze new hiring.

How Do I Learn More?

PROFESSIONAL ORGANIZATIONS

The following are organizations that provide information on geological technician careers, accredited schools, and employers:

American Association of Petroleum Geologists
PO Box 979
Tulsa, OK 74101
800-364-2274
http://www.aapg.org

American Geological Institute
4220 King Street
Alexandria, VA 22302-1502
703-379-2480
http://www.agiweb.org

Geological Society of America
PO Box 9140
Boulder, CO 80301-9140
303-447-2020
http://www.geosociety.org

U.S. Geological Survey
12201 Sunrise Valley Drive
Reston, VA 20192
http://www.usgs.gov

BIBLIOGRAPHY

The following is a sampling of materials relating to the professional concerns and development of geological technicians:

Day, Robert W. *Geotechnical Engineer's Portable Handbook.* New York: McGraw Hill, 1999.

Hyne, Norman J. et al. *Nontechnical Guide to Petroleum Geology, Exploration, Drilling and Production.* Tulsa, Okla.: Pennwell Books, 2001.

Montgomery, Carla W. *Fundamentals of Geology.* 3d ed. New York: McGraw Hill, 1996.

O'Reilly, Gerald. *Planning for Field Safety.* Alexandria, Va.: American Geological Institute, 1992.

HAZARDOUS WASTE MANAGEMENT TECHNICIANS

I t is late Friday morning, and Sam Borries receives a call from the Indiana Department of Environment Management (IDEM). A petroleum leak has been discovered in Hammond, Indiana. Gas is escaping a petroleum pipeline and is seeping into the Hammond sewer system. IDEM personnel fear that, if not quickly contained, the leak could result in a fire or explosion or could contaminate the Little Calumet River. Sam, an on-scene coordinator for the U.S. Environmental Protection Agency (EPA), calmly questions the caller. He agrees to help coordinate the cleanup.

On the scene, Sam quickly assesses the situation. The leak had been discovered on Thursday, after members of the community reported smelling gasoline odors. The responsible petroleum company had moved quickly to identify the leaking pipeline and block it off. Though unsure how much gas had escaped into the sewer system, they immediately notified the appropriate authorities and began recovery efforts. They mobilized huge vacuum recovery trucks to suck the gas out of the sewer system. Because the gas vapors were extremely dense, they also closed the street above the affected lines. The cleanup is well under way, but the threat of a fire or an explosion persists.

With Sam's assistance, the petroleum company, IDEM, and the Hammond Department of Environmental Management (HDEM) mobilize crews to dig up the road in order to locate the leaky gas line. As they search for the source of the leak, crews use sandbags to try to contain the escaping gas. They use a product called Biosolve to suppress gasoline vapors. In the afternoon, the team attempts to open the road above the sewer to one lane of traffic in each direction. When a passing motorist tosses a lit cigarette from his window, however, the team quickly realizes that this is too dangerous and closes the road until the response effort is completed.

The cleanup effort continues throughout the weekend. On Monday, the process is complicated by reports of gasoline odors in homes along the sewer lines. The team realizes that the incident is larger than first believed. They hire a local marine diving

Definition
Hazardous waste management technicians help identify, remove, and dispose of hazardous wastes. Technicians may collect water, soil, or other samples for laboratory analysis and monitor waste control systems.

Alternative Job Titles
Environmental technicians
Environmental technologists

High School Subjects
Biology
Chemistry
Earth science

Personal Skills
Leadership/management
Technical/scientific

Salary Range
$22,420 to $33,080 to $56,100

Minimum Educational Level
Some postsecondary training

Certification or Licensing
Voluntary

Outlook
Faster than the average

DOT
168

GOE
06.02.03

NOC
2263

O*NET-SOC
47-4041.00

company to find where the fuel is infiltrating the sewer line and to help devise a plan for plugging the leaks. By Wednesday, the petroleum company's pipeline has been repaired and is functioning normally. The emergency response team must still remove all the fuel and contaminated water from the sewer lines before repairing the road.

What Does a Hazardous Waste Management Technician Do?

Hazardous waste management technicians are trained to safely contain and remove highly toxic or volatile materials. Broadly defined, a hazardous waste is any substance that threatens human health or the environment.

Some hazardous waste management technicians respond to emergency situations, such as the petroleum leak in Hammond, Indiana. As an EPA employee, Sam's mandate is to respond to emergencies that pose "an immediate and substantial danger to human health and the environment." Sam, therefore, responds primarily to emergency situations, such as petroleum or chemical spills, although he also supervises ongoing cleanup efforts. Other hazardous waste management technicians clean up devastating industrial messes—ugly reminders of a time when our country did not monitor environmental contamination as closely as we do today. Such sites are specifically targeted for cleanup by the federal government under the Comprehensive Environmental Response, Compensation, and Liability Act (CERCLA) of 1980, known as "Superfund."

Since many of the worst Superfund sites have, today, been cleaned up, a larger number of hazardous waste management technicians are involved in lower priority cleanups. Many are cleaning up previously abandoned industrial sites, called brownfields, so that the land can once again be used. These sites do not pose an immediate threat to human health or the environment.

"As the country learns more about the effects of hazardous waste on the environment," notes Carl Patterson, a technician with the consulting firm CH2M Hill, "we're going in and cleaning up those kinds of sites, too."

The Environmental Careers Organization (ECO), a major environmental careers internship and job placement specialist in the United States, estimates that there are up to 33,000 municipal and industrial hazardous waste sites in the United States, plus 5,000 to 10,000 government-owned sites. In addition to helping clean up these kinds of sites, hazardous waste management technicians may identify, categorize, and dispose of hazardous waste, or help in efforts to lower the amount of hazardous waste produced in the first place. They also assist in other types of cleanup and pollution prevention efforts, including routine monitoring of air, soil, and water, to make sure hazardous substances are within acceptable limits.

Nearly every industry produces hazardous waste, from food, textiles, metals, petroleum, plastics, and paper manufacturing to dry cleaning services,

Lingo to Learn

Comprehensive Environmental Response, Compensation, and Liability Act (CERCLA) 1980 law (known as "Superfund") that mandated cleanup of private and government-owned hazardous waste sites.

Defense waste Radioactive waste from weapons research and development, decommissioned nuclear-powered ships and submarines, weapons material production, and other military waste; includes low- and high-level radioactive, hazardous, and mixed (radioactive and hazardous) waste.

Level A work Work involving hazardous substances that pose a high dermal (skin) threat.

National Priorities List U.S. EPA list of the worst hazardous waste sites in the country needing cleanup. Currently, there are 1,228 sites on the list, and cleanups of NPL sites are taking up to eight to ten years each.

Sampling Taking quantities of water, soil, or air from a site. Samples are tested in labs to check for the presence of hazardous substances.

U.S. Environmental Protection Agency (EPA) Federal agency responsible for overseeing the implementation of environmental laws, including those designed to monitor and control air, water, and soil pollution. State EPAs help carry out these laws.

printing, and more. Chemical companies produce up to 68 percent of all private industry hazardous waste. Petroleum companies are another significant source of hazardous waste. For example, one common hazardous waste is benzene, a component in fuel that has been identified as a carcinogen. Tanks of fuel around a gas station can leak, and substances from the fuel, including benzene, can seep into the ground and contaminate the groundwater, which we then drink. Other hazardous wastes include solvents used in paint, manufacturing, and service operations such as dry cleaners. Manufacturing processes also produce certain metals that are hazardous.

A hazardous waste management technician moves chemical recovery drums. *(Paul Shambroom/Photo Researchers Inc.)*

The federal government is also a leading generator of hazardous waste. According to the ECO, domestic military bases produce more hazardous waste than the top five chemical companies combined. The U.S. Department of Defense (DOD) spends about $5 billion per year on hazardous waste cleanups. Estimates vary, but all together, between 5,000 and 10,000 government-owned sites require cleanups— at a projected cost of $250 billion. The government usually hires private environmental consultants to carry out its cleanup jobs, which include military bases and military production sites.

The United States has some of the toughest environmental laws in the world. Beginning in the 1960s, people began to realize that this country's industry, including its military production industry, was producing vast amounts of pollution and waste that was ruining the environment and threatening human health and safety. Private industry, municipalities, and the government had been producing hazardous and other wastes for many years. A series of tough laws, including CERCLA, have been passed over the last 25 years to force the cleanup of old waste sites and discourage companies from creating new ones.

Although the cost of cleaning up our environment is high—billions of dollars have been spent to clean up hazardous waste sites—the cost of not cleaning up is potentially even higher.

What Is It Like to Be a Hazardous Waste Management Technician?

In his role as an on-site coordinator for the EPA, Sam Borries divides his time between his office and the sites of major spills. Sam's job is to coordinate the federal response to hazards. He typically coordinates his efforts with state and local authorities, including police and fire departments. If the responsible authority does not have the ability to adequately respond to a situation, however, Sam can step in and assume complete responsibility for the project. If local authorities have a situation under control, on the other hand, Sam may oversee the progress from his office.

"I respond to a lot of petroleum leaks," says Sam. "Under the Oil Pollution Act, I get involved when oil is released to a waterway. I may be working on a river, lake, wetland, or a storm sewer. It just depends on where the spill is."

When an emergency occurs, Sam's first priority is to put out any fires that occur. Once the fires have been extinguished, he tries to identify the source of the leak or spill in order to stop the release. The next step is to control and contain the hazardous material that has already been released. Once the substance has been contained, Sam and his colleagues devise a strategy for cleaning it up. "There are a variety of tools for cleaning up petroleum products," Sam notes. "We can use skimmers or vacuums to wick the petroleum off the water. We can run the water through an oil-water separator. Usually we try to treat the oil so that it can be reused. Sometimes we have to burn it off the water, though this is a less desirable method."

In addition to his technical responsibilities, Sam must perform public relations duties throughout emergency situations. "People want to know if there's a health threat," he explains. "Their first question is whether they've been exposed to anything and, if so, what they can do. Then they want to know how the situation will disrupt daily life. I've been in front of TV cameras more times than I can tell you."

Carl Patterson is a technician for CH2M Hill, one of the largest environmental consulting firms in the United States. CH2M Hill does every type of environmental analysis, cleanup, and follow-up project for private industrial companies, municipalities, and the government. CH2M Hill is also part of a global organization that does water plant and environmental projects all over the world.

Carl is based in the company's Deerfield Beach, Florida, offices. He helps to do the highly accurate measuring, monitoring, and sampling needed to be sure that a client is complying with environmental laws. Now in his sixth year with CH2M Hill, Carl focuses on projects to identify, correct, prevent, and monitor the contamination of water by hazardous substances. He is concerned with both surface water, such as lakes, streams, and canals, and with groundwater. When a fuel or chemical spills onto the ground, hazardous substances can soak through the soil and reach the groundwater, contaminating it. This is extremely dangerous, because groundwater is used for community water supplies.

"Water treatment facilities aren't designed to handle these kinds of hazardous substances," Carl says. "And in some places, like outlying rural areas, people are drinking groundwater, drawing it right out of the ground from wells. The efforts of federal, state, and local authorities to provide safe drinking water are really incredible, especially in this area. Florida's environment is very wet and marshy. The groundwater is very close to the surface, usually just a few feet. There's a high potential for problems. Also, there are miles of canals to control flooding, and that means a lot of exposed groundwater with potential for contamination."

Carl continues, "For example, there's a fuel storage facility near here. They have thousands of barrels of fuel. Obviously, there's a huge potential for a problem. The state requires the facility to monitor the groundwater around that site, so a daily task for us is to take groundwater samples from the monitoring wells there. CH2M Hill has its own labs; they run tests on the samples and see if there are hazardous substances in them. If so, and if there's more of the substance than allowed by federal, state, or local authorities, CH2M Hill can tell owners immediately. We also can help them develop a plan to clean up the problem and take steps to prevent other leaks."

To collect water samples, Carl uses a narrow, three-foot-long, tube-like instrument made of Teflon or stainless steel. Water is drawn in at the bottom of the instrument, following strict procedures defined by the EPA, the county in which the site is located, CH2M Hill, and sometimes the client. CH2M Hill's job is to be so precise with the retrieval procedures and in the analysis done back at the labs that the company produces "defendable data," such as data that can stand up in court. "I've never seen anything go to litigation," Carl says, "but that's how we operate, in terms of potentially defending in court the processes we used."

Accuracy is extremely important. "We work with very tiny numbers, very tiny compounds," he says. "For example, for benzene, one part per billion in the water is considered too much. When the test results are close, we'll go back and retest, particularly when there's a potential for very costly remedial projects. In fact, almost everything is triple redundancy [done three times]."

Altogether, Carl runs about 100 field tests a year. "Essentially, we do fieldwork for one to two months out of the year. The rest of the year is spent compiling data." Carl's work takes him to a wide variety of sites. "It's hard to express how broad it is, how there are projects almost everywhere," he says. "Sites are indoors and outdoors, and range from the obvious, like an oil refinery, to the less obvious, like a carpet factory. Metal manufacturing can create dust from cutting, bending, or other processes; when you sweep or wash the dust out of the plant, it has the potential to reach the groundwater and contaminate it."

Technicians who work in the field, testing and monitoring air, soil, or water, often enjoy being outdoors, free of the routine of office or lab work. But not all sites are outdoors, and many sites are unpleasant. "Some indoor sites are so noisy that you can't communicate. By the end of the day, you're frazzled," Carl says. "Some really smell bad. Some of these places are producing some really nasty effluents. I'm sometimes stunned at what people do with their wastes.

"Sometimes you're all bundled up, in special suits, a paper hat, a respirator," he continues. "The respirator's just an air-purifying mask with filters, but I'm claustrophobic and it bothers me. It makes it difficult to communicate. The ones I can't deal with are the zip-on suits. You're sealed in a suit from head to toe, like an astronaut. They're for Level A work, for substances with a very high dermal threat, those that will burn your skin." Luckily, he adds, CH2M Hill doesn't do Level A testing.

"There's lots of travel to this job, and sometimes real travel, all over the world," he says. "But sometimes you're traveling only to see the armpit of a country, the nasty side. And the workday is long."

Still, there is a lot about the job that Carl really likes. "Each project is almost a new world unto itself," he says. "And I like being part of the cleanup efforts; after all, it's my drinking water, too."

Do I Have What It Takes to Be a Hazardous Waste Management Technician?

Hazardous waste management technicians work with toxic and volatile materials. To ensure their own safety, and that of others, they must be extremely alert and accurate. They also must be able to follow orders. Some, but not all, positions require technical and scientific aptitude. Hazardous waste management technicians usually work in teams, so they must be able to cooperate and communicate well with others. Good reasoning skills, analytical thinking, and the ability to respond to unexpected conditions are also important.

In many ways, technicians must be rule followers, and they must be careful listeners. Regulations drive this industry; there are standards and guidelines that must be followed for every part of the hazardous waste management technician's job. If a standard requires the hazardous waste management technician to collect a half-liter sample, he or she must get

exactly that. When hazardous waste management technicians do not follow regulations, the price can be high. They can cost their employers or clients a great deal of money in fines, or, worse, they can endanger their lives and the lives of others.

"People in this profession must be motivated and they must have excellent people skills," says Sam Borries. "They also must be disciplined. They have to be willing to go to work at a moment's notice. Like most hazardous waste management technicians, I take turns being on call. Someone has to be on call 365 days a year. When I'm on call, I may get called in the middle of the night and, if I do, I go."

> Someone has to be on call 365 days a year. When I'm on call, I may get called in the middle of the night and, if I do, I go.

Good technicians also must be flexible, able to spot problems, and able to think quickly on their feet. "Sometimes, once you get out to the site, you find that the ground's not dirt like everyone expected—it's mud," Carl Patterson says. "There were plans for specific tests, but now it's pouring rain. Or there are power lines that the managers or engineers didn't anticipate. You have to be flexible and able to adapt to the conditions you find."

Good technicians are conscientious. "This job is all about details," Carl says. "But I also like to think about the big picture. For example, sometimes at a cleaned-up site there will be ground cleaners and incinerators. It's a standard setup: They'll have a system to drag water out of the ground, run it through stripping towers, and then pump it back in the ground. It helps to be able to picture how that's working. I need to know if a system is there, if it's on or off, and if it will change the way the tests should be done."

How Do I Become a Hazardous Waste Management Technician?

In the past, hazardous waste management technicians could find plenty of work with only a high school

In-depth

The *Exxon Valdez* Oil Spill

Just past midnight on March 24, 1989, an enormous oil tanker, the *Exxon Valdez*, ran aground on Bligh Reef in the northeastern part of beautiful Prince William Sound. Over the next few days, the tanker spilled more than 11,000,000 gallons of crude oil into the surrounding waters, creating an oil slick that measured seven miles long and seven miles wide. It was the largest oil spill in U.S. history.

More than 11,000 people, many of them hazardous waste management technicians, contributed to the cleanup effort. In the weeks and months that followed the spill, people worked around the clock to try to contain and remove the oil. They used an array of cleanup techniques, including burning, chemical dispersants, high-pressure/hot-water washing, cold-water washing, fertilizer-enhanced bioremediation, and manual and mechanical removal of oil and oil-laden sediments.

Despite the heroic efforts of these dedicated individuals, the formerly pristine waters of Prince William Sound were severely contaminated. Between 100,000 and 300,000 birds died. Nearly 3,000 sea otters were killed. Alaska's fisheries, a major source of income for local communities, were severely impaired. Today, the marine life and other wildlife of Prince William Sound are still recovering.

The *Exxon Valdez* tragedy illustrates a harsh reality of environmental hazards. No matter how sophisticated the techniques for remediation become, hazardous waste management technicians can never totally eradicate the damage caused by environmental contamination.

---

diploma. Hazardous waste management is becoming an increasingly sophisticated field, however, because of tighter regulations and advances in cleanup technology. More and more, a two-year diploma or degree in hazardous waste management is becoming important for many positions.

Whether or not a degree is required depends on the task, the company, and the nature of the problem, according to the Air and Waste Management Association. For some field or monitoring work, two-year degrees may be needed. Some of these jobs involve sophisticated work like chemical analyses or working under protocols.

On the other hand, other technicians are essentially moving waste, like forklift drivers, warehouse workers, or drivers. They will get some particular training or instruction from the company, but generally don't need a degree.

Experts see a trend toward higher educational requirements for environmental technicians overall than in the past. According to the Environmental Careers Organization, this is especially true in hazardous waste management. In this area, technical degrees, even graduate degrees, tend to be valued more than in some other areas, such as solid waste handling.

EDUCATION

High School

While still in high school, potential hazardous waste management technicians should take math and science, including biology, earth sciences, physics, and chemistry. To help develop strong communication skills, you also should take English, speech, and writing.

Postsecondary Training

The U.S. Environmental Protection Agency (EPA) provides grants for schools to develop and implement environmental training curricula. Today, there are hundreds of choices for those interested in pursuing postsecondary training in hazardous waste management. Options include community colleges, technical colleges, vocational institutes, and college outreach programs. Students should make sure the school is accredited and talk to the people in the placement office to find out where graduates have gone on to work.

INTERNSHIPS AND VOLUNTEERSHIPS

Students also should seek opportunities to gain firsthand experience by volunteering or participating in internships. Two national nonprofit groups help develop and place people in internships in the environmental industry: the Student Conservation Association (SCA) and the Environmental Careers Organization (ECO). The SCA focuses on internships in resource management, placing people in projects in federal, state, and private parks and natural lands. There is a three- to five-week summer internship program for 450 high school students each year.

The ECO encourages everyone to get experience while in school through internships, volunteering for local nonprofit or community organizations, and independent research and study projects. The ECO offers internship opportunities for those at the college level or above. Created in 1972 with a handful of interns, ECO today is a major environmental placement service that also holds career seminars, recruits on campus, and recently began staging an annual Environmental Workforce Symposium. College students, recent grads, and first-time job seekers are matched with paid internships in the environmental industry. Many of the interns are eventually hired full-time, and positions do include work in hazardous waste management. ECO publishes a book that outlines work throughout the environmental industry, *The New Complete Guide to Environmental Careers in the 21st Century*.

Another option is to contact a federal or local government agency directly about an internship. Many of the federal-level agencies have internship programs, including the EPA, National Park Service, and Bureau of Land Management. Programs are more informal at the local level; contact regional, county, or other local authorities and express your interest in an internship. In the private sector, an internship in a nonprofit organization is probably the easiest to come by. These groups include the National Wildlife Federation and the Natural Resources Defense Council. Opportunities exist at both the local tech national levels.

CERTIFICATION OR LICENSING

The Institute for Hazardous Materials Management gives a test for certifying people as hazardous materials managers. An applicant must have a bachelor's degree and at least three years of experience in the field. The National Environmental Health Association also has a certification process; those who pass the exam are Registered Hazardous Substances Specialists. An applicant must have completed a two-year program in hazardous materials/waste management.

Who Will Hire Me?

Hazardous waste management technicians are employed by chemical companies and other producers of hazardous waste, waste disposal companies and waste disposal consulting engineering firms, environmental consulting firms, government agencies, and other organizations. By far, the largest number of jobs is in the private sector. Private companies employ about 75 percent of all employees in hazardous waste management, and public organizations (federal, state, and local) employ 24 percent, according to ECO. Nonprofit organizations employ the remaining 1 percent. Following are some private-sector employers of hazardous waste management technicians:

In-house staffs. Private industry jobs can be found within large companies. Such companies generate waste and are likely to have their own in-house staff of environmentalists. This is especially true as regulations keep getting more and more complex. Medium-size companies may have smaller departments. Smaller companies may have a professional or two on staff, or hire outside consultants.

Consultants. Consulting companies are another good source of employment opportunities for hazardous waste management technicians. Some consulting companies advise companies how to handle a hazardous waste problem. Others also design a plan and provide the manpower to carry it out. Some have their own testing and laboratory services. There are about 100 very large environmental consulting firms in the United States, including companies like CH2M

The EPA is just one federal government agency that uses technicians. In fact, says ECO, the U.S. Forest Service, the National Park Service, the Bureau of Land Management, and the Fish and Wildlife Service probably employ more technicians and field personnel, while the EPA uses more scientists and other professionals. There also is a trend now toward increased work in hazardous waste management at the local level, by states, counties, and municipalities. Jobs here include technicians at municipal water plants and other public facilities.

According to the ECO, a growing part of the hazardous waste management field is the handling and disposal of medical wastes. Hospitals, labs, health care facilities, and pharmaceutical companies may have staff personnel to help them take care of their medical wastes. Or, they may hire consultants to do the job. Smaller generators of hazardous wastes include university research facilities and even households. Another source of hazardous waste is inactive mines: Hazardous minerals can leak into nearby surface and groundwater, creating potential health hazards.

Where Can I Go from Here?

Technicians typically do not go on to earn professional degrees, such as engineering or chemical degrees. However, there are several other advancement options that may be of interest to technicians. They may, for example, opt to specialize in the disposal of hazardous waste. These people conduct studies on hazardous waste management projects and provide information on treatment and containment of hazardous waste. At the government level, they help to develop hazardous waste rules and regulations.

"There also are *incident commanders*," says Mike Waxman. "An incident commander is the person who's in charge of and has ultimate responsibility for a hazardous waste site. They delegate tasks and interact with state and federal regulatory authorities as necessary. Basically, they carry the responsibility for the success or failure of the activity at the hazardous waste site."

Obtaining more education and training can help the technician earn more money and take on more responsibility. In some companies, additional education also will earn the technician a higher title. This is true at CH2M Hill, for example. "If I had a two-year associate's degree in one of the related scientific areas, my title would be different," Carl Patterson says. "If I had one in geology, for example, I'd be a geo-tech."

Some environmental professionals work in community relations or public affairs, helping to inform the public about what a company is doing

---

ADVANCEMENT POSSIBILITIES

Hazardous waste disposal specialists conduct studies on hazardous waste management projects and provide information on treatment and containment of hazardous waste.

Incident commanders have ultimate responsibility for a hazardous waste site. They delegate tasks and interact with state and federal regulatory authorities

---

with its wastes. The government also employs such professionals to help spread information about regulations and cleanup efforts.

What Are the Salary Ranges?

Salaries vary according to position, years of experience, geographic location, and educational background. The 2004 salary survey by *Environmental Protection*, a magazine for environmental professionals, listed salaries for a variety of positions in hazardous waste management. Plant level managers had average annual earnings of about $68,922, while plant level staff averaged about $62,468. Those working as health/safety supervisors reported incomes of around $56,254, and those working as regulatory compliance specialists made around $54,974.

According to the *Occupational Outlook Handbook*, hazardous materials removal workers had median annual earnings of $33,080 in 2003. Those in the lowest paid 10 percent earned $22,420 per year, and those in the highest paid 10 percent earned $56,100.

Technicians working in industry generally have benefits that include paid vacation and sick days, as well as health and life insurance. The consulting field may offer bonuses and better opportunities for advancement but generally provides fewer benefits.

What Is the Job Outlook?

"This field grew like gangbusters in the 1980s," says Sam Borries. "But it's leveling out now. I think the industry as a whole has matured." The U.S Department of Labor predicts that employment oppportunties will grow faster than the average through 2012 for hazardous materials removal workers.

While they can expect good job demand and stability, technicians also should expect changes during their careers because of advances in technology. "For example, the industry is looking at some things that would eliminate technicians going out as samplers," says Carl Patterson, "like fiber-optic detectors that tell you directly what constituents are in the groundwater, so you don't need to do it in the lab. It saves money: there's no shipping, no transporting, no lab."

"But I think technicians will always be able to move into another area," he adds. "And some testing will always require a human presence. For example, there are mobile rigs to dig 50 to 100 feet into the ground to take a sample. Someone needs to be there to be sure the rig is set up properly, with a tight seal, and be around when it's time to pull up the sample."

How Do I Learn More?

PROFESSIONAL ORGANIZATIONS

For information about scholarships, environmental careers and internships, certification, and volunteer opportunities contact the following organizations.

Air and Waste Management Association
One Gateway Center, 3rd Floor
Pittsburgh, PA 15222-1435
800-270-3444
info@awma.org
http://www.awma.org

Environmental Careers Organization
30 Winter Street
Boston, MA 02108
617-426-4375
http://www.eco.org

Institute of Hazardous Materials Management
11900 Parklawn Drive, Suite 450
Rockville, MD 20852-2624
301-984-8969
http://www.ihmm.org

National Environmental Health Association
720 South Colorado Boulevard, Suite 970-S
Denver, CO 80246-1925
303-756-9090
http://www.neha.org

Student Conservation Association
PO Box 550
689 River Road
Charlestown, NH 03603-0550
603-543-1700
http://www.thesca.org

BIBLIOGRAPHY

The following is a sampling of materials relating to the professional concerns and development of hazardous waste management technicians:

Blackman, William C., Jr. *Basic Hazardous Waste Management.* 3d ed. Boca Raton, Fla.: CRC Press, 2001.

Doyle, Kevin. *The Complete Guide to Environmental Careers in the 21st Century.* 4th ed. Washington, D.C.: Island Press, 1998.

Fanning, Odom. *Opportunities in Environmental Careers.* Revised ed. New York: VGM Career Books, 2002.

Fasulo, Michael, and Paul Walker. *Careers in the Environment.* Lincolnwood, Ill.: NTC/Contemporary Publishing Group, 2000.

Shah, Kanti L. *Basics of Solid and Hazardous Waste Management Technology.* Paramus, N.J.: Prentice Hall, 1999.

HEATING, AIR-CONDITIONING, AND REFRIGERATION TECHNICIANS

Stifling a yawn, Tom Gretka dials the combination to the shop padlock. It is six in the morning and the sky is just beginning to show a trace of light. The heavy metal doors rattle as he slides them up. Inside the shop, Tom walks past the large wooden worktables, past electric saws and power tools used to cut and join sheet metal, and past neat compartments of bolts, pipefittings, and electrical wiring stacked 15 feet to the ceiling. Beside a tall shelf, Tom pulls a piece of paper from a file and reads his work order for the day: "Project: Check duct runs in attic. Install 20-foot underground return air duct. Also 6-foot duct as per plan." Tom knows he has a big job ahead of him. He loads the tools he will need into a truck and begins driving, happy to get an early start on the day.

What Does a Heating, Air-Conditioning, and Refrigeration Technician do?

Heating, air-conditioning, and refrigeration technicians build, install, and maintain equipment necessary for comfortable, safe indoor environments. They provide heating and air-conditioning in facilities such as shops, hospitals, theaters, factories, restaurants, office buildings, and private homes. They may work to provide temperature-sensitive products such as computers, foods, medicines, and precision instruments with refrigerated climates. They may also provide cooling or heating systems in modes of transportation such as trucks, planes, and trains.

Heating, air-conditioning, and refrigeration technicians work for a variety of companies and businesses. They may be employed by heating and cooling contractors, manufacturers, dealers and distributors, utilities, or engineering consultants.

Definition
Heating, air-conditioning, and refrigeration technicians build, test, install, maintain, and repair heating, air-conditioning, and refrigeration systems and equipment.

Alternative Job Titles
Environmental control service technicians
Furnace installers
Heating, air-conditioning, and refrigeration mechanics

High School Subjects
Mathematics
Technical/shop

Personal Skills
Following instructions
Mechanical/manipulative

Salary Range
$21,900 to $35,700 to $55,600+

Minimum Educational Level
High school diploma; two-year technical school highly recommended

Certification or Licensing
Required for handling refrigerants

Outlook
Faster than the average

DOT
637

GOE
05.03.01

NOC
7313

O*NET-SOC
49-9021.00, 49-9021.01, 49-9021.02

When assembling and installing heating, air-conditioning, and refrigeration systems and equipment, technicians work from blueprints. Blueprints indicate how to assemble and install components. While working from the blueprints, technicians use algebra and geometry to calculate the sizes and contours of ductwork as they assemble it.

Heating, air-conditioning, and refrigeration technicians work with a variety of hardware, tools, and components. For example, in joining pipes and ductwork for an air-conditioning system, technicians may use soldering, welding, or brazing equipment, as well as sleeves, couplings, and elbow joints. Technicians handle and assemble motors, thermometers, burners,

Lingo to Learn

Blueprint A photographic print in blue and white used especially for mechanical drawings and architectural plans.

Chlorofluorocarbon (CFC) A chemical compound used for cooling in air-conditioning and refrigeration systems. The release of CFC contributes to stratospheric ozone layer depletion, and scientists are working to develop safer substitutes.

Duct A pipe or tube through which air or gases are carried in heating, air-conditioning, or refrigeration systems.

HVAC&R A common abbreviation for heating, ventilation, air-conditioning, and refrigeration.

Triangulation A trigonometric operation for finding a position or location by means of bearings from two fixed points a known distance apart.

Voltmeter An apparatus for measuring the quantity of electricity passed through a conductor by the amount of electrolysis produced.

compressors, pumps, and fans. They must join these parts together when building climate-control units, and then connect this equipment to the ductwork, refrigerant lines, and power source.

As a final step in assembly and installation, technicians run tests on equipment to ensure proper functioning. If the equipment is malfunctioning, technicians must investigate in order to diagnose the problem and determine a solution. At this time, they will adjust thermostats, reseal piping, and replace parts as needed.

Technicians who respond to service calls perform tests, diagnose problems, and make repairs. They calibrate controls, add fluids, change parts, clean components, and test the system for proper operation. For example, in performing a routine service call on a furnace, technicians will adjust blowers and burners, replace filters, clean ducts, and check thermometers and other controls.

Rather than work directly with the building, installation, and maintenance of equipment, some

technicians work in equipment sales. These technicians are usually employed by manufacturers or dealers and distributors and are hired to explain the equipment and its operation to prospective customers. Other technicians work for manufacturers in engineering laboratories, performing many of the same assembling and testing duties as technicians who work for contractors. They assist engineers with research, equipment design, and testing.

Technicians may also work for consulting firms, such as engineering firms or building contractors who hire technicians to help estimate costs, determine heating and air-conditioning load requirements, and prepare specifications for climate-control projects.

Heating, air-conditioning, and refrigeration technicians may also specialize on only one type of cooling, heating, or refrigeration equipment. *Air-conditioning and refrigeration technicians* install and service air-conditioning systems and a variety of refrigeration equipment, including walk-in coolers and frozen-food units in supermarkets.

Heating-equipment technicians or *furnace installers* install oil, gas, electric, solid-fuel, and multi-fuel heating systems. They also perform routine maintenance and repair work.

Technicians must also be aware of the potential hazards of dealing with chlorofluorocarbon (CFC) and hydrochlorofluorocarbon (HCFC) refrigerants, which are commonly used in refrigeration and air-conditioning systems. The release of HCFCs and CFCs into the atmosphere contributes to the depletion of the ozone layer, and therefore technicians must be careful to conserve, recycle, and recover these refrigerants. As of the year 2000, manufacturers can no longer produce CFC refrigerants, and regulations prohibit the discharge of HCFCs and CFCs.

What Is It Like to Be a Heating, Air-Conditioning, and Refrigeration Technician?

Tom Gretka has worked in the heating, air-conditioning, and refrigeration field for 20 years. For the last four years he has worked at the Carlson Company, a heating and cooling subcontractor in Tucson, Arizona. "We contract work from all kinds of places," says Tom, "restaurants, businesses, and private homes. We do installation on new structures and on renovations. We also do service calls." At

Carlson, Tom works a 40-hour week, from 7:00 A.M. to 3:30 P.M. or 6:00 A.M. to 2:30 P.M., Monday through Friday, depending on the season. "Of course, if it gets really busy, or if there's a deadline creeping up, I may work more, but 40 hours is typical," he says.

The first thing Tom does when he arrives at Carlson in the morning is to look at his work order. The work order tells Tom what he will be doing for the day. Some days Tom stays in the shop, building ductwork that will be installed later. "I work from a shop drawing or a blueprint," he says, "then I use a device called a ductolator that tells just about everything you need to know to size the ducts. The square footage of the structure determines how big the ducts should be. The ductolator helps with the figuring." When working with sheet metal to build the ducts, Tom operates brakes, shears, and other shop machines to bend and cut the material. He refers carefully to the blueprint and does quick geometric computations. Then he begins to solder. "Whether we fully assemble the ducts in the shop or put them all together at the site depends on how big they'll be. Knocked down [not assembled] the ducts might fit in one truck. Put together, they could take four.

"Basically, if you work for a contractor, you're going to be doing shopwork, fieldwork, or service work," says Tom. If his work order requires field or service work, Tom notes the name and address of the customer, which is printed clearly at the top of the order, so that he knows where he will be working. Then he reads the project description to determine the duties he will be performing and the equipment and tools he will need. "It might tell me I'm going to be removing a cooler and replacing it with a new one, or removing a gas or electric furnace, or adding air-conditioning to a house. There's a big variety, really."

Basically, if you work for a contractor, you're going to be doing shopwork, fieldwork, or service work.

"Once I'm at the job site," explains Tom, "I do whatever is necessary to fulfill the order. I install the ductwork, run refrigerant tubing, position the outdoor condensing unit, do all necessary electrical work. Really, it just depends on the work order."

To Be a Successful Heating, Air-Conditioning, and Refrigeration Technician, You Should . . .

○ have excellent communication skills

○ enjoy building and repairing things

○ have manual dexterity and be detail oriented

○ be confident using hand and power tools and be mechanically inclined

○ not be afraid of heights

After Tom has removed and replaced equipment per his work order, he runs tests on the system to make sure it functions properly. Once the tests are complete, Tom says, "We clean everything up and make it look nice. That's important. You can't just leave a bunch of exposed tubing. It might work fine, but no customer's going to be happy with the job if you leave things looking terrible." At the end of the workday, Tom drives back to Carlson, neatly replaces the tools in the shop, and washes up.

Do I Have What It Takes to Be a Heating, Air-Conditioning, and Refrigeration Technician?

"There's not much I don't like about my job," says Tom, "but anyone interested in doing it has to realize there will be some dirty, hot work. That comes with the territory." When heating, air-conditioning, and refrigeration technicians install equipment at construction sites, they will often be working outside in the elements, including summer heat, winter cold, rain, and snow. In addition, of course, the construction sites will not have a climate-control system running, since that is what the technicians are there to put in. "It's true," says Tom, "we don't always benefit from the results of our labor. By the time the air-conditioning system is up and running, our job is over. It's time for us to leave." Technicians face the same situation in doing repairs, where they may work in cold basements, hot attics, or stuffy refrigerated trucks to repair malfunctioning systems.

Besides being able to work in uncomfortable temperatures, you should have good manual dexterity if you are interested in becoming a heating, air-conditioning, and refrigeration technician. Working with motors, timers, and other components often means performing small, meticulous calibrations and adjustments. Precise, steady manipulative skills are an asset on this job.

You should also have confidence in using a variety of hand and power tools and be mechanically adept. This is particularly important if you wish to work in the installation and service facets of the field. Being in good physical condition is also important since this type of work can involve lifting and moving heavy equipment.

Heating, air-conditioning, and refrigeration technicians must also have people skills, since they often interact with customers and fellow employees. Communication skills and the ability to be courteous and tactful are crucial.

One reason Tom likes his job is that it offers him a variety of experiences. He works at different locations and performs different tasks every day. His favorite part of the job is remodeling. "I love going into an old house and putting in a new system. It's become like a hobby for me, really. Every single one is different, and it's great to get them up in working order again with a good system." If Tom were working in a lab or in sales, he speculates that his job might have less variety, which might appeal to some. "There are people who like to work in the same place, who don't want to have to haul equipment around and always wonder what their work setting will be later in the week." He suggests that these people would be happier working for manufacturers or dealers in the laboratory or sales office, or for institutions that employ their own heating, air-conditioning, and refrigeration staffs.

How Do I Become a Heating, Air-Conditioning, and Refrigeration Technician?

"I started at the bottom and worked my way up," says Tom. After high school, Tom took a job at an air-conditioning warehouse where he learned the names of the equipment while he took inventory, shelved and organized stock, and filled orders. He got promoted and became a helper to a technician who gave him such duties as carrying equipment, cleaning up, and insulating refrigerant lines. "My training was on the job. I was lucky enough to work with someone who told me, 'If you pay attention to me you can learn everything you need to know about this job.' My advice is to stick with whoever is willing to train you, watch what they're doing, and listen."

EDUCATION

High School

While in high school, you should take at least two years of advanced mathematics, including at least one year each of algebra and geometry if you are interested in becoming a heating, air-conditioning, and refrigeration technician. "When building and installing ducts, especially, we do an awful lot of figuring," says Tom. "We work with variables and use geometric concepts such as triangulation."

You should take metal and machine shop to become acquainted with construction, blueprints and shop drawings, sheet metal, and power and hand tools. Shop courses in electricity and electronics will provide a strong introduction into understanding circuitry and wiring and will teach you to read electrical diagrams, necessary when building, installing, and repairing climate-control systems. Students who study these subjects in high school will have an advantage when looking for on-the-job training or when studying at a technical college.

Courses in computer applications and programming, including computer-aided design (CAD), are also important for high school students interested in working in this field because much climate-control equipment is now being installed with microcomputers. Physics is an important subject for heating, air-conditioning, and refrigeration technicians, who need a solid background in a variety of physical principles to understand the purposes and functions of the equipment and the power sources they use.

Finally, English composition classes will provide you with the skills you will need to be able to follow detailed written directions and to write clear reports for employers and customers outlining how equipment has been installed, what tests have been run, and what maintenance procedures have been followed.

Postsecondary Training

Although postsecondary training is not mandatory to become a heating, air-conditioning, and refrigeration technician, employers prefer to hire technicians who have training from a technical school, junior college, or apprenticeship program.

Many technical schools and community colleges offer one- or two-year programs in which students can receive a degree or certificate as a heating, air-conditioning, and refrigeration technician. In these programs, students study physics and mathematics and how they apply to the climate-control field. The programs also cover equipment design, construction, installation, and electronics, providing hands-on experience as well as classroom demonstration and lecture. Most programs require additional courses such as English and computers. The armed forces also offer six-month to two-year training programs in heating, air-conditioning, and refrigeration.

Apprenticeship programs are another option for gaining education and training. These programs are often run by local professional organizations and unions, including the Air-Conditioning Contractors of America, the Mechanical Contractors Association of America, the National Association of Plumbing-Heating-Cooling Contractors, the Sheet Metal Workers' International Association, and others. These programs typically last four to five years and combine classroom instruction with on-the-job training. Students must receive a high school diploma or equivalent before applying to any of these programs.

CERTIFICATION OR LICENSING

Heating, air-conditioning, and refrigeration technicians who will be purchasing or handling refrigerants such as CFCs must pass an EPA-approved certification test. The written exam tests the applicant's knowledge about how refrigeration systems work, federal regulations and legislation regarding refrigerants, and the refrigerant products themselves. Certification is broken down into three areas, depending on the specialization area of the technician. Type I certification is for those who service small appliances. Type II certification is for technicians who deal with high-pressure refrigerants, and Type III certification is for those working with low-pressure refrigerants. The tests are administered by EPA-approved organizations, such as trade schools and unions.

Technicians enrolled in postsecondary certification programs will probably take this exam with the rest of their class at the end of the training period. Technicians who are not in collegiate, armed forces, or apprenticeship programs must find out how to obtain certification on their own. Tom's employer told him when and where to take the exam. He attended a seminar on the handling of chemical refrigerants and then took a test. Tom had to pay $150 to receive his certification, and after he passed the exam, he received a certification card. At Carlson, all employees who handle or purchase refrigerants must have certification cards on file in the office.

Voluntary certification for various specialties is available through professional associations. The heating and cooling industry recently adopted a standard certification program for experienced technicians. The Air Conditioning Excellence program is available to both installation and service technicians and is offered by North American Technician Excellence, Inc. Technicians must take and pass a core exam (covering safety, tools, soft skills, principles of heat transfer and total comfort, and electrical questions) and one specialty exam (covering installation, service, system components, and applied knowledge: regulations, codes and safety) of their choice. The five specialties available are: air conditioning, air distribution, gas heating, heat pumps, and oil heating. Technicians who become certified as a service technician are automatically certified as an installation technician without additional testing.

Technicians working in the industrial refrigeration industry may choose to become certified through the Refrigerating Engineers and Technicians Association's (RETA) program.

SCHOLARSHIPS AND GRANTS

Schools that offer programs in heating, air-conditioning, and refrigeration technology may provide scholarships as well. Contact your financial aid office or advisor for a complete list and additional details.

Professional associations frequently offer lists of scholarships, and some grant scholarship awards, such as the National Association of Plumbing-Heating-Cooling Contractors. Large manufacturers may also offer scholarship opportunities.

INTERNSHIPS AND VOLUNTEERSHIPS

With few exceptions, high school students lack the necessary training and work experience to be hired for summer jobs or internships in the field of heating, air-conditioning, and refrigeration. There are, however, still many ways for students interested in this field to begin developing some of the skills necessary for the job. Hobbies such as working on cars, bicycles, and small electrical appliances will help students gain confidence with tools, develop manual dexterity, practice assembling and repairing components, and learn about electronics.

High school students may also arrange to visit heating, air-conditioning, and refrigeration manufacturers, contractors, and dealers, as well as utilities companies to get a direct look at what the field entails. When visiting, students may talk to technicians, helpers, engineers, and contractors to discuss job possibilities in the field. High school students may also want to contact professional organizations and unions for information.

Internship opportunities may be available for students enrolled in technical schools or colleges. In fact, internships may be part of the curriculum, especially during the latter stages of the school program or during the summers.

LABOR UNIONS

Many technicians employed in the field of heating, air-conditioning, and refrigeration belong to a union. Two major unions for this field are the Sheet Metal Workers' International Association (http://www.smwia.org) and the United Association of Journeymen and Apprentices of the Plumbing and Pipe Fitting Industry of the United States and Canada (http://www.ua.org). Some employers require technicians to become members of a trade union. At Carlson, as with many other small shops or contractors, employees are not required to be union members. In addition to unions, technicians may join any of several professional associations that offer seminars, meetings, and publications for members.

Who Will Hire Me?

After about a year of on-the-job training as a helper, Tom became a technician, with his own truck and his own jobs. He got his job at Carlson by word of mouth. "Once you have your foot in the door, you hear about what's going on and who's hiring." Tom was interested in working for Carlson because he knew that Carlson frequently worked on house renovations, an aspect of the trade that Tom especially enjoys. David Carlson, Tom's boss and co-owner, knew Tom and was familiar with his work skills and background. When Tom applied for the job, David was glad to hire him.

Like Tom, more than half of all heating, air-conditioning, and refrigeration technicians are employed by cooling and heating contractors who are hired to install and maintain climate-control equipment in buildings and homes. "If you're willing and able to do shopwork, fieldwork, and service work for a contractor, you have a better chance of finding work." Technicians who are interested in specializing, however, should look for work with a contractor who has that specialty. For example, a technician who prefers service should apply for work with a service-oriented contractor.

While finding employment with contractors and dealers by word of mouth is routine, technicians can also find opportunities with manufacturers, utilities, contractors, and dealers in the classified section of the newspaper or on the Internet.

Technicians who attend technical or trade schools can often find employment through the school. Students may do an internship at a company between the first and second years of training and then be hired by that company after graduation. Even if the company does not have job openings, the people should be able to provide the student with references and possibly with information on a company that does have job openings. The school's job placement office is also an excellent way for students to find work. Sometimes these offices have job opening listings or bulletin boards that are even available to the general public. Prospective technicians who are not in a training program should contact local technical or junior colleges to see if such listings exist.

Local trade organizations are another way for prospective technicians to find employment. These organizations may publish newsletters that include job listings or may sponsor conferences at which employers meet with and interview job candidates. Tom's boss, David Carlson, recommends membership in the Refrigeration Service Engineers Society (RSES). RSES hosts local, national, and international meetings, and David notes that these meetings are a good way to break into the heating, air-conditioning, and refrigeration trade.

Where Can I Go from Here?

Over the last 20 years, Tom's advancement in the field of heating, air-conditioning, and refrigeration is evident through his steady increase in responsibilities and pay. At this point, Tom has become a master craftsman in his field and has the most responsibilities he can have as a technician. He goes out on his own jobs, creates his own work strategy for completing a task, and discusses the job directly with the customer. He is responsible for overseeing the work of helpers and less-experienced technicians and for writing up the work reports when a job is completed. Tom enjoys his job and plans to stick with it, learning all that he can about renovations of old houses. "Even after 20 years, I'm always learning," he says. "That keeps it fun."

If Tom did want to change jobs and alter his duties, there are many employment possibilities open to a skilled heating, air-conditioning, and refrigeration technician. Some technicians go into business for themselves, starting their own contracting or consulting firms. Others choose to switch to a different aspect of the trade, such as moving from service into sales or from installation into manufacturing. Technicians who start out in sales may move up to sales management. *Sales managers* promote and sell products, acting as liaisons between distributors and dealers.

Technicians at large companies or factories may get increases in responsibility and salary by being promoted to project manager or service manager. *Service managers* oversee other technicians who install and service equipment. Project managers

Advancement Possibilities

Inspectors ensure that equipment or systems are manufactured or installed according to approvals, specifications, or codes and that installations and equipment adhere to standards of companies, associations, and/or government agencies.

Service managers supervise service workers in the field, publish service information, and provide technical training to employees and customers.

Project managers oversee a specific project or projects, including engineering design, materials control, on-site problem solving, and coordination with other companies at the job site.

Sales managers work with distributors and dealers, promoting and selling manufacturer's products.

are responsible for specific projects and oversee the design aspect, materials control, troubleshooting, and overall coordination of projects.

Some technicians choose to leave the physical aspect of the job and move into administrative positions with contractors, dealers, or manufacturers. Some become *inspectors* and check on installations of equipment to make sure they meet specifications and codes. In addition, many technicians move into the related field of plumbing. Finally, it is possible for technicians to return to college to earn a four-year degree in electrical, mechanical, or civil engineering, which will open an even greater number of employment possibilities to them.

What Are the Salary Ranges?

Heating, air conditioning, and refrigeration mechanics and installers earned median annual salaries of $35,700 in 2003, according to the U.S. Department of Labor. The lowest paid 10 percent earned $21,900, while the top paid 10 percent earned $55,600. Heating and cooling apprentices usually earn about 50 percent of the wage rate paid to experienced workers. This percentage rises as apprentices gain experience and skill training in the field.

A 2005 Salary.com review of earnings nationwide for HVAC mechanics found that entry-level positions paid between $31,009 and $41,060 with a median of $35,793 annually. Those with experience, or senior-level HVAC mechanics, reported annual earnings between $43,474 and $53,805 with a median of $48,070.

Wages may vary by experience and employer size and location. Large companies and contractors generally provide benefits packages that include sick leave, medical benefits, pension plans, and paid vacations.

What Is the Job Outlook?

According to the *Occupational Outlook Handbook,* the outlook for employment in this field is expected to be good, growing faster than the average through 2012. Job opportunities are particularly good for skilled technicians. As technology advances, the use of microcomputer-controlled systems that regulate all building systems, including heating, air-conditioning, lighting, and security, will increase, and so will the need for skilled technicians to install and service these systems.

Rising energy costs and the desire to conserve energy are encouraging consumers to replace or upgrade their climate-control systems with more energy-efficient equipment, again creating work for technicians. In addition, the Clean Air Act, which took effect in 1993 and bans the discharge of CFC and HCFC refrigerants. That was followed in 2000 by regulations banning the production of CFC, ensuring that technicians will be needed to retrofit or replace existing equipment to meet new standards.

Maintenance and repair technicians' jobs are not as affected by the economy as some other jobs. While in bad economic times a consumer may postpone building a new house or installing a new air-conditioning system, existing units in homes, hospitals, restaurants, technical industries, and public buildings will still require skilled technicians to service their climate-control systems. Technicians who specialize in installation of systems have no cause for concern. With population growth and a good economy, there is often new construction of residential and commercial buildings, which means installation of climate-control systems is necessary.

Skilled technicians are also fortunate to have the opportunity for mobility. Climate-control services are needed worldwide and in a variety of settings. If technicians have difficulty finding work in one region or setting, they will almost certainly be needed in another.

How Do I Learn More?

PROFESSIONAL ORGANIZATIONS

For information on the industry, careers, certification, educational programs, and student chapters, contact the following organizations:

Air-Conditioning and Refrigeration Institute
4100 North Fairfax Drive, Suite 200
Arlington, VA 22203
703-524-8800
ari@ari.org
http://www.ari.org

Air Conditioning Contractors of America
2800 Shirlington Road, Suite 300
Arlington, VA 22206
703-575-4477
http://www.acca.org

American Society of Heating, Refrigerating and Air-Conditioning Engineers
1791 Tullie Circle, NE
Atlanta, GA 30329
800-527-4723
http://www.ashrae.org

Plumbing-Heating-Cooling Contractors Association
PO Box 6808
180 South Washington Street
Falls Church, VA 22040
800-533-7694
http://www.phccweb.org

National Institute for Metalworking Skills Inc.
3251 Old Lee Highway, Suite 205
Fairfax, VA 22030
703-352-4971
http://www.nims-skills.org

North American Technician Excellence Inc.
4100 North Fairfax Drive, Suite 210
Arlington, VA 22203
877-420-6283
http://www.natex.org

Refrigerating Engineers and Technicians Association
PO Box 1819
Salinas, CA 93902

831-455-8783
info@reta.com
http://www.reta.com

Cool Careers-Hot Jobs
PO Box 4361
Washington, DC 20044
info@coolcareers.org
http://www.coolcareers.org

BIBLIOGRAPHY

The following is a sampling of materials relating to the professional concerns and development of heating, air-conditioning, and refrigeration technicians:

Camenson, Blythe. *Real People Working in Mechanics Installation, and Repair.* Lincolnwood, Ill.: VGM Career Horizons, 1999.

Christopherson, Norm. *Pal's HVAC Technician Certification Exam Guide.* Pottstown, Pa.: Pal Publications, 2004.

HVAC Systems: Testing, Adjusting and Balancing. 2d ed. Atlanta: American Society of Heating, Refrigerating, and Air-Conditioning Engineers, 1999.

Meyer, Leo A. *HVAC Technician's Handbook.* Hayward, Calif.: LAMA Books, 2003.

Skimin, Gary K. *The Technician's Guide to HVAC Systems.* New York: McGraw-Hill, 1995.

HISTOLOGIC TECHNICIANS

The patient lies unconscious on the operating room table under a blaze of lights, surrounded by doctors and nurses. The chief surgeon peers at the patient's exposed stomach, looking for evidence of disease. She thinks cancer has caused the patient's symptoms, but she needs confirmation. She has taken a biopsy of the tissue, and the operation cannot be completed until the results come back from the laboratory.

Meanwhile, in the clinical pathology department of the large hospital, Jim Pond works swiftly with his cryostat, a special medical instrument that cuts the tissue sample into slices only three to six microns thick. He has stabilized the sample by freezing it. Now he arranges the paper-thin slices of tissue on microscope slides and quickly, carefully adds a chemical stain. Like magic, the stain turns some components of the specimen a different color. What was invisible suddenly becomes apparent. Jim passes the specimen to a pathologist, who examines the tissue under a microscope and verifies the surgeon's suspicions. The results are rushed to the operating room, and the surgery proceeds.

As a histologic technician, Jim sometimes works under pressure, but he handles it well. "I thrive on that," he says. "Sometimes we must work quickly, and sometimes we have more time, but we're always careful and pay close attention to detail. Patients depend on our work."

Definition

Histologic technicians prepare tissue specimens for microscopic examination. They process specimens to prevent deterioration and cut them using special laboratory equipment. They stain specimens with special dyes and mount the tissues on slides. Histologic technicians work closely with pathologists and other medical personnel to detect disease and illness.

High School Subjects

Biology
Chemistry
Health

Personal Skills

Artistic
Technical/scientific

Salary Range

$28,413 to $34,549 to $38,667

Minimum Educational Level

Some postsecondary training

Certification or Licensing

Required by certain states

Outlook

About as fast as the average

DOT

078

GOE

14.05.01

NOC

3211

O*NET-SOC

29-2012.00

What Does a Histologic Technician Do?

When a physician or researcher takes a tissue sample from a human, animal, or plant and sends it away for analysis, a team of laboratory workers prepares the specimen and studies it under a microscope. Cancer, leprosy, bacterial infections, and many other disorders can be detected in this way. The professional who performs basic laboratory procedures to prepare tissues for microscopic scrutiny is a *histologic technician*. Workers in this field use delicate instruments, which are often computerized. They also perform quality control tests and keep accurate records of their work.

After a tissue sample is taken, the first step in preparing it for study, known as "fixation," is usually performed by a pathologist or scientist. The specimen is examined, described, trimmed to the right size, and placed in special fluids to preserve it.

When the fixed specimen arrives at the histology lab, the technician removes the water from it. The water is replaced with melted wax, which moves into the tissue and provides support for the delicate cellular structure as it cools and hardens. Then the technician places small pieces of wax-soaked tissue in larger blocks of wax, a step called "embedding." Without the wax, the tissue would collapse during the next step of the process.

The technician sections the specimen by mounting it on a microtome, a scientific instrument with a very sharp blade. The microtome cuts thin slices of tissue, often only one cell thick, a procedure that requires precision, patience, and a steady hand. The technician cuts many sections of tissue, usually one after another so they form a ribbon, which is placed in warm water until it flattens out. Then the prepared sections are laid on microscope slides.

Next, the technician stains each tissue specimen by adding chemicals and places a coverslip over the sample to protect it. Different stains highlight different tissue structures or abnormalities in the cells, which helps pathologists, researchers, and other scientific investigators diagnose and study diseases.

A second, quicker technique is used to prepare samples and make diagnoses while the patient is still in the operating room. In these cases tissue specimens are frozen instead of being embedded in wax. It's important for a technician to work swiftly and accurately and to cooperate well with the rest of the team during this procedure, because the surgery cannot be completed until the test results are delivered.

Histologic technicians are part of a team of workers. They may be supervised by *histotechnologists,* who have more education; they perform complicated procedures, such as the staining of antigenic sites inside tissues. Some histotechnologists specialize in electron microscopy, which involves the precision cutting of tissues on such a small scale that the work is done under a microscope. Cytotechnologists are highly skilled and educated professionals who determine the presence of disease by studying slides prepared by histologic technicians; they sometimes supervise or educate technicians. *Pathologists* are medical doctors who interpret and diagnose the effect of disease on tissues, often by examining slides prepared by histologic technicians. The technician may also work closely with other physicians and researchers.

A laboratory team may include workers in other areas of specialization, such as medical and clinical laboratory technologists, who perform a variety of complex tests. For instance, they examine blood and other bodily substances under microscopes; make cultures to detect the presence of bacteria, fungi, and other micro-organisms; type and cross-match blood samples for transfusions; and determine a patient's cholesterol level. *Clinical chemistry technologists* prepare specimens and analyze the chemicals and hormones in bodily fluids. *Microbiology technologists* examine and identify microorganisms such as bacteria. *Blood bank technologists* collect blood,

Lingo to Learn

Biopsy   Removal of a section of tissue for medical examination and diagnosis.

Embedding   Placing prepared tissues into blocks of wax so that they may be cut and examined more precisely.

Fixing   Preserving tissue specimens from deterioration using special laboratory techniques.

Histology   The branch of science that deals with the structure and function of normal and abnormal tissue.

Microtome   Laboratory machine used to cut thin sections of tissue.

Pathology   The study of the nature of disease, its structure, and the changes produced by disease.

determine its type, and prepare it for transfusions. *Immunology technologists* study the way the human immune system protects itself from disease by responding to viruses and other foreign bodies.

What Is It Like to Be a Histologic Technician?

"My job as a histologic technician is never dull," says Jim Pond. "Just when I think I've seen it all, something new comes along, something medical or technical, and I get a chance to experience that. It may be working with large mechanical parts when I fix a problem with a machine, or it may be doing something new with tissue from a heart biopsy. Sometimes the specimens histologic technicians work with are so tiny that there's almost no room for error. When I'm able to solve a problem, big or small, that gives me pride in what I do."

Jim typically begins his day by receiving specimens and keeping track of each patient's identification number. "Then I process the tissue specimens and cut thin sections, using the microtome. Next, depending on the physician's instructions, I stain the tissue so that a diagnosis can be made," Jim says. He pauses

FYI

In 1664, Robert Hooke, an English scientist, used his penknife to slice pieces of cork. He placed these thin sections under the microscope. A few years later, the Dutch naturalist Anton van Leeuwenhoek used his shaving razor to carve thin sections from flowers, a writing quill, and a cow's optic nerve. Both men wanted to observe the microscopic structure of objects. Because of their investigations, the science of histology was born.

and nods his head. "The true histologic technician is able to do many things. Sure, we work with a lot of machines—robotic stainers, tissue processors, cover slippers—but in this lab, if every machine crashed tomorrow, we could do it all anyway. It would take longer, but we could do it."

A large part of Jim's day is spent working with people, often resident physicians in training, who are just learning about histopathology. "This hospital is part of a teaching institution," he explains, "so we get asked to do more stains and a larger variety as well, simply because the residents are learning which techniques work best."

Orders for histology procedures on common tissue specimens might include sampling gall bladders, tonsils, cardial sacs, and some of the more typical cancers. Rarer cancers might need an electron microscope workup, while unusual diseases like leprosy might need special stains.

"You have to know what you're doing in this job and be tactful, too," says Jim. "Over time, you gain a lot of experience and information as a histologic technician. Sometimes a resident will ask me to do a certain silver stain and I'll think that it's because he's searching for signs of a fungus, since we usually do silver stains for fungus. Then the resident might mention that he's concerned about the possibility of Alzheimer's disease, and so I might suggest that we try another stain, too.

"There are lots of ways to approach taking tissue samples, and each one provides a different kind of information. For instance, histologic technicians can take multiple samples at a certain level within the tissue, or we can reorient the tissue completely, or we cannot reorient it at all. Then there are all those different types of stains. One stain helps us look for infectious agents in the lungs, for example; another highlights connective tissue troubles; another tracks down inflammation in the blood vessels. The doctors make their diagnoses based on the information you and your techniques provide for them. Histologic technicians, through tact and craft, help physicians find out what's causing problems and confirm suspicions so that accurate diagnoses can be made."

Histologic technician Carol Bischof directs the program at Minnesota State Community and Technical College, Fergus Falls campus. Part of her day is spent working with students, either in the classroom or as they gain clinical experience in area hospitals. "I love it when I can get into the laboratory with students," she says. "Some of the stains histologic technicians use are so beautiful. Tri Chrome stain, for instance, is very pretty. Its colors could be used to design a quilt."

Carol explains that there is a significant amount of technique involved in staining tissue. "Your artistic abilities come out when you do this," she says. "Some stains need to be added gradually or removed slowly in order to bring out the correct details. Some stains differentiate between connective tissue and muscle tissue; others differentiate between brain and spinal tissue. It's a complex and beautiful procedure."

This is a fascinating and satisfying career, but it does have a few drawbacks. When histologic technicians work for large laboratories, they may spend a great deal of time standing or sitting in one position and performing one type of operation, but most are able to rotate the type of work they perform. Increasingly, they also must deal with governmental regulations designed to ensure quality control in laboratory work. A part of each day is spent complying with these rules. Some histologic technicians, especially those working for large hospitals, may work rotating shifts, including weekends and holidays.

Do I Have What It Takes to Be a Histologic Technician?

Lee G. Luna, a pioneer in histotechnology, said that histologic technicians need to be three things: scientist, mechanic, and artist. They need an interest in anatomy, biology, chemistry, and physics; an ability to repair equipment malfunctions; and an artistic eye for pattern, detail, and color. It's also important to have manual dexterity, patience, and the ability to work quickly and with precision.

As in most professions, histologic technicians tend to do a better job if they're willing to learn new techniques and concepts. Jim Pond says, "It helps to know when to ask questions, how to listen for answers, and how to store up information. Good pathologists will encourage histologic technicians to ask questions, and they will help them gain a bigger knowledge base so that the laboratory team can function even more efficiently."

As part of a team, technicians must also develop a sense of professional integrity. "It's essential, too, that you be professionally honest," says Eileen Nelson, former director of the University of North Dakota's histologic technician program at Grand Forks. "Sometimes the work is quite repetitive, and if you make a mistake, you don't cover it up. When you cut a slice wrong or misplace a piece of tissue, you have to say so. People's lives may depend on how well you do your job."

People's lives may depend on how well you do your job.

A lot of the work histologic technicians do uses standard procedures and is almost like following a recipe. Sometimes histologic technicians who work in larger laboratories may repeat the same part of a procedure all day long. Workers at a huge clinic might do cutting only, for example, or embedding only. This can be boring. Histologic technicians generally report that they are more satisfied with their jobs when they can spend time alternately cutting, staining, and charting tissues.

Histologic technicians work in laboratories that are well ventilated, and most of the tissue processors that they use are enclosed. This minimizes problems with odors and chemical fumes. Sometimes histologic technicians work with hazardous chemicals, but they wear protective clothing, as well as badges that will indicate overexposure and allow workers to seek immediate medical treatment should accidents occur. Histologic technicians also face the possibility of coming into contact with disease through tissue

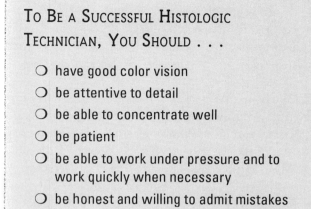

TO BE A SUCCESSFUL HISTOLOGIC TECHNICIAN, YOU SHOULD . . .

○ have good color vision
○ be attentive to detail
○ be able to concentrate well
○ be patient
○ be able to work under pressure and to work quickly when necessary
○ be honest and willing to admit mistakes

samples, but several of the steps involved in preparing specimens generally kill any living organisms.

How Do I Become a Histologic Technician?

Carol Bischof's path to histotechnology began with college in Mississippi and Ohio and led to a job in Minnesota. "While working on my master's degree in zoology, I did research for the Environmental Protection Agency," she says. "I studied how substances in paints and plastics affected rats and watched as histologic technicians processed and embedded the rodent tissues that we used. Then a friend called and said that the lab where she worked needed someone to do histology. I was familiar with laboratory techniques and so I got the job. Later on, I went back to school and got my certificate as a histologic technician."

EDUCATION

High School

Biology, chemistry, and other science courses are necessary if you wish to enter a histotechnology program after graduation. Mathematics and computer science courses are also important.

Postsecondary Training

There are three ways to become a histologic technician. While it is possible to enter the profession with a high school diploma and on-the-job training only, beginning in 2005, technicians seeking certification are required to hold a college degree or formal training through an institution such as a hospital, according to the American Society of Clinical Pathologists Board of Registry.

On-the-job training is still an acceptable entry into the field, according to Sumiko Sumida, a histologic technician and histotechnologist. Sumiko is technical director of the histology laboratory at the University of Washington Hospital Pathology Department in Seattle. She says, "Many laboratories will train people. It's an exciting field, because it has a lot of opportunities for people at the time they're just getting out of high school and maybe don't have the money to go to college. Most of the hospitals do require some college background, but opportunities do exist for on-the-job training," especially in rural areas.

The second way to enter the field involves completion of a one- to two-year certificate program at an accredited institution, usually a hospital. The certificate program includes classroom studies along with clinical and laboratory experience.

The third method involves earning an associate's degree from an accredited college or university and includes supervised, hands-on experience in clinical settings. General course work for histologic technicians includes classes in organic and inorganic chemistry, biochemistry, general biology, mathematics, medical terminology, and medical ethics. Additional classes include histology, quality control, instrumentation, microscopy, records and administration procedures, and studies in fixation, processing, and staining. College programs may also require core curriculum classes such as English, social science, and speech.

CERTIFICATION OR LICENSING

Certification is not required for entry-level histologic technicians. Some states do require that technicians be licensed. Histologic technicians become certified by passing a national examination offered by either the Board of Registry of the American Society of Clinical Pathologists (the main certifying organization) or by the National Credentialing Agency for Laboratory Personnel. Applicants may qualify for the Board of Registry exam by completing an accredited program in histotechnology or earning an associate's degree from an accredited college or university and combining it with one year of experience. The

National Accrediting Agency for Clinical Laboratory Sciences list 467 accredited programs for medical and clinical technology, including histologic technicians.

SCHOLARSHIPS AND GRANTS

Most colleges and universities offer general scholarships. The National Society for Histotechnology is the main source of information for scholarships specifically for students of histotechnology (see "How Do I Learn More?"). Several scholarships and awards are available each year through this organization. Occasionally, employers will provide educational funding for general laboratory workers who wish to enter the field of histotechnology.

Who Will Hire Me?

Jim Pond worked at three hospitals before deciding to study histotechnology. First, he had a job as a clerk. Then he moved to laboratory work in phlebotomy. His third job involved basic hematology and chemistry work. At each hospital, pathologists would note the quality of his work and encourage him to get additional schooling so he could advance into a position of more responsibility within the laboratory. "Finally, I listened to what they were recommending," Jim says. "The hospital where I was had a school for histologic technicians, and when the hospital said that they'd even pay me while I learned more about the field, I decided to give it a try."

A histologic technician has the opportunity to work in many fields of medicine and science. Most are employed by hospitals or by industrial laboratories that specialize in chemical, petrochemical, pharmaceutical, cosmetic, or household products. Some work for medical clinics, universities, or government organizations. Many biomedical companies hire histologic technicians to aid in research projects. Immunopathology, forensic medicine, veterinary medicine, marine biology, and botany are just a few of the options.

Sumiko Sumida says that people who have training in both histology and cytotechnology are in demand, especially in rural areas, which tend to have greater difficulty in attracting qualified technicians. That's partly due to the fact that salaries are often lower there. In addition, many histologic technicians are women, and it's sometimes hard for them to move their families to rural areas.

If you'd like to work part time in the field while you go to school, consider a job with a regional laboratory for large health systems. Histology is one of many fields that have been consolidated in recent years as health groups have pooled their resources to save money. For example, the average hospital used to employ a team of three to six histologic technicians, and smaller facilities often had only one. Now, many of these institutions have combined their resources. The result is laboratories with teams of perhaps 30 to 50 histologic technicians. Because these facilities operate seven days a week, 24 hours a day, there's a good chance you could be assigned to shifts that would not interfere with your classes at college.

Employers sometimes schedule recruiting visits to schools that offer histologic technician programs. You can also find leads on employment in professional journals.

Where Can I Go from Here?

Some histologic technicians become supervisors. Others specialize in certain areas of histotechnology, such as orthopedic implants or diseases of the lungs.

"If you have an interest in science, you can grow with the field and use it as a jumping-off point for the future. It's a field you can use as a stepping-stone to go in any direction. It's really up to the individual to take the plunge, take some risks," says Sumiko Sumida.

She suggests that a young person without much money could work as a histologic technician for a few years while attending college part time or completing a training program at a hospital, then use that experience and training to advance to a high-paying position as a pathologist's assistant. She strongly recommends taking a certification examination after working in the field for two years.

Technicians who have more education and experience are more apt to be promoted. With some employers, no matter how good your job skills might be, your chances of advancement are significantly smaller if you don't have formal training, including some college study. In the future an associate's degree will likely become the standard requirement for entering the field and being promoted. Returning to school, earning a bachelor's degree, and becoming a histotechnologist will boost your career even further and will probably increase your salary.

ADVANCEMENT POSSIBILITIES

Histotechnologists perform more complicated procedures than histologic technicians, such as enzyme histochemistry, electron microscopy, and immunofluorescence. Histotechnologists can teach, become laboratory supervisors, or become directors in schools for histologic technology.

Cytotechnologists analyze stained tissue samples for subtle clues that indicate disease. A cytotechnologist with more education and experience may advance to become a specialist and will typically supervise or educate other employees.

Categorical technologists focus on one field instead of rotating through various departments of the laboratory. They may be certified in microbiology, chemistry, blood banking, immunology, or hematology.

Pathologists are medical doctors who study the nature, cause, and development of diseases, and the structural and functional changes caused by them.

"If you go on to college, there are a lot of opportunities," Sumiko says. "You can go into management or become a technical representative." You could also earn an advanced degree and teach sciences.

What Are the Salary Ranges?

Geographic location, experience, level of education, employer, and work performed determine the salary ranges for histologic technicians. According to a 2003 wage survey conducted by the American Society of Clinical Pathologists (ASCP), for all positions the highest salaries were found in large hospitals in city or suburban areas located in the West. Wages were lower in small hospitals in rural areas in the South Central Atlantic and West South Central states.

According to the U.S. Department of Labor *Occupational Outlook Handbook*, the median salary for histologic technicians in 2002 was $34,549. The lowest paid 10 percent earned $28,413 and the highest paid 10 percent earned $38,667. Histologic technologists had higher wages: Beginning technologists had annual earnings of $41,122 to $45,760. Histologic supervisors had annual earnings of between $50,086 and $53,435.

Full-time technicians can expect benefits packages that include health insurance, paid vacation, and 401(k) plans.

What Is the Job Outlook?

According to the *Occupational Outlook Handbook*, employment of clinical laboratory workers is expected to grow about as fast as the average for all other occupations. As director of a histology program, Carol Bischof has seen the job market improve over the last few years. "There's going to continue to be a strong demand for well-trained histology technicians," she says. "There are many hospitals that have been giving sign-on bonuses, because there's a shortage of technicians. They want to hire them before they're even done with their clinical."

The 2003 wage and vacancy survey conducted by ASCP calculated the ratio of job openings to full-time histologic technicians and found that there were more job openings than people to fill them. The study found that histology vacancies rates varied depending on geographic location and facilities. Laboratories in large cities reported 7.7 percent vacancy rates. The South Central Atlantic and Far West regions had vacancy rates of 8.8 percent and 7.6 percent, respectively. Between 35 percent and 41 percent of laboratories reported problems recruiting staff. Small hospital staff vacancy rates were 6.7 percent. Vacancy rates for histology staff was higher than for supervisors.

"Right now, because of the consolidations that health care has been seeing in the last year or so, it's been pretty stable," Sumiko Sumida comments, but she adds, "There will probably be a huge outflux of people within the next five years," because a large number of professionals in the field are nearing retirement age. The ASCP survey found that 10 percent to 16 percent of laboratories reported an increase in staff turnover rates.

How Do I Learn More?

PROFESSIONAL ORGANIZATIONS

For career and certification information, and information about accredited programs, contact
 American Society of Clinical Pathologists
 2100 West Harrison Street
 Chicago, IL 60612
 312-738-1336
 info@ascp.org
 http://www.ascp.org

For career information, and information about accredited programs, contact
 National Accrediting Agency for Clinical Laboratory Sciences
 8410 West Bryn Mawr Avenue, Suite 670
 Chicago, IL 60631
 773-714-8880
 info@naacls.org
 http://www.naacls.org

For a free career brochure about histotechnology, contact
 National Society for Histotechnology
 4201 Northview Drive, Suite 502
 Bowie, MD 20716-2604
 301-262-6221
 histo@nsh.org
 http://www.nsh.org

BIBLIOGRAPHY

The following is a sampling of materials relating to the professional concerns and development of histologic technicians:

Berman, Irwin. *Color Atlas of Basic Histology*. New York: McGraw-Hill, 2003.

Carson, Freida L. *Histotechnology: A Self-Assessment Workbook*. 2d ed. Chicago: ASCP Press, 1997.

Cormack, David H. *Essential Histology*. 2d ed. Philadelphia: Lippincott, Williams & Willkins, 2001.

Kessel, Richard G. *Basic Medical Histology: the Biology of Cells, Tissues, and Organs*. New York: Oxford University Press, 1998.

Zhang, Shu-Xin. *An Atlas of Histology*. New York: Springer-Verlag, 1999.

HOME APPLIANCE AND POWER TOOL TECHNICIANS

Letting his truck warm up, Dave Allender goes back inside the shop to review his work tickets for the day. His 9:00 A.M. appointment is for a General Electric refrigerator that is not cooling, his 10:00 A.M. is a Maytag washing machine that will not drain, and his 11:00 A.M. is a stove built in 1952 that the customer wants repaired at any cost. Looking through the remainder of his appointments, Dave moves into the parts room to collect what he will need for the day's work.

Carrying the parts across the parking lot to load on his truck, he glances at his watch. It is 8:35. That refrigerator sounds like it may need a new compressor, and that will take some time. He decides to go a little early and get a head start on the day. That way, he will be sure to make his second appointment on time.

What Does a Home Appliance and Power Tool Technician Do?

From toasting bread, to washing clothes, to watching the latest release on video, almost everyone relies to some extent on household appliances. When something goes wrong with an appliance we depend on for frequent use, it can significantly disrupt our day. We then call on a *home appliance and power tool technician* to put things back on track.

Often called *service technicians* or *repair technicians,* these workers perform maintenance work on a number of different home appliances and power tools. Some service large appliances, such as washers, dryers, refrigerators, and ranges, making service calls to the customer's home.

Others repair smaller appliances and tools, such as irons, electric drills, toasters, food processors, and coffee makers. Repair work on such small, portable appliances and tools is usually done in a repair shop, as opposed to at the customer's home. Some techs install and service window air-conditioning units or central air systems, and some specialize in gas appliances, such as stoves and furnaces.

Definition

Home appliance and power tool technicians install and repair home appliances, such as ovens, washers, dryers, refrigerators, and vacuum cleaners, as well as power tools, such as saws and drills.

Alternative Job Titles

Appliance service representatives
Service technicians

High School Subjects

Chemistry
Physics
Technical/shop

Personal Skills

Following instructions
Mechanical/manipulative

Salary Range

$17,500 to $30,300 to $49,000+

Minimum Educational Level

Some postsecondary training

Certification or Licensing

Voluntary

Outlook

More slowly than the average

DOT

827

GOE

05.02.02

NOC

7332

O*NET-SOC

49-2092.00, 49-2092.01, 49-9031.00, 49-9031.01, 49-9031.02

Depending upon the individual, and his or her place of employment, the repair tech's work may include all types of appliances and tools or may be limited to a particular name brand or type of appliance.

When starting work on an appliance or tool, repair techs first determine the nature of the problem. They do this by first checking visually for visibly frayed electrical cords or broken connections. If possible, they run the machine to listen for odd noises or too much vibration and to look for fluid leaks or loose parts. In some cases, the appliance must be taken apart so that its internal parts can be examined.

In dealing with electrical systems, repair techs may need to consult wiring diagrams, or schematics,

Lingo to Learn

Ammeter An instrument for measuring current.

Ampere or **Amp** The base unit of electric current; the meter-kilogram-second unit of electric current.

Cellenoid valve An electric conductor wound as a spiral.

Circuit The complete path of an electric current.

Diode A device through which a current can pass in only one direction.

Electronics Science dealing with devices or systems involving the flow of electrons in a vacuum.

Schematic A generalized diagram or plan; in this case, used to refer to wiring diagrams.

Solid-state Pertaining to electronic devices, such as transistors or crystals, that can control currents without the use of moving parts.

Voltmeter A device for measuring the quantity of electricity passing through a conductor.

Watt The absolute meter-kilogram-second unit of power.

Wattmeter A calibrated instrument for measuring electric power in watts.

in order to understand the circuitry and to check for shorts or faulty wiring. They may also need to use specific testing devices, such as ammeters, voltmeters, or wattmeters. Some repairs may require the use of a service manual or troubleshooting guide.

After repair techs have discovered the nature of the problem, they work on correcting it. This may involve replacing or repairing defective parts, such as belts, switches, motors, circuit boards, heating elements, or gears. They may lubricate and clean the machinery, if necessary, or align and tighten it for maximum performance. Repair techs often use common hand tools, such as screwdrivers, pliers, and wrenches, but may also use special tools designed for work on particular appliances.

Those repair techs who service gas appliances may have to replace pipes, valves, or thermostats. They may also need to measure, cut, and thread pipes, and connect them to gas feeder lines, particularly when installing appliances. Installation could require that the repair tech saw holes in walls or floors or hang supports from beams in the house in order to place the pipes.

Gas-appliance installers and repair techs are often responsible for checking for gas leaks, explaining proper usage to customers, and answering emergency calls regarding leaks or other problems.

Although repair and maintenance of appliances and power tools is their primary duty, repair techs do have certain other responsibilities. They may answer questions and field complaints from customers. When making service calls to customer homes, they may also demonstrate or explain how to care for and use appliances or tools. Repair techs may also have to order parts from a catalog in order to complete some jobs. They must usually record the amount of time spent on a repair, the parts they have used, and whether the appliance is under a warranty. Sometimes they include a brief description of the work they have performed. Finally, repair techs may have to estimate the cost of the repairs, prepare bills, and collect payment for their work.

What Is It Like to Be a Home Appliance and Power Tool Technician?

Dave Allender is a technician for major household appliances. He is certified and experienced in refrigeration and air-conditioning units and, in his more than 11 years of experience, has worked on nearly every brand of every kind of appliance. "I work on any name you can think of," he says. "I work on anything in the market." He does not, however, repair power tools. He says that appliance repair has kept him so busy that he has not needed to look for any additional work.

Dave usually works 5.5 days each week, for a total of 44 hours. Occasionally he puts in extra time, if it is necessary to complete a job. In warm weather, he tends to work more hours due to the increased demand for repairs on air-conditioning and refrigeration units. "In the summers, I probably put in 50 to 55 hours a week to keep up with the refrigeration calls," he says. Because he is employed by an appliance dealership as an independent contractor, he does not receive extra compensation for overtime. As an independent contractor, he gets a flat percentage of the labor charges on each call, which adds up to a higher gross income, he says. However, he does not receive any of the benefits often associated with employment, such as health insurance, paid vacations, and sick leave. "This isn't for everyone," Dave says. "I started out in a hourly job. I could only do this after I got some experience."

For Dave, the workday starts at the office at 8:30 A.M. "Usually, first thing in the morning, we get five or six people calling in with questions, so I spend about 15 minutes on the phone." Then he looks at each work order for the day to assess the symptoms and makes sure he has all the necessary parts on his truck. "My first appointment is at 9:00 A.M., so I'm out of the office by 8:45 A.M.," he says. He usually spends the rest of the day out of the office, going from house to house to make service calls.

The nature of his day depends upon the nature of the individual service calls. Some problems take more time to repair than others. "Generally, I'm in and out of a customer's home within 15 minutes," Dave says. "That's about the average length." According to him, changing the compressor on a refrigerator/freezer is the most lengthy process, taking around 45 minutes. Often, the problem is something as simple as replacing a belt or unclogging a hose. Other times, the work is more physically demanding. "You should try pushing a full side-by-side refrigerator over carpet, by yourself," Dave says, laughing. "You get real strong, real quick." Some jobs also require more thought and skill than others, especially those that require the repair tech to read wiring diagrams to complete the job.

After each repair is complete, Dave writes up a brief description of the work he has done and the parts he has used and collects payment from the customer. Often, he also answers customers' questions. "They have lots of questions," he says. "Customers absolutely do not read their manuals. That's the number one rule." He says he tries to explain to the customers how to get better performance from their appliances.

Appointments are usually scheduled one hour apart, and on an average day, Dave makes six to nine calls. After his last call is complete, he heads back to the shop. "Every day, I come in, turn in my tickets, and pick up my tickets for tomorrow," he says. He also gives the parts manager his orders for any parts that need to be ordered.

In addition to his daily routine, Dave says he spends about one day every three months at a

> ## To Be a Successful Home Appliance and Power Tool Technician, You Should . . .
>
> ❍ have mechanical aptitude and work well with your hands
> ❍ enjoy communicating with people
> ❍ be able to work efficiently in a variety of settings
> ❍ be willing to learn about new techniques and products
> ❍ be able to work effectively with little or no supervision

manufacturers' seminar. Periodically, manufacturers invite the shop's servicers to a course on their new appliances. By attending these classes and reading the manuals, Dave is able to stay abreast of the latest products of many different appliance lines.

Do I Have What It Takes to Be a Home Appliance and Power Tool Technician?

The technician's most important responsibility, according to Dave, is to correct the problem properly the first time. "Any time you get a recall on the same appliance for the same problem," he says, "the customer doesn't get charged, and you don't get paid. Besides that, the customer stops trusting in your ability." He says repair techs must be very organized in their diagnosing and repairing, so as not to miss something that may result in another service call, or worse. "You may be held liable if the machine catches on fire within 30 days after you work on it," he says. "I've known two people who got sued, and lost." The repair tech must work responsibly.

A technician must also be able to deal courteously with all different sorts of people. "You've got to be a people person, mostly," Dave says. "You've got to be able to talk to them so that they have a certain amount of respect and trust for you." Occasionally, the repair tech must work in less than ideal conditions and still be able to maintain tact. "I hate to say it, but the worst part is when you walk into a really filthy house and then have to work on a refrigerator that's been closed up, not running, for two weeks," Dave says. "You just have to go right ahead and do the work and be polite about it."

Dave says that mechanical aptitude, or a genuine understanding of the way things work, is vital to successful repair work. "If you can't picture in your mind exactly how the stuff works, you can't operate on it," he says. The ability to read wiring diagrams, or schematics, is equally important. "If you don't know how to read schematics, you may as well walk away," he says.

> If you can't picture in your mind exactly how the stuff works, you can't operate on it.

Finally, it is necessary that repair techs be very self-directed because they will, in many cases, be working alone, with no supervision. "You're on your own the whole day," Dave says, "which I really enjoy." He says he likes having to rely only on himself to get the job done.

How Do I Become a Home Appliance and Power Tool Technician?

While still in high school, Dave started to tailor his education to get a good background for repair work. He took classes in building trades, industrial and electrical shop, and drafting. "I already knew what my base field would be when I was 16 years old," he says. Immediately after high school, he enrolled in a technical college, and received an associate's degree in heating, cooling, refrigeration, and electrical repair.

EDUCATION

High School

Most employers require that their repair techs at least have a high school diploma or its equivalent.

FYI

Most appliance repair techs agree that problems with self-cleaning ranges are the most complicated ones to diagnose. Also, because most of the new household appliances contain computerized or electronic components, technicians who can repair them will do well.

For those who plan to take further schooling at a vocational-technical school, graduation from high school is also a prerequisite.

Students who are interested in becoming home appliance and power tool technicians can start preparing while still in high school. Shop classes are extremely valuable at providing a good background for this job. A knowledge of electronics is becoming increasingly important, so electrical shop will be particularly valuable. Working with electrical and electronic systems or building electronic equipment from kits should give you a basic understanding of how the various systems function, as well as provide practice in reading diagrams.

Mathematics and physics are good choices to build a knowledge of mechanical principles. Chemistry classes are helpful if you plan to work on gas appliances. Finally, any classes that build communication skills are a good addition to the curriculum. Understanding the nature of the problem and explaining both the problem and its solution to the customer are crucial elements of the repair tech's job. This requires the ability to listen and communicate well.

You might want to talk to employees of local repair shops and appliance dealerships. These employees may be able to give you a clearer picture of the job. Another possibility is a summer or part-time job that allows you to observe or assist in repair work. Such a job would provide a firsthand knowledge of the industry, plus valuable experience and a potential job lead.

Postsecondary Training

Although it may be possible in some cases to find a job as a trainee with no further formal education, these opportunities are becoming increasingly rare.

Formal training, especially courses in electricity and electronics, are more and more necessary in the repair of today's technologically advanced appliances.

Most often, high school graduates who have an interest in appliance repair choose to take a training program at a vocational or technical school, or a community college. Such programs provide both classroom training and laboratory experience in the service and repair of appliances. The program length varies from school to school, with many lasting one to two years. Another means of obtaining an education in appliance repair is through correspondence courses, which often include both book and video training.

Finally, although it is less common, you may be able to get training on the job. In this case, you may be hired as a helper or apprentice to observe and assist experienced repair techs, either in the shop, or on-site, at customers' homes. Some appliance and power tool manufacturers and department store chains have formal training programs, where trainees work with demonstration appliances and other training equipment to acquire experience and skill.

Regardless of your educational background, you will almost certainly require some further training by your employer in order to be familiar with the specific work to be done. Also, as products change, so do the repair techniques, and the repair tech needs to stay up to date. Reading manuals and attending periodic courses given by manufacturers is a continuing responsibility of all technicians and servicers.

CERTIFICATION OR LICENSING

There is no national standard of testing for certification in this industry, and requirements vary from state to state. However, certification for appliance technicians is available from the National Appliance Service Technician Certification Program, which involves an exam. The Professional Service Association (PSA) also offers certification. Certification from PSA is valid for four years and requires continuing education credits for renewal.

Due to environmental concerns over the commonly used refrigerant, CFC (chlorofluorocarbon), since 1994 it is a federal requirement that all repair techs who work with refrigerant be certified for that type of work. In order to work legally, repair techs who plan to work with appliances that use refrigerant, such as air-conditioners, refrigerators, and freezers, must take and pass a federally mandated class and certification test. The Air Conditioning Contractors

of America (ACCA) offers a federally approved program, which consists of a one-day class and test.

Although the test is optional for those not working with CFC, it may be well worth your time, since the ability to work on refrigeration units will most likely make you a more valuable employee.

LABOR UNIONS

Some home appliance and power tool technicians choose to join the International Brotherhood of Electrical Workers.

Who Will Hire Me?

Dave found his first job through a classified ad. He says that even though he had completed the technical schooling, he lacked the hands-on experience that makes a repair tech valuable. "I went in to this guy," he says, "and I told him I was willing to take a job at starting pay, but in turn, he'd have to train me. That's how I got the job."

According to the *Occupational Outlook Handbook*, about half of the appliance repair techs in the workforce are employed by retail trade establishments, such as department stores, household appliance stores, and dealers that sell and service appliances and power tools. More than 15 percent are self-employed, and the remainder work for gas and electric utility companies, wholesalers, and electrical repair shops. Although there is a need for repair techs in almost every sort of community, the highest concentration of jobs will most likely be found in larger cities, where the population is high.

Technicians who have a formal education from a community college or vocational school will have the best prospects for finding jobs. Since few companies can afford to hire unskilled, untrained repair techs, employers increasingly are looking for workers who have learned the basic skills and just need to be trained on the specifics. If you have taken a technical training course, the school's placement office may be a good place to begin a job search. If the school you have attended does not offer a placement service, often teachers or administrators will have job leads or ideas about where to look.

In order to gain experience and break into the field, you might want to approach employers directly, offering to work for a substantially reduced wage

ADVANCEMENT POSSIBILITIES

Electrical-appliance-servicer supervisors supervise and coordinate activities of workers engaged in servicing, repairing, and installing electrical household appliances as well as order tools, supplies, and replacement parts.

Industrial gas servicers test, repair, and adjust all types of industrial gas equipment. They may advise customers on proper installation of equipment and may install and remove large industrial equipment.

Air-conditioner-installer supervisors supervise activities of workers engaged in fabricating, installing, and repairing air-conditioning systems in residential and commercial buildings. They inspect and measure to determine airflow requirements, plan and draw layouts of ductwork, get price quotes on materials and supplies, purchase equipment, and schedule installation times.

in exchange for on-the-job training. Some larger dealerships and department stores have in-house training programs and may be willing to train a promising applicant.

The job searcher might also want to watch the classified ads in all local newspapers, since repair tech jobs are sometimes listed. You might also send resumes to the personnel departments of larger retailers or manufacturers, or to the owners or managers of smaller repair shops or dealerships. Gas or electric utility companies may also be possibilities.

Finally, there are a number of publications targeted specifically toward the appliance repair business. These publications often carry classified job listings, and may be a source of leads.

Where Can I Go from Here?

Dave says he is happy with his employment situation for the present. However, the owner of the shop he works for is preparing to retire and may offer to sell him a part of the business. Dave is not sure that he wants to become involved in the hassles of running a business, but says he will decide when the time comes. "I don't know that I want to go any further than where I am," he says. "Essentially, I'm already self-employed, anyway."

An important factor in the advancement potential for the individual appliance repair tech is your place of employment. Those who are working in a small, privately owned repair business will probably not have many chances for rapid promotion. In such smaller businesses, there are usually not many levels of managerial or supervisory positions; often the owner or manager performs all administrative duties.

The repair tech who works for a large retailer, a factory service center, or a utility company will have more possibilities for promotion. Within these organizations, you could become a supervisor, assistant service manager, or service manager. The repair tech who demonstrates superior technical skills and the ability to deal well with customers and co-workers might eventually be promoted to a position such as regional service manager or parts manager.

Another career path for the experienced appliance repair tech involves teaching other repair techs at a factory service training school, technical school, or vocational school. This position would require a strong familiarity with a variety of products and their maintenance, as well as an aptitude for public speaking.

Repair techs who work for an appliance manufacturer might eventually move into a position in which they help write service manuals. Those employed by manufacturers might also have the opportunity to become salespersons or representatives to appliance dealerships.

Finally, some repair techs may eventually decide to open their own appliance repair businesses. With experience, a knowledge of business management, and the necessary funds to invest in equipment, repair techs can become owners and managers of their own shops.

What Are the Salary Ranges?

According to the *Occupational Outlook Handbook*, the median annual salary for home appliance repairers and installers was $30,300 in 2003. Those in the lowest paid 10 percent earned $17,500, while those in the highest paid 10 percent earned $49,000. In 2003, power tool repairers had median annual earnings of $32,800. The lowest paid 10 percent earned $19,600, and the highest paid 10 percent earned $54,200.

A 2005 review by Salary.com of earnings nationwide for electrical home appliance and power tool repairers reported annual earnings between $31,765 and $47,875 with a median of $39,398.

There is a difference in average pay between repair techs who service heating, air-conditioning, and refrigeration units and those who do not. The average starting salary for appliance repair techs who do not work in these areas is significantly lower than the salary for those who do.

In addition to skill level and type of equipment serviced, earnings vary significantly with the size of the repair tech's company. Larger companies, in general, pay higher wages than do smaller companies and frequently offer more comprehensive benefit programs as well.

Since the majority of repair techs are paid on an hourly basis, as opposed to being salaried, they are usually compensated for overtime work. In addition to their regular pay, some technicians may also receive commissions.

What Is the Job Outlook?

The U.S. Department of Labor expects employment of home appliance and power tool technicians to grow slower than the average for all occupations through 2012. The main reason for this decrease is that the appliances and tools that are currently being manufactured have been technologically improved to such a degree that they require much less repair work. The increasing use of electronic parts, such as solid-state circuitry, microprocessors, and sensing devices, has lead to a greater dependability in almost all appliances.

An additional factor is the increase of so-called "throwaway" appliances. Over the years, manufacturers have developed methods to produce various appliances much more cheaply than they originally could. This has reduced the cost of such appliances to such an extent that, in some cases, buying a new appliance is not much more expensive than repairing an existing one. Therefore, although Americans are buying increasing numbers of both home appliances

and power tools, there are fewer repairs being made now than have been necessary in the past.

Even so, there will continue to be some demand for well-trained repair techs, particularly those with a solid background in electronics. Most openings will arise as a result of workers switching occupations or retiring. Workers in this field are less affected by the overall economy than are those in many other professions. Thus the need for appliance repair remains relatively steady, even during economic downturns.

How Do I Learn More?

PROFESSIONAL ORGANIZATIONS

For information about the industry, training and educational programs, and certification contact the following organizations.

Air Conditioning Contractors of America
2800 Shirlington Road, Suite 300
Arlington, VA 22206
703-575-4477
http://www.acca.org

National Appliance Service Technician Certification
3608 Pershing
Fort Worth, TX 76107-4527
817-921-9101
http://www.nastec.org

Professional Service Association
71 Columbia Street
Cohoes, NY 12047
518-237-7777
http://www.psaworld.com

BIBLIOGRAPHY

The following is a sampling of materials relating to the professional concerns and development of home appliance and power tool technicians:

Davidson, Homer L. *Troubleshooting and Repairing Consumer Electronics without a Schematic.* New York: McGraw-Hill, 2004.

Kleinert, Eric. *Troubleshooting and Repairing Major Appliances.* New York: McGraw-Hill, 1995.

Langley, Billy C. *Major Appliances: Operation, Maintenance, Troubleshooting, and Repair.* Paramus, N.J.: Prentice-Hall, 1993.

Rowh, Mark, and Dick Glass. *Opportunities in Electronics Careers.* Lincolnwood, Ill.: VGM Career Horizons, 1999.

HORTICULTURAL TECHNICIANS

On a sunny afternoon in early May, Randy Abell steps carefully between rows of knee-high blue spruce trees. His head horticulturist, who is kneeling at the base of one of the trees, looks up at his approach.

"Mark, I think these look the best, right here," Randy says, pointing at a nearby row. "Which formula did we use on these?" He and Mark were trying to grow a blue spruce with an even bluer color than is usual, by varying the amounts of nitrogen, phosphorous, potassium, and sulfur in the nutrient formulas.

Mark wipes his hands on his pants and grins. "I thought those were the best ones, too," he says. "They got the first formula we made up, the one with the least nitrogen."

Randy nods his head. "Well, that's what we expected, then," he says. "Hey, I'll be out the rest of the afternoon. I'm going to meet with the City Planning Commission, and then I'm going out to Brookstone to start working up a design for the new phase of development. Why don't you up-pot those pin oaks?"

Mark stands up and stretches. "Sure will. Sounds like you've got a busy day." Squinting into the late afternoon sun, Randy smiles and nods. "Well, it's that time of year."

What Does a Horticultural Technician Do?

The beauty of a thick, green carpet of grass, perfectly sculpted shrubbery, and the bright, splashy colors of a flower bed are pleasures almost everyone has enjoyed, whether at their own homes, at a public park, or simply driving along a highway. Most of us have also seen the other end of the horticultural spectrum: overgrown lots, lawns taken over by weeds, and flowers or houseplants that just will not thrive. Although some may attribute success with plants to a green thumb, there is actually an art and a science to the placement, growth, and maintenance of trees, plants, and shrubs, as any *horticultural technician* can tell you.

Definition
Horticultural technicians plant, cultivate, and market plants to be used for ornamental purposes. They may also landscape and maintain both private and public grounds.

Alternative Job Titles
Arboriculture technicians
Floriculture technicians
Landscape development technicians
Nursery-operation technicians
Turf grass technicians

High School Subjects
Agriculture
Biology
Earth science

Personal Skills
Following instructions
Technical/scientific

Salary Range
$14,400 to $20,200 to $32,800 (Grounds maintenance workers)
$12,900 to $15,700 to $22,200 (Nursery and greenhouse workers)

Minimum Educational Level
High school diploma

Certification or Licensing
Voluntary

Outlook
Faster than the average (Grounds maintenance workers)
More slowly than the average (Nursery and greenhouse workers)

DOT
405

GOE
03.03.04

NOC
2225

O*NET-SOC
37-3011.00, 37-3012.00, 37-3013.00, 45-2092.00, 45-2092.01

Horticultural technology is typically broken down into the areas of floriculture, nursery operation, turf grass, arboriculture, and landscape development. Technicians may specialize in one of these areas, or may have responsibilities pertaining to several, or even all, areas. In every case, the technician must be well versed in the specific needs of the plants or trees with which he or she is working, including the methods of starting and growing them, soil conditions, temperature, moisture, and light requirements, pest and disease control, and appropriate fertilizers.

Both *floriculture technicians* and *nursery-operation technicians* work in nurseries or greenhouses to raise and sell plants. Floriculture technicians specialize in flowers, while nursery-operations technicians lean more toward shrubs, hedges, and trees. In many cases, however, the two areas may overlap. The duties of these technicians include planting seeds, transplanting seedlings, inspecting crops for problems, culling or pruning plants, and regulating the application of nutrients, herbicides, pesticides, and fungicides. They may also be responsible for planning growing schedules, quantities, and utilization of the growing space to achieve the best yield for the crops.

Technicians in the fields of floriculture and nursery operation sometimes hold a position known as *plant propagator*. Plant propagators initiate new kinds of plant growth, using techniques such as grafting, budding, layering, and rooting. They also develop and revise nutrient formulas for use on the new plants, select growth mediums, and prepare the containers to be used for growing. Other technicians may specialize in determining problems that are preventing plants from growing properly. Called *plant diagnosticians*, these technicians often work in retail nurseries solving problems for, and making recommendations to, customers who are having difficulties with their plants.

Turf grass technicians may work in either the private or the public sector. In the private sector, the technician is usually involved in providing lawn care services to homeowners' corporations or institutions with extensive grounds, like private colleges or country clubs. These services may include mowing, trimming, and irrigation, as well as insect, disease, and weed control and the proper use of fertilizers for particular types of grass and soil. In the public sector, technicians usually work for local, state, or federal government agencies to plan turf grass areas for parks, playing fields, or grassy areas along public highways.

Some technicians also work in the production of sod or in producing or selling seeds, fertilizers, insecticides, herbicides, and other equipment and supplies used in the area of horticulture. Finally, some work as *turf grass research and development technicians* for privately owned companies or local, state, or federal agencies.

Aboriculture technicians may also work in either the private sector, owning their own business

Lingo to Learn

B&B (Balled and burlapped) Refers to the method by which most large trees are transplanted, with their root balls covered in burlap.

Fungicide An agent applied to destroy fungi.

Herbicide A substance or preparation used for killing plants, especially weeds.

Mulch A covering of straw, leaves, or manure spread on the ground around plants to enrich the soil and prevent evaporation and erosion.

Pesticide A chemical preparation for destroying pests, such as mites.

Spreader roots A plant's smaller roots, which grow laterally.

Sod Ready-made squares of grass used to establish new lawns and renovate old ones.

Taproot A plant's main root, which descends downward.

Weed barrier A fabric, often used in landscaping, that permits air and moisture to pass through but prevents weed growth.

Up-pot To transfer a plant from one container into a larger container, to allow it more root room and further growth.

or working for an established company, or in the public sector, working for a park system, botanical garden, arboretum, or government agency. In both cases, technicians may plant, feed, prune, provide pest control, and diagnose problems or diseases for various types of trees. They may also use their knowledge of different tree types to determine where and how trees should be removed and planted. Some arboriculture technicians, known as *tree movers*, are responsible for the digging up, transportation, and replanting of trees, as well as estimating the cost of the removal. Others use their knowledge to sell trees, tools, fertilizers, peat moss, and other necessary equipment. These technicians also often work with customers to advise them about products and offer suggestions in planting and caring for their trees.

Landscape development technicians sketch and develop planting plans, using their knowledge of soil, temperature, and light conditions and of specific plant requirements. They also compile lists of materials needed and oversee or carry out the landscaping activities, including purchasing, planting, and caring for the decided-upon trees, shrubs, and plants.

These technicians may work for private companies that provide landscaping services directly to homeowners or businesses or for a city or county, designing landscaping for parks, parking lots, streets, or municipal buildings. Some technicians in this field may also work for landscape architects or begin their own businesses.

What Is It Like to Be a Horticultural Technician?

Randy Abell owns a small, "full-service" horticultural business. Full-service, as he defines it, means landscaping, groundskeeping, nursery, and garden center divisions. When Randy started Abell Nursery and Landscaping over six years ago, he was its sole employee. As a result, he has worked in, and developed a familiarity with, each area of service. Although part of his time is now spent on managerial responsibilities for his 10-employee, $450,000 business, he still works in all phases of the horticultural process. "My typical day depends on which area of the business I'm working in," he says. "If I'm working in the nursery or the garden center, I'm staying in one place, basically. If I'm doing landscaping or lawn care, I'm on site, wherever that may be."

If he will be working in the nursery, Randy's day begins in the greenhouse, with the task of trimming and up-potting certain plant specimens. By up-potting, or transferring plants from smaller into larger containers, he allows the roots space to expand, thereby producing a larger, more valuable plant.

He must also water all the plants with the appropriate liquid fertilizers. Randy says there are 150 different fertilizers used at his nursery. "Every one has a different formulation that will produce a different result in a plant," he says. "It's like cooking with spices. A dish can turn out 100 different ways, depending on the spices. So can a plant, depending on the nutrients." Randy works with one of his technicians to determine the most beneficial formulation for each plant. "That may involve a certain amount of research," he says.

> ### A dish can turn out 100 different ways, depending on the spices. So can a plant, depending on the nutrients.

On another day, Randy might work in the fields, planting seedlings. To ensure that the seedlings are planted in straight rows for precision in mowing and harvesting, a rope is stretched tightly from one end of a row to the other. Marks on the rope indicate where the seedlings should be planted. "Planting is one of the times when knowing a plant's characteristics is necessary. You need to know how far apart and how deep to plant," Randy says. "Of course, you also need to know what fertilizer type to use and when to harvest."

Harvesting the plants may be another of the nursery worker's responsibilities, although it requires a more specialized skill. "The tree digger removes the trees, balls, and burlaps them," Randy says. "To do that, you have to be able to look at a tree and know how big a root ball to dig. It's tricky."

Individualized care of various plant specimens is the order of the day when working in the nursery. Individualized lawn care is the business of the groundskeeping crews. "Working on a groundskeeping crew means following a schedule for fertilizing, mowing, trimming, and weed spraying," Randy says. "Every client, every lawn, has a set schedule and a page in the log book. Whenever we do work on that lawn, it gets documented."

Knowing the type, amount, and frequency of fertilizer and weed spray for a particular lawn is a part of the groundskeeping or turf grass technician's job. Another part is knowing when and how to mow. "You go to a job and check the conditions," Randy says. "Sometimes, you'll need to change the mowing height." For example, if the grass is wet, raising the mowing height creates less of a mess. If the ground is very dry, raising the mowing height prevents damage to the grass. If the ground is too wet, it might be wise to postpone mowing until another day. "You have to know what will do the best job," he says.

When working on a landscaping crew, Randy's responsibilities are more varied. Since every job is different, in terms of soil type, lay of the land, proportion of sun to shade, and the client's guidelines and budget, he must be able to plan and coordinate a number of factors to achieve the desired result.

Working from a landscaping design or blueprint, he reads the scale of the design to determine spacing of the plants he is installing. At present, Randy or a design architect are the only ones who develop the landscaping plans for his clients. Randy hopes that will not always be the case. "A technician with a good education and a good experience level could do design," he says. "You have to be aware of which plants will look good and grow well together. You also have to consider soil conditions and drainage and all that."

Once the design has been established, it is basically a matter of laying out the plants accordingly and planting them. "Once again, you have to know how to plant each type and what nutrients to add," Randy says. Some soil or drainage conditions require the application of extra materials, such as peat, or the installation of drainage pipes. Some jobs also require landscape construction. "I build retaining walls, borders. Sometimes I contract out for decks or patios," he says.

To finish up a landscaping job, Randy installs a fabric weed barrier on the ground around the plants, cutting a slit or an X for each plant to grow through. He then covers the weed barrier with the top dressing chosen by his client, which might be mulch, pine nuggets, or various types of crushed stone. A final duty involves explaining to the client how to care for his or her new plants.

The garden center workers must be the most knowledgeable technicians, according to Randy. "Working in there, you have to know everything."

The garden center is the retail side of the business, where customers come to buy trees, flowers, plants, equipment, and fertilizers. Usually, only one person works in the center at a time, dealing with all the customers who come in. Responsibilities include helping them select their plants and instructing them in planting and care, suggesting fertilizers, pesticides, and fungicides, helping them load up their purchases, and making delivery arrangements. Perhaps the most difficult part of working in the garden center is fielding questions. "I answer questions about why customers' plants aren't doing well, how they can get their flowers to bloom, how tall trees will be at their mature height, what plants look pretty together," Randy says. "I need to either know the answers or

---

TO BE A SUCCESSFUL HORTICULTURAL TECHNICIAN, YOU SHOULD . . .

- ○ enjoy growing and caring for plants and flowers
- ○ be willing to work outdoors, in varying weather conditions
- ○ be a good problem solver
- ○ have patience to perform detailed work
- ○ work well with your hands
- ○ be able to distinguish between hundreds, even thousands, of different plants

---

know where to look for the answers to all kinds of questions."

In addition to dealing with the customers, those technicians who work in the garden center often help out in the greenhouse or in the fields.

Do I Have What It Takes to Be a Horticultural Technician?

Horticultural technicians work very closely with various forms of plant life. They must be able to work effectively, on a basic, hands-on level, performing such activities as planting, watering, and pruning. They must also be able to understand the more theoretical and scientific aspects of horticulture, such as the chemical and biological, in order to determine the growth needs of specific plants.

"This job is anything but boring," Randy says. "There are so many different aspects of it. If you're working in lawn maintenance or landscaping, you're always in different places. If you're in the nursery, you're working with different plants in different stages of growth. If you're in the garden center, you're dealing with different customers and finding solutions to all kinds of problems."

The weather is also an aspect of this job that is variable. "Because of this, it is important for technicians, particularly those in turf grass management and landscaping, to be flexible," he says. "When your work is largely dependent on weather conditions, you have to be flexible. You can't get

FYI

According to an overview of the floral industry by the Society of American Florists, in 2004 there were 22,753 florist shops in the United States with average annual sales per shop of $290,000. Also in 2004, 70 percent of fresh cut flowers sold here were imported from other countries. Colombia accounted for 59 percent with Ecuador coming in a distant second at 19 percent. In 2003 California was the top flower grower in the United States, growing 72 percent of the cut flowers produced in this country.

with maybe 200," Randy says, "so there's a certain amount of fact-finding and research involved in answering some questions."

The horticultural technician's work may be physically demanding, depending upon the type of duties he or she is performing. Workers specializing in arboriculture, for example, may be required to climb trees. Many tasks include digging, bending, squatting, and lifting.

The hard work, however, is rewarding, Randy says. "In some jobs, you can't see the physical results of your work. This you can see, for years to come. It's gratifying to see your work all over town, to see trees that you started from seedlings." According to him, the business is pleasant, as well as rewarding. "You're always the good guy," he says. "Everyone likes trees and flowers, so you're doing something that makes people happy."

How Do I Become a Horticultural Technician?

Randy started his career with no formal training in horticulture. "I had some experience from working on my dad's tree farm. I'd say maybe I knew 5 percent of what I needed to know," he says, laughing. As his business developed, so did his knowledge of the field, partly through experience and partly through training classes and seminars he attended. "The state I live in has a Master Plantsman program through the local chapter of the American Association of Nurserymen," Randy says. "I used that to get a horticultural education, since my teaching degree wasn't going to help me very much in a nursery and landscaping business."

EDUCATION

High School

Entry-level horticultural technicians often begin their careers with only a high school diploma. While in high school, courses in biology and chemistry may be helpful in acquainting you with the workings of plant life and the effects of various nutrients. A background in geometry is also a useful tool, especially in landscape design and maintenance, where area, circumference, and square footage must frequently be determined.

really rigid about a schedule, because bad weather may come along and just blow that all to pieces." In some areas of the country, horticultural technicians, particularly those in turf grass management and landscaping, may find it difficult to find a job that lasts through the winter months. Conversely, the workload in the spring and summer is often quite heavy, requiring extra long days.

Weather conditions may prove to be a pro or a con of the job, depending upon the season, and the day. "Oh, in the spring, it's great to be in this business," Randy says. "Everyone's cooped up in their offices, and we're outside. But in late July, when it's 100 degrees, not too many people will be jealous of us." Depending upon the climate and temperatures of the region, and upon the area of specialization, horticultural technicians may have to work in rain, mud, or extreme heat or cold. According to Randy, unless the technician plans to work exclusively in a greenhouse or garden center, he or she should enjoy working outdoors and be able to tolerate varying weather conditions.

It is important for the technician to be able to think on his or her feet, and be a good problem solver. "Sometimes, if you're working in the nursery center," Randy says, "a customer will come in carrying just a little leaf, or a twig, and they'll say 'What is this? I want more of them.'" The technician also gets questions about planting, fertilizing, and caring for various plants. "We grow about 50 varieties and deal

English classes are recommended to increase verbal and written skills, and a background in Latin is very helpful, since those in the industry refer to many plants by their Latin names.

Finally, if classes in botany, horticulture, or agriculture are offered, take them. If these classes are unavailable at your high school, you might consider some other methods of obtaining the same information. Often, local chapters of horticultural associations, area nurseries, or greenhouses offer short classes or workshops in horticultural principles and techniques, which are open to the public for a small fee.

Postsecondary Training

There are a number of training choices in horticulture. The right path depends upon what type of work you hope to do.

If you are starting your first job straight out of high school, the majority of your training will take place on the job. This is especially common in the areas of turf grass management and landscaping, where entry-level jobs for high school grads are plentiful.

There are also a number of nondegree or certificate programs, which you could take before starting a career in horticulture, or after, in conjunction with on-the-job training. Many botanical gardens and arboreta offer educational programs as a community service. Many county cooperative extension offices also offer short courses geared toward the general public or the nursery trade, such as the Master Gardener Program.

A two-year associate's degree is yet another option for post-high school education. An associate's degree in horticultural technology generally requires classes that stress the technical or hands-on aspects of a specialized field. A sampling of possible classes includes plant propagation, lawn and turf management, nursery and garden center management, pest management, plant taxonomy, plant materials, landscape techniques, and fundamentals of horticulture. Many programs may also require some classes in English, computers, math, and science. If you want to enter the horticultural field at a technical or middle management level, an associate's degree is a good choice.

There are also a multitude of programs that lead to bachelor's, master's, and doctorate degrees in

various aspects of horticulture. For the student who is motivated to pursue higher education in this field, the sky is the limit.

CERTIFICATION AND LICENSING

There are no specific, standardized certification programs for horticultural technicians, but a few exist for those interested in certain aspects of the career. The Associated Landscape Contractors of America offers the title of Certified Landscape Technician-Interior to those who pass the multiple-choice exam; for Certified Landscape Technician-Exterior, techs must take a one-day, hands-on exam, choosing from the areas of installation, maintenance, or irrigation. Certification is also available from the Professional Lawn Care Association of America (PLCAA) for turfgrass and ornamental landscape professionals.

SCHOLARSHIPS AND GRANTS

Many schools that offer undergraduate degrees in horticulture also offer to qualified applicants financial aid in the form of scholarships and grants. The interested student should check with representatives of any given school to see what types of assistance may be available. The Society of American Florists also maintains a list of scholarships available to students specializing in floriculture.

Some scholarships or grants may be available through such sources as local civic groups, floriculture, horticulture, or garden organizations, and business

In-depth

Horticultural Therapy

Therapy for plants? No, therapy with plants! Horticultural therapists work with the emotionally and mentally handicapped, the blind and the disabled, senior citizens, and inner-city youth to grow and nurture plants. Through such therapy projects as growing and propagating flowers and houseplants, making flower arrangements, and starting terrariums, clients receive the physical and emotional benefits of working with living things. Therapists may also be involved in training the mentally retarded and other disabled persons for jobs in the field of horticulture.

For more information on education, jobs, and developments in the field of horticultural therapy, contact The American Horticultural Therapy Association at 800-634-1603, or visit their Web site, http://www.ahta.org.

||||||||||||||||||||||||||||||||||||||||||||||||||||||||||||

groups. Check directly with them for information on educational financial assistance.

INTERNSHIPS AND VOLUNTEERSHIPS

The American Association of Botanical Gardens and Arboreta (AABGA) has a very strong internship program. Offering a directory of internships in more than 100 public gardens throughout the United States, AABGA is a valuable resource for students who are interested in a practical experience in horticulture.

The length and content of internships vary from garden to garden, as do the wages paid, but most share certain features, such as rotating duties in several areas of the garden, formal and informal classes, field trips, garden programs, and special projects. Specialized internships focus on conservation of

rare plants, arid land horticulture, historic garden restoration, plant inventories, children's programs, and zoo horticulture.

The American Horticultural Society also offers internships. In addition, check with your neighbors to see if you can help them with their lawn care and gardening. A summer job mowing lawns is a good introduction into the field.

Who Will Hire Me?

Randy grew up primed for a horticultural career, living on his parents' tree farm until he went to college. Even so, he was certain that he did not want to join the family business, deciding instead, to get a bachelor's degree in education. It was not until he had completed his education and begun his first teaching job that he realized he was not going to be happy working inside. He decided to pursue a career in horticulture after all.

"I started out on the lawn maintenance side," he says, "because that was the easiest way to start, and I just expanded from there." Although he started his own business immediately, as opposed to first working for someone else, he now says he would not advise most people to do that. "I think it'd be much easier to work for someone else first and learn a little bit," he says. "I would especially suggest a job in a nursery or a garden center. That would be great experience."

The area of specialization that the prospective technician chooses to pursue will determine, to some degree, where he or she should look for a job. For those technicians who are interested in floriculture or nursery operation, a logical place to begin is by applying to all greenhouses and nurseries in the area. The job seeker should also remember that many large retail department stores have garden centers, which require knowledgeable staff members. Public botanical gardens and arboreta may also provide good opportunities for employment in these areas of specialization.

Technicians interested in the area of turf grass management might look in the local Yellow Pages under Lawn Care to get ideas for where to send resumes or applications. They might also check any area golf courses and cemeteries for entry-level openings. Finally, federal, state, and local government agencies may be a good source of possibilities, since they often employ turf grass technicians to maintain public areas.

Prospective arboriculture technicians should check with local park systems, botanical gardens, and arboreta for job openings. Also, like turf grass technicians, arboriculture techs are often hired by government agencies to maintain public areas. If the technician chooses to work in the private sector, he or she might check the Tree Service listings in the local phone book to compile a list of possible contacts. Likewise, landscape development technicians might want to check the phone book to compile a list of area landscape contractors and landscape architects.

Job seekers in all areas of horticulture should regularly check the classified advertising sections of all area newspapers. Entry-level horticultural jobs are frequently listed, especially in the spring and summer months. One particularly good way to break into the field might be for the high school student with an interest in horticulture to take an entry-level summer job in a nursery, public garden, lawn care or landscaping company, or a tree service business. This might provide you with an entry into the business on a permanent basis, as well as good job experience.

Technicians who decide to pursue formal schooling in horticulture may get assistance in finding a job through their college placement offices. Finally, there are a number of associations and publications geared toward the horticultural industry, which may be of help to the job seeker.

Where Can I Go from Here?

Randy has now achieved his most basic career goal, by owning his own full-service horticultural business. His plans are to expand and refine the existing facets of his company. "What I wanted was to be a full-service company, and now I am," he says. "But some areas of the business are still rudimentary, and I want to develop them much further."

Becoming the owner of their own businesses is a common goal for many workers in certain areas of horticulture, particularly those in turf grass management and landscape development. There are, however, a vast number of other career steps that the horticultural technician could take. Because the field is so wide and diverse, there is no set advancement pattern.

Technicians in the areas of floriculture and nursery operation might move into the position of

---

ADVANCEMENT POSSIBILITIES

Horticulturists conduct experiments and investigations into problems of breeding, production, storage, processing, and transit of fruit, nuts, berries, flowers, and trees; develop new plant varieties; and determine methods of planting, spraying, cultivating, and harvesting.

City foresters advise communities on the selection, planting schedules, and proper care of trees. They also plant, feed, spray, and prune trees and may supervise other workers in these activities.

Turf grass consultants analyze turf grass problems and recommend solutions. They also determine the best type of turf grass to use for specific areas, mowing schedules, and techniques.

---

horticultural inspector. Inspectors work for state or federal agencies to inspect plants being transported across state lines or entering the United States for insects, diseases, and legality. With additional experience and further schooling, these techs may also choose to become horticulturists, either at a research facility or a large firm.

Turf grass technicians might eventually become *greens superintendents*. Greens superintendents plan for and oversee the construction and maintenance of golf courses, including the supervision of other workers. Other possibilities in the area of turf grass are consulting, sod growing, and research and development positions.

Arboriculture technicians may, with further training, become tree surgeons or city foresters. Also, they may decide to start their own businesses, offering all types of tree services, including planting, pruning, spraying, and removal.

Technicians who pursue a career in landscape development often advance by becoming the manager or owner of their own small landscaping business. They might also move into supervisory positions at public parks, cemeteries, or botanical gardens. By returning to school to obtain a bachelor's degree, the technician could become a landscape architect.

Further schooling is also an option for horticultural technicians in other areas of specialization. Bachelor's, master's, or doctoral degrees in horticultural science will open up further possibilities for advancement in the areas of research or teaching.

What Are the Salary Ranges?

Since the field of horticulture encompasses so many different types of positions, salary levels for technicians vary significantly. In addition to the technician's chosen area of work, there are several other factors that influence the amount of compensation. When considering potential earnings, the technician should keep in mind that government agencies, colleges, and universities usually pay more than privately owned companies or gardens. Also, salaries may vary between regions of the country. As is the case in most areas of employment, the technician's levels of education and experience are significant factors. Finally, a worker who is able to specialize in a specific function, such as propagating plants, will likely command a higher salary.

According to the *Occupational Outlook Handbook,* Agricultural workers, which includes nursery and greenhouse workers, had annual earnings of between $12,900 and $22,200 with a median of $15,700 in 2003. Landscaping and groundskeeping laborers had annual salaries between $14,400 and $32,800 with a median of $20,200.

A 2005 review by Salary.com of earnings nationwide found nursery and greenhouse managers had annual salaries between $30,065 and $44,555. Entry-level groundskeepers earned between $21,610 and $29,597 annually, while senior-level groundskeepers, or those with experience and in supervisory positions, reported earnings between $25,768 and $35,343.

What Is the Job Outlook?

Depending on which area is chosen for employment, the job prospects for horticultural technicians vary. According to the U.S. Department of Labor, employment opportunities for landscaping and groundskeeping workers are expected to increase faster than the average for all occupations through the year 2012, while opportunities for nursery and greenhouse workers are expected to grow more slowly than average.

One major reason for the growth in jobs for landscaping and groundskeeping workers is the continued development and redevelopment of urban areas. With the construction of commercial and industrial buildings, shopping malls, homes, highways, parks, and recreational facilities, there should be an increasing demand for turf grass, arboriculture, and landscaping services. Potentially, this growth will also create a need for more trees, shrubs, and plants, which may eventually translate into an increased demand for nursery operation and floriculture technicians as well.

Another reason for the growth in job opportunities is America's increasing awareness of and commitment to preserving and maintaining the environment. The skills of educated and experienced horticultural technicians will be increasingly necessary to city planners and development committees in their efforts to retain the beauty of nature in the midst of urban expansion. Homeowners and developers are also increasingly using landscaping services to enhance the value and attractiveness of their properties, and many existing buildings and facilities are upgrading their landscaping, as well.

The number of horticultural technician jobs may also increase as American homeowners become more and more service oriented. In the past several years, there has been a trend toward homeowners hiring professionals to perform specific tasks as opposed to performing these tasks themselves. Landscaping, lawn care, and tree services are all examples of this, along with pest control, painting, decorating, repair work, and cleaning services.

How Do I Learn More?

PROFESSIONAL ORGANIZATIONS

Contact the following organizations for information about the industry, various internship opportunities, fellowships, education and training, and certification:

American Association of Botanical Gardens and
   Arboreta
100 West Tenth Street, Suite 614
Wilmington, DE 19801
302-655-7100
http://www.aabga.org

American Horticultural Society
7931 East Boulevard Drive
Alexandria, VA 22308
703-768-5700
http://www.ahs.org

American Horticultural Therapy Association
909 York Street
Denver, CO 80206
303-331-3862
http://www.ahta.org

Associated Landscape Contractors of America
950 Herndon Parkway, Suite 450
Herndon, VA 20170
800-395-2522
http://www.alca.org

American Nursery and Landscape Association
1000 Vermont Avenue, NW, Suite 300
Washington, DC 20005-4914
202-789-2900
http://www.anla.org

American Society for Horticultural Science (ASHS)
113 South West Street, Suite 200
Alexandria, VA 22314
703-836-4606
http://www.ashs.org

Professional Lawn Care Association of America
950 Herndon Parkway, Suite 450

Herndon, VA 20170
800-395-2522
http://www.plcaa.org

Society of American Florists
1601 Duke Street
Alexandria, VA 22314
800-336-4743
http://www.safnow.org

BIBLIOGRAPHY

Following is a sampling of materials relating to the professional concerns and development of horticultural technicians:

Goldberg, Jan. *Opportunities in Horticulture Careers.* Lincolnwood, Ill.: VGM Career Horizons Group, 1995.

Jozwik, Francis X. *How to Find a Good Job Working with Plants, Trees, and Flowers.* Mills, Wyo.: Andmar Press, 1994.

————. *Plants for Profit: Income Opportunities in Horticulture.* Mills, Wyo.: Andmar Press, 2000.

Preece, John E., and Paul E. Read. *The Biology of Horticulture: An Introductory Textbook.* New York: John Wiley & Sons, 1993.

Rice, Laura Williams, and Robert P. Rice Jr. *Practical Horticulture,* 5th ed. Paramus, N.J.: Prentice-Hall, 2002.

INDUSTRIAL ENGINEERING TECHNICIANS

‟**H**ey, John, are you finished with that relaying out project yet?" asks a supervisor through the office door. John Pena has been at his computer for three and a half hours examining floor plans. His relaying out project involves figuring out the fastest way to get finished product from the factory to the storage area so it will be ready to ship at a moment's notice to waiting buyers. He uses the material flow method, which will tell him how long it takes to move the product by a given route. John also must analyze the layout of the storage space to make sure the product gets shelved in the most efficient and safest way possible. He will spend a couple more hours on this project before he meets with his supervisors to report the results of his study and make his recommendations.

What Does an Industrial Engineering Technician Do?

With the birth of the industrial revolution, there arose a need for people to plan and monitor factories, making them as efficient as possible. This led to the development of industrial engineers, and then later in the 20th century, to *industrial engineering technicians*.

Originally, technicians functioned as assistants to the engineers, but as the manufacturing industry grew, technicians began to take on responsibilities of their own. They now occupy a large number of widely varied and specialized roles in private industry.

The kind of work done by industrial engineering technicians varies, depending on the size and type of company for which they work.

Methods engineering technicians analyze both new and existing products to determine the best way to make them at the lowest cost.

Materials handling technicians look at the workers' physical interaction with the materials used to make the products. These technicians study and compare methods of handling material and suggest changes that will reduce physical effort, thus reducing handling costs and damage to products.

Definition
Industrial engineering technicians study the use of personnel, materials, and machines in factories, stores, and offices to determine efficiency.

Alternative Job Titles
Methods-study analysts
Motion-study analysts
Pace analysts
Time-study analysts

High School Subjects
Computer science
Mathematics
Physics

Personal Skills
Mechanical/manipulative
Technical/scientific

Salary Range
$27,900 to $42,900 to $72,000

Minimum Educational Requirements
Associate's degree

Certification or Licensing
Voluntary

Outlook
About as fast as the average

DOT
012

GOE
02.08.02

NOC
2233

O*NET-SOC
17-3026.00

Plant layout technicians work in conjunction with materials handling and are the people most involved with plant facilities and their design. They study layouts of machinery and storage areas, and determine the most effective use of space and work progression. When a new piece of machinery is needed, they determine the best and most productive location for it. They may help with the layouts of new or redesigned buildings as work processes change.

Work measurement technicians study the production rate of a product and establish how much time is needed for all the relevant activities. They use films of workers in the factory, gather statistics, and time the motions needed to complete an operation. They help streamline and speed up production.

Lingo to Learn

Computer-Aided Drafting (CAD) Also called computer-aided design, or computer-aided design drafting; the use of computer software to draw or design such items as machine parts, products, or even buildings.

Computer-Aided Manufacturing (CAM) The use of computers to run the machines that make specific parts and products.

Computer-Integrated Manufacturing (CIM) An overall approach to planning, manufacturing, and selling and distributing products, where computers are used to track raw materials, produce the products, and track inventory and shipping in order to increase efficiency and reduce costs and inventory.

Material Requirement Planning (MRP) A system concerned with getting the right quantity of raw materials at the right time in order to keep inventory at a minimum and reduce costs.

Total Quality Management (TQM) A business concept aimed at improving quality, pleasing customers, eliminating errors and waste, empowering employees, and continually evaluating the entire process to improve performance.

A specialized form of work measurement is the *time-study technician*. This technician studies the different elements of work, their order, and the time needed to produce a part.

Many technicians work in control determination, or production control. This is the area of industrial engineering that regulates things such as production, inventory, budget, cost, and quality. *Production-control technicians* make sure that work schedules are met and that customers get the promised products on time. Working as coordinators, they follow the route of production through its many steps, keep inventories of materials, and try to anticipate and prevent delays. These technicians must be familiar with every aspect of production and the raw materials used. They often work in dispatching offices, issuing orders to production areas, overseeing the master schedule, and making progress reports to supervisors.

Making sure the factory is well supplied with all the necessary materials is the job of *inventory control technicians*. They keep inventories of raw materials, semifinished and completed products, packaging materials, and other relevant supplies.

Quality control technicians play a very important part in the manufacturing industry. They check incoming supplies and the work being produced, helping inspection departments to uphold quality standards. They inspect work in varying degrees of production, making sure the finished product meets specifications and does not vary from one to another in any significant way. They point out any sources of trouble and devise corrective procedures.

Cost control technicians monitor the costs of production. They analyze any discrepancies, propose corrective measures, and in general, make sure the company is operating within its budget.

Budgets are determined, in part, with the help of *budget technicians*. They gather facts and figures to determine break-even points and profit margins. These technicians present their findings to management in the form of charts and graphs that show the effects of production schedules on profitability.

Technicians can also be found working in the area of wage and job evaluation. They collect information on hourly wage employees, factoring in education, seniority, skill, and manual effort, which helps to set salary ranges and job descriptions.

What Is It Like to Be an Industrial Engineering Technician?

Factories and manufacturing companies have different work hours and shifts than regular offices do. The nine-to-five office schedule may not apply to industrial engineering technicians. John Pena gets to work around 6:30 A.M. and generally does not leave until 5:30 or 6:00 P.M. But, he points out, these are not the hours set by his employer. John chooses to stay as late as possible every day, to distinguish himself as a dedicated and effective worker. "It's what I want to do," he says.

He never really knows what he will be working on each day until he arrives at work. "Day-to-day duties change, depending on our needs," John says.

As a general rule, John devotes most of his morning to relaying out projects. That is, he analyzes the use of space, determining whether or not things are in the most efficient place possible.

For example, this morning John is examining a storage area and its layout. He looks at floor plans on his computer, using the CAD (computer-aided drafting) program as he tries to determine if products are being stored correctly, safely, and efficiently.

John uses what is called the material flow method, a technique to study the time it takes for a finished product to travel from the work cells—areas of production in the factory—to the storage area.

His job is to determine the quickest travel time and route so that the products get on the storage shelves as fast as possible. They will eventually be shipped out to waiting buyers.

"Once a week I have a relaying out project," he says. He works on plant layout for about half the day. The rest of his time is taken up with meetings and other projects as they arise.

This afternoon, John plans to visit another plant with a team of industrial engineers and technicians. They will observe and study other factories, their layout, and use of space. It is important for industrial engineering technicians to know what is going on in the rest of the industry and to keep up with new ideas and techniques.

Later, John will be expected to present and discuss his findings with managers and supervisors. He may apply some of these other methods to his own plant and its design.

To add to John's busy schedule, ongoing education is a constant in his life. "If you want to stay on top of things and increase your marketability as an employee, it's crucial," he says.

The more education, the better, for you and the company. You both benefit.

Throughout his tenure at his present job, John has continued to attend school. Many companies, John's included, will pay for their technicians to further their education. It increases the worth of the employee, instills loyalty to the company, and makes the business more profitable in the long run, John says. "The more education, the better, for you and the company. You both benefit."

Industrial engineering technicians generally work in offices and engineering laboratories. Depending on the type of work and specialty, they may spend a good deal of time in the plant or factory. This work can sometimes present the risk of injuries, so technicians must observe the same safety procedures as the plant workers.

Much of an industrial engineering technician's work involves computers. John spends a good deal of time at his computer terminal. "It's my most important tool," he says.

Other than the computer, John will use a few basic tools, such as a measuring tape and chalk. Industrial engineering technicians working in other areas might use video cameras, electrical recorders, and stopwatches. The computer is by far the most used tool of the trade, and knowledge of its functions and programs is essential in industrial engineering.

Do I Have What It Takes to Be an Industrial Engineering Technician?

Industrial engineering technicians often have heavy workloads and are given a lot of responsibility. As companies continually modernize and upgrade existing technology and manufacturing procedures, they are relying on these technicians in increasing amounts.

John works long hours and is often under pressure. Deadlines can be brutal, and he is often expected to get things done in near-impossible amounts of time.

"Often, when they come to me with a project, they want it yesterday," he says. Time constraints are the hardest requirements of his job. Gathering material, and planning, and organizing takes time that he is sometimes not given by his supervisors. Dealing with supervisors, foremen, and workers can be difficult as well, says John. "You have to really love working with lots of people, at all levels of authority in the company."

For industrial engineering technicians, patience really is a virtue. "Working with so many types of people, you have to have a lot of patience," says John. "Good communication and people skills are extremely important as well," he says. "To get a project completed, you have to interact with workers on all levels." It is crucial that an industrial engineering technician be able to converse and interact well with others.

Industrial engineering technicians occupy an intermediary type role in the workplace. In terms of both training and responsibility, they fall somewhere between professionally trained managers or engineers and the hourly workers involved in production. Associating with so many different types of people may be difficult and is one reason John emphasizes good communication skills. The wide exposure to all kinds of people is something that attracted John to this type of work to begin with. He loves the interaction, fast pace, and changeability of his work.

How Do I Become an Industrial Engineering Technician?

John knew fairly early on that he wanted to be an engineer, he just was not sure what kind. After high school, he attended his state university. Through the school, he got a part-time job that gave him his first taste of what engineering was all about.

"I really enjoyed what I was doing. My major was undeclared, but I had always been good with math and computers. I saw what the industrial engineering technicians were doing and just knew it was what I wanted," John recalls.

EDUCATION

High School

Preliminary courses in math and physics are essential at the high school level. "Take everything you can in math and the sciences," John advises. Algebra, geometry, trigonometry, calculus, chemistry, and physics are all recommended classes for students interested in pursuing a career as an industrial engineering technician.

Once again, knowledge of computers is stressed. Much of the industrial engineering technician's job relies on the use of computer programs. A good basic education in the uses of computers is crucial, so you need to be familiar and comfortable with them.

Other recommended course work includes drafting, mechanical drawing, metal shop, English, and speech. If available, you should also take classes in shop sketching, graph making, blueprint reading, and model making.

> ### TO BE A SUCCESSFUL INDUSTRIAL ENGINEERING TECHNICIAN, YOU SHOULD . . .
>
> ○ like working with computers, data, machines, and instruments
> ○ be curious about how things work
> ○ be very detail oriented and accurate in your work
> ○ have a lot of patience
> ○ like working with others and have good communication skills

Postsecondary Training

Study beyond the high school level is necessary for industrial engineering technicians. Most employers are interested in hiring graduates with at least a two-year degree in industrial engineering technology. Technical institutes, community colleges, vocational schools, and universities all offer this course of study.

The preferred course of study is the two-year program at a community college or technical institute that offers a certificate or degree in a science or engineering field. Many schools have specialized areas of study in industrial engineering technology or industrial management technology. Many students continue on after the two-year program and obtain a bachelor's degree in engineering technology.

College students in their first year can expect to take mathematics, blueprint reading, manufacturing processes, communications, introduction to numerical control, technical reporting, and computer-aided design.

In the second year, necessary courses include methods, operation, and safety engineering; production and quality control; computer control of industrial processes; facilities layout; materials handling; time study; and psychology and human relations.

When John started out, he was going for a two-year degree in industrial engineering technology, but he went on to earn his bachelor's degree in industrial engineering from his state university. He recommends that students continue to further their education. He is currently working toward his master's degree in business administration, taking night courses and even teaching a computer class at a local community college.

He also advises students to take more than just the basic industrial engineering courses. While in school, John tried to take as many classes in manufacturing as possible. "Don't put all your eggs in one basket," he says. "If you can get a strong grasp on another type of engineering, you can interplay both of them. It's really helped me."

CERTIFICATION OR LICENSING

Currently, there is no required certification process for industrial engineering technicians. The National Institute for Certification in Engineering Technologies has established a certification program that some industrial engineering technicians may choose to participate in. Those who do engage in the certification process may join the American Society of Certified Engineering Technicians.

SCHOLARSHIPS AND GRANTS

No specific scholarships or grants exist for industrial engineering technicians. Federal grants and student loans are available to students during their course of study.

INTERNSHIPS AND VOLUNTEERSHIPS

John did not participate in an internship program while he was in college. Like many other students in his field, he got a part-time job through his school's placement office. This allowed him to gain valuable experience and get paid at the same time.

Students are encouraged to pursue part-time and summer positions. It is a great way to learn more about your prospective career. In John's case, his first job helped him decide on a technician's specialty, pay for college, and eventually led to his current job.

LABOR UNIONS

Industrial engineering technicians are considered to be part of the engineering staff. They are not required to join any labor unions. Technicians must, however, observe all applicable rules and safety regulations when working in a plant.

Who Will Hire Me?

When John first entered college, he went to the job placement office at his technical school. "The very first interview they sent me on, I got the job," he recalls. He has been working for the same company ever since.

"It really helped me decide what area of engineering I wanted to go into," John says. The firsthand experience he gained through the part-time job allowed him to observe and evaluate the different areas of industrial engineering and the different technicians' roles.

John's boss became a kind of mentor to him, inspiring him to become a factory layout technician. The company also paid for John's continuing education, allowing him to obtain his bachelor's degree and go on for his master's.

Most technical schools, community colleges, and universities have job placement offices. Companies actively recruit employees while they are still in school or are nearing graduation. Because these job services are the primary source of entry-level jobs for industrial engineering technicians, you should check out a school's placement rate for your specific field before making a final decision about attending.

Newspaper want ads and employment services are other methods of getting jobs. Professional or trade magazines often have job listings and can be good sources for job seekers. Professional organizations are good for networking with other technicians and are up to date on industry advancement, changes, and areas of employment.

Most jobs for industrial engineering technicians are found in private manufacturing firms. These companies primarily manufacture electronic and electrical machinery and equipment, transportation equipment, industrial machinery, and office and computer equipment.

Any business involved in the production of materials will likely employ industrial engineering technicians. Factories are generally located outside of larger cities, in suburbs or in sparsely populated locations in just about any part of the United States.

Most of these employers are large companies that employ many people and use one, or a variety, of production systems. Some technicians do work for private consulting firms that hire out their services within the industry.

The federal government also employs industrial engineering technicians. The government agencies include the departments of Defense, Transportation,

Agriculture, and the Interior and the National Aeronautics and Space Administration (NASA). Some technicians are employed by state and local governments as well.

Where Can I Go from Here?

John is currently pursuing his master's degree in business administration and hopes to become a manager. He really enjoys working in his current area of factory and plant layout. As a manager, he would supervise all the department personnel, estimate costs, and work directly with other department heads to get the information needed by the layout department.

Most industrial engineering technicians begin as trainees, doing routine work supervised by engineers or other experienced technicians. As they gain knowledge and experience, they gradually acquire more responsibilities at work. If an industrial engineering technician pursues advanced education, other opportunities in management and supervision open up.

With increased education and job-related experience, an industrial engineering technician may become an industrial engineer in any of the related areas of specialization. You may go into civil engineering, production planning, chemical engineering, manufacturing engineering, materials engineering, or electrical engineering, for example.

The typical career path for industrial engineering technicians is to supervisory positions, industrial engineer, and eventually chief industrial engineer. The chief industrial engineer supervises all industrial engineering employees, consults with all department heads, directs all departmental projects, sets departmental budgets, and submits annual reports of his or her group's activities and accomplishments.

What Are the Salary Ranges?

According to the *Occupational Outlook Handbook*, the median annual earnings of industrial engineering technicians in 2003 were $42,900. The lowest paid 10 percent earned $27,900 and the highest paid 10 percent earned $72,000.

A 2005 review by Salary.com reported annual earnings nationwide for entry-level industrial engineering technicians of between $31,292 and

---

ADVANCEMENT POSSIBILITIES

Production engineers plan and coordinate production procedures in an industrial plant, direct the production department, and initiate programs to increase output.

Quality control managers supervise all inspections and quality control employees. They select and instruct employees in new techniques and meet with production people about manufacturing problems.

Manufacturing engineers plan, direct, and coordinate manufacturing processes in an industrial plant and develop, evaluate, and improve methods of manufacturing.

$38,017. Technicians with four or more years of experience earned between $43,407 and $67,269 annually.

Industrial engineering technicians usually work for large companies that provide benefits such as insurance, pension plans, paid holidays, and vacation time. In addition, many employers will pay tuition for their technicians who are attending school or pursuing advanced degrees in their field.

What Is the Job Outlook?

The U.S. Department of Labor expects employment of engineering technicians to grow about as fast as the average through 2012. This is despite the fact that most economists foresee a decline in the manufacturing industry during the 21st century. Not all aspects of the industry will be negatively affected; as one declines, another will increase in importance.

The manufacturing of computer equipment, industrial robotics, computer-aided technology, and health and medical supplies will all require the skills of trained technicians.

Technicians' careers and employment outlook are tied to rapidly changing technology. Computer-related fields and environmental technology are seen as areas of industrial engineering that will experience rapid growth.

As new environmental and safety regulations are passed, many companies will need to employ technicians to help them meet these standards. Factories and plants are trying to develop ways to reduce waste and pollution in a cost-effective manner, for example.

Many new and emerging technologies are changing the traditional ways that people do their jobs and that products are made. As this trend continues, industrial engineering technicians will be in demand. Automation technology, such as computer-aided design, numerically controlled machine tools, flexible manufacturing systems, and computer integrated manufacturing are areas in which technicians will be needed.

Technician jobs are also affected by changes in the economy. Federal government employees, especially technicians working for the Department of Defense, may be affected because of budget cutbacks in defense spending.

The rapid growth in the output of technical products will favor industrial engineering technicians. Employment opportunities will be good in the manufacturing of electronic parts, computer equipment, medical instruments, plastics, fiber optics, and telecommunications.

Prospective industrial engineering technicians should keep in mind that advances in technology and management techniques make this a rapidly changing field. Technicians will have to learn and change with the industry. Continuing education and training is the best, if not the only, way to take advantage of the opportunities open to industrial engineering technicians.

How Do I Learn More?

PROFESSIONAL ORGANIZATIONS

The following are organizations that provide information on industrial engineering technician careers, accredited schools and scholarships, certification, and employers:

Accreditation Board for Engineering and Technology
111 Market Place, Suite 1050
Baltimore, MD 21202
410-347-7700
http://www.abet.org

American Society of Certified Engineering Technicians
PO Box 1348
Flowery Branch, GA 30542
770-967-9173
http://www.ascet.org

IEEE Industry Applications Society
1828 L Street, NW, Suite 1202
Washington, DC 20036
202-785-0017
http://www.ieee.org

National Institute for Certification in Engineering Technologies
1420 King Street
Alexandria, VA 22314
888-476-4238
http://www.nicet.org

BIBLIOGRAPHY

The following is a sampling of materials relating to the professional concerns and development of industrial engineering technicians:

Kaydos, Will. *Measuring, Managing, and Maximizing Performance: What Every Manager Needs to Know About Quality and Productivity to Make Real Improvements in Performance.* Cambridge, Mass.: Productivity Press, 1991.

Kraget, Harmen, ed. *Enhancing Industrial Performance: Experiences with Integrating the Human Factor.* Boca Raton, Fla.: CRC Press, 1995.

Salvendy, Gavriel, ed. *Handbook of Industrial Engineering: Technology and Operations Management.* 3d ed. New York: John Wiley & Sons, 2001.

Turner, Wayne C. *Introduction to Industrial and Systems Engineering.* 3d ed. Englewood Cliffs, N.J.: Prentice-Hall, 1993.

Wrege, Charles D., and Ronald G. Greenwood. *Frederick W. Taylor, the Father of Scientific Management: Myth and Reality.* Homewood, Ill.: Irwin Professional Publishing, 1991.

Zandin, Kjell B., and Harold B. Maynard. *Maynard's Industrial Engineering Handbook.* New York: McGraw-Hill, 2001.

JOB TITLE INDEX